The purpose of the Cambridge Edition is to offer translations of the best modern German edition of Kant's work in a uniform format suitable for Kant scholars. When complete (fourteen volumes are currently envisaged), the edition will include all of Kant's published writings and a generous selection of his unpublished writings such as the *Opus postumum, handschriftliche Nachlass,* lectures, and correspondence.

This volume collects for the first time in a single volume all of Kant's writings on religion and rational theology. These works were written during a period of conflict between Kant and the Prussian authorities over his religious teachings. His final statement on religion was made after the death of King Frederick William II in 1797. The historical context and progression of this conflict is charted in the general introduction to the volume and in the translators' introductions to particular texts.

All the translations are new with the exception of *The Conflict of the Faculties,* where the translation has been revised and re-edited to conform to the guidelines of the Cambridge Edition. As is standard with all volumes in this edition there are copious linguistic and explanatory notes, and a glossary of key terms.

THE CAMBRIDGE EDITION OF THE WORKS OF IMMANUEL KANT

IMMANUEL KANT
Religion and Rational Theology

THE CAMBRIDGE EDITION OF THE WORKS OF IMMANUEL KANT

IMMANUEL KANT

Religion and Rational Theology

TRANSLATED AND EDITED BY

ALLEN W. WOOD
Yale University

GEORGE DI GIOVANNI
McGill University

 CAMBRIDGE
UNIVERSITY PRESS

CAMBRIDGE UNIVERSITY PRESS
Cambridge, New York, Melbourne, Madrid, Cape Town, Singapore, São Paulo

Cambridge University Press
40 West 20th Street, New York, NY 10011-4211, USA

www.cambridge.org
Information on this title: www.cambridge.org/9780521354165

© Cambridge University Press 1996

First published 1996
First paperback edition 2001
Reprinted 2004, 2005

A catalog record for this publication is available from the British Library.

ISBN-13 978-0-521-35416-5 hardback
ISBN-10 0-521-35416-1 hardback

ISBN-13 978-0-521-79998-0 paperback
ISBN-10 0-521-79998-8 paperback

Transferred to digital printing 2006

Contents

General editors' preface

Within a few years of the publication of his *Critique of Pure Reason* in 1781, Immanuel Kant (1724–1804) was recognized by his contemporaries as one of the seminal philosophers of modern times – indeed, as one of the great philosophers of all time. This renown soon spread beyond German-speaking lands, and translations of Kant's work into English were published even before 1800. Since then, interpretations of Kant's views have come and gone and loyalty to his positions has waxed and waned, but his importance has not diminished. Generations of scholars have devoted their efforts to producing reliable translations of Kant into English as well as into other languages.

There are four main reasons for the present edition of Kant's writings:

1. Completeness. Although most of the works published in Kant's lifetime have been translated before – the most important ones more than once – only fragments of Kant's many important unpublished works have ever been translated. These include the *Opus postumum*, Kant's unfinished *magnum opus* on the transition from philosophy to physics; transcriptions of his classroom lectures; his correspondence; and his marginalia and other notes. One aim of this edition is to make a comprehensive sampling of these materials available in English for the first time.

2. Availability. Many English translations of Kant's works, especially those that have not individually played a large role in the subsequent development of philosophy, have long been inaccessible or out of print. Many of them, however, are crucial for the understanding of Kant's philosophical development, and the absence of some from English-language bibliographies may be responsible for erroneous or blinkered traditional interpretations of his doctrines by English-speaking philosophers.

3. Organization. Another aim of the present edition is to make all Kant's published work, both major and minor, available in comprehensive volumes organized both chronologically and topically, so as to facilitate the serious study of his philosophy by English-speaking readers.

4. Consistency of translation. Although many of Kant's major works have been translated by the most distinguished scholars of their day, some of these translations are now dated, and there is considerable terminological disparity among them. Our aim has been to enlist some of the most accomplished Kant scholars and translators to produce new translations, freeing readers from both the philosophical and literary preconceptions of previous generations and allowing them to approach texts, as far as possible, with the same directness as present-day readers of the German or Latin originals.

In pursuit of these goals, our editors and translators attempt to follow several fundamental principles:

1. As far as seems advisable, the edition employs a single general glossary, especially for Kant's technical terms. Although we have not attempted to restrict the prerogative of editors and translators in choice of terminology, we have maximized consistency by putting a single editor or editorial team in charge of each of the main groupings of Kant's writings, such as his work in practical philosophy, philosophy of religion, or natural science, so that there will be a high degree of terminological consistency, at least in dealing with the same subject matter.

2. Our translators try to avoid sacrificing literalness to readability. We hope to produce translations that approximate the originals in the sense that they leave as much of the interpretive work as possible to the reader.

3. The paragraph, and even more the sentence, is often Kant's unit of argument, and one can easily transform what Kant intends as a continuous argument into a mere series of assertions by breaking up a sentence so as to make it more readable. Therefore, we try to preserve Kant's own divisions of sentences and paragraphs wherever possible.

4. Earlier editions often attempted to improve Kant's texts on the basis of controversial conceptions about their proper interpretation. In our translations, emendation or improvement of the original edition is kept to the minimum necessary to correct obvious typographical errors.

5. Our editors and translators try to minimize interpretation in other ways as well, for example, by rigorously segregating Kant's own footnotes, the editors' purely linguistic notes, and their more explanatory or informational notes; notes in this last category are treated as endnotes rather than footnotes.

We have not attempted to standardize completely the format of individual volumes. Each, however, includes information about the context in which Kant wrote the works that have been translated, an English–German glossary, an index, and other aids to comprehension. The general introduction to each volume includes an explanation of specific principles of translation and, where necessary, principles of selection of works included in that volume. The pagination of the standard German edition of Kant's works, *Kants gesammelte Schriften*, edited by the Royal Prussian (later German) Academy of Sciences (Berlin: Georg Reimer, later Walter deGruyter & Co., 1900–   ), is indicated throughout by means of marginal numbers.

Our aim is to produce a comprehensive edition of Kant's writings, embodying and displaying the high standards attained by Kant scholarship in the English-speaking world during the second half of the twentieth century, and serving as both an instrument and a stimulus for the further development of Kant studies by English-speaking readers in the century to come. Because of our emphasis on literalness of translation and on information rather than interpretation in editorial practices, we hope our edition will continue to be usable despite the inevitable evolution and occasional revolutions in Kant scholarship.

PAUL GUYER
ALLEN W. WOOD

General introduction

The subjects of religion and rational theology are integral to many of Kant's writings. Reflections on rational theology and the theological interpretation of nature were central to some of Kant's first important writings: the *Universal Natural History* and *Nova dilucidatio* (both 1755) and the *Only Possible Ground of Proof for a Demonstration of God's Existence* (1763). Rational theology and rational religious faith also figure prominently in all three *Critiques:* the Ideal of Pure Reason and Canon of Pure Reason in the first, the Dialectic of the second, and the Methodology of Teleological Judgment in the third. Although the writings translated in this volume do not therefore encompass the whole of his writings on religion and rational theology, they do contain the texts in which Kant dealt primarily with religion. They also document the history of one of the most critical and dramatic periods in Kant's professional life – the history of the process by which the philosopher came into collision with the Prussian authorities over the content of his teachings on religion.

Religious background

Kant received a strict religious upbringing from his parents, who were both devout pietists. Pietism was a seventeenth-century Christian revival movement that originated in Germany and was a powerful influence on German culture through the eighteenth century. It resembles in some ways other contemporary religious movements, such as the Quakers and Methodists in England or Chassidism among European Jews. Reacting to the ossified and sterile orthodoxy of mid-seventeenth-century Lutheran theology, the pietists regarded the Christian faith not as a set of doctrinal propositions but as a living relationship with God. They stressed above all the felt power of God's grace to transform the believer's life through a conversion or rebirth experience. Like orthodox Lutheranism, pietism exalted the authority of scripture above that of natural reason, but it was hostile to the intellectualization of Christianity even in the study of scripture, insisting instead that the Bible be read for inspiration and moral edification. Within schools and universities, pietists favored cultivation of piety and morality rather than theoretical study. In controversy, they urged, the aim should be not to achieve intellectual victory over one's opponents but instead to win over their hearts to godliness and righteousness. Some of the social tendencies within pietism were progressive, even radical. Emphasis on the immediacy and intimacy of religious experience was combined with a commitment to the priesthood of all believers, and this led to a Christian ethic that was strongly egalitarian in its import. For pietists, the visible church was less important than the church invisible, whose membership in principle includes the whole of humanity.

Kant's later attitude toward his pietist background was always ambivalent. When at the university he was drawn to the study of natural science, it was by a brilliant young Wolffian, Martin Knutzen, who was also a pietist. But pietism and the Wolffian rationalism of the German enlightenment were generally foes in Kant's milieu. The zeal pietists showed in their quest for inner, spiritual freedom could be turned against outward freedom when it challenged theological orthodoxy on rational grounds. It was at the instigation of pietists that Wolff had been driven from his professorship at Halle in 1723 on the order of King Frederick William I for teaching that the will, though free, is determined in accord with the principle of sufficient reason and for sympathetically studying the ethical theories of Confucius. His restoration to the same professorship under Frederick II (the Great) was widely perceived as a victory of rationalism over pietism. When Kant came into conflict with the attempt to enforce religious orthodoxy after Frederick's death, it was not pietists who led the repression, but Kant always tended to associate pietism with attacks on reason in religious matters.

Most of Kant's explicit pronouncements about pietism are negative. He sometimes equates "pietism" with the expression in behavior of a false devotion that pretends to despair of one's own powers and passively awaits grace from above; this pietism seems to him to a sign of a slavish cast of mind (*Religion* 6:184–5n). The pietist belief that one can experience divine grace in oneself seems to him an extravagant form of "enthusiasm" (*Schwärmerei*) (*Religion* 6:174). He rejects pietism's antiintellectualism, especially its antiintellectual inspirationalist attitude toward scripture (*Religion* 6:112–13).

Yet much in Kant's conception of true morality and religion amounts to a rationally purified version of pietism. About pietism, he is reported to have said in later years: "Even if the religious consciousness of that time and the conceptions of what is called virtue and piety were by no means clear or satisfactory, it yet contained the root of the matter. One may say about pietism what one will. Enough! The people who took it seriously were distinguished in a way which is worthy of greatest honor."[1]

---

[1] The report, by F. T. Rink, is quoted in Friedrich Paulsen, *Immanuel Kant, His Life and Doctrine* (New York: Scribner, 1902), p. 28; cf. Karl Vorländer, *Kants Leben* (Hamburg: Meiner, 1911), pp. 3–4.

Creeds, rituals, and the church.

Kant's education between the ages of eight and sixteen at the *Collegium Fridericianum* was made possible by his family pastor F. A. Schultz, who was also the principal of the school. Its emphasis was heavily religious. Each day began with half an hour of religious devotion, every class with a prayer, and an important part of the curriculum was drill in the religious catechism – about which Kant was later to remark that "in childhood we knew it by heart to the last detail and believed we understood it, but the older and more reflective we become, the less we understand of it, and hence we would deserve to be sent back to school, if only we could find someone there (other than ourselves) who understood it any better" (AK 8:323).

Along with whatever positive influences pietism may have had on Kant's moral and religious thought, it left him with a profound hostility to many traditional religious beliefs and practices. He came to regard catechisms and credal formulas as unconscionable impositions on our freedom of thought, destructive of the intellectual integrity required for any belief held in good conscience. As Kant wrote to J. C. Lavater in 1775:

> You ask for my opinion of your discussion of faith and prayer. Do you realize whom you are asking? A man who believes that, in the final moment only the purest candor concerning our most hidden inner convictions can stand the test and who, like Job, takes it to be a sin to flatter God and make inner confessions, perhaps forced out by fear, that fail to agree with what we freely think. (AK 10:176)

The effect of being told (or even of telling ourselves) what we *must* believe is never to alter our beliefs but only to constrain what we profess to believe (at first outer profession, but finally also our inner thoughts). This sort of religious faith can lead only to a systematic and habitual hypocrisy infecting all our thoughts and beliefs pertaining to the credal injunctions. For we dare not consider the grounds for what we believe, since we might find them inadequate; we dare not even inquire into the meaning of what we believe, because we might find that we do not believe all of what we profess; we dare not even ask ourselves sincerely what we do believe, because our sincere beliefs might not agree with the professions we have forced ourselves to make. Our best (perhaps our only) means of avoiding the dreaded crime of unbelief is simply to repeat our credal professions (outwardly and inwardly) without questioning, without even thinking, even if this means that we can't truly believe anything – least of all the creed we so ardently profess to believe.

Kant was persuaded that most of what passes for the religious service of God was "counterfeit service" (*Afterdienst*), "a pretension of honoring God through which we operate directly counter to the true service required by him" (*Religion* 6:168). The true service of God consists in nothing but morally good conduct in life. Ceremonial rituals, petitionary prayers, words of divine praise, penances, the observance of statutory laws prescribed by church traditions, none of these have any truly religious aim, but only serve as illusory substitutes for doing what a truly good God would demand of us: namely, our ordinary moral duty as human beings.

Ritual formulas that praise God treat him like an earthly despot whose favor his cringing minions may hope to win through self-abasing flattery; such formulas presuppose an image of our relationship to God which dishonors both him and ourselves. Prayer makes sense as long as it is seen as a way of bringing about a morally good disposition in ourselves; but prayer, "conceived as an inner ritual service of God and hence as a means of grace," is a "superstitious delusion" (*Religion* 6:194); as for petitionary prayer, it is "an absurd and at the same time impudent delusion to have a try whether, through the insistent intrusiveness of our prayer, God might not be diverted from the plan of his wisdom (to our present advantage)" (*Religion* 6:196n).

If religious rituals are seen as a way of conjuring up God's grace or divine aid in pursuing our earthly ends, then they are to be condemned as *fetishism*, the superstitious delusion of being able to produce supernatural effects (*Religion* 6:177).

Between a *shaman* of the Tunguses and the European prelate who rules over both church and state, or . . . between the wholly sensuous *Wogulite*, who in the morning lays the paw of a bear skin over his head with the short prayer "Strike me not dead!" and the sublimated *Puritan* and Independent of Connecticut, there certainly is a tremendous distance in the *style* of faith, but not in the *principle*; for as regards the latter, they all equally belong to one and the same class, namely of those who place their service of God in something . . . which cannot by itself constitute a better human being. (*Religion* 6:176)

Kant was convinced that the human species cannot fulfill its moral vocation apart from the existence of a "moral community" or "church," freely entered into by well-disposed individuals for the purpose of combatting the radical evil in human nature and strengthening their own and one another's disposition toward good (*Religion* 6:95–100). But the laws of this community must be inner and moral, not statutory or coercive; membership in it must be entirely free and equal. Existing churches or religious communities, if they are to perform their true function for the moral service of God and the destiny of the human race, must cease to be governed by a hierarchical political constitution and statutory religious laws:

In the end religions will gradually be freed of all empirical grounds of determination, of all statutes that rest on history and unite human beings provisionally for the promotion of the good. . . . The leading strings of holy tradition. . . . which in its time did good service, become little by little dispensable, yea finally when a human being enters upon his adolescence, turns into a fetter. . . . The degrading distinction between *laity* and *clergy* ceases, and equality springs from true freedom. . . . The very form of a church is dissolved: the vicar on earth enters the same class as the human beings who are now elevated to him as citizens of heaven, and so God is all in all. (*Religion* 6:121–2, 135)

Kant did not attend religious services. Several times he served as rector of the University of Königsberg, but was always "indisposed" when his official participation in religious observances would have been required.[2]

The Enlightenment and its enemies

Kant's views on religion posed no problem under the reign of Frederick the Great (1740–86), who was openly anticlerical and permitted, or even encouraged, all manner of religious freethinking. But the situation changed drastically with the accession of his nephew, Frederick William II. Frederick William was a religious fanatic. In the 1770s he had been associated with the "strict observance" freemasons, but around 1780 he came under the influence of the Königsberg figure J. A. Starck, founder of the *Klerikat* ("Clericalist") religious project, which sought a revival of religion in Prussian life.[3] Frederick William shortly became converted to a mystical form of Christianity, and during the early 1780s, he joined the Rosicrucian Society.[4] When he ascended the throne, some of his closest advisors, such as Johann Christoph Wöllner and Rudolf von Bischoffwerder, were chosen from among its members. The king's capricious nature opened him to manipulation by such men as well as to the influence of his mistresses. (In 1790 the king divorced his wife in order to marry the most prominent of these, the Countess von Dönhof; the scandal

---

[2] Vorländer, *Kants Leben*, p. 130.

[3] Starck is a complex and somewhat mercurial figure. He was a freemason, but became embroiled in controversy within the Order and was accused by his opponents of being a "crypto-Catholic." When this charge was made (probably by Kant's publisher, Biester) in the *Berlinische Monatschrift*, Starck filed a suit for defamation, which, however, was unsuccessful. Throughout his career Starck remained an opponent of theological rationalism. At the time of his first association with Friedrich Wilhelm, however, he was not aligned unambiguously with conservatism, as is indicated by the fact that in the controversy with Biester he was defended against Enlightenment critics by F. H. Jacobi, whose general political stance was liberal. It was only after the French Revolution that Starck (perhaps out of opportunism as much as conviction) charged the rationalists with aiming at the destruction of the existing social order. See Paul Konschel, *Hamanns Gegner, der Kryptokatholik D. Johann August Starck, Oberhofprediger und Generalsuperintendent von Ostpreussen: Ein Beitrag zur Geschichte der Aufklärungszeit*, Schriften der Synodalkommission fur ostpreussische Kirchengeschichte, No. 13 (Königsberg, 1912).

[4] On the history of Frederick William's religious views, see Paul Schwartz, *Der erste Kulturkampf in Preussen um Kirche und Schule (1788–1798)*, Monumenta Germaniae Paedagogica No. 58 (Berlin, 1925), chs. 2–3, and Johannes Schultze, "Die Rosenkreutzer und Friedrich Wilhelm II," *Forschungen zur brandenburgischen und preussischen Geschichte*, Veröffentlichungen der Historischen Kommission zu Berlin, No. 13 (Berlin, 1964), pp. 240–65.

was told to Kant by his former student, the royal tutor J. G. C. C. Kiesewetter, in a letter of April 20, 1790 (AK, 11:155–60).)

The concluding pages of Kant's *What Does It Mean to Orient Oneself in Thinking?*, which was written in the late summer and early autumn of 1786, shortly after Frederick's death, shows the philosopher was already aware of the nature of the political changes that were about to take place in Berlin, and what they might mean for freedom of thought and communication in Prussia. But the change of monarchs did not adversely affect Kant himself, at least in the short run. When the new king visited Königsberg in September, Kant was singled out for special favor. In November, only a month after the publication of the "Orientation" essay, Kant was elected a corresponding member of the Royal Academy of Sciences in Berlin, and as late as 1789 Zedlitz persuaded Wöllner to increase Kant's salary, making him the best paid professor in Königsberg.[5]

Kant was far from being the only figure in the German Enlightenment to entertain unorthodox religious opinions. Though German thinkers seldom went as far as the atheistic materialism current in the radical French Enlightenment, there flourished during Frederick's reign a wide variety of rationalist, deist, and liberal theological views, such as the "neologism" of J. S. Semler and other theologians, together with the beginnings of critical biblical scholarship through the work of such men as J. A. Ernesti and J. D. Michaelis. In 1778, G. E. Lessing – whose alleged "Spinozism" became the focus of the so-called "pantheism controversy" of 1785–86 – published the notorious *Wolffenbüttel Fragments* of the recently deceased H. S. Reimarus (see below, *Religion* 6:81n); these "fragments" rejected all supernatural revelation, denied both the existence and religious significance of miraculous events, and attacked the biblical histories themselves as contradictory, fraudulent, and generally unreliable.

By this time, many university chairs and church pulpits had come to be occupied by men who had been educated or influenced by such ideas, and their convictions deviated in various ways from Lutheran orthodoxy concerning such matters as the literal truth of scripture and the fundamentals of Christian doctrine (the trinity, the incarnation, the bodily resurrection). One especially notorious case was that of Karl Friedrich Bahrdt (see below, *Religion* 6:81n), an inspiring popular lecturer, who had been appointed to a theological lectureship in Leipzig, from which he denied the divinity of Jesus, preached a purely utilitarian ethic, debunked biblical miracle tales, offered naturalistic explanations of the events they reported, and developed his own esoteric theory of the meaning of the Gospels.[6]

---

[5] Steven Lestition, "Kant and the End of the Enlightenment in Prussia," *Journal of Modern History* 65 (March 1993), p. 73.
[6] See Klaus Epstein, *The Genesis of German Conservatism* (Princeton: Princeton University Press, 1966), pp. 118–20.

Religious conservatives such as the new king and his favorites regarded the whole situation as utterly intolerable. To put an end to it the king in 1788 replaced Baron Zedlitz (to whom Kant had dedicated the *Critique of Pure Reason*) as Minister of Education and Religious Affairs with J. C. Wöllner, a man whom Frederick the Great had described as "a deceitful, scheming parson." Even before the French Revolution of 1789, Prussian conservatives were taking steps to halt the spiritual contagion. The events in France, which many conservatives (such as Starck) were quick to explain as the diabolical work of freethinkers, confirmed their worst fears about the social effects of spiritual libertinism, and moved them to redouble their efforts.

The religious edicts

Wöllner's aim was to halt the spread of undisciplined apostasy among the clergy and to compel both spiritual and secular teachers to return to orthodoxy at least in their public instruction, if not in their private beliefs. On July 9, 1788, less than a week after his appointment, Wöllner promulgated an edict in the king's name covering the conduct of educators and ecclesiastics and the education of theological candidates. The edict was explicitly directed against "enlightenment" thought and pledged the removal from their offices, both ecclesiastical and professorial, of those who propagated it. Such measures were justified, it said, because "a conscienceless and evil man can never be a good subject, much less a true servant of the state in matters great or small"; it was therefore necessary to take action against "dangerous men and new teachers, who have it in mind to acquire followers and proselytes."[7] The edict noted with regret that "many pastors allow themselves unbridled liberty in the treatment of the dogma of their confession; they repudiate several essential parts and basic truths of the Protestant Church and indeed of the Christian religion. . . . They are not ashamed to warm up the miserable, long refuted errors of the Socinians, deists, naturalists and other sectarians, and to spread them among the people with impertinent impudence under the much abused banner of 'enlightenment'! They denigrate the respect in which the Bible has been hitherto held as the revealed word of God. . . . They throw suspicion on the mysteries of revealed religion, shaking the faith of Christians and indeed making Christianity appear ridiculous throughout the world."[8]

Wöllner's edict did not actually impose any significant censorship provisions that were not, at least in theory, already in force. But it served to

[7] Quoted by Lüdiger Lutkehaus, "Karl Friedrich Bahrdt, Immanuel Kant und die Gegenaufklärung in Preussen (1788–98)," *Jahrbuch des Instituts für deutsche Geschichte* 9 (1980), pp. 86–87.

[8] Quoted by Epstein, op. cit., pp. 143–4.

announce that the government intended to enforce new policies regarding schools and churches. All preachers who deviated from the creed of their Church, said the edict, would be peremptorily dismissed. All new appointments of preachers, teachers, and university professors would be "limited to subjects who provide no ground for questioning their inner adherence to the creed they are employed to teach."[9]

The religious edict put many liberal pastors in the position of choosing between losing their livelihood and teaching what they regarded as a set of outdated superstitions. Doubtful clergymen were assigned to preach on topics most likely to test them (for example, miracle stories) and their sermons were attended and reported on by state informants. Action was taken against university academics as well. Kant's friend and colleague, J. G. Hasse, was forced to choose between losing his post and recanting the contents of his treatise on "neology"; he chose the latter and was generally regarded as having disgraced himself;[10] for a time the fear was that the authorities would confront Kant with a similar choice.[11]

Unlike some of his associates, Wöllner was not unaware of the ugly aspects of what he was doing, but he was resolute in his enforcement of orthodoxy. The conservatives argued that public order required that the masses be taught a religion which is doctrinally uniform and orthodox, pure of subversive rationalistic glosses. Most people, they held, were incapable of understanding (or being motivated to comply with) the demands of morality except when presented in the form of divine commands with the threat of divine hatred attached to them as sanction. To allow individual thinkers to teach their own religious doctrines, contrary to traditional dogma, would lead inevitably to people's questioning the demands of morality, hence to the breakdown of that civil order which it was the government's duty to maintain.[12] Kant's enlightenment principle (de-

---

[9] Quoted by Epstein, ibid., p. 144.

[10] Vorländer, *Kants Leben,* pp. 181–2; cf. Arsenj Gulyga, *Kant: His Life and Thought,* trans. Marijan Despalatović (Boston: Birkhauser, 1987), pp. 210–11.

[11] See the letter to Kant of J. H. Campe, June 27, 1794, AK, 11:493–4.

[12] Epstein, op. cit., p. 362. The conservatives' defense was perhaps best articulated by D. J. Köppen:

> First: Religion provides the very strongest motive for good conduct, for man can have no higher interest than to have a satisfactory relationship to God. The morality to be expected of a man is ordinarily proportionate to the strength of this motive in his conduct.
>
> Second: It is not within the intellectual capacity of ordinary men to discover by philosophical reasoning the laws of ethics, their necessity and the appropriate motives for their certain observance – ordinary men simply lack the education to do this. The road to morality which relies upon higher authority and recognizes divine rewards and punishments is shorter, easier, and far better suited to ordinary human nature. The divine command: "Thou shalt not lie" with the adjoined motive, "because God hates liars," is far more effective than the deduction of both command and motive through

fended at the end of the "Orientation" essay) that all individuals have not only a right but a moral duty to think for themselves, obedient to the universal principles prescribed to them by their reason, thus seemed to the conservatives like a recipe for civil anarchy.

What in fact turned out to affect Kant most directly, however, was not the edict governing religious instruction, but a second religious edict of December 19, 1788, suppressing irreligious writings and empowering the Immediate Commission of Investigation to censor of all books and periodicals published in Berlin that dealt with moral or religious topics. The censors appointed were G. F. Hillmer and J. T. Hermes, both ignorant men so zealous in their religious conservatism that even Wöllner looked askance at some of the actions they took. Apparently, sometime in 1791, Kant was identified by the conservatives as someone who had to be silenced. In June of that year, Kiesewetter reported to the philosopher that the decision had been taken by T. C. G. Woltersdorf, the new chief consistory counsel, to forbid him to write any more (AK 11:264–6).

Nothing so drastic occurred right away, however. In fact, Wöllner had considerable difficulty enforcing the provisions of his religious edicts due to the opposition of the chief consistory of the Lutheran Church, the majority of whose members were religious rationalists, holdovers from the Zedlitz regime. In order to overrule them, he had been forced to appeal directly to the monarch. Because the Lutheran clergy were generally not in agreement with him, in order to enforce his policies Wöllner had to appoint to the Immediate Commission notorious religious bigots such as Hillmer and Hermes.[13]

In the meantime, at the end of 1790, Wöllner and Hermes used the Immediate Commission to put into practice a new system of testing for theological students. All theology candidates were subjected to a rigorous examination designed to ensure the orthodoxy of their opinions, supplemented by a solemn oath, whose violation in any particular would be

complicated and subtle philosophical reasoning – especially since it is not only a problem of cognition but of action based upon cognition. Hence religion is in fact the only reliable foundation of morality for the broad mass of mankind. . . .

It is difficult to understand how a man can be so arrogant as to believe that his own bright idea, even though it contradicts centuries of religious tradition, must be the absolute and unquestioned truth, and therefore justifies the abandonment of dogma; and that he is so infallible as to be compelled immediately to spread his opinion among the common people . . . If such men demand toleration, they must also claim toleration for every medical quack who peddles poison. They must argue that the government has no right to curb such a quack even though it should be convinced that he distributes harmful substances under benevolent names. (Köppen, *Das Recht der Fürsten, die Religionslehrer auf ein feststehendes Symbol zu verpflichten* (The Right of a Prince to Obligate Teachers of Religion to a Firm Creed) (Leipzig, 1789), pp. 46–64, 131, 85; cited by Epstein, op. cit., pp. 148–51)

[13] See Epstein, op. cit., pp. 362–7.

grounds for immediate dismissal. These steps outraged Kant, who saw them as ensuring nothing except that mendacity and hypocrisy would henceforth be among the necessary qualifications for being a theologian or cleric. He did not hesitate to express himself on the topic in an appendix to his essay *On the Miscarriage of All Philosophical Trials in Theodicy* (September 1791).

Kant's first open collision with the new censorship, however, came the following year, when he insisted on submitting the first part of his *Religion Within the Boundaries of Mere Reason* to the Berlin censorship. It was rejected by Hermes, but through the ruse of submitting the entire work to the judgment of the philosophy faculties at Königsberg and Jena, Kant managed to get it published in the spring of 1793.[14] One of the effects of the Berlin censorship was that two prominent journals left the city for a freer environment. In 1792, Friedrich Nicolai's *Allgemeine deutsche Bibliothek* moved to Kiel, and Johann Erich Biester's *Berlinische Monatschrift* moved to Jena. This made it possible for Kant, in June 1794, to publish *The End of All Things*, a bitterly satirical essay targeting the religious projects of Wöllner and the conservative ministers.

The royal reproof and Kant's response

This was apparently the last straw. Wöllner and Hermes were already outraged by the legerdemain through which Kant had circumvented the censorship of the *Religion*. The planned action against Kant finally took the form of an official letter from King Frederick William, dated October 1 and signed on his behalf by Wöllner's hand. It accused Kant, both in the *Religion* and in the shorter treatises, of "misusing" his philosophy to "distort and disparage many of the cardinal and basic teachings of the Holy Scriptures and Christianity"; and it demanded that the philosopher both "give an account of himself" and be guilty of no similar faults in the future, lest he be the object of "unpleasant measures" for his "continuing obstinacy" (AK 7:6; cf. AK 11:506).

By this time Kant's renown was such that he could have probably disregarded such an impudent and unenlightened command with impunity, as some of his friends urged him to do. But Kant had already anticipated what would be expected of him, and had decided to comply. In the letter to Biester accompanying *The End of All Things*, he stated his willingness to obey even commands forbidding him to express his opinions. A year earlier, in the second essay on theory and practice, Kant had even brought his compliance under a principle of right, declaring that subjects have no right to disobey even the unjust commands of the supreme authority in a state (AK 8:297–306; cf. AK 6:318–23). In the letter

---

[14] For the details of the way Kant got the *Religion* published, see the translator's introduction below.

to Biester, however, Kant gives a different rationale for offering his promise to the king, one not of juridical principle but rather of a resigned, weary, and cautious prudence: "Life is short, especially what is left to one who has already lived seventy years; what is to be found is a corner of the earth in which to bring it to an end free of cares" (AK 10:240–1).

On October 12, Kant returned the "account of himself" the king had demanded. As to the king's first point, Kant's alleged misconduct, the philosopher denied criticizing the Scriptures or harming the public religion of the land, either in his lectures or his published writings. He argued that since these were purely philosophical, they altogether avoided the science of biblical theology, hence attempted no evaluation of Holy Scripture or Christianity and therefore could not be guilty of disparaging either (AK 7:7; cf. AK 11:508). Regarding the second point, the guarantee that he would not similarly offend in future, Kant pledged "as your Majesty's most loyal subject," not to discourse publicly on any form of religion, whether natural or revealed, either in his lectures or his writings (AK 7:9–10; cf. AK 11:510–11).

Kant's defense of his treatment of religious topics in his lectures and publications was made to turn on what may seem a rather subtle point: that his treatment of religion was always *philosophical*, dealing exclusively with philosophical texts (such as Baumgarten's *Metaphysica*) and never mixing philosophical science with any other – specifically, with the science of biblical theology. It is significant to Kant, therefore, that his rational theology lectures on Baumgarten, as well as all four parts of the *Religion*, should have borne the title *"philosophical* doctrine of religion." The full significance of this point, however, can be appreciated only in light of a text on which Kant was working at the time that dealt with the structure of the university and the boundaries of competence and right proper to each of its four faculties: the three professional (or "higher") faculties of theology, law, and medicine, which perform functions regulated by the state; and the one philosophical (or "lower") faculty, whose duty is owed instead solely to reason, and which therefore should be free of any such professional regulation. Kant apparently began his treatise on this subject in 1794. He had even had an article on the subject solicited by the liberal theologian C. F. Stäudlin in Göttingen (AK 11:488). Kant replied that the treatise in question had already been finished for some time, though before October it had been submitted to Hillmer and Hermes, who refused permission to publish it. Stäudlin, who was beyond the reach of the Berlin censorship, promised Kant "unlimited freedom of the press," but to no avail. For since the relation of the philosophical faculty to the theological one clearly dealt with religious topics, Kant regarded his promise to the king as forbidding him to publish it (AK 11:513–15).

We may be tempted to agree with those of Kant's friends who urged him not to give in to Wöllner. We may see the philosopher's promise as a major victory for Wöllner and his religious struggle against enlightenment. Perhaps we are right to do so. But if we take a comprehensive look at the situation in which Wöllner found himself in October of 1794, we cannot regard him as triumphant. It is likely that Hermes, who had the ear of the royal household, had undermined Wöllner's credit with the king. Whatever the cause, in April 1794 Frederick William had reprimanded Wöllner in writing for not being aggressive enough in his attacks on the Enlightenment. The royal favor Wöllner had enjoyed since 1788 was never to be regained. When other royal favorites received estates after the Second Partition of Poland, Wöllner was conspicuously omitted from the division of the spoils. Wöllner's policies earned him enemies everywhere, and there was no organized party or faction to support his efforts or offer him personal protection. The only men he could find to implement his policies were fanatics with whom his relation was one of mutual mistrust but for whose extreme, often imprudent, actions he was usually held accountable. Wöllner had risen from poverty to political prominence; he died in the same condition in which he had been born. It is not surprising that Wöllner's censorship policies did not survive the ungrateful king he had tried to serve.[15]

Kant's last statement on religion

Three years passed; they were very productive years for Kant, especially considering that by the end of them he was well into his seventies. In 1795, he published *Toward Perpetual Peace*. After retiring from his teaching duties the following year, he worked to complete his ethical system and by July 1797 both parts of the *Metaphysics of Morals* had appeared. Then in November came the news: Frederick William II was dead.

In a spirit more wily than submissive, Kant now regarded himself no longer bound by his promise, which, he pointed out, had been made *"as your Majesty's most loyal subject,"* and had therefore been a personal promise to that particular monarch, from which the promisee's death freed him. Kant now took his work of 1794 on the structure of the university and the relation of philosophy to theology, and combined it with two other essays on different topics which he had written in the meantime. *The Conflict of the Faculties*, prefaced by the king's letter to him and his reply, and containing Kant's last major reflections on religion to appear in print, was published in the autumn of 1798.

Kant as a religious thinker

When we examine Kant's principal writings that deal primarily with religion, we find that they were produced largely during a time when enlightenment thinking was under political attack by religious conservatives; we

[15] See Epstein's comparatively sympathetic portrayal of Wöllner, op. cit., pp. 360–9.

cannot help noticing how their form and content were determined by Kant's response to that attack. This might tempt us to conclude that Kant's writings on religion were mainly writings *against* religion. Many popular conceptions of both Kantian ethics and metaphysics, however, often represent Kant's philosophy as merely an expression of, or at least fundamentally in harmony with, his Protestant and pietist religious background. There is an element of truth in both these conflicting images of Kant as a religious thinker. But the conflict between them should serve to warn us that each involves a fundamental distortion, and it should point us beyond both of them. For both images appeal to us only as long as we are unable to appreciate the distinctive religious sensibility of the Enlightenment, of which Kant was perhaps the greatest philosophical proponent.

Kant was a man of scientific temperament, whose chief concerns were the growth of human knowledge and the intellectual and moral development of the human species. He had no patience at all for the mystical or the miraculous. He was deeply skeptical of popular religious culture, severely disapproving of religious ceremonies, and downright hostile to the whole idea of ecclesiastical authority. In the context of Kant's time, however, this did not mean that he was unbelieving or irreligious; it merely signified that his religious temper was enlightened rather than conservative or enthusiastic. Although his principles, as applied to religion, were quite radical in their implications, his views and practices concerning their application to thought and culture were those not of a radical but of a moderate and a mediator.[16]

If Kant intensified his writing on religion during the period of Wöllner's repression, this certainly indicates that he did not shy away from confronting the authorities in pursuit of this reform. On the other hand, Kant's theory of the rightful spheres of the philosophy and theology faculties, and the legitimate role of state regulation in regard to the latter, represent a very moderate and conciliating stance with regard to existing religious authority. When the authorities moved against Kant himself he was willing to yield to their demands at least as far as was required by prudence and by his own principles of passive obedience. This is consistent with Kant's general political stance and his vision of historical progress: In religion, as in politics and social life generally, he thinks the human race has far to go, but it will sooner approach its ends through a process of cautious reform under the constant but mild pressure of open, rational reflection than by sudden and violent revolutions. In his view, we will find our way toward fundamental changes gradually, transforming what exists while remaining always at peace with it.

Moses Mendelssohn famously described Kant's criticism of the tradi-

---

[16] This is the main thesis of Steven Lestition, "Kant and the End of the Enlightenment in Prussia," loc. cit.

tional proofs for God's existence as "world-crushing"; but in fact, as we can see from his lectures on the subject, Kant's attitude toward traditional rational theology was on the whole highly favorable, and he took this rational theology to have vital religious importance. Thus if Kant denied that the existence of God could be proven on theoretical grounds, he still largely accepted the scholastic and rationalist conception of God and defended this conception against the nascent impulses, later to be so influential, which sought to replace it with a theology based on biblical revelation, or on a novel (for instance, Spinozist) metaphysics, or on religious feeling or mystical intuition.

Again, if Kant advocated that the existing church, like the existing state, needed to change its form quite radically in order to fulfill its proper vocation for the human species, he did not regard it in its present form either as evil and to be abolished or even as dispensable. On the contrary, he thought the human race could no more fulfill its moral vocation apart from organized religion than it could achieve justice through anarchy. Kant accepted the church as the necessary vehicle of genuine religious faith and hence our best hope for the moral progress of the human race. If it was an imperfect (in some respects even an unsuitable) vehicle, it was nevertheless indispensable, and its defects meant to Kant only that it was in need of gradual reform through persistent effort constantly guided by rational inquiry.

Finally, if Kant's account of the Christian faith and the church in the *Religion* – his judgment of it in light of the moral principles of pure reason – was largely a negative one, we should interpret this as his admission that while he thought he saw clearly the need for religious reform, he did not pretend to know what eventual shape religious life ought to take. Under these conditions, Kant gave the highest priority simply to maintaining and fostering a climate of thought and opinion in which critical thinking about the direction of the ongoing historical process of progressive religious change would be kept alive.

What does it mean to orient oneself
in thinking?

Translator's introduction

Was heisst: Sich im Denken orientiren? was first published in October 1786 in the *Berlinische Monatschrift* VIII, pp. 304–30.

The "Orientation" essay is Kant's contribution to the so-called pantheism controversy, one of the eighteenth century's most famous and influential philosophical disputes, whose course helped determine the course of German philosophy well into the following century. The principals in the dispute were F. H. Jacobi and Moses Mendelssohn, and its focus was the alleged Spinozism of Gotthold Ephraim Lessing. Mendelssohn and Lessing had been close friends for many years. After Lessing's death in 1781 Mendelssohn intended to write a laudatory character sketch of one of the eighteenth century's greatest and most respected German writers and thinkers, particularly on the topics of religion and art. Toward the end of his life, however, Lessing had also been acquainted with the much younger Jacobi, to whom (as Jacobi claimed) Lessing had confessed his allegiance to the philosophical principles of Spinoza. This was extremely disturbing, since Spinoza was widely regarded as an atheist and necessitarian whose principles were subversive of all religion and morality. The suggestion that the great rationalist Lessing might have been a secret Spinozist was both shocking to the learned public and at the same time profoundly ambiguous in its implications. On the one hand, it could mean that the principles of Enlightenment rationalism might in fact be morally and religiously subversive; on the other hand, it could mean that Spinozist pantheism was a more formidable philosophical position than rationalist orthodoxy allowed. Both conclusions were, in fact, widely accepted; both determined the course of philosophy in Germany throughout the period of German idealism.

In 1783, Jacobi initiated a correspondence with Mendelssohn mediated by Elise Reimarus (daughter of the deist theologian H. S. Reimarus), in which the two men debated the extent and nature of Lessing's Spinozism. It soon became clear that the real issues did not have as much to do with what Lessing's opinions were as with deeper philosophical differences over the ultimate implications of applying reason consistently to moral and religious questions. Mendelssohn defended an orthodox theology based on reason. He held that Lessing's agreement with Spinoza was only partial, and that it

3

not only need not but in fact did not extend to the more objectionable tenets of Spinozism. Jacobi argued that one cannot consistently embrace philosophical rationalism at all without committing oneself to the heterodox pantheism, necessitarianism, and even materialism for which Spinoza's philosophy was infamous. This, he thought, was the profoundest result attained by Lessing's courageous rationalism. Jacobi's position was that solely on the basis of philosophical reason, systematically developed, no morally and religiously tenable view of life is possible. A healthy human existence is attainable only through an attitude of faith rooted not in rational reflection but in the attitudes of moral practice.

This controversy became public in September 1785. Hearing rumors that Mendelssohn was about to publish a book touching on their disagreement, Jacobi quickly brought out *On the Doctrine of Spinoza in Letters to Mr. Moses Mendelssohn* (Breslau, 1785). This was indeed followed just a few weeks later by Mendelssohn's *Morning Hours* (Berlin, 1785), which contained a defense of rational theism along with reflections on maintaining a stable and consistent relationship between a speculative philosophy based on reason and the standpoint of healthy common sense. It also included a discussion of Lessing's theological opinions.

When Mendelssohn read Jacobi's account of Lessing's views and the account of his own correspondence with Jacobi, he was incensed and immediately penned a reply: *To Lessing's Friends: an Appendix to Mr. Jacobi's Correspondence on the Doctrine of Spinoza* (Berlin, 1786). Mendelssohn accused Jacobi of distorting Lessing's views and slandering his memory; he attacked Jacobi's recommendation of the "narrow path of faith" as a form of philosophical "enthusiasm" (*Schwärmerei*) that exalts authority over reason in matters of both religion and philosophy. This was to be Mendelssohn's last contribution to the controversy. In January 1786, he suddenly fell ill and died.

Within a month of this tragic event, Kant was urged by two of Mendelssohn's friends (and Kant's as well), Marcus Herz and Johann Erich Biester (editor of the *Berlinische Monatschrift*), to enter the struggle to avenge the death of the great Moses (see AK 10:431–3). The request was not out of place, for although Kant's critical views were at odds with Mendelssohn's Wolffian "dogmatism," the two philosophers had known and deeply respected one another's work for over twenty years. But some of Kant's own students had been urging him to enter the dispute on the other side, since they saw Mendelssohn's rational theology as contrary to critical principles and regarded Jacobi's moral faith as fundamentally continuous with Kantian principles. For the same reason, it was also apparently Jacobi's expectation that Kant would agree with him rather than with Mendelssohn.

After the publication of *To Lessing's Friends,* Jacobi defended his position in *Against Mendelssohn's Imputations in His Writing to Lessing's Friends*

(Leipzig, 1786). He protested that his aim had never been to accuse Lessing but rather to praise the integrity and consistency of his rationalism. In reply to the charge of "enthusiasm," Jacobi quoted passages from Kant's *Critique of Pure Reason*, denying the possibility of theoretical cognition of God and recommending instead an attitude of moral faith; he argued that the *Critique* expressed the same views as his own, and hence that he could no more be charged with "enthusiasm" than could the great *Aufklärer* of Königsberg.

Kant's reaction to Jacobi's position, and to Jacobi himself, was, however, anything but favorable. In April 1786, Kant wrote to Herz that the whole controversy "is nothing serious; it is only an affected *enthusiasm of genius* trying to make a name for itself"; but then added tantalizingly that he might write an essay for the *Berlinische Monatschrift* exposing the "humbug" (*Gaukelwerk*) (AK 10:442–3).

In June, Biester again appealed to Kant to join the controversy in opposition to Jacobi's "enthusiasm." In the meantime, in May, there had appeared a thoughtful defense of Jacobi's position: *Results of the Jacobian and Mendelssohnian Philosophy by a Volunteer* (Leipzig, 1786). Its author was Thomas Wizenmann, a young philosopher still in his twenties, who was to live only a year longer, and to whose criticisms of his views on moral faith Kant – with respect – replied in the *Critique of Practical Reason* (AK 5:143n). It may have been Wizenmann's intervention, more than anything else, that prompted Kant finally to address the issues between Jacobi and Mendelssohn, since Wizenmann went beyond Jacobi, holding in effect that healthy common sense itself was a function of religious faith and ultimately of revelation. This shifted the focus of the discussion, taking a position more directly opposed to Kant's on an issue that put Kant and Mendelssohn squarely in the same camp.

In the "Orientation" essay, published in October 1786, Kant did indeed take Mendelssohn's side in the controversy. He seized on Mendelssohn's idea, presented in the *Morning Hours*, of an "orientation" of philosophical speculation through rational common sense, reinterpreting this concept to accord with Kant's own doctrine that the shortcomings of theoretical speculation must be made good through rational faith on moral grounds. And Kant concurred in Mendelssohn's hostility to Jacobi's conception of faith regarding it, as a dangerous form of enthusiasm that denied the absolute authority of reason in matters of belief. The concluding pages of the "Orientation" essay also bring out an ominous *political* dimension to the controversy. Frederick the Great, the protector of Enlightenment, had died in August 1786; with the expected accession of Frederick William II, Kant could already see a troubled time ahead for all those who valued freedom of thought and rational inquiry in religious matters – and this, Kant insisted, must include not only philosophers such as Mendelssohn and himself, but also Jacobi and his supporters, whose lawless freedom to believe as inspiration prompted them would certainly place them among the earliest victims of repressive orthodoxy. The threat of this repression is implicit in the concluding paragraph's ardent plea for Jacobi and his friends not to abandon the cause of reason in its hour of peril.

Jacobi's disappointment with the "Orientation" essay seems to have led to a fateful redirection of his critical talents. Jacobi's attitude toward Kant was always ambivalent, and even his later writings praised Kant while criticizing him. But Jacobi had wanted to emphasize the continuity between their positions, especially on issues of faith and reason. In the "Orientation" essay, however, Jacobi found criticism not only of himself but also of great philosophers such as Leibniz and Spinoza, criticism which he regarded as unfair and founded on misunderstanding. From this point on, Jacobi's criticism of systematic philosophy focused on the argument that Kantian criticism is afflicted with internal inconsistencies regarding the "thing in itself" and leads inevitably to a skepticism even more corrosive than that to which it seeks to reply. These charges were first brought against Kant in Jacobi's *David Hume* (1787), but later they were turned against Fichte, whom Jacobi regarded as the most radical and dangerous of the Kantians. Jacobi's criticism of Kantian philosophy was extremely influential in determining its form during the 1790s and beyond.

The "Orientation" essay has been previously translated into English three times. The first translation was by John Richardson, a student of Jakob Sigismund Beck; it appeared in *Essays and Treatises on Moral, Political and Various Philosophical Subjects, by Emanuel Kant*, 2 volumes (London: William Richardson, 1798–9). The second translation was by Lewis White Beck in *Immanuel Kant, Critique of Practical Reason and other writings on moral philosophy* (Chicago: University of Chicago Press, 1949; reprinted: New York: Garland, 1976), pp. 293–305. The most recent translation is by H. B. Nisbet, in H. Reiss (ed.), *Kant's Political Writings*, second enlarged edition (Cambridge: Cambridge University Press, 1991), pp. 237–49.

What does it mean to orient oneself in thinking?

However exalted the application of our concepts, and however far up from sensibility we may abstract them, still they will always be appended to *image* representations,[a] whose proper function[b] is to make these concepts, which are not otherwise derived from experience, serviceable for *experiential use.* For how would we procure sense and significance for our concepts if we did not underpin them with some intuition (which ultimately must always be an example from some possible experience)? If from this concrete act of the understanding we leave out the association of the image – in the first place an accidental perception through the senses – then what is left over is the pure concept of understanding, whose range is now enlarged and contains a rule for thinking in general. It is in just such a way that general logic comes about; and many *heuristic* methods of thinking perhaps lie hidden in the experiential use of our understanding and reason; if we carefully extract these methods from that experience, they could well enrich philosophy with many useful maxims even in abstract thinking.

Of this kind is the principle to which the late Mendelssohn expressly subscribed for the first time, so far as I know, in his last writings (the *Morning Hours,* pp. 164–165 and the *Letters to Lessing's Friends,* pp. 33 and 67):[1] namely, the maxim that it is necessary to orient oneself in the speculative use of reason (which Mendelssohn otherwise trusted very much in respect of the cognition of supersensible objects, even so far as claiming for it the evidence of demonstration) by means of a certain guideline which he sometimes called *common sense* or *healthy reason* (in the *Morning Hours*), and sometimes *plain[c] understanding* (*To Lessing's Friends*). Who would have thought that this admission would not only have a destructive effect on his favorable opinion of the power of *speculative* reason when used in theological matters (which was in fact unavoidable), but that even common healthy reason, given the ambiguous position in which he left the employment of this faculty in contrast to speculation, would also fall into

[a] *bildliche Vorstellungen*
[b] *Bestimmung*
[c] *schlicht*

7

the danger of serving as a principle of enthusiasm in the dethroning of reason? And yet this happened in the controversy between Mendelssohn and Jacobi, chiefly through the not insignificant inferences of the acute author of the *Results;** even though I do not ascribe to either of the two the intention of bringing such a destructive way of thinking into currency; rather I prefer to regard the latter's*d* undertaking as an *argumentum ad hominem,e* which one is justified in using merely as a defensive weapon, so as to use one's opponent's vulnerabilities to his disadvantage. On the other hand, I will show that it was in fact *only* reason – not any alleged sense of truth, not any transcendent intuition under the name of faith, on which tradition and revelation can be grafted without reason's consent – which Mendelssohn affirmed, staunchly and with justified zeal; it was only that genuine pure human reason which he found necessary and recommended as a means of orientation. Yet here the high claims of reason's speculative faculty, chiefly its commanding authority (through demonstration), obviously falls away, and what is left to it, insofar as it is speculative, is only the task of purifying the common concept of reason of its contradictions, and defending it against its *own* sophistical attacks on the maxims of healthy reason. – The extended and more precisely determined concept of *orienting oneself* can be helpful to us in presenting distinctly the maxims healthy reason uses in working on its cognitions of supersensible objects.

In the proper meaning*f* of the word, to *orient* oneself means to use a given direction*g* (when we divide the horizon into four of them) in order to find the others – literally, to find the *sunrise*. Now if I see the sun in the sky and know it is now midday, then I know how to find south, west, north, and east. For this, however, I also need the feeling of a difference in my own subject, namely, the difference between my right and left hands. I call this a *feeling* because these two sides outwardly display no designatable difference*h* in intuition. If I did not have this faculty of distinguishing, without the need of any difference in the objects, between moving from left to right and right to left and moving in the opposite direction and thereby determining *a priori* a difference in the position of the objects, then in describing a circle I would not know whether west was right or left

8:135

---

* Jacobi, *Letters on the Doctrine of Spinoza.* Breslau, 1785. – Jacobi, *Against Mendelssohn's Imputations Regarding the Letters on the Doctrine of Spinoza.* Leipzig, 1786. – *The Results of the Jacobian and Mendelssohnian Philosophy Critically Investigated by a Volunteer* (ibid.).[2]
d i.e. Wizenmann, who in the *Results* had accused Mendelssohn, in his appeal to "healthy reason," of relying as much as Jacobi on religious faith.
e argument directed to the man
f Bedeutung
g Gegend
h keinen merklichen Unterschied

of the southernmost point of the horizon, or whether I should complete the circle by moving north and east and thus back to south. Thus even with all the objective data of the sky, I orient myself *geographically* only through a *subjective* ground of differentiation; and if all the constellations, though keeping the same shape and position relative to one another, were one day by a miracle to be reversed in their direction, so that what was east now became west, no human eye would notice the slightest alteration on the next bright starlit night, and even the astronomer – if he pays attention only to what he sees and not at the same time to what he feels – would inevitably become *disoriented*. But in fact the faculty of making distinctions through the feeling of right and left comes naturally to his aid – it is a faculty implanted by nature but made habitual through frequent practice. If only he fixes his eye on the Pole Star, he will be able not only to notice the alteration which has taken place, but in spite of it he will also be able to *orient* himself.

Now I can extend this geographical concept of the procedure of orienting oneself, and understand by it orienting oneself in any given space in general, hence orienting oneself merely *mathematically*. In the dark I orient myself in a room that is familiar to me if I can take hold of even one single object whose position I remember. But it is plain that nothing helps me here except the faculty for determining position according to a *subjective* ground of differentiation: for I do not see at all the objects[i] whose place I am to find; and if someone as a joke had moved all the objects around so that what was previously on the right was now on the left, I would be quite unable to find anything in a room whose walls were otherwise wholly identical. But I can soon orient myself through the mere feeling of a difference between my two sides, the right and left. That is just what happens if I am to walk and take the correct turns on streets otherwise familiar to me when I cannot right now distinguish any of the houses.   8:136

Finally, I can extend this concept even further, since it could be taken as consisting in the faculty of orienting myself not merely in space, i.e. mathematically, but in *thinking* in general, i.e. *logically*. By analogy, one can easily guess that it will be a concern of pure reason to guide its use when it wants to leave familiar objects (of experience) behind, extending itself beyond all the bounds of experience and finding no object[j] of intuition at all, but merely space for intuition; for then it is no longer in a position to bring its judgments under a determinate maxim according to objective grounds of cognition, but solely to bring its judgments under a determinate maxim according to a subjective ground of differentiation in the

i Objecte
j Object

9

determination of its own faculty of judgment.* This subjective means still remaining is nothing other than reason's feeling of its own need. One can remain safe from all error if one does not undertake to judge where one does not know what is required for a determinate judgment. Thus ignorance is in itself the cause of the limitations of our cognition, but not of the errors in it. But where it is not arbitrary*ᵐ* whether or not one will judge determinately, where there is some actual *need* – and moreover one attaching to reason in itself – which makes it necessary to judge, and yet we are limited by a lack of knowledge in respect of factors which are necessary for the judgment, there it is necessary to have a maxim according to which we may pass our judgment; for reason will be satisfied. For if it has been previously made out that here there can be no intuition of objectsⁿ or anything of the kind through which we can present a suitable object to our extended concepts and hence secure a real possibility for them, then there is nothing left for us to do except first to examine the concept with which we would venture to go beyond all possible experience to see if it is free of contradiction, and then at least to bring the *relation* of the object to objects of experience under pure concepts of the understanding – through which we still do not render it sensible, but we do at least think of something supersensible in a way which is serviceable to the experiential use of our reason. For without this caution we would be unable to make any use at all of such concepts; instead of thinking we would indulge in enthusiasm.

8:137

Yet through this, namely through the mere concept, nothing is settled in respect of the existence of this object and its actual connection with the world (the sum total of all objects of possible experience). But now there enters *the right* of reason's *need,* as a subjective ground for presupposing and assuming something which reason may not presume to know through objective grounds; and consequently for *orienting* itself in thinking, solely through reason's own need, in that immeasurable space of the supersensible, which for us is filled with darkᵒ night.

Many supersensible things may be thought (for objects of sense do not fill up the whole field of possibility) to which, however, reason feels no need to extend itself, much less to assume their existence. In the causes of the world, reason finds enough to keep it busy with those which are revealed by sense (or at least are of the same kind as those which reveal themselves to it), without having any necessity to make use of the influence of pure

---

* Thus to *orient* oneself in thinking in general means: when objective principlesᵏ of reason are insufficient for holding something true, to determine the matter according to a subjective principle.ˡ

ᵏ *Principien*

ˡ *Princip*

ᵐ *willkürlich*

ⁿ *Objecte*

ᵒ *dicker*

10

spiritual beings in nature; the assumption of these spiritual beings would rather be disadvantageous to the use of reason. For since we know nothing of the laws according to which they would operate, whereas we know – or at least we can hope to find out – a lot about the others, namely the objects of the senses, presupposing them would rather violate the use of reason. Thus that is not a need at all, but merely impertinent inquisitiveness straying into empty dreaming to investigate them – or play with such figments of the brain. It is quite otherwise with the concept of a first *original being* as a supreme intelligence and at the same time as the highest good. For not only does our reason already feel a need to take the *concept* of the unlimited as the ground of the concepts of all limited beings – hence of all other things* – ,   8:138
but this need even goes as far as the presupposition of its *existence,* without which one can provide no satisfactory ground at all for the contingency of the existence of things in the world, let alone for the purposiveness and order which is encountered everywhere in such a wondrous degree (in the small, because it is close to us, even more than in the large). Without assuming an intelligent author we cannot give any *intelligible ground* of it

---

* Since reason needs to presuppose reality as given for the possibility of all things, and considers the differences between things only as limitations arising through the negations attaching to them, it sees itself necessitated to take as a ground one single possibility, namely that of an unlimited being, to consider it as original and all others as derived. Since also the thoroughgoing possibility of every thing must be encountered within existence as a whole – or at least since this is the only way in which the principle of thoroughgoing determination makes it possible for our reason to distinguish between the possible and the actual – we find a subjective ground of necessity, i.e. a need in our reason itself to take the existence of a most real (highest) being as the ground of all possibility. Now this is how the Cartesian proof of God's existence arises, since subjective grounds for presupposing something for the use of reason (which always remains a ground only within an experiential use) is taken to be objective – hence *need is taken for insight.* Just as it is here, so it is also with all the proofs of the worthy Mendelssohn in his *Morning Hours.* They accomplish nothing by way of demonstration. But they are not for that reason by any means useless. For not to mention the fine occasion which such acute developments of the subjective conditions of the use of our reason provides for the complete cognition of this faculty of ours, of which they are lasting examples, a holding of something true on subjective grounds of the use of reason – if we lack objective ones and are nevertheless necessitated to judge – is always of great importance; only we must not give out what is in fact only a necessary *presupposition* as if it were a *free insight;* otherwise we needlessly offer the opponent with whom we are *arguing dogmatically* weaknesses which he can use to our disadvantage. Mendelssohn probably did not think about the fact that *arguing dogmatically* with pure reason in the field of the supersensible is the direct path to philosophical enthusiasm, and that only a critique of this same faculty of reasons can fundamentally remedy this ill. Of course, the discipline of the scholastic method (the Wolffian, for example, which he recommended for this reason) can actually hold back this mischief for a long time, since all concepts must be determined through definitions and all steps must be justified through principles; but that will by no means wholly get rid of it. For with what right will anyone prohibit reason – once it has, by his own admission, achieved success in this field – from going still farther in it? And where then is the boundary at which it must stop?

8:139

without falling into plain absurdities; and although we cannot *prove* the impossibility of such a purposiveness apart from an *intelligent cause* (for then we would have sufficient objective grounds for asserting it and would not need to appeal to subjective ones), given our lack of insight there yet remains a sufficient ground for *assuming* such a cause in reason's *need* to presuppose something intelligible in order to explain this given appearance, since nothing else with which reason can combine any concept provides a remedy for this need.

But one can regard the need of reason as twofold: *first* in its *theoretical*, second in its *practical* use. The first need I have just mentioned; but one sees very well that it is only conditioned, i.e. we must assume the existence of God *if* we *want to judge* about the first causes of everything contingent, chiefly in the order of ends which is actually present in the world. Far more important is the need of reason in its practical use, because it is unconditioned, and we are necessitated to presuppose the existence of God not only if we *want* to judge, but because we *have to judge*. For the pure practical use of reason consists in the precepts of moral laws. They all lead, however, to the idea of the *highest good* possible in the world insofar as it is possible only through *freedom: morality;*[p] from the other side, these precepts lead to what depends not merely on human freedom but also on *nature*, which is the greatest *happiness*, insofar as it is apportioned according to the first. Now reason *needs* to assume, for the sake of such a *dependent* highest good, a supreme intelligence as the highest *independent* good; not, of course, to derive from this assumption the binding authority of moral precepts or the incentives to observe them (for they would have no moral worth if their motive were derived from anything but the law alone, which is of itself[q] apodictically certain), but rather only in order to give objective reality to the concept of the highest good, i.e. to prevent it, along with morality, from being taken merely as a mere ideal, as it would be if that whose idea inseparably accompanies morality[r] should not exist anywhere.

8:140

Thus it is not *cognition* but a felt* *need* of reason through which Mendelssohn (without knowing it) oriented himself in speculative thinking. And since this guiding thread is not an objective principle[s] of reason, a principle of insight, but a merely subjective one (i.e. a maxim) of the only use of reason allowed by its limits – a corollary of its need – and since *by*

---

* Reason does not feel; it has insight into its lack and through the *drive for cognition* it effects the feeling of a need. It is the same way with moral feeling, which does not cause any moral law, for this arises wholly from reason; rather, it is caused or effected by moral laws, hence by reason, because the active yet free will needs determinate grounds.

[p] *Sittlichkeit*

[q] *für sich*

[r] *Moralität*

[s] *Princip*

itself alone' it constitutes the whole determining ground of our judgment about the existence of the highest being, and its use as a means of orientation in attempts to speculate on this same subject is only contingent, so Mendelssohn erred here in that he nevertheless trusted speculation to the extent of letting it alone settle everything on the path of demonstration. The necessity of the first means could be established only if the insufficiency of the latter is fully admitted: an admission to which his acuteness would ultimately have brought him if he had been granted, along with a longer life, also that application of mind, found more often in youth, which permits the alteration of old, habitual ways of thinking to accord with alterations in the state of the sciences. In any case, he retains the merit of insisting that the final touchstone of the reliability of judgment is to be sought in *reason alone,* whether in the choice of its propositions it is guided by insight or mere need and the maxim of what is advantageous to reason itself. He called reason in its latter use "common human reason"; for this always has its own interest before its eyes, whereas one must have left the course of nature behind if one is to forget this interest and look around idly among concepts from an objective viewpoint, merely so as to extend one's knowledge, whether or not it is necessary.

Since, however, in the question before us the expression: *pronouncement of healthy reason* always remains ambiguous and can always be taken either – as Mendelssohn himself misunderstood it – for a judgment of *rational insight* or – as the author of the *Results* appears to take it – for a judgment from *rational inspiration,* it will be necessary to give this source of judging another name, and none is more suitable than **rational belief or faith."** Every belief, even the historical, must of course be *rational* (for the final touchstone of truth is always reason); only a rational belief or faith is one grounded on no data other than those contained in *pure* reason. All believing is a holding true which is subjectively sufficient, but *consciously* regarded as objectively insufficient; thus it is contrasted with *knowing.* On the other hand, when something is held true on objective though consciously insufficient grounds, and hence is merely *opinion,* this *opining* can gradually be supplemented by the same kind of grounds and finally become a *knowing.* By contrast, if the grounds of holding true are of a kind that cannot be objectively valid at all, then the belief can never become a knowing through any use of reason. Historical belief, e.g., of the death of a great man, as reported in some letters, *can become a knowing* if his burial, testament, etc. are announced by the local authorities. Hence what is held true historically based on mere testimony – e.g. that somewhere in the world there is a city of Rome – can be believed, and yet someone who has never been there can say *I know* and not merely *I believe*

8:141

' *für sich allein*
" *Vernunftglaubens*

13

that Rome exists – these can very well be compatible. By contrast, pure *rational faith* can never be transformed into knowledge by any natural data of reason and experience, because here the ground of holding true is merely subjective, namely a necessary need of reason (and as long as we are human beings it will always remain a need) to *presuppose* the existence of a highest being, but not to demonstrate it. A need of reason to be used in a way which satisfies it *theoretically* would be nothing other than a pure *rational hypothesis,* i.e. an opinion sufficient to hold something true on subjective grounds simply because one can never expect to find grounds other than these on which to *explain certain given effects,* and because reason needs a ground of explanation. By contrast, *rational faith,* which rests on a need of reason's use with a *practical* intent, could be called a *postulate* of reason – not as if it were an insight which did justice to all the logical demands for certainty, but because this holding true (if only the person is morally good) is not inferior* in degree to knowing, even though

8:142 it is completely different from it in kind.

A pure rational faith is therefore the signpost or compass by means of which the speculative thinker orients himself in his rational excursions into the field of supersensible objects; but a human being who has common but (morally) healthy reason can mark out his path, in both a theoretical and a practical respect, in a way which is fully in accord with the whole end of his vocation; and it is this rational faith which must also be taken as the ground of every other faith, and even of every revelation.

The *concept* of God and even the conviction of his *existence* can be met with only in reason, and it cannot first come to us either through inspiration or through tidings communicated to us, however great the authority behind them. If I come across an immediate intuition of such a kind that nature, as I am acquainted with it, could not provide that intuition, then a concept of God must serve to gauge whether this appearance agrees with all the characteristics required for a Deity. Now even if I have no insight at all into how it is possible for any appearance to present, even as to quality, what can only be thought but never intuited, this much is still clear: that in order to judge whether what appears to me, what works internally or externally on my feelings, is God, I would have to hold it up to my rational concept of God and test it accordingly – not as to whether it is adequate to that concept, but merely whether it does not contradict it. In just the same way, even if nothing in what he discovered to me immediately contra-

---

* To the *firmness* of belief belongs the consciousness of its *unalterability.* Now I can be wholly certain that no one can ever refute the proposition *There is a God;* for where will he get this insight? Thus it is not the same with rational faith as with historical belief – where it is always possible that proofs of the contrary might be found out and where one must always harbor the reservation that one might alter one's opinion if our information about the matter should be extended.

dicted that concept, nevertheless this appearance, intuition, immediate revelation, or whatever else one wants to call such a presentation, never proves the existence of a being whose concept (if it is not to be vaguely^v determined and hence might be subject to association with every possible delusion) demands that it be of *infinite* magnitude as distinguished from everything created; but no experience or intuition at all can be adequate to that concept, hence none can unambiguously prove the existence of such a being. Thus no one can *first* be convinced of the existence of a highest being through any intuition; rational faith must come first, and then certain appearances or disclosures could at most provide the occasion for investigating whether we are warranted in taking what speaks or presents itself to us to be a Deity, and thus serve to confirm that faith according to these findings.   8:143

Thus if it is disputed that reason deserves the right to speak *first* in matters concerning supersensible objects such as the existence of God and the future world, then a wide gate is opened to all enthusiasm, superstition and even to atheism. And yet in the controversy between Jacobi and Mendelssohn, everything appears to overturn reason in just this way; I do not know whether it is directed only against *rational insight* and knowledge (through the supposed strength of speculation) or also against *rational faith*, so as to set up in opposition to it another faith which everyone can make up for himself as he likes. One would almost infer the latter intention when it is proposed that the Spinozist concept of God is the only one in agreement* with all the principles of reason and is never-   8:144

---

* It is hard to comprehend how the scholars just mentioned could find support for Spinozism in the *Critique of Pure Reason*.[3] The *Critique* completely clips dogmatism's wings in respect of the cognition of supersensible objects, and Spinozism is so dogmatic in this respect that it even competes with the mathematicians in respect of the strictness of its proofs. The *Critique* proves that the table of the pure concepts of the understanding has to contain all the material for pure thinking; Spinozism speaks of thoughts which themselves think, and thus of an accident that simultaneously exists for itself as a subject:[4] a concept that is not to be found in the human understanding and moreover cannot be brought into it. The *Critique* shows it does not suffice for the possibility even of a thought-entity that there is nothing self-contradictory in its concept (even though of course it then remains allowable, if necessary, to assume its possibility); but Spinozism alleges that it has insight into the impossibility of a being the idea of which consists solely of pure concepts of the understanding, which has been separated from all the conditions of sensibility, and in which a contradiction can never be met with;[5] and yet it has nothing at all by means of which to support this presumption, which transgresses all boundaries. It is just for this reason that Spinozism leads directly to enthusiasm. By contrast, there is not a single means more certain to eliminate enthusiasm from the roots up than that determination of the bounds of the pure faculty of understanding. – Likewise another scholar[6] finds *skepticism* in the *Critique*, even though precisely the starting point of the *Critique* is firmly to posit something certain and determinate in respect of the range of our cognition a priori. Similarly [he finds] a *dialectic* in the critical investigations, whereas the aim is to resolve and forever eliminate the unavoid-
^{v} *unsicher*

15

theless to be rejected.[8] For although it is wholly compatible with rational faith to concede that speculative reason itself is never in a position to have insight into the *possibility* of the being we must think of as God, it can't be reconciled with any faith, or with the holding true of any existence at all, to say that we could see clearly*ᵂ* the *impossibility* of an object and nevertheless could have cognition of its actuality through other sources.

Men of intellectual ability and broadminded disposition! I honor your talents and love your feeling for humanity. But have you thought about what you are doing, and where your attacks on reason will lead? Without doubt you want to preserve inviolate the *freedom to think;* for without that even your own free flights of genius would soon come to an end. Let us see what would naturally become of this freedom of thought if a procedure such as you are adopting should get the upper hand.

The freedom to think is opposed **first** of all to *civil compulsion.* Of course it is said that the freedom to *speak* or to *write* could be taken from us by a superior power, but the freedom to *think* cannot be. Yet how much and how correctly would we *think* if we did not think as it were in community with others to whom we *communicate* our thoughts, and who communicate theirs with us! Thus one can very well say that this external power which wrenches away people's freedom publicly to *communicate* their thoughts also takes from them the freedom to *think* – that single gem remaining to us in the midst of all the burdens of civil life, through which alone we can devise means of overcoming all the evils of our condition.

8:145 **Second,** freedom to think is also taken in a sense*ˣ* in which it is opposed to *compulsion over conscience;* even without having external power some citizens set themselves up as having the custody of others in religious affairs, and instead of arguing they know how to ban every examination of reason by their early influence on people's minds, through prescribed formulas of belief accompanied by the anxious fear of *the dangers of one's own investigation.*

Third, freedom in thinking signifies the subjection of reason to no laws except *those which it gives itself;* and its opposite is the maxim of a **lawless use** of reason (in order, as genius supposes, to see further than one can under the limitation of laws). The natural consequence is that if reason will not subject itself to the laws it gives itself, it has to bow under the yoke of laws given by another; for without any law, nothing – not even nonsense – can play its game for long. Thus the unavoidable consequence

able dialectic in which pure reason becomes involved and entangled when it is employed dogmatically everywhere. The Neoplatonists, who called themselves "eclectics" because they knew how to find their own conceits all over the place in other authors – if they had previously put them in there – proceeded in just this way; hence nothing new happens under the sun.[7]

ᵂ einsehen

ˣ Bedeutung

of *declared* lawlessness in thinking (of a liberation from the limitations of reason) is that the freedom to think will ultimately be forfeited and – because it is not misfortune but arrogance which is to blame for it – will be *trifled away*[y] in the proper sense of the word.

The course of things is roughly this. First *genius* is very pleased with its bold flights, since it has cast off the thread by which reason used to steer it. Soon it enchants others with its triumphant pronouncements and great expectations and now seems to have set itself on a throne which was so badly graced by slow and ponderous reason, whose language, however, it always employs. Then its maxim is that reason's superior lawgiving is invalid – we common human beings call this **enthusiasm,** while those favored by beneficent nature call its *illumination.* Since reason alone can command validly for everyone, a confusion of language must soon arise among them; each one now follows his own inspiration, and so inner inspirations must ultimately be seen to arise from the testimony of pre-served facts, traditions which were chosen originally but with time become *intrusive* documents – in a word, what results is the complete subjection of reason to facts, i.e. **superstition,** because this at least has the *form of law* and so allows tranquility to be restored.

Because, however, human reason always strives for freedom, when it first breaks its fetters the first use it makes of its long unaccustomed freedom has to degenerate into a misuse and a presumptuous trust in the independence of its faculties from all limitations, leading to a persuasion of the sole authority of speculative reason which assumes nothing except what it can justify by *objective* grounds and dogmatic conviction; everything else it boldly repudiates. Now the maxim of reason's independence of its *own need* (of doing without rational faith) is **unbelief.** This is not a histori-cal unbelief, for it is impossible to think of the latter as purposeful, hence it cannot be anything imputable (for everyone must believe a fact if it is sufficiently attested, just as he must believe a mathematical demonstra-tion, whether he wants to or not). It is rather an *unbelief of reason,*[z] a precarious[a] state of the human mind, which first takes from moral laws all their force as incentives to the heart, and over time all their authority, and occasions the way of thinking one calls **libertinism,**[b] i.e. **the principle of recognizing no duty at all.** At this point the authorities get mixed up in the game, so that even civil arrangements may not fall into the greatest disor-der; and since they regard the most efficient and emphatic means as the best, this does away with even the freedom to think, and subjects thinking,

8:146

---

[y] *verscherzt. Sich etwas verscherzen,* derived from *Scherz* = joke, means frivolously to lose or forfeit something.
[z] *Vernunftunglaube*
[a] *misslich*
[b] *Freigeisterei*

like other trades, to the country's rules and regulations. And so freedom in thinking finally destroys itself if it tries to proceed in independence of the laws of reason.

Friends of the human race and of what is holiest to it! Accept^c what appears to you most worthy of belief after careful and sincere examination, whether of facts or rational grounds; only do not dispute that prerogative of reason which makes it the highest good on earth, the prerogative of being the final touchstone of truth.* Failing here, you will become unworthy of this freedom, and you will surely forfeit it too; and besides that you will bring the same misfortune down on the heads of other, innocent parties who would otherwise have been well disposed and would have used their freedom *lawfully* and hence in a way which is conducive^d to what is best for the world!

---

* *Thinking for oneself* means seeking the supreme touchstone of truth in oneself (i.e. in one's own reason); and the maxim of always thinking for oneself is **enlightenment**. Now there is less to this than people imagine when they place enlightenment in the acquisition of *information;* for it is rather a negative principle in the use of one's faculty of cognition, and often he who is richest in information is the least enlightened in the use he makes of it. To make use of one's own reason means no more than to ask oneself, whenever one is supposed to assume something, whether one could find it feasible to make the ground or the rule on which one assumes it into a universal principle for the use of reason. This test is one that everyone can apply to himself; and with this examination he will see superstition and enthusiasm disappear, even if he falls far short of having the information to refute them on objective grounds. For he is using merely the maxim of reason's *self-preservation.* Thus it is quite easy to ground enlightenment in *individual subjects* through their education; one must only begin early to accustom young minds to this reflection. But to enlighten an *age* is very slow and arduous; for there are external obstacles which in part forbid this manner of education and in part make it more difficult.

^{c} *Nehme . . . an*

^{d} *zweckmässig*

18

On the miscarriage of all philosophical trials
in theodicy

Translator's introduction

This essay, "Über das Mißlingen aller philosophischen Versuche in der Theodicee," was first published in the *Berlinische Monatsschrift,* September 1791, 194–225. In a letter dated December 29, 1789, to its editor Johann Erich Biester, Kant had expressed his intention to contribute to the journal. In the letter, Kant had added: "I now have, however, a work of just about a month to complete. . . ."[a] Once that work, (undoubtedly the *Critique of Judgment*) had been completed, he planned to fill the time with some compositions perhaps suitable to Biester's journal. The present essay apparently represents the fulfillment of that plan.

It is difficult to state with certainty, for lack of any explicit statement on the part of Kant, what motivated him to write the essay. We know that it was the first of a series of writings on theological and religious matters (all published in this volume) that occupied Kant after the accession to the throne in Prussia of the reactionary Frederick William II.[b] That in writing the essay Kant was preoccupied by the repressive policies pursued by the new regime is clear from at least two places. The first is a passage (AK, 266) where Kant claims that Job would have stood little chance if judged before a synod or any other public body, "one alone excepted." The exception is obviously the Berlin High Consistory, a church tribunal still staffed by enlightened clerics who had been appointed to their posts prior to the new administration and were now obstructing the actions of the new minister of education and religious affairs, J. C. Wöllner. Kant's otherwise unintelligible qualification to his general statement is his vote of support for their resistance to the new oppressive regime.

The second place is the concluding remark appended to the essay, where Kant offers a series of reflections on the subject of "sincerity" and "professions of faith." The obvious background for these reflections is the 1790 edict requiring that candidates in theology be tested by means of a formal profession of faith – not only for their knowledge of Christian doctrine but also for their adherence. Kant's stated position in his reflections is that enlightened education and the self-discipline that freedom from external constraints alone can nurture will hopefully raise, in some

[a] AK 11:117
[b] For the historical details, and new constraints imposed on free thought, see the introduction to this volume and to *Religion within the Boundaries of Mere Reason.*

distant future, society's general level of sincerity. Obligatory professions of faith are counterproductive because they feed on the all-too-human propensity to self-deception and hence foster "a certain falsehood in a community's very way of thinking," especially when personal gain is at issue. Yet Kant concedes that, in the present spiritual state of society, the demand for such professions can be justified. In a long footnote (AK 8:268), he explains that, because of the real possibility of deception, it is fair under certain circumstances to submit citizens to the trial of "oath taking." In such trials, the sincerity of a profession of faith is tested by forcing the declarer to make the profession on the explicit admission that there *might* be a future judge of the world to whom the declarer will eventually have to answer. But, Kant adds, trials of this kind cannot be used when the professions extorted would entail a speculative commitment (such as that God exists) that in fact transcends theoretical insight and that therefore nobody could declare with a clear conscience. Such trials are permissible only when the source of the professions is "historical," i.e. (as Kant presumably means) only when a profession is directed to beliefs based on tradition and authority. The professions mandated by Wöllner with the 1790 edict clearly fell within this category. Kant's footnote can be read, therefore, as an attempt on his part to rationalize and excuse the edict. But it can equally be taken as an exercise in damage control. For Wöllner's intention was to reassert and protect from attacks the truth of ecclesiastical dogma, whereas Kant, by allowing that such dogma could indeed be the legitimate object of public professions of belief, was thereby implying that it had no theoretical content – that it was not "true" in any relevant sense, even though it could well have consequences so far as social discipline is concerned. While condoning the 1790 edict, Kant was in fact blunting its intended effect.

Against this politico-religious background, Kant's essay appears as an object lesson on the hypocrisy of those who, while pretending to uphold the cause of God, in fact use God to promote their own natural interests. But the essay can also be seen in another, more academic context. The essay was composed immediately after the *Critique of Judgment*, a work in part motivated by Kant's desire to meet the widely accepted criticisms moved from various quarters against his moral doctrine. It had been objected that, its unfortunate formalism apart, there was nothing new in this doctrine, since it made rationality of intention the fundamental criterion of conduct – a position to which no refined eudaemonist would want to object.ᶜ Even more effective had been Rehberg's denial that the idea of

---

ᶜ Examples of this eudaemonist reaction are J. G. H. Feder's review of Kant's *Groundwork of a Metaphysics of Morals*, in *Göttingische Anzeigen von gelehrten Sachen*, 3.172(1785), pp. 1739–44, and H. A. Pistorius' review of the same work in *Allgemeine Deutsche Bibliothek*, 66.2 (1786), pp. 447–63.

the law, though constituting the formal principle of morality as Kant had claimed, could by itself be an effective rule of conduct unless accompanied by other, more natural incentives.[d] In the context of these criticisms, the essay can be read as a figurative vindication of the effectiveness of Kant's moral principle despite its avowed formalism. Job can offer no reasons that would explain his unhappy situation. Yet, righteous man that he is, he stands by his undemonstrable inner conviction that in the eyes of God everything is as it ought to be. And at the end God justifies him. Just so with the idea of the law: Though empty of content so far as nature is concerned, it alone can generate a faith that promotes effective action in the world.

Whatever the motivation behind it, the essay is one of the more artistically successful pieces Kant ever produced. It was first translated into English by John Richardson, a student of Jakob Sigismund Beck. It was published in *Essays and Treatises on Moral, Political, and Various Philosophical Subjects, by Emanuel Kant*, 2 vols (London:[e] Printed for the Translator and Sold by William Richardson, 1798–99), Vol. 2, pp. 189–215, under the title, "On the Failure of All the Philosophical Essays in the Theodicée." I have checked the present translation against Richardson's and have adopted the occasional word and expression from it that I found especially apt. A more recent translation is included in Michel Despland's *Kant on History and Religion* (Montreal: McGill-Queen's, 1973), pp. 283–97, under the title "On the Failure of All Attempted Philosophical Theodicies."

---

[d] The most important document in this respect is August Wilhelm Rehberg's review of Kant's *Critique of Practical Reason*, in *Allgemeine Literatur-Zeitung*, Nr 188.a.b (August 6 1788), pp. 345–60. But Rehberg had already stated his position in *Über das Verhältniß der Metaphysik zur Religion* (Berlin: Mylius, 1787).

[e] Actually "printed in a remote part of Germany, where no better paper could possibly be got." Cf. Vol. 1, Preface, p. v, footnote. The place must have been Altenburg, where Richardson was employed in the household of the Count von Mühlen. Before leaving for Altenburg, Richardson had worked at his translations in Halle, as a guest of Professor Ludwig Heinrich Jacob from whom he received encouragement and clarification on difficult points. Jacob also acted as intermediary between Richardson and Kant. For the relevant documentation, see the following letters: May 10, 1797, AK 12:160; Sept. 8, 1797, AK 12:195–8; June 21, 1798, AK 12:242–3; and June 21, 1798, p. 244. Also AK 13:482. Of the title of his work, Richardson says: "Under the general title of *Essays* I have hidden much metaphysical material. Through this means I hope to stir my compatriots – as always still complacent in their empiricism – to study a better grounded and, in my humble opinion, the *one and only* well grounded philosophy." AK 12:242.

On the miscarriage of all philosophical trials[a] in theodicy

By "theodicy" we understand the defense of the highest wisdom of the creator against the charge which reason brings against it for whatever is counterpurposive[b] in the world. – We call this "the defending of God's cause," even though the cause might be at bottom no more than that of our presumptuous reason failing to recognize its limitations. This is indeed not the best of causes, yet one that can be condoned insofar as (aside from that self-conceit) the human being is justified, as rational, in testing all claims, all doctrines which impose respect upon him, before he submits himself to them, so that this respect may be sincere and not feigned.

Now for this vindication it is required that the would-be advocate of God prove *either* that whatever in the world we judge counterpurposive[c] is not so; *or*, if there is any such thing, that it must be judged not at all as an intended effect[d] but as the unavoidable consequence of the nature of things; *or*, finally, that it must at least be considered not as an intended effect[e] of the creator of all things but, rather, merely of those beings in the world to whom something can be imputed, i.e. of human beings (higher spiritual beings as well, good or evil, as the case may be).

The author of a theodicy agrees, therefore, that this juridical process be instituted before the tribunal of reason; he further consents to represent the accused side as advocate through the formal refutation of all the plaintiff's complaints; he is not therefore allowed to dismiss the latter in the course of the process of law through a decree of incompetency of the tribunal of human reason (*exceptio fori*),[f] i.e. he cannot dismiss the complaints with a concession of the supreme wisdom of the author of the world, imposed

upon the plaintiff, which would immediately explain away as groundless, even without examination, all doubts that might be raised against it; he must

---

[a] *Versuch:* a trial both in the sense of a scientific experiment and in the sense of putting somebody to the test.
[b] *das Zweckwidrige*
[c] *zweckwidrig*
[d] *Faktum.* The Latin *factum* literally means "something made or done."
[e] *Faktum*
[f] "An exception to the court," i.e., a challenge to the court's competence.

rather attend to the objections, and make comprehensible how they in no way derogate from the concept of the highest wisdom by clarifying and removing them.* – Yet there is one thing he need not attend to, namely a proof of God's wisdom from what the experience of this world teaches; for in this he would simply not succeed, since omniscience would be required to recognize in a given world (as gives itself to cognition in experience) that perfection of which we could say with certainty that absolutely none other is possible in creation and its government.

Now whatever is counterpurposive in the world, and may be opposed to the wisdom of its creator, is of a threefold kind:

I. The absolutely counterpurposive, or what cannot be condoned or desired either as end or means;

II. The conditionally counterpurposive, or what can indeed never co-exist with the wisdom of a will as end, yet can do so as means.

The *first* is the morally counterpurposive, evil proper[g] (sin); the *second,* the physically counterpurposive, ill[h] (pain). – But now, there still is a purposiveness[i] in the proportion of ill to moral evil, if the latter is once there, and neither can nor should be prevented – namely in the conjunction of ills and pains, as penalties, with evil, as crime. It is of this purposiveness in the world that one asks whether, in this respect, everyone in the world gets his due. Consequently, yet a   8:257

IIIrd kind of counterpurposiveness must be thinkable in the world, namely the disproportion between crimes and penalties in the world.   *punishment*

---

* Although the proper concept of *wisdom* represents only a will's property of being in agreement with the highest good as the *final end* of all things, whereas [the concept of] *art* represents only competence in the use of the suitable means toward *optional ends*, yet, when art proves itself adequate to ideas the possibility of which surpasses every insight of human reason (e.g. when means and ends reciprocally produce one another, as in organic bodies), as a *divine art,* it can also, not incorrectly, be given the name of wisdom – or rather, not to mix up concepts, the name of an *artistic wisdom* of the author of the world, in distinction from his *moral wisdom.* Teleology (and, through it, physicotheology) gives abundant proof in experience of this artistic wisdom. But from it no inference is allowed to the moral wisdom of the author of the world, for the natural law and the moral law require principles of entirely different kinds, and the demonstration of the latter wisdom must be carried out totally *a priori,* hence in no way be founded on the experience of what goes on in the world. Now since the concept of God suited to religion must be a concept of him as a moral being (for we have no need of him for natural explanation, hence for speculative purposes); and since this concept can just as little be derived from the mere transcendental concept of an absolutely necessary being – a concept that totally escapes us – as be founded on experience; so it is clear enough that the proof of the existence of such a being can be none other than a moral proof.

[g] *das eigentliche Böse*

[h] *Übel*

[i] *Zweckmäßigkeit*

The attributes of the world-author's supreme wisdom against which these [three kinds of] counterpurposiveness stand out as objections are, therefore, likewise three:

> First, the *holiness* of the author of the world, as *law-giver* (creator), in opposition to the moral evil in the world.
> Second, his *goodness*, as *ruler* (preserver), in contrast[j] with the countless ills and pains of the rational beings of the world.
> Third, his *justice*, as *judge*, in comparison to the bad state which the disproportion between the impunity of the depraved and their crimes seems to indicate in the world.*

8:258

The case against those three charges must be presented, therefore, along the three above mentioned kinds [of counterpurposiveness], and must be tested against their validity.

I. Against the complaint over the holiness of the divine will for the moral evil which disfigures the world, God's work, the first vindication consists in this:

a) There is no such thing as an absolute counterpurposiveness which we take the trespassing of the pure laws of our reason to be, but there are violations only against human wisdom; divine wisdom judges these accord-

---

* These three attributes, none of which can in any way be reduced to the others – as, for instance, justice to goodness, and so the whole to a smaller number – together constitute the moral concept of God. Nor can their order be altered (as by making benevolence, for instance, the supreme condition of world creation to which the holiness of legislation is subordinated) without doing violence to religion, which has this very concept for foundation. Our own pure (hence practical) reason determines this order of rank, for if legislation accommodated itself to benevolence, its dignity would no longer be there, nor a firm concept of duties. Indeed the human being wishes to be happy first; but then he sees, and (though reluctantly) accepts, that the worthiness to be happy, i.e. the conformity of the employment of his freedom with the holy law, must in God's decision be the condition of his benevolence, and must, therefore, necessarily precede it. For the wish that has the subjective end (self-love) for foundation cannot determine the objective end (of wisdom) prescribed by the law that unconditionally gives the will its rule. Moreover, punishment in the exercise of justice is founded in the legislating wisdom not at all as mere means but as an end: trespass is associated with ills not that some other good may result from it, but because this connection is good in itself, i.e. morally and necessarily good. Justice indeed presupposes the benevo-

8:258 lence of the legislator (for if his will were not directed to the well-being of his subjects, neither could he bind them under duty to obey him); yet justice is not goodness but rather essentially different from it, even though included in the general concept of wisdom. Hence also the lament over the lack of justice shown in the wrongs which are the lot of human beings here on earth is directed not at the *well-being* which does not befall the good, but at the *ill* which does not befall the evil (although, if well-being occurs to the evil, then the contrast makes the offence all the greater). For under divine rule even the best of human beings cannot found his wish to fare well on divine justice but must found it on God's beneficence, for one who only does what he owes[k] can have no rightful claim on God's benevolence.
[j] *Kontraste*
[k] *seine Schuldigkeit*

ing to totally different rules, incomprehensible to us, where, what we with right find reprehensible with reference to our practical reason and its determination might yet perhaps be in relation to the divine ends and the highest wisdom precisely the most fitting means to our particular welfare and the greatest good of the world as well; the ways of the most high are not our ways¹ (*sunt supris sua iura*),¹ and we err whenever we judge what is law only relatively to human beings in this life to be so absolutely, and thus hold what appears counterpurposive to our view of things from so lowly a standpoint to be such also when considered from the highest. – This apology, in which the vindication is worse than the complaint, needs no refutation; surely it can be freely given over to the detestation of every human being who has the least feeling for morality.

b) The second alleged vindication would indeed allow for the actuality of moral evil in the world, but it would excuse the author of the world on the ground that it could not be prevented, because founded upon the limitations of the nature of human beings, as finite. – However, the evil would thereby be justified, and, since it could not be attributed to human beings as something for which they are to be blamed, we would have to cease calling it "a moral evil."

8:259

c) The third rejoinder, that even conceding that it is really a matter of what we call moral evil, a guilt resting on the human being, yet no guilt may be ascribed to God, for God has merely tolerated it for just causes as a deed of human beings: in no way has he condoned it, willed or promoted it – this rejoinder incurs one and the same consequence as the previous apology (b) (even if we take no offense at the concept of a mere *tolerating* on the part of a being who is the one and sole creator of the world): namely, since even for God it was impossible to prevent this evil without doing violence to higher and even moral ends elsewhere, the ground of this ill (for so we must now truly call it) must inevitably be sought in the essence of things, specifically in the necessary limitations of humanity as a finite nature; hence the latter can also not be held responsible for it.

II. With respect to the complaint brought against divine goodness for the ills, namely the pains, in this world, its vindication equally consists

a) in this: It is false to assume in human fates a preponderance of ill over the pleasant enjoyment of life, for however bad someone's lot, yet everyone would rather live than be dead, and those few who opt for the latter, so long as they themeslves postpone it, thereby still confess to that preference; and if they are insane enough for it,ᵐ even then they simply pass over into the state of insensibility where pain as well cannot be felt. – But surely the reply to this sophistry may be left to the sentence of every human being of sound mind who has lived and pondered over the value of

---

¹ Those on high have their own laws.
ᵐ *zum letztern* (i.e., the "be dead" option)

life long enough to pass judgment, when asked, on whether he had any inclination to play the game of life once more, I do not say in the same circumstances but in any other he pleases (provided they are not of a fairy world but of this earthly world of ours).

8:260 b) To the second vindication – namely, the preponderance of painful feelings over pleasant ones cannot be separated from the nature of an animal creature such as the human being (in the vein of what Count Veri claims in his book on the nature of pleasure) – ² the retort to this is that, if that is the way it is, then another question arises, namely why the creator of our existence called us into life when the latter, in our correct estimate, is not desirable to us. Ill humor would reply here as that Indian woman did to Genghis Khan, who could neither give her satisfaction for violence suffered nor afford security for the future: "If you will not protect us, why do you then conquer us?"

c) The third way of untying the knot is supposed to be this: God has put us here on earth for the sake of a future happiness, hence out of his goodness; yet an arduous and sorrowful state in the present life must without exception precede that hoped-for superabundant blessedness – a state in which we are to become worthy of that future glory precisely through our struggle with adversities. – But, that before the highest wisdom this time of trial (to which most succumb, and in which even the best is not happy about his life) must without exception be the condition of the joy eventually to be savored by us, and that it was not possible to let the creature be satisfied with every stage of his life – this can indeed be pretended but in no way can there be insight into it; in this way one can indeed cut the knot loose through an appeal to the highest wisdom which willed it, but one cannot untie the knot, which is what theodicy claims to be capable of accomplishing.

III. To the last charge, namely against the justice of the world's judge,* is replied:

8:261 a) The pretension that the depraved go unpunished in the world is ungrounded, for by its nature every crime already carries with it its due punishment, inasmuch as the inner reproach of conscience torments the depraved even more harshly than the Furies. – But in this judgment there obviously lies a misunderstanding. For here the virtuous man lends to the depraved the characteristic of his own constitution, namely, a conscientiousness in all its severity which, the more virtuous a human being is, all

---

* It is remarkable that of all the difficulties in reconciling the course of world events with the divinity of their creator, none imposes itself on the mind as starkly as that of the semblance in them of a lack of *justice*. If it comes about (although it seldom happens) that an unjust, especially violent, villain does not escape unpunished from the world, then the impartial spectator rejoices, now reconciled with heaven. No purposiveness of nature will so excite him in admiration of it and, as it were, make him detect God's hand in it. Why? Because nature is here moral, solely of the kind we seldom can hope to perceive in the world.

the more harshly punishes him because of the slightest indiscretion frowned upon by the moral law in him. But where this attitude of mind and the accompanying conscientiousness are totally absent, so too is the tormentor of crimes committed; and the depraved, if only he can escape the external floggings for his heinous deeds, laughs at the scrupulousness of the honest who inwardly plague themselves with self-inflicted rebukes; the small reproaches which from time to time he might make to himself are, however, either made not through conscience at all or, if he still has some of this conscience within him, are abundantly upset and made good by the pleasure of the senses for which alone he has a taste. – If that charge shall be further

b) refuted by this: It is indeed not to be denied that there is absolutely no relation according to justice between guilt and punishment in this world, and in the ways of this world one must often witness" with indigna-tion a life led with crying injustice and yet happy to the end; this is not, however, something inherent in nature and deliberately promoted, hence not a moral dissonance, for it is a property of virtue that it should wrestle with adversities (among which is the pain that the virtuous must suffer through comparison of his own unhappiness with the happiness of the depraved), and sufferings only serve to enhance the value of virtue; thus this dissonance of undeserved ills resolves itself before reason into a glorious moral melody – the objection to this solution is that, although these ills, when they *precede* virtue or accompany it as its whetting stone, can indeed be represented as in moral harmony with it if at least the end of life crowns virtue and punishes the depraved; yet, if even such an end (as experience thereof gives many examples) fails against sense to material-ize, then the suffering seems to have occurred to the virtuous, not *so that* his virtue should be pure, but *because* it was pure (and accordingly contrary to the rules of prudent self-love); and this is the very opposite of the justice of which the human being can form a concept for himself. For as regards the possibility that the end of this terrestrial life might not perhaps be the end of all life, such a possibility cannot count as *vindication* of providence; rather, it is merely a decree of morally believing reason which directs the doubter to patience but does not satisfy him.

8:262

c) If, finally, an attempt is made at the third resolution to this disharmo-nious relation between the moral worth of human beings and the lot that befalls them, by saying: In this world we must judge all well-being and ill merely as the consequence of the use of the human faculties according to the laws of nature, in proprotion to the skill and the prudence of their application, and also in proportion to the circumstances they accidentally come by, but not according to their agreement with supersensible ends; in a future world a different order of things will obtain instead, and each will

" *wahrnehmen*

receive that which his deeds here below are worthy of according to moral judgment – [if this is said,] then this assumption too is arbitrary.*° Rather, unless reason, as a faculty of moral legislation, is pronouncing a decree in accordance with this legislative interest, it must find it probable, according to the mere laws of theoretical cognition, that the way of the world determines our fates in the future just as it does here, according to the order of nature. For what else does reason have as a guide for its theoretical conjecture except natural law? And though it allowed itself, as asked for above (item b), an appeal to patience, and the hope of a future improvement, how can it expect – since even for it the way of things according to the order of nature is a wise one here – that in a future world this way would be unwise according to the same laws? Since according to the same reason there is absolutely no comprehensible relation between the inner grounds of determination of the will (namely of the moral way of thinking) according to the laws of freedom, and the (for the most part external) causes of our welfare independent of our will according to the laws of nature, so the presumption remains that the agreement of human fate with a divine justice, according to the concepts that we construe of the latter, is just as little to be expected there as here.

· ·

8:263   Now the outcome of this juridical process before the forum of philosophy is this: Every previous theodicy has not performed what it promised, namely the vindication of the moral wisdom of the world-government against the doubts raised against it on the basis of what the experience of this world teaches – although, to be sure, as objections, so far as our reason's inherent insight regarding them goes, neither can these doubts prove the contrary. But again, whether in time yet more solid grounds of vindication will perhaps be found for the indicted reason – for absolving it not (as hitherto) merely *ab instantia*[p] – this still remains undecided; if we do not succeed in establishing with certainty that our reason is absolutely incapable of insight into *the relationship in which any world as we may ever become acquainted with through experience stands with respect to the highest wisdom,* then all further attempts by a putative human wisdom to gain insight into the ways of the divine wisdom are fully dismissed. Hence, in order to bring this trial to an end *once and for all,* it must yet be proven that at least a negative wisdom is within our reach – namely, insight into the necessary limitation of what we may presume with respect to that which is too high for us – and this may very well be done.

For in the arrangement of this world we have the concept of an *artistic wisdom* – a concept which, in order to attain to a physico-theology, is not

---

° willkürlich
p i.e., right there and then, without explanatory grounds

30

wanting in objective reality for our speculative faculty of reason. And we also have in the moral idea of our own practical reason a concept of a *moral wisdom* which could have been implanted in a world in general by a most perfect creator. – But of the *unity in the agreement* in a sensible world between that artistic and moral wisdom we have no concept; nor can we ever hope to attain one. For to be a creature and, as a natural being, merely the result of the will of the creator; yet to be capable of responsibility as a freely acting being (one which has a will independent of external influence and possibly opposed to the latter in a variety of ways); but again, to consider one's own deed at the same time also as the effect of a higher being – this is a combination of concepts which we must indeed think together in the idea of a world and of a highest good, but which can be intuited only by one who penetrates to the cognition of the supersensible (intelligible) world and sees the manner in which this grounds the sensible world. The proof of the world-author's moral wisdom in the sensible world can be founded only on this insight – for the sensible world presents but the appearance of that other [intelligible] world – and that is an insight to which no mortal can attain.

8:264

. .

All theodicy should truly be an *interpretation* of nature insofar as God announces his will through it. Now every interpretation of the declared will of a legislator is either *doctrinal*[q] or *authentic*. The first is a rational inference of that will from the utterances of which the law-giver has made use, in conjunction with his otherwise recognized purposes; the second is made by the law-giver himself.

As a work of God, the world can also be considered by us as a divine publication of his will's *purposes*. However, in this respect the world is *often* a closed book for us, and it is so *every time* we look at it to extract from it God's *final aim* (which is always moral) even though it is an object of experience. Philosophical trials in this kind of interpretation are doctrinal; they constitute theodicy proper – which we can therefore call "doctrinal." – Yet we cannot deny the name of "theodicy" also to the mere dismissal of all objections against divine wisdom, if this dismissal is a *divine decree*, or (for in this case it amounts to the same thing) if it is a pronouncement of the same reason through which we form our concept of God – necessarily and prior to all experience – as a moral and wise being. For through our reason God then becomes himself the interpreter of his will as announced through creation; and we can call this interpretation an *authentic* theodicy. But that is not the interpretation of a *ratiocinating* (speculative) reason, but of an *efficacious*[r] practical reason which, just as in legislating it commands absolutely

[q] *doktrinal*
[r] *machthabend*

31

without further grounds, so it can be considered as the unmediated definition and voice of God through which he gives meaning to the letter of his creation. Now I find such an authentic interpretation expressed allegorically in an ancient holy book.

8:265   Job is portrayed as a man whose enjoyment of life included everything which anyone might possibly imagine it as making it complete. He was healthy, well-to-do, free, master over others whom he can make happy, surrounded by a happy family, among beloved friends – and on top of all of this (what is most important) at peace with himself in a good conscience. A harsh fate imposed in order to test him suddenly snatched from him all these blessings, except the last. Stunned by this unexpected reversal, as he gradually regains his senses, he breaks out in lamentation over his unlucky star; whereupon a dispute soon develops between him and his friends – supposedly gathered to console him – in which the two sides expound their particular theodicy to give a moral explanation for that deplorable fate, each side according to its particular way of thinking (above all, however, according to its station). Job's friends declare themselves for that system which explains all ills in the world from God's *justice*, as so many punishments for crimes committed; and, although they could name none *for* which the unhappy man is guilty, yet they believed they could judge *a priori* that he must have some weighing upon him, for his misfortune would otherwise be impossible according to divine justice. Job – who idignantly protests that his conscience has nothing to reproach him for in his whole life; and, so far as human unavoidable mistakes are concerned, God himself knows that he has made him a fragile creature – Job declares himself for the system of *unconditional divine decision*. "He has decided," Job says, "He does as he wills."*

There is little worthy of note in the subtle or hypersubtle reasonings' of the two sides; but the spirit' in which they carry them out merits all the more attention. Job speaks as he thinks, and with the courage with which he, as well as every human being in his position, can well afford; his friends, on the contrary, speak as if they were being secretly listened to by the mighty one, over whose cause they are passing judgment, and as if gaining his favor through their judgment were closer to their heart than the truth. Their malice in pretending to assert things into which they yet must admit they have no insight, and in simulating a conviction which they in fact do not

8:266   have, contrasts with Job's frankness – so far removed from false flattery as to border almost on impudence – much to his advantage. "Will you defend God unjustly?" he asks;† "Will you give his person [special] consideration?

---

* Job 23:13.³
† Job 13:7–11, 16.⁴
' *was beide Theile vernünfteln oder übervernunfteln*
' *der Character*

Will you plead for God? He shall punish you, if you secretly have consideration for persons! – There will be no hypocrite before him!"

The outcome of the story actually confirms this. For God deigned to lay before Job's eyes the wisdom of his creation, especially its inscrutability. He allowed him glimpses into the beautiful side of creation, where ends comprehensible to the human being bring the wisdom and the benevolent providence of the author of the world unambiguously to light; but also, by contrast, into the horrible side, by calling out to him the products of his might, among which also harmful and fearsome things, each of which appears indeed to be purposively arranged for its own sake and that of its species, yet, with respect to other things and to human beings themselves, as destructive, counterpurposive, and incompatible with a universal plan established with goodness and wisdom. And yet God thereby demonstrates an order and a maintenance of the whole which proclaim a wise creator, even though his ways, inscrutable to us, must at the same time remain hidden – indeed already in the physical order of things, and how much more in the connection of the latter with the moral order (which is all the more impenetrable to our reason). – The conclusion is this: Since Job admits having hastily spoken about things which are too high for him and which he does not understand – not *as if wantonly*, for he is conscious of his honesty, but only unwisely – God finds against his friends, for (as conscientiousness goes) they have not spoken as well of God as God's servant Job. If we now consider the theoretical position" maintained by each side, that of Job's friends might convey more of an appearance of greater speculative reason and pious humility; before any court of dogmatic theologians, before a synod, an inquisition, a venerable congregation, or any higher consistory in our times (one alone excepted),[5] Job would have likely suffered a sad fate. Hence only sincerity of heart and not distinction of insight; honesty in openly admitting one's doubts; repugnance to pretending conviction where one feels none, especially before God (where this trick is pointless enough) – these are the attributes which, in the person of Job, have decided the preeminence of the honest man over the religious flatterer in the divine verdict.

8:267

The faith, however, which sprang in him for such a vexing resolution of his doubts – namely merely from being convicted of ignorance – could only arise in the soul of a man who, in the midst of his strongest doubts, could yet say (Job 27:5–6): "Till I die I will not remove mine integrity from me, etc."[6] For with this disposition he proved that he did not found his morality on faith, but his faith on morality: in such a case, however weak this faith might be, yet it alone is of a pure and true kind, i.e. the kind of faith that founds not a religion of supplication, but a religion of good life conduct.

" *die Theorie*

33

CONCLUDING REMARK

Theodicy, as has been shown here, does not have as much to do with a task in the interest of science as, rather, with a matter of faith. From the authentic theodicy we saw that in these matters, less depends on subtle reasoning than on sincerity in taking notice of the impotence of our reason, and on honesty in not distorting our thoughts in what we say, however pious our intention. – This leads to yet the following brief reflection on a big subject, namely sincerity, which is the principal requirement in matters of faith, as contrasted with the propensity to falsehood and impurity which is the principal affliction of human nature.

One cannot always stand by the *truth* of what one says to oneself or to another (for one can be mistaken); however, one can and must stand by the *truthfulness* of one's declaration or confession, because one has immediate consciousness of this. For in the first instance we compare what we say with the object in a logical judgment (through the understanding), whereas in the second instance, where we declare what we hold as true, we compare what we say with the subject (before conscience). Were we to make our declaration with respect to the former without being conscious of the latter, then we lie, since we pretend something else than what we are conscious of. – The observation that there is such an impurity in the human heart is not new (for Job already made it); yet one is tempted to believe that attention to it is new to the teachers of morality and religion, one so seldom finds them making a sufficient use of it despite the difficulty associated with a purification of the dispositions in human beings even when they *want* to act according to duty. We can call this truthfulness "formal conscientiousness"; "material conscientiousness" consists in the caution of not venturing anything on the danger that it might be wrong, whereas "formal" conscientiousness consists in the consciousness of having applied this caution in a given case. – Moralists speak of an "erring conscience." But an erring conscience is an absurdity;[v] and, if there were such a thing, then we could never be certain we have acted rightly, since even the judge in the last instance can still be in error. I can indeed err in the judgment *in which I believe* to be right, for this belongs to the understanding which alone judges objectively (rightly or wrongly); but in the judgment *whether I in fact believe* to be right (or merely pretend it) I absolutely cannot be mistaken, for this judgment – or rather this proposition – merely says that I judge the object in such-and-such a way.

Now the formal conscientiousness which is the ground of truthfulness consists precisely in the care in becoming conscious of this belief (or unbelief) and not pretending to hold anything as true we are not conscious of holding as true. Hence, if someone says to himself (or – what is one and the

8:268

[v] *Unding*

34

same in religious professions – before God) that *he believes*, without perhaps casting even a single glimpse into himself – whether he is in fact conscious of thus holding a truth or at least of holding it to some degree – *

^ʎ then such a person <u>lies</u>. And not only is his lie the most absurd (before a reader of hearts): it is also the most sinful, for it undermines the ground of   8:269 every virtuous intention. It is not difficult to see how quickly these blind and external *professions* (which can very easily be reconciled with an internal profession just as false) can, if they yield *means of gain*, bring about a certain falsehood in a community's very way of thinking. – Since a purification of this public way of thinking must in all likelihood be deferred to a distant future – until some day, perhaps under the protection of freedom of thought, it will become a general principle of upbringing and education – we may in the meantime dedicate yet a few lines to the consideration of that vice apparently so deeply rooted in human nature.

There is something moving and edifying in the depiction of a character which is sincere, and distant from all falsehood and deliberate^x dissemblance. But, since honesty (mere simplicity and straightforward-   8:270

---

* The means for extorting truthfulness in external declarations, *the oath* (*tortura spiritualis*),^ⱳ is held by any human court as not only permissible but as indispensable – a sad proof of the little respect of human beings for the truth even in the temple of public justice, where the mere idea of it should by itself instill the greatest respect. Human beings, however, also feign conviction – which is at least not of the kind, or in the degree, as they pretend – even in their inner profession; and since this dishonesty can also have external harmful consequences (for it gradually forges actual persuasion), this means for extorting truthfulness – the oath (which is, to be sure, only an internal means of extortion, i.e. the trial whether holding something as true can withstand the test of an internal hearing of the profession *under oath*) – can likewise   8:269 very well be used, if not to put a stop to the impudence of bold and in the end also externally violent assertions, at least to make it suspect. – Nothing more is expected by the human court from the conscience of one taking an oath than the admission that, *if there is* a future judge of the world (hence a God and a future life), the taker of the oath wills to answer to him for the truth of his external profession; there is no necessity for the court to require him to profess *that there is such a judge of the world*, because, if the first declaration cannot prevent a lie, a second false profession would cause even fewer scruples. By any such inner sworn statement one would be asking himself: Do you now, by everything which is dear and holy to you, venture to guarantee the truth of that important proposition of faith or of some other equally so held? At such an unreasonable demand conscience would be startled, because of the danger to which one is exposed of pretending more than one can assert with certainty – where holding something as true involves an object which is not attainable by way of knowledge (theoretical insight), though its assumption, while still always free, is commendable above all things because it alone makes possible the union into one system of the highest principles of practical reason with those of theoretical cognition of nature (hence reason's agreement with itself). – Professions of faith whose source is historical must, however, all the more be submitted to this trial of truthfulness by fire if they are set down as rules to others: for here the impurity and the simulated conviction is propagated among many, and the blame for it is the onus of whoever is the guarantor as it were of other consciences (for human beings are gladly passive with their conscience).[7]

^ⱳ Spiritual torture
^x *positiven*

ness of mind) is the least that we can possibly require of a good character (especially if we waive candor of heart) and it is therefore difficult to see on what that admiration which we reserve for such a character is based; it must be that sincerity is the property farthest removed from human nature – a sad comment, since all the remaining properties, to the extent that they rest on principles, can have a true inner value only through that one. None but a contemplative misanthrope (who wishes evil to nobody, yet is inclined to believe every evil of all) can hesitate whether to find human beings to *deserve hatred* or rather *contempt.* The properties for which he would judge them qualified for the first finding are those through which they do deliberate harm. That property, however, which appears to him to expose them to the second estimate, could be none other than a propensity which is *in itself evil* even if it harms no one – a propensity for something which cannot be used as means for any purpose; something which, objectively, is good in no respect.^y The first evil would indeed be none other than the evil of *hostility* (or, to put it mildly, of lack of love); the second can be none other than *mendacity* (falsity, even without any intention to harm). The *first* inclination has a purpose whose function^z is yet permissible and good in certain farther connections,^a e.g. hostility against incorrigible disturbers of the peace. The *second* propensity, however, is to use a means (the lie) which is good in no respect,^b whatever its aim, since it is evil and reprehensible in itself. The *evil* with which competence for good ends in certain external relations can yet be associated is in the constitution of a human being of the first kind;^c it is a sinning in means, which are not, however, reprehensible in every respect. The evil of the second kind is *baseness,*^d whereby all character is denied to the human being. – I am here restricting myself principally to the impurity that lies deep in what is hidden, where the human being knows how to distort even inner declarations before his own conscience. The inclination to external deception should be all the less surprising; it must then be that, although we are all aware of the falsity of the coin with which we trade, that coin still manages to maintain itself in circulation.

8:271   I remember reading in M. de Luc's *Letters concerning Mountain Ranges, the History of the Earth and Humanity* the following result of the author's partly anthropological voyage.[8] This philanthropist had set out presupposing the original goodness of our species, and sought verification of his

^y *zu nichts*
^z *Gebrauch*
^a *andern Beziehungen.* A few lines later, with respect to the same inclination, Kant speaks of *äußern Verhältnissen.* One wonders if this earlier *andern* is a printer's error and ought to be read, rather, as *äußern,* i.e., "external."
^b *zu nichts*
^c i.e., as deserving hate
^d *Nichtswürdigkeit*

36

presupposition in places where urban luxury cannot have such influence as to corrupt minds – in mountain ranges, from the Swiss mountains all the way to the Harz[9] and, after his faith in an unselfish inclination to help became somewhat shaky through an experience on the Swiss side,ᶜ yet at the ends he draws this conclusion: *As regards benevolence the human being is good enough* (no wonder, since benevolence rests on an innate inclination of which God is the creator) *provided that no bad propensity to subtle deception dwells in him* (which is also not to be wondered at, because to refrain from deception rests on the character which the human being himself must build within himself). And this result of the investigation is one which, even without traveling to the mountains, everyone could have met with among his fellow citizens – indeed, yet closer to home, in his own heart.

ᶜ *in den erstern*

Religion within the boundaries of mere reason

Translator's introduction

Dilthey's reconstruction in 1890 of the events that led to the publication of Kant's *Die Religion innerhalb der Grenzen der bloßen Vernunft* is now a classic on which every subsequent account has depended.[a] In brief, this is what happened. In February 1792, Kant sent to J. E. Biester, the editor of the *Berlinische Monatsschrift*,[b] an essay entitled "Concerning Radical Evil in Human Nature." Kant's letter to Biester is lost. However, we learn from another letter that Kant wrote the following year to C. F. Stäudlin[c] that he had intended the essay as the first of four pieces on religion to be published in Biester's journal.[d] The essay was approved in Berlin for publication by the philosophy censor, G. F. Hillmer, on the ground that (as Biester reported to Kant) "after careful reading he [Hillmer] had found this writing, like the rest of Kant's, only intended for, and of appeal to, the thoughtful scholar, adept to enquiry and distinctions – not any reader in

[a] "Der Streit Kants mit der Zensur über das Recht freier Religionsforschung" (Kant's Dispute with Censorship over the Right of Free Research in Religion), *Archiv für Geschichte der Philosophie*, 3(1890), pp. 418–50; republished in *Gesammelte Schriften*, Vol. 4 (Stuttgart: Teubner, Vandenhoech & Ruprecht, 2nd ed., 1959), pp. 285–309. I am very much indebted to this study by Dilthey; also to Emil Fromm, *Immanuel Kant und die preussische Censur, nebst kleiner Beiträgen zur Lebensgeschichte Kants* (Hamburg und Leipzig: Voss, 1894), and Emil Arnoldt, *Beiträge zu der Material der Geschichte von Kants Leben und Schriftstellertätigkeit in bezug auf seine 'Religionslehre' und seine Konflikt mit der preussischen Regierung*, in *Altpreussische Monatsschrift*, 34.5/6 (1894); 35.1/2(1895); republished in book form in Königsberg i. Pr.: Beyer, 1898, and also included in *Emil Arnoldt: Gesammelte Schriften*, Vol. 4 (Berlin: Cassirer, 1909), from which we shall cite. See also Emil Fromm's important review of Arnoldt's work, in "Zur Vorgeschichte der Königlichen Kabinetsordre an Kant vom 1. Oktober 1794," *Kant-Studien*, 3(1899): 142–7.
[b] *The Berlin Monthly*. Johann Erich Biester (1749–1816). A reference to the essay is perhaps found in Kant's letter to C. L. Reinhold of September 21, 1791, where Kant diplomatically excuses himself for again postponing a public judgment on Reinhold's new theory of representation on the ground that "I am presently working on a small yet taxing job, and also on a revision of the *Critique of Judgment* for a second edition, due to be published next Easter, not reckoning my university affairs – altogether overburdened and overextended for what little strength I now have" (AK 11: 288–9). The "small but taxing job" is presumably the essay.
[c] May 4, 1793; AK 11:414–15. Stäudlin (1761–1826) was professor of theology at Göttingen. Kant later dedicated his *Der Streit der Fakultäten* (1798, *The Conflict of the Faculties*) to him.
[d] He had probably been working on them for some time. Cf. the letter to Biester, December 29, 1789, AK 11:117.

general."[e] The second essay to be sent, however, was not so fortunate, and its eventual rejection by the censors is what occasioned Kant's famous confrontation with censorship.

Preventive censorship had been an accepted political fact in Kant's Prussia even under the relatively enlightened reign of Frederick II. In 1749 a royal edict (revised and made more stringent in 1772) had established a Berlin Censorship Commission to which all writing printed in the realm had to be submitted for prior examination and approval. Even after its later revision, however, the edict allowed for considerable latitude. For instance, it exempted from the commission's jurisdiction all writing executed and printed in the universities, and subjected it rather to the judgment of the appropriate academic faculties. Only writing that bore directly on state affairs could not avail itself of this privilege. The edict had been intended, in other words, as a weapon ready at hand in case of need but in fact seldom to be used.[f]

The situation changed with the accession to the throne in 1786 of Frederick William II. A new censorship edict promulgated in 1788 did not, as Dilthey points out, "strengthen Frederick's provisions in any considerable way."[g] It even reasserted the privilege earlier granted to academic writing of being examined for approval by academic authorities. It was not the letter of the law, however, but the new spirit in which it would be applied, and the personality of the people on whom the task of applying it would devolve, that was to make the difference. The members of the old Berlin Commission, although all drawn from the church hierarchy, were men of learning, deeply imbued with the spirit of the Enlightenment and not likely to cooperate with the reactionary policies of the new government. It was only a matter of time, however, before they would be replaced by more pastorally inclined colleagues, and the new censorship edict, though not substantially different in the letter from the earlier, would bring about totally different practical results.

As things turned out, it was precisely the friction between Wöllner (the conservative new minister of religion) and the liberal members of the church Superior Consistory in Berlin,[h] exacerbated by the antiliberal backlash caused by the French Revolution, that precipitated events. To counteract the Consistory's obstruction to his conservative measures, Wöllner had created a new Immediate[i] Commission of Investigation;[j] one of its duties

---

[e] March 6, 1792; AK 11:316.

[f] Dilthey reports that a censor, in 1759, wondered whether anyone still bothered submitting anything to censorship, because such a long time had passed since anything had crossed his desk. Cf. *Gesammelte Schriften*, 4, p. 287.

[g] P. 287.

[h] Cf., *On the Miscarriage of All Philosophical Trials in Theodicy*, p. 33, editorial note 5.

[i] i.e. directly answerable to the sovereign.

[j] *Immediat-Examinationskommission*.

was to be specifically the censorship of all books in theology and morality, of all periodical articles and occasional writings in morality and philosophy, to be published in Berlin. Named head censor was G. F. Hillmer, a sometime high-school teacher and a notoriously intolerant bigot. In matters theological, however, Hillmer was to enlist the help of J. T. Hermes, an equally fanatical local pastor.[k] The net result was that two of the oldest organs of the Enlightenment left Berlin. Nicolai moved the production of the *Allgemeine deutsche Bibliothek* to Kiel, and Biester that of his *Berlinische Monatsschrift* to Jena.[l] Although Biester gave a very circumspect explanation of his move to Kant (in a letter of March 6, 1792), his true intention as well as that of Nicolai had obviously been to circumvent the new censorship. The reach of Wöllner's censors did not extend outside Prussia, and there was nothing in the law that forbade the importation of books printed elsewhere. As Biester said to Kant: "To have printing done externally has never been forbidden here."[m]

When in 1792, therefore, Kant sent his first essay on religion to Biester, and in the (now lost) accompanying letter asked him (as it transpires from Biester's reply)[n] to submit it to the censors, he was abiding by the spirit of Wöllner's legislation more scrupulously than the letter of the law required. According to Borowski (Kant's earliest biographer) Kant's intention had been to avoid giving "even the least semblance of wanting to follow some devious literary route,[o] and of expressing so-called bold opinions only by deliberately circumventing the strict Berlin censorship."[p]

[k] Dilthey, p. 289.

[l] Another immediate result was the resignation from the *Berlinmonatsschrift* of Friedrich Gedike (1754–1803), its chief editor up to that point.

[m] AK 11:315–16. Later in life, in his autobiography, Biester was to be much more candid about the reason for the journal's move. He then wrote: "Herr von Wöllner was ill disposed to the monthly journal, which continued publication in its usual style but, because of the severity of censorship or, more to the point, because of the unreasonableness of censor Hillmer, had been published outside the realm since January 1792 (when Gedike resigned the editorship). The Minister had personally told the publisher [i.e. Gedike] that his journal was offensive, and for that reason he [Gedike] had no hope of becoming a member of the Academy, to which he had been nominated by Count von Herzberg." Cited after Norbert Hinske, *Was ist Aufklärung? Beiträge aus der Berlinischen Monatsschrift; Augsewählte Beiträge aus den Jahren 1783–1786* (Darmstadt: Wissenschaftliche Buchgesellschaft, 1973), p. xxxv. The reason for Gedike's resignation is clear.

[n] i.e. the letter of March 6, 1793.

[o] *eine literarische Schleichweg.* According to Dilthey, this is an echo of the 1788 edict, which made an author (as contrasted to a publisher) accountable only if he had obtained his permission to print by devious means (*erschlichen*). Dilthey, p. 290.

[p] "Kant's Censorship Troubles," Appendix 4 to L. E. Borowski, *Darstellung des Lebens und Characters Immanuel Kants*, 1804, ed. F. Gross (*Depiction of the Life and Character of Immanuel Kant;* Berlin: Deutsche Bibliothek, 1912), p. 103. According to Arnoldt, because of internal inconsistencies and discrepancies with what Kant says elsewhere, this report, which Borowski claims to be drawing from Kant's own "writ," cannot be accepted without due criticism. *Gesammelte Schriften,* pp. 29–31.

Biester himself – though he dutifully abided by Kant's request and in his letter of reply professed nothing but respect for both the law and Kant's judgment – could not avoid conveying a muted note of skepticism. One could hardly blame him for that. Kant had asked him to go through a legal procedure which Kant had carefully taken steps to circumvent. At the end of the letter, Biester wanted to know "quite definitely: whether in the future [he] should still submit his [i.e. Kant's] essays for the Berlin monthly to the censorship *here* [i.e. in Berlin]."[q]

It is apparent that Kant did not sway from his chosen course of action, for on June 18, 1792, after wondering aloud just "why [Kant] had throughout insisted on the [Berlin] censorship," Biester sadly reported to Kant that his manuscript (obviously the second of the planned essays) had been rejected. He had submitted it to Hillmer for approval in keeping with Kant's instructions. Since the manuscript dealt with biblical theology, Hillmer had enlisted Hermes's cooperation according to regulations, and had finally concurred with Hermes's decision to "*refuse the imprimatur.*"[r]

Dismayed by this outcome, Biester immediately took steps in an effort to reverse it. He wrote to Hermes asking him whether the refusal had been based on something in Kant's essay allegedly contrary to the universal truths of religion, or on some unpublicized censorship regulation.[s] Hermes laconically replied that "the royal edict had been his guide in this case; more he could not explain."[t] Thereupon Biester made a direct appeal to the King's cabinet. Since he saw nothing reprehensible in Kant's essay and the essay was, on the contrary, an earnest and honest attempt to search for the truth; moreover, since it was not the purpose of censorship to hinder any such search, Biester pointedly asked again whether there were rules regulating the otherwise very elastic domain of the censors' jurisdiction which editors and authors did not know about. Biester also insisted that the appeal be heard in a plenary session of the cabinet. Unfortunately, the timing was not very propitious for his cause. The ministers were under pressure from various quarters to take steps to halt every possible inroad of French revolutionary ideas into the realm, and had recently been reprimanded by the King himself for encouraging the so-called *Aufklärer* with their disagreements.[u] Not unexpectedly, therefore, the cabinet unanimously voted to turn down Biester's appeal.

Kant immediately decided on a new course of action. He wrote to Biester asking him to return his manuscript immediately.[v] He had no

[q] AK 11:316.
[r] AK 11:329–30.
[s] Dilthey, p. 290.
[t] Cf. Biester's letter to Kant, June 18, 1792; AK 11:330.
[u] Cf. Dilthey, p. 293.
[v] Letter of July 30, 1792, AK 11:336. Cf. Biester's reply, September 22, 1792, AK 11:357.

intention of letting his first essay stand without the following pieces. But neither did he see any point in publishing the latter outside Berlin, because, granted the legal restrictions under which Biester's magazine now operated, the censors could accuse Kant of devious conduct and cause him troubles. Instead, what he had decided to do – though he did not say this to Biester – was to collect the first essay already published and the other three yet to appear into a single book, and to publish them together in this form. Since the planned book was a work done within the ambit of a university, Kant could avail himself of the old privilege of having it judged by a university faculty. However, since Hillmer had passed Kant's second essay on to Hermes, on the ground that it dealt with biblical matters and therefore fell within the competence of a theologian, Kant now took the point of contention to be whether a philosophical work dealing with religious matters was to be judged by philosophers (according to philosophical criteria of truth) or by theologians. He later related to Stäudlin, to explain the context of some otherwise singular passages in the Preface of his just published book,[w] that he had thereupon submitted the manuscript to a theological faculty to determine whether it fell within its competence or not. We learn from Borowski that Kant at first hesitated as to which institution to submit it, seriously considering Göttingen and Halle at first, but eventually settling for Königsberg.[x] The reply he received was the one he had sought. – Since the manuscript was of a philosophical nature, the philosophical faculty had jurisdiction over it. Accordingly, Kant submitted it for examination to the appropriate academic body at Jena,[y] and, the approval having been granted, had it published by

---

[w] AK 11:415.

[x] Leben, p. 104.

[y] At Jena, and not at Königsberg as both Dilthey and Fromm presumed. The reason for assuming, as Arnoldt does, that Kant chose to submit his manuscript to the faculty of philosophy at Jena is a compelling one. The copy-edited texts of Parts 2, 3, and 4 of Religion are all extant (at least in significant portions) and each sheet bears some variation of the notation "Vidi JC. Hennings," i.e. "I saw [and approved], JC. Hennings." J. Ch. Hennings was at the time the dean of the faculty of philosophy at Jena, and it was apparently to him that the manuscript was submitted. As Arnoldt also points out, there were good reasons why Kant would not have turned either to Königsberg or to Halle (the obvious alternative to Königsberg, since it too was in Prussia). The dean of philosophy at Königsberg at the time was Christian Jakob Kraus, Kant's sometime student and later colleague and friend. To submit the manuscript to him would have been tantamount to Kant submitting it to himself. On the other hand, the philosophy dean at Halle was the same J. A. Eberhard who only a few years before had attacked Kant's Critique of Pure Reason. Kant would not have found a very sympathetic forum there. Just why Kant chose Jena, though it lay outside Prussian jurisdiction, is not however as clear. We know that both the first two editions of the eventual book, although published by Nicolovius in Königsberg, were printed in Jena. Perhaps Nicolovius suggested Jena to Kant for business reasons, since the book would be printed there. But then, the contrary hypothesis, that Nicolovius printed the book in Jena because it had been submitted for censorship there, is equally possible. Cf. Arnoldt: Gesammelte Schriften, pp. 32–7.

Nicolovius in Königsberg. It was ready for the public in book form at the Easter fair of 1793.

Some important documents relating to this very phase in the publication saga of Kant's book came to light only with the recovery of the Rostock Kant manuscripts. Two of them are drafts of a letter very likely addressed by Kant to the faculty of theology at Königsberg concerning his freedom to publish.[z] Written on the margin of one of the two (presumably the earlier one), there is a brief exposition of Kant's main ideas in the order in which they are found further developed in the other (and presumably later) draft. This third exposition was one of two texts[a] that Dilthey published as part of his 1890 account of the events. It reads in part:

> I have the honor, Honorable Sirs, of submitting three philosophical treatises, . . . not indeed for censorship but for a judgment, whether the faculty of theology would take it upon itself to surrender censorship of it, so that the philosophical faculty may without worry exercise its right over it, in conformity to the title of the script.[b] – For although philosophical theology is here presented also in relation to the biblical (how far it trusts itself to approximate the latter by pursuing its own attempts at scriptural interpretation; where reason, on the contrary, does not reach, or is unable to follow the accepted interpretation of the church), to do so is indisputably within its competence, in which it stays within its boundaries and does not intrude on biblical theology any more than the latter can be accused of intruding on the domain of another science just because, to justify and explain itself, it makes use of as many philosophical ideas as it deems suitable to the purpose.[c]

This claim became for Kant a fundamental thesis. We find it stated in the Preface to the first edition of the published book, in a section for which Kant prepared at least two drafts (also recovered among the Rostock manuscripts) before settling for the final text.[d] And we find it again as the main theme of *The Conflict of the Faculties*, which Kant published in 1798[e] at a time when the political climate had again changed in favor of a less restrictive censorship.[f]

---

[z] "Very likely," but not with absolute certainty, because, as Dilthey points out, the actual letter was not found in the University archives, which are unfortunately incomplete (p. 293), and nowhere is the addressee explicitly mentioned in the extant text.

[a] Cf. note reference below.

[b] i.e., "Philosophical Doctrine of Religion"; cf. below, p. 51.

[c] Dilthey, p. 294. Cf. also AK 11:344–5.

[d] The more masterly of the two, in which Kant states his case much more forcefully than in the published version, is the second of the two texts incorporated by Dilthey in his 1890 study (pp. 299–305).

[e] AK 7.

[f] Kant had first discussed the issue of censorship in the essay, "An Answer to the Question: What Is Enlightenment?" published in the *Berlinische Monatschrift*, 4/1784, 481–94. He had there distinguished between what he called a "public" and a "private" use of reason, where by "public use" he meant the use that a scientist makes of reason in keeping with reason's

It took some time, however, for this change to occur. In 1793 the situation actually took a turn for the worse, in reaction to the worsened situation in France.[g] Kant knew that, despite his philosophical fine distinctions and his legal niceties, he was provoking the government.[h] And he did not, in fact, escape censure. On October 4, 1794, he received a royal rescript in which he was accused of having for some time "abused his philosophy for the purpose of distorting and disparaging several principal and fundamental doctrines of Holy Scripture and of Christianity," and of having done so in his "book, *Religion within the Boundaries of Mere Reason*, as well as in other smaller treatises."[i] The rescript further enjoined him to refrain from similar conduct in the future.

universal (hence "public") requirements, and, by "private," the use that an official of the state makes of it in the discharge of his office (which is limited by historical circumstances and hence "private"). While Kant advocated unlimited freedom of thought and expression in the "public" use of reason, he defended the state's right to impose restrictions on the "private" use. His position, in other words, could be summed up in the adage, "Think as you wish, but obey," which in fact reflected the position of Frederick the Great. This position had been clearly formulated on the basis of the king's own public statements in an article anonymously published, also in the *Berlinische Monatschrift*, only a few months before Kant's essay was published ("On the Freedom of Thought and Expression: To Princes, Ministers, Writers," 3/1783, 312–30. The relevant texts are reproduced in Hinske, *Was ist Aufklärung?* Cf. also Hinske's comments, p. lvi). Arnoldt excuses Kant's eventual docile profession of obedience to the king (about which more later) on the ground that, as a state official, he was duty bound to obey the king according to his own moral standards. (Cf. *Anroldt: Gesammelte Schriften*, pp. 169–207.) On the other hand, this is what Hamann had to say of Kant's position at the time of the publication of the 1784 essay: "The distinction between public and private use of reason is [altogether] comic. . . . To be sure, the issue is how to unite the two natures of one under age and of his guardian. But how to make contradictory hypocrites of both is no *mystery* in need of preaching; the knot of the whole political enterprise lies precisely there. Of what use is to me the festive dress of freedom if I wear the costume of the slave at home? Does Plato belong to the gentler sex? Women ought to be silent in the parish. . . . In their own home (i.e. at the lectern and on the stage and at the pulpit) they might [run the risk of] chatter[ing] at their hearts' instigation. There they speak as individuals under age; they must forget and contradict all as soon as, in their self-incurred dotage, they are to do the community work of the state. [Kant's] public use of reason and freedom is nothing but a dessert, a randy dessert. The private use is the *daily bread* we should do without because of the other." Cf. *Johann Georg Hamann Briefwechsel*, ed. A. Henkel, Vol. 5 (Wiesbaden and Frankfurt/M.: Insel, 1965), Letter to C. J. Kraus, December 18, 1784, p. 292. Hamann had little use for a "public" reason exercised in abstraction from all social contexts.
[g] Dilthey, p. 306.
[h] Cf. the anxiety expressed to Biester in the letter of May 18, 1794; AK 11:481–2.
[i] AK 7:6. The fact that the rescript was promulgated only after the publication of the second edition of *Religion*, and that Wöllner had received the publication of the first in silence and had not prevented the second, led Arnoldt to speculate that Kant's smaller writings (also mentioned in the royal rescript) had in fact been the cause of the condemnation, and that "The End of All Things," published in the *Berlinische Monatschrift* just before the rescript arrived, had precipitated it. These writings all contained political views that could be deemed dangerous. Kant's condemnation in "The End of All Things" of the efforts of those who would bring about the perfection of the world (hence the end of time) through human means

Kant replied by arguing that his book could not have been detrimental to the public order, since it had not been intended for the general public.[j] His intention, moreover, had not been to evaluate Christianity (which he could not, therefore, have disparaged) but to evaluate natural religion;[k] and if, within the context of the latter, reason "speaks as if it were sufficient onto itself – and revealed doctrine, therefore, superfluous – this is nothing but an expression of reason's estimate of its own [moral capacity]," with respect to which revelation must indeed be considered an external and accidental doctrine, "yet not an unnecessary or superfluous one, since it serves to compensate for the *theoretical* lack of rational faith . . . in such questions as the origin of evil."[l] Kant also insisted that in his book he had shown nothing but respect for the biblical content of Christian faith, since he had repeatedly declared that the Bible is the best available guide to be followed in public religious instruction for the establishment and preservation of a national religion truly conducive to the improvement of souls.[m] All this notwithstanding, in order to deflect every possible suspicion, Kant docilely concluded by declaring that, as "His Majesty's *loyal subject*," he would henceforth refrain from "any public pronouncement concerning religion (be it natural or revealed) whether in lectures or in writings."[n] And Kant faithfully abided by this promise until the death of Frederick William II (November 16, 1797), and the abrogation (under the new king, Frederick William III) of Wöllner's edict, when he deemed himself released from it.[o] He then proceeded to make public both the royal rescript of censure and his reply to it by including the texts of the two documents in the Preface to the already mentioned *Conflict of the Faculties*.

could be taken, moreover, as a veiled satire at the efforts of Wöllner and company to reform society (*Arnoldt: Gesammelte Schriften*, pp. 105–46). Although appealing, this hypothesis was however rejected by Fromm in his review of Arnoldt's book (as cited in footnote *a*, p. 41). Fromm argues, on the strength of official records, that Kant's condemnation had been in the works for some time, and had only been delayed because of external circumstances.

[j] AK 7:8.

[k] AK 7:8.

[l] AK 7:8–9.

[m] AK 7:9.

[n] AK 7:10. Cf. footnote *f*, p. 47. At the time of receiving the rescript silencing him, Kant wrote down the following note on a scrap of paper later found among his manuscripts: "To recant or deny one's inner conviction is despicable, but to be silent in a case like the present is the duty of a subject; and although everything one says must be true, to declare every truth publicly is not for that reason also a duty." As cited by Fromm, *Kant und die preussische Censur*, p. 49.

[o] Cf. Borowski, p. 59. Borowski claims that Kant deliberately affixed "loyal subject" to his signature at the bottom of his reply to the king in order to make it clear that his promise held good only between himself and the king.

We have seen that Kant had apparently worked for some time on his four pieces on religion before writing to Biester in 1792. Unfortunately, his early biographers differ on how much attention Kant paid to religious and theological literature after his early pietist education.[p] According to Borowski, Kant read on all subjects; he "only did not touch theological enquiries, of any kind, but especially those dealing with exegesis and dogmatics."[q] According to Jachmann, on the contrary, he "combined with all the [other] sciences [that he knew] a precise knowledge of the religious doctrines of the Christians, the Jews, and of other peoples, and much theological learning."[r] Which of these two testimonies deserves more credence is, of course, for scholars to decide. On whichever side, however, scholarly opinion will eventually come down, there is no doubt about Kant's motive for writing his four essays on religion.[s] In the already mentioned letter to Stäudlin,[t] Kant wrote:

> The plan that I made for myself some time ago as I prepared to work in the field of pure philosophy called for the resolution of three problems: (1) What can I know? (metaphysics); (2) What ought I to do? (morality); (3) What may I hope for? (religion) – [the last of] which should be followed at the end by a fourth, "What is humankind?" (anthropology, [a subject] on which I have lectured every year for over twenty years). – With the enclosed monograph, *Religion within the Boundaries etc.*, I have tried to complete the third portion of my plan. Conscientiousness and true respect for the Christian religion have been my guide in this work, but also the principle of a befitting candor: to conceal nothing but rather to lay open how I believe that I see a possible union of the Christian religion with the purest practical reason.

To explore the limits of pure reason even in matters of faith was Kant's purpose, and just *how* he thought he saw a possible union between the religion of Christianity and that of reason he had already stated almost two decades earlier, in 1775, in a letter to Lavater:

> My presupposition is that no book, whatever its authority – yes, even a revelation taking place before my own senses – can impose upon my religion (of dispositions) something which has not already become a duty for me through the holy law in me (in accordance with which I must answer for everything I do); and I must not dare

---

[p] For Kant's pietist early education, cf. R. B. Jachmann, *Immanuel Kant geschildert in Briefen an einem Freund*, 1804, ed. F. Groß (*Immanuel Kant Depicted in Letters to a Friend;* Berlin: Deutsche Bibliothek, 1912), pp. 123–4.

[q] Borowski, p. 79.

[r] *Kant Depicted in Letters to a Friend*, p. 138 (Letter 5).

[s] In a masterful study of the theological and dogmatic sources of Kant's book on religion, Joseph Bohatec gives definite evidence in favor of Jachmann's assessment. Cf. *Die Religionsphilosophie Kants in der "Religion innerhalb der Grenzen der bloßen Vernunft," mit besonderer Berücksichtigung ihrer theologisch-dogmatischen Quellen* (Hamburg: Hoffmann & Campe, 1939; photographic reproduction, Darmstadt, 1966).

[t] May 4, 1793; AK 11:414.

to cram my soul with devotional testimonies, confessions, and so on, which do not spring from the unfeigned and infallible precepts of the law (for *statutes* can indeed produce *external observances* but not *dispositions* of the heart). I, therefore, seek in the Gospel not the ground of my faith but its fortification; and in the moral spirit of the Gospels I find the report of how that faith was disseminated, and of the means of its introduction into the world – in brief, of what is *incumbent* upon me – clearly distinguished from what *God does* for me. Hence nothing new is imposed [by the Gospel] upon me; rather (whatever the state of those reports) *new* strength and confidence is given to my good dispositions.["]

Once published in 1793, Kant's book on religion quickly went through a succession of reprints and new editions. Within the year it was reprinted in Frankfurt/Leipzig and in Neuwied. A second edition, to which Kant added a new preface and many important new notes, came out in 1794 and was reprinted in the same year in Frankfurt/Leipzig.[v] In 1794 F. Grillo published a volume of excerpts in spite of censorship obstacles.[w] Another volume of extracts by an anonymous editor was published in 1796,[x] as was, the following year, the second volume of F. G. Born's *Kantii opera*, which included a Latin translation of *Religion*.

And it was not long before the book began to be publicized in Great Britain as well. A. F. M. Willich gave a brief exposition of its content in his *Elements of the Critical Philosophy* (1798),[y] referring to it both as "Religion within the Limits of Pure Reason" (p. 9), and as "Religion considered within the Bounds of Mere Reason" (p. 114). In 1799, in Volume II of *Essays and Treatises on Moral, Political, and Various Philosophical Subjects, by Emanuel Kant*, John Richardson included the translation of a text entitled "The Religion under the Sphere of Naked Reason."[z] This text was not, however (nor did the translator claim that it was), that of Kant's *Religion*. It was rather the edited version of the fourth and last part of a volume entitled, *The Principles of Critical Philosophy, Selected from the Works of Emanuel Kant, and Expounded by James Sigismund Beck*,[a]

["] To J. C. Lavater, after April 28, 1775; AK 10:179–80. Cf. also the letter of April 28, 1775; AK 10:176–9.

[v] AK 6:501.

[w] *Aphoristische Darstellung der Religion innerhalb der Gränzen der bloßen Vernunft des Herrn Immanuel Kant* (Rostock/Leipzig: Stiller, 1794; reprinted in Ætas Kantiana). Cf. Kiesewetter's letter to Kant of November 23, 1793, AK 11:451.

[x] *Kant's Theorie der rein moralischen Religion mit Rücksicht auf das reine Christentum kurz dargestellt* (Riga, 1796; reprinted in Ætas Kantiana).

[y] The full title reads: *Elements of the Critical Philosophy, containing a concise account of its origin and tendency; a view of all the works published by its founder, Professor Immanuel Kant, and a glossary for an explanation of terms and phrases*, by A. F. M. Willich, M.D. (London: Printed for T. N. Longman, 1798).

[z] Pp. 367–422. For Richardson and his *Essays and Treatises*, cf. above, p. 23.

[a] London: Sold by J. Johnson, W. Richardson. In *Immanuel Kant in England, 1793–1838* (Princeton, 1931), p. 15, René Wellek states that Richardson's *Principles of Critical Philosophy*

which Richardson had published in 1797 and which, as the title clearly led one to expect, contained only an assortment of Kantian excerpts and glosses arranged by Richardson's sometime teacher Beck. Richardson had decided to republish in *Essays and Treatises* an amended version of the part of the earlier volume dealing with religion because, as he noted, "several inaccuracies, which disfigure it, having unfortunately creeped in, the translator deemed a subject of such sublimity and importance worthy of this revisal."[b] The first complete and direct translation of Kant's book must be attributed, therefore, to the Scottish barrister J. William Semple, who published it at Edinburgh in 1838, with the title, "Religion within the Boundary of Pure Reason."[c] A new translation of Part I was made by T. K. Abbott and included in his *Kant's Theory of Ethics or Practical Philosophy.*[d] The English title that Abbott gave to the text, "First Part of the Philosophical Theory of Religion," was a faithful translation of the heading, "Der philosophischen Religionslehre," which Kant had prefaced to each of the four parts of his work and which he had very likely intended as the title for the whole volume right up to publication. A new, complete translation by Theodore M. Greene and Hoyt H. Hudson was published in 1934, with the title, "Religion within the Limits of Reason Alone."[e] It was reissued with slight revisions and a new introductory essay by John R. Silber in 1960.[f]

The present translation of the 1794 edition of "Religion" is based on the Academy text established by Georg Wobbermin,[g] whose editorial notes I have at times also used (as duly acknowledged at the appropriate places). In my work, I have consulted throughout Greene and Hudson's

---

is a translation of Beck's *Erläuternder Auszug aus den critischen Schriften des Herrn Prof. Kant, auf Anrathen desselben* (*Explanatory Extract of the Writings of Mr. Kant, Professor, at His Advice;* Riga, 1793; reprinted in Ætas Kantiana), presumably Volume 1. I can detect, however, nothing but the vaguest resemblances between the two texts.

[b] Volume 2, p. 369, note. The last pages especially are heavily edited and enlarged. The text originally bore the title of "Part IV: More Elaborate Discussion of Moral Religion."

[c] *Religion Within the Boundary of Pure Reason,* tr. J. W. Semple, Advocate (Edinburgh: Thomas Clark, 1838), x–276. For Semple's contribution to the diffusion of Kant in English, cf. Wellek, pp. 248ff.

[d] London: Longmans, Green, Reader and Dyer, 1873. The same work, still including Kant's essay, was republished in 1879 in a much enlarged form, with the title, *Kant's Critique of Practical Reason and Other Works on the Theory of Ethics* (London: Longmans, Green, and Co.). In the preface to this second edition, Abbott translates the title of Kant's whole work as *Religion, so far as it lies within the limits of Reason alone,* p. iv, footnote.

[e] Chicago, London: Open Court.

[f] New York: Harper & Row. The passage from Kant's book allegedly translated in 1845 "by an anonymous writer from Book Three, Part One, Section VI," to which Greene and Hudson refer (p. cxxxv), is in fact a word-for-word reproduction of pp. 140–143 of Semple's translation. The passage is reproduced in Article I of *The British Quarterly Review,* November 1, 1845, pp. 310–12.

[g] AK 6.

English text as well as the Italian one by Poggi and Olivetti.[h] With respect to the former, I can repeat what its translators say with reference to Abbott's translation of Part I – that I "could not avoid, without falling into mere singularity, reproducing words and phrases."[i]

This translation is, however, completely new. Kant's language poses peculiar challenges to the translator, mostly because of the diffuseness of its syntax even by German standards. Kant tends to pile up clauses upon clauses recklessly, sometimes holding them together by but the barest of syntactical threads. The temptation of the translator is to make these clauses into full sentences, and in this way turn Kant's otherwise unwieldy structures into more manageable separate parts. The shortfall of this strategy, however, is that it risks not conveying in English the rhetorical force of Kant's German. What Kant's long sentences lack in syntactical cohesiveness, they make up in rhetorical unity. And this unity is in turn a function of the singleness of thought that animates every sentence of Kant. Clauses pile up upon clauses, not haphazardly but as comments displaying the full complexity of the one point Kant is nonetheless trying to make. The progression of Kant's arguments often relies on precisely this unremitting march of clauses, and to halt its advance with undue stops risks trading off diffuseness of syntax for diffuseness of meaning.

For this reason, I have sought to make the German of Kant as transparent through the English as possible, hence to multiply dependent clauses in English too, even at the risk of having to thread at times at the extreme limits of accepted form. In those cases where the strategy failed and Kant's full sentence had to be broken down, I have tried to run the resulting sentences together with such opening connectives as "And," "For," "So," "But," "Yet," or, occasionally, to set them in opposition by means of a colon separating them. I suggest that the best way of reading Kant is to "hear" him speak. The force of his rhetoric is that of the spoken word. Kant is the teacher forever pursuing an elusive thought before his audience of students, adding comments to comments, now raising his voice and now lowering it, often retrieving points previously made but again relevant and perhaps forgotten, and not letting up until the full thought or the full image has finally been expressed. As in spoken language, so too in Kant's writing – what counts at the end is not syntactical elegance but rhetorical strength.

Greene and Hudson's translation of the title, "Religion within the Limits of Reason Alone," has been widely accepted in the Kant literature. It was only after long deliberation that I decided, therefore, to amend it. I replaced "limits" with "boundaries" in order to make more explicit the

[h] *La religione entro i limiti della sola ragione,* trans. Alfredo Poggi, ed. Marco M. Olivetti (Roma/Bari: Laterza, 1985).
[i] P. cxxxvi (1960 edition).

image of "confines" or "borders" (as of a territory or country) clearly conveyed by the German *die Grenzen*. The expression *bloße Vernunft* presented special difficulties. Several translations have been offered in the past. Willich has both "pure reason" and "mere reason." Semple renders it as "pure reason" in the title but in the text itself refers to it repeatedly as "naked reason" (pp. 7, 11, 133). Richardson has "naked reason" in one place,[j] and "bare reason" in another.[k] Then there is, of course, Greene and Hudson's "reason alone." To this list one could also add "unassisted reason," "unsupported reason," and "sheer reason." With the exception of "pure reason" – which is misleading at best[l] – all these translations are in principle possible, because they all accurately render at least one possible meaning of the dense German *bloß*. Because they all are too specialized, however, they all fail to capture all the allusions that Kant could convey with just one German word; hence they all end up saying too much and yet not enough. Faced by this difficulty, and unable to find in English any equally supple and rich word, I finally decided after much hesitation to revert to Willich's "mere reason." I made this choice because, in spite of the negative connotations which "mere" nowadays tends to have, according to its dictionary definition the word still means "pure, unmixed, undiluted," which is also the meaning of the original Latin *merus* (see the *Oxford English Dictionary, s.v.*); it is at least this mixture of traits which Kant meant to convey by *bloß*. I made the choice also because of the legal, albeit somewhat antiquated, meaning of "mere." In a legal context, "mere" denotes an action "performed or exercised by a person without the aid of anyone else," and, with reference to a "right," it denotes the right itself as distinguished from possession. Certainly, it was Kant's intention to examine religion in the light of unaided reason: to establish its "mere" rights as contrasted with those it had acquired historically. "Mere reason" thus seems to me to convey at least the basic metaphors elicited by *bloße Vernunft*. Of course, I recognize that "mere" still falls short of *bloß*. But here is where translation runs up against its limits, and the translator has no choice but to submit to them graciously.[m] I also hope that with "mere reason" I have retained the rhetorical punch of Kant's *bloße Vernunft*, which Greene and Hudson were also sensitive to preserve.

[j] Cf. footnote z, p. 50.
[k] *Metaphysical Works of the Celebrated Immanuel Kant, with a Sketch of His Life and Writings* (London: Printed in 1819 but published [posthumously] in 1836), *The Logic*, p. 233.
[l] Cf. Abbott, 1879, p. iv, footnote.
[m] "Mere reason" conveys Kant's intention in *Religion* as stated in the sketch of a letter to Reuß: "The issue here is not the faith which alone would be possible to a human individual in general, but the faith of someone who bases himself solely [*bloß*] on reason – which thereby rests entirely on grounds *a priori*, and asserts its validity under all forms of faith." May 1793 (approx.) AK 11:416. Maternus Reuß (1751–98), Benedictine professor of philosophy at Würzburg.

I took care of the *Willkür-Wille* distinction – which Silber found particularly troublesome" – by translating *Willkür* as "power of choice" and *Wille* as "will," and in the editorial footnotes by alerting the reader to the few cases where I diverge from this practice. *Sinnlichkeit* and *sinnlich* also presented problems because of the nuances that "sensibility" and "sensible" have taken up in modern English usage. "Sensibility" tends to blend with "sensitivity," and "sensible" with "good sense." Since both terms have assumed technical meaning in Kantian literature, I have not hesitated using them. However, I have at times replaced them with circumlocutions employing "the senses," or with the adjectival use of the noun "sense." For instance, I have sometimes said "sense experience" rather than "sensible experience," or "the world of the senses" instead of "the sensible world," or again, "something that the senses can hold on to" instead of "something that can be sensibly held on to." In all cases, since the meaning is clear from context, I have let rhetorical appropriateness rather than any rigorously formulated principle govern my practice. I have also occasionally used "sensory" for *sinnlich*, and I have indicated in footnotes the instances in which I translate it as "sensuous," and I have also faithfully entered in footnotes a German term whenever my translation is somewhat eccentric (and hence possibly misleading). Finally, I have translated with "principle" both *Grundzatz* and *Prinzip*, even though *Grundsatz* has logical whereas *Prinzip* causal connotations (as in "first proposition" as contrasted with "first cause of evil"). The difference between the two is clear in context.

Any word or phrase in square brackets has been added to Kant's text by the translator. Unless otherwise specified, the translations of texts cited in the notes are mine. Scriptural citations are from the King James Version of the Bible.

G. di G.

" Green/Hudson, 1960 edition, p. cxxxix.

Religion within the boundaries of mere reason

Preface to the first edition

So far as morality is based on the conception of the human being as one who is free but who also, just because of that, binds himself through his reason to unconditional laws, it is in need neither of the idea of another being above him in order that he recognize his duty, nor, that he observe it, of an incentive other than the law itself. At least it is the human being's own fault if such a need is found in him; but in this case too the need could not be relieved through anything else: for whatever does not originate from himself and his own freedom provides no remedy for a lack in his morality. – Hence on its own behalf morality in no way needs religion (whether objectively, as regards willing, or subjectively, as regards capability) but is rather self-sufficient by virtue of pure practical reason. – For, since its laws bind through the mere form of universal lawfulness of the maxims to be adopted in accordance with this lawfulness as the highest condition (itself unconditional) of all ends, morality needs absolutely no material determining ground of the free power of choice,* that is no end, either in order to recognize what duty is or to impel its performance; on the contrary, when duty is the issue, morality can perfectly well abstract from ends altogether, and ought so to do. For example, to know whether I should (or even can) be truthful in my testimony before a court of justice, or faithful when someone else's goods entrusted to me are being re- 6:4

---

* Those for whom the merely formal determining ground as such (lawfulness) will not suffice as the determining ground in the concept of duty, nonetheless admit that this ground is not to be found in *self-love* directed to one's own *comfort.* But then there are only two determining grounds left: one that is rational, namely, one's own *perfection;* and another that is empirical, the *happiness* of others.[1] Now, if by the first they do not already understand moral perfection, which can only be one thing (namely a will unconditionally obedient to the law), in which case they would however be defining in a circle, then they must mean the human being's natural perfection inasmuch as it is capable of enhancement; and of this perfection there can be many aspects (such as skill in the arts and the sciences, taste, physical agility, etc.). But these are always only conditionally good, that is, good only on condition that their use does not conflict with the moral law (which alone commands unconditionally); hence natural perfection cannot be, when made into an end, the principle of the concepts of duty. The same also applies to an end when associated with the happiness of other human beings. For an action must first be weighed in itself according to the moral law before it can be associated with the happiness of others. The action's promotion of this happiness, therefore, is duty only conditionally, and cannot serve as the supreme principle of moral maxims.

claimed, there is no need to demand an end which I might perhaps propose to myself to realize by my declaration, for what sort of end this would be does not matter at all; rather, one who still finds it necessary to look around for some end when his testimony is rightfully demanded of him, is in this respect already contemptible.

But although on its own behalf morality does not need the representation of an end which would have to precede the determination of the will, it may well be that it has a necessary reference to such an end, not as the ground of its maxims but as a necessary consequence accepted in conformity to them. – For in the absence of all reference to an end no determination of the will can take place in human beings at all, since no such determination can occur without an effect, and its representation, though not as the determining ground of the power of choice nor as an end that comes first in intention, must nonetheless be admissible as the consequence of that power's determination to an end through the law (*finis in consequentiam veniens*);[a] without this end, a power of choice which does not [thus] add to a contemplated action the thought of either an objectively or subjectively determined object (which it has or should have), instructed indeed as to *how* to operate but not as to the *whither,* can itself obtain no satisfaction. So morality really has no need of an end for right conduct; on the contrary, the law that contains the formal condition of the use of freedom in general suffices to it. Yet an end proceeds from morality just the same; for it cannot possibly be a matter of indifference to reason how to answer the question, *What is then the result of this right conduct of ours?* nor to what we are to direct our doings or nondoings, even granted this is not fully in our control, at least as something with which they are to harmonize. And this is indeed only the idea of an object that unites within itself the formal condition of all such ends as we ought to have (duty) with everything which is conditional upon ends we have and which conforms to duty (happiness proportioned to its observance), that is, the idea of a highest good in the world, for whose possibility we must assume a higher, moral, most holy, and omnipotent being who alone can unite the two elements of this good. This idea is not (practically considered) an empty one; for it meets our natural need, which would otherwise be a hindrance to moral resolve, to think for all our doings and nondoings taken as a whole some sort of final end which reason can justify. What is most important here, however, is that this idea rises out of morality and is not its foundation; that it is an end which to make one's own already presupposes ethical principles. It cannot be a matter of indifference to morality, therefore, whether it does or does not fashion for itself the concept of a final end of all things (although, to be sure, harmonizing with this end does not increase the number of morality's duties but rather provides

6:5

___

[a] an end occurring by way of consequence.

58

these with a special point of reference for the unification of all ends); for only in this way can an objective practical reality be given to the combination, which we simply cannot do without, of the purposiveness [deriving] from freedom and the purposiveness of nature. Assume a human being who honors the moral law, and who allows himself to think (as he can hardly avoid doing) what sort of world he would *create*, were this in his power, under the guidance of practical reason – a world within which, moreover, he would place himself as a member. Now, not only would he choose a world precisely as the moral idea of the highest good requires, if the choice were entrusted to him alone, but he would also will the very existence of [such] a world, since the moral law wills that the highest good possible through us be actualized, even though, in following this idea, he   6:6
might see himself in danger of forfeiting much in the way of personal happiness, for it is possible that he might not be adequate to what reason makes the condition for it. He would thus feel himself compelled by reason to acknowledge this judgment with complete impartiality, as if rendered by somebody else yet at the same time his own, and in this way the human being evinces the need, effected in him by morality, of adding to the thought of his duties a final end as well, as their consequence.

Morality thus inevitably leads to religion, and through religion it extends itself* to the idea of a mighty moral lawgiver outside the human

---

* The proposition, "There is a God, hence there is a highest good in the world," if it is to proceed (as proposition of faith) simply from morality, is a synthetic *a priori* proposition; for although accepted only in a practical context, it yet exceeds the concept of duty that morality contains (and which does not presuppose any matter of the power of choice, but only this power's formal laws), and hence cannot be analytically evolved out of morality. *But how is such a proposition* a priori *possible?* Agreement with the mere idea of a moral lawgiver for all human beings is indeed identical with the moral concept of duty in general, and to this extent the proposition commanding the agreement would be analytic. But the acceptance of the existence of this lawgiver means more than the mere possibility of such an object. I can only indicate here, but without developing it, the key to the resolution of this task, as far as I believe myself to have insight into it.[2]

An *end* is always the object of an *inclination*, that is, of an immediate desire to possess a thing by means of one's action, jut as a *law* (which commands practically) is the object of *respect*. An objective end (i.e. an end which we ought to have) is one which is assigned to us as such by reason alone. The end that contains the inescapable, and at the same time sufficient, condition of all other ends is the *final end*. One's own happiness is the subjective final end of rational beings belonging to the world (they each *have* this end by virtue of their nature which is dependent upon sensible objects; it would therefore be otiose to say of that end that one *ought to* have it), and all practical propositions that have this ultimate end as their ground are synthetic yet at the same time empirical. But that every human being ought   6:7
to make the highest possible *good* in the world his own *final end* is a synthetic practical proposition a priori, that is, an objective-practical proposition given through pure reason, since it is a proposition that exceeds the concept of the duties in this world, and adds a consequence (an effect) of these duties that is not contained in the moral laws and cannot, therefore, be evolved out of them analytically. For these laws command absolutely, whatever their consequences; indeed, they even require that we abstract from such consequences

59

being, in whose will the final end (of the creation of the world) is what can and at the same ought to be the final human end.

. .
.

6:7   If morality recognizes in the holiness of its law an object worthy of the highest respect, at the level of religion it represents an object of *worship* in the highest cause that brings this law to fruition, and thus morality appears in its majesty. Everything, however, even the most sublime object, is diminished under the hands of human beings whenever they apply its idea

6:8 to their use. That which can be venerated truthfully only so far as respect for it is free, is forced to accommodate itself to forms which can be given authority only through coercive laws; and that which of itself exposes itself to the public criticism of all, must submit to a criticism which has coercive power, i.e., to a censorship.

However, since the command: Obey authority! is also a moral one and

entirely whenever a particular action is concerned, and thereby they make of duty an object of the highest respect, without proposing to us, or assigning, an end (and a final end) such as would constitute some sort of inducement for it and an incentive to the fulfillment of our duty. All human beings could sufficiently partake of this incentive too if they just adhered (as they should) to the rule of pure reason in the law. What need have they to know of the outcome of their doings and nondoings that the world's course will bring about? It suffices for them that they do their duty, even if everything were to end with life in this world, and in this life too happiness and desert perhaps never converge. Yet it is one of the inescapable limitations of human beings and of their practical faculty of reason (perhaps of that faculty in all other worldly beings as well) to be concerned in every action with its result, seeking something in it that might serve them as an end and even prove the purity of their intention – which result would indeed come last in practice (*nexu effectivo*)[b] but first in representation and intention (*nexu finali*).[c] Now, in this end human beings seek something that they can *love*, even though it is being proposed to them through reason alone. Hence the law that only inspires *respect* in them, though it does not recognize this sought-after something as [its own] need, nonetheless extends itself on its behalf to include the moral final end of reason among its determining grounds. That is, the proposition, "Make the highest possible good in this world your own final end," is a synthetic proposition *a priori* which is introduced by the moral law itself, and yet through it practical reason reaches beyond the law. And this is possible because the moral law is taken with reference to the characteristic, natural to the human being, of having to consider in every action, besides the law, also an end (this characteristic of the human being makes him an object of experience). The proposition itself is possible (just like the theoretical yet synthetic propositions *a priori*) only because it contains the *a priori* principle of the cognition of the determining grounds of a power of free choice in experience in general, so far as experience, by exhibiting the effects of morality in its ends, gives an objective, although only practical, reality to the concept of morality as having causality in the world. – But now, if the strictest observance of the moral laws is to be

6:8 thought of as the cause of the ushering in of the highest good (as end), then, since human capacity does not suffice to effect happiness in the world proportionate to the worthiness to be happy, an omnipotent moral being must be assumed as ruler of the world, under whose care this would come about, i.e., morality leads inevitably to religion.

[b] according to the concatenation of efficiency
[c] according to the concatenation of finality

its observance, like that of any duty, can be extended to religion, it is fitting that a treatise dedicated to the definition of the concept of religion should itself offer an example of this obedience – which, however, cannot be demonstrated merely by attending to the law in a single state regulation while [remaining] blind to all others, but concomitantly, only through coherent respect for all regulations. Now the theologian who judges on books can be appointed either as one who is to care simply for the welfare of souls, or as one who at the same time is to care for the welfare of the sciences: the first judges simply as divine, the second as scholar as well. It rests with the latter, as a member of a public institution to which (under the name of "university") all the sciences are entrusted for cultivation and protection against encroachments, whether to restrict the prerogatives of the first so that his censorship shall not disrupt the field of the sciences. And if the two are biblical theologians, then primacy in censorship pertains to the second as a member of the university in a faculty charged with the treatment of this theology; for, as regards the first concern (the welfare of souls), both have one and the same mandate, whereas, as regards the second (the welfare of the sciences), the theologian in the capacity of university scholar has in addition another special function to discharge. If we deviate from this rule things must finally come to the pass where they have already once been (for example, at the time of Galileo), namely that the biblical theologian, to humble the pride of the sciences and spare himself effort on them, might venture incursions even into astronomy or   6:9 other sciences such as the ancient history of the earth, and [thus] take charge of all the endeavors of the human understanding – just like those peoples who, finding in themselves neither ability nor resolution enough to defend themselves against threats of attack, transform all about them into a wilderness.

Over against biblical theology, however, there stands on the side of the sciences a philosophical theology which is a property held in trust by another faculty. This theology must have complete freedom to expand as far as its science reaches, provided that it stays within the boundaries of mere reason and makes indeed use of history, languages, the books of all peoples, even the Bible, in order to confirm and explain its propositions, but only for itself, without carrying these propositions over into biblical theology or wishing to modify its public doctrines, which is a privilege of divines. And although the right of censorship of the theologian (considered as a divine) cannot be disputed where it has been established that philosophical theology has truly trespassed across its boundaries and encroached on biblical theology, yet, as soon as this is in doubt again and the question therefore arises whether the trespass has occurred through a writing or some other public dissertation of the philosopher, the superior censorship can only fall to the biblical theologian as *member of his faculty;*

for as such he[d] has also been charged with the care of the second interest of the community, namely the flourishing of the sciences, and has been appointed with just as much validity as [has] the first.[e]

Indeed, in a case like this the primary censorship is the prerogative of this faculty [of theology] and not of the faculty of philosophy; for with respect to certain doctrines the former alone holds privilege, whereas the latter deals with its own openly and freely; only the former, therefore, can make complaints that its exclusive right has been impinged upon. However, in spite of the verging of the two bodies of doctrine on one another and the anxiety about a transgression of boundaries by philosophical theology, doubt about an encroachment can easily be averted if it is only borne in mind that any such mischief does not occur because the philosopher *borrows* something from biblical theology to use for his own purpose (for biblical theology itself will not want to deny that it contains much in common with the doctrines of mere reason and, in addition, much that belongs to the science of history or linguistic scholarship and is subject to the censorship of these [disciplines]); rather, even granted that the philosopher uses whatever he borrows from biblical theology in a meaning suited to mere reason but perhaps not pleasing to this theology, [the mischief occurs] only because the philosopher *brings* something *into* biblical theology itself and thereby seeks to fit it for other ends than it is fitted for. – Thus we cannot say, for instance, that the teacher of natural right encroaches on the Codex of Roman Law[3] just because he borrows from it many a classical expression and formula for his philosophical doctrine of natural right, even when, as often happens, he employs them in not quite the same sense in which, according to the interpreters of the Codex, they are to be taken, so long as he does not wish that the jurists proper, or perhaps the courts of law, should also use them that way. For if that were not within his competence, we could conversely also accuse the biblical theologian, or the statutory jurist, of having countless times encroached upon the domain of philosophy, because both must often borrow from it, though only to their respective advantage, since they cannot do without reason nor, where science is at issue, without philosophy. And, were the biblical theologian to consider having absolutely nothing to do wherever possible with reason in things religious, we can easily foresee on which side the loss would be; for a religion that rashly declares war on reason will not long endure against it. – I will even venture to ask whether it would not be beneficial, upon completion of the academic instruction in

6:10

---

[d] "as such he" = *dieser* (i.e. "this")

[e] *der erstere*, literally, "the first." Kant's text is ambiguous. The Greene/Hudson translation glosses, "the theologian regarded as divine." Although this is a likely interpretation, the "first" could just as well refer to the "philosophical theologian." Cf. the sentence immediately following.

biblical theology, always to add by way of conclusion, as requisite to the complete preparation of the candidate, a special course on the pure *philosophical* doctrine of religion (which would avail itself of everything, the Bible included) somewhat along the lines of this book (or any other, if a better one of the same kind can be had). – For the sciences profit simply from being set apart, insofar as each science first constitutes a whole by itself; only after that shall the experiment be made of considering them in association. Now whether the theologian agrees with the philosopher or believes himself obliged to oppose him: let him just hear him out. For in this way alone can the theologian be forearmed against all the difficulties that the philosopher may cause him. To conceal these difficulties, however, or indeed to decry them as ungodly is a mean expedient that will not wash; to mix the two [disciplines] and for the biblical theologian to direct only the occasional fleeting glance at [philosophy], constitutes a lack of thoroughness where in the end nobody knows exactly how they stand in the whole with respect to the doctrine of religion.

6:11

Of the following four essays in which, to make apparent the relation of religion to a human nature partly laden with good dispositions and partly with evil ones, I represent the relationship of the good and the evil principles as two equally self-subsisting transient causes affecting men, the first was already inserted in the *Berlin Monthly* of April 1792[4] but could not be omitted here, because of the rigorous coherence of the materials in this work which, in the three essays now to be added, contains the complete development of the first. –

The reader will excuse the orthography (different from mine) of the first sheets in view of the different hands that have worked on the copy, and the shortness of the time left to me for revision.

Preface to the second edition

Except for misprints and certain few expressions that have been corrected, nothing has been altered in this edition. Newly added supplements have been placed at the foot of the text, marked with a dagger (†).

Regarding the title of this work (since doubts have been expressed also regarding the intention hidden behind it) I note: Since, after all, *revelation* can at least comprise also the pure *religion of reason,* whereas, conversely, the latter cannot do the same for what is historical in revelation, I shall be able to consider the first as a *wider* sphere of faith that includes the other, a *narrower* one, within itself (not as two circles external to one another but as concentric circles); the philosopher, as purely a teacher of reason (from mere principles *a priori*), must keep within the inner circle and, thereby, also abstract from all experience. From this standpoint I can also make this second experiment, namely, to start from some alleged revelation or other and, abstracting from the pure religion of reason (so far as it constitutes a system on its own), to hold fragments of this revelation, as a *historical system,* up to moral concepts, and see whether it does not lead back to the same pure *rational system* of religion [from which I have abstracted]. The latter, though not from the theoretical point of view (under which must also be reckoned the technicopractical point of view of pedagogical method, as a *technology*) may yet, from the morally practical point of view, be independent and sufficient to genuine religion, which, as a rational concept *a priori* (remaining after everything empirical has been removed), only obtains in this relation. If this is the case, then we shall be able to say that between reason and Scripture there is, not only compatibility but also unity, so that whoever follows the one (under the guidance of moral concepts) will not fail to come across the other as well. Were this not so, we would either have two religions in one person, which is absurd, or a *religion* and a *cult,* in which case, since the latter is not (like religion) an end in itself but has value only as a means, the two would have to be often shaken up together that they might, for a short time, combine; like oil and water, however, they would soon have to separate again and let the purely moral religion (the religion of reason) float to the top.

I noted in the first Preface that this unification, or the attempt at it, is a task to which the philosophical researcher of religion has perfect right, and not an encroachment on the exclusive right of the biblical theologian.

Since then I have found this claim advanced in the *Ethics*[5] (Part I, pp. 5–11) of the late Michaelis – a man well versed in both disciplines – and applied throughout his entire work, without the higher faculty finding anything in this prejudicial to its rights.

In this second edition I have not been not able to take cognizance, as I would have wished to do, of the judgments passed upon this text by worthy men, named and unnamed, since (as with all foreign literature) these arrive in our regions very late. [I say this] especially with reference to the *Annotationes quaedam theologicae etc.* of the renowned Hr. Dr. Storr of Tübingen,[6] who has examined the text with his accustomed sagacity and with a diligence and fairness deserving the greatest thanks; I plan a reply to him, but do not venture to promise it because of the difficulties that old age poses especially in the way of working with abstract ideas. – But there is a review in Number 29 of *Recent Critical News*, from Greifswald, which I can dispose of just as expeditiously as the reviewer did the text itself.[7] For in his opinion my writing is nothing but the answer to this question which I myself posed to myself: "How is the ecclesiastical system of dogmatics possible, in its concepts and doctrines, according to pure (theoretical and practical) reason?" – Hence this investigation is of no concern at all to those who have no more acquaintance and understanding of his (Kant's) system than desire to be capable of them; for them the system might as well not exist. – To this I answer: Only common morality is needed to understand the essentials of this text, without venturing into the critique of practical reason, still less into that of theoretical reason. For instance, whenever virtue, as a facility in *actions* conforming to duty (according to their legality), is called *virtus phaenomenon* but, as a constant *disposition* toward such actions from *duty* (because of their morality), is called *virtus noumenon*, these expressions are used only because of the schools; the matter itself is contained, though in other words, in the most popular instruction for children or in sermons, and is easily understood. If only one could boast as much regarding the mysteries of divine nature, which are considered part of religious doctrine and are imported into the catechisms as though they were entirely popular but must eventually be transformed into moral concepts if they are to become intelligible to everyone.

6:14

Königsberg, 26 January 1794.

Table of contents

Part I: Concerning the indwelling of the evil principle alongside the good, or, Of radical evil in human nature.

Part II: Concerning the struggle of the good with the evil principle for dominion over the human being.

Part III: Concerning the victory of the good over the evil principle and the founding of a Kingdom of God on earth.

Part IV: Concerning service and counterfeit service*ƒ* under the dominion of the good principle, or, Of Religion and Priestcraft.

ƒ Service = *Dienst;* counterfeit service = *Afterdienst. After* in German can mean "anus."

The philosophical doctrine of religion
Part one

Part One

Concerning the indwelling of the evil principle alongside the good

or

Of the radical evil in human nature

That "the world lieth in evil"[8] is a complaint as old as history, even as old as the older art of poetic fiction; indeed, just as old as that oldest among all fictions, the religion of the priests. All allow that the world began with something good: with the Golden Age, with life in Paradise, or an even happier life in communion with heavenly beings. But then they make this happiness disappear like a dream, and they spitefully hasten the decline into evil (moral evil, with which the physical always went hand in hand) in an accelerating fall,* so that now (this "now" is, however, as old as history) we live in the final age; the Last Day and the destruction of the world are knocking at the door, and in certain regions of India the Judge and Destroyer of the world, Rutra (otherwise known as Shiva or Shiwa), already is worshipped as the God now holding power, after Vishnu, the Sustainer of the World, grown weary of the office he had received from Brahma the Creator, resigned it centuries ago.[9]

More recent, though far less widespread, is the opposite heroic opinion,[10] which has gained standing only among philosophers and, in our days, especially among the pedagogues: that the world steadfastly (though hardly noticeably) forges ahead in the very opposite direction, namely from bad to better; that at least there is in the human being the predisposition to move in this direction. But surely, if the issue is *moral* good or evil (not just growth in civilization), they have not drawn this view from experience, for the history of all times attests far too powerfully against it; and we may

6:20

Aetas parentum peior avis tulit
Nos nequiores, mox daturos
Progeniem vitiosiorem.
Horace[f]

[f] *Odes*, III, 6: "The age of our parents (who were worse than our forefathers) brought us forth yet more dishonest, and we are now ready to issue an even more vicious progeny."

69

presume that it is, rather, just an optimistic presupposition on the part of the moralists, from Seneca to Rousseau, intended to encourage the indefatigable cultivation of that seed of goodness that perhaps lies in us, if one could only count on any such natural foundation of goodness in the human kind. Yet this is also to be said: Since we must assume that the human being is sound of body by nature (i.e., in the way he is usually born), there is no cause not to assume that he is equally sound and good of soul by nature as well. Nature itself would then be promoting the cultivation in us of this ethical predisposition toward goodness.[11] As Seneca says: *Sanabilibus aegrotamus malis, nosque in rectum genitos natura, si sanari, velimus, adiuvat.*[h]

But since it well may be that we have erred in both these ways of reading experience, the question arises whether a middle ground may not at least be possible, namely that, as a species, the human being can neither be good nor evil, or, at any rate, that he can be the one just as much as the other, partly good, partly evil. – We call a human being evil, however, not because he performs actions that are evil (contrary to law), but because these are so constituted that they allow the inference of evil maxims in him. Now through experience we can indeed notice unlawful actions, and also notice (at least within ourselves) that they are consciously contrary to law. But we cannot observe maxims, we cannot do so unproblematically even within ourselves; hence the judgment that an agent is an evil human being cannot reliably be based on experience. In order, then, to call a human being evil, it must be possible to infer *a priori* from a number of consciously evil actions, or even from a single one, an underlying evil maxim, and, from this, the presence in the subject of a common ground, itself a maxim, of all particular morally evil maxims.

But lest anyone be immediately scandalized by the expression *nature*, which would stand in direct contradiction to the predicates *morally* good or *morally* evil if taken to mean (as it usually does) the opposite of the ground of actions [arising] from *freedom*, let it be noted that by "the nature of a human being" we only understand here the subjective ground – wherever it may lie – of the exercise of the human being's freedom in general (under objective moral laws) antecedent to every deed that falls within the scope of the senses. But this subjective ground must, in turn, itself always be a deed [i] of freedom (for otherwise the use or abuse of the human being's power of choice with respect to the moral law could not be imputed to him, nor could the good or evil in him be called "moral"). Hence the ground of evil cannot lie in any object *determining* the power of choice through inclination, not in any natural impulses, but only in a rule that the power of choice itself produces for the exercise of its freedom,

[h] *De ira,* II:13.1: "We are sick with curable diseases, and if we wish to be cured, nature comes to our aid, *for we are born to health.*" The quote is also found on the title page of J.-J. Rousseau's *Émile.*
[i] *Actus*

i.e., in a maxim. One cannot, however, go on asking what, in a human being, might be the subjective ground of the adoption of this maxim rather than its opposite. For if this ground were ultimately no longer itself a maxim, but merely a natural impulse, the entire exercise of freedom could be traced back to a determination through natural causes – and this would contradict freedom. Whenever we therefore say, "The human being is by nature good," or, "He is by nature evil," this only means that he holds within himself a first ground* (to us inscrutable) for the adoption of good or evil (unlawful) maxims, and that he holds this ground *qua* human, universally – in such a way, therefore, that by his maxims he expresses at the same time the character of his species.

We shall say, therefore, of one of these [two] characters (which distinguish the human being from other possible rational beings) that it is *innate* in him; and yet we shall always be satisfied that nature is not to blame for it (if the character is evil), nor does it deserve praise (if it is good), but that the human being is alone its author. But since the first ground of the   6:22 adoption of our maxims, which must itself again lie in the free power of choice, cannot be any fact[j] possibly given in experience, the good or the evil in the human being is said to be innate (as the subjective first ground of the adoption of this or that maxim with respect to the moral law) only *in the sense* that it is posited as the ground antecedent to every use of freedom given in experience (from the earliest youth as far back as birth) and is thus represented as present in the human being at the moment of birth – not that birth itself is its cause.

Remark

At the basis of the conflict between the two hypotheses presented above there lies a disjunctive proposition: *The human being is* (by nature) *either morally good or morally evil.* It will readily occur to anyone to ask, however, whether this disjunction is accurate; and whether some might not claim that the human being is by nature neither of the two, others, that he is both at once, that is, good in some parts and evil in others. Experience even seems to confirm this middle position between the two extremes.

It is of great consequence to ethics in general, however, to preclude, so far as possible, anything morally intermediate, either in actions (*adia-*

---

* That the first subjective ground of the adoption of moral maxims is inscrutable can be seen provisionally from this: Since the adoption is free, its ground (e.g. why I have adopted an evil maxim and not a good one instead) must not be sought in any incentive of nature, but always again in a maxim; and, since any such maxim must have its ground as well, yet apart from a maxim no *determining ground* of the free power of choice ought to, or can, be adduced, we are endlessly referred back in the series of subjective determining grounds, without ever being able to come to the first ground.

[j] *Factum* (i.e. "something done")

phora)^k or in human characters; for with any such ambiguity all maxims run the risk of losing their determination and stability. Those who adhere to this strict way of thinking are commonly called *rigorists* (a name intended to carry reproach, but in fact a praise); so we can call *latitudinarians* those at the opposite extreme. These latter, again, are either latitudinarians of neutrality and may be called *indifferentists*, or latitudinarians of coalition and can then be called *syncretists*.[12]*

6:23   On the rigorist's criteria,† the answer to the question just posed is

---

* If the good = a, the opposite contradicting it is the not-good. Now, this not-good is the consequence either of the mere lack of a ground of the good, = o, or of a positive ground antagonistic to the good, = −a; in this latter case, the not-good can also be called positive evil. (With respect to pleasure and pain there is a similar middle term, whereby pleasure = a, pain = −a, and the state in which neither of the two obtains is indifference, = o.) Now, if the moral law in us were not an incentive of the power of choice, the morally good (the agreement of the power of choice with the law) would be = a, and the not-good, = o; the latter, however, would be just the consequence of the lack of a moral incentive, = a × o. In us, however, the law is incentive, = a. Hence the lack of the agreement of the power of choice with it (= o) is possible only as the consequence of a real and opposite determination of the power of choice, i.e. of a *resistance* on its part, = −a; or again, it is only possible through an evil power of choice. And so between an evil and a good disposition (the inner principle of maxims) according to which the morality of an action must be judged, there is no intermediate position.[13]

†A morally indifferent action (*adiaphoron morale*) would be one that merely follows upon the laws of nature, and hence stands in no relation at all to the moral law as law of freedom – for such an action is not a *factum*,^{l} and with respect to it neither *command*, nor *prohibition*, nor yet *permission* (*authorization* according to law), intervenes or is necessary.

† Professor Schiller, in his masterful treatise on *gracefulness* and *dignity* in morality (*Thalia*, 1793, 3rd issue),[14] disapproves of this way of representing obligation, because it carries with it the frame of mind of a Carthusian. Since we are however at one upon the most important principles, I cannot admit disagreement on this one, if only we can make ourselves clear to one another. – I readily grant that I am unable to associate *gracefulness* with the *concept of duty*, by reason of its very dignity. For the concept of duty includes unconditional necessitation, to which gracefulness stands in direct contradiction. The majesty of the law (like the law on Sinai) instills awe (not dread, which repels; and also not fascination, which invites familiarity); and this awe rouses the respect of the subject toward his master, except that in this case, since the master lies in us, it rouses a *feeling of the sublimity* of our own vocation that enraptures us more than any beauty. – But *virtue*, i.e. the firmly grounded disposition to fulfill one's duty strictly, is also *beneficent* in its consequences, more so than anything that nature or art might afford in the world. Hence the glorious picture of humanity, as portrayed in the figure of virtue, does allow the attendance of the *graces*, who, however, maintain a respectful distance when duty alone is at issue. And if we consider the gracious consequences that virtue would spread throughout the world, should it gain entry everywhere, then the morally oriented reason (through the imagination) calls sensibility into play. Hercules becomes *Musagetes*^{m} only after subduing monsters, a labor at which those good sisters^n shrink back in fear and trembling. These same attendants of Venus Urania^o become wanton sisters in the train of

^{k} morally indifferent

^{l} "deed," in the sense of "something done."

^{m} leader of the muses

^{n} i.e. the muses

^{o} Heavenly Venus

based on the morally important observation that freedom of the power of choice has the characteristic, entirely peculiar to it, that it cannot be determined to action through any incentive *except so far as the human being has incorporated it into his maxim* (has made it into a universal rule for himself, according to which he wills to conduct himself); only in this way can an incentive, whatever it may be, coexist with the absolute spontaneity of the power of choice (of freedom). But the moral law is itself an incentive in the judgment of reason, and whoever makes it his maxim is *morally* good. Now, if the law fails nevertheless to determine somebody's free power of choice with respect to an action relating to it, an incentive opposed to it must have influence on the power of choice of the human being in question; and since, by hypothesis, this can only happen because this human being incorporates the incentive (and consequently also the deviation from the moral law) into his maxim (in which case he is an evil human being), it follows that his disposition as regards the moral law is never indifferent (never neither good nor bad).[15]

6:24

Nor can a human being be morally good in some parts, and at the same time evil in others. For if he is good in one part, he has incorporated the moral law into his maxim. And were he, therefore, to be evil in some other part, since the moral law of compliance with duty in general is a single one and universal, the maxim relating to it would be universal yet particular at the same time: which is contradictory.*

6:25

Venus Dione[p] as soon as they meddle in the business of determining duties and try to provide incentives for them – Now, if we ask, "What is the *aesthetic* constitution, the *temperament* so to speak *of virtue*: is it courageous and hence *joyous*, or weighed down by fear and dejected?" an answer is hardly necessary. The latter slavish frame of mind can never be found without a hidden *hatred* of the law, whereas a heart joyous in the *compliance* with its duty (not just complacency in the *recognition* of it) is the sign of genuineness in virtuous disposition, even where *piety* is concerned, which does not consist in the self-torment of a remorseful sinner (a torment which is very ambiguous, and usually only an inward reproach for having offended against prudence), but in the firm resolve to improve in the future. This resolve, encouraged by good progress, must needs effect a joyous frame of mind, without which one is never certain of having *gained* also a *love* for the good, i.e. of having incorporated the good into one's maxim.

* The ancient moral philosophers, who have pretty well exhausted all that can be said concerning virtue, have also not left the two questions above untouched. They expressed the first thus: Whether virtue must be learned (the human being, therefore, would by nature be indifferent to virtue and vice?) The second was: Whether there is more than one virtue (and hence the human being can perhaps[q] be virtuous in some parts, and vicious in others)? To both they replied with rigoristic precision in the negative; and rightly so, for they were considering virtue *in itself*, in the *idea* of reason (how the human being ought to be). If, however, we want to pass moral judgment on this moral being, the human being *as he appears*, such as experience lets us cognize him, we can then answer both questions in the positive. For then he would be judged, not by the scales of pure reason (before a divine court of justice), but according to empirical standards (by a human judge). More about this in what follows.

6:25

[p] Venus as mother
[q] The text reads "nicht etwa." I am omitting the "nicht," which does not seem to make any difference.

Moreover, to have the one or the other disposition by nature as an innate characteristic does not mean here that the disposition has not been earned by the human being who harbors it, i.e. that he is not its author, but means rather that it has not been earned in time (that he has been the one way or the other *always, from his youth on*). The disposition, i.e. the first subjective ground of the adoption of the maxims, can only be a single one, and it applies to the entire use of freedom universally. This disposition too, however, must be adopted through the free power of choice, for otherwise it could not be imputed. But there cannot be any further cognition of the subjective ground or the cause of this adoption (although we cannot avoid asking about it), for otherwise we would have to adduce still another maxim into which the disposition would have to be incorporated, and this maxim must in turn have its ground.′ Hence, since we cannot derive this disposition, or rather its highest ground, from a first act of the power of choice in time, we call it a characteristic of the power of choice that pertains to it by nature (even though the disposition is in fact grounded in freedom). However, that by the "human being" of whom we say that he is good or evil by nature we are entitled to understand not individuals (for otherwise one human being could be assumed to be good, and another evil, by nature) but the whole species, this can only be demonstrated later on, if it transpires from anthropological research that the grounds that justify us in attributing one of these two characters to a human being as innate are of such a nature that there is no cause for exempting anyone from it, and that the character therefore applies to the species.

I

CONCERNING THE ORIGINAL PREDISPOSITION TO GOOD IN HUMAN NATURE

We may justifiably bring this predisposition, with reference to its end, under three headings, as elements of the determination of the human being:

1. The predisposition to the *animality* of the human being, as a *living being;*
2. To the *humanity* in him, as a living and at the same time *rational* being;
3. To his *personality,* as a rational and at the same time *responsible* being.*16

---

* We cannot consider this predisposition as already included in the concept of the preceding one, but must necessarily treat it as a special predisposition. For from the fact that a being

′ I have amended the text by moving the closing parenthesis from the end of the sentence, where it is in the Academy text, to after "asking about it." The clause starting with "for otherwise" provides no explanation why we should not be asking about the cause, but it makes sense as an explanation of why no further cause can be known.

74

1. The predisposition to animality in the human being may be brought under the general title of physical or merely *mechanical* self-love, i.e. a love for which reason is not required.[17] It is threefold: *first*, for self-preservation; *second*, for the propagation of the species, through the sexual drive, and for the preservation of the offspring thereby begotten through breeding; *third*, for community with other human beings, i.e. the social drive. – On these three can be grafted all sorts of vices (which, however, do not of themselves issue from this predisposition as a root). They can be named vices of the *savagery* of nature, and, at their greatest deviation from the natural ends, are called the *bestial vices of gluttony, lust and wild lawlessness* (in relation to other human beings).

6:27

2. The predispositions to humanity can be brought under the general title of a self-love which is physical and yet *involves comparison* (for which reason is required); that is, only in comparison with others does one judge oneself happy or unhappy. Out of this self-love originates the inclination *to gain worth in the opinion of others*, originally, of course, merely *equal worth*: not allowing anyone superiority over oneself, bound up with the constant anxiety that others might be striving for ascendancy; but from this arises gradually an unjust desire to acquire superiority for oneself over others.[18] – Upon this, namely, upon *jealousy* and *rivalry*, can be grafted the greatest vices of secret or open hostility to all whom we consider alien to us. These vices, however, do not really issue from nature as their root but are rather inclinations, in the face of the anxious endeavor of others to attain a hateful superiority over us, to procure it for ourselves over them for the sake of security, as preventive measure; for nature itself wanted to use the idea of such a competitiveness (which in itself does not exclude reciprocal love) as only an incentive to culture. Hence the vices that are grafted upon this inclination can also be named vices of *culture*, and in their extreme degree of malignancy (where they are simply the idea of a maximum of evil that surpasses humanity), e.g. in *envy, ingratitude, joy in others' misfortunes*, etc., they are called *diabolical vices*.

has reason does not at all follow that, simply by virtue of representing its maxims as suited to universal legislation, this reason contains a faculty of determining the power of choice unconditionally, and hence to be "practical" on its own;[f] at least, not so far as we can see. The most rational being of this world might still need certain incentives, coming to him from the objects of inclination, to determine his power of choice. He might apply the most rational reflection to these objects – about what concerns their greatest sum as well as the means for attaining the goal determined through them – without thereby even suspecting the possibility of such a thing as the absolutely imperative moral law which announces to be itself an incentive, and, indeed, the highest incentive. Were this law not given to us from within, no amount of subtle reasoning on our part would produce it or win our power of choice over to it. Yet this law is the only law that makes us conscious of the independence of our power of choice from determination by all other incentives (of our freedom) and thereby also of the accountability of all our actions.

[f] *für sich*

3. The predisposition to personality is the susceptibility to respect for the moral law *as of itself a sufficient incentive to the power of choice*. This susceptibility to simple respect for the moral law within us would thus be the moral feeling, which by itself does not yet constitute an end of the natural predisposition but only insofar as it is an incentive of the power of choice. But now this is possible only because the free power of choice incorporates moral feeling into its maxim: so a power of choice so constituted is a good character, and this character, as in general every character of the free power of choice, is something that can only be acquired; yet, for its possibility there must be present in our nature a predisposition onto which nothing evil can be grafted. The idea of the moral law alone, together with the respect that is inseparable from it, cannot be properly called a *predisposition to personality;* it is personality itself (the idea of humanity considered wholly intellectually). The subjective ground, however, of our incorporating this incentive into our maxims seems to be an addition to personality, and hence seems to deserve the name of a predisposition on behalf of it.

If we consider the three predispositions just named according to the conditions of their possibility, we find that the *first* does not have reason at its root at all; that the *second* is rooted in a reason which is indeed practical, but only as subservient to other incentives; and that the *third* alone is rooted in reason practical of itself, i.e. in reason legislating unconditionally. All these predispositions in the human being are not only (negatively) *good* (they do not resist the moral law) but they are also predispositions *to the good* (they demand compliance with it). They are *original,* for they belong to the possibility of human nature. The human being can indeed use the first two inappropriately, but cannot eradicate either of the two. By the predispositions of a being we understand the constituent parts required for it as well as the forms of their combination that make for such a being. They are *original* if they belong with necessity to the possibility of this being, but *contingent* if the being in question is possible in itself also without them. It should be noted, finally, that there is no question here of other predispositions except those that relate immediately to the faculty of desire and the exercise of the power of choice.

II.
CONCERNING THE PROPENSITY TO EVIL IN HUMAN NATURE

By *propensity (propensio)* I understand the subjective ground of the possibility of an inclination (habitual desire, *concupiscentia*), insofar as this possibility is contingent for humanity in general.* It is distinguished from a

---

*† *Propensity* is actually only the *predisposition* to desire an enjoyment which, when the subject has experienced it, arouses *inclination* to it. Thus all savages have a propensity for intoxi-

predisposition in that a propensity can indeed be innate yet *may* be represented as not being such: it can rather be thought of (if it is good) as *acquired*, or (if evil) as *brought* by the human being *upon* himself. – Here, however, we are only talking of a propensity to genuine evil, i.e. moral evil, which, since it is only possible as the determination of a free power of choice and this power for its part can be judged good or evil only on the basis of its maxims, must reside in the subjective ground of the possibility of the deviation of the maxims from the moral law. And, if it is legitimate to assume that this propensity belongs to the human being universally (and hence to the character of the species), the propensity will be called a *natural* propensity of the human being to evil. – We can further add that the will's" capacity or incapacity arising from this natural propensity to adopt or not to adopt the moral law in its maxims can be called *the good or the evil heart.*

We can think of three different grades of this natural propensity to evil. *First*, it is the general weakness of the human heart in complying with the adopted maxims, or the *frailty* of human nature; *second*, the propensity to adulterate moral incentives with immoral ones (even when it is done with good intention, and under maxims of the good), i.e. *impurity; third*, the propensity to adopt evil maxims, i.e. the *depravity* of human nature, or of the human heart.

First, the frailty (*fragilitas*) of human nature is expressed even in the complaint of an Apostle: "What I would, that I do not!"[19] i.e. I incorporate the good (the law) into the maxim of my power of choice; but this good, which is an irresistible incentive objectively or ideally (*in thesi*), is subjectively (*in hypothesi*) the weaker (in comparison with inclination) whenever the maxim is to be followed.

Second, the impurity (*impuritas, improbitas*" of the human heart consists   6:30
in this, that although the maxim is good with respect to its object (the intended compliance with the law) and perhaps even powerful enough in practice, it is not purely moral, i.e. it has not, as it should be [the case], adopted the law *alone* as its *sufficient* incentive but, on the contrary, often (and perhaps always) needs still other incentives besides it in order to

---

cants; for although many of them have no acquaintance at all with intoxication, and hence absolutely no desire for the things that produce it, let them try these things but once, and there is aroused in them an almost inextinguishable desire for them. – Between propensity and inclination (the latter presupposes acquaintance with the object of desire) there is yet *instinct*. It is a felt need to do or enjoy something of which we still do not have a concept (such as the drive in animals to build' or the drive to sex). Above inclination there is, finally, still another level of the faculty of desire, *passion* (not *emotional agitation*, for this belongs to the feeling of pleasure and aversion), or an inclination that excludes mastery over oneself.

' *kunsttrieb*
" *Willkür*
" *improbitas:* disgracefulness

determine the power of choice for what duty requires; in other words, actions conforming to duty are not done purely from duty.

Third, the depravity (*vitiositas,*[m] *pravitas*) or, if one prefers, the *corruption* (*corruptio*) of the human heart is the propensity of the power of choice to maxims that subordinate the incentives of the moral law to others (not moral ones). It can also be called the *perversity* (*perversitas*) of the human heart, for it reverses the ethical order as regards the incentives of a *free* power of choice; and although with this reversal there can still be legally good (*legale*) actions, yet the mind's attitude is thereby corrupted at its root (so far as the moral disposition is concerned), and hence the human being is designated as evil.

It will be noted that the propensity to evil is here established (as regards actions) in the human being, even the best; and so it also must be if it is to be proved that the propensity to evil among human beings is universal, or, which here amounts to the same thing, that it is woven into human nature.

So far as the agreement of actions with the law goes, however, there is no difference (or at least there ought to be none) between a human being of good morals (*bene moratus*)[x] and a morally good human being (*moraliter bonus*), except that the actions of the former do not always have, perhaps never have, the law as their sole and supreme incentive, whereas those of the latter *always* do. We can say of the first that he complies with the law according to the *letter* (i.e. as regards the action commanded by the law); but of the second, that he observes it according to the *spirit* (the spirit of the moral law consists in the law being of itself a sufficient incentive). *Whatever is not of this faith is sin*[20] (in attitude). For whenever incentives other than the law itself (e.g. ambition, self-love in general, yes, even a kindly instinct such as sympathy) are necessary to determine the power of choice to *lawful* actions, it is purely accidental that these actions agree with the law, for the incentives might equally well incite its violation. The maxim, by the goodness of which all the moral worth of the person must be assessed, is therefore still contrary to law, and the human being, despite all his good actions, is nevertheless evil.

6:31

The following elucidation is also necessary in order to define the concept of this propensity. Every propensity is either physical, i.e. it pertains to a human's power of choice as natural being; or moral, i.e. it pertains to a human's power of choice as moral being. – In the first sense, there is no propensity to moral evil, for the latter must originate from freedom; a physical propensity (one based on sensory inducements) to whatever use of freedom, be it for good or evil, is a contradiction. Hence a propensity to evil can only attach to the moral faculty of choice.[y] Nothing

[m] being given to vice
[x] well behaved
[y] *dem moralischen Vermögen der Willkür*

is, however, morally (i.e. imputably) evil but that which is our own deed. And yet by the concept of a propensity is understood a subjective determining ground of the power of choice *that precedes every deed,* and hence is itself not yet a *deed.* There would then be a contradiction in the concept of a simple propensity to evil, if this expression could not somehow be taken in two different meanings, both nonetheless reconcilable with the concept of freedom. Now, the term "deed" can in general apply just as well to the use of freedom through which the supreme maxim (either in favor of, or against, the law) is adopted in the power of choice, as to the use by which the actions themselves (materially considered, i.e. as regards the objects of the power of choice) are performed in accordance with that maxim. The propensity to evil is a deed in the first meaning (*peccatum originarium*),[z] and at the same time the formal ground of every deed contrary to law according to the second meaning, [i.e. of a deed] that resists the law materially and is then called vice (*peccatum derivativum*);[a] and the first indebtedness remains even though the second may be repeatedly avoided (because of incentives that are not part of the law). The former is an intelligible deed, cognizable through reason alone apart from any temporal condition; the latter is sensible, empirical, given in time (*factum phenomenon*).[b] Now the first one is said to be a bare propensity especially when compared with the second, and to be innate, because it cannot be eradicated (for the supreme maxim for that would have to be the maxim of the good, whereas in this propensity the maxim has been assumed to be evil). But the chief reason is   6:32 that we are just as incapable of assigning a further cause for why evil has corrupted the very highest maxim in us, though this is our own deed, as we are for a fundamental property that belongs to our nature. – In what has just been said can be found the reason why in this section, from the very start, we sought the three sources of moral evil solely in that which affects the ultimate ground for the acceptance or the observance of our maxims according to the laws of freedom, not in what affects sensibility (as receptivity).

III.

THE HUMAN BEING IS BY NATURE EVIL
VITIIS NEMO SINE NASCITUR, HORACE [c]

In view of what has been said above, the statement, "The human being is *evil,*" cannot mean anything else than that he is conscious of the moral law and yet has incorporated into his maxim the (occasional) deviation from it.

---

[z] original sin
[a] derivative sin
[b] phenomenal deed
[c] *Satires* I:iii.68. Nobody is born without vice.

"He is evil *by nature*" simply means that being evil applies to him considered in his species; not that this quality may be inferred from the concept of his species ([i.e.] from the concept of a human being in general, for then the quality would be necessary), but rather that, according to the cognition we have of the human being through experience, he cannot be judged otherwise, in other words, we may presuppose evil as subjectively necessary in every human being, even the best. Now, since this propensity must itself be considered morally evil, hence not a natural predisposition but something that a human being can be held accountable for, consequently must consist in maxims of the power of choice contrary to the law and yet, because of freedom, such maxims must be viewed as accidental, a circumstance that would not square with the universality of the evil at issue unless their supreme subjective ground were not in all cases somehow entwined with humanity itself and, as it were, rooted in it: so we can call this ground a natural propensity to evil, and, since it must nevertheless always come about through one's own fault, we can further even call it a *radical* innate *evil* in human nature (not any the less brought upon us by ourselves).

We can spare ourselves the formal proof that there must be such a corrupt propensity rooted in the human being, in view of the multitude of woeful examples that the experience of human *deeds* parades before us. If we wish to draw our examples from that state in which many a philosopher especially hoped to meet the natural goodliness of human nature, namely from the so-called *state of nature*, let one but compare with this hypothesis the scenes of unprovoked cruelty in the ritual murders of Tofoa, New Zealand, and the Navigator Islands,[21] and the never-ending cruelty (which Captain Hearne reports)[22] in the wide wastes of northwestern America from which, indeed, no human being derives the least benefit,* and we find vices of savagery more than sufficient to distance us from any such opinion. If we are however disposed to the opinion that we can have a better cognition of human nature known in its civilized state (where its predispositions can be more fully developed), we must then hear out a long melancholy litany of charges against humankind – of secret falsity even in the most intimate friendship, so that a restraint on trust in the

6:33

---

*† Thus the perpetual war between the Arathapescaw Indians and the Dog Rib Indians has no other aim than mere slaughter. In the savages' opinion, bravery in war is the highest virtue. In the civilized state too, bravery is an object of admiration and one reason for the special respect commanded by that estate in which bravery is the sole merit; and this is not without basis in reason. For that a human being should be capable of possessing and adopting as his goal something (honor) which he values more highly still than his life, and of sacrificing all self-interest to it, this surely bespeaks a certain sublimity in his predisposition. Yet we see in the complacency with which the victors boast of their grandiose deeds (the butchery, the merciless killing, and the like) that it is in their mere superiority, and in the havoc that they can wreak, with no other end, that they really place their good.

mutual confidence of even the best friends is reckoned a universal maxim of prudence in social dealings; of a propensity to hate him to whom we are indebted, to which a benefactor must always heed; of a hearty goodwill that nonetheless admits the remark that "in the misfortunes of our best friends there is something that does not altogether displease us"[23]; and of many other vices yet hidden under the appearance of virtue, let alone those of which no secret is made, for to us someone already counts as good when *his evil is common to a class*[24] – and we shall have enough of the vices of *culture* and civilization (the most offensive of all) to make us rather turn our eyes away from the doings of human beings, lest we be dragged   6:34 ourselves into another vice, namely that of misanthropy. And if we are not satisfied yet, we need but consider a state wondrously compounded from both the others, namely that of a people in its external relations, where civilized peoples stand vis-à-vis one another in the relation of raw nature (the state of constant war) and have also firmly taken it into their heads not to get out of it, and we shall become aware of fundamental principles in the great societies we call *states** directly in contradiction to official policy yet never abandoned, principles which no philosopher has yet been able to bring into agreement with morality or else (what is terrible) suggest [how to replace with][d] better ones, reconcilable with human nature: So *philosophical chiliasm,* which hopes for a state of perpetual peace based on a federation of nations united in a world-republic, is universally derided as sheer fantasy as much as *theological chiliasm,* which awaits for the completed moral improvement of the human race   ~never~ ~be~ ~peace~

Now, the ground of this evil cannot (1) be placed, as is commonly done, in the sensuous nature[e] of the human being, and in the natural inclinations   6:35 originating from it. For not only do these bear no direct relation to evil (they rather give the occasion for what the moral disposition can demon-

---

*† If we look at the history of these simply as a phenomenon of inner predispositions of humanity for the most part concealed from us, we then become aware of a certain machinelike progression of nature according to ends which are not theirs (the peoples') but nature's own. So long as a state has a neighboring one which it can hope to subdue, it strives to aggrandize itself by subjugating it. It thus strives for a universal monarchy – a state constitution in which all freedom would necessarily expire, and, together with it, virtue, taste and science (which follow upon freedom). Yet after this monster (in which the laws gradually lose their force) has swallowed up all its neighbors, it ultimately disintegrates all by itself. It divides through rebellion and factionalism into many smaller states which, instead of striving after a union of states (a republic of free federated peoples), in turn begin the same game all over again, so that war (that scourge of the human race) will not cease. Although not so incurably evil as the grave of universal despotism (or even as a federation of nations pitted against the relaxation of despotism in any state), war, as an ancient said,[25] nonetheless creates more evil men than it takes away.

[d] I am adding "[how to replace with]" in an effort to retain Kant's loose sentence structure yet abide by English syntax.

[e] *Sinnlichkeit*

81

strate in its power, for virtue): we also cannot presume ourselves responsible for their existence (we cannot because, as conatural to us, natural inclinations do not have us for their author), though we can well be responsible for the propensity to evil which, since it concerns the morality of the subject and hence is to be found in the latter as a freely acting being, must be capable of being imputed to the subject as itself guilty of it – this despite the deep roots the propensity has in the power of choice, on account of which we must say that it is found in the human being by nature. – The ground of this evil can also not be placed (2) in a *corruption* of the morally legislative reason, as if reason could extirpate within itself the dignity of the law itself, for this is absolutely impossible. To think of oneself as a freely acting being, yet as exempted from the one law commensurate to such a being (the moral law), would amount to the thought of a cause operating without any law at all (for the determination according to natural law is abolished on account of freedom): and this is a contradiction. – *Sensuous nature*[f] therefore contains too little to provide a ground of moral evil in the human being, for, to the extent that it eliminates the incentives originating in freedom, it makes of the human a purely *animal* being; a reason exonerated from the moral law, an *evil reason* as it were (an absolutely evil will), would on the contrary contain too much, because resistance to the law would itself be thereby elevated to incentive (for without any incentive the power of choice cannot be determined), and so the subject would be made a *diabolical* being. – Neither of these two is however applicable to the human being.

But even though the existence of this propensity to evil in human nature can be established through experiential demonstrations of the actual resistance in time of the human power of choice against the law, these demonstrations still do not teach us the real nature of that propensity or the ground of this resistance; that nature rather, since it has to do with a relation of the free power of choice (the concept of which is not empirical) to the moral law (of which the concept is equally purely intellectual), must be cognized *a priori* from the concept of evil, so far as the latter is possible according to the laws of freedom (of obligation and imputability). What follows is the development of this concept.

6:36   The human being (even the worst) does not repudiate the moral law, whatever his maxims, in rebellious attitude (by revoking obedience to it). The law rather imposes itself on him irresistibly, because of his moral predisposition; and if no other incentive were at work against it, he would also incorporate it into his supreme maxim as sufficient determination of his power of choice, i.e. he would be morally good. He is, however, also dependent on the incentives of his sensuous nature[g] because of his equally

---

[f] *Sinnlichkeit*
[g] *Sinnlichkeit*

innocent natural predisposition, and he incorporates them too into his maxim (according to the subjective principle of self-love). If he took them into his maxim *as of themselves sufficient* for the determination of his power of choice, without minding the moral law (which he nonetheless has within himself), he would then become morally evil. But now, since he naturally incorporates both into the same maxim, whereas he would find each, taken alone, of itself sufficient to determine the will, so, if the difference between maxims depended simply on the difference between incentives (the material of the maxims), namely, on whether the law or the sense impulse provides the incentive, he would be morally good and evil at the same time – and this is a contradiction (as we saw in the Introduction). Hence the difference, whether the human being is good or evil, must not lie in the difference between the incentives that he incorporates into his maxim (not in the material of the maxim) but in their *subordination* (in the form of the maxim): *which of the two he makes the condition of the other*. It follows that the human being (even the best) is evil only because he reverses the moral order of his incentives in incorporating them into his maxims. He indeed incorporates the moral law into those maxims, together with the law of self-love; since, however, he realizes that the two cannot stand on an equal footing, but one must be subordinated to the other as its supreme condition, he makes the incentives of self-love and their inclinations the condition of compliance with the moral law – whereas it is this latter that, as *the supreme condition* of the satisfaction of the former, should have been incorporated into the universal maxim of the power of choice as the sole incentive.

In this reversal of incentives through a human being's maxim contrary to the moral order, actions can still turn out to be as much in conformity to the law as if they had originated from true principles – as when reason uses the unity of the maxims in general, which is characteristic of the moral law, merely to introduce into the incentives of inclination, under the name of *happiness*, a unity of maxims which they cannot otherwise have. (For example, when adopted as principle, truthfulness spares us the anxiety of maintaining consistency in our lies and not being entangled in their serpentine coils.) The empirical character is then good but the intelligible character still evil.

Now if a propensity to this [inversion] does lie in human nature, then there is in the human being a natural propensity to evil; and this propensity itself is morally evil, since it must ultimately be sought in a free power of choice, and hence is imputable. This evil is *radical*, since it corrupts the ground of all maxims; as natural propensity, it is also not to be *extirpated* through human forces, for this could only happen through good maxims – something that cannot take place if the subjective supreme ground of all maxims is presupposed to be corrupted. Yet it must equally be possible to *overcome* this evil, for it is found in the human being as acting freely.

6:37

The depravity of human nature is therefore not to be named *malice,*[h] if we take this word in the strict sense, namely as a disposition (a subjective *principle* of maxims) to incorporate evil *qua evil* for incentive into one's maxim (since this is *diabolical*), but should rather be named *perversity* of the heart, and this heart is then called *evil* because of what results. An evil heart can coexist with a will which in the abstract[i] is good. Its origin is the frailty of human nature, in not being strong enough to comply with its adopted principles, coupled with its dishonesty in not screening incentives (even those of well-intentioned actions) in accordance with the moral guide, and hence at the end, if it comes to this, in seeing only to the conformity of these incentives to the law, not to whether they have been derived from the latter itself, i.e. from it as the sole incentive. Now, even though a lawless action and a propensity to such contrariety, i.e. *vice,* do not always originate from it, the attitude of mind that construes the absence of vice as already being conformity of the *disposition* to the law of duty (i.e. as *virtue*) is nonetheless itself to be named a radical perversity in the human heart (for in this case no attention at all is given to the incentives in the maxim but only to compliance with the letter of the law).

6:38   This *innate* guilt (*reatus*), which is so called because it is detectable as early as the first manifestation of the exercise of freedom in the human being, but which must nonetheless have originated from freedom and is therefore imputable, can be judged in its first two stages (those of frailty and impurity) to be unintentional guilt (*culpa*); in the third, however, as deliberate guilt (*dolus*), and is characterized by a certain *perfidy* on the part of the human heart (*dolus malus*) in deceiving itself as regards its own good or evil disposition and, provided that its actions do not result in evil (which they could well do because of their maxims), in not troubling itself on account of its disposition but rather considering itself justified before the law. This is how so many human beings (conscientious in their own estimation) derive their peace of mind when, in the course of actions in which the law was not consulted or at least did not count the most, they just luckily slipped by the evil consequences; and [how they derive] even the fancy that they deserve not to feel guilty of such transgressions as they see others burdened with, without however inquiring whether the credit goes perhaps to good luck, or whether, on the attitude of mind they could well discover within themselves if they just wanted, they would not have practiced similar vices themselves, had they not been kept away from them by impotence, temperament, upbringing, and tempting circumstances of time and place (things which, one and all, cannot be imputed to us). This dishonesty, by which we throw dust in our own eyes and which hinders the establishment in us of a genuine moral disposition, then extends itself also

[h] depravity = *Bösartigheit;* malice = *Bösheit*
[i] *im Allgemeinen*

externally, to falsity or deception of others. And if this dishonesty is not to be called malice, it nonetheless deserves at least the name of unworthiness. It rests on the radical evil of human nature which (inasmuch as it puts out of tune the moral ability to judge what to think of a human being, and renders any imputability entirely uncertain, whether internal or external) constitutes the foul stain of our species – and so long as we do not remove it, it hinders the germ of the good from developing as it otherwise would.

A member of the English Parliament exclaimed in the heat of debate: "Every man has his price, for which he sells himself."[26] If this is true (and everyone can decide by himself), if nowhere is a virtue which no level of temptation can overthrow, if whether the good or evil spirit wins us over only depends on which bids the most and affords the promptest pay-off, then, what the Apostle says might indeed hold true of human beings universally, "There is no distinction here, they are all under sin – there is none righteous (in the spirit of the law), no, not one."[27]*

6:39

IV.
CONCERNING THE ORIGIN OF EVIL
IN HUMAN NATURE

Origin (the first origin) is the descent of an effect from its first cause, i.e. from that cause which is not in turn the effect of another cause of the same kind. It can be considered as either *origin according to reason*, or *origin according to time*. In the first meaning, only the effect's *being*[l] is considered; in the second, its *occurrence*, and hence, as an event, it is referred to its *cause in time*. If an effect is referred to a cause which is however bound to it according to the laws of freedom, as is the case with moral evil, then the determination of the power of choice to the production of this effect is

---

* The appropriate proof of this sentence of condemnation by reason sitting in moral judgment is contained not in this section, but in the previous one. This section contains only the corroboration of the judgment through experience – though experience can never expose the root of evil in the supreme maxim of a free power of choice in relation to the law, for, as *intelligible*[j] deed, the maxim precedes all experience. – From this, i.e. from the unity of the supreme maxims under the unity of the law to which it relates, we can also see why the principle of the exclusion of a mean between good and evil must be the basis of the intellectual judgment of humankind, whereas, for the empirical judgment, the principle can be laid down on the basis of *sensible*[k] *deed[s]* (actual doing or not doing) that there is a mean between these extremes – on the one side, a negative mean of indifference prior to all education; on the other, a positive mean, a mixture of being partly good and partly evil. This second judgment, however, concerns only human morality as appearance, and in a final judgment must be subordinated to the first.

[j] *intelligibile*
[k] *sensibler*
[l] *Dasein*

85

6:40

thought as bound to its determining ground not in time but merely in the representation of reason; it cannot be derived from some *preceding* state or other, as must always occur, on the other hand, whenever the evil action is referred to its natural cause as *event* in the world. To look for the temporal origin of free actions as free (as though they were natural effects) is therefore a contradiction; and hence also a contradiction to look for the temporal origin of the moral constitution of the human being, so far as this constitution is considered as contingent, for constitution here means the ground of the *exercise* of freedom which (just like the determining ground of the free power of choice in general) must be sought in the representations of reason alone.

Whatever the nature, however, of the origin of moral evil in the human being, of all the ways of representing its spread and propagation through the members of our species and in all generations, the most inappropriate is surely to imagine it as having come to us by way of *inheritance* from our first parents; for then we could say of moral evil exactly what the poet says of the good: *genus et proavos, et quoae non fecimus ipsi, vix ex nostra puto.*ᵐ* – We should note further that, when we enquire into the origin of evil, at the beginning we still do not take into account the propensity to it (as *peccatum in potentia*)ⁿ but only consider the actual evil of given actions according to the evil's inner possibility, and according to all that must conspire within the power of choice for such actions to be performed.

6:41

Every evil action must be so considered, whenever we seek its rational origin, as if the human being had fallen into it directly from the state of innocence. For whatever his previous behavior may have been, whatever the natural causes influencing him, whether they are inside or outside

---

* The three so-called "higher faculties" (in the universities) would explain this transmission each in its own way, namely, either as *inherited disease*, or *inherited guilt*, or *inherited sin*. (1) The Faculty of Medicine would represent the inherited evil somewhat as it represents the tapeworm, concerning which certain natural scientists are actually of the opinion that, since it is not otherwise found either in an element outside us nor (of this same kind) in any other animal, it must already have been present in our first parents. (2) The *Faculty of Law* would regard it as the legal consequence of our accession to an *inheritance* bequeathed to us by these first parents but weighted down because of a serious crime (for to be born is just to inherit the use of the goods of the earth, inasmuch as these are indispensable to our survival). We must therefore make payment (atone) and, at the end, shall still be evicted (by death) from this possession. This is how the justice of law works! (3) The *Theological Faculty* would regard this evil as the personal participation by our first parents in the *fall* of a condemned rebel: either we were at the time ourselves accomplices (though not now conscious of it); or even now, born under the rebel's dominion (as Prince of this World), we prefer his goods to the supreme command of the heavenly master and lack sufficient faith to break loose from him, hence we shall eventually have to share in his doom.

ᵐ Ovid, *Metamorphoses*, XIII:140–141: "Race and ancestors, and those things which we did not make ourselves, I scarcely consider as our own."

ⁿ potential sin

them, his action is yet free and not determined through any of these causes; hence the action can and must always be judged as an *original exercise of his power of choice*. He should have refrained from it, whatever his temporal circumstances and entanglements; for through no cause in the world can he cease to be a free agent. It is indeed rightly said that to the human being are also imputed the *consequences* originating from his previous free but lawless actions. All that is thereby meant, however, is this: It is not necessary to get sidetracked into the prevarication of establishing whether such actions may have been free or not, since there is already sufficient ground for the imputation in the admittedly free action which was their cause. However evil a human being has been right up to the moment of an impending free action (evil even habitually, as second nature), his duty to better himself was not just in the past: it still is his duty *now;* he must therefore be capable of it and, should he not do it, he is at the moment of action just as accountable, and stands just as condemned, as if, though endowed with a natural predisposition to the good (which is inseparable from freedom), he had just stepped out of the state of innocence into evil. – Hence we cannot inquire into the origin in time of this deed but must inquire only into its origin in reason, in order thereby to determine and, where possible, to explain the propensity [to it], if there is one, i.e. the subjective universal ground of the adoption of a transgression into our maxim.

Now, the mode of representation which the Scriptures use to depict the origin of evil, as having a *beginning* in human nature, well agrees with the foregoing; for the Scriptures portray this beginning in a narrative, where what must be thought as objectively first by nature[o] (without regard to the condition of time) appears as a first in time. Evil begins, according to the Scriptures, not from a fundamental propensity to it, for otherwise its beginning would not result from freedom, but from *sin* (by which is understood the transgression of the moral law as *divine command*); the state of human beings prior to any propensity to evil is however called the state of innocence. The moral law moved forward in the form of *prohibition* (Genesis II:16–17),[28] as befits a being who, like the human, is not pure but is tempted by inclinations. But, instead of following this law absolutely as sufficient incentive (which alone is unconditionally good, and with which there cannot be further hesitation), the human being looked about for yet other incentives (III:6)[29] which can be good only conditionally (i.e. so far as they do not infringe the law). And he made it his maxim – if one thinks of action as originating from freedom with consciousness – to follow the law of duty, not from duty but, if need be, also with an eye to other aims. He thereby began to question the strin-

6:42

---

[o] *der Natur der Sache nach*

gency of the command that excludes the influence of every other incentive, and thereupon to rationalize* downgrading his obedience to the command to the status of the merely conditional obedience as a means (under the principle of self-love), until, finally, the preponderance of the sensory inducements over the incentive of the law was incorporated into the maxim of action, and thus sin came to be (III:6). *Mutato nomine de te fabula narratur.* It is clear from the above that this is what we do daily, and that hence "in Adam we have all sinned"[31] and still sin – except that a prior innate propensity to transgression is presupposed in us but not in the first human being, in whom rather innocence is presupposed with respect to time; hence his transgression is called a *fall into sin*, whereas ours is represented as resulting from a prior innate depravity of our nature. This propensity, however, means nothing more than this: if we wish to engage in an explanation of evil with respect to its *beginning in time*, we must trace the causes of every deliberate transgression in a previous time of our life, all the way back to the

6:43   time when the use of reason had not yet developed, hence the source of evil back to a propensity (as natural foundation) to evil which is therefore called innate; in the case of the first human being, who is represented with full control of the use of his reason from the beginning, this is neither necessary nor expedient, for otherwise the foundation [of sin] (the evil propensity) would have to be co-created; hence we construe his sin as generated directly from innocence. – We must not however seek an origin in time of a moral character for which we are to be held accountable, however unavoidable this might be if we want to *explain* the contingent existence of this character (hence the Scriptures, in accordance with this weakness of ours, have perhaps so portrayed its origin in time).

The rational origin, however, of this disharmony in our power of choice with respect to the way it incorporates lower incentives in its maxims and makes them supreme, i.e. this propensity to evil, remains inexplicable to us, for, since it must itself be imputed to us, this supreme ground of all maxims must in turn require the adoption of an evil maxim. Evil can have originated only from moral evil (not just from the limitations of our nature); yet the original predisposition (which none other than the human being himself could have corrupted, if this corruption is to be imputed to him) is a predisposition to the good; there is no conceivable ground for us, therefore, from which moral evil could first have come in us. – The

---

* Any profession of reverence for the moral law which in its maxim does not however grant to the law – as self-sufficient incentive – preponderance over all other determining grounds of the power of choice is hypocritical, and the propensity to it is inward deceit, i.e. a propensity to lie to oneself in the interpretation of the moral law, to its prejudice (III:5); wherefore the Bible too (the Christian part of it) calls the author of evil (who is even within us) the Liar from the beginning,[30] and thus characterizes the human being as regards what seems to be the main ground of evil in him.

ᵖ Horace, *Satires*, I:1: "Change but the name, of you the tale is told."

Scriptures express this incomprehensibility in a historical narrative,* which adds a closer determination of the depravity of our species, by projecting evil at the beginning of the world, not, however, within the human being, but in a *spirit* of an originally more sublime destiny.[32] The absolutely *first* beginning of all evil is thereby represented as incomprehensible to us (for whence the evil in that spirit?); the human being, however, is represented as having lapsed into it only *through temptation*,[33] hence not as corrupted *fundamentally* (in his very first predisposition to the good) but, on the contrary, as still capable of improvement, by contrast to a tempting *spirit*, i.e. one whom the temptation of the flesh cannot be accounted as a mitigation of guilt. And so for the human being, who despite a corrupted heart yet always possesses a good will, there still remains hope of a return to the good from which he has strayed.

6:44

⟶ predisposition to good ⟶ evil incomprehensible

General remark
Concerning the restoration to its power of the original predisposition to the good

The human being must make or have made *himself* into whatever he is or should become in a moral sense, good or evil. These two [characters] must be an effect of his free power of choice, for otherwise they could not be imputed to him and, consequently, he could be neither *morally* good nor evil. If it is said, The human being is created good, this can only mean nothing more than: He has been created for the *good* and the original *predisposition* in him is good; the human being is not thereby good as such, but he brings it about that he becomes either good or evil, according as he either incorporates or does not incorporate into his maxims the incentives contained in that predisposition (and this must be left entirely to his free choice). Granted that some supernatural cooperation is also needed to his becoming good or better, whether this cooperation only consist in the diminution of obstacles or be also a positive assistance, the human being must nonetheless make himself antecedently worthy of receiving it; and

---

* What is being said here must not be regarded as though intended for Scriptural exegesis, which lies outside the boundaries of the competence of mere reason. We can explain how we put a historical account to our moral use without thereby deciding whether this is also the meaning of the writer or only our interpretation, if this meaning is true in itself, apart from all historical proof, and also the only meaning according to which we can derive something edifying from a text which would otherwise be only a barren addition to our historical cognition. We should not quarrel over an issue unnecessarily, and over its historical standing, when, however we understand it, the issue does not contribute anything to our becoming a better human being – if what can make a contribution in this respect is just as well known without historical demonstration and must even be known without it. Historical cognition that has no intrinsic relation, valid for everyone, to this [moral improvement], belongs among the *adiaphora*, which each may treat as one finds edifying.

6:44

he must *accept* this help (which is no small matter), i.e. he must incorporate this positive increase of force into his maxim: in this way alone is it possible that the good be imputed to him, and that he be acknowledged a good human being.

6:45   How it is possible that a naturally evil human being should make himself into a good human being surpasses every concept of ours. For how can an evil tree bear good fruit? But, since by our previous admission a tree which was (in its predisposition) originally good but did bring forth bad fruits,* and since the fall from good into evil (if we seriously consider that evil originates from freedom) is no more comprehensible than the ascent from evil back to the good, then the possibility of this last cannot be disputed. For, in spite of that fall, the command that we *ought* to become better human beings still resounds unabated in our souls; consequently, we must also be capable of it, even if what we can do is of itself insufficient and, by virtue of it, we only make ourselves receptive to a higher assistance inscrutable to us. – Surely we must presuppose in all this that there is still a germ of goodness left in its entire purity, a germ that cannot be extirpated or corrupted. And it certainly cannot be self-love,† which, when

---

* The tree, good in predisposition, is not yet good in deed; for, if it were so, it surely could not bring forth bad fruit. Only when a human being has incorporated into his maxim the incentive implanted in him for the moral law, is he called a good human being (the tree, a good tree absolutely).

† Words susceptible of two entirely different meanings often long delay the achievement of conviction on even the clearest grounds. Like *love* in general, *self-love* too can be divided into love of *good will* and love of *good pleasure* (*benevolentiae et complacentiae*), and both (as is self-evident) must be rational. To incorporate the first into one's maxim is natural (for who would not want that things always go well for him?). This love is however rational to the extent that with respect to the end only what is consistent with the greatest and most abiding well-being is chosen, and that also the most apt means for each of these components of happiness are chosen. Reason only occupies here the place of a servant of natural inclination; the maxim that one adopts has absolutely no relation to morality. Let this maxim, however, become an unconditional principle of the power of choice, and it is the source of an incalculably great resistance to morals. – A rational love of *good pleasure in oneself* can be understood in either [of two senses: in one,] that we take pleasure in those maxims, already mentioned, which have for end the satisfaction of natural inclination (so far as this end can be attained by complying with them); and then it is one and the same with the love of good will toward oneself: one takes pleasure in oneself, just as a businessman who has done well in his business speculations rejoices over his good discernment because of the maxims he adopted

6:46 in them. [In the second sense,] the maxim of self-love, of *unconditional good pleasure* in oneself (independent of gain or loss resulting from action), is however the inner principle of a contentment only possible for us on condition that our maxims are subordinated to the moral law. No human being, to whom morality is not indifferent can take pleasure in himself, or can even avoid a bitter sense of dislike about himself, if he is conscious of such maxims in him as do not conform to the moral law. We could call this love a *rational love* of oneself that prevents any adulteration of the incentives of the power of choice by other causes of contentment consequent upon one's actions (under the name of happiness to be procured through them). But, since this denotes unconditional respect for the law, why needlessly

adopted as the principle of all our maxims, is precisely the source of all evil. *is still a seed of good*

The restoration of the original predisposition to good in us is not   6:46
therefore the acquisition of a *lost* incentive for the good, since we were
never able to lose the incentive that consists in the respect for the moral
law, and were we ever to lose it, we would also never be able to regain it.
The restoration is therefore only the recovery of the *purity* of the law, as
the supreme ground of all our maxims, according to which the law itself is
to be incorporated into the power of choice, not merely bound to other
incentives, nor indeed subordinated to them (to inclinations) as conditions, but rather in its full purity, as the self-*sufficient* incentive of that
power. The original good is *holiness of maxims* in the compliance to one's
duty, hence merely out of duty, whereby a human being, who incorporates
this purity into his maxims, though on this account still not holy as such   6:47
(for between maxim and deed there still is a wide gap), is nonetheless
upon the road of endless progress toward holiness.[34] When the firm resolve to comply with one's duty has become a habit, it is called *virtue* also
in a legal sense, in its *empirical character* (*virtus phaenomenon*). Virtue here
has the abiding maxim of *lawful* actions, no matter whence one draws the
incentives that the power of choice needs for such actions. Virtue, in this
sense, is accordingly acquired *little by little*, and to some it means a long
habituation (in the observance of the law), in virtue of which a human
being, through gradual reformation of conduct and consolidation of his
maxims, passes from a propensity to vice to its opposite. But not the
slightest *change of heart* is necessary for this; only a change of *mores.*[q] A
human being here considers himself virtuous whenever he feels himself
stable in his maxims of observance to duty – though not by virtue of the
supreme ground of all maxims, namely duty, but [as when], for instance,
an immoderate human being converts to moderation for the sake of
health; a liar to truth for the sake of reputation; an unjust human being to
civic righteousness for the sake of peace or profit, etc., all in conformity
with the prized principle of happiness. However, that a human being
must conform to duty

render more difficult the clear understanding of the principle with the expression *rational
self-love*, when this self-love is however *moral* only under the latter condition, and we thus go
around in a circle (for we can love ourselves morally only to the extent that we are conscious
of our maxim to make respect for the law the highest incentive of our power of choice)? For
us – dependent as we are on objects of the senses – happiness is by *nature* the first that we
desire and desire unconditionally. Yet by our nature (if this is how we want to name
something innate in us) as a substance endowed with reason and freedom, this very happiness is not the first by far, nor is it indeed the object of our maxims unconditionally: this is
rather the *worthiness of being happy*, i.e., the agreement of all our maxims with the moral law.
Now, that this worthiness is objectively the condition under which alone the wish for
happiness can conform with the law-giving reason, in this consists every ethical advance; and
in the disposition to wish only under such condition, the ethical frame of mind.
[q] *Sitten*

should become not merely *legally* good, but *morally* good (pleasing to God) i.e. virtuous according to the intelligible character [of virtue] (*virtus noumenon*) and thus in need of no other incentive to recognize a duty except the representation of duty itself – that, so long as the foundation of the maxims of the human being remains impure, cannot be effected through gradual *reform* but must rather be effected through a *revolution* in the disposition of the human being (a transition to the maxim of holiness of disposition). And so a "new man"[35] can come about only through a kind of rebirth, as it were a new creation (John, 3:5;[36] compare with Genesis, 1:2[37]) and a change of heart.

But if a human being is corrupt in the very ground of his maxims, how can he possibly bring about this revolution by his own forces and become a good human being on his own? Yet duty commands that he be good, and duty commands nothing but what we can do. The only way to reconcile this is by saying that a revolution is necessary in the mode of thought' but a gradual reformation in the mode of sense' (which places obstacles in the way of the former), and [that both] must therefore be possible also to the human being. That is: If by a single and unalterable decision a human being reverses the supreme ground of his maxims by which he was an evil human being (and thereby puts on a "new man"),[38] he is to this extent, by principle and attitude of mind, a subject receptive to the good; but he is a good human being only in incessant laboring and becoming i.e. he can hope – in view of the purity of the principle which he has adopted as the supreme maxim of his power of choice, and in view of the stability of this principle – to find himself upon the good (though narrow) path of constant *progress* from bad to better. For him who penetrates to the intelligible ground of the heart (the ground of all the maxims of the power of choice), for him to whom this endless progress is a unity, i.e. for God, this is the same as actually being a good human being (pleasing to him); and to this extent the change can be considered a revolution. For the judgment of human beings, however, who can assess themselves and the strength of their maxims only by the upper hand they gain over the senses in time, the change is to be regarded only as an ever-continuing striving for the better, hence as a gradual reformation of the propensity to evil, of the perverted attitude of mind.

From this it follows that a human being's moral education must begin, not with an improvement of mores, but with the transformation of his attitude of mind and the establishment of a character, although it is customary to proceed otherwise and to fight vices individually, while leaving their universal root undisturbed. But now, even the most limited human being is capable of all the greater a respect for a dutiful action the

6:48

' *Denkungsart*
' *Sinnesart*

92

more he removes from it, in thought, other incentives which might have influence upon its maxim through self-love. And even children are capable of discovering even the slightest taint of admixture of spurious incentives: for in their eyes the action then immediately loses all moral worth. This predisposition to the good is cultivated in no better way than by just adducing the *example* of good people (as regards their conformity to law), and by allowing our apprentices in morality to judge the impurity of certain maxims on the basis of the incentives actually behind their actions. And so the predisposition gradually becomes an attitude of mind, so that *duty* merely for itself begins to acquire in the apprentice's heart a noticeable importance. To teach only *admiration* for virtuous actions, however great a sacrifice these may have cost, falls short of the right spirit that ought to support the apprentice's feeling' for the moral good. For, however virtuous someone is, all the good that he can ever perform still is   6:49
merely duty; to do one's duty, however, is no more than to do what lies in the common moral order and is not, therefore, deserving of wonder. This admiration is, on the contrary, a dulling of our feeling for duty, as if to give obedience to it were something extraordinary and meritorious.

Yet there is one thing in our soul which, if we duly fix our eye on it, we cannot cease viewing with the highest wonder, and for which admiration is legitimate and uplifting as well. And that is the original moral predisposition in us, as such. – What is this in us (one can ask oneself) in virtue of which we, beings ever dependent on nature through so many needs, are at the same time elevated so far above it in the idea of an original predisposition (in us) that we would hold the whole of nature as nothing, and ourselves as unworthy of existence, were we to pursue the enjoyment of nature – though this alone can make our life desirable – in defiance of a law through which our reason commands us compellingly, without however either promising or threatening anything thereby? Every human being who has been instructed in the holiness that lies in the idea of duty, even one of the most ordinary ability, must feel the force of this question deeply within himself, though he has not presumed to investigate the concept of freedom which first and foremost derives from this law.* The   6:50
very incomprehensibility of this predisposition, proclaiming as it does a

* We can quickly be convinced that the concept of the freedom of the power of choice does not precede in us the consciousness of the moral law but is only inferred from the determinability of our power of choice through this law as unconditional command. We have only to ask whether we are certainly and immediately conscious of a faculty enabling us to overcome, by firm resolve, every incentive to transgression, however great (*Phalaris licet imperet, ut sis falsus, et admoto dictet periuria tauro*)." Everybody must admit that *he does not*
' *Gemüt*
" Juvenal, *Satires* VIII:81–82: "[. . . T]hough Phalaris himself should command you to be false and, having brought up his bull, should dictate perjuries." Phalaris was a tyrant of Agrigent. According to legend, he tortured his enemies by putting them inside a hollow bull cast in iron ore, which was then heated red hot.

divine origin, must have an effect on the mind, even to the point of exaltation, and must strengthen it for the sacrifices which respect for duty may perhaps impose upon it. Often to arouse this feeling of the sublimity of our moral vocation is especially praiseworthy as a means of awakening moral dispositions, since it directly counters the innate propensity to pervert the incentives in the maxims of our power of choice. Thus it works, in the unconditional respect for the law which is the highest condition of all the maxims to be adopted, for the restoration of the original ethical order among the incentives and, thereby, for the restoration to its purity of the predisposition in the human heart to the good.

But does not the thesis of the innate corruption of the human being with respect to all that is good stand in direct opposition to this restoration through one's own effort? Of course it does, so far as the comprehensibility of, i.e. our *insight* into, its possibility is concerned, or, for that matter, the possibility of anything that must be represented as an event in time (change) and, to this extent, as necessary according to nature, though its opposite must equally be represented, under moral laws, as possible through freedom; it is not however opposed to the possibility of this restoration itself. For if the moral law commands that we *ought* to be better human beings now, it inescapably follows that we must be *capable* of being better human beings. The thesis of innate evil is of no use in moral *dogmatics*, for the precepts of the latter would include the very same duties, and retain the same force, whether there is in us an innate propensity to transgression or not. In moral *discipline*, however, the thesis means more, yet not more than this: We cannot start out in the ethical training of our conatural moral predisposition to the good with an innocence which is natural to us but must rather begin from the presupposition of a depravity of our power of choice in adopting maxims contrary to the original ethical predisposition; and, since the propensity to this [depravity] is inextirpable, with unremitting counteraction against it. Since this only leads to a pro-

6:51

know whether, were such a situation to arise, he would not waver in his resolve. Yet duty equally commands him unconditionally: he *ought* to remain true to his resolve; and from this he rightly *concludes* that he must also *be able* to do it, and that his power of choice is therefore free. Those who pretend that this inscrutable property is entirely within our grasp concoct an illusion through the word *determinism* (the thesis that the power of choice is determined through inner sufficient grounds) as though the difficulty consisted in reconciling these grounds with freedom – [an issue] that does not enter into anyone's mind. Rather, what we want to discern, but never shall, is this: how can *pre-determinism* co-exist with freedom, when according to predeterminism freely chosen[v] actions, as occurrences, have their determining grounds *in antecedent time* (which, together with what is contained therein, no longer lies in our control), whereas according to freedom the action, as well as its contrary, must be in the control of the subject at the moment of its happening.

6:50

† There is no difficulty in reconciling the concept of *freedom* with the idea of God as a

[v] *willkürlich*

94

gression from bad to better extending to infinity, it follows that the transformation of the disposition of an evil human being into the disposition of a good human being is to be posited in the change of the supreme inner ground of the adoption of all the human being's maxims in accordance with the ethical law, so far as this new ground (the new heart) is itself now unchangeable. Assurance of this cannot of course be attained by the human being naturally, neither via immediate consciousness nor via the evidence of the life he has hitherto led, for the depths of his own heart (the subjective first ground of his maxims) are to him inscrutable. Yet he must be able to *hope* that, by the exertion of *his own* power, he will attain to the road that leads in that direction, as indicated to him by a fundamentally improved disposition. For he ought to become a good human being yet cannot be judged *morally* good except on the basis of what can be imputed to him as done by him.

Against this expectation of self-improvement, reason, which by nature finds moral labor vexing, now conjures up, under the pretext of natural impotence, all sorts of impure religious ideas (among which belongs falsely imputing to God the principle of happiness as the supreme condition of his commands). All religions, however, can be divided into *religion of rogation* (of mere cult) and *moral religion*, i.e. the religion of *good life-conduct*. According to the first, the human being either flatters himself that God can make him eternally happy (through the remissions of his debts) without any necessity on his part *to become a better human being;* or else, if this does not seem possible to him, that *God* himself *can make him a better human being* without his having to contribute more than to *ask* for it, and, since before an omniscient being asking is no more than *wishing*, this would amount in fact to doing nothing, for, if improvement were a matter of mere wishing, every human being would be good. According to moral religion, however (and, of all the public religions so far known, the Christian alone is of this type), it is a fundamental principle that, to become a better human being, everyone must do as much as it is in his powers to do; and only then, if a human being has not buried his innate talent (Luke 19:12–16),[39] if he has made use of the original predisposition to the good in order to become a better human being, can he hope that what does not lie in his power will be made good by cooperation from above. Nor is it absolutely necessary that the human being know in what this cooperation

6:52

---

necessary being, for freedom does not consist in the contingency of an action (in its not being determined through any ground at all), i.e. not in indeterminism ([the thesis] that God must be equally capable of doing good or evil, if his action is to be called free) but in absolute spontaneity. The latter is at risk only with predeterminism, where the determining ground of an action lies *in antecedent time*, so that the action is no longer in *my* power but in the hands of nature, which determines me irresistibly; since in God no temporal sequence is thinkable, this difficulty has no place.

consists; indeed, it is perhaps unavoidable that, were the way it occurs revealed at a given time, different people would, at some other time, form different conceptions of it, and that in all sincerity. For here too the principle holds, "It is not essential, and hence not necessary, that every human being know what God does, or has done, for his salvation"; but it is essential to know *what a human being has to do himself* in order to become worthy of this assistance.

†This General Remark is the first of four which are appended, one to each Part of this writing, and which could bear the labels 1) Of Effects of Grace; 2) Miracles; 3) Mysteries; and 4) Means of Grace. – These are, as it were, *parerga* to religion within the boundaries of pure reason; they do not belong within it yet border on it. Reason, conscious of its impotence to satisfy its moral needs, extends itself to extravagant ideas which might make up for this lack, though it is not suited to this enlarged domain. Reason does not contest the possibility or actuality of the objects of these ideas; it just cannot incorporate them into its maxims of thought and action. And if in the inscrutable field of the supernatural there is something more than it can bring to its understanding, which may however be necessary to make up for its moral impotence, reason even counts on this something being made available to its good will even if uncognized, with a faith which (with respect to the possibility of this something) we might call *reflective*, since the *dogmatic* faith which announces itself to be a *knowledge* appears to reason dishonest or impudent: for to remove difficulties that obstruct what stands firm on its own (practically), when these difficulties touch upon transcendent questions, is only a secondary occupation (*parergon*). As regards the disadvantages that result from these ideas (which are also *morally* transcendent), when we wish to introduce them into religion, their effects, in the order of the four classes mentioned above, are as follows: (1) supposed inner experience (effects of grace), *enthusiasm*; (2) alleged outer experiences (miracles), *superstition;* (3) presumed enlightenment of the understanding with respect to the supernatural (mysteries), *illumination,* the delusion of the initiates; (4) adventurous attempts at influencing the supernatural (means of grace), *thaumaturgy,* sheer aberrations of a reason that has strayed beyond its limits, indeed for a supposed moral aim (one pleasing to God). – Regarding this General Remark to the first Part of our treatise in particular, the summoning of the *effects of grace* belongs to the last class and cannot be incorporated into the maxims of reason, if the latter keeps to its boundaries; nor, in general, can anything supernatural, because all use of reason ceases precisely with it. – For it is impossible to make these effects *theoretically* cognizable (that they are effects of grace and not of immanent nature), because our use of the concept of cause and effect cannot be extended beyond the objects of experience, and hence beyond nature; moreover, the presupposition of a *practical* employment of this idea is wholly self-contradictory. For the

6:53

employment would presuppose a rule concerning what good we ourselves must *do* (with a particular aim [in mind]) in order to achieve something; to expect an effect of grace means, however, the very contrary, namely that the good (the morally good) is not of our doing, but that of another being – that we, therefore, can only *come by* it by *doing nothing,* and this contradicts itself. Hence we can admit an effect of grace as something incomprehensible but cannot incorporate it into our maxims for either theoretical or practical use.

The philosophical doctrine of religion
Part two

Part two
Concerning the battle of the good against the evil principle for dominion over the human being

To become a morally good human being is not enough simply to let the germ of the god which lies in our species develop unhindered; there is in us an active and opposing cause of evil which is also to be combatted. It was especially the Stoics who among the ancient moralists called attention to this through their watchword *virtue*, which designates courage and valor (in Greek as well as in Latin)[40] and hence presupposes the presence of an enemy. In this respect the name *virtue* is a glorious one, and the fact that people have often boastfully misused and derided it (as of late the word "Enlightenment") can do it no harm. – For to require courage is already halfway to instilling it; whereas the lazy and timid cast of mind (in morality and religion), which has not the least trust in itself and waits for external help, unharnesses all the forces of a human being and renders him unworthy even of this help.

However, those valiant men [the Stoics] mistook their enemy, who is not to be sought in the natural inclinations, which merely lack discipline and openly display themselves unconcealed to everyone's consciousness,[41] but is rather as it were an invisible enemy, one who hides behind reason and hence all the more dangerous. They send forth *wisdom* against *folly*, which lets itself be deceived by inclinations merely because of carelessness, instead of summoning it against the *malice* (of the human heart) which secretly undermines the disposition with soul-corrupting principles.*

[handwritten: ⌐evil embedded]

* These philosophers derived their universal moral principle from the dignity of human nature, from its freedom (as an independence from the power of the inclinations), and they could not have laid down a better or nobler principle for foundation.[42] They then drew the moral laws directly from reason, the sole legislator, commanding absolutely through its laws. And so was everything quite correctly apportioned – objectively, as regards the rule, and also subjectively, with respect to the incentive – provided that one attributes to the human being an uncorrupted will, unhesitatingly incorporating these laws into its maxims. The mistake of those philosophers, however, lay in just this last presupposition. For no matter how far back we direct our attention to our moral state, we find that this state is no longer *res integra*,^ᵚ and
ᵚ i.e. a complete thing

101

6:58 *Considered in themselves* natural inclinations are *good*, i.e. not reprehensible, and to want to extirpate them would not only be futile but harmful and blameworthy as well; we must rather only curb them, so that they will not wear each other out but will instead be harmonized into a whole called happiness. Now the reason that accomplishes this is called *prudence*. Only what is unlawful is evil in itself, absolutely reprehensible, and must be eradicated. And the reason which teaches this, all the more so when it also puts it in actual practice, alone deserves the name of *wisdom*, in comparison to which vice may indeed also be called *folly*, but only when reason feels enough strength within itself to *despise* it (and every stimulation to it), not just to *hate* it as something to be feared, and arm itself against it.

6:59 Thus when the Stoic thought of the human moral battle simply as a human being's struggle with his inclinations, so far as these (innocent in themselves) must be overcome as obstacles in the compliance to his duty, he could locate the cause of the transgression only in the *omission* to combat them, since he did not assume any special positive principle (evil in itself);44 since this omission is, however, itself contrary to duty (a transgression) and not just a natural error, and its cause cannot in turn be sought (without arguing in a circle) in the inclinations but, on the contrary, only in that which determines the power of choice as free power of choice (in the first and inmost ground of the maxims which are in agreement with the inclinations), we can well understand how philosophers – to whom the basis of an explanation remains forever shrouded in darkness† and, though absolutely

that we must rather start by dislodging from its possession the evil which has already taken up position there (as it could not have done, however, if it had not been incorporated by us into our maxims). That is, the first really good thing that a human being can do is to extricate himself from an evil which is to be sought not in his inclinations but in his perverted maxims, and hence in freedom itself. Those inclinations only make more difficult the *execution* of the good maxims opposing them; whereas genuine evil consists in our *will* not to resist the inclinations when they invite transgression, and this disposition is the really true enemy. The inclinations are opponents of the basic principles only in general (be these principles good or bad), and to this extent that high-minded principle of morality [of the Stoics] is beneficial as a preliminary exercise (the discipline of the inclinations in general) that renders the subject tractable at the hand of basic principles. But, to the extent that specific principles of *moral-goodness* ought to be present yet, as maxims, are not, we must presuppose in the subject somebody else opposing them, in the struggle with which virtue must hold its own; without it all virtues, though indeed not splendid *vices*, as one Church Father has it,43 would certainly be *splendid frailties*, for through them rebellion is indeed often stilled, though never the rebel himself conquered and extirpated.

† It is a very common presupposition of moral philosophy that the presence in the human being of moral evil can very easily be explained, namely by the power of the incentives of sensibility, on the one hand, and the impotence of the incentive of reason (respect for the law) on the other, i.e. by *weakness*. But then the moral good in him (in his moral predisposition) would have to be even more easily explainable, for to comprehend the one without comprehending the other is quite unthinkable. Now reason's ability to become master over all the inclinations striving against it through the mere idea of a law is absolutely inexplicable; hence it is also incomprehensible how the senses could have the ability to become master

necessary, is nonetheless unwelcome – could mistake the real opponent of goodness with whom they believed they had to stand in combat.*

We should not therefore be disconcerted if an apostle represents this *invisible* enemy – this corrupter of basic principles recognizable only through his effects upon us – as being outside us, indeed as an evil *spirit:* "We have to wrestle not against flesh and blood (the natural inclinations) but against principalities and powers, against evil spirits.[45] This expression does not appear to be intended to extend our cognition beyond the world of the senses but only to make intuitive, *for practical use,* the concept of something to us unfathomable. It is at any rate all the same to us, so far as this practical use is concerned, whether we locate the tempter simply in   6:60 ourselves, or also outside us; for guilt touches us not any the less in the latter case than in the former, inasmuch as we would not be tempted by him were we not in secret agreement with him.* – We will divide this whole examination into two sections.

Section one.
Concerning the rightful claim^y^ of the good principle to dominion over the human being

A. THE PERSONIFIED IDEA OF THE GOOD PRINCIPLE

That which alone can make a world the object of divine decree and the end of creation is *Humanity* (rational being in general as pertaining to the world)^z^ *in its full moral perfection,*[46] from which happiness follows in the will of the Highest Being directly as from its supreme condition. – This hu-

---

over a reason which commands with such authority on its side. For if all the world proceeded in accordance with the precept of the law, we would say that everything occurred according to the order of nature, and nobody would think even of inquiring after the cause.

* It is a peculiarity of Christian morality to represent the moral good as differing from the moral evil, not as heaven from *earth,* but as heaven from *hell.* This is indeed a figurative representation and, as such, a stirring one, yet not any the less philosophically correct in meaning – For it serves to prevent us from thinking of good and evil, the realm of light and the realm of darkness, as bordering on each other and losing themselves into one another by gradual steps (of greater and lesser brightness); but rather to represent them as separated by an immeasurable gap. The total dissimilarity of the basic principles by which one can be subject to either one or the other of these two realms, and also the danger associated with the illusion of a close relationship between the characteristics that qualify somebody for one or the other, justify this form of representation which, though containing an element of horror, is nonetheless sublime.

^x^ Kant's sentence does not parse. I have had to drop a comma and a *welcher* to make sense of it.

^y^ *Rechtsanspruch; Recht* also translates as "law."

^z^ *Weltwesen* = . . . being . . . as pertaining to the world

man being, alone pleasing to God, "is in him from all eternity";[47] the idea of him proceeds from God's being; he is not, therefore, a created thing but God's only-begotten Son, "the *Word*" (the *Fiat!*) through which all other things are, and without whom nothing that is made would exist[48] (since for him, that is, for a rational being in the world, as can be thought according to its moral determination, everything was made). – "He is the reflection of his glory."[49] – "In him God loved the world,"[50] and only in
6:61 him and through the adoption of his dispositions can we hope "to become children of God";[51] etc.

Now it is our universal human duty to *elevate* ourselves to this ideal of moral perfection, i.e. to the prototype of moral disposition in its entire purity, and for this the very idea, which is presented to us by reason for emulation, can give us force. But, precisely because we are not its authors but the idea has rather established itself in the human being without our comprehending how human nature could have even been receptive of it, it is better to say that that *prototype* has *come down* to us from heaven, that it has taken up humanity (for it is not just as possible to conceive how the *human being, evil* by nature, would renounce evil on his own and *raise* himself up to the ideal of holiness, as it is that the latter take up humanity – which is not evil in itself – by *descending* to it). This union with us may therefore be regarded as a state of *abasement* of the Son of God[52] if we represent to ourselves this God-like human being, our prototype, in such a way that, though himself holy and hence not bound to submit to sufferings, he nonetheless takes these upon himself in the fullest measure for the sake of promoting the world's greatest good. The human being, on the contrary, who is never free of guilt even when he has taken on the very same disposition, can regard himself as responsible for the sufferings that come his way, whatever the road, and hence unworthy of the union of his disposition with such an idea, even though this idea serves him as prototype.

We cannot think the ideal of a humanity pleasing to God (hence of such moral perfection as is possible to a being pertaining to this world and dependent on needs and inclinations) except in the idea of a human being willing not only to execute in person all human duties, and at the same time to spread goodness about him as far wide as possible through teaching and example, but also, though tempted by the greatest temptation, to take upon himself all sufferings, up to the most ignominious death, for the good of the world and even for his enemies. – For human beings cannot form for themselves any concept of the degree and the strength of a force like that of a moral disposition except by representing it surrounded by obstacles and yet – in the midst of the greatest possible temptations – victorious.

6:62 In the *practical faith in this Son of God* (so far as he is represented as having taken up human nature) the human being can thus hope to become pleasing to God (and thereby blessed); that is, only a human being conscious of such a moral disposition in himself as enables him to *believe* and

104

self-assuredly trust that he, under similar temptations and afflictions (so far as these are made the touchstone of that idea), would steadfastly cling to the prototype of humanity and follow this prototype's example in loyal emulation, only such a human being, and he alone, is entitled to consider himself not an unworthy object of divine pleasure.

B. THE OBJECTIVE REALITY OF THIS IDEA

From the practical point of view this idea has complete reality within itself. For it resides in our morally-legislative reason. We *ought* to conform to it, and therefore we must also *be able* to. If we had to demonstrate in advance that it is possible to be a human being conforming to this prototype, as is absolutely necessary in the case of concepts of nature (lest we run the risk of being stalled by empty concepts), we would have to entertain reservations about allowing even to the moral law the authority of unconditional and yet sufficient determining ground of our power of choice. For how it is possible that the mere idea of conformity to law in general be an even more powerful incentive of that power than any conceivable as deriving from [individual] advantages, can neither be understood by reason nor verified by examples from experience. For, as regards the first, the law commands unconditionally; and, as regards the second, even if there never had been one human being capable of unconditional obedience to the law, the objective necessity that there be such a human being would yet be undiminished and self-evident. There is no need, therefore, of any example from experience to make the idea of a human being morally pleasing to God a model to us; the idea is present as model already in our reason. – If anyone, in order to accept for imitation a human being as such an example of conformity to that idea, asks for more than what he sees, i.e. more than a course of life entirely blameless and as meritorious as indeed one may ever wish; and if, in addition, he also asks for miracles as credentials, to be brought about either through that human being or on his behalf – he who asks for this thereby confesses to his own moral *unbelief,* to a lack of faith in virtue which no faith based on miracles (and thus only historical) can remedy, for only faith in the practical validity of the idea that lies in our reason has moral worth. (And moreover, such faith alone can validate miracles, if need be, as effects coming from the good principle; it cannot borrow its validation from them.)

6:63

Just for this reason an experience must be possible in which the example of such a human being is given (to the extent that one can at all expect and ask for evidence of inner moral disposition from an external experience). For, according to the law, each and every human being should furnish in his own self an example of this idea. And the required prototype always resides only in reason, since outer experience yields no example adequate to the idea; as outer, it does not disclose the inwardness of the disposition but only allows inference to it, though not with strict certainty. (Indeed, even a human being's inner experience of himself does not allow him so to fathom the depths of his heart as to be able to attain, through self-observation, an entirely reliable cognition of the basis of the maxims which he professes, and of their purity and stability).

Now if a human being of such a truly divine disposition had descended, as it were, from heaven to earth at a specific time, and had he exhibited in his self, through teaching, conduct, and suffering, the *example* of a human being well-pleasing to God, to the extent that such an example can at all be expected from outer experience (for, in fact, the *prototype* of any such human being is nowhere to be sought except in our reason); had he brought about, through all this, an incalculably great moral good in the world, through a revolution in the human race: even then we would have no cause to assume in him anything else except a naturally begotten human being (because he too feels to be under the obligation to exhibit such an example in himself). Not that we would thereby absolutely deny that he might indeed also be a supernaturally begotten human being. But, from a practical point of view[a] any such presupposition is of no benefit to us, since the prototype which we see embedded in this apparition must be sought in us as well (though natural human beings), and its presence in the human soul is itself incomprehensible enough that we should also assume, besides its supernatural origin, its hypostatization in a particular human being. On the contrary, the elevation of such a Holy One above every frailty of human nature would rather, from all that we can see, stand in the way of the practical adoption of the idea of such a being for our imitation. For let the nature of this human being well-pleasing to God be thought as human, inasmuch as he is afflicted by just the same needs and hence also the same sufferings, by just the same natural inclinations and hence also the same temptations to transgression, as we are. Let it also be thought as superhuman, however, inasmuch as his unchanging purity of will, not gained through effort but innate, would render any transgression on his part absolutely impossible. The consequent distance from the natural human being would then again become so infinitely great that the divine human being could no longer be held forth to the natural human being as *example*. The natural human being would say: If I were given a perfectly holy will, every temptation to evil would of itself founder in me; if I were given the most complete inner assurance that, after a short life on earth, I should at once become partaker (by virtue of this holiness) in all the eternal glory of the Kingdom of Heaven, I would then take all sorrows upon myself, however grave they might be, even to the most ignominious death, not only willingly but also joyfully, since I would have the glorious and imminent outcome before my eyes. To be sure, the thought that this

6:64

[a] *in praktischer Absicht*

106

divine human being had actual possession of his eminence and blessedness from eternity (and did not need to earn them first through such sorrows), and that he willingly divested himself of them for the sake of plainly unworthy individuals, even for the sake of his enemies, to deliver them from eternal damnation – this thought must attune our mind to admiration, love and thankfulness toward him. Likewise the idea of a conduct in accordance with so perfect a rule of morality could no doubt also be valid for us, as a precept to be followed. Yet he himself could *not* be presented to us *as an example to be emulated*, hence also not as proof that so pure and exalted a moral goodness can be practised and attained *by us.**

Yet such a divinely disposed teacher, though in fact totally human,   6:65
would nonetheless be able to speak truly of himself as if the ideal of   6:66
goodness were displayed incarnate in him (in his teaching and conduct).

---

* It is plainly a limitation of human reason, one which is ever inseparable from it, that we cannot think of any significant moral worth in the actions of a person without at the same time   6:65
portraying this person or his expression in human guise, even though we do not thereby mean to say that this is how things are in themselves ($\chi\alpha\tau'\,\dot\alpha\lambda\acute\eta\vartheta\varepsilon\iota\alpha\nu$)[b] for we always need a certain analogy with natural being in order to make supersensible characteristics comprehensible to us. Thus a philosophical poet assigns to the human being, inasmuch as he has to do battle against a propensity to evil within himself, just because he might overpower it, a higher rung on the moral ladder of beings than to the very inhabitants of heaven who, by virtue of the holiness of their nature, are raised above all possibility of being led astray ("The world with its defects/ is better than a realm of will-less angels."[53]) – The Scriptures too, to make the extent of God's love for the human race comprehensible to us, adapt themselves to this manner of representation, by attributing to God the highest sacrifice a living being can ever perform in order to make even the unworthy happy ("Therefore hath God loved the world, etc."[54]), although through reason we cannot form any concept of how a self-sufficient being could sacrifice something that belongs to his blessedness, thus robbing himself of a perfection. We have here (as means of elucidation) a *schematism of analogy*, with which we cannot dispense. To transform it, however, into a *schematism of object-determination* (as means for expanding our cognition) constitutes *anthropomorphism*, and from the moral point of view (in religion) this has most injurious consequences. – Here I also want to remark incidentally that, in the ascent from the sensible to the supersensible, we can indeed *schematize* (render a concept comprehensible through analogy with something of the senses) but in no way infer by analogy that what pertains to the sensible must also be attributed to the supersensible (thus *expanding* the concept of the latter): we cannot, for the utterly simple reason that it would run *counter* to all analogy to conclude that, since we must necessarily use a schema for a concept to render it comprehensible to us (to support it with an example), this schema must necessarily belong to the object too as its predicate. Thus I cannot say: Just as I cannot make the cause of a plant *comprehensible* to me (or the cause of any organic creature, or in general of the purposive world) in any other way than on the analogy of an artificer in relation to his work (a clock), namely by attributing understanding to the cause, so too must the cause itself (of the plant, of the world in general) *have* understanding; i.e. attributing understanding to it is not just a condition of my capacity to comprehend but of the possibility itself to be a cause. But between the relationship of a schema to its concept and the relationship of this very schema of the concept to the thing itself there is no analogy, but a formidable leap ($\mu\varepsilon\tau\acute\alpha\beta\alpha\sigma\iota\varsigma\,\varepsilon\acute\iota\varsigma\,\acute\alpha\lambda\lambda o\,\gamma\acute\varepsilon\nu o\varsigma$)[c] which leads straight into anthropomorphism. Of this I have given proof elsewhere.

[b] according to truth
[c] passage into another genus

For he would be speaking only of the disposition which he makes the rule of his actions but which, since he cannot make it visible as an example to others in and of itself, he places before their eyes externally through his teachings and actions: "Which of you convinceth me of sin?"[55] And it is only proper that, in the absence of proof to the contrary, a teacher's irreproachable example of what he teaches – when this is, moreover, a matter of duty for everyone – be attributed to no other disposition in him except the purest one. Now, when expressed in thought as the ideal of humankind, such a disposition, in conjunction with all the sufferings undertaken for the sake of the world's highest good, is perfectly valid for all human beings, at all times, and in all worlds, before the highest righteousness, whenever a human being makes his own like unto it, as he ought. To be sure, it will ever remain a righteousness which is not our own, inasmuch as ours would have to come into existence in a life conduct completely and unfailingly in accord with that disposition. Yet an appropriation of it for the sake of our own must be possible, provided that ours is associated with the disposition of the prototype, even though rendering this appropriation comprehensible to us is still fraught with great difficulties. These difficulties we now want to consider.

C. DIFFICULTIES THAT STAND IN THE WAY OF THE REALITY OF THIS IDEA, AND THEIR SOLUTION

The first difficulty which makes doubtful the possibility of realizing in us the idea of a humanity well-pleasing to God, considering the *holiness* of the Lawgiver and the lack of righteousness on our part, is the following. The law says: "Be ye holy (in the conduct of your lives) as your Father in Heaven is holy,"[56] for this is the ideal of the Son of God which is being placed before us as model. The distance between the goodness which we ought to effect in ourselves and the evil from which we start is, however, infinite, and, so far as the deed is concerned – i.e. the conformity of the conduct of one's life to the holiness of the law – it is not exhaustible in any time. Nevertheless, the human being's moral constitution ought to agree with this holiness. The latter must therefore be assumed in his disposition, in the universal and pure maxim of the agreement of conduct with the law, as the germ from which all good is to be developed – [in a disposition] which proceeds from a holy principle adopted by the human being in his supreme maxim. And this is a change of heart which must itself be possible because it is a duty. – Now the difficulty lies here: How can this disposition count for the deed itself, when this deed is *every time* (not generally, but at each instant) defective? The solution rests on the following: According to our mode of estimation, [to us] who are unavoidably restricted to temporal conditions in our conceptions of the relation-

6:67

108

ship of cause to effect, the deed, as a continuous advance *in infinitum* from a defective good to something better, always remains defective, so that we are bound to consider the good as it appears in us, i.e. according to the *deed*, as *at each instant* inadequate to a holy law. But because of the *disposition* from which it derives and which transcends the senses, we can think of the infinite progression of the good toward conformity to the law as being judged by him who scrutinizes the heart (through his pure intellectual intuition) to be a perfected whole even with respect to the deed (the life conduct).* And so notwithstanding his permanent deficiency, a human being can still expect to be *generally* well-pleasing to God, at whatever point in time his existence be cut short. ℙ look at me whole

⅃ The *second* difficulty that arises whenever we consider the human being, as he strives toward the good, with respect to the relation of his moral good to the divine *goodness*, has to do with *moral happiness*, by which we do not here mean the assurance of the everlasting possession of contentment in one's *physical state* (freedom from evils and enjoyment of ever mounting pleasures), i.e. *physical happiness*, but the assurance of the reality and *constancy* of a disposition that always advances in goodness (and never falters from it). For, *if one were absolutely assured of the unchangeableness of such a disposition*, the constant "seeking after the Kingdom of God" would be equivalent to knowing oneself already in possession of this kingdom, inasmuch as a human being thus disposed would from himself derive the confidence that "all things else (i.e. what relates to physical happiness) will be added to him."57

6:68

Now one could indeed refer a human being anxious on this score, and his wish, to: "His (God's) Spirit gives witness to our spirit,"58 etc.; that is, whoever possesses as pure a disposition as is required will feel of himself that he can never fall so low as to regain a liking for evil. There is, however, something awkward about such feelings of a presumed supernatural origin: one is never more easily deceived than in what promotes a good opinion of oneself. Moreover, it seems never advisable to be encouraged to such a state of confidence but much more beneficial (for morality) to "work out one's salvation with *fear* and *trembling*"59 (a hard saying which, if misunderstood, can drive one to the darkest enthusiasm). Yet

---

* It must not be overlooked that we do not thereby mean to say that the disposition should serve to *compensate* for any lack of conformity to duty, hence for the actual evil, in this infinite series (the presupposition is rather that the human moral constitution pleasing to God is actually to be found in the series), but rather that the disposition, which takes the place of the totality of the series of approximations carried on *in infinitum*, makes up only for the deficiency which is in principle inseparable from the existence of a temporal being, [namely] never to be able to become quite fully what he has in mind.*d* For as regards the compensation for the transgressions incurred in this progression, we shall consider it in connection with the solution to the *third* difficulty.

d im Begriffe

without *any* confidence in the disposition once acquired, perseverance in it would hardly be possible. We can, however, find this confidence, without delivering ourselves to the sweetness or the anxiety of enthusism, by comparing our life conduct so far pursued with the resolution we once embraced. – For [take] a human being who, from the time of his adoption of the principles of the good and throughout a sufficiently long life henceforth, has perceived the efficacy of these principles on what he does, i.e. on the conduct of his life as it steadily improves, and from that has cause to infer, but only by way of conjecture, a fundamental improvement in his disposition: [he] can yet also reasonably hope that in this life he will no longer forsake his present course but will rather press in it with ever greater courage, since his advances, provided that their principle is good, will always increase his *strength* for future ones; nay, if after this life another awaits him, that he will persevere in it (in all appearances under different circumstances, yet according to the very same principle) and come ever closer to his goal of perfection, though it is unattainable; for, on the basis of what he has perceived in himself so far, he can legitimately assume that his disposition is fundamentally improved. By contrast, one who has always found himself unable to stand fast by his often repeated resolutions to be good but has always relapsed into evil, or who has been forced to acknowledge that in the course of his life he has gone from bad to worse, slipping ever further down as though on a slope: [such a one]

6:69   can reasonably entertain no hope of improving, even if he still had to live longer in this world, or a future life stood ahead of him, for, from all indications, he would have to regard the corruption as rooted in his disposition. Now, the first is a glimpse into a *boundless* future which is, however, desirable and happy; the second, by contrast, into a *misery* which is just as *boundless*, i.e. for human beings, from what they can judge, the two [glimpse] into either a blessed or a cursed[c] *eternity*. And these are representations powerful enough to serve to one part [of humanity] as reassurance and confirmation in the good, and, to the other, for rousing conscience to judgment, to make yet a break with evil so far as is possible, hence as incentives, without any necessity to presuppose *dogmatically*, as an item of doctrine, that an eternity of good or evil is the human lot also objectively:* with supposed cognitions and assertions of this sort reason

---

* Among those questions which, even if they could be answered, would not in the least enlighten the questioner (and which we may therefore call *childish questions*) is this: Will the punishment of hell be finite or everlasting? Teach the first alternative, and there is cause to fear that many would say (like all those who believe in purgatory, or like the sailor in Moore's *Travels*[60]): "Well, I hope that I will be able to last it out." Assert the second instead, and count it as tenet of faith, and the unintended result may be the hope of complete impunity after a most dastardly life. For a clergyman, though sought for advice and consolation only in the brief moments of a belated remorse at the end of such a dastardly life, must yet find it cruel
[c] *unselig*

110

simply transgresses the limitations of its insight. The good and pure   6:70
disposition of which we are conscious (and which we can call a good spirit   6:71
that presides over us) thus carries confidence in its own perseverance and
stability, though indirectly, and is our Comforter (Paraclete) whenever our

and inhuman to proclaim eternal damnation to the [dying] one; and since the clergyman
admits no middle ground between eternal damnation and complete absolution (on the
contrary, either there is eternal punishment or no punishment at all), he will have to hold out
to him the hope of not being punished at all, i.e. he must promise to transform him in a hurry
into a human being well-pleasing to God; but, since there is no time left then for the
conversion to a life of good conduct, professions of remorse, formulas of faith, even vows of
a new life just in case the end of the present one is somewhat delayed, will have to take the
place of the means. – Such is the unavoidable consequence when the *eternity* of [one's]
future destiny, conformable to the conduct of [one's] present life, is set forth as *dogma*, and a
human being is not rather instructed to form a concept of his future moral state on the basis
of his state up to the present, and to come *on his own* to a conclusion regarding it as the
[totality of the] naturally foreseeable consequences of his present one. For then the *immeasur-
ableness* of the series of such consequences under the dominion of evil will work on him the
same moral effect (of inciting him before the end of his life to undo whatever has happened
as much as he can, through reparation or compensation proportionate to his actions) as can
be expected from proclaiming the eternity of the evil, without however entailing the disadvantages of the dogma of this eternity (which, moreover, is warranted by neither rational insight
nor scriptural exegesis), namely that the wicked human being counts in advance, even *during*   6:70
his life, on an easily obtainable pardon, or that, at life's close, he believes he only has to
reckon with the claims of heavenly justice upon him, and these he can satisfy with words
alone, and human rights are meanwhile left begging, and nobody will get back what belongs
to him (this is an outcome so common to this kind of expiation that an example to the
contrary is almost unheard of). – Furthermore, should anyone fear that his reason, through
conscience, will judge him too leniently, he errs, I believe, seriously. For reason is incorruptible just because it is free, and must pass judgment over him (the human being) precisely as
reason; and if we simply tell him, under such circumstances, that it is at least possible that
soon he must stand before a judge, we need but leave him to his own reflection, which will in
all probability judge him with the greatest severity. – To this I want to add a couple of further
comments. The common saying, "All's well that ends well," can indeed be applied to moral
cases, but only if by the "good ending" we understand that a human being becomes a
genuinely good human being. Yet where is he to recognize himself to be such, since he can
draw this conclusion only from the constancy of his consequent good conduct, and, at the
end of life, there is no time left for this? With respect to *happiness* the saying can more easily
be conceded, but here too only by assuming the standpoint of someone who looks at his life,
not from the starting point, but at its close, and reviews it from there. Griefs once endured,
when we feel safe from them, leave no painful reminiscences behind but rather a feeling of
gladness that makes the enjoyment of the supervening good fortune all the sweeter. For
pleasure and pain (since they belong to the senses) are both included in the temporal series,
and disappear with it; they do not constitute a totality with the present enjoyment of life but
are rather displaced by it as it succeeds them. If we however apply the same saying to the
judgment of the moral worth of the life we have led up to the present, we may be wide of the
truth in our judgment, even if, in conclusion, we have given to our life a totally good new
turn. For the moral subjective principle of the *disposition* by which our life is to be judged is
(as transcending the senses) not of the kind that its existence can be thought as divisible into
temporal segments but rather only as an absolute unity. And since we can draw inferences
regarding the disposition only on the basis of actions (which are its appearances), for the

111

lapses make us anxious about its perseverance. Certainty with respect to the latter is neither possible to the human being, nor, so far we can see, morally beneficial. For (be it well noted) we cannot base this confidence upon an immediate consciousness of the immutability of our disposition, since we cannot see through to the latter but must at best infer it from the consequence that it has on the conduct of our life. And since our inference is drawn from perceptions that are only appearances of a good or bad disposition, our inference never reveals with any certainty especially the *strength* of the disposition, least of all when, in the face of impending death, we think that we have improved ours. For then, in the absence of further conduct upon which to base our judgment of our moral worth, even those empirical proofs of the genuineness of an improved disposition are entirely lacking, and the unavoidable consequence of a rational estimate of our moral state is a feeling of hopelessness (which, however, human nature itself, because of the obscurity of all views that transcend the limits of this life, takes care that it does not turn into wild despair).

The *third* and apparently the greatest difficulty – which would have[f]

6:72   every human being, even after he has entered upon the path of goodness, still a reprobate in the sentencing of his entire life conduct before a divine *righteousness* – is as follows. – Whatever his state in the acquisition of a good disposition, and, indeed, however steadfastly a human being may have persevered in such a disposition in a life conduct conformable to it, *he nevertheless started from evil,* and this is a debt which is impossible for him to wipe out. He cannot regard the fact that, after his change of heart,

---

purpose of a [moral] estimate our life is to be viewed only as a *temporal unity,* i.e. a *whole.* But then the reproaches [arising] from the first part of our life (before the improvement) join in with just as loud a voice as the approval in the *concluding* part, and might indeed dampen the triumphant tone of the "All's well that ends well." – Finally, closely related to this doctrine

6:71   regarding the duration of punishment in another world, though not identical with it, is yet another, namely, that "All sins must be forgiven here," that at the end of life our account must be completely closed, and nobody may hope somehow to make up there for what was neglected here. This doctrine can no more proclaim itself to be dogma than the previous one, but is rather only a principle by which practical reason regulates itself in its use of the concept of the supersensible, while at the same time granting that it knows nothing of the objective composition of the latter. Practical reason is in fact saying only this much: We can conclude that we are human beings pleasing to God, or not, only on the basis of the conduct of the life we have led so far; and since this conduct ends with our life, so too does the reckoning, the balance of which alone must yield whether we may regard ourselves as justified or not. – In general, if, instead of [extending it to] the *constitutive* principles of the cognition of supersensible objects into which we cannot in fact have any insight, we restricted our judgment to the *regulative* principles, which content themselves with only their practical use, human wisdom would be better off in a great many respects, and there would be no breeding of would-be knowledge of something of which we fundamentally know nothing – groundless though indeed for a while glittering sophistry that it is, at the end unmasked as a detriment to morality.
[f] *vorstellt*

he has not incurred new debts as equivalent to his having paid off the old ones. Nor can he produce, in the future conduct of a good life, a surplus over and above what he is under obligation to perform each time; for his duty at each instant is to do all the good in his power. – Moreover, so far as we can judge by our reason's standards of right, this original debt, or at any rate the debt that precedes whatever good a human being may ever do (this, and no more, is what we understood by *radical* evil; cf. the first Section), cannot be erased by somebody else. For it is not a *transmissible* liability which can be made over to somebody else, in the manner of a financial debt (where it is all the same to the creditor whether the debtor himself pays up, or somebody else for him), but the *most personal* of all liabilities, namely a debt of sins which only the culprit, not the innocent, can bear, however magnanimous the innocent might be in wanting to take the debt upon himself for the other. – Now, moral evil (transgression of the moral law, called sin when the law is taken *as divine command*) brings with it an *infinity* of violations of the law, and hence an *infinity* of guilt (though it is otherwise before a human court, which takes only the individual crime into account, hence only the act and anything related to it, not the universal disposition), not so much because of the *infinity* of the highest lawgiver whose authority is thereby offended (for we understand nothing of such intangible relations of the human being to the highest being) but because the evil is in the *disposition* and the maxims in general (in the manner of *universal principles* as contrasted with individual transgressions): consequently, every human being has to expect *infinite* punishment and exclusion from the Kingdom of God. ~~evil disposition~~

The resolution to this difficulty rests on the following consideration. The judicial verdict of one who knows the heart of the accused must be thought as based on the universal disposition of the latter, not on the appearances of his disposition, [i.e.] on actions that either diverge from the law or agree with it. In this respect, however, we now presuppose in the human being a good disposition which has the upper hand over the evil principle dominant in him. So the question is whether the moral consequence of his earlier disposition, [i.e.] punishment, (or in other words: the effect on the subject of God's displeasure) can be extended to reach even his present state, in his improved disposition in which he already is an object of divine pleasure. Now, since the question here is not whether, also *before* the human being's conversion, the punishment imposed upon him accorded with divine justice (as there is no doubt about this), the punishment *is not* to be thought (in this inquiry) as fully exacted before the human being's improvement. Also *after his conversion*, however, since he now leads a new life and has become a "new man,"[61] the punishment cannot be considered appropriate to his new quality (of thus being a human being well-pleasing to God). Yet satisfaction must be rendered to Supreme Justice, in whose sight no one deserving of punishment can go

6:73

113

unpunished. But, since neither *before* nor *after* conversion is the punishment in accordance with divine wisdom but is nevertheless necessary, the punishment must be thought as adequately executed in the situation of conversion itself. We must therefore see whether, by means of the very concept of moral conversion, we can think that situation as entailing such ills as the new human being, whose disposition is good, can regard as having been incurred by himself (in a different context) and, [therefore], as *punishment** whereby satisfaction is rendered to divine justice. – Now conversion is an exit from evil and an entry into goodness, "the putting off of the old man and the putting on of the new,"[64] since the subject dies unto sin (and thereby also the subject of all inclinations that lead to sin) in order to live unto justice. As an intellectual determination, however, this conversion is not two moral acts separated by a temporal interval but is rather a single act, since the abandonment of evil is possible only through the good disposition that effects the entrance into goodness, and *vice-versa*. The good principle is present, therefore, just as much in the abandonment of the evil as in the adoption of the good disposition, and the pain that by rights accompanies the first derives entirely from the second. The emergence from the corrupted disposition into the good is in itself already sacrifice (as "the death of the old man,"[65] "the crucifying of the flesh"[66]) and entrance into a long train of life's ills which the new human being undertakes in the disposition of the Son of God, that is, simply for the sake of the good, yet are still fitting *punishment* for someone else, namely the old human being (who, morally, is another human being). – *Physically* ([i.e.] considered in his empirical character as a sensible being) he still is the same human being liable to punishment, and he must be judged as such before a moral tribunal of justice and hence by himself as well. Yet, in his new disposition (as an intelligible being), in the sight of a divine judge for whom the disposition takes the place of the deed, he is *morally* another being. And this disposition which he has incorporated in

6:74

---

* We cannot assume that the hypothesis that all evils in the world are generally to be regarded as punishments for transgressions committed was devised for the sake of a theodicy or as a contrivance for the purposes of priestly religion (cult), for it is too common to have been artificially excogitated; we must rather presume that the hypothesis is closely allied to human reason, which is inclined to link the course of nature with the laws of morality, and hence quite naturally comes up with the idea that we should seek to become better human beings first, before we can request to be freed from the ills of life, or to be compensated for them with a superior good. – Hence the first man is represented (in Holy Scriptures) as condemned to work if he wishes to eat, his wife to bear children in pain, and both to die, *all on account of their transgression,* although there is no telling how animal creatures, fitted with their bodily limbs, could have expected any other destiny even if these transgressions had not been perpetrated.[62] For the Hindus human beings are but spirits (called "Dewas") locked up in animal bodies as punishment for previous crimes, and even a philosopher (Malebranche) preferred to attribute no soul, and hence no feelings, to nonrational animals rather than to admit that horses had to withstand so much torment "without having ever eaten of forbidden hay."[63]

all its purity, like unto the purity of the Son of God – or (if we personify this idea) this very **Son of God** – bears as *vicarious substitute* the debt of sin for him, and also for all who believe (practically) in him: as *savior*, he satisfies the highest justice through suffering and death, and, as *advocate*, he makes it possible for them to hope that they will appear justified before their judge. Only we must remember that (in this way of imagining) the suffering which the new human being must endure* while dying to the *old* human being throughout his life is depicted in the representative of the human kind as a death suffered once and for all. – Here, then, is that   6:75 surplus over the merit from works for which we felt the need earlier, one which is imputed to us *by grace*. For what in our earthly life (and perhaps even in all future times and in all worlds) is always only in mere *becoming* (namely, our being a human being well-pleasing to God) is imputed to us as if we already possessed it here in full. And to this we indeed have no rightful claim† (according to the empirical cognition we have of ourselves), so far as we knowˢ ourselves (estimate our disposition not directly

(handwritten: no right to grace)

* Even the purest moral disposition elicits in the human being, regarded as a worldly creature, nothing more than the continuous becoming of a subject well pleasing to God in   6:75 actions (such as can be met with in the world of the senses). In quality (since it must be thought as supersensibly *grounded*) this disposition can indeed be, and ought to be, holy and conformable to the archetype's disposition. In degree, however, (in terms of its manifestations in actions) it always remains deficient and infinitely removed from that of the archetype. Nevertheless, as an intellectual unity of the whole, the disposition takes *the place of* perfected *action*, since it contains the ground of its own steady progress in remedying its deficiency. But now it can be asked: Can he "in whom there is no condemnation,"[67] or [in whom there] must be [none], believe himself justified and, at the same time, count *as punishment* the sufferings that befall him on the way to an ever greater goodness, thus professing to deserve punishment and, by the same token, also to have a disposition displeasing to God? Yes indeed, but always in his quality as the "man" he is continually putting off. Whatever is due to him as punishment in that quality, i.e. as "the old man" (and this includes all the sufferings and ills of life in general) he gladly takes upon himself in his quality as "the new man," solely for the sake of the good; consequently, to that extent and as such a "new man," those sufferings are not ascribed to him as "punishments" but the term here rather means only this: In his quality as "the new man" he willingly takes upon himself, as so many opportunities to test and exercise his disposition for the good, all the ills and sufferings that befall him; these "the old man" would have to impute to himself as punishment, and he too actually imputes them to himself as such inasmuch as he still is in the process of dying to "the old man." This punishment is itself the cause and at the same time the effect of his disposition for the good, hence also of the contentment and *moral happiness* inherent in the consciousness of his progress in the good (and this progress is one and the same act as the abandonment of evil). In the old disposition, by contrast, these very ills would have counted exclusively as punishment, and would also have had to be *felt* as such, since, even when considered as mere ills, they would still be opposed to what, in the form of *physical happiness*, a human being in such a disposition takes as his exclusive goal.

†† Rather, *receptivity* is all that we, on our part, can attribute to ourselves, whereas a superior's decision to grant a good for which the subordinate has no more than (moral) receptivity is called *grace*.

ˢ *erkennen*

6:76 but only according to our deeds), so that the accuser within us would still be more likely to render a verdict of guilty. It is always therefore only a decree of grace when we are relieved of all responsibility for the sake of this good in which we believe, though fully in accord with eternal justice (because based on a satisfaction that for us consists only in the idea of an improved disposition of which, however, God alone has cognition).

It can further be asked whether this deduction of the idea of a *justification* of a human being who is indeed guilty but has passed into a disposition well-pleasing to God has any practical use at all, and what such use could be. It is hard to see what *positive* use can be made of it for religion and for the conduct of life, for the fundamental condition of the inquiry is that the individual in question already actually is in the required good disposition for the sake of which (its development and encouragement) every practical employment of moral concepts is truly directed as end; as regards comfort, such a good disposition already brings it with it (as comfort and hope, not as certainty) to anyone conscious of it in himself. Thus the investigation is only an answer to a speculative question, but one that cannot therefore be passed over in silence, since reason could then be accused of being absolutely incapable of reconciling the human being's hope of absolution from his guilt with divine justice, and this accusation might be disadvantageous to reason in many respects, most of all morally. However, the *negative* use that can be derived from the investigation for religion and morality, on behalf of each and every human being, is very far-reaching. For from the deduction as adduced we see that it is possible to think of absolution for a human being burdened with guilt, before heavenly justice, only on the assumption of a total change of heart; that, therefore, no expiations, be they of the penitential or the ceremonial sort, no invocations or exaltations (even those of the vicarious ideal of God's Son) can make up for the lack of this change of heart or, if the change is there, in the least increase its validity before the heavenly tribunal; for that ideal must be adopted in our disposition before it can stand in place of the deed.[–]A different issue is raised by the question, What can a human being expect *at the end of his life,* or what can he fear, in virtue of his conduct during it? For this a human being must first of all have cognition of his own character, at least to some extent. Thus, though he may believe that

6:77 there has been an improvement in his disposition, he must be equally able to take the old (corrupted) one into consideration, the one from which he started, and examine what and how much of this disposition he has cast off, as well as the *quality* (whether pure or still impure) and the *grade* of the supposed new disposition for overcoming the old one and preventing relapse into it; he will thus have to look at his disposition throughout his whole life. But, since he can derive no certain and definite concept of his real disposition through immediate consciousness but only from the conduct he has actually led in life, he shall not be able to think of any other condition of being delivered to the verdict of a future judge (that is, his awakening consciousness, together with the empirical self-cognition produced by it) than that *his whole life* be one day placed before the judge's eyes, and not just a segment of it, perhaps the last and to him still the most advantageous; to it he would of his own accord add the prospect in a life further extended (without fixing limits for himself on this score), in case it lasted longer. Here he cannot allow the previously recognized disposition to take the place of the deed but, on the contrary, he must extract his disposition from the deed before him. What verdict, does the reader think, will this mere thought lead a human being to pronounce upon his future life on the base of his conduct so far, when this thought brings back to his recollection (though he is not of the worst sort) much which he has otherwise easily forgotten, even if no more were said to him than that he has cause to believe that one day he will stand before a judge? Address this question in a human being to the judge within him, and the human being will pronounce a stern judgment upon himself, for he cannot bribe his reason; but represent for him another judge, of whom news will be had through sources of information elsewhere, and he will have much with which to counter the judge's severity under the pretext of human frailty; he will think he can get around him, whether by forestalling his punishment through remorseful self-inflicted torments that do not, however, originate in any genuine disposition toward improvement or by mollifying him with prayers and entreaties, even with incantations and self-proclaimed professions of faith. And give him now encouragement (as with the proverb, "All is well that ends well") and from early on he will make his plans accordingly, with a view not to forfeit too much of life's pleasures unnecessarily and, by life's end, to settle his accounts with speed and to his advantage.*   6:78

---

*† The aim of those who have a clergyman summoned to them at the end of life is normally to find in him a *comforter*, not on account of their *physical* sufferings brought on by the last illness or even by the natural fear in the face of death (for on this score death itself, which puts an end to life, can be the comforter) but because of the *moral* sufferings, the reproaches of their conscience. At such time, however, conscience ought rather to be *stirred up* and *sharpened*, in order that whatever good yet to be done, or whatever consequences of past evil still left to be undone (repaired for), will not be neglected, in accordance with the warning, "Agree with thine adversary" (with him who has a legal right against you) "quickly, while thou art in the way with him" (i.e. so long as you still live), "lest he deliver thee to the judge" (after death), etc.[68] But to administer opium to conscience instead, as it were, is to be guilty of a crime against the human being himself and against those who survive him, and is totally contrary to the purpose for which such support given to conscience at life's end can be held necessary.

117

Section two
Concerning the evil principle's rightful claim to dominion over the human being, and the struggle of the two principles with one another

The Holy Scriptures (the Christian portion thereof) convey this intellectual moral relation in the form of a story in which two principles, opposed to each other like heaven to hell and represented as two persons outside the human being, not only test their respective power in him but also seek (the one party as his prosecutor, the other as advocate) to establish their claims *through law,*[h] as it were before a supreme judge.

The human being was originally appointed the proprietor of all the goods of the earth (Genesis 1:28),[69] though he was to have only their usufruct (*dominium utile*)[i] under his Creator and Lord as the supreme proprietor (*dominus directus*).[j] At the same time an evil being is introduced (we have no cognition of how he became so evil as to betray his master, for originally he was good) who, through his fall, has lost whatever estate he might have had in heaven and now wants to acquire another on earth. But, since earthly and corporeal objects give him no pleasure (he is a being of a higher species – a spirit), he seeks to establish dominion *over minds* by causing our first parents to rebel against their overlord and become dependent on him. And so he succeeds in setting himself up as the supreme proprietor of all the goods on earth, i.e. as the prince of this world. Now, one might well wonder why God did not avail himself of his power against this traitor,* and did not prefer to destroy the kingdom which he intended to found at its very inception. But, in his domination and government over rational beings the Supreme Being deals with them in accordance with the principle of their freedom, and whatever good or evil befalls them, it ought to be theirs to ascribe to themselves. A Kingdom of Evil was thus set up here on earth in defiance of the good principle, and all of Adam's (natural) descendants were subjugated to it – and this with their own free consent, since the false show of this world's goods diverted their gaze from the abyss of perdition in store for them. Because of its rightful claim to dominion over the human being, the good principle did indeed retain a hold through the establishment of a form of government solely directed to

6:79

---

* Father Charlevoix reports that when he told his Iroquois catechumen the story of all the evil that the evil spirit wrought on a creation originally good, and how this spirit is still constantly seeking to thwart the best divine arrangements, the catechumen asked him with indignation: But why does not God strike the Devil dead? to which question he candidly admits that he was unable, on the spot, to find an answer.[70]

[h] Law = *Recht*

[i] The right to the enjoyment of the advantages of a property belonging to another, so far as may be had without damage or prejudice to the property.

[j] the immediate lord

the public and exclusive veneration of its name (in the *Jewish* theocracy). But, since in this government the subjects remained attuned in their minds to no other incentive except the goods of this world and only wished, therefore, to be ruled through rewards and punishments in this life – nor were they in this respect capable of other laws except such as were in part imposed by burdensome ceremonies and observances, in part indeed ethical but only inasmuch as they gave rise to external compulsion, hence were only civil, and the inferiority of the moral disposition was in no way at issue – so this institutional order did no substantial injury to the realm of darkness but only served to keep ever in remembrance the imprescriptible right of the first proprietor. – Now there suddenly appeared among these very people, at a time when they were feeling the full measure of all the evils of a hierarchical constitution, and were feeling it as well, perhaps, because of the Greek sages' moral doctrines on freedom which, unsettling as they were for the slavish mind, had gradually gained influence over them and had induced most of them to reflection – they were thus ripe for a revolution – a person whose wisdom, even purer than that of the previous philosophers, was as though descended from heaven; and he announced himself indeed as a true human being, so far as his doctrines and example were concerned, yet also as an envoy of heavenly origin who was not implicated, at the time of original innocence, in the bargain with the evil principle into which the rest of the human race had entered through their representative (their first progenitor);* "in him,

6:80

---

*† To conceive the possibility of a person free from innate propensity to evil by having him born of a virgin mother is an idea of reason consistent with, as it were, a moral instinct difficult to explain and yet undeniable. For, since natural generation cannot take place without sensual pleasure on both sides and yet seems to relate us to the mating of animals generally far too closely (for human dignity), we look upon it as something to *be ashamed* of – an attitude[k] which certainly was the real cause of the belief in the sanctity of the monastic state – and imagine it, therefore, as something immoral, something not reconcilable with the perfection of a human being, yet grafted in his nature and hence also passed on to his followers as an evil predisposition. – Now, the idea of the birth, independent of any sexual intercourse (virginal), of a child untainted by moral blemish is well suited to this obscure representation (merely sensible on one side, yet moral and hence intellectual on the other), though not without its theoretical difficulties (with respect to which, however, it is not at all necessary to determine anything from a practical point of view). For, according to the hypothesis of epigenesis, the mother, who descended from her parents through *natural* birth, would still be tainted with this moral blemish and would pass it on to her child, at least half of it, even in a supernatural birth. To escape this consequence, therefore, we would have to assume the theory that the seeds [of the descendants] *pre-exist* in the progenitors, not, however, the theory that these seeds develop on the *female* side (for then the consequence is not escaped) but on the *male* side alone (not on the part of the *ova* but of the *spermatozoa*). So, since the male side has no part in a supernatural pregnancy, this mode of representation could be defended as theoretically consistent with the idea [of virginal birth]. – But what is the use of all this theorizing *pro* or *contra*, when it suffices for practical purposes to hold the idea itself before us as model, as symbol of humankind raising itself above temptation to evil (and withstanding it victoriously)?

[k] *Vorstellung*

119

therefore, the prince of this world had no part."[71] The sovereignty of this
6:81 prince was thereby put in jeopardy. For were this human being well-
pleasing to God to resist his temptations also to enter into that bargain [with
him], and were other human beings to believe in him and adopt his same
disposition, then the prince of the world would lose just that many subjects,
and his kingdom would run the risk of being totally destroyed. The prince
offered, therefore, to make him the vassal lord of his whole kingdom, if he
just would pay homage to him as the owner of it.[72] But, since this attempt did
not succeed, not only did he take away from this stranger in his territory
anything that could make his earthly life agreeable (to the point of direst
poverty): he also provoked against him every persecution by which evil
human beings could embitter him – sufferings that only one well disposed
can truly feel with depth, [such as] the slandering of his teaching's pure
intention (in order to deprive him of a following) – and he finally pursued
him to the most ignominious death, without achieving anything in the least
against him by this onslaught by unworthy people upon his steadfastness
and honesty in teaching, and example for the sake of the good. And now to
the outcome of this combat. Its result can be viewed in *legal*[l] terms, or in
physical terms. If one views the physical result (which belongs to the senses),
then the good principle is the worsted party; after enduring many sufferings, he had to give up his life in combat,* for he had provoked a revolt in a
6:82 foreign dominion (which, as such, had coercive power). However, since the
realm in which *principles* (be they good or evil) have power is not one of
nature but of freedom, i.e. it is a realm in which one can control things only
to the extent that one rules over minds, and where nobody is therefore slave

---

*† Not that (as in Dr. Bahrdt's fanciful fiction)[73] he *sought* death in order to promote a worthy
purpose through a shining and sensational example; that would be suicide. For one may
indeed dare something at the risk of losing one's life, or even endure death at the hand of
another, when one cannot avoid it, without betraying an irremissible duty. But one cannot
dispose of oneself and one's life as a means, whatever the end, and thus be the *author* of
one's death. – Nor (as the Wolfenbüttel fragmentarist suspects)[74] did he *stake* his life for just
a political though illegal purpose, and not a moral one, perhaps that of overthrowing the rule
of the priests in order to establish himself in their place with supreme temporal power. For in
opposition to this stands the admonition, "Do this in remembrance of me,"[75] which he gave
to his disciples at the last supper, when he had already given up the hope of attaining any
such power. This admonition, if intended as the remembrance of a worldly design that had
come to nought, would have been an offensive exhortation, such as to provoke ill-will against
its originator, and hence self-defeating. However, the remembrance could just as well refer
to the failure of a very good and purely moral design of the Master, namely, to bring about in
his own lifetime a *public* revolution (in religion), by overthrowing a morally repressive ceremonial faith and the authority of its priests (the preparations for the gathering together at Easter
of his disciples, scattered all over the land, might well have had this as end). And we may
6:82 indeed even now regret that the design did not succeed, even though it was not in vain, for
after the Master's death it gave way to a religious transformation that quietly spread everywhere, though in the midst of many sufferings.
l rechtlicher

120

(bondsman) but who wills to be one, and only so long as he wills it: so the master's very death (the last extreme of a human being's suffering) was the manifestation of the good principle, that is, of humanity in its moral perfection, as example for everyone to follow. The representation of this death ought to have had, and could have had, the greatest influence on human hearts at that time – indeed, so it can at any time – for it most strikingly displays the contrast between the freedom of the children of heaven and the bondage of a mere son of earth. However, the good principle did not descend among humans from heaven at one particular time but from the very beginning of the human race, in some invisible way (as anyone must grant who attentively considers the holiness of the principle, and the incomprehensibility as well of the union of this holiness with human sensible nature in the moral disposition) and has precedence of domicile in humankind by right. And, since the principle appeared in an actual human being as example for all others, this human being "came unto his own, and his own received him not, but as many as received him, to them gave he power to be called the sons of God, even to them that believe on his name";[76] that is, by exemplifying this principle (in the moral idea) that human being opened the doors of freedom to all who, like him, choose to die to everything that holds them fettered to earthly life to the detriment of morality; and among these he gathers unto himself "a people for his possession, zealous of good works,"[77] under his dominion, while he abandons to their fate all those who prefer moral servitude.

So the moral outcome of this conflict, on the part of the hero of the story (up to his death), is not really the *conquering* of the evil principle – for its kingdom still endures and, in any case, a new epoch must yet come in which it is to be destroyed – but only the breaking up of its controlling power in holding against their will those who have so long been subject to it, now that another moral dominion (since the human being must be subject to some dominion or other) has been revealed to them as freedom, and in it they can find protection for their morality if they want to forsake the old one. Moreover, the evil principle is still called the prince of this world, and those in this world who adhere to the good principle should always be prepared for physical sufferings, sacrifices, and mortifications of self-love, all of which are portrayed in this world by the evil principle as persecutions, since in his kingdom he has rewards only for those who have made earthly goods their ultimate aim.

It is easy to see, once we divest of its mystical cover this vivid mode of representing things, apparently also the only one at the time *suited to the common people*, why it (its spirit and rational meaning) has been valid and binding practically, for the whole world and at all times: because it lies near enough to every human being for each to recognize his duty in it. Its meaning is that there is absolutely no salvation for human beings except in the innermost adoption of genuine moral principles in their disposition,

6:83

121

[and] that to interfere with this adoption is surely not the so often blamed sensibility but a certain self-incurred perversity or, as we might otherwise also call this wickedness, fraud (*faussité*, the satanic guile through which evil came into the world): [this is] a corruption that lies in all human beings and cannot be overcome except through the idea of the moral good in its absolute purity, combined with the consciousness that this idea belongs to our original predisposition and we only need to be assiduous in keeping it free of any impure mixture, and to accept it deeply in our disposition, to become convinced by the gradual influence that it has on the mind that the dreaded powers of evil have nothing to muster against it ("the gates of hell shall not prevail")[78] and, lest we happen to compensate for a deficiency in this trust *by way of superstition*, through expiations that presuppose no change of heart, or *by way of enthusiasm*, through alleged (merely passive) inner illuminations, and thus ever be kept distant from the good based on self-activity, that we should not ascribe to this good any other distinguishing trait except that of a well-ordered conduct of life. –

6:84 Finally, any attempt like the present to find a meaning in Scriptures in harmony with the *most holy* teachings of reason must be held not only as permissible but as duty;* and we may be reminded at this point of what the *wise teacher* said to his disciples regarding someone who went his own way, by which, however, he would have had eventually to come to the same goal: "Forbid him not; for he who is not against us is for us."[79]

General remark

If a moral religion (to be cast not in dogmas and observances but in the heart's disposition to observe all human duties as divine commands) must be established, eventually all the *miracles* which history connects with its inception must themselves render faith in miracles in general dispensable. For we betray a culpable degree of moral unbelief if we do not grant sufficient authority to duty's precepts, as originally inscribed in the heart by reason, unless they are in addition authenticated through miracles: "Except ye see signs and wonders, ye will not believe."[80] Yet, when a religion of mere cult and observances has run its course and one based on the spirit and the truth (on moral disposition) is to be introduced in its place, it is entirely conformable to the ordinary human way of thinking, though not required by the [new] religion, if the historical introduction of the latter be accompanied and as it were adorned by miracles, to announce the end of the previous one which without miracles would not have had any authority at all: indeed, even in such a way that, to win over the adherents of the earlier religion to the recent revolution, the older religion is interpreted as the ancient prefiguration, now come to fulfill-

*† And it may be admitted that it is not the only one.

ment, of the final end of providence in the new. And it would not pay under these circumstances to contest those narratives or interpretations, now that the true religion, which in its time needed introduction through such aids, is finally here and from now on is able to hold its own on rational grounds. For we would then have to accept that the mere faith in things incomprehensible and their repetition (of which anyone is capable without being for that reason a better human being, or ever becoming one thereby) is a way, indeed the only way, of pleasing God – a claim that we   6:85 must dispute with all our might. It might well be that the person of the teacher of the one and only religion, valid for all worlds, is a mystery; that his appearance on earth, as well as his translation from it, his eventful life and his passion, are all but miracles – indeed, that the history that ought to testify to the account of these miracles is itself a miracle (a supernatural revelation). So we may leave the merit of these miracles, one and all, undisturbed; nay even venerate the external cover that has served to bring into public currency a doctrine whose authentication rests on a document indelibly retained in every soul and in need of no miracle: provided, however, that, as regards the use of these historical reports, we do not make it a tenet of religion that knowing, believing, and professing them are themselves something by which we can make ourselves well-pleasing to God.

As for miracles in general, there are rational human beings who, though not disposed to renounce belief in them, never allow this belief to intervene in practical matters; and this is as much as to say that, *in theory,* they do indeed believe that there are miracles, but avow none *in their practical affairs.* For this reason wise governments have always granted that miracles did occur *in ancient times,* and have even received this opinion among the doctrines of official religion, but have not tolerated *new* miracles.* For ancient miracles have already been little by little so defined and   6:86

---

* In this respect even those teachers of religion who link their articles of faith to the authority of the government (i.e. the orthodox) follow the same maxim as the latter does. Hence Herr Pfenniger,[81] in defending the claim of his friend Herr Lavater[82] that a faith in miracles is still possible, rightly accuses of inconsistency the orthodox (for he explicitly excepted those of a *naturalistic* bend of mind on this point), because, although they assert miracles that occurred in the Christian community some seventeen centuries ago, they are unwilling to sanction more now, without being able to prove from the Scriptures either that, or if, miracles ought at some point to cease altogether (for the subtle argument that miracles are no longer necessary presumes a greater insight than any human being ought to be thought capable of), and this is a proof which they still owe to him. It was therefore only a maxim of reason not to grant or allow miracles now, not an objective insight that there are none. But is not this maxim, which in this instance is directed to the threat of civil mischief, also valid for the fear of a similar mischief in the philosophical community and the rational community at large? – Those who do not grant *great* (sensational) miracles but freely allow *little* ones, under the title of *special [divine] governance* (since these last are merely for guidance and require only a little   6:86 application of force on the part of the supernatural cause), do not bear in mind that what

restricted by the authorities that they can cause no disturbance among the community, whereas there must be concern about new miracle workers, on account of the effects that they can have upon the public peace and the established order. If we however ask: What is to be understood by the word *miracles?* they can then be defined (since what really matters to us is only to know what they are *for us,* i.e. for our practical employment of reason) as events in the world, the causes and *effects* of which are absolutely unknown to us and so must remain. And we can think of either *theistic* or *demonic* miracles – the latter being divided into *angelic* miracles (miracles of good spirits) and *satanic* miracles (miracles of evil spirits), though of the demonic miracles only the satanic really come into question, for the *good* angels (I know not why) give us little or nothing at all to say about them.

Regarding *theistic* miracles, we can of course form a concept of the laws governing the actions of their cause (as an omnipotent etc. and hence moral being), but only a *general* concept, so far as we can think of him as the creator and ruler of the world, according to the order of nature as well as the moral order, for we can obtain immediate and independent cognition of the laws of these orders, and reason can then employ them for its own use. Should we, however, accept that from time to time, and in special cases, God allows nature to deviate from such laws, then we do not have the least conception, nor can we ever hope to attain one, of the law according to which God promotes any such occurrence (apart from the *general moral* law that whatever God does will all be good, in virtue of which, however, nothing precise is established with respect to the particular event). Here reason is as paralyzed, for it is held back in its affairs according to recognized laws while not being instructed in a new one; and neither can it ever hope to be thus instructed in the world. Among miracles, however, the demonic are the ones most irreconcilable with the employment of our reason. For, as regards the *theistic* miracles, reason can at least have a negative criterion at its disposal, namely, if something is represented as commanded by God in a direct manifestation of him yet is directly in conflict with morality, it cannot be a divine miracle despite every appearance of being one (e.g. if a father were ordered to kill his son who, so far as he knows, is totally innocent);[83] whereas in the case of a supposed demonic miracle even this criterion fails to apply, and should we, in these cases, seize upon the contrary positive criterion to put at reason's disposal – namely, if through the miracle there comes an invita-

6:87

---

matters here is not the effect or its magnitude but the form of the course of worldly events, i.e. the *way in which the effect occurs,* whether naturally or supernaturally, and that for God no distinction of easy or difficult is to be thought of. And as regards the *mystery* of supernatural influences, any such deliberate concealment of the importance of an occurrence of this kind is even less proper.

tion to a good action which in itself we already recognize as duty, this invitation has not come from an evil spirit – even then we could be mistaken, for the evil spirit often acts the part, as they say, of an angel of light.

In practical affairs, therefore, we cannot possibly count on miracles, or in any way take them into consideration in the employment of our reason (which is necessary in all circumstances of life). A judge (however much he might believe in miracles in the church) hears a delinquent's allegations of diabolical temptations to which he was subjected as though nothing were said, despite the fact that, if the judge regarded a case of this sort possible, it would be well worth some consideration that a simple-minded ordinary human being has fallen into the snares of a cunning villain. But the judge cannot summon the villain; he cannot have the two confront one another; in a word, he can make absolutely nothing rational out of the case. The rational clergyman will therefore be well on guard against cramming the heads of those committed to his spiritual care with stories from *The Hellish Protheus*,[84] and making their imagination run wild. Concerning, however, the good sort of miracles, these are used by people in practical affairs as mere turns of phrase. Thus the doctor says: Nothing will help the sick man, short of a miracle, i.e. he will surely die. – Now, to practical affairs also belongs the natural scientist's search for the causes of events in their own natural laws; in the natural laws of these events, I say, which he can therefore verify through experience, even though he must   6:88 renounce cognition of that which brings about effects according to these laws, in itself, or of what these laws might be for us relative to some other possible sense. A human being's moral improvement is likewise a practical affair incumbent upon him, and heavenly influences may indeed always cooperate in this improvement, or be deemed necessary to explain its possibility. Yet he has no understanding of himself in the matter: neither how to distinguish with certainty such influences from the natural ones, nor how to bring them and so, as it were, heaven itself down to himself. And, since he knows not what to do with them, in no case does he *sanction** miracles but rather, should he pay heed to the precept of reason, he conducts himself as if every change of heart and all improvement depended solely on the application of his own workmanship. But that, through the gift of a *firm* theoretical faith in miracles, the human being himself could perform them and thus storm heaven, is a senseless notion that strays too far outside the limits of reason to dwell on.†

---

*† Which is the same as saying: He does not incorporate faith in miracles in his maxims (either of theoretical or practical reason), without however contesting their possibility or actuality.

† It is a common ruse of those who dupe the gullible with the arts of *magic*, or who at least want to render such people in general prone to believe, that they appeal to the scientists' own admission of *ignorance*. After all, they say, we have no cognition of the *cause* of gravity, of magnetic force and the like. – Yet we have cognition of the laws of these forces in sufficient

detail within determinate limitations on the conditions under which alone certain effects occur; and that is enough for the rational employment of the forces as well as the explanation of their appearances, *secundum quid,*[p] [i.e.] for the *regressive* employment of their laws in the ordering of experiences under them, though not *simpliciter,*[q] [i.e.] to gain insight into the causes themselves of the forces operating according to the laws. – From this an inner phenomenon of the human understanding becomes comprehensible: why so called "miracles of nature", i.e. sufficiently attested though absurd appearances or characteristics of things that show up unexpectedly contrary to the hitherto recognized[r] laws of nature, are eagerly received and *stimulate* the mind so long as they are still held to be natural, whereas the announcement of a real miracle *dejects* the mind. The reason is that the first open up the prospect of a new acquisition of nourishment for reason; that is, they give *hope* of discovering new laws of nature, whereas the other arouses apprehension that we might lose confidence also in those already accepted in cognition.[s] When reason is deprived of the laws of nature, it no longer is of any use in the resulting magical world, not even for moral employment in complying in it with our duty; for we no longer know whether, unbeknown to us, changes have occurred in our very moral incentives due to miracles, and nobody can decide whether to attribute these changes to ourselves or to some other obscure cause. – Those, whose judgement in these matters inclines them to the opinion that without miracles they can manage nothing, believe that they moderate reason's offence at miracles by assuming that they only happen *seldom.* If they thereby mean that this is already implicit in the concept of a miracle (for if any such event happened regularly, it could no longer be defined as miracle), we can, if necessary, let them get away with this sophistry (of transforming an objective question about what a thing is into a subjective one of what we mean by the word with which we signify it) and still ask: *How often?* Once in a hundred years perhaps? Or, indeed, in ancient times but no more now? We can determine nothing here on the basis of the cognition of the object (for on our own admission, the object escapes us) but only on the basis of the necessary maxims of our reason's employment: either miracles are to be admitted as *daily* [events] (though hidden under the appearance of natural occurrences), or *never,* and in this last case they are not to be used as foundation either of our rational explanations or of the maxims of our actions; and since the first [alternative] is in no way compatible with reason, nothing remains but to accept the latter maxim – for this principle always remains only a maxim of judgement, not a theoretical assertion. Nobody can have so exaggerated a conceit of his insight as to make bold to assert definitely that, for instance, the most admirable conservation of the species in the plant and animal kingdom, where every spring a new generation once more displays it original undiminished, with all the inner perfection of mechanism, and even (as in the vegetable kingdom) with all the always so delicate beauty of colour, without the forces of inorganic nature, otherwise so destructive in the bad weather of autumn and winter, being able at this point to harm the seed – that this, I say, is a mere consequence of natural laws, and pretend to *understand* whether the creator's direct influence is not rather needed for it each time. – But these are experiences; *for us,* therefore, they are nothing other than effects of nature, and *ought* never to be judged otherwise. For this is what modesty requires of reason's claims, and to transcend these boundaries is presumptuousness and immodesty, even though in asserting miracles people often purport to demonstrate a humble and self-renouncing way of thinking.

[p] in a certain respect
[q] i.e. absolutely
[r] *bekannt*
[s] *als bekannt*

The philosophical doctrine of religion
Part three

Part three
The victory of the good principle over the evil principle, and the founding of a kingdom of God on earth

The battle that every morally well-disposed human being must withstand in this life, under the leadership of the good principle, against the attacks of the evil principle, can procure him, however hard he tries, no greater advantage than freedom from the *dominion* of evil. That he be *free*, that he "relinquish the bondage under the law of sins, to live for righteousness,"[85] this is the highest prize that he can win. He still remains not any the less exposed to the assaults of the evil principle; and, to assert his freedom, which is constantly under attack, he must henceforth remain forever armed for battle.

The human being is nevertheless in this perilous state through his own fault; hence he is *bound* at least to apply as much force as he can muster in order to extricate himself from it. But how? That is the question. – If he searches for the causes and the circumstances that draw him into this danger and keep him there, he can easily convince himself that they do not come his way from his own raw nature, so far as he exists in isolation, but rather from the human beings to whom he stands in relation or association. It is not the instigation of nature that arouses what should properly be called the *passions*, which wreak such great devastation in his originally good predisposition. His needs are but limited, and his state of mind in providing for them moderate and tranquil. He is poor (or considers himself so) only to the extent that he is anxious that other human beings will consider him poor and will despise him for it. Envy, addiction to power, avarice, and the malignant inclinations associated with these, assail his nature, which on its own is undemanding, *as soon as he is among human beings*. Nor is it necessary to assume that these are sunk into evil and are examples that lead him astray: it suffices that they are there, that they surround him, and that they are human beings, and they will mutually corrupt each other's moral disposition and make one another evil. If no means could be found to establish a union which has for its end the prevention of this evil and the promotion of the good in the human

129

being – an enduring and ever expanding society, solely designed for the preservation of morality by counteracting evil with united forces – however much the individual human being might do to escape from the dominion of this evil, he would still be held in incessant danger of relapsing into it. – Inasmuch as we can see, therefore, the dominion of the good principle is not otherwise attainable, so far as human beings can work toward it, than through the setting up and the diffusion of a society in accordance with, and for the sake of, the laws of virtues – a society which reason makes it a task and a duty of the entire human race to establish in its full scope. – For only in this way can we hope for a victory of the good principle over the evil one. In addition to prescribing laws to each individual human being, morally legislative reason also unfurls a banner of virtue as rallying point for all those who love the good, that they may congregate under it and thus at the very start gain the upper hand over evil and its untiring attacks.

An association of human beings merely under the laws of virtue, ruled by this idea, can be called an *ethical* and, so far as these laws are public, an *ethico-civil* (in contrast to a *juridico-civil*) society, or an *ethical community*. It can exist in the midst of a political community and even be made up of all the members of the latter (indeed, without the foundation of a political community, it could never be brought into existence by human beings). It has however a special unifying principle of its own (virtue) and hence a form and constitution essentially distinct from those of the other. There is nevertheless a certain analogy between the two, when considered in general as two communities, and with respect to this analogy the ethical community can also be called an *ethical state*, i.e. a *kingdom* of virtue (of the good principle). The idea of such a state has an entirely well-grounded, objective reality in human reason (in the duty to join such a state), even though we cannot subjectively ever hope of the good will of human beings that these will work harmoniously toward this end.

6:95

Division one
Philosophical representation of the victory of the good principle in the founding of a Kingdom of God on earth

I. CONCERNING THE ETHICAL STATE OF NATURE

A *juridico-civil* (political) *state* is the relation of human beings to each other inasmuch as they stand jointly under *public juridical laws* (which are all coercive laws). An *ethico-civil* state is one in which they are united under laws without being coerced, i.e. under *laws of virtue* alone.

Now, just as the rightful (but not therefore always righteous) *state of nature,* i.e. the *juridical state of nature,* is opposed to the first, so is the *ethical state of nature* distinguished from the second. In these two [states of nature] each individual prescribes the law to himself, and there is no external law to which he, along with the others, acknowledges himself to be subject. In both each individual is his own judge, and there is no effective *public* authority with power to determine legitimately, according to laws, what is in given cases the duty of each individual, and to bring about the universal execution of those laws.

In an already existing political community all the political citizens are, as such, still in the *ethical state of nature,* and have the right to remain in it; for it would be a contradiction (*in adjecto*)[q] for the political community to compel its citizens to enter into an ethical community, since the latter entails freedom from coercion in its very concept. Every political community may indeed wish to have available a dominion over minds as well, according to the laws of virtue; for where its means of coercion do not reach, since a human judge cannot penetrate into the depths of other human beings, there the dispositions to virtue would bring about the 6:96
required result. But woe to the legislator who would want to bring about through coercion a polity directed to ethical ends! For he would thereby not only achieve the very opposite of ethical ends, but also undermine his political ends and render them insecure. – The citizen of the political community therefore remains, so far as the latter's lawgiving authority is concerned, totally free: he may wish to enter with his fellow citizens into an ethical union over and above the political one, or rather remain in a natural state of this sort. Only insofar as an ethical community must rest on *public* laws and have a constitution based on them, must those who freely commit themselves to enter into this state, not [indeed] allow the political power to command them how to order (or not order) such a constitution internally, but allow limitations, namely the condition that nothing be included in this constitution which contradicts the duty of its members as *citizens of the state* – even though, if the ethical bond is of the genuine sort, this condition need not cause anxiety.

Further, since the duties of virtue concern the entire human race, the concept of an ethical community always refers to the ideal of a totality of human beings, and in this it distinguishes itself from the concept of a political community. Hence a multitude of human beings united in that purpose cannot yet be called the ethical community as such but only a particular society that strives after the consensus of all human beings (indeed, of all finite rational beings) in order to establish an absolute ethical whole of which each partial society is only a representation or schema; for each of these societies can in turn be represented, in relation

[q] i.e., a contradiction generated by the juxtaposition of two mutually exclusive terms.

to others of this kind, as situated in the natural state, with all the imperfections of the latter (as is also the case with separate political states not bound together through a public international law).

II.

THE HUMAN BEING OUGHT TO LEAVE THE ETHICAL STATE OF NATURE IN ORDER TO BECOME A MEMBER OF AN ETHICAL COMMUNITY

6:97 Just as the juridical state of nature is a state of war of every human being against every other, so too is the ethical state of nature one in which the good principle, which resides in each human being, is incessantly attacked by the evil which is found in him and in every other as well. Human beings (as we remarked above) mutually corrupt one another's moral predisposition and, even with the good will of each individual, because of the lack of a principle which unites them, they deviate through their dissensions from the common goal of goodness, as though they were *instruments of evil*, and expose one another to the danger of falling once again under its dominion. Further, just as the state of a lawless external (brutish) freedom and independence from coercive laws is a state of injustice and of war, each against each, which a human being ought to leave behind in order to enter into a politico-civil state,* so is the ethical state of nature a *public* feuding between the principles of virtue and a state of inner immorality which the natural human being ought to endeavor to leave behind as soon as possible.

Now, here we have a duty *sui generis*,^{v} not of human beings toward human beings but of the human race toward itself. For every species of

---

* Hobbes's statement,[86] *status hominum naturalis est bellum omnium in omnes*,^{r} has no other fault apart from this: it should say, *est status belli . . . etc.*^{s} For, even though one may not concede that actual *hostilities* are the rule between human beings who do not stand under external and public laws, their condition (*status iuridicus*),^{t} i.e. the relationship in and through which they are capable of rights (of their acquisition and maintenance) is nonetheless one in which each of them wants to be himself the judge of what is his right vis-à-vis others, without however either having any security from others with respect to this right or offering them any: and this is a condition of war, wherein every man must be constantly armed against everybody else. Hobbes's second statement,[87] *exeundum esse e statu naturali*,^{u} follows from the first: for this condition is a continual violation of the rights of all others through the presumption of being the judge in one's own affairs and of not allowing any security to other human beings in theirs save one's own power of choice.
^{r} the natural state of men is a war of all against all
^{s} is a state of war . . . etc.
^{t} juridical state
^{u} one must exit from the natural state
^{v} of a unique kind

rational beings is objectively – in the idea of reason – destined to a common end, namely the promotion of the highest good as a good common to all. But, since this highest moral good will not be brought about solely through the striving of one individual person for his own moral perfection but requires rather a union of such persons into a whole toward that very end, [i.e.] toward a system of well-disposed human beings in which, 6:98
and through the unity of which alone, the highest moral good can come to pass, yet the idea of such a whole, as a universal republic based on the laws of virtue, differs entirely from all moral laws (which concern what we know to reside within our power), for it is the idea of working toward a whole of which we cannot know whether as a whole it is also in our power: so the duty in question differs from all others in kind and in principle. – We can already anticipate that this duty will need the presupposition of another idea, namely, of a higher moral being through whose universal organization the forces of single individuals, insufficient on their own, are united for a common effect. First of all, however, we must follow up the leading thread of that moral need and see where it will lead us.

III.
THE CONCEPT OF AN ETHICAL COMMUNITY IS THE CONCEPT OF A PEOPLE OF GOD UNDER ETHICAL LAWS

If an ethical community is to come into being, all individuals must be subjected to a public legislation, and all the laws binding them must be capable of being regarded as commands of a common lawgiver. Now if the community to be founded is to be a *juridical* one, the mass of people joining in a union must itself be the lawgiver (of constitutional laws), because legislation proceeds from the principle of *limiting the freedom of each to the conditions under which it can coexist with the freedom of everyone else, in conformity with a universal law,* * and the universal will thus establishes an external legal constraint. If, however, the community is to be an *ethical* one, the people, as a people, cannot itself be regarded as legislator. For in such a community all the laws are exclusively designed to promote the *morality* of actions (which is something *internal*, and hence cannot be subject to public human laws) whereas these public laws (and in this they 6:99
constitute a juridical community) are on the contrary directed to the *legality* of actions, which is visible to the eye, and not to (inner) morality which alone is at issue here. There must therefore be someone other than the people whom we can declare the public lawgiver of an ethical community. But neither can ethical laws be thought of as proceeding *originally*

* This is the principle of all external right.

merely from the will of this superior (as statutes that would not be binding without his prior sanction), for then they would not be ethical laws, and the duty commensurate to them would not be a free virtue but an externally enforceable legal duty. Therefore only such a one can be thought of as the supreme lawgiver of an ethical community, with respect to whom all *true duties*, hence also the ethical,* must be represented as *at the same time* his commands; consequently, he must also be one who knows the heart,[89] in order to penetrate to the most intimate parts of the dispositions of each and everyone and, as must be in every community, give to each according to the worth of his actions. But this is the concept of God as a moral ruler of the world. Hence an ethical community is conceivable only as a people under divine commands, i.e. as a *people of God*,[90] and indeed *in accordance with the laws of virtue*.

We might of course also think of a people of God *in accordance with statutory laws*, that is to say, such laws as do not involve the morality of actions but only their legality. This would be a juridical community, of which God would indeed be the lawgiver (hence its *constitution* would be a theocracy) – though priests, as human beings who receive their orders directly from him, would run an aristocratic *government*. Such a constitution, however, whose existence and form rest entirely on historical grounds, does not constitute the problem of a morally legislative reason which alone we are to bring to a resolution here. It will come up for examination in the historical section, as an institution under politico-civil laws, of which the lawgiver, though God, is yet external, whereas we only have to do here with an institution, of which the lawgiver is purely internal, a republic under laws of virtue, i.e. with a people of God "zealous of good works."[91]

To such a *people* of God we can oppose the idea of a *band* under the evil principle – a union of those who side with that principle for the propagation of evil. It is in the interest of evil to prevent the realization of the other union, even though here too the principle that battles the dispositions of virtue resides in our very self and is only figuratively represented as an external power.

6:100

---

* As soon as something is recognized as duty, even if it should be a duty imposed through the purely arbitrary will[a] of a human lawgiver, obeying it is equally a divine command. Of course we cannot call statutory civil laws divine commands; but if they are legitimate, their *observance* is equally a divine command. The proposition, "We ought to obey God rather than men,"[88] means only that when human beings command something that is evil in itself (directly opposed to the ethical law), we may not, and ought not, obey them. But, conversely, if an alleged divine statutory law is opposed to a positive civil law not in itself immoral, there is then cause to consider the alleged divine law as spurious, for it contradicts a clear duty, whereas that it is itself a divine command can never be certified sufficiently on empirical evidence to warrant violating on its account an otherwise established duty.
[a] *Willkür*

134

IV.
THE IDEA OF A PEOPLE OF GOD CANNOT BE REALIZED (BY HUMAN ORGANIZATION) EXCEPT IN THE FORM OF A CHURCH

The sublime, never fully attainable idea of an ethical community is greatly scaled down under human hands, namely to an institution which, at best capable of representing with purity only the form of such a community, with respect to the means for establishing a whole of this kind is greatly restricted under the conditions of sensuous[x] human nature. But how could one expect to construct something completely straight from such crooked wood?[92]

To found a moral people of God is, therefore, a work whose execution cannot be hoped for from human beings but only from God himself. Yet human beings are not permitted on this account to remain idle in the undertaking and let Providence have free rein, as if each could go after his private moral affairs and entrust to a higher wisdom the whole concern of the human race (as regards its moral destiny). Each must, on the contrary, so conduct himself as if everything depended on him. Only on this condition may he hope that a higher wisdom will provide the fulfillment of his well-intentioned effort.   6:101

The wish of all well-disposed human beings is, therefore, "that the kingdom of God come, that His will be done on earth";[93] but what preparations must they make in order that this wish come to pass among them?

An ethical community under divine moral legislation is a *church* which, inasmuch as it is not the object of a possible experience, is called the *church invisible* (the mere idea of the union of all upright human beings under direct yet moral divine world-governance, as serves for the archetype of any such governance to be founded by human beings). The *church visible* is the actual union of human beings into a whole that accords with this ideal. So far as every society under public laws entails a subordination of its members (in the relation of those who obey the society's laws with respect to those who oversee their observance), the mass of people united into that whole (of the church) is a *congregation* under superiors who (under the name of teachers or shepherds of souls) only administer the affairs of the church's invisible supreme head, and, in this respect, are called *servants* of the church, just as, in a political community, the visible head occasionally calls himself the supreme servant of the state, even though he does not acknowledge any other human being above himself (and, as a rule, not even the people as a whole). The true (visible) church is one that displays the (moral) kingdom of God on earth inasmuch as the latter can be realized through human beings. The requisites for a true church, and also its marks, are the following:[94]

---

[x] *sinnlichen*

1. *Universality*, whence its numerical unity, for which it must be internally predisposed; to wit: though indeed divided and at variance with itself in accidental opinions, yet, as regards its essential purpose, it is founded on principles that necessarily lead it to universal union in a single church (hence, no sectarian schisms).

2. Its *make-up* (quality), i.e. *purity*: union under no other incentives than moral ones (cleansed of the nonsense of superstition and the madness of enthusiasm).

3. *Relation* under the principle of *freedom:* the internal relation of its members among themselves as well as the external relation of the church to the political power, both in a *free state* (hence neither a *hierarchy*, nor an *illuminatism* – which is a kind of *democracy* through individual inspirations, which can vary greatly from one another, according to each mind).

4. Its *modality*, the *unchangeableness* of its *constitution* – exception however made for the accidental regulations that only concern the *administration* of the church and must change according to times and circumstances, for which, however, the church must already possess secure principles within itself *a priori* (in the idea of its end, and hence in the form of primordial laws publicly laid down for instruction once and for all, as it were through a book of laws, not through arbitrary creeds which, since they lack authority, are fortuitous, exposed to contradiction, and changeable).

6:102

As church, therefore, i.e. considered as the mere *representative* of a state [ruled] by God, an ethical community really has nothing in its principles that resembles a political constitution. Its constitution is neither *monarchical* (under a pope or patriarch), nor *aristocratic* (under bishops and prelates), nor *democratic* (as of sectarian *illuminati*). It could best of all be likened to the constitution of a household (a family) under a common though invisible moral father, whose holy son, who knows the father's will and yet stands in blood relation with all the members of the family, takes his father's place by making the other members better acquainted with his will; these therefore honor the father in him and thus enter into a free, universal and enduring union of hearts.

V.

THE CONSTITUTION OF EACH AND EVERY CHURCH ALWAYS PROCEEDS FROM SOME HISTORICAL (REVEALED) FAITH, WHICH WE CAN CALL ECCLESIASTICAL FAITH; AND THIS IS BEST FOUNDED ON A HOLY SCRIPTURE

6:103

The only faith that can found a universal church is *pure religious faith*, for it is a plain rational faith which can be convincingly communicated to everyone, whereas a historical faith, merely based on facts, can extend its influence no further than the tidings relevant to a judgment on its credibility can reach. Yet, due to a peculiar weakness of human nature, pure faith can never be relied on as much as it deserves, that is, [enough] to found a Church on it alone.

Conscious of their impotence in the cognition of supersensible things, and though they allow every honor to be paid to faith in these things (as the faith which must carry conviction for them universally), human beings are yet not easily persuaded that steadfast zeal in the conduct of a morally good life is all that God requires of them to be his well-pleasing subjects in his Kingdom. They cannot indeed conceive their obligation except as directed to some *service* or other which they must perform for God – wherein what matters is not the intrinsic worth of their actions as much as, rather, that they are performed for God to please him through passive obedience, however morally indifferent the actions might be in themselves. It does not enter their heads that, whenever they fulfill their duties toward human beings (themselves and others), by that very fact they also conform to God's commands; hence, that in all their doings and non-doings, so far as these have reference to morality, they are *constantly in the service of God;* and that it is absolutely impossible to serve him more intimately in some other way (for they can act and exercise their influence on no other than earthly beings, not on God). Since every great lord of this world has a special need of being *honored* by his subjects, and of being *praised* through signs of submissiveness; nor can he expect, without this, as much compliance with his orders from his subjects as he needs to rule over them effectively; and, in addition, however reasonable a human being may be, he always finds an immediate pleasure in attestations of honor: so we treat duty, to the extent that it is equally God's command, as the transaction of an *affair* of God, not of humans; and thus arises the concept of a religion of *divine service* instead of the concept of a purely moral religion.

Since all religion consists in this, that in all our duties we look upon God as the lawgiver to be honored universally, the determination of religion, so far as the conformity of our conduct with it is concerned, comes down to knowing *how God wills* to be honored (and obeyed). – Now a divine legislative will commands either through laws in themselves *merely statutory* or through *purely moral* laws. As regards the latter, each individual can recognize by himself, through his own reason, the will of God which lies at the basis of his religion; for the concept of the Divinity actually originates solely from the consciousness of these laws and from reason's need to assume a power capable of procuring for them the full effect possible in this world in conformity with the moral final end. The concept of a divine will, determined merely according to purely moral laws, allows us to think of only *one* religion which is purely moral, just as of *only one*

6:104

God. If, however, we assume statutory laws of such a will, and put our religion in observing them, then cognition of these laws is possible not through our own mere reason but only through revelation. And, whether given to each individual secretly or publicly – that it may be propagated among human beings through tradition or scripture – this revelation would be a *historical* and not a *purely rational faith*. – And even assuming divine statutory laws (laws which let us recognize them as obligatory, not of themselves, but only inasmuch as they are the revealed will of God), even then pure *moral* legislation, through which God's will is originally engraved in our hearts, is not only the unavoidable condition of all true religion in general but also that which actually constitutes such religion, and for which statutory religion can contain only the means to its promotion and propagation.

So if the question How does God wish to be honored? is to be answered in a way universally valid for every human being, *each considered simply as a human being*, there is no second thought that the legislation of his will might not be simply *moral*. For a statutory legislation (which presupposes a revelation) can be regarded only as contingent, as something that cannot have reached, nor can reach, every human being, hence does not bind all human beings universally. Thus, "not they who say Lord! Lord! But they who do the will of God,"[95] those, therefore, who seek to become well-pleasing to him, not through loud praises of him (or of his envoy, as a being of divine origin) according to revealed concepts which not every human being can have, but through a good life conduct, regarding which everyone knows his will – these will be the ones who offer to him the true veneration that he desires.

If, however, we regard ourselves as duty-bound to behave not just as human beings but also as *citizens* within a divine state on earth, and to work for the existence of such an association under the name of a church, then the question How does God will to be honored in *a church* (as a congregation of God)? appears unanswerable by mere reason, but to be in need of a statutory legislation only proclaimed through revelation, hence of a historical faith which we can call "ecclesiastical" in contradistinction to pure religious faith. For in pure religious faith it all comes down to what constitutes the matter of the veneration of God, namely the observance in moral disposition of all duties as his commands. On the other hand, a church which is the union in a moral community of many human beings of equally many dispositions, needs a *public* form of obligation, some ecclesiastical form that depends on experiential conditions and is intrinsically contingent and manifold, hence cannot be recognized as duty without divine statutory laws. However, we should not therefore forthwith presume that the determination of this form is a task of the divine lawgiver; there is rather reason to assume that it is God's will that we should ourselves carry out the idea of such a community. And, though human

6:105

138

beings might have indeed tried out many a form of church with unhappy result, yet they ought not to cease striving after this end, if need be through renewed attempts which as much as possible avoid the mistakes of previous ones, since the task, which for them is at the same time a duty, is left entirely up to them. We therefore have no reason, in founding and informing any church, to hold its laws straightaway as divine and *statutory;* it is, rather, presumptuous to declare them such, in order to spare ourselves the trouble of improving the church's form further, or, perhaps, even an usurpation of higher authority, in order to impose a yoke upon the multitude by means of ecclesiastical statutes, under the pretense of divine authority. But it would be just as arrogant peremptorily to deny that the way a church is organized may perhaps also be a special divine dispensation, if, so far as we can see, the church is in perfect harmony with moral religion, and if, in addition, we cannot see how it could ever have made its appearance all at once without the requisite preparatory advances of the public in religious concepts. Now, in the hesitation over this task – whether God or human beings themselves should found a church – there is proof of the human propensity to a *religion of divine service (cultus)*, and, since such a religion rests on arbitrary precepts, to faith in statutory divine laws based on the assumption that some divine legislation, not to be discovered through reason but in need of revelation, must supervene to even the best life conduct (a conduct that the human being could always adopt under the guidance of the pure moral religion); attention is thereby given to the veneration of the supreme being directly (and not by way of that compliance to his commands already prescribed to us through reason). Thus it happens that human beings will never regard either union into a church, or agreement over the form to be given to it, or likewise any *public* institution for the promotion of the moral [content] of religion, as necessary in themselves but only for the purpose of, as they say, serving their God, by means of festivities, professions of faith in revealed laws, and the observance of precepts that belong to the form of the church (which is however itself a means). Although all these observances are at bottom morally indifferent actions, yet, precisely for this reason, they are deemed to be all the more pleasing to God, since they are supposed to be carried out just for his sake. Thus in the molding of human beings into an ethical community, ecclesiastical faith naturally* precedes pure religious faith: there were *temples* (buildings consecrated to public service) before *churches* (places of assembly for instruction and inspiration in moral dispositions); *priests* (consecrated stewards in the practices of piety) before *ministers* (teachers of pure moral religion), and for the most part they still come first in the rank and value accorded to them by the crowd at large.

Now once it stands as unalterable that a statutory *ecclesiastical faith* is

6:106

---

*† Morally speaking it ought to happen the other way around.

not added to the pure faith of religion as its vehicle and the means for the public union of human beings in promoting it, we must also concede that the preservation of this pure faith unchanged, its universal and uniform diffusion, and even the respect for the revelation assumed within it, can hardly be adequately provided for through *tradition*, but only through *scripture;* which, again, as a revelation to present and future generations, must be the object of the highest respect, for this is what human need requires in order to be certain of the duty to divine service. A holy book commands the greatest respect even among those (indeed, among these most of all) who do not read it, or are at least unable to form any coherent concept of religion from it; and no subtle argument can stand up to the knockdown pronouncement, *Thus it is written.* Hence also the passages in it that are to lay down a point of faith are simply called *sayings.* The appointed interpreters of such scripture are themselves, by virtue of their very occupation, consecrated persons, as it were; and history proves that never could a faith based on scripture be eradicated by even the most devastating political revolutions, whereas a faith based on tradition and ancient public observances meets its downfall as soon as the state breaks down. How fortunate,* when one such book, fallen into human hands, contains complete, besides its statutes legislating faith, also the purest moral doctrine of religion, and this doctrine can be brought into the strictest harmony with those statutes (which [in turn] contribute to its introduction). In this event, both because of the end to be attained thereby and the difficulty of explaining by natural laws the origin of the enlightenment of the human race proceeding from it, the book can command an authority equal to that of a revelation.

6:107

· ·
·

And now something more relating to this concept of a revealed faith.

There is only *one* (true) *religion;* but there can be several kinds of *faith.* – We can say, further, that in the various churches divided from one another because of the difference in their kinds of faith, one and the same true religion can nevertheless be met with.

6:108

It is therefore more appropriate (as it in fact is more customary) to say: This human being is of this (Jewish, Mohammedan, Christian, Catholic, Lutheran) *faith,* than: He is of this or that religion. This last expression ought in justice not to be used at all in addressing the larger public (in catechisms and sermons), for it is too learned and unintelligible for them; indeed, modern languages provide no word for it of equivalent meaning.

---

* An expression for everything wished for, or worthy of being wished for, but which we can neither foresee nor bring about through our effort according to the laws of experience; for which, therefore, if we want to name a ground, can adduce no other than a generous providence.

The ordinary human being will every time understand by it his own ecclesiastical faith, which is the one that falls within the grasp of his senses, whereas religion hides inside him and depends on moral dispositions. We do most people too much honor when we say of them that they profess this or that religion, for they know[y] none and demand none; statutory ecclesiastical faith is all that they understand by the word. So too the so-called religious struggles, which have so often shaken the world and spattered it with blood, have never been anything but squabbles over ecclesiastical faiths. And the oppressed have never really complained for being hindered from adhering to their religion (for no external power can do this), but for not being allowed to practice their ecclesiastical faith publicly.

Now whenever, as usually happens, a church passes itself off as the only universal one (even though it is based on faith in a particular revelation which, since it is historical, can never be demanded of everyone), whoever does not acknowledge its (particular) ecclesiastical faith is called an *unbeliever,* and is wholeheartedly hated; whoever deviates from it only in part (in nonessentials), is called an *erring believer* and is at least shunned as a source of infection. Finally, if someone declares himself for this church yet deviates from its faith in something essential (something made out to be so), especially if he propagates his errant belief, he is called a *heretic (Ketzer)** and, like a rebel, is held more punishable than an external foe and is expelled from the church through excommunication (like that which the Romans pronounced on him who crossed the Rubicon without the consent of the Senate) and given over to all the gods of hell. The correctness of belief that the teachers or heads of a church claim solely for themselves in matters of ecclesiastical faith is called *orthodoxy,* which we may perhaps divide into *despotic (brutal)* and *liberal.* – If a church which claims that its ecclesiastical faith is universally binding is to be called *catholic,* and *protestant* a church that protests against such claims of others (though it would often gladly exercise them itself, if it could), then the attentive observer will come across many a renowned example of protestant catholics and, by contrast, still more offensive examples of arch-catholic protestants: the first are human beings whose frame of mind (though this is not that of their church) is given to *self-expansion;* by comparison with these the second clearly stand out, but not at all to their advantage, with the *narrowness* of theirs.

6:109

---

* According to Georgius (*Alphab. Tibet.,* p. 11),[96] the Mongols call Tibet *Tangut-Chazar,* i.e. the land of the house-dwellers, in order to distinguish these from themselves, nomads who live in deserts under tents; hence the name "Chazars," and from this *Ketzer*[z] since the Mongols adhered to the Tibetan faith (of the Lames), which conforms to Manicheism and perhaps originated from it, and they spread this name in their incursions into Europe; hence too the names *Haeretici* and *Manichaei* were used as synonymous some time ago.[97]

6:109

[y] *kennen*

[z] i.e. heretic

VI.

ECCLESIASTICAL FAITH HAS THE PURE FAITH
OF RELIGION FOR ITS SUPREME INTERPRETER

We have noted that, although a church sacrifices the most important mark
of its truth, namely the legitimate claim to universality, whenever it bases
itself upon a faith of revelation which, as historical faith, (even if more
widely spread and more firmly secured for the remotest posterity through
scripture) is incapable of a transmission that commands conviction universally,[98] yet, because of the natural need of all human beings to demand for
even the highest concepts and grounds of reason something that *the senses
can hold on to*, some confirmation from experience or the like, (a need
which must also be seriously taken into account when the intention is *to
introduce* a faith universally) some historical ecclesiastical faith or other,
usually already at hand, must be used.

6:110   Now to unite the foundation of a moral faith (be this faith an end or
merely an auxiliary means) with such an empirical faith which, to all
appearances, chance has dealt to us, we require an interpretation of the
revelation we happen to have, i.e. a thoroughgoing understanding of it in a
sense that harmonizes with the universal practical rules of a pure religion
of reason. For the theoretical element of ecclesiastical faith cannot be of
moral interest to us, if it does not work toward the fulfillment of all human
duties as divine commands (which constitutes the essential of every religion). This interpretation may often appear to us as forced, in view of the
text (of the revelation), and be often forced in fact; yet, if the text can at all
bear it, it must be preferred to a literal interpretation that either contains
absolutely nothing for morality, or even works counter to its incentives.* –

*† To illustrate this with an example, take Psalm 59: vv. 11–16,[99] where we find a *prayer* for
revenge that borders on the horrific. Michaelis (*Ethic*, Part II, p. 202)[100] approves of this prayer
and adds: "The psalms are *inspired;* if they pray for revenge, then it cannot be wrong: *We should
not have a holier morality than the Bible.*" I pause here at this last statement and ask whether
morality must be interpreted in accordance with the Bible, or the Bible, on the contrary, in
accordance with morality. – Without now considering the passage of the New Testament, "It
was said to our fathers, etc., but I say to you, Love your enemies, *bless those who curse you,*
etc."[101] – how this passage, which is also inspired, can hold along with the other – I shall try
either to fit that passage to those of my moral principles which stand on their own (for instance,
that here are understood not corporeal enemies but, symbolized by them, the invisible ones
which are much more pernicious to us, namely the evil inclinations which we must wish to
bring under our feet completely), or, if this will not do, I shall rather assume that this passage is
to be understood, not at all in a moral sense, but in terms of the relation that the Jews
considered themselves to have toward God as their political regent – as also another passage
of the Bible, where it is said: "Vengeance is mine; I shall repay! saith the Lord,"[102] which is
commonly interpreted as a moral warning against private revenge, though it apparently only
refers to the law in force in every state that one should seek satisfaction for insults in the court
of justice of the overlord, where the judge's permission to the plaintiff to propose any punishment he wishes, however harsh, is not to be taken as approval of the plaintiff's vindictiveness.

We shall also find that this is how all types of faith – ancient and new, some written down in holy books – have always been treated, and that rational and thoughtful teachers of the people have kept on interpreting them until, gradually, they brought them, as regards their essential con- 6:111 tent, in agreement with the universal principles of moral faith. The moral philosophers among the Greeks and, later, among the Romans, did exactly the same with their legends concerning the gods. They knew in the end how to interpret even the coarsest polytheism as just a symbolic representation of the properties of the one divine being; and how to invest all sorts of depraved actions, and even the wild yet beautiful fancies of their poets, with a mystical meaning that brought popular faith (which it would never have been advisable to destroy, for the result might perhaps have been an atheism even more dangerous to the state) close to a moral doctrine intelligible to all human beings and alone beneficial. Late Judaism, and Christianity too, consist of such in part highly forced interpretations, yet, [in] both [instances], directed to ends undoubtedly good and necessary to every human being. The Mohammedans know very well (as Reland shows)[103] how to inject a spiritual meaning in the description of their paradise, otherwise dedicated to every sensuality, and the Indians do the same with the interpretation of their *Vedas*,[104] at least for the more enlightened part of their people. – [105] That this, however, can be done without ever and again greatly offending against the literal meaning of the popular faith is due to the fact that, long before this faith, the predisposition to moral religion lay hidden in human reason; and, though its first raw expressions were indeed intent on just the practice of divine service and, for its sake, gave rise to those alleged revelations, yet they thereby also implanted in their poetic fabrications, though unintentionally, something of the character of their supersensible origin. – Nor can we charge such interpretations with dishonesty, provided that we do not wish to claim that the meaning we give to the symbols of a popular faith, or even to holy books, is exactly as intended by them, but leave this issue open and only assume the *possibility* that their authors may be so understood. For the final purpose of even the reading of these holy books, or the investigation of their content, is to make better human beings; whereas their historical element, which contributes nothing to this end, is something in itself quite indifferent, and one can do with it what one wills. – (Historical faith is "dead, being alone,"[106] i.e. of itself, considered as declaration, contains nothing, nor does it lead to anything that would have a moral value for us.)

Hence, though a scripture is accepted as divine revelation, its supreme 6:112 criterion will nonetheless be something like this: "Every scripture given by inspiration of God is profitable for doctrine, for reproof, for correction, etc.";[107] and, since this last – namely the moral improvement of human beings – constitutes the true end of all religion of reason, it will also

143

contain the supreme principle of all scriptural exegesis. This religion is "the Spirit of God, who guides us into all truth."[108] And this it is which in *instructing* us also *animates* us with basic principles for action, and relates whatever the scripture may yet contain for historical faith entirely to the rules and incentives of pure moral faith, which alone constitutes true religion in each ecclesiastical faith. All investigation and interpretation of Scripture must proceed from the principle that this spirit is to be sought in it, and "eternal life can be found therein only so far as Scripture testifies to this principle."[109]

Now placed besides this interpreter of Scripture, but subordinated to him, is another, namely the *scriptural scholar.* The authority of Scripture, as the worthiest and in the enlightened world now the only instrument of union of all human beings into one church, establishes the ecclesiastical faith which, as popular faith, cannot be ignored, since no doctrine exclusively based on reason would seem to the people to make an unalterable norm; they demand a divine revelation, hence also a historical authentication of its authority through the deduction of its origin. Now human art and wisdom cannot climb up to heaven to ascertain for itself the credentials of the mission of the first teacher but must be satisfied with signs which, the content apart, can yet be gathered from the way the faith was introduced, i.e. with human reports which we must eventually trace back to very ancient times, and in languages now dead, to evaluate their historical credibility. Hence *scriptural scholarship* is required to preserve the authority of a church based on holy Scripture, though not that of a religion (for to have universality a religion must always be based on reason), even if such scholarship establishes nothing more than that there is nothing in the Scripture's origin which would make its acceptance as immediate divine revelation impossible. And this would be enough not to disturb

6:113 those who fancy that they find in this idea [of revealed Scripture] a special strengthening of their moral faith and, therefore, gladly accept it. – Yet not only the *certification* of holy Scripture, but its *exposition* as well, requires scholarship, and for the same reason. For how will the unlearned, who can read it only in translation, be certain of its meaning? Hence the expositor, who has control of the underlying language, must also have a broad acquaintance with history and critical judgment, in order to draw from the situation, the customs and beliefs (the popular religion) of an earlier time the means with which to unlock the understanding of the church community.

Religion of reason and scriptural scholarship are, therefore, the properly appointed interpreters and trustees of a sacred document. It is self-evident that they must not on any account be hindered by the secular arm in the public use of their insights and discoveries in this field, or be bound to certain dogmas; for otherwise the *laity* would be forcing the *clerics* to fall in line with their opinion which they hold, however, only because of the instruction of the clerics. When the state takes care that there is no lack of scholars and of individuals of morally good standing to govern over the entire church body, to whose consciences it can entrust this task, it has already done all that its duty and authority entail.[110] That the lawgiver extend this [duty and authority] into the schools, and attend to their quarrels (which, so long as they are not carried on from the pulpit, leave the church-public totally undisturbed), is an unreasonable demand, which the public cannot make on him without presumption, for it is beneath his dignity.

Yet a third claimant to the office of interpreter steps forward, one who needs neither reason nor learning to recognize both the true meaning of Scripture and its divine origin, but only an inner *feeling*. Now we certainly cannot deny that "whoever follows the light of Scripture and *does* what it prescribes, will surely discover that it is of God,"[111] and that the very impulse to good actions and uprightness of life, which the human being who reads Scripture or listens to it must feel, would have to convince him of its divine nature: for this impulse is but the effect of the moral law which fills the human being with heartfelt respect, and hence deserves to   6:114 be considered also as divine command. But just as we cannot derive or convey the recognition of laws, and that they are moral, on the basis of any sort of feeling, equally so and even less can we derive or convey on the basis of a feeling sure evidence of a direct divine influence: for the same effect can have more than one cause, whereas in this case the morality alone of the law (and of the doctrine), recognized through reason, is the cause of the effect. And even on the assumption that this origin is merely a possibility, our duty is yet to construe it in this sense, if we do not wish to open wide the gates to every kind of enthusiasm, and even cause the unequivocally moral feeling to lose dignity through association with all sorts of other fanciful ones. – Feeling is private to each individual and cannot be expected of others, even when we have advance cognition of the law from which or according to which it arises; thus we cannot extol it as a touchstone for the genuineness of a revelation, since it teaches absolutely nothing but only contains the manner in which a subject is affected as regards his pleasure or displeasure, and no cognition whatever can be based on this. –

There is, therefore, no norm of ecclesiastical faith except Scripture, and no other expositor of it except the *religion of reason* and *scholarship* (which deals with the historical element of Scripture). And, of these two, the first alone is *authentic* and valid for the whole world, whereas the second is merely *doctrinal;* its aim is the transformation of the ecclesiastical faith for a given people at a given time into a definite and self-maintaining system. As regards ecclesiastical faith, there is no avoiding the fact that historical faith ultimately becomes just a faith in scholars and in their insight – a circumstance that does not, indeed, particularly redound to the honour of human nature, but which can be made good through public freedom of thought. And this freedom is all the more justified since only if scholars submit their interpretations to public scrutiny, and themselves remain always open and receptive to better insight, can they count on the community's confidence in their decisions.

VII.
THE GRADUAL TRANSITION OF ECCLESIASTICAL FAITH TOWARD THE EXCLUSIVE DOMINION OF PURE RELIGIOUS FAITH IS THE COMING OF THE KINGDOM OF GOD

The distinguishing mark of the true church is its *universality;* and the sign of this, in turn, is the church's necessity and its determinability in only one possible way. Now historical faith (which is based upon revelation as experience) has only particular validity, namely for those in contact with the history on which the faith rests, and, like all cognition based on experience, carries with it the consciousness not that the object believed in *must* be so and not otherwise but only that it *is* so; hence it carries at the same time the consciousness of its contingency. This faith can therefore indeed suffice as an ecclesiastical faith (of which there can be several); but only the pure faith of religion, based entirely on reason, can be recognized as necessary and hence as the one which exclusively marks out the *true* church. – Thus, even though (in accordance with the unavoidable limitation of human reason) a historical faith attaches itself to pure religion as its vehicle, yet, if there is consciousness that this faith is merely such and if, as the faith of a church, it carries a principle for continually coming closer to pure religious faith until finally we can dispense of that vehicle, the church in question can always be taken as the *true* one; but, since conflict over historical dogmas can never be avoided, it can be named only church *militant*, though with the prospect at the end of flowering into the unchanging and all-unifying church *triumphant!* We call the faith of every individual receptive to (worthy of) eternal happiness, a *saving* faith. This too can be but one faith, and, despite the diversity of ecclesiastical faiths, it can yet be met in any in which, tending to its goal of pure religious faith, it is practical. The faith of a religion of service is, on the contrary, a *slavish* and mercenary faith (*fides mercenaria, servilis*) and cannot be considered as saving, because it is not moral. For moral faith must be a free faith, founded on pure dispositions of the heart (*fides ingenua*).[112] The one faith fancies to please God through actions (of *cultus*) which (though laborious) yet possess no moral worth in themselves, hence are actions extracted only

through fear or hope, the kind which also an evil human being can perform, whereas for that the other faith presupposes as necessary a morally good disposition.

Saving faith holds two conditions for its hope of blessedness: the one with respect to what it itself cannot bring about, namely the lawful undoing (before a judge) of actions done; the other with respect to what it can and should bring about, namely the conversion to a new life conformable to its duty. The first is faith in satisfaction (reparation for guilt, redemption, reconciliation with God); the second, faith in the ability to become well-pleasing to God in a future good conduct of life. – The two conditions add up to one faith; they belong together necessarily. The necessity of a connection cannot be seen, however, unless we assume that one faith can be derived from the other, i.e. that according to the law of morally efficient causes either the faith in absolution from the debt resting upon us will elicit a good life conduct, or the true and active disposition of a good life conduct – one to be pursued at all times – will elicit faith in that absolution.

Here now appears a remarkable antinomy of human reason with itself, the resolution of which – or, if this is not possible, at least its settlement – can alone determine whether a historical (ecclesiastical) faith must always supervene as an essential portion of saving faith over and above the pure religious one, or whether, as mere vehicle, historical faith will finally pass over, in however distant a future, into pure religious faith.

1. If it is presupposed that satisfaction has occurred for the sins of humankind, it is indeed understandable that each and every sinner would gladly bring it to bear upon himself and, if this depended simply on *faith* (it would amount to a declaration on the sinner's part of his intention that the satisfaction occur also for him), he would not for an instant suffer misgivings on that account. It is totally inconceivable, however, how a rational human being who knows himself to deserve punishment could seriously believe that he only has to believe the news of a satisfaction having been rendered for him, and (as the jurists say) accept it *utiliter,*[a]113 in order to regard his guilt as done away with, indeed, to such an extent (to its very roots) that a good life conduct, for which he has not made the least effort so far, would be even for the future the unavoidable consequence of   6:117 his faith and his acceptance of the proffered relief. No thoughtful person can bring himself to this faith, however much self-love often transforms into a hope the mere wish for a good, for which one does nothing or can do nothing, as though the object were to come on its own, lured by the mere yearning for it. One cannot think any such thing possible unless a human being considers this faith itself as heavenly instilled in him, as something, therefore, for which his reason has no need to account fur-

---

[a] for one's advantage

ther. If a human being is not capable of this, or if he is still too upright to affect any such confidence in him simply as a means of ingratiating himself, despite all the respect for such an overflowing satisfaction, despite every wish that it were also accessible to him, yet he cannot but regard it as only conditional, that is, consider the improvement of his life conduct, as much as lies in his power, as having to come first, before he gives even the least credit to the hope that the favor from on high will redound to his good. – If, therefore, historical cognition of this favor belongs to ecclesiastical faith, whereas the improved life conduct belongs to pure moral faith as a condition, then *the pure moral faith must take precedence over the ecclesiastical.*

2. But if humankind is corrupt by nature, how can a human being believe that on his own, try hard as he will, he can make a "new man"[114] of himself, one well-pleasing to God, when, conscious of the transgressions of which he has so far been guilty, he still stands in the power of the evil principle and finds no capacity in him sufficient to improve things in the future? If he cannot regard the justice, which he has himself aroused against himself, as reconciled through foreign satisfaction, and, through this faith, himself as reborn, as it were, and thus capable for the first time to undertake a new life conduct – which would then be the consequence of his union with the good principle – on what would he base his hope of becoming a human being well-pleasing to God? – Faith in a merit which is not his own, but through which he is reconciled with God, would therefore have to precede any striving for good works, and this contradicts the previous proposition. This conflict cannot be mediated through insight into the causal determination of the freedom of a human being, i.e. into the causes that make a human being become good or bad: in other

6:118 words, it cannot be resolved theoretically, for this question totally surpasses the speculative capacity of our reason. Practically, however, where the question is not what comes first in the use of our free will physically, but morally, whence, in other words, we are to make our start, whether from faith on what God has done for our sake, or from what we ought to do in order to become worthy of it (whatever this may be), there is no hesitation in deciding for the second alternative.

For the acceptance of the first requisite for salvation, namely faith in a vicarious satisfaction, is in any case only necessary for the theoretical concept; we cannot *make* the removal of sin *comprehensible* in any other way. By contrast, the necessity of the second principle is practical and, indeed purely moral: surely we cannot hope to partake in the appropriation of a foreign satisfying merit, and thus in salvation, except by qualifying for it through our zeal in the compliance with every human duty, and this must be the effect of our own work and not, once again, a foreign influence to which we remain passive. For since the command to do our duty is unconditional, it is also necessary that the human being make the command, as a maxim, the basis of his faith, i.e. that he begin with the improvement of his life as the supreme condition under which alone a saving faith can occur.

Ecclesiastical faith, being historical, rightly begins with the first principle. But, since it contains only the vehicle for the pure faith of religion (in which the true end lies), what in this faith (as practical) constitutes the condition, namely the maxim of *action,* must come first: the maxim of *knowledge* or theoretical faith must only bring about the consolidation and completion of that maxim of action.

In this connection it can also be remarked that, according to the first principle, faith (namely, faith in vicarious satisfaction) is accounted to the human being as duty, whereas faith in a good life conduct, such as is brought about in him through a higher influence, is accounted to him as grace. – According to the second principle the reverse holds true. For according to it, a *good life conduct* is (as supreme condition of grace) unconditional *duty,* whereas the satisfaction from on high is merely a *matter of grace.* – The first principle is accused (often not unjustly) of ritual *superstition,* which knows how to reconcile a criminal life conduct with religion; the second, of *naturalistic unbelief,* which combines indifference 6:119 or, indeed, even antagonism to all revelation with an otherwise perhaps exemplary conduct of life. – This, however, would be like cutting the knot (by means of a practical maxim) instead of disentangling it (theoretically), something which is after all permitted in religious questions. – At any rate, by way of satisfying the theoretical preoccupation, the following can be of use. – The living faith in the prototype of a humanity well-pleasing to God (the Son of God) refers, *in itself,* to a moral idea of reason, insofar as the latter serves for us not only as guideline but as incentive as well; it is, therefore, all the same whether I start out from it (as *rational* faith) or from the principle of a good life conduct. By contrast, faith in this very same prototype *according to its appearance* (faith in the God-man) is not, as *empirical* (historical) faith, one and the same as the principle of a good life conduct (which must be totally rational); and it would therefore be something quite different to wish to start with such a faith* and derive a good life conduct from it. To this extent there would be a contradiction between the two propositions above. However, in the appearance of the God-man, the true object of the saving faith is not what in the God-man falls to the senses, or can be cognized through experience, but the prototype lying in our reason which we put in him (since, from what can be gathered from his example, the God-man is found to conform to the prototype), and such a faith is all the same as the principle of a good life conduct. – Hence we do not have two principles here that differ in themselves, so that to start from the one or the other would be to enter on opposite paths, but

---

*† Which would have to justify the existence of such a person on historical evidence.

only one and the same practical idea from which we proceed: once, so far as this idea represents the prototype as situated in God and proceeding from him; and again, so far as it represents it as situated in us; in both cases, however, so far as it represents the prototype as the standard measure of our life conduct. And the antinomy is therefore only apparent: for only through a misunderstanding does it regard the very same idea, only taken in different relations, as two different principles. – However, if one wished to make the historical faith in the actuality of an appearance, such as has only once occurred in the world, the condition of the one saving 6:120 faith, then there would indeed be two entirely different principles (the one empirical, and the other rational), and there would arise over them a true conflict of maxims, whether to proceed from the one or the other as starting point, which no reason would ever be able to settle. – [Take] the proposition: We must believe that there once was a human being (of whom reason tells us nothing) who has done enough through his holiness and merit, both for himself (with respect to his duty) and for all others (and their deficiency as regards their duty), to hope that we ourselves can become blessed in the course of a good life, though only in virtue of this faith. This proposition says something quite different from the following: We must strive with all our might after the holy intention of leading a life well-pleasing to God, in order to be able to believe that God's love for humankind (already assured to us through reason) will somehow make up, in consideration of that honest intention, for humankind's deficiency in action, provided that humankind strives to conform to his will with all its might. – What's said in the first does not lie in the power of every human being (including the unlearned). History testifies that all forms of religion have been ruled by this conflict between the two principles of faith; for all religions have had their expiations, however they have construed them. On the other hand, moral disposition has not failed, for its part, to make its demands heard. Yet the priests have at all times complained more than the moralists. They have moaned loudly (and in the form of demands on the authorities to combat the problem) over the neglect of the service of God, which was instituted to reconcile the people with heaven and ward off misfortune from the state. The moralists, by contrast, have complained about the decay of morals, which they very much blame on those means of remission of sin with which the priests have made it easy for everyone to be reconciled with the Divinity over the grossest vices. In fact, if for the repayment of debts already incurred or yet to be incurred an inexhaustible fund is already at hand, to which we only need to help ourselves to make us blameless (and, in spite of all claims made by conscience, we shall no doubt help ourselves to it first and foremost), whereas we can postpone our commitment to a good life conduct until, because of this repayment, we have first sorted ourselves out, then it is not easy to conceive other consequences for such a faith. – Yet, were this faith so portrayed, as if it had such a peculiar force and such a mystical (or magical) influence that, however much we ought to regard it, from what we know, merely as historical, it would nonetheless be in a position of improving the whole human being radically (of making a new man[115] out of him) if he just holds on to it and to all the feelings bound with it, then such a faith would have to be regarded as itself imparted and inspired directly by heaven (with and within the historical faith), and everything, the moral constitution of humankind included, would then be reduced to an unconditional decree of God: "He hath mercy on whom he will, and whom he will he *hardeneth*,"[116]* and this, taken according to the letter, is the *salto mortale* of human reason.[117]

6:121

It is therefore a necessary consequence of the physical and, at the same time, the moral predisposition in us – the latter being the foundation and at the same time the interpreter of all religion – that in the end religion will gradually be freed of all empirical grounds of determination, of all statutes that rest on history and unite human beings provisionally for the promotion of the good through the intermediary of an ecclesiastical faith. Thus at last the pure faith of religion will rule over all, "so that God may be all in all."[118] – The integuments within which the embryo is first formed into a human being must be laid aside if the latter is to see the light of day. The leading-string of holy tradition, with its appendages, its statutes and observances, which in its time did good service, become bit by bit dispensable, yea, finally, when a human being enters upon his adolescence, turn into a fetter. So long as he (the human species) "was a child, he was as clever as a child"[119] and knew how to combine learning too, and even a philosophy helpful to the church, with propositions imposed upon him without any of his doing: "But when he becomes a man, he puts away the childish things."[120] The degrading distinction between *laity* and *clergy* ceases, and equality springs from true freedom, yet without anarchy, for each indeed obeys the law (not the statutory one) which he has prescribed for himself, yet must regard it at the same time as the will of the world ruler as revealed to him through reason, and this

6:122

---

* That [text] can, indeed, be interpreted as follows: No human being can say with certainty why this human being becomes good, that one evil (both comparatively), for we often seem to find the predisposition that makes for the distinction already at birth, and even contingencies of life over which nobody has any control are at times the decisive factor; and just as little can we say what will become of either. In this matter we must therefore entrust judgment to the All-seeing; and this is so expressed in the text as if he pronounces his decree upon them before they are born, thus prescribing to each the role that he will eventually play. For the world creator, if he is conceived in anthropopathic terms, *prevision* in the order of appearance is at the same time also *predestination*. But in the supersensible order of things in accordance with the laws of freedom, where time falls away, there is just one *all-seeing knowledge*, without the possibility of explaining why one human being behaves in this way, another according to opposite principles, and yet, at the same time, of reconciling the why with freedom of the will.

ruler invisibly binds all together, under a common government, in a state inadequately represented and prepared for in the past through the visible church. – All this is not to be expected from an external revolution, which produces its effect, very much dependent on fortuitous circumstances, in turbulence and violence: what is thus for once put in place at the establishment of a new constitution is regrettably retained for centuries to come, for it is no longer to be altered, not, at least, except through a new revolution (which is always dangerous). – The basis for the transition to the new order of things must lie in the principle of the pure religion of reason, as a revelation (though not an empirical one) permanently taking the place within all human beings, and this basis, once grasped after mature reflection, will be carried to effect, inasmuch as it is to be a human work, through gradual reform; for, as regards revolutions, which can shorten the advance of the reform, they are left up to Providence and cannot be introduced according to plan without damage to freedom. –

We have reason to say, however, that "the Kingdom of God is come into us,"[121] even if only the principle of the gradual transition from ecclesiastical faith to the universal religion of reason, and so to a (divine) ethical state on earth, has put in roots universally and, somewhere, also *in public* – though the actual setting up of this state is still infinitely removed from us. For since this principle contains the basis for a continual approximation to the ultimate perfection, there lies in it (invisibly) – as in a shoot that develops and will in the future bear seeds in turn – the whole that will one day enlighten the world and rule over it. But truth and goodness (and in the natural predisposition of every human being there lies the basis both for insight into these and for heartfelt sympathy for them) do not fail, once made public, to propagate everywhere, in virtue of their natural affinity with the moral predisposition of rational beings. The obstacles due to political and civil causes, which might interfere with their spread from time to time, serve rather to make all the more profound the union of minds with the good (which never leaves the thoughts of human beings after these have once cast their eyes upon it).*

6:123

· ·
·

* Without either refusing the service of ecclesiastical faith or feuding with it, we can retain its useful influence as a vehicle yet equally deny to it – as the illusion of a duty to serve God ritually – every influence on the concept of true (viz. moral) religion. And so, in spite of the diversity of statutory forms of faith, we can establish tolerance among their adherents through the basic principles of the one religion of reason, with reference to which teachers ought to expound all the dogmas and observances of their various faiths; until, with time, by virtue of a true enlightenment (an order of law originating in moral freedom) which has gained the upper hand, the form of a degrading means of compulsion can be exchanged, with everybody's consent, for an ecclesiastical form commensurate to the dignity of a moral religion, viz. a free faith. – To reconcile ecclesiastical unity of faith with freedom in matters

Such is therefore the work of the good principle – unnoticed to human 6:124
eye yet constantly advancing – in erecting a power and a kingdom for itself
within the human race, in the form of a community according to the laws
of virtue that proclaims the victory over evil and, under its dominion,
assures the world of an eternal peace.

Division two
Historical representation of the gradual establishment of the dominion of the good principle on earth

We cannot expect to draw a *universal history* of the human race from
religion on earth (in the strictest meaning of the word); for, inasmuch as it
is based on pure moral faith, religion is not a public condition; each
human being can become conscious of the advances which he has made in
this faith only for himself. Hence we can expect a universal historical
account only of ecclesiastical faith, by comparing it, in its manifold and
mutable forms, with the one, immutable, and pure religious faith. From
this point onward, where ecclesiastical faith publicly acknowledges its
dependence on the restraining conditions of religious faith, and its necessity to conform to it, the *church universal* begins to fashion itself into an
ethical state of God and to make progress toward its fulfillment, under an
autonomous principle which is one and the same for all human beings and

---

of faith is a problem which the idea of the objective unity of the religion of reason constantly
urges us to resolve through the moral interest that we take in it, but which, if we turn for it to
human nature, we have little hope of bringing about in a visible church. The idea is one of
reason which is impossible for us to display in an intuition adequate to it but which, as
practical regulative principle, has nonetheless the objective reality required to work toward
this end of unity of the pure religion of reason. It is the same here as with the political idea of
the right of a state,[b] insofar as this right ought at the same time to be brought into line with
an international law[c] which is universal and *endowed with power*. Experience refuses to allow
us any hope in this direction. There seems to be a propensity in human nature (perhaps put
there on purpose) that makes each and every state strive, when things go its way, to subjugate
all others to itself and achieve a universal monarchy but, whenever it has reached a certain
size, to split up from within into smaller states. So too each and every church entertains the
proud pretension of becoming a universal one; as soon as it has propagated and acquires
ascendancy, however, a principle of dissolution and schism into various sects makes its
appearance.

† If we are allowed to assume a design of providence here, the premature and hence
dangerous (since it would come before human beings have become morally better) fusion of
states into one is averted chiefly through two mightily effective causes, namely the difference
of languages and the difference of religions.

[b] *Staatsrecht*
[c] *Völkerrecht*

for all times. – We can see in advance that this history will be nothing but the narrative of the enduring conflict between the faith of divine service and the faith of moral religion, the first of which, as historical faith, human beings are constantly inclined to place higher, while the second has, for its part, never relinquished its claim to the preeminence that pertains to it as the only faith which improves the soul – a claim which, at the end, it will surely assert.

6:125 This history can have unity, however, only if merely restricted to that portion of the human race in which the predisposition to the unity of the universal church has already been brought close to its development. For here the question at least of the distinction between a rational and a historical faith is already being openly stated, and its resolution made a matter of the greatest moral concern; whereas the history of the dogmas of various peoples, whose faiths are in no way connected, is no guarantee of the unity of the church. Nor can the fact that at some point a certain new faith arises in one and the same people, substantially different from the previously dominant one, be counted as [indication] of this unity, even if, inherent in the previous faith, were the *occasional* causes of the new production. For we must have a principle of unity if we are to count as modifications of one and the same church the succession of different forms of faith which replace one another – and it is really with the history of that church that we are now concerned.

For this purpose, therefore, we can deal only with the history of the church which from the beginning bore within it the germ and the principles of the objective unity of the true and *universal* religious faith to which it is gradually being brought nearer. – And it is apparent, first of all, that the *Jewish* faith stands in absolutely no essential connection, i.e. in no unity of concepts, with the ecclesiastical faith whose history we want to consider, even though it immediately preceded it and provided the physical occasion for the founding of this church (the Christian).

The *Jewish faith*, as originally established, was only a collection of merely statutory laws supporting a political state; for whatever moral additions were *appended* to it, whether originally or only later, do not in any way belong to Judaism as such. Strictly speaking Judaism is not a religion at all but simply the union of a number of individuals who, since they belonged to a particular stock, established themselves into a community under purely political laws, hence not into a church;[122] Judaism was rather *meant* to be a purely secular state, so that, were it to be dismembered through adverse accidents, it would still be left with the political faith (which pertains to it by essence) that this state would be restored to it (with the advent of the Messiah). The fact that the constitution of this state was based on a theocracy (visibly, on an aristocracy of priests or leaders who boasted of instructions directly imparted to them from God), and that God's name was therefore honored in it (though only as a secular regent with absolutely no rights over, or claims upon, conscience), did not make that constitution religious. The proof that it was not to have been a religious constitution is clear. *First*, all its commands are of the kind which 6:126 even a political state can uphold and lay down as coercive laws, since they deal only with external actions. And although the Ten Commandments would have ethical validity for reason even if they had not been publicly given, yet in that legislation they are given with no claim at all on the *moral disposition* in following them (whereas Christianity later placed the chief work in this) but were rather directed simply and solely to external observance. And this is also clear from the fact that, *second*, all the consequences of fulfilling or transgressing these commandments, all rewards or punishments, are restricted to the kind which can be dispensed to all human beings in this world indifferently. And not even this is done in accordance with ethical concepts, since both rewards and punishments were to extend to a posterity which did not take any practical part in the deeds or misdeeds, something which in a political state may indeed be a clever device for fostering obedience, but would be contrary to all equity in an ethical one. Moreover, whereas no religion can be conceived without faith in a future life, Judaism as such, taken in its purity, entails absolutely no religious faith. This can be further supported by the following remark. It can hardly be doubted that, just like other peoples, even the most savage, the Jews too must have had a faith in a future life, hence had their heaven and hell, for this faith automatically imposes itself upon everyone by virtue of the universal moral predisposition in human nature. Hence it must have come about *intentionally* that the lawgiver of this people, though portrayed as God himself, did not *wish* to show the least consideration for the future life – an indication that his intention was to found only a political and not an ethical community, for to speak in a political community of rewards and punishments not visible in this life would be, on this assumption, a totally inconsequential and improper procedure. Now, although it can also hardly be doubted that the Jews subsequently produced, each for himself, some sort of religious faith which they added to the articles of their statutory faith, yet such a faith never was an integral part of the legislation of Judaism. *Third*, far from establishing an age suited to the 6:127 achievement of the *church universal*, let alone establishing it itself in its time, Judaism rather excluded the whole human race from its communion, a people especially chosen by Jehovah for himself, hostile to all other peoples and hence treated with hostility by all of them. In this connection also we should not place too much weight on the fact that this people set up, as universal ruler of the universe, a one and only God who could not be represented by any visible image. For we find in most other peoples that their doctrine of faith equally tended in this direction, and incurred the suspicion of polytheism only because of the *veneration* given to certain mighty undergods subordinated to the one God. For a God who wills only obedience to commands for which absolutely no improvement of moral disposition is required cannot truly be that moral being whose concept we find necessary for a religion. Religion is rather more likely to occur with a faith in many such mighty invisible beings, if a people were somehow to think of them as uniting, in spite of their "departmental" differences, in deeming worthy of their pleasure only those human beings who adhere to virtue with all their heart, than when faith is dedicated to but one being, who, however, makes of a mechanical cult the main work.

We cannot, therefore, begin the universal history of the Church (inasmuch as this history is to constitute a system) anywhere but from the origin of Christianity, which, as a total abandonment of the Judaism in which it originated, grounded on an entirely new principle, effected a total revolution in doctrines of faith.[123] The care that the teachers of Christianity take, and may even have taken from the very beginning, to link it to Judaism with a connecting strand, in wishing to have the new faith regarded as only a continuation of the old one which contains all its events in prefiguration, shows all too clearly that their only concern in this matter is, and was, about the most apt means of *introducing* a pure moral religion in place of an old cult to which the people were much too well habituated, without, however, directly offending against their prejudices. The subsequent discarding of the corporeal sign which served wholly to separate this people from others is itself warrant for the judgment that the new faith, not bound to the statutes of the old, nor, indeed, to any statute at all, was to contain a religion valid for the world and not for one single people.

6:128 Thus from Judaism – but from a Judaism no longer patriarchal and uncontaminated, no longer standing solely on a political constitution (which also had already been shattered); from a Judaism already mingled, rather, with a religious faith because of the moral doctrines which had gradually gained public acceptance within it; at a juncture when much foreign (Greek) wisdom had already become available to this otherwise still ignorant people, and this wisdom presumably had had the further effect of enlightening it through concepts of virtue and, in spite of the oppressive burden of its dogmatic faith, of making it ready for revolutions which the diminution of the priests' power, due to their subjugation to the rule of a people indifferent to every foreign popular faith, occasioned – it was from a Judaism such as this that Christianity suddenly though not unprepared arose. The teacher of the Gospel announced himself as one sent from heaven while at the same time declaring, as one worthy of this mission, that servile faith (in days of divine service, in professions and practices) is inherently null; that moral faith, which alone makes human beings holy "as my father in heaven is holy"[124] and proves its genuineness by a good life-conduct, is on the contrary the only one which sanctifies. And, after he had given in his very person, through teaching and suffering even to undeserved

yet meritorious death,* an example conforming to the prototype of a   6:129
humanity well-pleasing to God, he was represented as returning to the
heaven from which he came. For, though he left his last will behind him by
word of mouth (as in a testament), yet, as regards the power of the memory
of his merit, his teaching and example, he was able to say that "he (the ideal
of a humanity well-pleasing to God) would still be with his disciples, even to
the end of the world."¹²⁵ To this teaching – which would indeed need
confirmation through miracles if it had to do only with *historical faith* in the
descent and the possibly supramundane rank of his person, but which, as
part of a moral and soul-saving faith, can dispense with all such proofs of its
truth – to this teaching there are nonetheless added in a holy book miracles
and mysteries, and the propagation of these is itself a miracle requiring a
historical faith which cannot be authenticated or secured in meaning and
import except through scholarship.

Every faith which, as historical, bases itself on books, needs for guarantee a *learned public* in whom it can be controlled, as it were, through
writers who were the contemporaries of the faith's first propagators yet in

---

* With which the public record of his life (which can therefore also serve universally as an
example for imitation) ends. The more esoteric story of his *resurrection* and *ascension* (which,
simply as ideas of reason, would signify the beginning of another life and the entrance into
the seat of salvation, i.e. into the society of all the good), added as sequel and witnessed only
by his intimates, cannot be used in the interest of religion within the boundaries of mere
reason, whatever its historical standing. This is not just because it is a historical narrative (for
so also is the story of what went before), but because, taken literally, it implies a concept
which is indeed very well suited to the human sense mode of representation but is very
troublesome to reason's faith concerning the future, namely the concept of the materiality of
all the beings of this world – a *materialism* with respect to human *personality*, which would be
possible only on the condition of one and the same *body* (psychological materialism), as well
as a *materialism* with respect to *existence*ᵈ in general in a world, which, on this principle, could
not be but *spatial* (cosmological materialism). By contrast, the hypothesis of the spirituality of
the rational beings of this world, according to which the body can remain dead on earth and
yet the same person still be living, or the hypothesis that the human being can attain to the
seat of the blessed in spirit (in his non-sensuousᵉ quality) without being transposed to some
place in the infinite space surrounding the earth (which we also call heaven) – this hypothesis is more congenial to reason, not merely because it is impossible to conceive a matter
endowed with thought, but, most of all, because of the contingency to which our existence   6:129
after death would be exposed if we made it rest merely on the coherence of a certain clump
of matter under a certain form, whereas we can conceive the permanence of a simple
substance as natural to it. – On the latter presupposition (of spirituality) reason can, however, neither find an interest in dragging along, through eternity, a body which, however
purified, must yet consist (if personality rests on its identity) of the same material which
constitutes the body's organic basis and which, in life, the body itself never quite grew fond
of; nor can it render comprehensible what this calcareous earth, of which the body consists,
should be doing in heaven, i.e. in another region of the world where other matters might
presumably constitute the condition of the existence and preservation of living beings.

ᵈ *Gegenwart*
ᵉ *nicht-sinnlich*

157

no way suspect of special collusion with them, and whose connection with our present authors has remained unbroken. The pure faith of reason, on the contrary, does not need any such documentation but is its own proof. Now at the time of the revolution in question, there already was among the people who ruled over the Jews and had spread in their very homeland 6:130 (among the Romans) a learned public from whom the history of the political events of the time has been transmitted to us through an unbroken series of writers, and this people, though little concerned with the religious faiths of their non-Roman subjects, was not at all unreceptive to public miracles allegedly occurring among them; yet its writers made no mention, neither of the miracles nor of the equally public revolution which these caused (with respect to religion) among that people subjected to them, though they were contemporary witnesses. Only later, after more than one generation, did they institute research into the nature – but not into the history of the origin – of this change in faith which had hitherto remained unrecognized by them (and had occurred not without public commotion), in an effort to find it in their own annals. Hence, from its origin until the time when Christianity developed a learned public of its own, its history is obscure, and we thus have still no cognition of what effect its doctrine had upon the morality of its adherents, whether the first Christians were individuals truly improved morally or just people of ordinary cast. At any rate, from the time that Christianity itself became a learned public, or became part of the universal one, its history, so far as the beneficial effect which we rightly expect from a moral religion is concerned, has nothing in any way to recommend it. – How mystical enthusiasm in the life of hermits and monks and the exaltation of the holiness of the celibate state rendered a great number of individuals useless to the world; how the alleged miracles accompanying all this weighed down the people with the heavy chains of a blind superstition, how, with the imposition of a hierarchy upon free human beings, the terrible voice of *orthodoxy* rose from the mouth of self-appointed canonical expositors of scripture, and this voice split the Christian world into bitter parties over opinions in matters of faith (upon which, without recourse to pure reason as the expositor, no universal agreement can possibly be attained); how in the East, where the state itself, in an absurd manner, attended to the articles of faith of priests and their priestdom, instead of holding these priests within the narrow confines of a simple teacher's station (out of which they are at all times inclined to transgress into that of ruler) – how at the end, I say, this state inevitably had to become the prey of external enemies who finally put an end to the dominion of its faith; 6:131 how in the West, where faith erected a throne of its own independent of secular power, the civil order was wrecked and rendered impotent, together with the sciences (which support it), by a self-proclaimed vicar of God; how the two parts of the Christian world were overcome by barbarians, like plants and animals which, on the verge of disintegration through disease, attract destructive insects to complete the process; how, again in the West, the spiritual leader just mentioned ruled over kings and chastised them like children by means of the magic wand of his threat of excommunication, and incited them to foreign wars (the Crusades) which would depopulate another portion of the world, and to feuds among themselves, and the subjects to rebellion against those in authority over them and to bloodthirsty hatred against their otherwise-minded confreres in one and the same so-called universal Christianity; how the root of this strife, which even now is kept from violent outbreaks only through political interest, lies hidden in the fundamental principle of an ecclesiastical faith which rules despotically, and still occasions apprehension over the replaying of similar scenes: This history of Christianity (which, so far as it was to be erected on a historical faith, could not have turned out otherwise), when beheld in a single glance, like a painting, could indeed justify the outcry, *tantum religio potuit suadere malorum!,*[f] did not the fact still clearly enough shine forth from its founding that Christianity's true first purpose was none other than the introduction of a pure religious faith, over which there can be no dissension of opinions; whereas all that turmoil which has wrecked the human race, and still tears it apart, stems from this alone: because of a bad propensity in human nature, what should have served at the beginning to introduce this pure faith – i.e. to win over to the new faith, through its own prejudices, the nation which was accustomed to its old historical faith – this was subsequently made the foundation of a universal world-religion.

Should one now ask, Which period of the entire church history in our ken up to now is the best? I reply without hesitation, *The present.* I say this because one need only allow the seed of the true religious faith now being sown in Christianity – by only a few, to be sure, yet in the open – to grow unhindered, to expect from it a continuous approximation to that church, ever uniting all human beings, which constitutes the visible representation (the schema) of the invisible Kingdom of God on earth. – In matters 6:132 which ought to be moral and soul improving by nature, reason has wrest itself free from the burden of a faith constantly exposed to the arbitrariness[g] of its interpreters, and, in all the lands on our part of the world, universally among those who truly revere religion (though not everywhere openly), it has accepted, in the *first* place, the principle of reasonable *moderation* in claims concerning anything that goes by the name of revelation. To wit: Since no one can dispute the *possibility* that a scripture which, in its practical content, contains much that is godly may also be regarded (with respect to what is historical in it) as divine revelation; more-

---

[f] "Such evil deeds could religion prompt!" Lucretius, *De rerum natura,* I:101.
[g] *Willkür*

over, since the union of human beings into one religion cannot feasibly be established and given permanence without a holy book and an ecclesiastical faith based on it; since also, given the present situation of human insight, some new revelation ushered in through new miracles can hardly be expected, the most reasonable and the fairest thing to do, once a book is already in place, is to use it from then on as the basis for ecclesiastical instruction, and not to weaken its value through useless or malicious attacks, yet at the same time not to force faith in it upon any human being, as requisite for his salvation. A *second* principle is this: Since the sacred narrative is only adopted for the sake of ecclesiastical faith, and, by itself alone, it neither could, nor ought to, have any influence whatever on the reception of moral maxims but is rather given to this faith only for the vivid presentation of its true object (virtue striving toward holiness), it should at all times be taught and expounded in the interest of morality, and the point should thereby also be stressed, carefully and (since espe-

6:133   cially the ordinary human being has in him a constant propensity to slip into passive* faith) repeatedly, that true religion is not to be placed in the knowledge or the profession of what God does or has done for our salvation, but in what we must do to become worthy of it; and this can never be anything but what possesses an unquestionably *unconditional* value, hence is alone capable of making us well-pleasing to God, and every human being can at the same time be fully certain of its necessity without the slightest scriptural learning. – Now it is the duty of the rulers not to hinder the public diffusion of these principles; on the contrary, much is risked, and at one's own responsibility, when we intrude upon the way of divine providence by favoring certain historical ecclesiastical doctrines, which at best have in their favor only an appearance of truth to be established by scholars, and, through the offer or withdrawal of certain civil advantages otherwise available to everyone, by exposing the subjects'

6:134   conscience to temptation – † all of which, apart from the harm which

---

* One cause of this propensity lies in the principle of security, namely that the mistakes of a religion in which I was born and brought up, in which I was instructed without any choice of mine, and in which I did not alter anything through any ratiocination of mine, are not charged on my account but on that of my educators or of the teachers publicly appointed to that task – a reason too why we do not readily approve of somebody's public change of religion, to which, to be sure, yet another (and deeper) is added, namely, that with the uncertainty which we all privatively feel regarding which, among the historical faiths, is the right one, whereas moral faith is everywhere the same, we find it highly unnecessary to cause a sensation on this score.

† If a government does not wish to be regarded as doing violence to conscience because it only prohibits *the public declaration* of one's religious opinions while not hindering anyone from *thinking* in secret whatever he sees fit, then we make fun of this, saying that no freedom is thereby granted by the government, since thought cannot be prevented anyway. But what the secular supreme power cannot do, the spiritual power can. It can prohibit even thought, and actually hinder it as well; indeed, it can exercise this coercion (namely the prohibition even to think otherwise than it prescribes) upon its mighty authorities themselves. – For

thereby befalls a freedom which is in this case holy, can hardly produce good citizens for the state. Who, among those who conspire to hinder such a free development of the divine predispositions to the world's highest good, or even promote its hindrance, would wish, upon reflection in consultation with conscience, to answer for all the evil which can arise from such violent interventions and hamper, perhaps for a long time to come, or indeed even set back the advance in goodness envisaged by the world's government, even though no human power or institution could ever abolish it entirely?

As regards its guidance by Providence, the Kingdom of Heaven is finally represented in this history not only as coming nearer, in an approach delayed indeed at certain times yet never entirely interrupted, but as being ushered in as well. Now the Kingdom of Heaven can be interpreted as a symbolic representation aimed merely at stimulating greater hope and courage and effort in achieving it, if to this narrative there is attached a prophecy (just as in the Sibylline books)[126] of the consummation of this great cosmic revolution, in the image of a visible Kingdom of God on earth (under the governance of his representative and vicar, who has again come down [from heaven]), and of the happiness which is to be enjoyed here on earth under him after the separation and expulsion of the rebels who once again make an attempt at resistance; together with the total extirpation of these rebels, and of their leader (as in the Apocalypse),[127] so that the *end of the world* constitutes the conclusion of the story. The teacher of the Gospel manifested the Kingdom of God on earth to his disciples only from its glorious, edifying, and moral side, namely in terms of the merit of being citizens of a divine state; and he instructed them as to what they had to do, not only that they attain to it themselves, but that they be united in it with others of like mind, and if possible with

---

because of their propensity to a servile faith of divine worship, to which they are spontaneously inclined not to give the greatest importance, above moral faith (which is the service of God above all through the observance of their duties), but also the only importance, one that compensates for any other deficiency, it is always easy for the custodians of orthodoxy, as the shepherds of souls, to instill into their flock such a pious terror of the slightest deviation from certain propositions of faith based on history, indeed the terror of any investigation, that they will not trust themselves to allow a doubt to arise even in thought alone regarding these propositions imposed on them, since this would amount to lending a ear to the evil spirit. True, to be free of this coercion one needs only *to will* (and this is not the case with the coercion to public confessions imposed by a sovereign); but it is precisely this willing on which a bar is being applied internally. Yet, though this true coercion of conscience is bad enough (since it leads to inner hypocrisy), it is not as bad as the restriction of external freedom of faith, because, through the advancement of moral insight and of our awareness of freedom, from which alone true respect of duty can arise, internal coercion must gradually 6:134 disappear on its own, whereas external coercion hinders all spontaneous advances in the ethical communion of the believers, which constitutes the essence of the true church, and totally subjects its form to political ordinances.

the whole human race. But as regards happiness, which constitutes the other part of the human being's unavoidable desire, he told them from the beginning that they could not count on it during their life on earth. He prepared them instead to be ready for the greatest tribulations and sacrifices; yet (since total renunciation of the physical element of happiness cannot be expected of a human being, so long as he exists) he added: "Rejoice and be exceeding glad: for great is your reward in Heaven."[128] The addition to the history of the church that deals with its future final destiny represents it, however, as finally *triumphant,* i.e. as crowned with happiness here on earth, after having overcome all obstacles. – The separation of the good from the evil, which would not have been conducive to the church's end in the course of its advance to perfection (since the mingling of the two was necessary precisely for this reason, in part to sharpen the virtue of the good, and in part to turn the other away from their evil through the example of the good), is represented as the final consequence of the establishment of the divine state after its completion. And here yet a last proof of the stability of this state, regarded as power, is added: its victory over all external foes, who are also considered [as assembled] in one state (the state of hell), whereby all earthly life then comes to an end, as "the last enemy (of good human beings), death, is destroyed,"[129] and immortality commences on both sides, to the salvation of the one, and the damnation of the other; the very form of a church is dissolved; the vicar on earth enters the same class as the human beings who are now elevated to him as citizens of Heaven, and so God is all in all.[130]*

    This representation in a historical narrative of the future world, which is not itself history, is a beautiful ideal of the moral world-epoch brought about by the introduction of the true universal religion and *foreseen*[h] in faith in its completion – one which we do not *see directly*[i] in the manner of an empirical completion but *have a glimpse of*[j] in the continuous advance and approximation toward the highest possible good on earth (in this there is nothing mystical but everything proceeds naturally in a moral

---

* This expression (if we set aside its element of mystery, which transcends the bounds of possible experience and only belongs to the sacred *history* of mankind, hence does not concern us practically) can be so understood: historical faith, which, as ecclesiastical, needs a holy book to guide human beings but, precisely for this reason, hinders the church's unity and universality, will itself cease and pass over into a pure religious faith which illumines the whole world equally; and we should diligently work for it even now, through the continuous development of the pure religion of reason out of its present still indispensable shell.

    † Not that it "will cease" (for it might always be useful and necessary, perhaps, as vehicle) but that "it can cease"; whereby is intended only the intrinsic firmness of pure moral faith.

[h] *ausgesehenen*
[i] *absehen*
[j] *hinaussehen*

way), i.e. we can make preparation for it. The appearance of the Anti-christ, the millennium, the announcement of the proximity of the end of the world, all take on their proper symbolic meaning before reason. And the last of them, represented (like the end of life, whether far or near) as an event which we cannot see in advance, expresses very well the necessity for us always to be ready for it, yet (if we ascribe to this symbol its intellectual meaning) in fact always to consider ourselves as actually the chosen citizens of a divine (ethical) state. "When, therefore, cometh the Kingdom of God?" – "The Kingdom of God cometh not in visible form. Neither shall they say: Lo here; or lo there! *For behold, the Kingdom of God is within you!*" (Luke, 17, 21–22).*

---

*† A kingdom of God is here represented not according to a particular covenant ([it is] not a messianic kingdom) but according to a *moral* one (available to cognition through mere reason). A messianic kingdom (*regnum divinum pactitium*)ᵏ would have to draw its proof from history, and there it is divided into the *messianic* kingdom of the *old* and of the *new* covenant. Now it is worthy of notice that the worshippers of the former (the Jews) have preserved their identity though dispersed throughout the world, whereas the adherents of other religions have normally assimilated their faith with that of the people among whom they scattered. This phenomenon strikes many as being so remarkableˡ that, in their judgment, it certainly could not have been possible by nature but only as an extraordinary event designed for a divine purpose. – But a people in possession of a written religion (sacred books) never assimilates in faith with a people which (like the Roman Empire, i.e. the whole civilized world at the time) has nothing of the kind but only has customs; it rather sooner or later makes proselytes. Hence the Jews too, after the Babylonian captivity (when, as it appears, their sacred books were read publicly for the first time), were no longer accused of their propensity to run after false gods, at the very time when the Alexandrian culture, which must have had an influence on them too, could have made it easy for them to give these gods a systematic form. So too the Parsees, followers of the religion of Zoroaster, have until now retained their faith in spite of their dispersion, because their *dustoors*ᵐ possessed the Zendavesta. Those Hindus, on the other hand, who under the name of "Gypsies" have scattered far and wide, have not avoided the mixture of foreign faith, since they came from the scum of the population (the Pariahs, to whom it is even forbidden to read their sacred books). However, what the Jews would not have achieved on their own, the Christian and later the Mohammedan religion, but the Christian especially, did for them, since these religions presuppose the Jewish faith and the sacred books pertaining to it (although the Mohammedan religion claims that they have been distorted). For the Jews could always rediscover their ancient documents among the Christians (who had issued from them) if in their wanderings, where the skill to read them and hence the desire to possess them may have repeatedly died out, they just retained memory of having at one time possessed them. Hence we do not run across Jews outside the lands indicated, if we except the few on the coast of Malabar and perhaps one community in China (and of these the first were able to be in continual business relation with their fellow believers in Arabia), although there is no doubt that they must have spread in those rich lands as well but, because of the lack of any affinity between their faith and the local, ended up forgetting theirs completely. At any rate, it is quite awkward to base edifying considerations upon this preservation of the Jewish people and their religion in circumstances so disadvantageous to them, for both parties

6:137

ᵏ a divine kingdom secured by covenant

ˡ *wundersam*

ᵐ high priests

General remark

Investigation into all forms of faith that relate to religion invariably runs across a *mystery* behind their inner nature, i.e. something *holy*, which can indeed be *cognized*[n] by every individual, yet cannot be *professed*[o] publicly, i.e. cannot be communicated universally. – As something *holy* it must be a moral object, hence an object of reason and one capable of being sufficiently recognized[p] internally for practical use; yet, as something *mysterious*, not for theoretical use, for then it would have to be communicable to everyone and hence also capable of being externally and publicly professed.

Now faith in something which, however, we yet regard as a holy mystery can either be looked upon as *divinely dispensed* or as a *pure faith of reason*. Unless impelled by the most extreme need to accept the first kind, we shall make it a maxim to abide by the second. – Feelings are not cognitions; they are not, therefore, the marks of a mystery; and, since mystery relates to reason yet is not something that can be imparted universally, each individual will have to look for it (if there is any such thing) in his own reason.

It is impossible to determine, *a priori* and objectively, whether there are such mysteries or not. Hence we shall have to look directly into the inner, the subjective, part of our moral predisposition in order to see whether any can be found in us. We shall not, however, be allowed to count among the holy mysteries the *grounds* of morality, which are inscrutable to us, but only what is given to us in cognition yet is not susceptible of public disclosure; for morality allows of open communication, even though its cause is not given to us. Thus freedom – a property which is made manifest to the human being through the determination of his power of choice by the unconditional moral law – is no mystery, since cognition of it can be *communicated* to everyone; the ground of this property, which is inscrutable to us, is however a mystery, since it is *not given* to us in cognition. This very freedom, however, when applied to the final object of practical reason

---

believe that they find confirmation in it. One sees in the preservation of the people to which it belongs, and of its ancient faith that has remained unadulterated in spite of the dispersion among so many peoples, the proof of a special beneficent providence which is saving this people for a future kingdom on earth; the other sees in it nothing but the admonishing ruins of a devastated state which stands in the way of the Kingdom of Heaven to come but which a particular providence still sustains, partly to preserve in memory the old prophecy of a messiah issuing from this people, and partly to make of it an example of punitive justice, because, in its stiffneckedness, that people wanted to make a political and not a moral concept of this messiah.

[n] *gekannt*
[o] *pekannt*
[p] *erkannt*

(the realization of the final moral end), is alone what inevitably leads us to holy mysteries. – *

Since by himself the human being cannot realize the idea of the su-   6:139
preme good inseparably bound up with the pure moral disposition, either with respect to the happiness which is part of that good or with respect to the union of the human beings necessary to the fulfillment of the end, and yet there is also in him the duty to promote the idea, he finds himself driven to believe in the cooperation or the management of a moral ruler of the world, through which alone this end is possible. And here there opens up before him the abyss of a mystery regarding what God may do, whether *anything* at all is to be attributed to him and *what* this something might be in particular, whereas the only thing that a human being learns from a duty is what he himself must do to become worthy of that fulfillment, of which he has no cognition or at least no possibility of comprehension.

This idea of a moral ruler of the world is a task for our practical reason. Our concern is not so much to know what he is in himself (his nature) but what he is for us as moral beings; even though for the sake of this relation we must think the divine nature by assuming it to have the full perfection required for the execution of his will (e.g. as the will of an immutable, omniscient, all-powerful, etc. being). And apart from this relation we can cognize nothing about him.

Now, in accordance with this need of practical reason, the universal true religious faith is faith in God (1) as the almighty creator of heaven

---

* The *cause* of the universal gravity of all matter in the world is equally unknown to us, so much so that we can even see that we shall never have cognition of it, since its very concept presupposes a first motive force unconditionally residing within it. Yet gravity is not a mystery; it can be made manifest to everyone, since its *law* is sufficiently cognized. When Newton represents it as if it were the divine presence in appearance (*omnipraesentia phaenomenon*),ᵠ this is not an attempt to explain it (for the existence of God in space involves a contradiction) but a sublime analogy in which the mere union of corporeal beings into a cosmic whole is being visualized, in that an incorporeal cause is put underneath them – and so too would fare the attempt to comprehend the self-sufficient principle of the union of rational beings in the world into an ethical state, and to explain this union from that principle. We recognize only the duty that draws us to it; the possibility of the intended effect in obeying this duty lies outside the bounds of all our insight. – There are mysteries that are   6:139 hidden things of nature (*arcana*), and there are mysteries of politics (things kept secret, *secreta*); yet we *can* still become acquaintedʳ with either, inasmuch as they rest on empirical causes. With respect to that which is universal human duty to have cognition of (namely anything moral) there can be no mystery; but with respect to that which God alone can do, for which to do anything ourselves would exceed our capacity and hence also our duty, there we can have a genuine, i.e. a holy, mystery of religion (*mysterium*). And it might perhaps be useful only to know and to understand that there is such a mystery rather than to have insight into it.

ᵠ phenomenal omnipresence
ʳ *können . . . uns bekannt werden*

and earth, i.e. morally as *holy* lawgiver; (2) as the preserver of the human race, as its *benevolent* ruler and moral guardian; (3) as the administrator of his own holy laws, i.e. as *just* judge.

6:140 This faith really contains no mystery, since it expresses solely God's moral bearing toward the human race. It is also by nature available to all human reason and is therefore to be met with in the religion of most civilized peoples.* It is also inherent in the concept of a people regarded as a community, where such threefold superior power (*pouvoir*) is always to be thought, except that the people is here represented as ethical, and hence the threefold quality of the moral head of the human race, which in a juridico-civil state must of necessity be distributed among three different subjects, † can be thought as united in one and the same being.

6:141 But since this faith, which purified the moral relation of human beings to the highest being from harmful anthropomorphism on behalf of universal religion and brought it up to measure with the true morality of a people of God, was first set forth in a certain doctrine of faith (the Christian one) and made public to the world only in it, its promulgation can well be called

---

* In the sacred prophetic story of the "last things," the *judge of the world* (really he who will take as his own under his dominion those who belong to the kingdom of the good principle, and will separate them out) is represented and spoken of not as God but as the Son of man.[131] This seems to indicate that *humanity itself,* conscious of its limitation and fragility, will pronounce the sentence in this selection. And this is a generosity which does not, however, violate justice. – In contrast, when represented in his Divinity (the Holy Spirit), i.e. as he speaks to our conscience with the voice of the holy law which we ourselves recognize and in terms of our own reckoning, the judge of human beings can be thought of only as passing judgment according to the rigor of the law, for we ourselves know absolutely nothing of how much can be credited in our behalf to the account of our frailty but have only our trespasses before our eyes, together with the consciousness of our freedom and of the violation of our duty for which we are wholly to be blamed, and hence have no ground for assuming generosity in the judgment passed on us.

† It is hard to give a reason why so many ancient peoples hit upon this idea, unless it is that the idea lies in human reason universally whenever we want to think of the governance of a people and (on the analogy of this) of world governance. The religion of Zoroaster had these three divine persons, Ormuzd, Mithra, and Ahriman,[132] the Hindu religion had Brahma, Vishnu, and Shiva[133] – but with only this difference, that the religion of Zoroaster represents its third person as the creator not just of *evil* as punishment but also of the *moral evil* itself for which humans are being punished, whereas the Hindu religion represents it only as judging and punishing. The religion of Egypt had its Ptha, Kneph, and Neith,[134] of whom, so far as the obscurity of the reports from those ancient times allow us to surmise, the first was to represent spirit, distinguished from matter, as *world-creator;* the second, a generosity which sustains and *rules;* the third, a wisdom which limits this generosity, *i.e. justice.* The Goths

6:141 revered their Odin (father of all), their Freya (also Freyer, goodness), and Thor, the judging (punishing) God. Even the Jews seem to have pursued these ideas in the final period of their hierarchical constitution. For in the charge of the Pharisees that Christ had called himself a *Son of God,* they do not seem to put any special weight of blame on the doctrine that God has a son, but only on Christ's claim to be the Son of God.[135]

the revelation of something which had hitherto remained a mystery for human beings through their own fault.

This revelation says, *first*, that we should represent the supreme lawgiver, neither as *merciful* and hence *forbearing* (indulgent) toward human weakness, nor as *despotic* and ruling merely according to his unlimited right; and his laws not as arbitrary, totally unrelated to our concepts of morality, but as directed at the holiness of the human being. *Second,* we must place his goodness, not in an unconditional *benevolence* toward his creatures, but in that he first sees to their moral constitution through which they are *well-pleasing* to him, and only then makes up for their incapacity to satisfy this requirement on their own. *Third,* his justice cannot be represented as *generous* and *condoning* (for this implies a contradiction), and even less as dispensed by the lawgiver in his quality of holiness (for before it no human being is justified), but only as restricting his generosity to the condition that human beings abide by the holy law, to the extent that as *sons of men*[136] they can measure up to it. – In a word, God wills to be served as morally qualified in three specifically different ways, for which the designation of different (not physically, but morally) personalities of one and the same being is not a bad expression. And this creed of faith at the same time expresses the whole of pure moral religion which, without this distinction of personalities, would run the danger of degenerating into an anthropomorphic servile faith, because of the human propensity to think of the Divinity as a human authority* (who does not usually   6:142 separate in his rule [the parts of] this threefold quality but rather often mixes or interchanges them).

But, if this very faith (in a divine Trinity) were to be regarded not just as the representation of a practical idea, but as a faith that ought to represent what God is in himself, it would be a mystery surpassing all human concepts, hence unsuited to a revelation humanly comprehensible, and could only be declared in this respect as mystery. Faith in it as an extension of theoretical cognition of the divine nature would only be the profession of a creed of ecclesiastical faith totally unintelligible to human beings or, if they think that they understand it, the profession of an anthropomorphic creed, and not the least would thereby be accomplished for moral improvement. – Only what we can indeed thoroughly understand and penetrate in a practical context, but which surpasses all our concepts for theoretical purposes (for the determination of the nature of the object in itself), is mystery (in one context) and can yet (in another) be revealed. Of this kind is the above mentioned mystery, which can be divided into three mysteries revealed to us through our own reason:

1. The mystery of the *call* (of human beings to be citizens of an ethical

---

* *Oberhaupt*

state). – We can form a concept of the universal and *unconditional* subjection of human beings to the divine legislation only insofar as we also consider ourselves his *creatures;* just so can God be considered the ultimate source of all natural laws only because he is the creator of natural things. It is, however, totally incomprehensible to our reason how beings can be *created* to use their powers freely, for according to the principle of causality we cannot attribute any other inner ground of action to a being, which we assume to have been produced, except that which the producing cause has placed in it. And, since through this ground (hence through an external cause) the being's every action is determined as well, the being itself cannot be free. So through our rational insight we cannot reconcile the divine and holy legislation, which only applies to free beings, with the concept of the creation of these beings, but must simply presuppose the latter as already existing free beings who are determined to citizenship in the divine state, not in virtue of their creation, but because of a purely moral necessitation, only possible according to the laws of freedom, i.e. through a call. So the call to this end is morally quite clear; for speculation, however, the possibility of beings who are thus called is an impenetrable mystery.

6:143

2. The mystery of *satisfaction.* The human being, so far as we have cognition of him, is corrupted and of himself not in the least adequate to that holy law. However, if the goodness of God has called him as it were into being, i.e. has invited him to a particular kind of existence (to be a member of the Kingdom of Heaven), he must also have a means of compensating, from the fullness of his own holiness, for the human being's inadequacy with respect to it. But this goes against the spontaneity (presupposed in every moral good or evil which a human being might have within himself), according to which the required goodness must stem from a human being himself, not from someone else, if it is to be imputable to him. – Inasmuch as reason can see, therefore, no one can stand in for another by virtue of the superabundance of his own good conduct and his merit; and if we must *assume* any such thing, this can be only for moral purposes, since for ratiocination it is an unfathomable mystery.

3. The mystery of *election.* Even if we admit such a vicarious satisfaction as possible, a morally believing acceptance of it is itself a determination of the will toward the good that already presupposes in the human being a disposition well-pleasing to God – one which the human being, in his natural corruption, cannot however bring about on his own within himself. But that a heavenly *grace* should work in him to grant this assistance to one human being, yet denies it to another, not according to the merit of works but through some unconditional *decree,* and elects one part of our race to salvation, the other to eternal reprobation: this again does not yield the concept of a divine justice but must at best be deferred to a wisdom whose rule is an absolute mystery to us.

Now regarding these mysteries, so far as they touch the moral life-history of every human being – namely how does it happen that there is a moral good or evil in the world at all, and (if evil is in every human being and at all times) how is it that good will still originates from it and is restored in a human being; or why, when *this* happens in some, are others however excluded from it – regarding this God has revealed nothing to us, nor can he reveal anything, for we would not *understand* it.* It would be as if from the human being, through his freedom, we wanted to *explain* and *make comprehensible* to us what happens; regarding this God has indeed revealed his will through the moral law in us but has left the *causes* whereby a free action occurs or does not occur on earth in the same obscurity in which everything must remain for human investigation; all this ought to be conceived, as history, according to the law of cause and effect yet also from freedom.† Regarding the objective rule of our conduct, however, all that we need is sufficiently revealed (through reason and Scripture), and this revelation is equally understandable to every human being.

6:144

That the human being is called to a good life conduct through the moral law; that, through an indelible respect for this law which lies in him, he also finds in himself encouragement to trust in this good spirit and to hope that, however it may come about, he will be able to satisfy this spirit; finally, that, comparing this expectation with the rigorous command of the law, he must constantly test himself as if summoned to accounts before a judge – reason, heart, and conscience all teach this and drive us to it. It is presumptuous to require that more be made manifest to us, and if this were to happen, we must not regard it as a universal human need.

6:145

But, although that great mystery which encompasses in one single formula all those we have mentioned can be made comprehensible to

---

*† We normally have no misgivings in asking novices in religion to believe in mysteries, since the fact that we do not *comprehend* them, i.e. that we have no insight into the possibility of their object, could just as little justify our refusal to accept them as it could the refusal to accept (say) the capacity of organic matter to procreate – a capacity which likewise no one comprehends yet, though it is and will remain a mystery for us, no one can refuse to accept. We do, however, *understand* what this expression means, and have an empirical concept of its object together with the consciousness that it contains no contradiction. – Now we can with right require of every mystery proposed for belief that we *understand* what is meant by it. And this does not happen just because we understand *one by one* the words with which the mystery is enunciated, i.e. by attaching a meaning to each separately, but because, when combined together in one concept, the words still allow a meaning and do not, on the contrary, thereby escape all thought. – It is unthinkable that God could make this cognition come to us through *inspiration*, if we for our part do not fail earnestly to wish for it, for such cognition could simply not take hold in us, since the nature of our understanding is incapable of it.
†† Hence in a practical context (whenever duty is at issue), we understand perfectly well what freedom is; for theoretical purposes, however, as regards the causality of freedom (and equally its nature) we cannot even formulate without contradiction the wish to understand it.

every human being through his reason, as an idea necessary in practice, yet we can say that, to become the moral foundation of religion, and particularly of a public one, it was revealed at the time when it was *publicly* taught for the first time, and was made into the symbol of a totally new religious epoch. *Solemn formulas* normally contain a language of their own, sometimes mystical and not understood by everyone, intended only for those who belong to a particular society (a brotherhood or community), a language which properly (out of respect) ought to be used only for a ceremonial act (as, for instance, when someone is to be initiated in an exclusive society as member). The highest goal of the moral perfection of finite creatures, never completely attainable by human beings, is, however, the love of the Law.

In conformity with this idea, "God is love"[137] would be a principle of faith in religion: In God we can *revere* the loving one (whose love is that of moral *approbation* of human beings so far as they conform to his holy laws), the Father; in God also, so far as he displays himself in his all-encompassing idea, which is the prototype of the humanity generated and beloved by him, we can *revere* his *Son;* and, finally, so far as he makes his approbation depend upon the agreement of human beings with the condition of his love of approbation, the *Holy Spirit;** but we cannot truly *call*

6;146

* This Spirit, through whom the love of God as author of salvation (really, our corresponding love proportionate to his) is united to the fear of God as lawgiver, i.e. the conditioned with the condition, and which can therefore be represented "as proceeding from both,"[138] besides "leading to all truth (observance of duty),"[139] is at the same time the true Judge of human beings (at the bar of conscience). For "judging" can be taken in a twofold sense: as concerning either merit and the lack of merit, or guilt and nonguilt. God, considered as *love* (in his Son), judges human beings insofar as a merit can yet accrue to them over and above their guilt, and here his verdict is: *worthy* or *unworthy*. He separates out as his own those to whom such merit can still be imputed. The rest go away emptyhanded. On the other hand, the sentence of the judge according to *justice* (of the judge properly so called, under the name of Holy Spirit) upon those to whom no merit can accrue, is: *guilty* or *not guilty*, i.e. damnation or absolution. – In the first instance the *judging* means the *separating out* of the meritorious from the unmeritorious, the two sides both competing for the one prize (salvation). But by *merit* we do not understand here a moral advantage before the law (for with respect to the latter no surplus of observance to duty can accrue to us over and above what is due), but only in comparison to other human beings, relative to their moral disposition. *Worthiness* has moreover always only negative meaning (not-unworthiness), that is, moral receptivity to such goodness. – Hence he who judges under the first qualification (as *brabeuta*)[1] pronounces a judgment of election between *two* persons (or parties) competing for the same prize (salvation); while he who judges under the second (the judge in the proper sense) passes sentence upon *one and the same* person before a court (conscience) that decides between prosecution and defense. – Now if it is assumed that, although all human beings are indeed guilty of sin, to some there can nonetheless accrue a merit, then the pronouncement of the judge proceeds *from love*, a lack of which can lead only to *a judgment of rejection* and its inevitable consequence of a *judgment of condemnation* (since the human being is now handed over to the *just* judge). – It is thus, in my opinion, that the apparently contradictory propositions, "The

6:146

[1] an arbiter of games (Greek)

upon him in this multiform personality (for this would imply a diversity of
beings, whereas God is always only a single object), though we can indeed   6:147
in the name of that object which he himself loves and reveres above all
else, and with which it is both a wish and a duty to enter in moral union.[142]
For the rest, the theoretical profession of faith in the divine nature under
this threefold quality belongs to the mere classical formula of an ecclesiastical faith, to distinguish it from other forms derived from historical
sources – a formula to which few human beings are in a position of
attaching a clear and distinct concept (one not exposed to misunderstanding); its examination pertains rather to teachers in their relation to one
another (as philosophical and erudite expositors of a holy book), that they
may agree on its meaning, not all of which is suited to the general capacity
of comprehension or to the needs of the time, while mere literal faith
hurts rather than improves the true religious disposition.

Son will come again to judge the quick and the dead,"[140] but also, "God sent not his Son into
the world to condemn the world; but that the world through him might be saved" (John 3:7),
can be reconciled; and they can agree with the other where it is said, "He that believeth not
in him is condemned *already*" (John 3:18), namely by the Spirit, of whom it is said, "He will
judge the world because of sin and righteousness."[141] – The anxious solicitude over such
distinctions as we are instituting here in the domain of mere reason, strictly for reason's sake,
might well be regarded as useless and burdensome subtlety; and so they would be indeed, if
they were directed to an inquiry into the divine nature. But since in their religious affairs
human beings are constantly inclined to turn to the divine goodness on account of their
faults without, however, being able to circumvent his justice, and yet a *generous judge* in one
and the same person is a contradiction, it is obvious that their concepts on this subject must
be very wavering and inherently inconsistent even from a practical point of view, hence their
justification and exact determination of great practical importance.

The philosophical doctrine of religion
Part four

Part four
Concerning service and counterfeit service[u] under the dominion of the good principle, or, Of religion and priestcraft

It is already a beginning of the dominion of the good principle and a sign "that the Kingdom of God is at hand,"[143] even if only the principles of its constitution begin to become *public;* for in the world of the understanding something is already there when the causes, which alone can bring it to pass, have taken root generally, even though the complete development of its appearance in the world of the senses is postponed to an unseen distance. We have seen that to unite in an ethical community is a duty of a special kind (*officium sul generis*), and that, though we each obey our private duty, we might indeed thereby derive an *accidental agreement* of all in a common good, without any special organization being necessry for it, yet that such a universal agreement is not to be hoped for, unless a special business is made of resisting the attacks of the evil principle (which human beings themselves otherwise tempt each other to serve as tools) by the union of all with one another for one and the same end, and the establishment of one community under moral laws, as a federated and therefore stronger force. – We have also seen that such a community, **as a Kingdom of God,** can be undertaken by human beings only through *religion,* and, finally, that in order for religion to be public (a requisite for a community), this *Kingdom* is represented in the visible form of a *church,* 6:152 the founding of which therefore devolves on human beings as a work which is entrusted to them and can be required of them.

To erect a church as a community under religious laws, however, seems to require more wisdom (of insight as well as of good disposition) than human beings can be thought capable of; it seems that the moral goodness especially, which is aimed at through such an organization, must for this purpose be *presupposed* in them already. Nonsensical is in fact even

[u] Counterfeit service = *Afterdienst*

175

the expression that *human beings* should *found* a Kingdom of God (as we might well say of them that they can establish the kingdom of a human monarch); God must himself be the author of his Kingdom. Since we do not know, however, what God may directly do to display in actuality the idea of his Kingdom, in which to be citizens and subjects we discover the moral vocation within us, yet know very well what we must do to make ourselves fit to be members of it, this idea, whether aroused and made *public* in the human race through reason or through Scripture, still binds us to the formation of a church, of which God himself is in the last instance the author of the *constitution* as founder, whereas human beings, as members and free citizens of this kingdom, are in all instances the authors of the *organization;* thus those among them who manage the public affairs of the church in accordance with this organization will constitute the church's *administration,* as ecclesiastical servants, while the rest will make up a fellowship, the *congregation,* subject to their laws.

Now, since a pure religion of reason, as a public religious faith, admits only the mere idea of a church (that is, an invisible church), and since only the visible one, founded on laws, is in need of and susceptible to an organization by human beings, it follows that service under the dominion of the good principle in the invisible church cannot be considered as ecclesiastical service, and that the religion of reason does not have legal servants who act as the *officials* of an ethical community; the members of this community receive their orders from the highest lawgiver individually, without intermediary. But, since with respect to our duties (which, taken collectively, we must at the same time look upon as divine commands) we nevertheless are at all times at the service of God, the *pure religion of reason* will have all right-thinking human beings as its *servants* (yet without being *officials*); but to this extent they cannot be called servants of a church (that is, of a visible one, which alone is at issue here). – However, since every church erected on statutory laws can be the true church only to the extent that it contains within itself a principle of constantly coming closer to the pure faith of religion (which, when operative,[v] is what truly constitutes religion in every faith) and of eventually being able to dispense with ecclesiastical faith (in its historical aspect), we shall nonetheless be able to posit in these laws, and among the officials of the church founded on them, a *service* of the church (*cultus*), provided that these officials direct their teaching and order to that final end (a public religious faith). By contrast the servants of a church who do not take this end into consideration but rather declare the maxim of constant approximation to it as damnable, while dependence on the historical and statutory part of the church's faith as alone salvific, can justly be accused of *counterfeit service* of the church or the ethical community under the dominion of the good principle (which is represented through the church). – By a

6:153

[v] *praktisch*

176

"counterfeit service" (*cultus spurius*) is meant the persuasion that we are serving someone with deeds which, in fact, go counter to his intention. This comes about in a community when that which has value only as means for satisfying the will of a superior, is given out to be, and is substituted for, what would make us well-pleasing to him *directly*, and the superior's intention is thereby frustrated.

First part
Concerning the service of God in a religion in general

Religion is (subjectively considered) the recognition of all our duties as divine commands.* That religion, in which I must first know that some- 6:154 thing is a divine command in order that I recognize it as my duty, is *revealed* religion (or a religion which requires a revelation); by contrast, that religion in which I must first know that something is duty before I can acknowledge it as a divine command is *natural religion*. Anyone who de-

---

* With this definition some erroneous interpretations of the concept of a religion in general is obviated. *First*, so far as theoretical cognition and profession of faith are concerned, no assertoric knowledge is required in religion (even of the existence of God), since with our lack of insight into supersensible objects any such profession can well be hypocritically feigned; speculatively, what is required is rather only a *problematic* assumption (hypothesis) 6:154 concerning the supreme cause of things, whereas with respect to the object toward which our morally legislative reason bids us work, what is presupposed is an *assertoric* faith, practical and hence free, that promises a result for the final aim of religion; and this faith needs only *the idea of God* which must occur to every morally earnest (and therefore religious) pursuit of the good, without pretending to be able to secure objective reality for it through theoretical cognition. Subjectively, the *minimum* of cognition (it is possible that there is a God) must alone suffice for what can be made the duty of every human being. *Second*, this definition of a religion in general obviates the erroneous representation of religion as an aggregate of *particular* duties immediately relating to God, and thereby prevents that we take on (as human beings are inclined to do anyway) *works of courtly service* over and above the ethico-civil duties of humanity (of human beings to human beings) and subsequently seek to make up for the very deficiency in the latter by means of the former. There are no particular duties toward God in a universal religion; for God cannot receive anything from us; we cannot act on him or for him. Should we want to transform our guilt-inspired awe before him into a particular duty, we would forget that such an awe is not a particular act of religion but the religious disposition which universally accompanies all our actions done in conformity to duty. Even when it is said: "One ought to obey God before human beings," this only means that whenever statutory commands, regarding which human beings can be both legislators and judges, conflict with duties which reason prescribes unconditionally – and God alone can judge whether they are observed or transgressed – the former must yield precedence to the latter. Would we, on the contrary, understand by that in which God must be obeyed before human beings the statutory commands of God as alleged by a church, the principle would then easily become the often heard war-cry of hypocritical and ambitious clerics inciting revolt against their civil authority. For anything permissible, which civil authority commands, is *certainly* a duty; whereas, whether something which is indeed permissible in itself yet cognizable by us only through divine relation is truly commanded by God, this is (at least for the most part) highly uncertain.

clares natural religion as alone morally necessary, i.e. a duty, can also be called *rationalist* (in matters of faith). If he denies the reality of any supernatural divine revelation, he is called *naturalist;* should he, however, allow

6:155 this revelation, yet claim that to take cognizance of it and accept it as actual is not necessarily required for religion, then he can be named *pure rationalist;* but, if he holds that faith in divine revelation is necessary to universal religion, then he can be called pure *supernaturalist* in matters of faith.

By virtue of his very title, the rationalist must of his own accord hold himself within the limits of human insight. Hence he will never deny in the manner of a naturalist, nor will he ever contest either the intrinsic possibility of revelation in general or the necessity of a revelation as divine means for the introduction of true religion; for no human being can determine anything through reason regarding these matters. The point of dispute can therefore concern only the reciprocal claims of the pure rationalist and the supernaturalist in matters of faith, or what either accepts as necessary and sufficient, or only as accidental, to the one and only true religion.

If religion is divided not according to its first origin and inner possibility (for then it divides into natural and revealed) but simply according to the characteristic that renders it capable of *external communication*, it can be of two different kinds. It is either the *natural religion*, of which (once it is there) every human being can be convinced through his reason; or it is a *learned religion*, of which one can convince others only by means of erudition (in and through which the others have to be guided). – This distinction is very important, for from the origin of a religion alone we cannot draw any conclusion regarding its suitability or unsuitability to be a universal religion of humanity, but we can on the basis of its constitution as universally communicable, or not; the first property constitutes, however, the essential characteristic of the religion which ought to bind every human being.

Accordingly a religion can be *natural*, yet also *revealed*, if it is so constituted that human beings *could and ought to have* arrived at it on their own through the mere use of their reason, even though they *would* not have come to it as early or as extensively as is required, hence a revelation of it at a given time and a given place might be wise and very advantageous to the human

6:156 race, for then, once the thereby introduced religion is at hand and has been made publicly known, everyone can henceforth convince himself of its truth by himself and his own reason. In this case the religion is *objectively* a natural one, though *subjectively* one-revealed; hence it truly deserves also the first title. For that there once was such a supernatural revelation might well subsequently be entirely forgotten without the religion in question losing the least thereby, either in comprehensibility or certainty, or in its power over minds. It is otherwise, however, with a religion which on account of its intrinsic constitution cannot be considered but as revealed. If it were not preserved in a totally secure tradition or in holy books as records, it would disappear from the world; and a supernatural revelation would have to come about, either one publicly repeated from time to time or one continuously enduring within each human being, without which the spread and propagation of any such faith would not be possible.

But every religion in part at least, even a revealed religion, must also contain certain principles of natural relgion. For revelation can be added in thought to the concept of a *religion* only through reason, since this very concept is one of pure reason, being derived from an obligation under the will of a *moral* lawgiver. We too shall therefore consider a revealed religion as yet *natural*, on the one hand, but on the other hand, as *learned* religion; we shall test it and be able to sort out what, and how much, it is entitled to from the one source or the other.

We cannot however do this, if our intention is to talk about a revealed religion (or at least one presumed to be so), without selecting some examples from history, for to be understood we would still have to think up instances as examples, and the possibility of these instances could otherwise be contested to us. But we cannot do better than adopt, as medium for the elucidations of our ideas of a revealed religion in general, some book which contains [instances] of that sort, especially a book inextricably interwoven with teachings that are ethical and hence related to reason, and then hold it before us, one among a variety of books dealing with religion and virtue accredited to a revelation, as an example of the prac-   6:157
tice, useful in itself, without thereby wanting to intrude into the business of those to whom is entrusted the interpretation of this very book as an aggregate of positive doctrines of revelation, or to challenge their exegesis based on scholarship. The practice is, on the contrary, advantageous to scholarship, since the latter proceeds toward one and the same end as the philosophers, namely the moral good; [they aim,] through their own rational grounds, to bring scholarship to precisely where it itself expects to arrive by another road. – In our case this book can be the New Testament, as the source of the Christian doctrine of faith. In keeping with our intent, we now wish to expound the Christian religion in two sections – first, as natural religion, and then, second, as learned religion – with reference to its content and the principles found in it.

FIRST SECTION
OF THE FIRST PART
THE CHRISTIAN RELIGION AS
NATURAL RELIGION

Natural religion, as morality (with reference to the freedom of the subject), combined with the concept of that which can actualize its ultimate end (the concept of *God* as moral originator of the world), and referred to a duration of the human being proportionate to the entirety of this end (immortality), is a pure practical concept of reason which, despite its infinite fruitfulness, yet presupposes only so little a capacity for theoretical reason that, practically, we can sufficiently convince every human being of it and everyone can expect its effect at least, as duty. This religion possesses the great prerequisite of the true church, namely the qualification for universality, inasmuch as by universality we mean validity for every human being (*universitas vel omnitudo distributiva*),[m] i.e. communality of insight.[x] To propagate and preserve itself as world religion in this sense, it requires indeed a staff ministering (*ministerium*) to the purely invisible church, but no officials (*officiales*), i.e. teachers but no dignitaries, for by virtue of the rational religion of single individuals no church in the sense of a universal union (*omnitudo collectiva*)[y] is yet in place, nor is any such church really contemplated through that idea. – But since such a commu-

6:158 nality of insight could not of itself preserve itself, nor, without taking on the form of a visible church, [could it] propagate itself to its [full] universality, but [could] only [do so] if a collective universality, or the union of the believers in one (visible) church according to principles of a pure religion of reason, is added to it, yet this church would not originate from that communality of insight of itself, nor, were it to be established, would it be brought by its free adherents (as was shown above) to a permanent state as a *community* of believers (because none of these enlightened individuals believes himself in need of fellowship in such a church for his religious convictions) unless certain statutory ordinances – which, however, have standing (authority) as law – are added to the natural laws which reason alone can recognize, what constitutes a special duty of human beings and a means to their higher end is still lacking, namely their permanent union in a visible church; but the said authority, to be the founder of such a church, presupposes a fact[z] and not just a concept of pure reason.

If we now assume a teacher of whom the story (or, at least, a general opinion which is not in principle disputable) has it that he was the first to advocate a pure and compelling religion, one within the grasp of the whole world (i.e. a natural religion) and of which the doctrines, as preserved for us, we can therefore test on our own; [that he did so] publicly and even in defiance of a dominant ecclesiastical faith, oppressive and devoid of moral scope (a faith whose cult can serve as example of the type of faith, essentially statutory, that at the time was the norm in the world); if we find that he made this universal religion of reason the supreme and indispensable condition of each and every religious faith, and then added certain statutes to it containing forms and observances intended to serve as means for the establishment of a church founded upon those principles: then, de-

[m] universality or distributive totality
[x] *allgemeine Einhelligkeit*
[y] collective totality
[z] *Factum*

180

spite the accidentality and arbitrariness[a] of what he ordained to this end, we cannot deny to the said church the name of the true universal church, nor can we deny to him the authority due to one who called human beings to union in this church, which he did without wishing to add to their fatih with new and onerous ordinances, or to turn actions first instituted by him into special holy practices, obligatory in themselves as constitutive elements of religion.

After this description one will not fail to recognize the person who can be revered, not indeed as the *founder* of the *religion* which, free from every dogma, is inscribed in the heart of all human beings (for there is nothing arbitrary in the origin of this religion), but as the founder of the first true *church*. – For accreditation of his dignity as of divine mission, we shall adduce some of his teachings as indubitable documents of a religion in general, let their historical status be what it may (for in the idea itself is already present the sufficient ground for accepting them); they can surely be none other than pure doctrines of reason, for these alone are teachings that carry their own proof and on which, therefore, the accreditation of any other must principally rest. 6:159

First, he maintains that not the observance of external civil or statutory ecclesiastical duties but only the pure moral disposition of the heart can make a human being well-pleasing to God (Matthew, 5.20–48); that sins in thought are regarded in the eyes of God as equivalent to deed (5.28)[144] and that holiness is above all the goal for which the human being should strive (5.48);[145] that, for example, to hate in one's heart is tantamount to killing (5.22);[146] that an injustice brought upon a neighbor can be made good only through satisfaction rendered to the neighbor himself, not through acts of divine service (5.24),[147] and that, on the point of truthfulness, the civil instrument for extracting it,* the oath, detracts from respect for truth itself (5.34–37);[148] – that the natural but evil propensity of the 6:160

---

* It is not easy to understand why religious teachers hold as so insignificant this clear prohibition against a means of forcing confession before a civil tribunal which is based upon mere superstition, not upon conscientiousness. For that we are here counting most on the efficacy of superstition can be recognized from the fact that a human being whom we do not trust to tell the truth in a solemn declaration, on the truthfulness of which rests the judgment of human justice (the one sacred thing in the world), we yet believe will be persuaded to do so through a formula which does not contain anything over and above that declaration itself except the invocation of divine punishments upon himself (punishments which he cannot escape anyway, because of his lie), as if it depended on him whether or not he renders account to this supreme tribunal. – In the cited passage of Scripture, this kind of attestation is presented as an *absurd* presumption – wanting to make actual, as though through magic words, things that are not within our power. – It is easy to see, however, that the wise teacher, who here says that whatever goes beyond Yea, Yea, and Nay, Nay, in the attestation of truth comes of evil, had in view the bad effect that oaths bring in their train, namely that the greater importance attributed to them almost sanctions the common lie.

[a] *des Willkürlichen*

human heart ought to be completely reversed, that the sweet feeling of revenge must be transformed into tolerance (5.39.40)[149] and the hatred of one's enemies into beneficence (5.44).[150] Thus he says, he does intend to satisfy the Jewish law in full (5.17),[151] whence it is obvious that not scholarship but pure religion of reason must be its interpreter, for, taken according to the letter, the law allows the very opposite of all this. – Furthermore, with his signposts of the strait gate and narrow way he does not leave unnoticed the misinterpretation of the law which human beings allow themselves in order to evade their true moral duty and make up for it by fulfilling the ecclesiastical duty (7.13).[152]* He nevertheless requires of these pure dispositions that they should also be demonstrated in *deeds* (5.16),[154] and, by contrast, he rebuffs the crafty hope of those who, through invocation and praise of the supreme lawgiver in the person of his envoy, would make up for their lack of deeds and ingratiate themselves into his favor (7.21).[155] And he wants these works to be performed also in public, as an example for imitation (5.16),[156] in an attitude of cheerfulness, not as actions extorted from slaves (6.16),[157] in such a way that, from a small beginning in the communication and propagation of such dispositions, religion will gradually grow into a kingdom of God through its inner power, like a seed in good soil or a ferment of goodness (13.31,32,33).[158] – Finally, he sums up all duties (1) into one *universal* rule (which includes the internal as well as the external moral relation of human beings), namely, Do your duty from no other incentive except the unmediated appreciation of duty itself, i.e. love God (the Legislator of all duties) above all else; (2) and into a *particular* rule, one namely that concerns the human being's external relation to other human beings as universal duty, Love every one as yourself, i.e. promote his welfare from an unmediated goodwill, one not derived from selfish incentives. And these commands are not merely laws of virtue but precepts of *holiness* which we ought to strive after, yet in view of them the striving itself is called *virtue*. – He therefore rebuffs every hope of those who would wait quite passively for this moral goodness, with hands in their lap, as if it were a heavenly gift from above. And he confronts anyone who leaves unused the natural disposition to goodness that lies in human nature (as a capital entrusted to him), in lazy confidence that surely a higher moral influence will somehow make up for his lack in moral constitution and perfection, with the threat that even the good which he might have done by natural predisposition may not come about in him because of this neglect (25.29).[159]

6:161

Concerning the expectation, very natural to the human being, that as

---

* The *strait gate* and the narrow way, which leads to life, is that of a good life-conduct; the *wide gate* and the broad way frequented by the many is the *church*.[153] Not as if it were up to the church and its dogmas whether the human being is lost, but because the *entrance* into it and the profession of its statutes or the celebration of its rites are regarded as the manner in which God truly wants to be served.

regards happiness his lot will be proportionate to his moral conduct, especially in view of the many sacrifices of happiness that must be undertaken for the sake of moral conduct, this teacher promises (5.11,12)[160] a reward for such sacrifices in a future world, but, in accordance with the different dispositions behind moral conduct, of a different kind for those who did their duty *for the sake of the reward* (or also for release from a deserved punishment) that for those better human beings who performed it for its own sake. When one ruled by self-interest – the God of this world – only refines it by the use of reason and extends it outside the narrow bounds of the present without renouncing it, he is represented as one who takes it upon himself to defraud his master and wins from him sacrifices on behalf of duty (Luke, 16.3 – 9).[161] For if it occurs to him that eventually, perhaps soon, he must abandon this world, and that he can take nothing with him of what he possesses to the next, he may well decide to write off his account what he or his master, self-interest, could legitimately require of needy human beings here on earth, and thereby procure for himself as it were transfer bills payable in another world; in this, as regards the incentives of such beneficent actions, he indeed acts *prudently* rather than *morally*, yet in conformity with the moral law, at least according to its letter, and he can legitimately hope that for this too he will not remain unrewarded in the future.* Compare with this what is said of beneficence toward the needy motivated simply by duty (Matt., 25.35– 40),[162] where the judge of the world declares as the true elects to his   **6:162** kingdom those who extended help to the needy without it even entering their minds that what they were doing was also worthy of recompense, or that they were perhaps binding heaven to a recompense, so to speak, precisely because they were acting without attention to it, and we can then clearly see that when the teacher of the Gospel speaks of a recompense in the world to come, he did not mean thereby to make this recompense an incentive of actions but only (as an uplifting representation of the consummation of divine goodness and wisdom in the guidance of the human race) an object of the purest admiration and greatest moral approval for a reason which passes judgment upon human destiny as a whole.

Here we then have a complete religion, which can be proposed to all human beings comprehensibly and convincingly through their own rea-

---

* We know nothing about the future, nor ought we to look for more than what stands in rational connection with the incentives of morality and their end. Here belongs the belief   **6:162** that there is no good action which will not also have its good consequence in the world to come for him who performs it; that, therefore, however reprehensible a human being might find himself at the end of his life, he must not on that account allow himself to stop short of doing at least *one* more good action which is in his power; and that, in doing it, he has cause to hope that, in proportion as he now harbors a purely good intention, it will yet be of greater worth to him than those deedless absolutions which are supposed to make up for the lack of good actions without contributing anything to the lessening of the guilt.

son; one, moreover, whose possibility and even necessity as a prototype for us to follow (so far as human beings are capable of it) has been made visible in an example, without either the truth of those teachings or the authority and the worth of the teacher requiring any other authentication (for which scholarship or miracles, which are not matters for everyone, would be required). The appeals which we here find to older (Mosaic) legislation and prefiguration, as though these were to serve the teacher as authentication, were not given in support of the truth of the teachings [as objects of] thought, but only for their introduction among people who, without exception and blindly, clung to the old. And this must always be more difficult among human beings whose heads, filled with statutory dogmas of faith, have been made almost incapable of receiving the religion of reason than when this religion is to be brought to the reason of

6:163 unlearned yet also unspoiled human beings. Hence no one should be disconcerted to find an exposition, which accommodated itself to the prejudices of the times, now enigmatic and in need of careful interpretation; though it everywhere lets a religious doctrine shine forth, and often even points to it explicitly, which must be comprehensible to every human being and must convince without expenditure of learning.

SECOND SECTION
THE CHRISTIAN RELIGION AS A LEARNED RELIGION

Inasmuch as a religion propounds as necessary dogmas of faith of which we cannot have cognition through reason as such but which must yet be transmitted unadulterated (according to the essential content) to all human beings for all future times, it must be regarded (if we do not wish to assume a continuous miracle of revelation) as a sacred possession entrusted to the care of the *learned.* For although this religion, accompanied by miracles and deeds, could *at the beginning* find entry everywhere, even with respect to things not validated by reason, yet the report itself of these wonders, as well of the doctrines dependent on them for their validation, would *in the passage of time* necessitate a written, documented, and unchanging instruction to posterity.

The acceptance of the principles of a religion is preeminently called *faith (fides sacra).*[b] We shall have to consider the Christian faith, therefore, on the one hand as pure *rational faith,* and on the other as *revealed faith (fides statutaria).*[c] The first may be considered as a faith freely accepted by everyone *(fides elicita),*[d] the second as a commanded faith *(fides imperata).*[e]

---

[b] sacred faith
[c] statutory faith
[d] elicited faith
[e] commanded faith

Of the evil that lies in the human heart and of which nobody is free; of the impossibility of ever retaining ourselves justified before God on the basis of our life-conduct and yet of the necessity of such a valid justification before him; of the futility of substituting ecclesiastical observances and pious servile works for the lack of righteousness and yet of the inescapable obligation to become a new man: [of all this] everyone can be convinced through his reason, and to be convinced of it is part of religion.[163]

But from the point where Christian doctrine is built upon facts[f] and not   6:164
upon mere concepts of reason, it is no longer called simply the Christian *religion*, but the Christian *faith*, which has been made the foundation of a church. The service of a church consecrated to such a faith has therefore two sides. On the one side, it is the service that must be rendered to the church in accordance with its historical faith; on the other side, it is the service due to it according to the practical and moral faith of reason. Neither side can stand in the Christian church on its own, separated from the other: the second not from the first, because the Christian faith is a religious faith; and the first not from the second because it is a learned faith.

The Christian faith, as a *learned* faith, rests on history, and, to the extent that erudition (objectively) is at its base, it is not in itself a *free* faith or one derived from insight into theoretically sufficient grounds of demonstration (*fides elicita*). Were it a pure faith of reason, it would still have to be regarded as a free faith even though the moral laws upon which it is based as faith in a divine legislator command unconditionally – in the way it was also represented in the first section. Indeed, if only this believing were not made into a duty, even as historical faith it could be a theoretically free faith, if all human beings were learned. If, however, it is to be valid for all human beings, even the unlearned, it is a faith not merely commanded but one which obeys the command blindly (*fides servilis*),[g] i.e., it does not investigate whether the command is acutally divine.

In Christian revealed doctrine, however, we cannot by any means begin with an *unconditional faith* in revealed propositions (of themselves hidden to reason) and then have erudite cognition follow behind, somewhat like a mere defense against an enemy attacking the rear train; for then the Christian faith would not just be *fides imperata* but *fides servilis* as well. Hence it must always be taught at least as *fides historica elicita*,[h] i.e. *erudition* would have to constitute in it, as a revealed doctrine of fiath, not the rearguard but the vanguard, the small number of scriptural scholars (the clerics), who also cannot totally dispense with profane learning, dragging behind them the long train of the unlearned (the laity) who are on their   6:165
own uninformed about Scripture (among whom even the civil authorities

[f] *Facta*
[g] slavish faith
[h] elicited historical faith

belong). – If this is not however to happen, universal human reason must be recognized and honored as supreme commanding principle in a natural religion within the Christian doctrine of faith; whereas the doctrine of revelation, upon which a church is founded and which stands in need of scholars as interpreters and preservers, must be cherished and cultivated as a mere means, though a most precious one, for giving meaning, diffusion, and continuity to natural religion even among the ignorant.

This is the true *service* of the church under the dominion of the good principle; but that service in which revealed faith is to come ahead of religion is a *counterfeit service* through which the moral order is totally reversed, and what is mere means is unconditionally commanded (as an end). Faith in propositions, of which the unlearned cannot be made sure either through reason or Scripture (inasmuch as the latter would have first to be authenticated), would then be made into an absolute duty (*fides imperata*) and, as slavish service, it would be elevated, together with other observances connected with it, to the rank of saving faith, though it has no morally determining ground of actions. – A church founded upon this last principle does not have true *servants* (*ministri*), like those of the first constitution, but commanding high *officials* (*officiales*), and these, although (as in a Protestant church) they do not display themselves in hierarchical splendor as spiritual officials clothed with external power but even protest in words against any such thing, in fact wish to be regarded as the exclusive chosen interpreters of a holy Scripture, having robbed the pure religion of reason of its due dignity as at all times its highest interpreter, and having commanded scriptural scholarship for use solely in the interests of ecclesiastical faith. Thus they transform *service* of the church (*ministerium*) into a *domination* of its members (*imperium*), even though, to hide this presumptuousness, they make use of the modest title of the former. The maintenance of this domination, however, which to reason would have been easy, costs the church dearly in outlay of great erudition. For, "blind with respect to nature, it scrambles to gather the whole antiquity above its head and buries itself under it."[164] – The course which things take, once brought to this pass, is as follows:

First, the procedure prudently followed by the first propagators of Christ's doctrine to procure for it introduction among their people is taken to be a part of religion itself, valid for all times and all peoples, so that we ought to believe that *every Christian must be a Jew, whose Messias has come;* it is not however altogether coherent to say that a Christian is not really bound by any law of Judaism (as statutory) yet must accept the entire holy book of this people on faith as divine revelation given to all human beings.* – But the authenticity of this book at once poses a big difficulty

6:166

*† Mendelssohn very ingeniously makes use of this weak point of the customary picture of Christianity to preempt any suggestion of religious conversion made to a son of Israel. For, as

(and this authenticity is far from being established by the fact that passages in it, indeed the entire history narrated there, is used in the books of the Christians for just this end). Prior to the beginning of Christianity, and even before its considerable advance, Judaism had yet to penetrate among the *learned public,* i.e. it was yet to be known to the learned contemporaries of other peoples, its history yet to be controlled so to speak, and its sacred book thus brought to historical credibility because of its antiquity. And, even if this were all sorted out, it does not suffice to be acquainted with[i] the book in translation and transmit it to posterity in this form. The security of the ecclesiastical faith based on it rather requires that there should be learned individuals knowledgeable in the Hebrew language (so far as this is possible for a language of which we have only one single book) at all times and among all peoples. And it ought not to be merely a   6:167 concern of historical science, but one on which hangs the salvation of humankind, that there should be individuals sufficiently knowledgeable in this language to secure the true religion for the world.

The Christian religion suffers indeed from a similar fate, [namely] that although its sacred events occurred openly under the very eyes of a learned people yet its history was already more than one generation past before it penetrated among its learned public; hence the authentication of those events must do without the corroboration of contemporaries. Yet Christianity has the great advantage over Judaism of being represented as coming *from the mouth of the first teacher* not as a statutory but as a moral religion. And since it thereby treads in the closest proximity to reason, it was capable through reason to propagate with the greatest assuredness by itself, even without historical scholarship, at all times and among all peoples. But the first founders of *congregations* found it yet necessary to intertwine the history of Judaism with it, and this, granted the founders' situation at the time, was the sound thing to do, though only sound

---

he said, since the faith of the Jews is, according to the admission of the Christians, the lower floor upon which Christianity rests as the floor above, any such suggestion would be tantamount to asking someone to demolish the ground floor in order to feel at home on the second.[165] His true opinion, however, shines through quite clearly. He means to say: first remove Judaism from your *religion* (though in the historical teaching of faith it may always remain as an antiquity) and we shall be able to take your proposal under advisement. (In fact nothing would then be left over, except pure moral religion unencumbered by statutes.) Our burden will not be lightened in the least by throwing off the yoke of external observances, if another is imposed in its place, namely the yoke of a profession of faith in sacred history, which, for the conscientious, is an even more onerous burden. – In any case, the sacred books of this people will no doubt always be preserved and attended to, though not for the sake of religion, yet for scholarship. For the history of no other people dates with any pretension of credibility as far back as this – back to epochs of prehistory within which we can fit all the profane history known to us (even to the beginning of the world). And so the great blank which profane history necessarily leaves open is filled by sacred history.
[i] *kennen*

perhaps with respect to that situation; and so, that history has come down to us together with the founders' sacred legacy. These founders of the *church*, however, took up those fortuitous means of advocacy into the essential articles of faith themselves, and either augmented them with tradition and interpretations, which acquired legal force from the councils, or authenticated them through scholarship. And there still is no foreseeing how many alterations still lie ahead of faith because of this scholarship, or its extreme opposite, the inner light to which every layman can lay claim. And this cannot be avoided so long as we seek religion not within us but from the outside.

Second part
Concerning the counterfeit service of God in a statutory religion

6:168

The one and true religion contains nothing but laws, i.e. practical principles, of whose unconditional necessity we can become conscious and which we therefore recognize as revealed through pure reason (not empirically). Only for the sake of a church, of which there can be different and equally good forms, can there be statutes, i.e. ordinances held to be divine, though to our purely moral judgment they are arbitrary and contingent. Now to deem this statutory faith (which is in any case restricted to one people and cannot contain the universal world religion) essential to the service of God in general, and to make it the supreme condition of divine good pleasure toward human beings, is a *delusion of religion,** and acting upon it constitutes counterfeit service, i.e. a pretension of honoring God through which we act directly contrary to the true service required by him.

---

* Delusion is the mistake of regarding the mere representation of a thing as equivalent to the thing itself. For a rich miser, for instance, the delusion of *parsimony* is to regard the representation of being able to make use of his riches at will as sufficient substitute for never using them. The delusion of *honor* posits praise in others, which is at bottom only the external representation of their esteem (which internally they perhaps do not entertain at all), the value that ought to be attributed to the esteem itself; to this delusion also belongs, therefore, the obsession for titles and decorations, since these are only external representations of preeminence over others. *Madness*ʲ too is so called because it is the habit of taking a mere representation (of the imagination) for the presence of the thing itself, and to value it as such. – Now the consciousness of possessing a means to a certain end (before we have availed ourselves of it) is the possession of this end in representation only; hence to be satisfied with this consciousness, as though it could count as possession of the end, is a *practical delusion*, which is all that is at issue here.
ʲ *Wahnsinn;* cf. *Wahn* = delusion

§ I
CONCERNING THE UNIVERSAL SUBJECTIVE
GROUND OF RELIGIOUS DELUSION

Anthropomorphism, which is hardly to be avoided by human beings in their theoretical representation of God and his being, but is also harmless enough (provided that it does not influence concepts of duty), is highly dangerous with respect to our practical relation to his will and to our very morality; for, since *we are making a God for ourselves,* * we create him in the way we believe that we can most easily win him over to our advantage, and ourselves be dispensed from the arduous and uninterrupted effort of affecting the innermost part of our moral disposition. The principle that the human being usually coins to justify this behavior is that in everything we do solely for the sake of pleasing God (provided that it does not run directly counter to morality, though not contributing to it in the least) we demonstrate to God our willingness to serve him as his obedient and, because obedient, well-pleasing subjects: therefore, we are also serving him (*in potentia*).[l] – There need not always be sacrifices for the human being to believe that he is rendering this service to God: festivals too, or even public games, as among the Greeks and Romans, have often had to serve, and still serve, to make the Divinity favorable to a people, or also to individuals, in keeping with their delusion. Yet sacrifices (penances, castigations, pilgrimages, etc.) have always been regarded as more powerful, more likely to work on the favor of heaven, and more apt to remove sin, since they more forcefully serve to indicate unbounded (though not moral) subjection to the will of heaven. The more useless such self-inflicted torments are, the less aimed at the universal moral improvement of the human being, the holier they seem to be. For, just because they have absolutely no use in the world, and yet cost effort, they seem to be aimed solely at attesting devotion to God. – Although, it is said, God has in no respect been served through the deed, he nonetheless sees good will

6:169

*† Although it certainly sounds questionable, it is in no way reprehensible to say that every human being *makes a God* for himself, indeed, he must make one according to moral concepts (attended by the infinitely great properties that belong to the faculty of exhibiting an object in the world commensurate to these concepts) in order to honor in him *the one who made him.* For in whatever manner a being has been made known[k] to him by somebody else, and described as God, indeed, even if such a being might appear to him in person (if this is possible), a human being must yet confront this representation with his ideal first, in order to judge whether he is authorized to hold and revere this being as Divinity. Hence, on the basis of revelation alone, without that concept being *previously* laid down in its purity at its foundation as touchstone, there can be no religion, and all reverence for God would be *idolatry.*[166]

6:169

[k] *bekannt*
[l] potentially

in it, a heart which is indeed too weak to obey his moral commands but makes up for this lack by its demonstrated eagerness to obey. Visible here is the propensity to a form of conduct which has no moral value in itself, except perhaps as a means of elevating the sensible faculty of representation for the purpose of harmonizing it with the ideas of the end, or of

6:170 repressing it in case it works counter to these ideas.* Yet in our mind we attribute to this conduct the value of the end itself, or, what amounts to the same thing, we attribute to the mind's readiness to take on attitudes of dedication to God (called *devotion*) the value of these attitudes themselves. And this way of doing things is, therefore, a mere delusion of religion, which can assume all kinds of forms, in some appearing closer to the moral form than in others, yet in all not merely an unpremeditated deception but a maxim by which we attribute intrinsic value to the means rather than the end. And, because of this maxim, the delusion is equally absurd in all its forms, and, as a hidden inclination to deceit, equally to be condemned.

§ 2

THE MORAL PRINCIPLE OF RELIGION OPPOSED
TO THE DELUSION OF RELIGION

To begin with I accept the following proposition as a principle requiring no proof: *Apart from a good life-conduct, anything which the human being supposes that he can do to become well-pleasing to God is mere religious delusion*

6:171 *and counterfeit service of God.* – I say, anything that *the human being* believes that he can do, for we are not thereby denying that, beyond all that *we* can do, there might yet be something in the mysteries of the supreme wisdom which only God can do to make us human beings well-pleasing to him.

---

* For those who believe[167] that in the critique of pure reason they are faced by intrinsic contradictions whenever they stumble upon the distinctions between the sensible and the intelligible, I here remark that, whenever mention is made of sensuous*^m* means to promote the intellectual side (of the purely moral disposition), or of the obstacles which these means put in its way, the influence of these two so unlike principles must never be thought as *direct*. For, as beings of the senses, we can have effect only with respect to the *appearances of the intellectual principle*, i.e. with respect to the determination of our physical powers through the *power of free choice* as exhibited in actions, whether in opposition to the law or in its favor, so that cause and effect are represented as in fact of like kind. But as regards what transcends the senses (the subjective principle of morality in us which lies hidden in the incomprehensible property of freedom), for example the pure religious disposition, we have no insight into anything in it which touches upon the relation in the human being of cause to effect apart from its law (though this is enough by itself); i.e. we cannot *explain* to ourselves the possibility of actions as events in the world of the senses from a human being's moral constitution as [something] imputable to them, precisely because these actions are free, whereas the grounds of explanation of any event must be drawn from the world of the senses.
^m sinnlich

190

But if the church should proclaim such a mystery as in some sense revealed, then the opinion that to *believe* in this revelation, as related to us in sacred history, and to *profess* it (whether internally or externally) is something which in itself can make us well-pleasing to God, is itself a dangerous religious delusion. For this faith, as the inner profession of what a human being firmly hold to be true, is a *deed* so patently extracted through fear that a sincere human being might sooner agree to any other condition than to this one; for in all other compulsory works he would only be doing something superfluous at most, whereas here, by making a declaration of whose truth he is not convinced, something contrary to his conscience. That confession, therefore, regarding which he persuades himself that of itself (as the acceptance of a good offered to him) it can make him well-pleasing to God, is something which he fancies himself capable of rendering over and above his good life-conduct in obedience to the moral laws which are to be practiced in the world, insasmuch as with his service he turns directly to God.

In the *first* place, reason does not leave us altogether without comfort with respect to the lack of a righteousness of our own (which is valid before God). Reason says that whoever does, in a disposition of true devotion to duty, as much lies within his power to satisfy his obligation (at least in a steady approximation toward complete conformity to the law), can legitimately hope that what lies outside his power will be supplemented by the supreme wisdom *in some way or other* (which can render permanent the disposition to this steady approximation), without reason thereby presuming to determine the way or know in what it consists, for God's way can perhaps be so mysterious that, at best, he could reveal it to us in a symbolic representation in which the practical import alone is comprehensible to us, whereas, theoretically, we could not in the least grasp what this relation of God to the human being is in itself, or attach concepts to it, even if God wanted to reveal such a mystery to us. – Suppose now that a certain church were to claim that it knows precisely the way in which God makes up for that moral lack in the human race, and were at the same time to sentence to eternal damnation all human beings who do not know in any natural way that means of justification of which reason has no cognition, and hence also to fail to elevate it to a principle of religion and to profess it as such: Who is the unbeliever in this case? he who has confidence, without knowing how what he hopes for will come to pass; or he who must know precisely the way human beings are released from evil or, failing this, give up all hope of this redemption? – At bottom the latter does not set much store by the knowledge of this mystery (for his reason already teaches him that it is totally useless for him to know something about which he can do nothing) but only wants to know it so that he can make for himself (even if it happens only inwardly) a divine service of the belief, of the acceptance, the profession, and the glorifica-

6:172

tion of all that is revealed, and this divine service might win for him the favor of heaven prior to any expenditure of his own powers toward a good life-conduct, hence quite gratuitously, and would indeed elicit this conduct in a totally supernatural fashion, or, where he may have perhaps gone against it, would at least make up for the transgression.

Second: if the human being strays even slightly from the above maxim, there are *no bounds* left for the counterfeit service of God (superstition)," for everything is arbitrary past that maxim (provided that it does not contradict morality directly). From a sacrifice by lip service, which costs him the least, to the sacrifice of natural goods, which might otherwise better be used to the advantage of humanity, yea, even to the immolation of his own person by losing himself to the world (in the ranks of hermits, fakirs or monks), he offers everything to God, except his moral disposition; and when he says that he brings his heart too to him, he does not mean by this the disposition of a life-conduct well-pleasing to him but a heartfelt wish that his sacrifice may be accepted as payment in place of this disposition (*natio gratis anhelans, multa agendo nihil agens.* Phaedrus).[168]

Finally, when once we go over to the maxim of a service presumed to be of itself well-pleasing to God and also, if need be, conciliatory, yet not purely moral, there is no essential difference among the ways of serving him as it were mechanically which would give one way an advantage over another. In worth (or rather worthlessness) they are all the same, and it would be mere affectation to regard oneself as privileged, because of a *more refined* deviation from the one intellectual principle of genuine respect of God, over those who allow themselves to become guilty of an assumedly coarser debasement to sensuality. Whether the devout individual makes his statutory visit at *church* or undertakes a pilgrimage to the sanctuaries in Loretto or Palestine; whether he takes his formulas of prayer to the heavenly authority with his *lips,* or by means of a *prayer-wheel,* like the Tibetan (who believes that his wishes, even if set out in writing, will reach their end just as well, only provided that they be *set in motion* by some thing or another, by the wind, for instance, if written on flags, or by the hand, if enclosed in a canister as though in a slinging device),[169] or whatever the surrogate for the moral service of God might be, it is all the same and of equal worth. – Differences of external form here count equally for nothing but everything depends, rather, upon the acceptance or the forsaking of the one single principle of becoming well-pleasing to God – [upon] whether [we do it] through moral disposition alone, so far as the latter manifests its vitality in actions which are its appearance, or through pious play-acting and nothing-doing.* But is there not also perhaps a dizzying *delusion of virtue,* rising

6:173

---

* It is a psychological phenomenon that the adherents to a confession in which there is somewhat less of the statutory to believe, feel themselves as it were ennobled thereby and
" *die Superstition*

above the bounds of human capacity, and might it not well be reckoned, together with groveling delusion of religion, in the general class of self-deceptions? No. The disposition of virtue has to do with something *actual,* which is in itself well-pleasing to God and conforms to what is best for the world. True, a delusionary sense of superiority may attach itself to it – the delusion of regarding oneself adequate to the idea of one's holy duty. But this is only accidental. And to place the highest value in that disposition is not a delusion, as it is, for instance, to place it in the ecclesiastical exercises of devotion, but an absolutely efficacious contribution to the world's highest good.

It is furthermore customary (at least in the church) to call *nature* what can be done by the human being on the strength of the principle of virtue, and *grace* what only serves to supplement the deficiency of all his moral capacity and, since adequacy in this respect is also duty for us, can be only wished or also hoped and prayed for; to regard the two as together effective causes of a disposition sufficient to a conduct of life well-pleasing to God; and not merely to distinguish the two but, rather, to set them well against one another.

6:174

The persuasion that we can distinguish the effects of grace from those of nature (virtue), or even to produce these effects in us, is *enthusiasm;* for nowhere in experience can we recognize a supersensible object, even less exert influence upon it to bring it down to us, though there do occur from time to time in the mind movements that work toward morality but which we cannot explain, and about which are forced to admit our ignorance: "The wind bloweth where it listeth. . . . but canst not tell whence it cometh, etc."[170] To want to *perceive* heavenly influences is a kind of madness in which, no doubt, there can also be method (since those alleged inner revelations must always attach themselves to moral, and hence rational, ideas), but which nonetheless always remains a self-deception detrimental to religion. To believe that grace may have its effects, and that perhaps there must be such effects to supplement the imperfection of our striving for virtue, is all that we can say on the subject; for the rest, we are not capable of determining anything concerning their distinguishing marks and even less of doing something toward their production.

The delusion that through religious acts of cult we can achieve anything in the way of justification before God is religious *superstition,* just as the delusion of wanting to bring this about by striving for a supposed

more enlightened, though they have still retained enough of statutory faith that, from their fancied pinnacle of purity, they should not look down with contempt (as they in fact do) upon their brothers in ecclesiastical delusion. The reason for this is that, however little, they do thereby find themselves somewhat nearer to pure moral religion, though they yet depend on the delusion wanting to supplement it through pious observances in which reason is only less passive.

contact with God is religious *enthusiasm.* – It is superstitious delusion to want to become well-pleasing to God through actions that any human being can do without even needing to be a good human being (e.g. by the profession of statutory articles of faith, the observance of ecclesiastical practice and discipline, etc.). And it is called superstitious because it is a choosing of merely natural (not moral) means which on their own can have absolutely no effect on something which is not nature (i.e. the ethical good). – But a delusion is called enthusiastic when the imagined means themselves, being supersensible, are not within the human being's power, even without considering the unattainability of the supersensible end intended through them; for this feeling of the immediate presence of the highest being, and the distinguising of it from any other, even from the moral feeling, would constitute the receptivity of an intuition for which there is no sense[faculty] in human nature. – Since superstitious delusion contains means in themselves suitable to many individuals, and possible to them as well, at least to counteract the obstacles that stand in the way of a disposition well-pleasing to God, it is to this extent yet related to reason and only accidentally reprehensible, i.e.. only inasmuch as it transforms what can only be a means into an object immediately well-pleasing to God. Enthusiastic religious delusion is, on the contrary, the moral death of the reason without which there can be no religion, because, like all morality in general, religion must be founded on principles.

6:175

Thus the principle in an ecclesiastical faith which rectifies or prevents every religious delusion is this: ecclesiastical faith must contain within itself, besides the statutory articles which it yet cannot quite dispense with, another principle as well, of bringing about the religion of good life conduct as its true goal, in order at some future time to be able to dispense with statutory articles altogether.

§ 3
CONCERNING PRIESTCRAFT* AS A REGIME IN THE COUNTERFEIT SERVICE OF THE GOOD PRINCIPLE

The veneration of mighty invisible beings, which was wrung from the helpless human being because of the fear naturally rooted in the con-

6:176

---

*† This name,° which designates only the authority of a spiritual father (πάππα), takes on the sense of a reproach only through the related concept of the spiritual despotism found in all ecclesiastical forms, however unpretentious and popular they declare themselves. Hence in comparing sects I do not want in any way to be understood as meaning to disparage the usages and ordinances of one as contrasted to any other. They all deserve equal respect, so far as their forms are attempts by poor mortals to give sensible representation to the Kingdom of God on earth, but equal blame as well, when (in a visible church) they mistake the form of the representation of this idea for the thing itself.
° *Pfaffenthum*

sciousness of his powerlessness, did not immediately begin with a religion but with the servile worship of God (or gods) which, whenever it received a certain public and legal form, became a *temple service;* and it became an *ecclesiastical service* only after the moral culture of human beings gradually came to be associated with these laws: at the foundation of both lies a historical faith, until we finally begin to regard them as provisional, and we begin to see in them the symbolic representation and the means of furtherance of a pure faith of religion.

Between a *shaman* of the Tunguses and the European prelate who rules over both church and state, or (if, instead of the heads and leaders, we only want to look at the faithful and their ways of representation) between the wholly sensuous[p] *Wogulite,* who in the morning lays the paw of a bear skin over his head with the short prayer, "Strike me not dead!"[171] and the sublimated *Puritan* and Independent[172] in Connecticut, there certainly is a tremendous distance in the *style* of faith, but not in the *principle;* for, as regards the latter, they all equally belong to one and the same class, namely of those who place their service of God in something (faith in certain statutory articles, or the observance of certain arbitrary practices) which cannot by itself constitute a better human being. Only those whose intention is to find this service solely in the disposition to good life-conduct distinguish themselves from those others by crossing over into an entirely different principle, one exalted[q] far above the other, namely the principle whereby they profess themselves members of a (invisible) church which encompasses all right-thinking people within itself and alone, in virtue of its essential composition, can be the true church universal.

The one aim which they all have in common is to steer to their advantage the invisible power which presides over human destiny; they are of different minds only over how to go about it. If they hold that power to be an intelligent being and, therefore, attribute to him a will from which they await their lot, their effort can then be directed only to the choice of the manner in which, as beings subject to his will, they can become pleasing to him through their doings or nondoings. If they think of him as a moral being, then their own reason will easily persuade them that the condition of earning his favor must be their morally good life-conduct, especially the pure disposition which is the subjective principle of the latter. Yet it is 6:177
possible that the highest being may perhaps wish, in addition, to be served in a manner which we cannot recognize through mere reason, namely through actions in which, on their own, we cannot indeed detect anything moral but which we arbitrarily take upon ourselves nonetheless, either because commanded by him, or else in order to attest our submissiveness to him, and which, in either mode of procedure, if they constitute a whole

[p] *sinnlichen*
[q] *erhabenen*

of systematically ordered activities, would thus establish a *service* of God in general. – Now if the two are to be joined, then either we must accept each as a direct way of pleasing God or take one of them as only the instrument of the other, which is the true service of God. It is self-evident that the moral service of God (*officium liberum*)ʳ pleases him directly. We could not however recognize it as the supreme condition of all that is pleasing in the human being (as already stipulated also by the concept of morality) if it were possible to regard the services of wages (*officium mercenarium*)ˢ as well-pleasing to God *on its own;* for nobody would then know which service is to be given precedence in any given case, in order to direct our judgment regarding our duties accordingly, or how the two supplement one another. Hence actions which have no moral value in themselves will have to be accepted as well-pleasing to God only to the extent that they serve as means in the furtherance of what, with respect to them, is good unmediatedly (for morality), i.e., *for the sake of the moral service of God.*

Now the human being who makes use of actions that in themselves contain nothing well-pleasing to God as means nevertheless for gaining God's unmediated favor, and therewith the fulfillment of his wishes, is under the delusion of possessing an art of achieving a supernatural effect through entirely natural means. Attempts of this sort are normally called *sorcery,* a word for which we however wish to substitute the otherwise familiar word *fetishism* (for "sorcery" carries with it the attendant concept of commerce with the evil principle, whereas the attempts at issue can also conceivably be undertaken through misunderstanding, with good moral intent). However, the thought of a supernatural effect on the part of a human being could occur to anybody only on the supposition that he works upon God and makes use of him as a means to produce an effect in the world for which his own powers alone, yea, even his insight into whether the effect is well-pleasing to God, do not suffice. And this entails an absurdity in its very conception.

But if, in addition to what makes him the object of divine favor directly (through the active disposition to a good life-conduct), a human being seeks also by means of certain formalities to make himself *worthy* of a supplement to his impotence through supernatural assistance, and to this purpose his only intention is to make himself *receptive* to the attainment of the object of his morally good wish through observances which have indeed no unmediated value yet serve as means to the furtherance of that moral disposition, then, to be sure, he is counting on something *supernatural* to supplement his natural impotence, yet not something which is an *effect* of the *human being* (through influence upon the divine will) but

6:178

ʳ free service
ˢ mercenary service

196

something *received*, which he can hope for but not produce himself. – But if actions, which, so far as we can see, do not contain in themselves anything moral and well-pleasing to God are nevertheless intended by him to serve him as means, indeed as conditions by which to expect support for his wishes from God directly, he must then be under a delusion, namely that, although he possesses neither the physical faculty nor the moral receptivity for the supernatural, he can nevertheless bring it about through actions which are *natural*, though not in themselves at all related to morality (actions which require no disposition well-pleasing to God for their exercise, and which can therefore be performed by the most wicked human being just as well as by the best), through formulas of invocation, through professions of a servile faith, through ecclesiastical observances, and the like, and that he can thus *conjure up* as it were God's support; for between merely physical means and a morally efficacious cause there is no connection at all according to a law, of which reason can form a thought, and according to which the moral cause can be represented as determinable to certain effects through the physical means.

Whoever therefore gives precedence to the observance of statutory laws, requiring a revelation as necessary to religion, not indeed merely as a means to the moral disposition but as the objective condition for becoming well-pleasing to God directly, and whoever places the striving for a good life-conduct behind the historical faith (whereas the latter, as something which can only be well-pleasing to God *conditionally*, ought to be directed to the former, which alone pleases God *absolutely*) – whoever does this transforms the service of God into mere *fetishism;* he engages in a counterfeit service, which sets back all the work leading to true religion. So much depends, when we wish to join two good things, on the order in which we combine them! – But it is in this distinction that true *enlightenment* consists; through it does the service of God for the first time become a free and hence moral cult. If, however, the human being departs from it, the yoke of a (statutory) law will be imposed on him instead of the freedom of the children of God, and this yoke, since it is an unconditional coercion to believe in something of which we can have cognition only historically and hence cannot carry conviction with everyone, can be much more burdensome* to conscientious human beings than the whole business of

6:179

---

* "That yoke is easy, and the burden is light"[173] where the duty incumbent upon every human being can be regarded as imposed upon him by himself and through his own reason, and to this extent he takes it upon himself freely. Only moral laws, as divine commands, are however of this kind, and of them alone the founder of the pure church could say: "My commands are not grievous,"[174] for these commands do not weigh down, because everyone sees the necessity of following them on his own; hence nothing is here being forced upon him; whereas ordinances despotically imposed upon us by command, of which we cannot see any use though imposed for our best interests (yet not through our own reason), are like vexations (drudgery) to which we subject ourselves only because forced to. In themselves,

piously ordained observances could ever be, for the celebration of these observances is enough to be in harmony with an established ecclesiastical community without anyone needing to profess either inwardly or outwardly that he believes them to be part of an order *founded by God*, for it is by this profession that conscience is really harassed.

Priestcraft is therefore the constitution of a church to the extent that a *fetish-service* is the rule; and this always obtains wherever statutory commands, rules of faith and observances, rather than principles of morality, make up the groundwork and the essence of the church. Now there are indeed many ecclesiastical forms in which the fetishism is so manifold and mechanical that it appears to drive out nearly all of morality, hence also religion, and to usurp their place, and thus borders very closely on paganism. Here, however, where worth or the lack thereof rests on the nature of one principle which binds above all others, there is no question of a more or less. If that principle imposes humble submission to a constitution as compulsory service and not rather the free homage due to the moral law *in general*, then, however few the imposed observances, let them but be declared as unconditionally necessary and it is enough for a fetish-faith through which the masses are ruled and robbed of their moral freedom through obedience to a church (not to religion). The constitution of this church (hierarchy) can be monarchical or aristocratic or democratic: this is merely a matter of organization; its constitution still is and remains under any of these forms always despotic. Where articles of faith are included in the constitutional law, a *clergy* rules which believes that it can actually dispense with reason, and ultimately with scriptural scholarship itself, because, since it is the single authoritative guardian and interpreter of the will of the invisible lawgiver, it has the exclusive authority to administer the prescriptions of faith; hence, thus equipped with this absolute power, it need not convince but *only give orders*. – Now, since apart from this clergy all that is left is the *laity* (the head of the political commonwealth not excepted), the church finally rules the state, not indeed through force, but through influence over minds, and also, in addition, through pretense of the benefit which the state could allegedly derive from the unconditional obedience to which a spiritual discipline has habituated the very *thinking* of the people. Thus the habit of hypocrisy undermines, unnoticed, the integrity and loyalty of the subjects; sharpens them in the simulation of service also in civil duties, and, like all wrongly accepted principles, brings about exactly the opposite of what was intended.

· ·
·

however, regarded in the purity of their source, the actions commanded to us through those moral laws are precisely the ones which the human being finds the hardest. We would gladly undertake the most burdensome of pious drudgery in their stead, if it were only possible to offer this in payment for them.

This is, however, the inevitable consequence of at first sight an apparently harmless transposition of the principles of the one sanctifying religious faith, for the issue was to which of the two one should concede priority of place as supreme condition (to which the other is subordinated). It is fair, it is reasonable, to assume that not just the "wise after the flesh,"[175] the learned or skilled at ratiocination, are called to this enlightenment concerning their true well-being – for the whole human race should be capable of this faith – but that rather "the foolish things of the world,"[176] even the ignorant or those most limited conceptually, must be able to lay claim to such instruction and inner conviction. Now it might indeed seem that a historical faith is precisely of this sort, especially if the concepts which it needs for expressing its message are entirely anthropological and quite suited to the senses. For what is easier than to grab and to partake with others of a narrative made so accessible to the senses and so simple, or to repeat the words of mysteries when there is absolutely no necessity to attach any meaning to them! And how easily does this sort of thing find access everywhere, especially in conjunction with the promise of a great advantage, and how deeply rooted does faith in truth of such a narrative become when the latter bases itself, moreover, upon a document long recognized as authentic, and faith in it is thus certainly suited even to the commonest human capacities! Now though news of such an event, as well as the faith in rules of conduct based on it, are not intended solely or primarily for the learned or the wise of the world, these latter are yet not excluded from them. And thus arise so many doubts, partly concerning the truth of the event, partly the sense in which its exposition is to be taken, that to accept faith in it, subjected as it would be to so many (however well intentioned) controversies, as the supreme condition of a universal and exclusively saving faith, would be the most absurd thing conceivable. – There is, on the other hand, a practical cognition which, though resting solely upon reason and not in need of any historical doctrine, yet lies as close to every human being, even the simplest, as though it had been literally inscribed in his heart – a law, which we need only name in order immediately to agree with everybody else about its authority, and which carries with it *unconditional* binding force in everyone's consciousness, namely the law of morality. And, what is more, this cognition either already leads of itself alone to faith in God, or at least determines the concept of him as that of a moral legislator, thus guiding toward a pure religious faith which is not only within the grasp of every human being but also in the highest degree worthy of respect. Indeed, it leads so naturally to this that, if one wanted to make the experiment, he would find that this faith can be elicited from every human being, upon questioning, in its entirety, without any of it having ever been taught to him. It is, therefore, not only an act of prudence to begin with this faith, and to let a historical faith consistent with it follow after it, but also duty to make it the

6:181

6:182

supreme condition under which alone we can hope to partake of whatever salvation a historical faith might ever promise, in such a way indeed that we can and may concede validity to the latter as universally binding only according to the interpretation given to it by pure religious faith (because it contains universally valid doctrine), whereas the moral believer still is always open to historical faith to the extent that he finds it beneficial to the vitality of his pure religious disposition; only in this way does this historical faith have a pure moral worth: because it is free and not coerced through any threat (for then it can never be sincere).

But even when the service of God in a church is preeminently directed to the pure moral veneration of God according to the laws prescribed to humanity in general, we can yet ask whether, in the church in question, the *doctrine of divine blessedness* alone or the pure *doctrine of virtue* as well, each separately, should make up the content of the religious instruction. The first of these designations, namely the *doctrine of divine blessedness*, perhaps best expresses the meaning of the word *religio* (as understood nowadays) in an objective sense.

Divine blessedness comprises two determinations of the moral disposition in relation to God. The *fear* of God is this disposition in obedience to his commands from *imposed* duty (the duty of a subject), i.e. from respect for the law. The *love* of God is instead [obedience] from one's own *free choice* and from pleasure in the law (from the duty of a child). Both contain, therefore, over and above morality, the concept of a supersensible being endowed with the properties required for the attainment of the highest good which is aimed at through morality but transcends our faculties. And the concept of the *nature* of this being, whenever we go beyond the moral relation of his idea to us, is always in danger of being thought by us anthropomorphically and hence in a manner often directly prejudicial 6:183 to our ethical principles. Its idea cannot therefore stand on its own in speculative reason but bases its very origin, and more still its force, entirely on its reference to our self-subsistent determination to duty. Now, which is more natural in the first instruction of youth, or also in the ministration of the pulpit: to expound the doctrine of virtue ahead of the doctrine of divine blessedness, or that of divine blessedness ahead of the doctrine of virtue (perhaps even without mentioning the latter at all)? The two obviously stand in necessary connection with each other. This is not however possible, since they are not *of one kind,* except [in this way]: one must be conceived and expounded as end and the other merely as means. But the doctrine of virtue stands on its own (even without the concept of God); the doctrine of divine blessedness contains the concept of an object which we represent to ourselves, with reference to our morality, as a cause supplementing our incapacity with respect to the final moral end. Hence divine blessedness cannot of itself constitute the final end of moral striving but can only serve as a means of strengthening what in itself makes for a better human being, [i.e.] virtuous disposition; and this it does by holding out to this striving and guaranteeing for it (as striving after goodness, even after holiness) the expectation of the final end for which it is itself powerless. The concept of virtue, by contrast, is derived from the soul of the human being. It is already within him in full, though undeveloped, and, unlike the concept of religion, is not in need of ratiocination through inferences. In the purity of this concept; in the awakening to consciousness of a capacity otherwise never surmised by us, of being able to become master over the greatest obstacles within us; in the dignity of the humanity which the human being must respect in his own person and personal vocation, and which he strives to achieve – there is in this something that so uplifts the soul, and so leads it to the very Deity, which is worthy of adoration only in virtue of his holiness and as the legislator of virtue, that the human being, even when still far removed from allowing this concept the power of influencing his maxims, is yet not unwiling to be supported by it. For through this idea he already feels himself to a degree ennobled, whereas the concept of a world ruler, who makes of this duty a commandment for us, still lies far removed from him, and, were he to begin with it, he would run the risk of dashing his courage (which is an essential component of virtue) and of transforming divine blessedness into a fawning slavish subjection to the commands of a despotic might. The courage to stand on one's own feet is itself strengthened through the doctrine of   6:184 atonement which follows from it. For this doctrine represents what cannot be altered as wiped out, and opens up for the path to a new conduct of life; whereas, when the doctrine is made to come first, the futile endeavor to render undone what has been done (expiation), the fear concerning the imputation of expiation, the representation of our total incapacity for the good, and the anxiety lest we slip back into evil, must take the courage away from the human being,* and must reduce him to a state of groaning

---

* The different kinds of faith among peoples gradually impart to the latter a character which also distinguishes them externally in their civic bond, and is later attributed to them as though it were a generalized temperamental trait. Thus in its first establishment Judaism drew upon itself the charge of *misanthropy*, for a people was to cut itself off from all other peoples and avoid intermingling with them by means of every conceivable – and in some cases painful – observance. Mohammedanism is distinguished by its *pride*, because it finds confirmation of its faith in victories and in the subjugation of many peoples rather than in miracles, and because its devotional practices are all of a fierce kind. †The Hindu faith gives its adherents the character of *pusillanimity*, for reasons directly opposite to those just mentioned. – Now surely it is not because of the inner nature of the Christian faith, but because of the manner in which people's minds are introduced to it, that a similar charge can be brought against it with respect to those who are the most serious about it but who, starting with human corruption and despairing of all virtue, place their religious principle solely in *piety* (by which is understood the principle of conducting oneself passively in view of the divine blessedness expected through a power from above). For these [individuals] never place any reliance in themselves but constantly look about them in constant anxiety for a

6:185 moral passivity where nothing great and good is undertaken but instead everything is expected from wishing for it. – As regards moral disposition, everything depends upon the highest concept to which the human being subordinates his duties. If reverence for God comes first, and the human being therefore subordinates virtue to it, then this object [of reverence] is an *idol*, i.e. it is thought as a being whom we may hope to please not through morally upright conduct in this world but through adoration and ingratiation; religion is then idolatry. Thus divine blessedness is not a surrogate for virtue, a way of avoiding it, but its completion, for the sake of crowning it with the hope of the final success of all our good ends.

§ 4
CONCERNING THE GUIDING THREAD OF
CONSCIENCE IN MATTERS OF FAITH

The question here is not, how conscience is to be guided (for conscience does not need any guide; to have a conscience suffices), but how conscience itself can serve as guiding thread in the most perplexing moral decisions. –

Conscience is a consciousness which is of itself' a duty. But how can we think such a consciousness, when the consciousness of all our representations seems to be necessary only for logical purposes, hence only conditionally, whenever we want to clarify our representation; hence cannot be unconditional duty?

It is a moral principle, requiring no proof, that we *ought to venture*

---

supernatural assistance, and even think that in this self-contempt (which is not humility) they possess a means of obtaining favor. The outward expression of this (in pietism or false piety) is indeed a sign of a *slavish* cast of mind.

† This remarkable phenomenon (of an ignorant though intelligent people's pride in its faith) may also have its origin from the fancy of its founder that he alone had once again restored in the world the concept of God's unity and of his supersensible nature – a concept which would have indeed ennobled his people by freeing it from the subjugation to images and the anarchy of polytheism if he could with justice credit himself with this contribution. – Concerning the characteristic of the third class of religious fellowship, which is based upon a badly understood humility, the abatement of self-conceit in the evaluation of one's own moral worth through confrontation with the holiness of the law should not bring about contempt for oneself but rather the resolution to bring ourselves ever nearer to conformtiy to

6:185 that law according to this noble predisposition in us. Virtue, which truly consists in the courage for this, has instead been relegated to paganism as a name already suspect of self-conceit, and in opposition to it the grovelling courting of favor is being extolled. – *False devotion (bigotterie, devotio spuria)* is the habit of placing the exercise of piety, not in actions well-pleasing to God (in the fulfillment of human duties) but in direct commerce with God through manifestations of awe; this exercise must thus be counted as *compulsory service (opus operatum)*, except that to superstition it adds also the delusion of allegedly supersensible (heavenly) feelings.

' *für sich selbst*

nothing where there is danger that it might be wrong (quod dubitas, ne feceris![u]   6:186
Pliny).*[177]* So the *consciousness* that an action *which I want to undertake* is
right, is unconditional duty. Now it is understanding, not conscience,
which judges whether an action is in general right or wrong. And it is not
absolutely necessary to know, of all possible actions, whether they are
right or wrong. With respect to the action that *I* want to undertake,
however, I must not only judge, and be of the opinion, that it is right; I
must also be *certain* that it is. And this is a requirement of conscience to
which is opposed *probabilism,* i.e., the principle that the mere opinion that
an action may well be right is itself sufficient for undertaking it. – *[178]*
Conscience could also be defined as *the moral faculty of judgment, passing
judgment upon itself,* except that this definition would be much in need of
prior clarification of the concepts contained in it. Conscience does not
pass judgment upon actions as cases that stand under the law, for this is
what reason does so far as it is subjectively practical (whence the *casus
conscientiæ* and casuistry, as a kind of dialectic of conscience). Rather, here
reason judges itself, whether it has actually undertaken, with all diligence,
that examination of actions (whether they are right or wrong), and it calls
upon the human being himself to witness *for* or *against* himself whether
this has taken place or not.

Take, for instance, an inquisitor who clings fast to the exclusiveness
of his statutory faith even to the point, if need be, of martyrdom, and
who has to pass judgment upon a so-called heretic (otherwise a good
citizen) charged with unbelief. Now I ask: if he condemns him to death,
whether we can say that he has passed judgment according to his conscience (though erroneous), or whether we can rather accuse him of
plain *lack of conscience;* whether he simply erred or consciously did wrong;
since we can always tell him outright that in such a situation he could
not have been entirely certain that he was not perhaps doing wrong. He
was indeed presumably firm in the belief that a supernaturally revealed
divine will (perhaps according to the saying, *compellite intrare*)*[v][179]* permitted him, if not even made a duty for him, to extirpate supposed unbelief
together with the unbelievers. But was he really as strongly convinced of
such a revealed doctrine, and also of its meaning, as is required for
daring to destroy a human being on its basis? That to take a human
being's life because of his religious faith is wrong is certain, unless (to   6:187
allow the most extreme possibility) a divine will, made known to the
inquisitor in some extraordinary way, has decreed otherwise. But that
God has ever manifested this awful will is a matter of historical documentation and never apodictically certain. After all, the revelation reached
the inquisitor only through the intermediary of human beings and their

---

[u] do not do what you are doubtful about
[v] compel them to come in

203

interpretation, and even if it were to appear to him to have come from God himself (like the command issued to Abraham to slaughter his own son like a sheep),[180] yet it is at least possible that on this point error has prevailed. But then the inquisitor would risk the danger of dong something which would be to the highest degree wrong, and on this score he acts unconscientiously. – Now such is the situation with every historical or phenomenal faith, namely that the *possibility* is always there of coming across an error; consequently it is unconscientious to act upon it, granted this possibility that what it requires or permits is perhaps wrong, i.e. at the risk of violating a human duty in itself certain.

More still: even if an action commanded by such a positive (allegedly) revealed law were in itself allowed, the question yet arises whether, in accordance with their presumed conviction, spiritual authorities or teachers may impose it upon the people to profess it as an *article of faith* (on penalty of forfeiting their status). Since conviction in this matter has no other grounds of proof except historical ones, and in the judgment of the people (if they just subject themselves to the least test) there always is the absolute possibility that an error has crept into these [proofs] or in their classical interpretation, the cleric would be compelling the people to profess as true, at least inwardly, as though it were a matter of their belief in God, i.e. as if in his presence, something which they however do not know with certainty to be such; for instance, to recognize the allocation of a certain day for the periodic public promotion of divine blessedness as part of a religion directly commanded by God; or to profess firm belief in a mystery which they do not even understand. Here the people's spiritual authority would himself be acting against his conscience, by forcing upon others a belief in something of which he cannot himself be ever wholly convinced; therefore he should consider well what he is doing, for he must answer for all the abuse arising from such servile faith. – Thus there can perhaps be truth in what is believed, yet at the same time untruthfulness in the belief (or even in the purely inward profession of it), and this is in itself damnable.

6:188   Although, as noted above,[181] human beings who have made but the slightest beginning in freedom of thought,* for they previously were un-

---

* I admit that I am not comfortable with this way of speaking, which even clever men are wont to use: "A certain people (intent on establishing civil freedom) is not ripe for freedom"; "The bondmen of a landed proprietor are not yet ripe for freedom"; and so too, "People are in general not yet ripe for freedom of belief." For on this assumption freedom will never come, since we cannot *ripen* to it if we are not already established in it (we must be free in order to be able to make use of our powers purposively in freedom). To be sure, the first attempts will be crude, and in general also bound to greater hardships and dangers than when still under the command but also the care of others; yet we do not ripen to freedom otherwise than through our *own* attempts (and we must be free to be allowed to make them). I raise no objections if those in power, being constrained by the circumstances of the time, put

der a slavish yoke of faith (e.g. the Protestants), immediately consider themselves ennobled as it were the less they need to believe (of what is positive and belongs to priestly precepts), the very reverse holds of those who have not been capable of, or have not willed, any attempt of this kind; for this is their principle: It is advisable to believe too much rather than too little. For what we do over and above what we owe does at least no harm and might even perhaps help. – Upon this delusion, which makes of dishonesty in religious professions a fundamental principle (to which it is all the easier to commit oneself, since religion makes good every mistake, consequently also that of dishonesty) is based the so-called security maxim in matters of fatih (*argumentum a tuto*):*ᵂ* If what I profess regarding God is true, I have hit the mark; if not true but not something in itself otherwise forbidden, I have merely believed it superfluously, and though this was of course not necessary, I have only burdened myself perhaps with an inconvenience which is no crime. The danger arising from the dishonesty of his pretension – *the violation of conscience* in proclaiming as certain, even before God, something of which he is yet conscious that, its nature being what it is, cannot be asserted with unconditional confidence – this *the hypocrite regards as a mere nothing.* – The genuine maxim of safety, alone consistent with religion, is exactly the reverse: Whatever, as means or condition of blessedness, can be made [object of] my cognition not through my own reason but only through revelation, and can be introduced into my profession solely through the intermediary of a historical faith, for the rest does not however contradict the pure principles of morality – this I cannot indeed believe and assert as certain, but just as little can I reject it as certainly false. At the same time, without determining anything in this regard, I count on the fact that whatever saving content it may have, it will come to good for me only so far as I do not render myself unworthy of it through a defect of the moral disposition in a good life-conduct. In this maxim is true moral safety, namely safety before conscience (and more cannot be required of a human being); by contrast, the greatest danger and unsafety attend the supposedly prudential device of craftily avoiding the detrimental consequences which might befall me from withholding profession, for by holding out for both parties I spoil my standing with both. –

6:189

Let the author of a creed or the teacher of a church, indeed; let every

---

off relinquishing these three bonds far, very far, into the future. But to make it a principle that those who are once subjected to them are essentially not suited to freedom, and that one is justified in keeping them from it for all time, this is an intrusion into the prerogatives of Divinity itself, which created human beings for freedom. It certainly is more convenient to rule in state, household, and church, if one succeeds in imposing such a principle. But is it also more just?
ᵂ argument from security

human being, so far as he inwardly stands by the conviction that certain propositins are divinely revealed, ask himself: Do you really dare to avow the truth of these propositions in the sight of him who scrutinizes the heart, and at the risk of relinquishing all that is valuable and holy to you? I would have to have a very unfavorable conception of human nature (which is, after all, at least not altogether incapable of good) not to suppose that

6:190 even the boldest teacher of the faith must quake at the question.* But if this is so, how does it accord with conscientiousness to insist nevertheless on such a declaration of faith, which admits of no restriction, and to pass off the presumptuousness of such avowals even as a duty and service to God, when the freedom of human beings which is absolutely required for everything moral (such as the adoption of a religion) is thereby being totally trampled under foot, and no place is even left for the good will which says: "Lord, I believe; help thou mine unbelief!"[181†]

General remark

Whatever good the human being can do on his own, according to the laws of freedom, as compared with the faculty available to him only through supernatural help, can be called *nature*, in distinction from *grace*. Not that by the former expression we understand a physical property distinct from freedom; rather, we use it only because we at least have cognition of the *laws* of this faculty (the laws of *virtue*) and, on the *analogy of nature*, reason

---

*† The very man who has the temerity to say: He who does not believe in this or that historical doctrine as a precious truth, *that one is damned,* would also have to be ready to say: If what I am now relating to you is not true, *let me be damned!* – Were there anyone capable of such a dreadful declaration, I should advise dealing with him according to the Persian proverb concerning a *hadji:* If someone has been in Mecca once (as a pilgrim), leave the house where he dwells with you; if he has been there twice, leave the street where he resides; and if he has been there three times, then leave the city, or even the land, where he lives![182]
†† *Oh sincerity!* You Astræa,[184] who have fled from the earth to heaven, how are you (the foundation of conscience, and hence of all inner religion) to be drawn down from there to us again? I can admit, though it is much to be deplored, that straightforwardness (saying the *whole* known truth) is not to be found in human nature. But we must be able to demand *sincerity* (that *everything said* be said with truthfulness) of every human being, and if in our nature there were no predisposition to it, whose cultivation is only being neglected, the human race would have to be in its own eyes an object of deepest contempt. This required quality of the mind is one, however, exposed to many temptations, and costs many a sacrifice, and hence also calls for moral strength, i.e. virtue (which must be earned), yet must be guarded and cultivated earlier than any other, for the opposite propensity is the hardest to extirpate if it is just allowed to take root. – Now contrast with it our manner of upbringing, especially in matters of religion or, better, doctrines of faith, where fidelity of memory in answering questions concerning them, without regard for fidelity of profession (which is never put to the test), is accepted as already sufficient to make a believer of him who does not understand even what he professes as holy, and one will no longer wonder at the lack of sincerity that produces nothing but inward hypocrites.

thus possesses a visible and comprehensible clue to it. On the other hand, whether, if and when, or how much, *grace* has effect on us – this remains totally hidden to us, and in this matter, as in general in all things supernatural (to which morality, as *holiness*, belongs), reason is bereft of any information of the laws according to which it might occur.

The concept of a supernatural intervention into our moral though deficient faculty, and even into our not totally purified or at least weak disposition, to satisfy our duty in full – this is a transcendent concept, merely in the idea of whose reality no experience can assure us. – But even to accept it as idea for a purely practical intent is very risky and hard to reconcile with reason; for what is to be accredited to us as morally good conduct must take place not through foreign influence but through the use of our own powers. Yet its impossibility (that the two may not occur side by side) cannot be proven either, since freedom itself, though not containing anything supernatural in its concept, remains just as incomprehensible to us according to its possibility as the supernatural [something] we might want to assume as surrogate for the independent yet deficient determination of freedom.

But since we are at least acquainted with* the (moral) *laws* of freedom according to which the latter is to be determined, whereas of a supernatural assistance – whether a certain moral strength perceivable in us in fact comes from it, or also on what occasions, and under what conditions this is to be expected – we can have not the least cognition,* so apart from the general presupposition that grace will work in us what nature cannot if we have just made use of that nature (i.e., of our own forces) according to possibility, we cannot make any further use of this idea at all, neither for determining how (over and above the constant striving for a good life-conduct) we might draw down upon us the cooperation of this grace, nor on what occasions we might expect it. – This ideal totally escapes us; and it is, moreover, salutary to keep ourselves at a respectful distance from it, as from a sacred thing, lest, under the delusion that we do miracles ourselves, or that we perceive miracles in us, we render ourselves unfit for all use of reason, or let ourselves be tempted into a state of inertia where in passive idleness we expect from above what we ought to be seeking within us.

Now *means* are all the intermediate causes which the human being *has within his power*, whereby to effect a certain intent. But there is no other means (nor can there be any) by which to become worthy of heavenly assistance, except the earnest endeavor to improve his moral nature in all possible ways, thereby making himself capable of receiving a nature fully fit – as is not in his power – for divine approval, since the expected divine

---

* *kennen*
* *erkennen*

assistance itself has only his morality for its aim. That the impure human being would not seek this assistance here but rather in certain sensuous practices[z] (which certainly are within his power but cannot on their own make him a better human being, yet this is what in some supernatural way they are to effect) was indeed already to be expected *a priori*, and so it also happens in fact. The concept of a so-called *means of grace*, though self-contradictory (according to what has just been said), still serves here as a means of self-deception, which is as common as it is detrimental to true religion.

The true (moral) service of God, which the faithful must render as subjects belonging to his kingdom but no less also as its citizens (under laws of freedom), is itself just as invisible as the kingdom, i.e. it is a *service of the heart* (in spirit and truth), and can consist only in the disposition of obedience to all true duties as divine commands, not in actions determined exclusively for God. Yet for the human being the invisible needs to be represented through something visible (sensible), indeed what is more, it must be accompanied by the visible for the sake of praxis[a] and, though intellectual, made as it were an object of intuition (according to a certain analogy); and although this is only a means of making intuitive for ourselves our duty in the service of God – to be sure an indispensable means yet at the same time one subject to the danger of misconstruction – yet, through a *delusion* which creeps upon us, it is easily taken for the *service of God* itself and is also commonly given this name.

This alleged service of God, when brought back to its spirit and its true meaning, namely, to a disposition ordained to the kingdom of God within us and outside us, can be divided, even by reason, into four observances of duty; and certain formalities, which do not stand in necessary connection with them, have however been appointed to correspond to them, because these formalities have from antiquity been found to be good sensible intermediaries that serve as schemata for the duties, thus awakening and sustaining our attention to the true service of God. They are based, one and all, upon the aim of promoting the moral good: (1) of establishing *this good firmly within us*, and repeatedly to awaken in our heart the disposition for it (private prayer); (2) of *propagating* it *externally* through public assembly on days legally consecrated thereto, in order that religious doctrines and wishes (together with dispositions of the same kind) be loudly proclaimed and thereby fully shared (church-going); (3) of *transmitting* it to posterity through the reception of new members joining the fellowship of faith, it being a duty also to instruct them in this faith (in the Christian religion, *baptism*); (4) of *maintaining this fellowship* through repeated public formalities which stabilize the union of its members into an ethical body –

6:193

---

[z] *sinnlichen Veranstaltungen*
[a] *des Praktischen*

this, according to the principle of the mutual equality of the members' rights and their sharing in all the fruits of moral goodness (communion).

Every beginning in religious matters, when not undertaken in a purely moral spirit but as a means *in itself* capable of propitiating God and thus, through him, of satisfying all our wishes, is a *fetish-faith*. This is the persuasion that what cannot effect a certain thing, either according to *nature* or the moral laws of reason, will through it alone nonetheless effect the thing wished for, if only we firmly believe that it will indeed effect it, and we accompany our belief with certain formalities. Even where the conviction has already taken hold that everything in these matters depends on the moral good, which can originate only in action, the sensuous[b] human being still searches for an escape route by which to circumvent that arduous condition; namely that if only he observes *the custom* (the formalities), God will surely accept that for the act itself, and this would of course have to be called an instance of God's superabundant grace, were it not rather a grace dreamed up in slothful trust, or itself perhaps an instance of hypocritical trust. Thus in every type of public faith the human being has devised certain practices for himself, as *means of grace*, even though such practices are not related in all faiths, as in the Christian, to practical concepts and to dispositions conformable to them. (For instance, of the five great commands of the Mohammedan faith – washing, praying, fasting, almsgiving, and the pilgrimage to Mecca – almsgiving alone would deserve to be excepted, if it occurred from a truly virtuous and at the same time religious disposition to human duty, and would thus also truly deserve to be regarded as a means of grace; but in fact, since in this faith alsmgiving can well coexist with the extortion from others of things which are offered to God in the person of the poor, it does not deserve to be thus exempted.)

6:194

Specifically there can be three kinds of *delusory faith* in overstepping the boundaries of our reason with respect to the supernatural (which according to the laws of reason is neither an object of theoretical or practical use). *First*, the belief that we have cognition of something through experience which we in fact cannot accept as happening according to objective laws of experience (faith *in miracles*). *Second*, the delusion that we must include among our concepts of reason, as necessary to what is morally best for us, that of which we ourselves can form no concept through reason (faith *in mysteries*). *Third*, the delusion that through the use of purely natural means we can bring about an effect which is a mystery to us, namely the influence of God upon our morality (faith in *means of grace*). – We have already dealt with the first two of these forms of fictitious faith in the General Remarks at the end of the two immediately preceding parts of this work. It still remains for us, therefore, to treat of the means of grace (which are further distinguished from the *effects of*

[b] *sinnlich*

209

grace,* i.e. supernatural moral influences to which we are merely passively related; to pretend to experience these influences is, however, an enthusiastic delusion pertaining merely to feeling).

1. *Praying,* conceived as an *inner ritual* service of God and hence as a means of grace, is a superstitious delusion (a fetish-making); for it only is the *declaring of a wish* to a being who has no need of any declaration regarding the inner disposition of the wisher, through which nothing is therefore accomplished nor is any of the duties incumbent on us as commands of God discharged; hence God is not really served. A sincere 6:195 wish to please God in all our doings and nondoings, i.e. the disposition, accompanying all our actions, to pursue these as though they occurred in the service of God, is the *spirit of prayer,* and this can and ought to be in us "without ceasing."[185] But to clothe† this wish in words and formulas

---

*† See General Remark at the end of *Part One.*

† In that wish, which is the spirit of prayer, the human being only seeks to work upon himself (to give life to his dispositions by means of the *idea of God*), whereas in the other, where he declares himself in words, hence externally, he seeks to work *upon* God. In the first sense of prayer can be offered with perfect sincerity, even though a human being does not pretend to be capable of asserting God's existence as wholly certain; in the second form, as an *address,* a human being assumes that this supreme object is present in person, or at least he poses (even inwardly) as though he were convinced of its presence, reckoning that, suppose this is not so, his posing can at least do no harm but might rather gain him favor; hence sincerity cannot be found in as perfect a form in this latter (verbal) prayer as it can in the former (the pure spirit of prayer). – Anyone will find the truth of this last remark confirmed if he imagines a pious and well-meaning individual, but one otherwise limited with respect to these purified religious concepts, being caught unawares by somebody else, I do not say praying aloud, but gesturing in a way which indicates praying. Everyone will naturally expect, without my saying so, that this individual will fall into confusion or embarrassment, as though caught in a situation of which he should be ashamed. But why? Because a human being found talking to himself immediately gives rise to the suspicion that he is having a slight fit of madness; and so we would also judge him (not altogether unjustly) if, though alone, we find him occupied in practices or gestures that we expect only of one who sees somebody else before him, whereas this is not the case in the adduced example. – The teacher of the gospel, however, has superbly expressed the spirit of prayer in a formula that at once renders prayer dispensable and by the same token itself as well (as a verbal formula). One finds nothing in it but the resolution to good life-conduct which, combined with the consciousness of our frailty, carries with it the standing wish to be a worthy member in the Kingdom of God; hence contains no actual request for something that God in his wisdom might perhaps refuse but a wish instead which, if earnest (efficacious), will itself bring about its objective (to become a human being well-pleasing to God). Even the wish for the means of preserving our existence for one day (the wish for bread), since it is explicitly not directed to the continuance of that existence but is only the effect of a merely felt animal need, is more an admission of what *nature wills* in us than a specially considered request for what the human being *wills* – the kind which would be for bread for another day, which is clearly enough excluded here. – 6:196 Only the kind of prayer made in moral disposition (animated only through the idea of God), since as the spirit of prayer it itself brings about its object (to be well-pleasing to God), can be made in *faith,* by which we mean no more than the assurance in us that the prayer *can be answered;* but nothing in us except morality is of this kind. For even if the request did not go

(though it be only inwardly) can, at best, only carry with it the value of a means for the continual stimulation of that disposition within us; it can- 6:196 not, however, have any direct reference to divine satisfaction, and just because of this it also cannot be duty for everyone. For a means can be 6:197

further than today's bread, nobody can yet be assured that it can be answered, i.e. that its being granted to the petitioner is necessarily bound to God's wisdom; it might perhaps better conform to this wisdom that a human being be allowed to die on this day for lack of bread. It is, further, an absurd and at the same time impudent delusion to have a try at whether, through the insistent intrusiveness of our prayer, God might not be diverted from the plan of his wisdom (to our present advantage). We cannot therefore be sure that any prayer which does not have a moral object, can be answered, i.e. we cannot pray for anything *in faith*. Indeed, even though the object may be moral yet possible only through supernatural influence (or at least such as we only expect from this source, since we have no wish to exert ourselves about it, as for example a change of heart, the putting on of the new man,[186] called rebirth), it is nonetheless so uncertain whether God will find it conformable to his wisdom to make up for our (self-incurred) deficiency supernaturally, that we rather have cause to expect the contrary. Even in this respect a human being cannot therefore pray in faith. – From this we can clarify what might be the meaning of a faith which works miracles (a faith which would still be associated with inner prayer). Since God can lend a human being no power to produce effects supernaturally (since that is a contradiction); since, on his part, according to the concepts that he forms for himself of the good ends possible in this world, a human being cannot determine how divine wisdom judges in these matters and hence cannot, by means of the wish that he nurtures in and by himself, make use of the divine power for his purposes, it follows that a gift of miracles, specifically one which is up to the human being himself whether he has it or not ("If ye had faith as a grain of mustard-seed, etc."),[187] is not, taken literally, in any way to be thought of. Such a faith, therefore, if it has to have any meaning at all, is simply an idea of the preponderance that the moral constitution of the human being, if a human being were to possess it in the full perfection pleasing to God (which he however never reaches), would have over all other moving causes which God in his supreme wisdom might have; hence a ground for being confident that, if we were or would ever become *all* that we should be and (in continued approximation) can be, nature would have to obey our wishes which, however, would in this case never be unwise.

As regards the *edification* which is the purpose of churchgoing, here too public prayer is not a means of grace but a moral solemnity, whether it be celebrated with the communal singing of the hymn of faith, or with the *address* formally directed to God through the mouth of the clergyman in the name of the whole congregation and embracing within itself every moral con- 6:197 cern of human beings. This address, since it makes these concerns visible as a public issue, where the wish of each human being should be represented as united with the wishes of all toward one and the same end (the ushering in of the Kingdom of God), not only can elevate emotions to the point of moral exaltation (whereas private prayers, since they are absolved without this sublime idea, gradually lose their influence upon the mind through habituation) but also possesses a stronger rational basis than the other[c] for clothing the moral wish, which constitutes the spirit of prayer, in the guise of a formal address, yet without any thought of evoking the presence of the supreme being, or some special power of this rhetorical figure, as means of grace. For there is a special purpose here, namely, all the more to excite the moral incentives of each individual through an external solemnity which portrays the *union of all human beings* in the shared desire for the Kingdom of God; and this cannot more appropriately be accomplished than by addressing the head of this kingdom as though he were especially present in that place.

[c] *die erstere*, i.e. private prayer

211

prescribed only to one who *needs* it for certain ends, yet hardly everyone finds this means necessary (to converse within oneself and in fact *with oneself,* though allegedly all the more comprehensibly *with God*). It is rather necessary to endeavor that, through progressive purification and elevation of the moral disposition, the spirit of prayer alone should be sufficiently stimulated within us, and that its letter (at least so far as we are concerned) should finally fall away. For the letter, like everything which is trained at a given end indirectly, rather weakens the effect of the moral idea (which, subjectively regarded, is called *devotion*). Thus the consideration of the profound wisdom of divine creation in the smallest things and of its majesty in the great whole, such as was indeed already available to human beings in the past but in more recent times has widened into the highest admiration – this consideration not only has such a power as to transport the mind into that sinking mood, called *adoration,* in which the human being is as it were nothing in his own eyes, but is also, with respect to the human moral determination, such a soul-elevating power, that in comparison words, even if they were those of King David in prayer (and David knew little of all those marvels), would have to vanish as empty sound, because the feeling arising from such a vision of the hand of God is inexpressible. – [188] Human beings are moreover prone, when disposed to religion, to transform anything in fact only connected with their personal moral improvement into a courtly service in which the expressions of humiliation and glorification are, as a rule, all the less morally felt the more verbose they are. Hence it is all the more necessary, especially in the earliest practice of prayer imposed upon children who still are in need of the letter, carefully to impress that speech (even when inwardly uttered; indeed, even the attempts to attune the mind to the comprehension of the idea of God, which is to come closer to an intuition) has here no value in itself, but the only chore is rather the enlivening of the disposition to a life-conduct well-pleasing to God, and to this [end] speech serves only as an instrument of the imagination. For otherwise all those devout attestations of awe risk producing nothing but hypocritical veneration of God instead of a practical service of him which, as such, does not consist in mere feelings.

6:198

2. *Church-going,* thought of as the solemn *general external worship of God* in a church, inasmuch as it is a sensuous*d* display to the community of believers, is not only a means valuable to each *individual* for his own *edification** but also a duty obligating them *collectively,* as citizens of a

---

* If we are looking for a meaning appropriate to this term, none is likely to be found other than that by it we understand the *moral consequence of devotion upon a subject.* Now this consequence does not consist in emotion (which as such is already comprised in the concept of devotion), though most of those who think themselves devoted (and for this reason are
d sinnlich

divine state which is to be represented here on earth; provided, that this   6:199
church does not contain formalities that might lead to idolatry and can
thus burden the conscience, e.g. certain forms of adoration of God personified as infinite goodness under the name of a human being, for such
sensuous[j] portrayal of God is contrary to the command of reason: "*Thou
shalt not make unto thee any graven image,* etc."[191] But to wish to use it as in
itself a *means of grace,* as though God were directly served by it and had
attached special *graces* to the celebration of these solemnities (which are
mere sensuous[k] representations of the *universality* of religion), is a delusion which might indeed suit the mentality of a good *citizen* in a *political
community,* and external propriety, yet not only contributes nothing to the
quality of the citizen as *citizen in the Kingdom of God* but rather debases it
and serves to hide under a deceptive veneer, from the eyes of others and
even from his own, the bad moral content of his disposition.

    3. The one-time solemn *initiation* into the church-community, i.e. the
first reception *of a member into a church* (in the Christian church through
baptism), is a solemnity rich in meaning which imposes grave obligations
either upon the initiate, if he is himself in a position to profess his faith, or
upon the witnesses who take upon themselves the care of his education in it;
it has something holy for its end (the formation of a human being as a citizen
in a divine state) but is not, in itself, a holy action performed by others
effecting holiness and receptivity for divine grace in this subject, hence not
a *means of grace,* however extravagant in the early Greek Church was its
reputation of being capable of washing away all sins at once – a delusion
that openly betrayed its ties to an almost more than pagan superstition.

    4. The oft-repeated solemn ritual of *renewal, continuation,* and *propaga-
tion of this church-community* under the laws of *equality (communion),* which

---

also called *sanctimonious*)[e] put it entirely there; hence the word *edification* must signify the
consequence that devotion has upon the actual improvement of the human being. But this
improvement will not obtain unless the human being systematically sets to work, lays firm
principles deep in his heart in accordance with well-understood concepts, erects thereupon
dispositions appropriate to the relative importance of the duties connected with these principles, strengthens them and secures them against the attack of the inclinations and, as it were,
builds up[f] a new man as a *temple of God.*[189] One can easily see that this construction can
progress but slowly; yet it must at least be possible to see that something has been *performed.*
But human beings believe themselves to be duly *edified*[g] (through listening or reading or
singing) while absolutely nothing has been *built,*[h] indeed, when hand has yet to be put to the
work, presumably because they hope that that moral edifice[i] will rise up of itself, like the
walls of Thebes, to the music of sighs and of ardent wishes.[190]

[e] *Andächtler;* cf. *Andächtig* = devoted
[f] *erbaut*
[g] *erbaut*
[h] *gebaut*
[i] *Gebäude*
[j] *sinnlich*
[k] *sinnlich*

after the example of the founder of such a church (and at the same time in memory of him) may well assume the form of a ritual communal partaking at the same table, has in it something great which expands people's narrow, selfish and intolerant cast of mind, especially in religious matters, to

6:200 the idea of a cosmopolitan *moral community,* and it is a good means of enlivening a community to the moral disposition of brotherly love which it represents. But to boast that God has attached special graces to the celebration of this solemn ritual, and to incorporate among the articles of faith the proposition that the ritual, though a purely ecclesiastical action, is in addition a *means of grace* – this is a delusion of religion which cannot but work counter to the spirit of religion – *Priestcraft* would thus be, in general, the dominion which the clergy has usurped over minds by pretending to have exclusive possession of the means of grace.

. .

All such artificially induced self-deceptions in religious matters have a common ground. Of the divine moral properties – holiness, mercy, and justice – the human being normally appeals directly to the second in order to avoid the forbidding condition of conforming to the requirements of the first. It is arduous to be a good *servant* (here one always hears only talk of duties); hence the human being would rather be a *favorite,* for much is then forgiven him, or, where duty has been too grossly offended against, everything is again made good through the intercession of some one else who is favored in the highest degree, while he still remains the undisciplined servant[1] he always was. But, in order to satisfy himself with some show of likelihood that this plan of his is workable, he usually transfers his conception of a human being (his faults included) over to the Divinity; and so, just as among the best *rulers of our race* legislative rigor, benevolent grace and scrupulous justice do not work their moral effect upon the actions of the subject separately and each on its own (as they should), but they rather tend to *blend* together in the mind of the human sovereign as he renders his decisions, hence one need only try to get the better of one of these properties, [namely] the fallible wisdom of the human will, to bring the other into compliance: so too does the human being hope to achieve the same thing with God by appealing exclusively to his *grace.* (For this reason the separation in thought of the properties of God, or rather of his relations to the human being, through the idea of a threefold personality, on whose analogy that separation is apparently to be thought, was

6:201 important also for religion, in order to make each relation knowable as distinct.) To this end the human being busies himself with every formality he can think of, to give sign of how much he *respects* the divine commands, in order that it will not be necessary for him to *observe* them. And, that his

[1] *der lose Knecht*

214

ineffective wishes may also serve to compensate for the disobedience of these commands, he cries out, "Lord! Lord!" in order that it will not be necessary for him to "do the will of his heavenly Father."[192] And so, he construes a concept of the solemn rituals surrounding the use of certain means for enlivening truly practical dispositions as though they were means of grace in themselves; he even makes out the belief that that's what they are as itself an essential element of religion (the common man: even the whole of religion) and leaves it up to the all-gracious Providence to make a better human being of him, while he busies himself with *piety* (which is a passive respect of the divine law) rather than with *virtue* (which is the deployment of one's forces in the observance of the duty which he respects), though in fact it is this virtue, *combined with piety,* which alone can constitute the idea we understand by the word *divine blessedness* (true *religious disposition*). – If the delusion of this supposed favorite of heaven reaches heights of enthusiasm, to the point of imagining that he feels the special effects of faith within him (or even has the impertinence of trusting in a supposed hidden *familiarity* with God), virtue finally becomes loathsome to him and an object of contempt. No wonder, then, that the complaint is to be heard publicly, that religion still contributes all too little to the improvement of human beings, and that the inner light ("under a bushel")[193] of these chosen individuals fails also to shine forth outwardly, through good works. And indeed, by comparison with other naturally honest human beings who carry their religion without fuss, not as substitute for but as a furtherance of the virtuous disposition which manifests its efficacy in a good life-conduct, it fails to shine forth *pre-eminently* (as we could well demand in view of their pretensions). Yet the teacher of the Gospel has himself put into our hands these external evidences of external experience as a touchstone by which we can recognize human beings, and each of them can recognize himself, by their fruits. But thus far we cannot see how those who, in their opinion, have been exceptionally favored (the elect) might in the slightest outdo the naturally honest human beings, who can be relied upon in daily affairs, in business and in need; on the contrary, taken as a whole, they can hardly withstand comparison with him, which proves that the right way to advance is not from grace to virtue but rather from virtue to grace.

6:202

The end of all things

Translator's introduction

Das Ende aller Dinge was first published in June 1794 in the *Berlinische Monatschrift* 23, pp. 495–522.

By 1792 J. E. Biester, editor of the *Berlinische Monatschrift*, had moved his publication to Jena to avoid the Prussian religious censors. On April 10, 1794, Kant wrote him criticizing the political philosophy of the Hanover conservative August Rehberg and connecting it with the censorship activities of Hermes and Hillmer, who "have taken their positions as overseers of secondary schools and have thereby acquired influence over the universities with respect to how and what is supposed to be taught there." Then he abruptly ends the letter with this final paragraph: "The essay I will send you soon is entitled 'The End of All Things,' which will be partly plaintive and partly funny to read" (AK 11:496–7).

Having endured the difficulties with the censors in getting the *Religion* published, Kant's outlook was anything but sanguine regarding the prospects for free thought and discussion of religious topics in Prussia. "The End of All Things" is a plea for Christians to be true to what is best in their religion by adopting a "liberal" way of thinking; but because it is a plea directed at the Prussian religious authorities, it is one Kant expects to fall on deaf ears. Thus it is couched in the form of a sly, bitter satire, which approaches its political theme only indirectly.

Chiliastic imagery was common at the time. It was used not only by enthusiasts such as Lavater, but also by rationalists, and by the French revolutionaries in particular, who pictured themselves as ushering in a new world by enthroning reason. Kant's aim, as usual, is to bring chiliastic speculation within the bounds of reason. His criticism of those who would meddle in God's affairs is a more or less open criticism of the orthodox in Prussia, who were trying to impose their vision of religious truth by political means. But the choice of the end of the world as his topic might also be seen simply as a way for Kant to express an attitude of black despair regarding the immediate prospects in Prussia for free communication and enlightened education in matters of religion.

In the essay's final pages (8:336–9), Kant rues the counterproductive folly of those who seek to promote Christianity (a religion whose greatness lies in the way it puts love in the service of morality) through the use of earthly threats and rewards, since these means can only corrupt morality and put an end to love. It is transparent that these criticisms allude to the projects of J. C. Wöllner and his associates; hence Kant could expect this essay only to increase the hostility the authorities had already shown toward him.

When, on May 18, the philosopher finally transmitted to Biester the text of "The End of All Things," he accompanied it with a resigned letter in which he avows that he will "punctiliously obey" any laws which "*command* what is not opposed to my principles," or even those which "*forbid* making known my principles in their entirety, as I have done up to now (and for which I am not sorry in the least)" (AK 11:240–1). These remarks seem already to anticipate the royal reproof of his writings on religion which he was to receive in October of that year, and which led to Kant's promise to the King to refrain from any further writing on religious subjects. The decision to prohibit Kant from writing on religion had been taken by C. G. Woltersdorf, the *Oberkonsistorialrath*, as early as June 1791, and this fact had been reported promptly to Kant by his former student, the royal tutor J. G. Kiesewetter (AK 11:264–6). By 1794 the philosopher must have known that royal action against him could not be delayed much longer.

"The End of All Things" has been translated into English twice previously. The first translation, by Robert E. Anchor, appeared in Lewis White Beck, Emil Fackenheim, and Robert E. Anchor (eds.), *Kant on History* (New York: Bobbs-Merrill, 1963). The second, by Ted Humphrey, appeared in Ted Humphrey (ed.), *Perpetual Peace and Other Essays* (Indianapolis: Hackett, 1983).

The end of all things

It is a common expression, used chiefly in pious language, to speak of a person who is dying as going *out of time into eternity*.

This expression would in fact say nothing if *eternity* is understood here to mean a time proceeding to infinity; for then the person would indeed never get outside time but would always progress only from one time into another. Thus what must be meant is an *end of all time* along with the person's uninterrupted duration; but this duration (considering its existence as a magnitude) as a magnitude (*duratio Noumenon*) wholly incomparable with time, of which we are obviously able to form no concept (except a merely negative one). This thought has something horrifying about it because it leads us as it were to the edge of an abyss: for anyone who sinks into it no return is possible ("But in that earnest place/ Him who holds nothing back/ Eternity holds fast in its strong arms." Haller);[1] and yet there is something attractive there too: for one cannot cease turning his terrified gaze back to it again and again (*nequeunt expleri corda tuendo.* Virgil).[a] It is frighteningly *sublime* partly because it is obscure, for the imagination works harder in darkness than it does in bright light. Yet in the end it must also be woven in a wondrous way into universal human reason, because it is encountered among all reasoning peoples at all times, clothed in one way or another. – Now when we pursue the transition from time into eternity (whether or not this idea, considered theoretically as extending cognition, has objective reality), as reason does in a moral regard, then we come up against the *end of all things* as temporal beings and as objects of possible experience – which end, however, in the moral order of ends, is at the same time the beginning of a duration of just those same beings as *supersensible*, and consequently as not standing under conditions of time; thus that duration and its state will be capable of no determination of its nature[b] other than a moral one.

Days are as it were the children of time, because the following day, with what it contains, is an offspring of the previous one. Now just as the last child of its parents is called the youngest child, so the German language likes to call the last day (the point in time which closes all time) the

---

[a] "They cannot satisfy their hearts with gazing" (Virgil, *Aeneid* 8:265).
[b] *Beschaffenheit*

youngest day.^c The last day thus still belongs to time, for on it something or other *happens* (and not to eternity, where nothing happens any more, because that would belong to the progress of time): namely, the settling of accounts for human beings, based on their conduct in their whole lifetime. It is a *judgment day;* thus the judgment of grace or damnation by the world's judge is therefore the real^d end of all things in time, and at the same time the beginning of the (blessed or cursed) eternity, in which the lot that has fallen to each remains just as it was in the moment of its pronouncement (of the sentence). Thus the last day also contains in itself simultaneously the *last judgment.* – Now if among the *last things* there should yet be counted the end of the world as it appears in its present shape, namely the falling of the stars from heaven, considered as a vault, and the collapse of this heaven itself (or its disappearance, as a scroll when it is rolled up),² both being consumed in flames, with the creation of a new earth and a new heaven as the seat of the blessed and of hell as that of the damned,³ then that judgment day would obviously not be the last day; instead, different days would follow upon it, one after another. Yet since the idea of an end of all things takes its origin from reasonings not about the *physical* but rather about the moral course of things in the world, and is occasioned only by it, while the latter alone can be referred to the supersensible (which is to be understood only morally) – and it is the same with the idea of eternity – so consequently the representation of those last things which are supposed to come *after* the last day are to be regarded only as a way of making sensible this latter together with its moral consequences, which are otherwise not theoretically comprehensible to us.

But it is to be noted that from the most ancient times there have been two systems pertaining to the future eternity: one is that of the *unitists,*^e awarding eternal blessedness to all human beings (after they have been purified by a longer or shorter penance), while the other is the system of the *dualists,** which awards blessedness to *some* who have been elected,

8:329

---

* In the ancient Persian religion (of Zoroaster), such a system was grounded on the assumption of an eternal struggle between two original beings, the good principle Ormuzd and the evil Ahriman. – It is strange that in the naming of these two original beings the language of two lands distant from each other, and still farther removed from the present seat of the German language, is German. I remember reading in Sonnerat that in Ava (the land of the Burmese) the good principle^f is called "Godeman"^g (which appears also to lie in the name *Darius Codomannus;* and the word "Ahriman" sounds very similar to [the German for] "wicked man"^h – present day Persian also contains a lot of originally German words; so it
^c *Jüngster Tag* is the German term for what we call (the biblical) "judgment day"; this term will be translated henceforth as "last day."
^d *eigentliche*
^e *Unitarier*
^f *Princip*
^g "Godeman" sounds similar to the German *"guter Mann"*
^h *arge Mann*

but eternal damnation to all *the rest.* For there would probably be no room for a system according to which all were predestined[i] to be *damned,* because then there would be no ground which could justify their being created at all; but the *annihilation* of all would indicate a defective wisdom, one which is dissatisfied with its own work and knows no other way of remedying the flaws except to destroy it. – Just the same difficulty stands in the way of the dualists as the obstacle to thinking the eternal damnation of everyone; for why, one could ask, were even a few created – Why even a single individual? – if he is supposed to exist only to be rejected for eternity? For that is worse than never having been at all.

Indeed, as far as we have insight into it, as far as we can investigate it ourselves, the dualistic system (but only under *one* supremely good original being) has – for the *practical* aims of every human being judging himself (though not for being warranted to judge others) – a preponderant ground for it: for as far as he is acquainted with himself, reason leaves him no other prospect for eternity than that which his conscience opens up for him at the end of this life on the basis of the course of his life as he has led it up to then. But this ground, as a judgment of mere reason, is far from sufficient for making this into a *dogma,* hence a theoretical proposition which is valid in itself (objectively). For what human being knows[j] himself or others through and through? Who knows enough to decide whether if we subtract from the causes of a presumably well-led course of life everything which is called the merit of fortune – such as an innately kind temperament, the naturally greater strength of his higher powers (of the understanding and reason, to tame his drives), besides that also his opportunity, the times when contingency fortunately saved him from many temptations which struck another – who knows if he separates all these from his actual character (from which he must necessarily subtract them if he is to evaluate it properly, since as gifts of fortune he cannot ascribe them to his own merit) – who will then decide, I say, whether before the all-seeing eye of a world-judge one human being has any superiority over another regarding his inner moral worth? And, on the basis of this superficial self-knowledge,[k] might it not perhaps be absurd self-conceit to pronounce any judgment at all to one's own advantage concerning one's own moral worth or that of others (or of the fates they deserve)? – Hence the unitist's system, as much as the dualist's, considered as dogma, seems to transcend completely the speculative faculty of human reason; and everything brings us back to limiting those ideas of reason

8:330

might be a task for those who do research into antiquity to use the guiding thread of *linguistic* affinity to inquire into the origin of the present day *religious* conceptions of many peoples. (See Sonnerat's *Travels,* Book 4, Chapter 2, B.)[4]

[i] *bestimmt*

[j] *kennt*

[k] *Selbsterkenntnis*

223

absolutely to the conditions of their practical use only. For we see nothing before us now that could teach us about our fate in a future world except the judgment of our own conscience, i.e. what our present moral state, as far as we are acquainted with it, lets us judge rationally concerning it: namely, that those principles[l] we have found ruling in ourselves during the course of our life (whether they be good or evil) will continue after death, without our having the slightest ground to assume that they will alter in that future. Hence for eternity we would have to anticipate for ourselves the consequences suiting that merit or guilt under the dominion of the good or evil principle; in this respect, consequently, it is wise to act *as if* another life – and the moral state in which we end this one, along with its consequences in entering on that other life – is unalterable. Thus from a practical point of view,[m] the system to be assumed will have to be the dualistic one – especially since the unitistic system appears to lull us too much into an indifferent sense of security – yet we might not try to make out which of the two systems deserves superiority from a theoretical and merely speculative point of view.

But why do human beings expect *an end* of the world *at all?* And if this is conceded to them, why must it be a terrible end (for the greatest part of the human race)? . . . The ground of the first point appears to lie in the fact that reason says to them that the duration of the world has worth only insofar as the rational beings in it conform to the final end of their existence; if, however, this is not supposed to be achieved, then creation itself appears purposeless to them, like a play having no resolution and affording no cognition of any rational aim. The latter point is grounded on our opinion about the corrupt nature[n] of the human race,* which corrup-

8:331

---

* In all ages self-styled sages (or philosophers), without paying enough attention to the worth of the disposition to good in human nature, have exhausted themselves in repellent, partly disgusting parables, which represent our earthly world, the dwelling place of humanity, as contemptible: (1) As an inn (caravansarai), as that dervish regards it, where everyone arriving there on his life's journey must be prepared to be driven out soon by his successor; (2) as a *penitentiary* – an opinion to which the Brahmanists, Tibetans and other sages of the Orient (and even Plato) are attached – a place of chastisement and purification for fallen spirits driven out of heaven, who are now human or animal souls; (3) as a *madhouse*, where each not only annihilates his own intents, but where each adds every thinkable sorrow to the other, and moreover holds the skill and power to do this to be the greatest honor; finally (4), as a *cloaca*, where all the excrement from the other worlds has been deposited. The latter notion is in a certain way original, and for it we have a Persian wit to thank; he transposed paradise, the dwelling place of the first human couple, into heaven, where there was a garden with ample trees richly provided with splendid fruits, whose digested residue, after the couple's enjoyment of them, vanished through an unnoticed evaporation; the exception was a single tree in the middle of the garden, which bore a fruit which was delicious but did not dry up in this way. As it now happened, our first parents now lusted after it, despite the prohibition

[l] *Principien*
[m] *Absicht*
[n] *Beschaffenheit*

tion is great to the point of hopelessness; this makes for an end, and indeed a terrible one, the only end (for the greatest part of humanity) that accords with highest wisdom and justice, employing any respectable standard. – Hence the *omens of the last day* (for where the imagination has been excited by great expectations, how can there fail to be signs and miracles?) are all of a terrible kind. Some see them in increasing injustice, oppression of the poor by the arrogant indulgence of the rich, and the   8:332 general loss of fidelity and faith; or in bloody wars igniting all over the earth, and so forth; in a word, in the moral fall and the rapid advance of all vices together with their accompanying ills, such as earlier times – they think – have never seen. Others, by contrast, [find them] in unusual alterations in nature – in earthquakes, storms and floods, or comets and atmospheric signs.

In fact it is not without cause that human beings feel their existence a burden, even if they themselves are the cause. The ground of this appears to me to lie in this. – In the progress of the human race the culture of talents, skill and taste (with their consequence, luxury) naturally runs ahead of the development of morality; and this state is precisely the most burdensome and dangerous for morality just as it is for physical well-being, because the needs grow stronger than the means to satisfy them. But the moral disposition of humanity – which (like Horace's *poene pede claudo*)⁰ always limps behind, tripping itself up in its hasty course and often stumbling – will (as, under a wise world governor, one may hope) one day overtake it; and thus, even according to the experimental proofs of the superior morals of our age as compared with all previous ones, one should nourish the hope that the last day might sooner come on the scene with Elijah's ascension⁵ than with the like descent of Korah's troops into hell,⁶ and bring with it the end of all things on earth. Yet this heroic faith in virtue does not seem, subjectively, to have such a generally powerful influence for converting people's minds as a scene accompanied by terrors, which is thought of as preceding the last things.

∵

Note. Here we have to do (or are playing) merely with ideas created by reason itself, whose objects (if they have any) lie wholly beyond our field of vision; although they are transcendent for speculative cognition, they

---

against tasting it, and so there was no other way to keep heaven from being polluted except to take the advice of one of the angels who pointed out to them the distant earth, with the words: "There is the toilet of the whole universe," and then carried them there in order to relieve themselves, but then flew back to heaven leaving them behind. That is how the human race is supposed to have arisen on earth.

⁰ "Punishment with a lame foot"; the line actually reads: *Raro antecedentem scelestum/ Deseruit pede Poena claudo* ("Rarely does punishment fail to catch the guilty, though it runs with a lame foot"), Horace, *Odes* 3.2.32.

are not to be taken as empty, but with a practical intent they are made available to us by lawgiving reason itself, yet not in order to brood over their objects as to what they are in themselves and in their nature, but rather how we have to think of them in behalf of moral principles directed toward the final end of all things (through which, though otherwise they would be entirely empty, acquire objective practical reality): hence we have a *free* field before us, this product of our own reason, the universal concept of an end of all things, to divide it up and to classify what stands under it according to the relation it has to our faculty of cognition.

8:333

Accordingly, the whole will be brought about, divided up and represented under three divisions: (1) the *natural** end of all things according to the order of divine wisdom's moral ends, which we therefore (with a practical intent) can *very well understand;* (2) their *mystical* (supernatural) end in the order of efficient causes, of which we *understand nothing,* and (3) the *contranatural* (perverse) end of all things, which comes from us when we *misunderstand* the final end; the first of these has already been discussed, and what follows now is the remaining two.

. .
.

In the *Apocalypse* (10:5–6): "An angel lifts his hand up to heaven and swears by the one who lives from eternity to eternity who has created heaven, etc.: *that henceforth time shall be no more.*"[7]

If one does not assume that this angel "with his voice of seven thunders" (v. 3) wanted to cry nonsense, then he must have meant that henceforth there shall be no *alteration;* for if there were still alteration in the world, then time would also exist, because alteration can take place only in time and is not thinkable without presupposing it.

8:334

Now here is represented an end of all things as objects of sense – of which we cannot form any concept at all, because we will inevitably entangle ourselves in contradictions as soon as we try to take a single step beyond the sensible world into the intelligible; that happens here since the moment which constitutes the end of the first world is also supposed to be the beginning of the other one, hence the former is brought into the same temporal series with the latter, which contradicts itself.

But we also say that we think of a duration as *infinite* (as an eternity) not because we have any determinate concept of its magnitude – for that is impossible, since time is wholly lacking as a measure – but rather because that concept – since where there is time, *no end* can come about – is merely a negative one of eternal duration, by which we come not one step

---

* *Natural (formaliter)* means what follows necessarily according to laws of a certain order of whatever sort, hence also the moral order (hence not always the physical order). Opposed to it is the *nonnatural,* which can be either supernatural or contranatural. What is necessary from *natural causes* is also represented as maternally natural (physically necessary).

further in our cognition, but we will have said only that reason in its (practical) intent toward its final end can never have done enough on the path of constant alterations; and if reason attempts this with the principle[p] of rest and immutability of the state of beings in the world, the result is equally unsatisfactory in respect of its *theoretical* use; on the contrary, it would fall into total thoughtlessness, and nothing would remain for it but to think as the final end an alteration, proceeding to infinity (in time) in a constant progression, in which the *disposition* (which is not a phenomenon, like the former, but something supersensible, hence not alterable with time) remains the same and is persisting. The rule for the practical use of reason in accord with this idea thus says no more than that we must take our maxims as if, in all alterations from good to better going into infinity, our moral condition, regarding its disposition (the *homo Noumenon*, "whose change takes place in heaven") were not subject to any temporal change at all.

But that at some point a time will arrive in which all alteration (and with it, time itself) ceases – this is a representation which outrages the imagination. For then the whole of nature will be rigid and as it were petrified: the last thought, the last feeling in the thinking subject will then stop and remain forever the same without any change. For a being which can become conscious of its existence and the magnitude of this existence (as duration) only in time, such a life – if it can even be called a life – appears equivalent to annihilation, because in order to think itself into such a state it still has to think something in general, but *thinking* contains a reflecting, which can occur only in time. – Hence the inhabitants of the other world will be represented, according to their different dwelling places (heaven or hell), as striking up always the same song, their "Alleluia!," or else eternally the same wailing tones ([Rev.] 19:1–6; 20:15): by which is indicated the total lack of all change in their state.   8:335

Likewise this idea, however far it surpasses our power to grasp it, is very closely related to reason in its practical reference. Even assuming a person's moral-physical state here in life at its best – namely as a constant progression and approach to the highest good (marked out for him as a goal) – , he still (even with a consciousness of the unalterability of his disposition) cannot combine it with the prospect of *satisfaction* in an eternally enduring alteration of his state (the moral as well as the physical). For the state in which he now is will always remain an ill compared with a better one which he always stands ready to enter; and the representation of an infinite progression toward the final end is nevertheless at the same time a prospect[q] on an infinite series of ills which, even though they may be outweighed by a greater good, do not allow for the possibility of

[p] *Princip*
[q] *Prospect*

227

contentment; for he can think that only by supposing that the *final end* will at sometime be *attained*.

Now the person who broods on this will fall into *mysticism* (for reason, because it is not easily satisfied with its immanent, i.e. practical use, but gladly ventures into the transcendent, also has its mysteries), where reason does not understand either itself or what it wants, but prefers to indulge in enthusiasm rather than – as seems fitting for an intellectual inhabitant of a sensible world – to limit itself within the bounds of the latter. From this comes the monstrous system of Lao-kiun[8] concerning the *highest good*, that it consists in *nothing*, i.e. in the consciousness of *feeling* oneself swallowed up in the abyss of the Godhead by flowing together with it, and hence by the annihilation of one's personality; in order to have a presentiment of this state Chinese philosophers, sitting in dark rooms with their eyes closed, exert themselves to think and sense their own nothingness. Hence the *pantheism* (of the Tibetans and other oriental peoples); and in consequence from its philosophical sublimation *Spinozism* is begotten, which is closely akin to the very ancient *system of emanation* of human souls from the Godhead (and their final reabsorption into it). All this because people would like at last to have an *eternal tranquillity* in which to rejoice, constituting for them a supposedly blessed end of all things; but really[r] this is a concept in which the understanding is simultaneously exhausted and all thinking itself has an end.

8:336

· ·
· ·

The end of all things which go through the hands of human beings, even when their purposes are good, is *folly*, i.e. the use of means to their ends which are directly opposed to these ends. *Wisdom*, that is, practical reason using means commensurate to the final end of all things – the highest good – in full accord with the corresponding rules of measure, dwells in God alone; and the only thing which could perhaps be called human wisdom is acting in a way which is not visibly contrary to the idea of that [divine] wisdom. But this assurance against folly, which the human being may hope to attain only through attempts and frequent alteration of his plans, is rather a "gem which the best person can only follow after, even though he *may* never *apprehend* it";[s] but he may never let the self-indulgent persuasion befall him – still less may he proceed according to it – that he *has grasped* it. – Hence too the projects – altering from age to age and often absurd – of finding suitable means to make *religion in a whole people pure and at the same time powerful,* so that one can well cry out: Poor mortals, with you nothing is constant except inconstancy![9]

---

[r] *eigentlich*
[s] cf. Philippians 3:12: "Not as though I had already attained, either were already perfect, but I follow after, if that I may apprehend that for which I also am apprehended of Christ Jesus."

If, meanwhile, these attempts have for once finally prospered far enough that the community is susceptible and inclined to give a hearing not merely to the received pious doctrines but also to a practical reason which has been illuminated by them (which is also absolutely necessary for a religion); if the sages (of a human sort) among the people – not through an undertaking among themselves (as a clergy) but as fellow citizens – draw up projects and for the most part agree – which proves in a way that is above suspicion that they are dealing with the truth – and if the people at large also takes an interest in it (even if not in every detail) through a need, generally felt and not based on authority, directed to the necessary cultivation of its moral disposition: then nothing seems to be more advisable than to let those sages go ahead and pursue their course, since for once, as regards the *idea* they are following, they are on a good path; but as regards the success of the means they have chosen to the best final end, since this – as it may turn out in the course of nature – always remains uncertain, it is advisable always to leave it to *providence*. For however incredulous one may be, one must – where it is absolutely impossible to foresee with certainty the success of certain means taken according to all human wisdom (which, if they are to deserve their name, must proceed solely toward morality) – believe in a practical way in a concurrence of divine wisdom with the course of nature, unless one would rather just give up one's final end. – Of course it will be objected: It has often been said that the present plan is the best, one must stay with it from now on, that is the state of things for eternity. "Whoever (according to this concept) is good, he is good for always, and whoever (opposed to him) is evil, is evil for ever" (Rev. 22:11): just as if eternity, and with it the end of all things, might now have already made its entrance; – and likewise since then new plans, among which the newest are often only the restoration of an old one, have always been trotted out; and henceforth too there will be no lack of *more ultimate* projects.

8:337

I am so very conscious of my incapacity to make a new and fortunate attempt here that I, who obviously possess no great power of invention, would rather advise that we leave matters as they last stood, and as for nearly a generation they have proven themselves tolerably good in their consequences. But since this may not be the opinion of men who are either of great or else of enterprising spirit, let me modestly note not so much what they would have to do as what they will have to take care that they will be up against, because otherwise they would act against their own intention (even if that were of the best).

Christianity has, besides the greatest respect that the holiness of its laws irresistibly instills, something about it which is *worthy of love.* (Here I mean not the worthiness of love of the person who obtained it for us with great sacrifices, but that of the cause itself: namely, the moral constitution which he founded, for the former [worthiness] may be inferred only from

229

8:338

the latter.) Respect is without doubt what is primary, because without it no true love can occur, even though one can harbor great respect for a person without love. But if it is a matter not merely of the representation of duty but also of following duty, if one asks about the *subjective* ground of actions from which, if one may presuppose it, the first thing we may expect is what a person *will do* – and not a matter merely of the *objective* ground of *what he ought to do* – then love, as a free assumption of the will of another into one's maxims, is an indispensable complement to the imperfection of human nature (of having to be necessitated to that which reason prescribes through the law). For what one does not do with liking' he does in such a niggardly fashion – also probably with sophistical evasions from the command of duty – that the latter as an incentive, without the contribution of the former, is not very much to be counted on.

Now if to Christianity – in order to make good on it – one adds any sort of authority (even a divine one), even if one's intention in doing so is well-meaning and the end is actually just as good, then its worthiness to be loved has nevertheless disappeared: for it is a contradiction to *command* not only that someone should do something but that he should do it *with liking.*

Christianity has the intention of furthering love out of concern for the observance of duty in general; and it produces it too, because its founder speaks not in the quality of a commander demanding obedience to *his will,* but in that of a friend of humanity who appeals to the hearts of his fellow human beings on behalf of their own well-understood will, i.e. of the way they would of themselves voluntarily act if they examined themselves properly.

Thus it is from the *liberal* way of thinking – equally distant from a slavish cast of mind and from licentiousness – that Christianity expects the *effect* of its doctrine, through which it may win over the hearts of human beings when their understanding has already been illuminated by the representation of their duty's law. The feeling of freedom in the choice of the final end is what makes the legislation worthy of its love. – Thus although the teacher of this end also announces *punishments,* that is not to be understood – or at least it is not suited to the proper nature" of Christianity so to explain it – as though these should become the incentives for performing what follows from its commands; for to that extent it would cease to be worthy of love. Rather, one may interpret this only as a

8:339

loving warning, arising out of the beneficence of the lawgiver, of preventing the harm that would have to arise inevitably from the transgression of the law (for: *lex est res surda et inexorabilis.* Livy.);" because it is not

---

' *gern*

" *eigentümliche Beschaffenheit*

" "The law is deaf and inexorable"; the whole passage reads: *Leges rem surdam, inexorabilem esse, salubriorem, melioremque inopi quam potenti* ("The laws are deaf things, inexorable, more salutary and better to the powerless than to the powerful"); Livy, *History of Rome* 2.3.4.

Christianity as a freely assumed maxim of life but the law which threatens here; and the law, as an unchanging order lying in the nature of things, is not to be left up to even the creator's arbitrary will*w* to decide its consequences thus or otherwise.

If Christianity promises *rewards* (e.g. "Be joyful and consoled, for everything will be repaid you in heaven"),[10] this must not be interpreted – according to the liberal way of thinking – as if it were an offer, through which the human being would be *hired*, as it were, to a good course of life; for then Christianity would, once again, not be in itself*x* worthy of love. Only the expectation*y* of such actions arising from unselfish motives can inspire respect in the person toward the one who has the expectation; but without respect there is no true love. Thus one must not take that promise in this sense, as if the rewards are to be taken for the incentives of the actions. Love, through which a liberal way of thinking is bound to the benefactor, is not directed toward the good received by the needy person, but instead merely to the benefactor's generosity of *will* which is inclined to confer it, even if he does not have the resources or is prevented from carrying it out by other motives which come from a regard for what is universally best for the world.

That is the moral worthiness to be loved which Christianity carries with it, which still glimmers through the many external constraints which may be added to it by the frequent change of opinions; and it is this which has preserved it in the face of the disinclination it would otherwise have encountered, and (what is remarkable) this shows itself in all the brighter light in an age of the greatest enlightenment that was ever yet among human beings.

If Christianity should ever come to the point where it ceased to be worthy of love (which could very well transpire if instead of its gentle spirit it were armed with commanding authority), then, because there is no neutrality in moral things (still less a coalition between opposed principles*z*), a disinclination and resistance to it would become the ruling mode of thought among people; and the *Antichrist*, who is taken to be the forerunner of the last day, would begin his – albeit short – regime (presumably based on fear and self-interest); but then, because Christianity, though supposedly *destined* to be the world religion, would not be *favored* by fate to become it, *the* (perverted) *end of all things*, in a moral respect, would arrive.

---

w *Willkür*
x *für sich*
y *Ansinnen*
z *Principien*

The conflict of the faculties

Editor's introduction

Der Streit der Fakultäten first appeared in the autumn of 1798, published by Friedrich Nicolovius in Königsberg.

The Conflict of the Faculties brings together three different essays Kant had written at various times. Sometime between June and October 1794, Kant wrote an essay on the prerogatives of the philosophical faculty in relation to the theological faculty of the university. Clearly it was at least partly an attempt to justify the manner in which he had circumvented the censors in publishing the *Religion* (see the Translator's Introduction to that work). After Wöllner's letter of reproof and Kant's subsequent promise not to lecture or publish on religious subjects (see General Introduction and below, AK 7:5–11), the liberal theologian C. F. Stäudlin in Göttingen offered the philosopher the opportunity to publish this new essay free of the Prussian censorship (AK 11:488). But Kant regarded this as a violation of his promise to the king, and therefore felt duty bound to decline Stäudlin's invitation (AK 11:513–15).

After the death of King Frederick William II, however, Kant chose to regard himself as released from his promise and free to publish his essay on the relation of the philosophical and theological faculties. But he expanded the scope of his original essay to include the relation of the "lower" faculty (of philosophy) to all three of the university's "higher" faculties (of theology, law, and medicine). Based on his account of freedom of expression given in "What Is Enlightenment?" (1784), Kant maintains that the three "higher" faculties have duties to the state. Hence (in the terminology of "What Is Enlightenment?"), their activities belong to the "private" use of reason and are thus subject to state regulation. The function of the philosophy faculty, by contrast, is directed solely to the cosmopolitan world of learning and scholarship. It concerns the "public" use of reason and hence should be free of such regulation.

In order to supplement his treatment of the relation of philosophy to theology, in accordance with this expanded scope, Kant now adds two other short essays, ostensibly pertaining to the relation between philosophy and the other two "higher" or professional faculties. "An Old Question Raised Again" was apparently written in 1795. The date is significant because it means that Kant's sympathetic participation in the spirit of the French Revolution must have still continued in 1798 when the essay was

235

published, but his sober (even pessimistic) assessment of the likely outcome of the revolution itself probably dates from at least as early as 1795.
Unlike many of his contemporaries, Kant never placed his hopes on
popular insurrection as a vehicle for progressive change (he even regarded
resistance to an unjust government as contrary to right); but the aging
philosopher stood firm in his historical optimism – in his sympathy with
what the French Revolution meant, the deeper ideals it stood for – even
after younger enthusiasts had become disillusioned with it. The third
essay in *The Conflict of the Faculties*, "The Power of the Mind to Master
Morbid Feelings," was written in 1796, after Kant received from C. F.
Hufeland a copy of his book *Macrobiotics* (1796).

Within ten years of its original publication, this Third Part had already
been translated into English by John C. Colquhoun, appearing in John
Sinclair, *The Code of Health and Longevity* (Edinburgh, 1807). The Second
Part, "An Old Question Raised Again," was translated by Robert E.
Anchor, and first appeared in Lewis White Beck, Emil Fackenheim, and
Robert Anchor (eds.), *Kant on History* (Indianapolis: Bobbs-Merrill,
1963). "An Old Question Raised Again" has since been translated again
by H. B. Nisbet, in Hans Reiss (ed.), *Kant's Political Writings* (Cambridge:
Cambridge University Press, 1970). *The Conflict of the Faculties* as a whole
has been translated only once, by Mary J. Gregor (New York: Abaris
Books, 1979; reprinted Lincoln, NB: University of Nebraska Press,
1992), using Anchor's translation of "An Old Question Raised Again."
The present text is a slight revision of Gregor's version.

The conflict of the faculties

Preface

An enlightened government, which is releasing the human spirit from its chains and deserves all the more willing obedience because of the freedom of thought it allows, permits the present pages to be published; this accounts for the freedom I take to add, as a preface, a brief account of what concerns me personally in this turn of events.

King Frederick William II – a courageous, sincere, benevolent and – except for certain peculiarities of temperament – an altogether excellent ruler, who knew me personally and, from time to time, gave me expressions of his favor – issued in 1788 a *religious edict,* followed shortly afterward by an edict of censorship which sharply restricted literary activity in general and so reinforced the earlier decree; this he did at the instigation of a clergyman,[1] later promoted to Minister of Spiritual Affairs; and to him, again, we have no just grounds for imputing any but good intentions based on his inner convictions. It cannot be denied that certain signs, which preceded this explosion, must have warned the government that reform was needed in that field – a reform that should have been carried out quietly, through the academic instruction of those who were to become the people's public teachers; for young clergymen had been preaching their sermons in such a tone that no one with a sense of humor would let himself be converted by teachers like *that.*

It was while the religious edict was exercising a lively influence on native as well as foreign writers that my treatise entitled *Religion within the Boundaries of Mere Reason** appeared. And since I sign my name to all my writings, so that I cannot be accused of using underhanded means, the following royal proclamation was issued to me in the year 1794. It should be noted that, since I let only my most trusted friend know of its existence,[2] it has never been made public before.

Frederick William, by the Grace of God King of Prussia, etc., etc.,

---

* My purpose in formulating this title was to prevent a misinterpretation to the effect that the treatise deals with religion *from* mere reason (without revelation). That would be claiming too much, since reason's teachings could still come from men who are supernaturally inspired. The title indicates that I intended, rather, to set forth as a coherent whole everything in the Bible – the text of the religion believed to be revealed – that can *also* be recognized *by mere reason.*

First, our gracious greetings, worthy, most learned, dear and loyal subject! Our most high person has long observed with great displeasure how you misuse your philosophy to distort and disparage many of the cardinal and basic teachings of the Holy Scriptures and of Christianity; how you have done this particularly in your book *Religion within the Boundaries of Mere Reason*, as well as in other shorter treatises. We expected better things of you, as you yourself must realize how irresponsibly you have acted against your duty as a teacher of youth and against our paternal purpose, which you know very well. We demand that you give at once a most conscientious account of yourself, and expect that in the future, to avoid our highest disfavor, you will be guilty of no such fault, but rather, in keeping with your duty, apply your authority and your talents to the progressive realization of our paternal purpose. Failing this, you must expect unpleasant measures for your continuing obstinacy.

 With our favorable regards.

Berlin, 1 October 1794
By *special*, most gracious order
of His Majesty
Woellner

7:7

addressed – To our worthy and most learned Professor, dear and loyal
 Kant

at
Königsberg in Prussia
delivered 12 October 1794

To which, for my own part, I replied most obediently as follows:[3]
 Most Gracious etc., etc.

 The supreme order of Your Majesty, issued on October 1 and delivered to me on October 12, charges me, as my most humble duty: *first*, "to give a most conscientious account of myself for having misused my philosophy to distort and disparage many of the cardinal and basic teachings of the Holy Scriptures and of Christianity, particularly in my book *Religion within the Boundaries of Mere Reason*, as well as in other shorter treatises, and for having, by this, incurred the guilt of transgressing my duty as a teacher of youth and opposing the highest paternal purpose, which I know very well"; and, *secondly*, "to be guilty of nothing of the sort in the future." With regard to both these points I shall not fail to put before Your Majesty proof of my most submissive obedience, by the following declaration.

 As for the *first* – that is, the charge brought against me – my conscientious account is as follows:

 As a *teacher of youth* – that is, I take it, in my academic lectures – I never have and never could have mixed any evaluation of the Holy Scriptures and of Christianity into my lectures. The text of Baumgarten, which

240

is the basis of my lectures and the only thing that could be at all relevant to such a discourse, are sufficient to prove this. For, being purely philosophical, these texts do not and cannot contain a single heading referring to the Bible or to Christianity; and since I have always censured and warned against the mistake of straying beyond the boundaries of the science at hand or mixing one science with another, this is the last fault I could be reproached with.

Again, as a *teacher of the people* – in my writings and particularly in my book *Religion within the Boundaries etc.* – I have not in any way offended against the highest paternal purpose, which I know: in other words, I have done no harm to the public *religion of the land.* This is already clear from the fact that the book in question is not at all suitable for the public: to them it is an unintelligible, closed book, only a debate among scholars of the faculty, of which the people take no notice, but the faculties themselves remain free to judge it publicly, according to the best of their knowledge and their conscience; it is only those who are appointed to teach the people (in the schools and from the pulpits) who are bound to uphold whatever outcome of the debate the crown sanctions for them to expound *publicly;* for they cannot think out their own religious belief *by themselves,* but can only have it handed down to them by the same route – namely, its examination and rectification by the competent faculties (of theology and philosophy), hence the crown is entitled not only to permit but even to require the faculties to let the government know, by their writings, everything they consider beneficial to a public religion of the land.

Since, in the book mentioned, I make no *appraisal* of Christianity, I cannot be guilty of *disparaging* it. In fact, it is only natural religion that I appraise: The only possible occasion for this misunderstanding is the fact that I cite some biblical texts to corroborate certain purely rational teachings in religion. But the late *Michaelis,*[4] who uses the same practice in his moral philosophy, explains that his purpose in doing this is neither to put anything biblical into philosophy nor to draw anything philosophical out of the Bible, but only to clarify and confirm his rational propositions by their real or supposed agreement with the judgments of others (poets, perhaps, and orators). – But when reason speaks, in these matters, as if it were sufficient to itself and as if revealed teachings were therefore superfluous (an assertion which, were it to be taken objectively, would have to be considered a real disparagement of Christianity), it is merely expressing its appraisal of itself – not in terms of its [theoretical] ability [but] in terms of what it prescribes us to do[a] insofar as it alone is the source of the *universality,* *unity,* and *necessity* in the tenets of faith that are the essence of

7:8

7:9

---

[a] Here the text has been amended following Klaus Reich (Hamburg Mether Verlag, 1959): "*nicht nach ihrem theoretischen Vermögen, sondern nach dem, wessie als zu thun vorschreibt . . .* "

241

any religion as such, which consists in the morally practical (in what we *ought* to do). On the other hand, what we have cause to believe on historical grounds (where "*ought*" does not hold at all) – that is, revelation as contingent tenets of faith – it regards as nonessential. But this does not mean that reason considers it idle and superfluous; for revelation is useful in making up the *theoretical* deficiency which our pure rational belief admits it has (in the questions, for example, of the origin of evil, the conversion from evil to good, the human being's assurance that he has become good, etc.) and helps – more or less, depending on the times and the person concerned – to satisfy a rational need.

Further, I have evidenced my great respect for Christianity in many ways – among others, by my account of the Bible in the book mentioned, where I praised it as the best and most adequate means of public instruction available for establishing and maintaining indefinitely a state religion that is truly conducive to the soul's improvement; hence I censured the temerity of raising objections and doubts, in the schools and pulpits and in popular writings, about the theoretical teachings of the Bible and the mysteries these contain (for in the faculties this must be permitted). But this is not yet the highest tribute of respect to Christianity. Its best and most lasting eulogy is its harmony, which I demonstrated in this book, with the purest moral belief of religion, since it is by this, and not by historical scholarship, that Christianity, so often debased, has always been restored; and only by this can it again be restored when, in the future, it continues to meet a similar fate.

Finally, as I have always and above all recommended to other believers a conscientious sincerity in not professing or obtruding on others, as articles of faith, more than they themselves are sure of, so, when composing my writings, I have always pictured this judge as standing at my side to keep me not only from error that corrupts the soul, but even from any careless expression that might give offense; for which reason now, in my seventy-first year, when I can hardly help thinking that I may well have to answer for this very soon to a judge of the world who scrutinizes men's hearts, I can frankly present this account of my teachings, which you demand of me, as composed with the utmost *conscientiousness*.

7:10

Regarding the second point – not to be guilty in the future of (as I am charged) distorting and disparaging Christianity – I believe the surest way, which will obviate the least suspicion, is for me to declare solemnly, *as Your Majesty's most loyal subject,** that I will hereafter refrain altogether from discoursing publicly, in lectures or writings, on religion, whether natural or revealed.

With deepest devotion I remain for life, etc.

---

* This expression, too, I chose carefully, so that I would not renounce my freedom to judge in this religious suit *forever,* but only during His Majesty's lifetime.

The further history of this incessant drive toward a faith ever more estranged from reason is well known.

The examination of candidates for ecclesiastical offices was now entrusted to a *Commission of Faith,* which based the examination on a Pietistic *Schema Examinationis.* This drove conscientious candidates in theology away from ecclesiastical offices in flocks and overpopulated the faculty of law – a kind of emigration which, by the way, may have had its advantages. – To give some idea of the spirit of this Commission: their claim that an overwhelming remorse must precede forgiveness required a profound affliction of repentance (*maeror animi*)[b] on the human being's part, and they asked whether he could attain this grief by himself. *Quod negandum ac pernegandum,*[c] was the answer: the repentant sinner must especially beg this repentance from heaven. – Now it seems perfectly obvious that anyone who still has to beg for this *repentance* (for his transgressions) does not really *repent* of his deeds; this looks just as contradictory as the statement about *prayer:* if it is to be heard, it must be made in faith. For if the petitioner has faith, he does not need to ask for it; but if he does not have faith, his petition cannot be heard.

This nonsense has now been brought under control. A happy event has recently taken place that will not only promote the civil good of the commonwealth in general, for which religion is a primary political need, but benefit the sciences in particular, by means of a Higher School Commission established for their advancement. The choice of a wise government has fallen upon an enlightened statesman[5] who has, not a one-sided predilection for a special branch of science (theology), but the vocation, the talent, and the will to promote the broad interests of the entire scholastic profession and who will, accordingly, secure the progress of culture in the field of the sciences against any new invasions of the obscurantists.

7:11

. .

Under the general title *The Conflict of the Faculties* I am now issuing three essays that I wrote for different purposes and at different times. They are, however, of such a nature as to form a systematic unity and combine in one work, though it was only later that I realized that they could be suitably brought together in one volume (in order to prevent scattering them) as the conflict of the *lower* faculty with the three *higher* faculties.

[b] grief of soul
[c] which should be denied and denied altogether

First part
The conflict of the philosophy faculty with the
theology faculty

Introduction

Whoever it was that first hit on the notion of a university and proposed that a public institution of this kind be established, it was not a bad idea to handle the entire content of learning (really, the thinkers devoted to it) *like a factory*, so to speak – by a division of labor, so that for every branch of the sciences there would be a public teacher or *professor* appointed as its trustee, and all of these together would form a kind of learned community called a *university* (or higher school). The university would have a certain autonomy (since only scholars can pass judgment on scholars as such), and accordingly it would be authorized to perform certain functions through its *faculties** (smaller societies, each comprising the university specialists in one main branch of learning): to admit to the university students seeking entrance from the lower schools and, having conducted examinations, by its own authority to grant degrees or confer the universally recognized status of "doctor" on free teachers (that is, teachers who are not members of the university) – in other words, *to create doctors.*

In addition to these *incorporated* scholars, there can also be scholars *at large*, who do not belong to the *university* but simply work on part of the great content of learning, either forming independent organizations, like various workshops (called *academies* or *scientific societies*), or living, so to speak, in a state of nature so far as learning is concerned, each working by himself, as an *amateur* and without public precepts or rules, at extending and propagating [his field of] learning.

We must distinguish, further, between scholars proper and those members of the *intelligentsia* (university graduates) who are instruments of the government, invested with an office for its own purpose (which is not exactly the progress of the sciences). As such, they must indeed have been educated at the university; but they may well have forgotten much of what they learned (about theory), so long as they retain enough to fill a civil

7:18

---

* Each of which has its *Dean*, who is the head of the faculty. This title, taken from astrology, originally meant one of the three astral spirits that preside over a sign of the zodiac (of 30 degrees), each governing 10 degrees. From the stars it was transferred to the military camp (*ab astris ad castra*,*ᵈ* see *Salmasius de annis climacteriis*, page 561),⁶ and finally to the university, where, however, the number 10 (of professors) was not taken into account. Since it was the scholars who first thought up most of the honorific titles with which state officials now adorn themselves, they can hardly be blamed for not having forgotten themselves.

ᵈ from star to camp

office. While only the scholar can provide the principles underlying their functions, it is enough if they retain empirical knowledge of the statutes relevant to their office (hence what has to do with practice). Accordingly they can be called the *businesspeople* or technicians of learning. As tools of the government (clergymen, magistrates, and physicians), they have legal influence on the public and form a special class of the intelligentsia, who are not free to make public use of their learning as they see fit, but are subject to the censorship of the faculties, so the government must keep them under strict control, to prevent them from trying to exercise judicial power, which belongs to the faculties; for they deal directly with the people, who are incompetent (like the clergyman in relation to the layman), and share in the executive, though certainly not the legislative, power in their field.

GENERAL DIVISION OF THE FACULTIES

The faculties are traditionally divided into two ranks: *three higher* faculties and *one lower* faculty. It is clear that this division is made and this terminology adopted with reference to the government rather than the learned professions; for a faculty is considered higher only if its teachings – both as to their content and the way they are expounded to the public – interest the government itself, while the faculty whose function is only to look after the interests of science is called lower because it may hold whatever propositions about science it finds good. Now the government is interested primarily in means for securing the strongest and most lasting influence on the people, and the subjects which the higher faculties teach are just such means. Accordingly, the government reserves the right itself to *sanction* the teachings of the higher faculties, but those of the lower faculty it leaves up to the scholars' reason. – But even when the government sanctions teachings, it does not itself *teach;* it requires only that the respective faculties, *in expounding a subject publicly,* adopt certain teachings and exclude their contraries. For the government does not teach, but it commands those who, in accepting its offices,* have contracted to teach what it wants (whether this be true or not). – If a government were to concern itself with [the truth of] these teachings, and so with the growth or progress of the sciences, then it

7:19

---

* It is a principle in the British Parliament that the monarch's speech from the throne is to be considered the work of his ministers (since the House must be entitled to judge, examine, and attack the content of the speech and it would be beneath the monarch's dignity to let himself be charged with error, ignorance, or untruth). And this principle is quite acute and correct. It is in the same way that the choice of certain teachings which the government expressly sanctions for public exposition must remain subject to scholarly criticism; for this choice must not be ascribed to the monarch but to a state official whom he appoints to do it – an official who, it is supposed, could have misunderstood or misrepresented his ruler's will.

would, in the highest person, be trying to play the role of scholar, and its pedantry would only undermine the respect due it. It is beneath the government's dignity to mingle with the people (in this case, the people in the learned professions), who cannot take a joke and deal impartially with everyone who meddles in the sciences.

It is absolutely essential that the learned community at the university also contain a faculty that is independent of the government's command with regard to its teachings;* one that, having no commands to give, is free to evaluate everything, and concerns itself with the interests of the sciences, that is, with truth: one in which reason is authorized to speak out publicly. For without a faculty of this kind, the truth would not come to light (and this would be to the government's own detriment); but reason is by its nature free and admits of no command to hold something as true (no imperative "Believe!" but only a free *credo*ʿ). – The reason why this faculty, despite its great prerogative (freedom), is called the lower faculty lies in human nature; for a human being who can give commands, even though he is someone else's humble servant, is considered more distinguished than a free man who has no one under his command.

7:20

---

* A minister of the French government summoned a few of the most eminent merchants and asked them for suggestions on how to stimulate trade – as if he would know how to choose the best of these. After one had suggested this and another that, an old merchant who had kept quiet so far said: "Build good roads, mint sound money, give us laws for exchanging money readily, etc.; but as for the rest, leave us alone!"⁷ If the government were to consult the Philosophy Faculty about what teachings to prescribe for scholars in general, it would get a similar reply: just don't interfere with the progress of understanding and science.
ʿ I believe

I.
On the relation of the faculties

First section
The concept and division of the higher faculties

Whenever an artificial institution is based on an Idea of reason (such as that of a government) which is to prove itself practical in an object of experience (such as the entire field of learning at the time), we can take it for granted that the experiment was made according to some principle contained in reason, even if only obscurely, and some plan based on it – not by merely contingent collections and arbitrary combinations of cases that have occurred. And a plan of this sort makes a certain kind of division necessary.

We can therefore assume that the organization of a university into classes and faculties did not depend entirely on chance. Without attributing premature wisdom and learning to the government, we can say that by its own felt need (to influence the people by certain teachings) it managed to arrive *a priori* at a principle of division which seems otherwise to be of empirical origin, so that the *a priori* principle happily coincides with the one now in use. But this does not mean that I shall advocate [the present system] as if it had no faults.

According to reason (that is, objectively), the following order exists among the incentives that the government can use to achieve its end (of influencing the people): first comes the *eternal* well-being of each, then his *civil* well-being as a member of society, and finally his *physical* well-being (a long life and health). By public teachings about the *first* of these, the government can exercise very great influence to uncover the inmost thoughts and guide the most secret intentions of its subjects. By teachings regarding the *second*, it helps to keep their external conduct under the reins of public laws, and by its teachings regarding the *third*, to make sure that it will have a strong and numerous people to serve its purposes. So the ranks customarily assigned to the higher faculties – *theology* first, *law* second, and *medicine* third – are in accordance with reason. According to *natural instinct*, however, human beings consider the physician most important, because he prolongs their *life*. Next to him comes the jurist, who promises to secure their contingent *possessions*. And only last (almost at the point of death) do they send for the clergyman, though it is their salvation that is in question; for even the clergyman, no matter how highly he commends the happiness of the world to come, actually perceives nothing of it and hopes fervently that the doctor can keep him in this vale of tears a while longer.

. .

All three higher faculties base the teachings which the government entrusts to them on *writings,* as is necessary for a people governed by learning, since otherwise there would be no fixed and universally accessible norm for their guidance. It is self-evident that such a text (or book) must comprise *statutes,* that is, teachings that proceed from the power of choice of an authority (that do not issue directly from reason); for otherwise it could not demand obedience simply, as something the government has sanctioned. And this holds true of the entire code of laws, even those of its teachings, to be expounded to the public, which could also be derived from *reason:* the code takes no notice of their rational ground, but bases itself on the command of an external legislator. The code of laws is the canon, and as such it is quite distinct from those books which the faculties write as (supposedly) complete summaries of the spirit of the code, so that the community (of the learned and the ignorant) may grasp its concepts more easily and use them more safely – the *symbolic books,* for example. These can claim only the respect due to the *organon,* which gives easier access to the canon, and have no authority whatsoever; even if the most eminent scholars in a certain field should agree to give such a book the weight of norm for their faculty, it would derive no authority from this: for the scholars are not entitled to do this, but only to establish the book as a pedagogical method for the time being – a method that can always be changed to suit the times and, in any case, concerns only the way they lecture [on the code], without in any way affecting the content of the legislation.

7:23

So the biblical theologian (as a member of a higher faculty) draws his teachings not from reason but from the *Bible;* the professor of law gets his, not from natural law, but from the *law of the land;* and the medical expert does not draw his *method of therapy as practiced on the public* from the physiology of the human body but from *medical regulations.* As soon as one of these faculties presumes to mix with its teachings something it treats as derived from reason, it offends against the authority of the government that issues orders through it and encroaches on the territory of the philosophy faculty, which mercilessly strips from it all the shining plumes that were protected by the government and deals with it on a footing of equality and freedom. The higher faculties must, therefore, take great care not to enter into a misalliance with the lower faculty, but must keep it at a respectful distance, so that the dignity of their statutes will not be damaged by the free play of reason.

A.

THE DISTINCTIVE CHARACTERISTIC OF THE
THEOLOGY FACULTY

The biblical theologian proves the existence of God on the grounds that He spoke in the Bible, which also discusses His nature (and even goes so far into it that reason cannot keep up with the text, as when, for example, it speaks of the incomprehensible mystery of His threefold personality). But the biblical theologian as such cannot and need not prove that God Himself spoke through the Bible, since that is a matter of history and belongs to the philosophy faculty. [Treating it] as a matter of faith, he will therefore base it – even for the scholar – on a certain (indemonstrable and inexplicable) *feeling* that the Bible is divine. But the question of the divine origin of the Bible (in the literal sense) must not be raised at all in public discourses directed to the people; since this is a scholarly matter, they would fail completely to understand it and, as a result, would only get entangled in impertinent speculations and doubts. In such matters it is much safer to rely on the people's confidence in their teachers. – The biblical theologian can also have no authority to ascribe a nonliteral – for example, a moral – meaning to statements in the text, and since there is no human interpreter of the Scriptures authorized by God, he must rather count on a supernatural opening of his understanding by a spirit that guides to all truth than allow reason to intervene and (without any higher authority) maintain its own interpretation. – Finally, as far as our will and its fulfillment of God's commands is concerned, the biblical theologian must not rely on nature – that is, on the human being's own moral power (virtue) – but on grace (a supernatural but, at the same time, moral influence), which the human being can obtain only by an ardent faith that transforms his heart – a faith that itself, in turn, he can expect only through grace. – If the biblical theologian meddles with his reason in any of these tenets, then, even granting that reason strives most sincerely and earnestly for that same objective, he leaps (like Romulus's brother) over the wall of ecclesiastical faith, the only thing that assures his salvation, and strays into the free and open fields of private judgment and philosophy. And there, having run away from the Church's government, he is exposed to all the dangers of anarchy. – But note well that I am here speaking only of the *pure (purus, putus)*[f] biblical theologian, who is not yet contaminated by the ill-reputed spirit of freedom that belongs to reason and philosophy. For as soon as we allow two different callings to combine and run together, we can form no clear notion of the characteristic that distinguishes each by itself.

7:24

[f] pure and clean (a Latin idiom)

B.

THE DISTINCTIVE CHARACTERISTIC OF THE
FACULTY OF LAW

The jurist, as an authority on the text, does not look to his reason for the laws that secure the *Mine* and *Thine,* but to the code of laws that has been publicly promulgated and sanctioned by the highest authority (if, as he should, he acts as a civil servant). To require him to prove the truth of these laws and their conformity with right, or to defend them against reason's objections, would be unfair. For these decrees first determine what is right, and the jurist must straightaway dismiss as nonsense the further question of whether the decrees themselves are right. To refuse to obey an external and supreme will on the grounds that it allegedly does not conform with reason would be absurd; for the dignity of the government consists precisely in this: that it does not leave its subjects free to judge what is right or wrong according to their own notions, but [determines right and wrong] for them by precepts of the legislative power.

    In one respect, however, the faculty of law is better off in practice than the theology faculty: it has a visible interpreter of the law – namely, a judge or, if his decision is appealed, a legal commission, and (as the highest appeal) the legislator himself. The theological faculty is not so well provided for, when the sayings of its sacred book have to be interpreted. But this advantage is offset by a disadvantage at least equal to it: namely, that any secular code of laws always remains subject to change, as experience brings more or better insight, whereas the sacred code decrees that there will be no change (either by subtraction or addition), and maintains that it is closed forever. Furthermore, biblical theologians do not join in the jurist's complaint that it is all but vain to hope for a precisely determined norm for the administration of justice (*ius certus*); for they reject the claim that their dogma lacks a norm that is clear and determined for every case. Moreover, if the practicing lawyer (counsel or attorney-at-law) has harmed a client by giving him bad advice, he refuses to be held responsible for it (*ob consilium nemo tenetur*[g]); but the practicing theologian (preacher or spiritual adviser) does not hesitate to take the responsibility on himself and to guarantee – at least to hear him talk – that any decision passed in the next world will correspond exactly with his decisions in this one. But he will probably decline if he is invited to declare formally that he will stake his soul on the truth of everything he would have us believe on the Bible's authority. And yet, the nature of the principles maintained by these public teachers permits no doubt whatsoever that their assurances are correct – assurances they can give all the

7:25

7:26

---

[g] no one is bound by the advice he receives

more safely because they need not fear that experience will refute them in this life.

C.
THE DISTINCTIVE CHARACTERISTIC OF THE
FACULTY OF MEDICINE

Although medicine is an art, it is an art that is drawn directly from nature and must therefore be derived from a science of nature. So the physician, as a man of learning, must come under some faculty by which he must have been trained and to whose judgment he must remain subject. – But since the way physicians deal with the people's health must be of great interest to the government, it is entitled to supervise their dealings with the public through an assembly chosen from the businessmen of this faculty (practicing doctors) – *a board of public health* – and through medical regulations. Unlike the other higher faculties, however, the faculty of medicine must derive its rules of procedure not from orders of the authorities but from the nature of things themselves, so that its teachings must have also belonged originally to the philosophy faculty, taken in its widest sense. And because of this special characteristic of the medical faculty, medical regulations deal not so much with what doctors should do as with what they should not do: they ensure, *first*, that there will be doctors for the public and, *secondly*, that there will be no spurious doctors (no *ius impune occidendi*,[h] according to the principle: *fiat experimentum in corpori vili*[i]). By the first of these principles, the government watches over the public's *convenience*, and by the second, over the public's *safety* (in the matter of the people's health). And since these two services are the function of a *police force*, all medical regulations really have to do only with *policing the medical profession*.

The medical faculty is, therefore, much freer than the other two higher faculties and closely akin to the philosophy faculty. Indeed, it is altogether free with regard to the teachings by which physicians are trained, since its texts cannot be sanctioned by the highest authorities but can be drawn only from nature. It can also have no laws strictly speaking (if by laws we mean the unalterable will of the legislator), but only regulations (*edicts*); and since learning requires [as its object] a systematic content of teachings, knowledge of these regulations does not constitute the learning [of the medical faculty]. This faculty does indeed possess such learning; but since the government does not have the authority to sanction it (because it is not contained in any *code of laws*), it must leave this to the faculty's discretion and concern itself only with helping medical practitioners to be

7:27

[h] right to kill with impunity
[i] may experiments be done on worthless bodies

of service to the public, by establishing dispensaries and hospitals. – These practitioners (physicians), however, remain subject to the judgment of their faculty in matters which concern the medical police and so interest the government.

Second section
The concept and division of the lower faculty

The lower faculty is the rank in the university that occupies itself with teachings which are not adopted as directives by order of a superior, or in so far as they are not so adopted. Now we may well comply with a practical teaching out of obedience, but we can never accept it as true simply because we are ordered to (*de par le Roi*).[j] This is not only objectively impossible (a judgment that *ought not* to be made), but also subjectively quite impossible (a judgment that no one *can* make). For he who, as he says, wants to err does not really err and, in fact, accept the false judgment as true; he merely declares, falsely, an assent that is not to be found in him. – So when it is a question of the *truth* of a certain teaching to be expounded in public, the teacher cannot appeal to a supreme command nor the pupil pretend that he believed it by order. This can happen only when it is a question of *action*, and even then the pupil must recognize by a *free* judgment that such a command was really issued and that he is obligated or at least entitled to obey it; otherwise, his acceptance of it would be an empty pretense and a lie. – Now the power to judge autonomously – that is, freely (according to principles of thought in general) – is called reason. So the philosophy faculty, because it must answer for the truth of the teachings it is to adopt or even allow, must be conceived as free and subject only to laws given by reason, not by the government.

But a department of this kind, too, must be established at a university; in other words, a university must have a faculty of philosophy. Its function in relation to the three higher faculties is to control them and, in this way, be useful to them, since *truth* (the essential and first condition of learning in general) is the main thing, whereas the *utility* the higher faculties promise the government is of secondary importance. – We can also grant the theology faculty's proud claim that the philosophy faculty is its handmaid (though the question remains, whether the servant *carries her lady's torch before or her train behind*), provided it is not driven away or silenced. For the very *modesty* [of its claim] – merely to be free, as it leaves others free, to discover the truth for the benefit of all the sciences and to set it

7:28

---

[j] by the king's [command]

before the higher faculties to use as they will – must commend it to the government as above suspicion and, indeed, indispensable.

Now the philosophy faculty consists of two departments: a department of *historical cognition* (including history, geography, philology and the humanities, along with all the empirical knowledge contained in the natural sciences), and a department of *pure rational cognition* (pure mathematics and pure philosophy, the metaphysics of nature and of morals). And it also studies the relation of these two divisions of learning to each other. It therefore extends to all parts of human cognition (including, from a historical viewpoint, the teachings of the higher faculties), though there are some parts (namely, the distinctive teachings and precepts of the higher faculties) which it does not treat as its own content, but as objects it will examine and criticize for the benefit of the sciences.

The philosophy faculty can, therefore, lay claim to any teaching, in order to test its truth. The government cannot forbid it to do this without acting against its own proper and essential purpose; and the higher faculties must put up with the objections and doubts it brings forward in public, though they may well find this irksome, since, were it not for such critics, they could rest undisturbed in possession of what they have once occupied, by whatever title, and rule over it despotically. – Only the businesspeople of the higher faculties (clergymen, legal officials, and doctors) can be prevented from contradicting in public the teachings that the government has entrusted to them to expound in fulfilling their respective offices, and from venturing to play the philosopher's role; for the faculties alone, not the officials appointed by the government, can be allowed to do this, since these officials get their cognition from the faculties. If, that is to say, these officials – for example, clergymen and legal officials – should want to put before the public their objections and doubts about ecclesiastical and civil laws that have been given, they would be inciting the people to rebel against the government. The faculties, on the other hand, put their objections and doubts only to one another, as scholars, and the people pay no attention to such matters in a practical way, even if they should hear of them; for, agreeing that these subtleties are not their affair, they feel obliged to be content with what the government officials, appointed for this purpose, announce to them. – But the result of this freedom, which the philosophy faculty must enjoy unimpaired, is that the higher faculties (themselves better instructed) will lead these officials more and more onto the way of truth. And the officials, for their own part, also more enlightened about their duty, will not be repelled at changing their exposition, since the new way involves nothing more than a clearer insight into means for achieving the same end. And such a change can well come about without polemics and attacks, that only stir up unrest, on the traditional way of teaching, when [it is seen that] the content to be taught is preserved in its entirety.

7:29

Third section
On the illegal conflict of the higher faculties with the lower faculty

A public conflict of views, hence a scholarly debate, can be illegal by reason of its matter or its form. It would be illegal by reason of its *matter* if it were not permissible to *debate*, in this way, about a public proposition because it was not permissible to *judge* publicly this proposition and its opposite. It would be illegal by reason of its *form*, or the way in which the debate is carried on, if one of the parties relied, not on objective grounds directed to his adversary's reason, but on subjective grounds, trying to determine his judgment through his *inclinations* and so to gain his assent by fraud (including bribery) or force (threats).

Now the faculties engage in public conflict in order to influence the   7:30
people, and each can acquire this influence only by convincing the people that it knows best now to promote their welfare. But as for the way they propose to accomplish this, the lower faculty is diametrically opposed to the higher faculties.

The people conceive of their welfare, not primarily as freedom, but as [the realization of] their natural ends and so as these three things: being *happy* after death, having their *possessions* guaranteed by public laws during their life in society, and finally, looking forward to the physical enjoyment of *life* itself (that is, health and a long life).

But the philosophy faculty can deal with all these wishes only by precepts it derives from reason. It depends, accordingly, on the principle of freedom and limits itself to saying what the human being himself can and should do toward fulfilling these wishes – live *righteously*, commit no *injustice*, and, by being *moderate* in his pleasures and patient in his illnesses, rely primarily on the self-help of nature. None of this, indeed, requires great learning; but in these matters we can, for the most part, dispense with learning if we would only restrain our inclinations and be ruled by our reason. But since this requires self-exertion, it does not suit the people.

So the people (who find the philosophy faculty's teaching a poor substitute for their inclination to *enjoyment* and their aversion from *working* for it) invite the higher faculties to make them more acceptable proposals. And the demands they make on these scholars run like this. "As for the *philosophers'* twaddle, I've known that all along. What I want you, as scholars, to tell me is this: if I've been a *scoundrel* all my life, how can I get an eleventh-hour ticket to heaven? If I've *broken* the law, how can I still win my case? And even if I've used and *abused* my physical powers as I've pleased, how can I stay healthy and live a long time? Surely this is why you have studied – so that you would know more than someone like ourselves (you call us idiots), who can claim nothing more than sound under-

257

standing." – But now the people are approaching these scholars as if they were soothsayers and magicians, with knowledge of supernatural things; for if an unlearned person expects something from a scholar, he readily forms exaggerated notions of him. So we can naturally expect that if someone has the effrontery to give himself out as such a miracle-worker, the people will flock to him and contemptuously desert the philosophy faculty.

7:31

But the businesspeople of the three higher faculties will always be such miracle-workers, unless the philosophy faculty is allowed to counteract them publicly – not in order to overthrow their teachings but only to deny the magic power that the public superstitiously attributes to these teachings and the rites connected with them – as if, by passively surrendering themselves to such skillful guides, the people would be excused from any activity of their own and led, in ease and comfort, to achieve the ends they desire.

If the higher faculties adopt such principles (and it is certainly not their function to do this), then they are and always will be in conflict with the lower faculty; but this conflict is also *illegal;* for the higher faculties, instead of viewing transgressions of the law as hindrances, welcome them as occasions for showing their great art and skill in making everything as good as ever, and, indeed, better than it would otherwise have been.

The people want to be *led,* that is (with the language of the demagogues), they want to be *duped.* But they want to be led not by the scholars of the faculties (whose wisdom is too high for them), but by the businessmen of the faculties – clergymen, legal officials, and doctors – who understand a botched job (*savoir faire*)[k] and have the people's confidence. And so the government, which can work on the people only through these practitioners, will itself be *led* to obtrude on the faculties a theory that arises, not from the pure insight of their scholars, but from calculations of the influence their practitioners can exert on the people by it. For the people naturally adhere most to doctrines which demand the least self-exertion and the least use of their own reason, and which can best accommodate their duties to their inclinations – in theology, for example, the doctrine that they can be saved merely by a literal "faith," without having to examine (or even really know) what they are supposed to believe, or that their performance of certain prescribed rites will itself wash away their transgressions; or in law, the doctrine that compliance with the letter of the law exempts them from examining the legislator's intentions.

7:32

[If the higher faculties adopt such principles], they are involved in an essential and irreconcilable conflict with the lower faculty, and this conflict is illegal because, if the government legislated for the higher faculties according to the principle attributed to it [in the preceding paragraph], its

[k] know-how

258

own principle would authorize anarchy itself. – For *inclination* and, in general, what someone finds useful for his *private aim* can never qualify as a law, and so cannot be set forth as a law by the higher faculties; hence a government that sanctioned such principles would offend against reason itself and, by this, bring the higher faculties into conflict with the lower faculty – a conflict that cannot be tolerated because it would completely destroy the philosophy faculty; this, admittedly, is the quickest way of ending a conflict; but it is also (in medical terms) a *heroic* means – one that endangers life.

Fourth section
On the legal conflict of the higher faculties with the lower faculty

Regardless of their content, any teachings that the government may be entitled to sanction for public exposition by the higher faculties can be accepted and respected only as statutes proceeding from [the government's] choice and as human wisdom, which is not infallible. But the government cannot be completely indifferent to the truth of these teachings, and in this respect they must remain subject to reason (whose interests the philosophy faculty has to safeguard). Now this is possible only if complete freedom to examine these teachings in public is permitted, so since arbitrary propositions, though sanctioned by the supreme authority, may not always harmonize with the teachings reason maintains as necessary, there will be a conflict between the higher and lower faculties which is, first, *inevitable*, but second, *legal* as well; for the lower faculty has not only the title but also the duty, if not to state the *whole* truth in public, at least to see to it that *everything* put forward in public as a principle is true.

If the source of a sanctioned teaching is *historical*, then – no matter how highly it may be commended as sacred to the unhesitating obedience of faith – the philosophy faculty is entitled and indeed obligated to investigate its origin with critical scrupulosity. If the teaching, though presented in the manner of historical knowledge (as revelation), has a *rational* origin, the lower faculty cannot be prevented from investigating, in the historical narrative, the rational basis of this legislation and also evaluating it as either technically or morally practical. Finally, the source of a teaching proclaimed as law may be only *aesthetic:* in other words, the teaching may be based on a feeling connected with it (for example, a pious feeling of supernatural influence – although, since feeling yields no objective principle,[1] it is only subjectively valid and cannot provide the basis for a universal law). In this

7:33

[1] *Princip*

259

case the philosophy faculty must be free to examine in public and to evaluate with cold reason the source and content of this alleged basis of doctrine, unintimidated by the sacredness of the object which has supposedly been experienced and determined to bring this alleged feeling to concepts. The following paragraphs contain the formal principles of procedure for such a conflict and the consequences resulting from it.

1) This conflict cannot and should not be settled by an amicable accommodation (*amicabilis compositio*), but (as a lawsuit) calls for a verdict, that is, the decision of a judge (reason) which has the force of law. For the dispute could be settled only through dishonesty, by [the lower faculty's] concealing the cause of the dissension and letting itself be persuaded; but a maxim of this kind is directly opposed to the spirit of a *philosophy* faculty, which has the public presentation of truth as its function.

2) This conflict can never end, and it is the philosophy faculty that must always be prepared to keep it going. For there must always be statutory precepts of the government regarding teachings to be set forth in public, since unlimited freedom to proclaim any sort of opinion publicly is bound to be dangerous both to the government and to the public itself. But because all the government's statutes proceed from human beings, or are at least sanctioned by them, there is always the danger that they may be erroneous or unsuitable; and this applies also to the statutes that the government's sanction supplies to the higher faculties. Consequently, the philosophy faculty can never lay aside its arms in the face of the danger that threatens the truth entrusted to its protection, because the higher faculties will never give up their desire to rule.

7:34   3) This conflict can never detract from the dignity of the government. The conflict is not between the faculties and the government but between one faculty and another, and the government can look on unmoved. Though it has indeed taken certain tenets of the higher faculties under its own protection, by directing the businessmen of these faculties to expound them to the public, it is not protecting the higher faculties, as learned societies, on account of the truth of these teachings, views and opinions they are to expound publicly, but only for the sake of its (the government's) own advantage; for it would be beneath the government's dignity to decide about the intrinsic truth of these tenets and so to play the role of scholar. – The higher faculties, in other words, must answer to the government only for the instruction and information they give their businessmen to expound to the public; for these circulate among the people as a *civil* community and, because they could impair the government's influence over it, are subject to its sanction. On the other hand, the teachings and views that the faculties, as theorists, have to settle with one another are directed to a different kind of public – a *learned* community devoted to the sciences; and since the people are resigned to understanding nothing about this, the government does not see fit to intervene in scholarly

discussions.* The rank of the higher faculties (as the right side of the   7:35
parliament of learning) supports the government's statutes; but in as free a
system of government as must exist when it is a question of truth, there
must also be an opposition party (the left side), and this is the philosophy
faculty's bench. For without its rigorous examinations and objections, the
government would not be adequately informed about what could be to its
own advantage or detriment. – But if the businesspeople of the faculties
should want, on their own initiative, to make changes in the decrees given
for them to expound publicly, then the government in its vigilance could
lay claim to [jurisdiction over] them as *innovators* who could be dangerous
to it. It could not, however, pass judgment on them directly, but only in
accordance with the most loyal verdict drawn from the higher faculties,
since it is only *through the faculty* that the government can direct these
businesspeople to expound certain teachings.

4) This conflict is quite compatible with an agreement of the learned
and civil community in maxims which, if observed, must bring about a
constant progress of both ranks of the faculties toward greater perfection,
and finally prepare the way for the government to remove all restrictions
that its choice has put on freedom of public judgment.

In this way, it could well happen that the last would some day be first
(the lower faculty would be the higher) – not, indeed, in authority, but in
counseling the authority (the government). For the government may find
the freedom of the philosophy faculty, and the increased insight gained
from this freedom, a better means for achieving its ends than its own
absolute authority.

RESULT

So this antagonism, that is, this *conflict* of two parties united in [their
striving toward] one and the same final end (*concordia discors, discordia*

---

* On the contrary, if the businesspeople of the faculties (in their role of practitioners) bring   7:34
the conflict before the civil community (publicly – from the pulpits, for example), as they are
prone to do, they drag it illegitimately before the judgment seat of the people (who are not
competent to judge in scholarly matters), and it ceases to be a scholarly debate. And then
begins the state of illegal conflict mentioned above, in which doctrines in keeping with the
people's inclinations are set forth, the seeds of insurrection and factions are sown, and the
government is thereby endangered. These self-appointed tribunes of the people, in doing
this, renounce the learned professions, encroach on the rights of the civil constitution (stir
up political struggles), and really deserve to be called *neologists*. This justly hated name is
badly misused when it is applied indiscriminately to every author of innovations in doctrine
and pedagogical method (for why should the old always be better than the new?). But those
who introduce a completely different form of government, or rather a lack of any government (anarchy), by handing over scholarly questions to the decision of the people, really
deserve to be branded neologists; for they can steer the judgment of the people in whatever
direction they please, by working on their habits, feelings, and inclinations, and so win them
away from the influence of a legitimate government.

concors),*ᵐ* is not a *war*, that is, not a dispute arising from conflicting final aims regarding the *Mine* and *Thine* of learning. And since, like the political Mine and Thine, this consists in *freedom* and *property*, with freedom necessarily preceding property as its condition, any right granted to the higher faculty entails permission for the lower faculty to bring its scruples about this right before the learned public.

Appendix
The conflict between the theology and philosophy faculties, as an example to clarify the conflict of the faculties

I.
SUBJECT MATTER OF THE CONFLICT

A biblical theologian is, properly speaking, one *versed in the Scriptures* with regard to *ecclesiastical faith*, which is based on statutes – that is, on laws proceeding from another person's act of choice. A rational theologian, on the other hand, is one *versed in reason* with regard to *religious* faith, which is based on inner laws that can be developed from every human being's own reason. The very concept of religion shows that it can never be based on decrees (no matter how high their source); for religion is not the sum of certain teachings regarded as divine revelations (that is called theology), but the sum of all our duties regarded as divine *commands* (and, on the subject's part, the maxim of fulfilling them as such). As far as its matter, i.e. object*ⁿ* is concerned, religion does not differ in any point from morality, for it is concerned with duties as such. Its distinction from morality is a merely formal one: that reason in its legislation uses the Idea of God, which is derived from morality itself, to give morality influence on man's will to fulfill all his duties. This is why there is only one religion. Although there are indeed different varieties of belief in divine revelation and its statutory teachings, which cannot spring from reason – that is, different forms in which the divine will is represented sensibly so as to give it influence on our minds – there are not different religions. Of these forms Christianity, as far as we know, is the most adequate. Now Christianity, as found in the Bible, is composed of two heterogeneous elements, one of which comprises the canon of religion and the other its organon or vehi-

7:37 cle. The canon of religion can be called *pure religious faith* (which has no statutes and is based on mere reason); its vehicle can be called *ecclesiastical faith*, which is based entirely on statutes that need to be revealed in order

---

ᵐ discordant concord, concordant discord
ⁿ object

to hold as sacred doctrines and precepts for conduct. – But since we have a duty to use ecclesiastical faith too (provided we can adopt it as divine revelation) as a guide to our end of pure religious faith, we can see why the term "religious faith" commonly includes dogma based on Scripture as well.

The biblical theologian says: "Search the Scriptures, where you think you find eternal life."[8] But since the moral improvement of the human being is the sole condition of eternal life, the only way we can find eternal life in any Scripture whatsoever is by putting it there. For the concepts and principles required for eternal life cannot really be learned from anyone else: the teacher's exposition is only the occasion for him to develop them out of his own reason. But the Scriptures contain more than what is in itself required for eternal life; part of their content is a matter of historical belief, and while this can indeed be useful to religious faith as its mere sensible vehicle (for certain people and certain eras), it is not an essential part of religious faith. Now the faculty of biblical theologians insists on this historical content as divine revelation as strongly as if belief in it belonged to religion. The philosophy faculty, however, opposes the theology faculty regarding this confusion, and what divine revelation contains that is true of religion proper.

A *method of teaching*, too, is connected with this vehicle (that is, with what is added on to the teachings of religion). This method is not to be taken as divine revelation but as something left to the apostles' discretion. However, we can accept it as valid in relation to the way of thinking in the apostles' times ($\chi\alpha\tau'$ $\dot{\alpha}\nu\theta\rho\omega\pi o\nu$),[o] not as a part of doctrine itself ($\chi\alpha\tau'$ $\alpha\lambda\eta\theta\epsilon\iota\alpha\nu$)[p]: having value either in a negative way, as a mere concession to certain erroneous but widely held views, so that the apostles need not offend against a prevalent illusion that was not essentially opposed to religion (for example, belief in diabolical possession), or also in a positive way, as taking advantage of a people's partiality to its old ecclesiastical faith, which was now to end, in introducing the new (for example, interpreting the history of the old covenant as a prototype for the events of the new – though if we make the mistake of including [these remnants of] Judaism in the tenets of faith, they can well make us moan: *nunc istae reliquias nos exercent* – Cicero).[q]   7:38

For this reason scriptural erudition in Christianity is subject to many difficulties in the art of exegesis, and the higher faculty (of biblical theologians) is bound to come into conflict with the lower faculty over it and its principle.[r] For the higher faculty, being concerned primarily for theoreti-

[o] for the human being
[p] for the truth
[q] now these remains weary us[9]
[r] *Princip*

cal biblical knowledge, suspects the lower faculty of philosophizing away all the teachings that must be considered real revelation and so taken literally, and of ascribing to them whatever sense suits it. On the other hand the lower faculty, looking more to the practical – that is, more to religion than to dogma – accuses the higher of so concentrating on the means, dogma, that it completely loses sight of the final end, inner religion, which must be moral and based on reason. And so, when conflict arises about the sense of a scriptural text, philosophy – that is, the lower faculty, which has truth as its end – claims the prerogative of deciding its meaning. The following section contains the philosophical principles of scriptural exegesis. By this I do not mean that the interpretation must be philosophical (aimed at contributing to philosophy), but only that the *principles* of interpretation must be philosophical. For any principle – even those exegetical principles having to do with historical or grammatical criticism – must always be dictated by reason; and this is especially true here, since what the text yields for religion can be only an object of reason.'

II.

PHILOSOPHICAL PRINCIPLES OF SCRIPTURAL EXEGESIS FOR SETTLING THE CONFLICT

I. If a scriptural text contains certain *theoretical* teachings which are proclaimed sacred but which *transcend* all rational concepts (even moral ones), it *may* be interpreted in the interests of practical reason; but if it contains statements that contradict practical reason, it *must* be interpreted in the interests of practical reason. Here are some pertinent examples.

7:39
  a) The doctrine of the Trinity, taken literally, has *no practical relevance at all*, even if we think we understand it; and it is even more clearly irrelevant if we realize that it transcends all our concepts. – Whether we are to worship three or ten persons in the Deity makes no difference: the pupil will implicitly accept one as readily as the other because he has no concept at all of a number of persons in one God (hypostases), and still more so because this distinction can make no difference in his rules of conduct. On the other hand, if we read a moral meaning into this article of faith (as I have tried to do in *Religion within the Boundaries* etc.), it would no longer contain an inconsequential belief but an intelligible one that refers to our moral vocation. The same holds true of the doctrine that one person of the Godhead became *human*. For if we think of this God-

---

' following Vorländer's emendation: "*weil, was aus Schriftstellen für die Reltgion auszumitteln sei, bloß ein Gegenstand der Vernunft.*"

man, not as the Idea of humanity in its full moral perfection, present in God from eternity and beloved by him* (cf. *Religion*, p. 73 ff),[10] but as the Deity "dwelling incarnate"[11] in a real human being and working as a second nature in him, then we can draw nothing practical from this mystery: since we cannot require ourselves to rival a God, we cannot take him as an example. And I shall not insist on the further difficulty – why, if such a union is possible in one case, God has not let all human beings participate in it, so that everyone would necessarily be pleasing to him. Similar considerations can be raised about the stories of the resurrection and ascension of this God-man.

For practical purposes we can be quite indifferent as to whether we   7:40 shall live merely as souls after death or whether our personal identity in the next world requires the same matter that now forms our body, so that our soul is not a distinct substance and our body must be restored to life. For who is so fond of his body that he would want to drag it around with him for eternity, if he can get along without it? So the apostle's conclusion: "If Christ had not risen" (if his body had not come to life), "neither would we rise again"[13] (we would not continue to live after death) is not valid. But it may not be a conclusion (for one does not argue on the basis of an inspiration); he may have meant only that we have reason to believe Christ is still alive and that our faith would be in vain if even so perfect a man did not continue to live after (bodily) death. This belief, which reason suggested to him (as to all human beings), moved him to historical belief in a public event, which he accepted in good faith as true and used as a basis of proof for moral belief in the future life, failing to realize that, apart from his moral belief, he himself would have found it hard to credit this tale. In this way the moral purpose would be achieved, though the apostle's way of representing it bears the mark of the school of thought in which he was trained. – Moreover, there are serious objections to that event: by establishing the Lord's Supper (a sad colloquy) as a commemoration of himself, Christ seems to be taking formal leave of his disciples (not looking forward to a speedy reunion with them). His complaints on the cross

---

* The enthusiasm of *Postellus*,[12] a sixteenth-century Venetian, on this point is of a highly original kind and serves as an excellent example of the sort of aberration, and indeed *logical* raving people can fall into if they transform the perceptible rendering of a pure idea of reason into the representation of an object of the senses. For if we understand by that Idea not humanity in the abstract but a real human being, this person must be of one or the other sex. And if this divine offspring is of the male sex (a son), he has masculine frailties and has taken on himself the guilt of human beings. But since the frailties as well as the transgressions of the other sex are specifically different from those of the male, we are, not without reason, tempted to suppose that the female sex will also have its special representative (a divine daughter, as it were) as its expiatress. And Postellus thought he had found her, in the person of a pious Venetian maiden.

express failure in his purpose (to lead the Jews to the true religion in his lifetime), whereas we should rather have expected satisfaction in an aim accomplished. Finally, the disciples' words according to Luke: "We had thought he would redeem Israel,"[14] do not imply that they were expecting a reunion with him in three days, still less that any word of his resurrection had reached their ears, – But when we are dealing with religion, where the faith instilled by reason with regard to the practical is sufficient to itself, why should we get entangled in all these learned investigations and disputes because of a historical narrative that should always be left in its proper place (among matters that are indifferent)?

7:41   b) It seems to violate outright the highest rule of exegesis that reason feels entitled to interpret the text in a way it finds consistent with its own principles, even when it is confronted with a text where no other meaning can be ascribed to the sacred author, as what he actually intended by his words, than one which contradicts reason: [in other words], that we should not interpret the text literally, unless we are willing to charge it with error. – Yet this is what has always happened, with the approval of the most eminent theologians. In their interpretation of scriptural texts which literally contradict our rational concept of God's nature and will, biblical theologians have long made it their rule that what is expressed in human terms ($\alpha\nu\theta\rho\omega\pi\sigma\pi\alpha\theta\omega\zeta$)['] must be *interpreted* in a sense worthy of God ($\theta\epsilon\sigma\pi\rho\epsilon\pi\omega\zeta$).["] By this they quite clearly confess that in matters of religion reason is the highest interpreter of the scriptures. – They followed this rule with regard to St. Paul's teaching on predestination, which clearly shows that his personal view must have been that human beings are predestined in the strictest sense of the term.[15] Although a major Protestant church, following him, adopting this teaching into its creed, a great part of that church later abandoned the doctrine or, as far as possible, changed its meaning, because reason finds that predestination cannot be reconciled with its own teachings on freedom and the imputation of action, and so with the whole of morality. – Even when belief in scriptural teachings would involve no offense against moral principles but only against rational maxims for judging natural phenomena, scriptural exegetes, with almost unanimous approval, have proceeded in the same way. Many biblical stories – about diabolical possession (demoniacs), for example – have been interpreted in such a way that reason can hold its own with them (so as not to open the door to every kind of superstition and imposture); and the right to do this

['] suited to human feelings
["] proper to God

has not been challenged, even though the scriptures relate these tales in the same historical style as the rest of sacred history and it is almost certain that their author thought they were literally true.

II. With regard to scriptural teachings that we can know only by revelation, faith is not in itself *meritorious,* and lack of such faith, and even doubt opposed to it, in itself involves no *guilt.* The only thing that matters in religion is *deeds,* and this final aim and, accordingly, a meaning appropriate to it, must be attributed to every biblical dogma.   7:42

Dogma is now what we ought to believe (for faith admits of no imperative), but what we find it possible and useful to admit for practical (moral) purposes, although we cannot demonstrate it and so can only believe it. If we ignore this moral consideration and admit as a principle[v] faith merely in the sense of theoretical assent – assent, for example, to what is based historically on the testimony of others, or to some assumption or other without which I cannot explain certain given phenomena – such faith is no part of religion because it neither makes nor gives proof of a better human being; and if such belief is feigned in the soul, thrust upon it only by fear and hope, then it is opposed to sincerity and so to religion as well. – And so, if certain texts seem to regard faith in revealed doctrine as not only meritorious in itself but even superior to morally good works, we must interpret them as referring only to moral faith, which improves and elevates the soul by reason – although, admittedly, the literal meaning of such texts as "he who believes and is baptized will be saved" etc. goes against this interpretation. Doubt concerning these statutory dogmas and their authenticity, therefore, cannot disturb a morally well-disposed soul. – Yet these same propositions can be considered essential requirements for *expounding* a certain *ecclesiastical faith.* But since ecclesiastical faith, as the mere vehicle of religious faith, is mutable and must remain open to gradual purification until it coincides with religious faith, it cannot be made an article of faith itself. This does not mean that it may be attacked publicly in the churches or even passed over dry-shod; for it comes under the protection of the government, which watches over public unity and peace. However, the teacher should warn [the people] not to ascribe holiness to dogma itself but to pass over, without delay, to the religious faith it has introduced.

III. Action must be represented as issuing from the human being's own use of his moral powers, not as an effect [resulting] from the influence of an external, higher cause by whose activity the human being is passively healed. The interpretation of scriptural texts which, taken literally, seem to contain the latter view must therefore be deliberately directed toward making them consistent with the former view.   7:43

[v] *Princip*

If by nature we mean the principle*ᵐ* that impels us to promote our *happiness,* and by grace the incomprehensible moral disposition in us – that is, the principle*ˣ* of *pure morality* – then nature and grace not only differ from each other but often come into conflict. But if by nature (in the practical sense) we mean our ability to achieve certain ends by our own powers in general, then grace is none other than the nature of the human being insofar as he is determined to actions by a principle*ʸ* which is intrinsic to his own being, but supersensible (the thought of his duty). Since we want to explain this principle, although we know no further ground for it, we represent it as a stimulus to good produced in us by God, the predisposition to which we did not establish in ourselves, and so, as grace. – That is to say, sin (evil in human nature) has made penal law necessary (as if for slaves); grace, however, is the hope that good will develop in us – a hope awakened by belief in our original moral predisposition to good and by the example of humanity as pleasing to God in his son. And grace can and should become more powerful than sin in us (as free beings), if only we let it act in us or let our disposition to the kind of conduct shown in that holy example become active. – Scriptural texts which seem to enjoin a merely passive surrender to an external power that produces holiness in us must, then, be interpreted differently. It has to be made clear from them that *we ourselves must work* at developing that moral predisposition, although this predisposition does point to a divine source that reason can never reach (in its theoretical search for causes), so that our possession of it is not meritorious, but rather the work of grace.

IV. If the human being's own deeds are not sufficient to justify him before his conscience (as it judges him strictly), reason is entitled to adopt on faith a supernatural supplement to fill what is lacking to his justification (though not to specify in what this consists).

7:44

That reason has this title is self-evident. For the human being must be able to become what his vocation requires him to be (adequate to the holy law); and if he cannot do this naturally by his own powers, he may hope to achieve it by God's cooperation from without (whatever form this may take). – We can add, further, that faith in this supplement for his deficiency is sanctifying, for only by it can man cease to doubt that he can reach his final aim (to become pleasing to God) and so lay hold of the courage and firmness of attitude he needs to lead a life pleasing to God (the sole condition of his hope for eternal life). – But we need not be able to understand and state exactly what the means of this replenishment is (for the final analysis this is transcendent and, despite all that God Himself might tell us about it, inconceivable to us); even to lay claim to this

ᵐ Princip
ˣ Princip
ʸ Princip

268

knowledge would, in fact, be presumptuous. Accordingly, scriptural texts that seem to contain such a specific revelation must be interpreted as concerning, not moral faith (for all human beings), but only the vehicle of that moral faith, designed to fit in with the creed which a certain people already held about it, hence they have to do with mere ecclesiastical faith (for Jewish Christians, for example), which requires historical evidence that not everyone can share, whereas religion (because it is based on moral concepts) must be complete in itself and free from doubt.

. .

But I hear biblical theologians cry out in unison against the very idea of a philosophical interpretation of Scripture. Philosophical exegesis, they say, aims primarily at a natural religion, not Christianity. I *reply* that Christianity is the Idea of religion, which must as such be based on reason and to this extent be natural. But it contains a means for introducing this religion to human beings, the Bible, which is thought to have a supernatural source; and insofar as the Bible (whatever its source may be) promotes moral precepts of reason by propagating them publicly and strengthening them within men's souls, we can consider it the vehicle of religion and accept it, in this respect, as supernatural revelation. Now only a religion that makes it a principle not to admit supernatural revelation can be called *naturalistic.* So Christianity is not a naturalistic religion – though it is a merely natural one – because it does not deny that the Bible may be a supernatural means for introducing religion and that a church may be established to teach and profess it publicly: it simply takes no notice of this source where religious doctrine is concerned.

7:45

III.
OBJECTIONS CONCERNING THE PRINCIPLES OF SCRIPTURAL EXEGESIS, ALONG WITH REPLIES TO THEM

Against these rules of exegesis I hear the outcry, *first,* that they are all judgments of the philosophy faculty, which, by giving them, presumes to interfere in the biblical theologian's business. – I *reply* that whereas dogma requires historical scholarship, reason alone is sufficient for religious faith. Reason does, it is true, claim to interpret dogma, in so far as it is the vehicle of religious faith. But since the value of dogma is only that of a means to religion as its final end, could such a claim be more legitimate? And can there be any principle higher than reason for settling arguments about truth? Moreover, the philosophy faculty does theologians no harm if it uses their statutes to corroborate its own teachings by showing that they are consistent with these statutes; one would rather expect the theology faculty to feel honored by this. But if the two faculties still find themselves in thoroughgoing conflict about interpreting the Bible, I can suggest only this compromise: *If biblical theologians will stop using reason for their purposes, philosophical theologians will stop using the Bible to confirm their propositions.* But I seriously doubt that biblical theologians would agree to this settlement. – *Second,* these interpretations are allegorical and mystical, and so neither biblical nor philosophical. My *reply* is that the exact opposite is true. If the biblical theologian mistakes the husk of religion for religion itself, [it is he who must interpret the scriptures allegorically:] he must explain the entire Old Testament, for example, as a continuous *allegory* (of prototypes and symbols) of the religious state still to come – or else admit that true religion (which cannot be truer than true) had already appeared then, making the New Testament superfluous. As for the charge that rational interpretation of the Scriptures is mystical, the sole means of avoiding mysticism (such as Swedenborg's[16]) is for philosophy to be on the lookout for a moral meaning in scriptural texts and even to impose it on them. For unless the supersensible (the thought of which is essential to anything called religion) is anchored to determinate concepts of reason, such as those of morality, fantasy inevitably gets lost in the transcendent, where religious matters are concerned, and leads to an illuminism in which everyone has his private, inner revelations, and there is no longer any public touchstone of truth.

7:46

But reason has its own objections to a rational interpretation of the Bible, which we shall note briefly and try to resolve according to the list of interpretive rules cited above. a) *Objection:* As *revelation,* the Bible must be interpreted in its own terms, not by reason; for the source of the knowledge it contains lies elsewhere than in reason. *Reply:* Precisely because we accept this book as divine revelation, we cannot give a merely theoretical interpretation of it by applying the principles proper to the study of history (that it must be consistent with itself); we must interpret this book in a practical way, according to rational concepts. For the kind of characteristics that experience provides can never show us that a revelation is divine: the mark of its divinity (at least as the *conditio sine qua non*) is its harmony with what reason pronounces worthy of God. – b) *Objection:* A theory must always precede anything practical; and if the theory in question is a revealed doctrine, it could contain purposes of the divine will which we might be obligated to promote even though we cannot penetrate them. So it seems that faith in these theoretical propositions is obligatory in itself and that doubt concerning them involves guilt. *Reply:* This can be granted in the case of ecclesiastical faith, whose concern with practice goes no further than the formalities it enjoins, where the fact that the dogma of a church is not impossible is all that its members need in order to accept it as true. But we cannot have religious faith unless we are *convinced* of its truth, and its truth cannot be certified by statutes (declaring themselves divine pronouncements); for, again, only history could be used to prove that these statutes are divine, and history is not entitled to pass itself off as divine revelation. And so for religious faith, which is directed solely to the morality of conduct, to deeds, acceptance of historical – even biblical – teachings has in itself no positive or negative moral value and comes under the heading of adraphoral. – c) *Objection:* How can the call "Arise and walk"[17] come to someone spiritually dead unless it is accompanied by a supernatural power to restore him to life? *Reply:* This call comes to the human being through his own reason, insofar as it contains the supersensible principle[z] of moral life. It is true that this may not immediately restore him to life so that he can arise by himself: [at first] perhaps it awakens him only to stir himself and strive toward a good life (like one whose powers are merely dormant and not extinct). But this striving is already a deed, which requires no external influence and, if it continues, can produce the kind of conduct intended. – d) *Objection:* To believe that God, by an act of kindness, will in some unknown way fill what is lacking to our justification is to assume gratuitously a cause that will satisfy the need we feel (it is to commit a *petitio principii*); for when we expect something by the grace of a superior, we cannot assume that we must get it as a matter of course; we can expect it only if it was actually promised to us, and hence only by acceptance of a definite promise made to us, as in a formal contract. So it seems that we can hope for that supplement and assume that we shall get it only insofar as it has been actually pledged through divine *revelation*, not as a stroke of luck. *Reply:* A direct revelation from God embodied in the comforting statement "Your sins are forgiven you"[18] would be a supersensible experience, and this is impossible. But it is also unnecessary with regard to what (like religion) is based on moral principles of reason and is therefore certain a priori, at least for practical purposes. There is no other way we can conceive the decrees of a holy and benevolent lawgiver with regard to frail creatures who are yet striving with all their might to fulfill whatever they recognize as their duty; and if, without the aid of a definite, empirically given promise, we have a rational faith and trust in his help, we show better evidence of a pure moral attitude and so of our receptivity to the manifestation of grace we hope for than we could by empirical belief.

7:47

7:48

∴

It is in this way, according to the principle of the morality which revelation has in view, that we must interpret the Scriptures *insofar as they have to do with religion;* otherwise our interpretations are either empty of practical content or even obstacles to the good. – Only a moral interpretation, moreover, is really an *authentic* one – that is, one given by the God within us; for since we cannot understand anyone unless he speaks to us through

[z] *Princip*

271

our own understanding and reason, it is only by concepts of *our* reason, insofar as they are pure moral concepts and hence infallible, that we can recognize the divinity of a teaching promulgated to us.

General remark: On religious sects

In what really deserves to be called religion, there can be no division into sects (for since religion is one, universal and necessary, it cannot vary). But there can well be division into sects with regard to ecclesiastical faith, whether it is based merely on the Bible or on tradition as well, to the extent that belief in what is merely the vehicle of religion is taken as an article of religion.

If Christianity is understood as belief in a *messiah*, merely to enumerate its sects would be a Herculean task, and a thankless one as well; for Christianity so understood is itself merely a sect* of messianic faith, as distinguished from *Judaism* in the narrower sense (in the final period of its undivided dominion over the people), when the question was raised: "Are you he who was to come, or shall we look for another?" And this is how the Romans at first took Christianity. But Christianity in this sense would be the faith of a certain people, based on dogmas and Scriptures, and we could not know whether it is directly valid for all human beings, the final revelation by which we must henceforth abide, or whether we can expect the future to bring other divine statutes that will approximate still more closely to the end.

So if we are to divide ecclesiastical faith into sects according to a determinate plan, we cannot begin with what is given empirically. We must rather begin with distinctions that reason can think a priori, in order to determine the step, in the series formed by different opinions in matters of faith, at which a distinction would give rise to different sects.

According to the *accepted* view, the principle*a* of division in matters of faith is either *religion* or *paganism* (which are opposed to each other as A to non-A). Those who profess religion are commonly called *believers;* those who profess paganism, *infidels.* Religion is the kind of faith that locates the *essence* of all divine worship in the human being's morality; paganism is the kind that does not, either because it lacks the concept of a supernatural

7:49

---

* It is a peculiarity of the German use (or abuse) of language that the followers of our religion call themselves *Christen*, as if there were more than one Christ and each believer were a Christ. They should rather call themselves *Christianer* – But "Christian" would immediately be regarded as the name of a sect, people of whom one could say many evil things (as happens in *Peregrinus Proteus*).[19] – So a critic in the *Halle Scientific Journal* maintains that the name Jehovah should be pronounced "Yahweh." But if the name were altered in this way, it would seem to designate a merely national deity, not the Lord of the World.
a Princip

moral being (*Ethnicismus brutus*)[b] or because it makes something other than the attitude of living a morally good life, hence something nonessential to religion, a part of religion (*Ethnicismus speciosus*).[c]

Now tenets of faith which are also to be conceived as divine commands are either merely *statutory* doctrines, which are contingent for us and [must be] revealed [if we are to know them], or *moral* doctrines, which involve consciousness of their necessity and can be recognized a priori – that is, *rational doctrines*. The sum total of statutory teachings comprises *ecclesiastical faith* [or dogma]; that of moral teachings, pure *religious* faith.*

To claim *universal validity* for a dogma (*catholicismus hierarchius*)[d] involves a contradiction: for unconditioned universality presupposes necessity, and since this occurs only where reason itself provides sufficient grounds for the tenets of faith, no mere statute can be universally valid.   7:50
Pure religious faith, on the other hand, can justly claim universal validity (*catholicismus rationalis*).[e] So a division into sects can never occur in matters of pure religious belief. Wherever sectarianism is to be found, it arises from a mistake on the part of ecclesiastical faith: the mistake of regarding its statutes (even if they are divine revelations) for essential parts of religion, and so substituting empiricism in matters of faith for rationalism and passing off what is merely contingent as necessary in itself. But since, in contingent doctrines, there can be all sorts of conflicting articles or interpretations of articles, we can readily see that mere dogma will be a prolific source of innumerable sects in matters of faith, unless it is rectified by pure religious faith.

To indicate precisely how religious belief purifies dogma, I think the following proposition is the most convenient touchstone we can use: to the extent that any dogma gives out merely statutory teachings of faith as essential religious teachings, it contains a certain *admixture of paganism;* for paganism consists in passing off the externals (non-essentials) of religion as essential. This admixture can be present to such a degree that it turns the entire religion into a mere dogma, which raises practices to the status of laws, and so becomes sheer paganism.† And [a church] cannot

---

* I do not say that this division is either precise or in keeping with ordinary usage; but it may stand for the time being.

† *Paganism*, according to its etymology, is the religious superstition of people in the woods – that is, of a group whose religious belief has no ecclesiastical system of government and hence no public law. The Jews, Mohammedans, and Hindus, however, refuse to recognize as a law anything that differs from theirs, and give other peoples, who do not have exactly the same ecclesiastical rites as theirs, the title of reprobation (Goj, Dschaur, etc.) – that is, of infidels.

[b] crude ethnicism
[c] specious ethnicism
[d] hierarchical catholicism
[e] rational catholicism

escape this pejorative name by saying that its doctrines are, nevertheless, divine revelations. For it is not because of such statutory doctrines and ecclesiastical duties themselves that this sort of faith deserves to be called pagan, but rather because of the unconditioned value it attributes to them (as parts of religion itself and not its mere vehicle, although they have no intrinsic moral content; and so what counts, here, is not the matter of revelation but the way in which this is adopted [by a church] in its practical attitude). Ecclesiastical authority to pronounce salvation or damnation according to this sort of faith would be called priestcraft. And self-styled Protestants should not be deprived of this honorific title if they insist on making the essence of their creed belief in tenets and rites which reason says nothing about, and which the most evil and worthless human being can profess and observe as well as the best – even if they add on an imposing rear guard of virtues that spring from the wondrous power of these tenets and rites (and so have no roots of their own).

7:51

As soon, then, as ecclesiastical faith begins to speak with authority on its own and forgets that it must be rectified by pure *religious faith*, sectarianism sets in. For, since pure religious faith (as practical rational faith) cannot lose its influence on the human soul – an influence that involves consciousness of our freedom – while ecclesiastical faith uses force on our conscience, everyone tries to put into or get out of dogma something in keeping with his own view.

This power of dogma occasions three types of movement: a mere separation from the church, that is, abstention from public association with it (by separatists); a public rift regarding the form of the church, although the dissidents accept the content of its doctrines (by schismatics); or a union of dissenters from certain doctrines of faith into particular societies which, though not always secret, are not sanctioned by the state (sectarians). And some of these sects (cliques of the pious, so to speak) fetch from the same treasury still more particular, secret doctrines not intended for the great audience of the public. Finally, false peacemakers (syncretists) arise, who want to satisfy everyone by melting down the different creeds. These syncretists are even worse than sectarians, because they are basically indifferent to religion in general and take the attitude that, if the people must have dogma, one is as good as another so long as it lends itself readily to the government's aims. This principle is quite correct and even wise when the ruler states it in his capacity as ruler. But as the judgment of the subject himself, who must ponder this matter in his own – and indeed his moral – interest, it would betray the utmost contempt for religion; for religion cannot be indifferent to the character of its vehicle which we adopt in our dogma.

7:52

On the subject of sectarianism (which, as in Protestantism, goes so far as to multiply churches), we are accustomed to say that it is desirable for many kinds of religion (properly speaking, kinds of ecclesiastical faith) to exist in a state. And this is, in fact, desirable to the extent that it is a good sign – a sign, namely, that the people are allowed freedom of belief. But it is only the government that is to be commended here. In itself, such a public state of affairs in religion is not a good thing unless the principle^f underlying it is of such a nature as to bring with it universal agreement on the essential maxims of belief, as the concept of religion requires, and to distinguish this agreement from conflicts arising from its non-essentials. Differences of opinion about the relative efficacy of the vehicle of religion in promoting its final aim, religion itself (that is, the moral improvement of human beings), may therefore produce, at most, different church sects, but not different religious sects; for this is directly opposed to the unity and universality of religion (and so of the invisible church). Enlightened Catholics and Protestants, while still holding to their own dogmas, could thus look upon each other as brothers in faith, in expectation (and striving toward this end): that, with the government's favor, time will gradually bring the formalities of faith closer to the dignity of their end, religion itself (and for this reason the faith in question cannot be faith that we can obtain God's favor or pardon by anything other than a pure moral attitude of will). – Without dreaming of a conversion of all Jews* (to Christianity in the sense of a *messianic* faith), we can consider it possible even in their case if, as is now happening, purified religious concepts awaken among them and throw off the garb of the ancient cult, which now serves no purpose and even suppresses any true religious attitude. Since they have long had *garments without a man* in them (a church without religion) and since, moreover, a *man without garments* (religion without a church) is not well protected, they need certain formalities of a church – the church best able to lead them, in their present state, to the final end. So we can consider the proposal of Ben Davie,[21] a highly intelligent Jew, to adopt publicly the religion of *Jesus* (presumably with its vehicle, the *Gospel*), a most fortunate one. Moreover it is the only plan which, if carried out, would leave the Jews a distinctive faith and yet quickly call attention to them as an educated and civilized people who are ready for all the rights of citizenship and whose faith could also be sanctioned by the government. If this were to happen, the Jews would have to be left free, in their interpretation of the Scriptures (the Torah and the Gospels), to distin-

7:53

---

* Moses Mendelssohn rejects this demand in a way that does credit to his *cleverness* (by an *argumentatio ad hominem*).[20] Until (he says) God, from Mount Sinai, revokes our law as solemnly as He gave it (in thunder and lightning) – that is, until the end of time – we are bound by it. By this he apparently meant to say: Christians, first get rid of the Judaism in *your own* faith, and then we will give up ours. – But it is for his co-religionists to decide whether this does credit to his good will; for by this stern challenge he cut off their hope for any relief whatsoever from the burden that oppresses them, though he apparently considered only the smallest part of it essential to his faith.

^{f} *Princip*

guish the way in which Jesus spoke as a Jew to Jews from the way he spoke as a moral teacher to human beings in general. – The euthanasia of Judaism is pure moral religion, freed from all the ancient statutory teachings, some of which were bound to be retained in Christianity (as a messianic faith). But this division of sects, too, must disappear in time, leading, at least in spirit, to what we call the conclusion of the great drama of religious change on earth (the restoration of all things), when there will be only one shepherd and one flock.

. .
.

But if we ask not only what Christianity is but also how to set about teaching it so that it will really be present in the hearts of human beings (and this is one with the question of what to do so that religious faith will also make human beings better), there can be no division into sects regarding the end, since this is always the same. But our choice of means to the end can bring about a division of sects; since we can conceive of more than one cause for the same effect, we can hold different and conflicting views as to which means is fitting and divine and so disagree in our principles,^{g} even in those having to do with what is essential (in a subjective sense) in religion as such.

7:54

Now the means to this end cannot be empirical – since empirical means could undoubtedly affect our actions but not our attitude – hence, for one who thinks that the *supersensible* must also be *supernatural,* the above problem turns into the question: how is rebirth (resulting from a conversion by which one becomes an other, new man) possible by God's direct influence, and what must man do to bring it about? I maintain that, without consulting history (which can say only that certain opinions have been held but not that they arose necessarily), we can predict a priori that people who consider it a trifling matter to call in a supernatural cause for a natural effect must inevitably divide into sects over this problem. Indeed, I maintain that this division is the only one that entitles us to speak of two different religious sects, since other so-called religious sects are merely church sects, and their divisions do not concern the core of religion. In handling any problem, however, one must first *state* the problem, then *solve* it, and finally *prove* that the solution does what was required of it. Accordingly:

1. The problem (which the valiant Spener[22] called out fervently to all ecclesiastical teachers) is this: the end of religious instruction must be to make us *other* human beings and not merely better human beings (as if we were already good but only negligent about the degree of our goodness). This thesis was thrown in the path of the *orthodox* (a not inappropriate name), who hold that the way to become pleasing to God consists in

^{g} *Principien*

276

believing pure revealed doctrine and observing the practices prescribed by the church (prayer, churchgoing, and the sacraments) – to which they add the requirement of honorable conduct (mixed, admittedly, with transgressions, but these can always be made good by faith and the rites prescribed). – The problem, therefore, has a solid basis in reason.

2. But the solution turns out to be completely *mystical,* as one might expect from supernaturalism in principles of religion; for, according to it, the original, incorruptible moral predisposition in human nature, though *supersensible,* is still to be called flesh because its effect is not *supernatural* 7:55 as well; only if spirit (God) were the direct cause of the human being's improvement would this effect be a supernatural one. So the human being, being by nature dead in sin, cannot hope to improve by his own powers, not even by his moral predisposition. – Now those who believe in a mystical solution to the difficulty divide into two sects with regard to the *feeling* of this supernatural influence: according to one sect, it has to be the kind that *dashes the heart to pieces* (crushes it with remorse): according to the other, the kind that *melts the heart* (so that the human being dissolves in blessed communion with God). Thus the solution to the problem (of making good human beings out of bad) begins from two opposed standpoints ("where the volition is indeed good, but its fulfillment is wanting").[23] In one sect it is only a question of *freeing* ourselves from the power of evil within us, and then the good principle will appear of itself; in the other, of admitting the good principle in our attitude of will, and then, by a supernatural influence, there is no longer room for the evil, and the good rules alone.

The idea of a moral metamorphosis of the human being that could yet take place only by supernatural influence may well have been *rumbling around* in believers' heads for a long time; but only in more recent times has it been clearly enunciated and given rise to a division of sects between the followers of *Spener* and *Franck*[24] (Pietists) and the *Moravian Brethren of Zinzendorf*[25] (*Moravians*) on the doctrine of conversion.

According to the Pietist hypothesis, the operation that separates good from evil (of which human nature is compounded) is a supernatural one – a breaking and crushing of the heart in *repentance,* a grief (*maeror animi*)[h] bordering on despair which can, however, reach the necessary intensity only by the influence of a heavenly spirit. The human being must himself beg for this grief, while grieving over the fact that his grief is not great enough (to drive the pain completely from his heart). Now as the late Hamann[26] says: "This descent into the hell of self-knowledge paves the way to deification." In other words, when the fire of repentance has reached its height, the amalgam of good and evil *breaks up* and the purer metal of the *reborn* gleams through the dross, which surrounds but does

[h] grief of soul

not contaminate it, ready for service pleasing to God in good conduct. –
7:56   This radical change, therefore, begins with a *miracle* and ends with what we would ordinarily consider natural, since *reason* prescribes it: namely, a morally good course of life. But even in the highest flight of a mystically inclined imagination, one cannot exempt man from doing anything himself, without making him a mere machine; and so what man has to do is *pray* fervidly and incessantly (insofar as we are willing to count prayer as a *deed*), and only from this can he expect that supernatural effect. But since prayer, as they say, can be heard only if it is made in faith, and faith itself is an effect of grace – that is, something the human being cannot achieve by his own powers – the scruple arises that this view gets involved in a vicious circle with its means of grace and, in the final analysis, really does not know how to handle the thing.

According to the *Moravian* view, as the human being becomes aware of his sinful state he takes the first step toward his improvement quite naturally, by his *reason;* for as reason holds before him, in the moral law, the mirror in which he sees his guilt, it leads him, using his moral disposition to the good, to decide that from now on he will make the law his maxim. But his carrying out of this resolution is a *miracle.* In other words, it is an easy thing for the human being to turn his back on the banner of the evil spirit and set out under that of the good; but what he is naturally incapable of doing is to persevere in this, not to relapse into evil but, on the contrary, to advance constantly in goodness. For this, he needs nothing less than the feeling of supernatural communion with a heavenly spirit and even continuous awareness of intercourse with it. It is true that in this latter, one side cannot fail to reprove and the other to beg forgiveness; but one need not worry about an estrangement or a relapse (from grace), if only he takes care to cultivate, without interruption, this intercourse which is itself a continuous prayer.

Here we have two mystical theories of feeling offered as keys to the problem of becoming a new man. What is at issue between them is not the *object*[i] and end of all religion (which, both agree, is conduct pleasing to God), but the *subjective* conditions which are necessary for us to acquire the power to work out that theory in ourselves. The subjective condition in question cannot be virtue (which is an empty name to them), but only
7:57   *grace;* for both sides agree that we cannot acquire this power naturally. But their theories then diverge, since one side thinks we can escape from the dominion of the evil spirit only by a *fearful* struggle with it, whereas the other finds this quite unnecessary and even censures it as hypocritical; instead, it straightway concludes an alliance with the good spirit, since the earlier pact with the evil spirit (as *pactum turpe*)[j] can give rise to no

---

[i] *object*
[j] wrongful contract

278

objection to this. When the kinds of feeling involved in the human being's rebirth are as sharply contrasted as in the theories of these two parties, their different theories of rebirth, as a supernatural and radical spiritual revolution that takes place once and for all, may well appear outwardly as a division of sects.*

3. The *proof:* that number 2 happens, so that the problem posed in number 1 is solved. – This proof is impossible. For we would have to prove that we have had a supernatural experience, and this is a contradiction in terms. The most that could be granted is that the human being has experienced a change in himself (new and better volitions, for example) which he does not know how to explain except by a miracle and so by something supernatural. But an experience which he cannot even convince himself is actually an experience, since (as supernatural) it cannot be traced back to any rule in the nature of our understanding and established by it, is an-interpretation of certain sensations that one does not know what to make of, not knowing whether they are elements in cognition and so have real objects or whether they are mere fancies. To claim that we *feel*   7:58
as such the immediate influence of God is self-contradictory, because the idea of God lies only in reason. – Here, then, we have a problem along with a solution to it, for which no proof of any kind is possible; and so we can never make anything rational out of it.

Now we still have to inquire whether the Bible may not contain another principle for solving Spener's problem – a principle, different from the sectarian principles we have just discussed, which could replace the unfruitful ecclesiastical principle of sheer orthodoxy. As a matter of fact, it not only leaps to the eye that there is such a principle in the Bible; it is also conclusively certain that only by this principle and the Christianity it contains could the Bible have acquired so extensive a sphere of efficacy and achieved such lasting influence on the world, an effect that no revealed doctrine (as such), no belief in miracles, and no number of the faithful crying out in unison could ever have produced, because in that case it would not have been drawn from the human being's own soul and must, accordingly, always have remained foreign to him.

---

* If it were possible for a whole people to be brought up in one of these sects, what sort of national physiognomy would this people be likely to have? For there is no doubt that such a physiognomy would emerge, since frequently repeated mental impressions, especially if they are contrary to nature, express themselves in one's appearance and tone of voice, and facial expressions eventually become permanent features. *Sanctified* or, as Herr Nicolai[27] calls them, *divinely blessed* faces would distinguish such a people from other civilized and enlightened peoples (not exactly to its advantage); for this is a caricature of piety. But it was not contempt for piety that made "Pietist" a sect name (and a certain contempt is always connected with such a name); it was rather the Pietists' fantastic and – despite all their show of humility – proud claim to be marked out as supernaturally favored children of heaven, even though their conduct, as far as we can see, is not the least bit better in moral terms than that of the people they call children of the world.

For there is something in us that we cannot cease to wonder at when we have once seen it, the same thing that raises *humanity* in its idea to a dignity we should never have suspected in the human being as an object of experience. We do not wonder at the fact that we are beings subject to moral laws and destined by our reason to obey them, even if this means sacrificing whatever pleasures may conflict with them; for obedience to moral laws lies objectively in the natural order of things as the object of pure reason, and it never occurs to ordinary, sound understanding to ask where these laws come from, in order, perhaps, to put off obeying them until we know their source, or even to doubt their vaildity. – But we do wonder at our *ability* so to sacrifice our sensuous nature to morality that we *can* do what we quite readily and clearly conceive we *ought* to do. This ascendancy of the *supersensible* human being in us over the *sensible*, such that (when it comes to a conflict between them) the sensible is *nothing*, though in its own eyes it is

7:59   *everything*, is an object of the greatest *wonder;* and our wonder at this moral predisposition in us, inseparable from our humanity, only increases the longer we contemplate this true (not fabricated) ideal. Since the *supersensible* in us is inconceivable and yet practical, we can well excuse those who are led to consider it *supernatural* – that is, to regard it as the influence of another and higher spirit, something not within our power and not belonging to us as our own. Yet they are greatly mistaken in this, since on their view the effect of this power would not be our deed and could not be imputed to us, and so the power to produce it would not be our own. – Now the real solution to the problem (of the new man) consists in putting to use the idea of this power, which dwells in us in a way we cannot understand, and impressing it on human beings, beginning in their earliest youth and continuing on by public instruction. Even the Bible seems to have nothing else in view: it seems to refer, not to supernatural experiences and fantastic feelings which should take reason's place in bringing about this revolution, but to the spirit of Christ, which he manifested in teachings and examples so that we might make it our own – or rather, since it is already present in us by our moral predisposition, so that we might simply make room for it. And so, between *orthodoxy* which has no soul and *mysticism* which kills reason, there is the teaching of the Bible, a faith which our reason can develop out of itself. This teaching is the true religious doctrine, based on the *criticism* of practical reason, that works with divine power on the hearts of all human beings toward their fundamental improvement and unites them in one universal (though invisible) church.

. .

But the main purpose of this note is really to answer the question: could the government confer on a mystical sect the sanction of a church or could it, consistently with its own aim, tolerate and protect such a sect, without giving it the honor of that prerogative?

280

If we admit (as we have reason to do) that it is not the government's business to concern itself with the future happiness of the subjects and show them the way to it (for it must leave that to the subjects, since the ruler usually gets his own religion from the people and their teachers), 7:60 then the government's purpose with regard to ecclesiastical faith can be only to have, through this means too, subjects who are tractable and morally good.

With this end in view the government will, first, refuse to sanction any kind of *naturalism* (ecclesiastical faith without the Bible); for naturalism would not provide the form of a church subject to the government's influence, and this contradicts our supposition. – It will, therefore, bind the public teachers of the people to biblical orthodoxy; and these teachers, again, will be subject to the judgment of the relevant faculties with regard to orthodoxy, since otherwise priestcraft would spring up – that is, the working men of ecclesiastical faith would assume control and rule the people according to their own purposes. But the government would not endorse *orthodoxy* by its authority; for orthodoxy – the view that belief in dogma is sufficient for religion – regards the natural principles of morality as of secondary importance, whereas morality is rather the mainstay on which the government must be able to count if it wants to trust the people.* Least of all can the government raise mysticism, as the people's view that they themselves can share in supernatural inspiration, to the rank of a public ecclesiastical faith, because mysticism has nothing public about it and so escapes entirely the government's influence.

7:61

Conclusion of peace and settlement of the conflict of the faculties

In any conflict having to do only with pure but practical reason, no one can dispute the prerogative of the philosophy faculty to make the report and, as far as the formal rules of procedure are concerned, *draw up* the

---

* In religious matters the only thing that can interest the state is: to what doctrines it must bind teachers of religion in order to have useful citizens, good soldiers, and, in general, faithful subjects. Now if, to that end, it chooses to enjoin orthodox statutory doctrines and means of grace, it can fare very badly. For it is an easy thing for a human being to accept these statutes, and far easier for the evil-minded human being than for the good, whereas the moral improvement of his attitude of will is a long and difficult struggle. And so, if a human being is taught to hope for salvation primarily from these statutes, he need not hesitate greatly about transgressing his duty (though cautiously), because he has an infallible means at hand to evade God's punitive justice (if only he does not wait too long) by his orthodox belief in every mystery and his urgent use of the means of grace. On the other hand, if the teaching of the church were directed straight to morality, the judgment of his conscience would be quite different: namely, that he must answer to a future judge for any evil he has done that he cannot repair, and that no ecclesiastical means, no faith or prayer extorted by dread, can avert this fate (*desine fata deum flecti sperare pecando* [cease hoping that you will alter the divine will by prayer]). – With which belief, now, is the state more secure?

case. But with regard to its content, the theology faculty occupies the armchair, the sign of precedence – not because it can claim more insight than the others in matters of reason, but because it deals with the human being's most important concern and is therefore entitled the *highest* faculty (yet only as *prima inter pares*).[k] But it does not speak according to laws of pure rational religion which can be known a priori (for then it would degrade itself and descend to the philosophers' bench): it speaks, rather, according to *statutory* precepts of faith contained in a book, particularly the book called the *Bible* – that is, in a code that reveals an old and a new covenant which the human being concluded with God many centuries ago. Its authenticity, as an object of historical belief (not moral belief, since that could also be drawn from philosophy), can be better established by the effect its reading can produce in the hearts of the human beings than by proofs based on critical examination of the teachings and tales it contains. Its interpretation, moreover, is not left to laypeople's reason, but reserved for the acumen of experts.*

7:62   Biblical faith is historical belief in a *messiah*, which has as its basis a book of God's covenant with Abraham. It consists in a *Mosaic-messianic* and an *evangelical-messianic* dogma, and gives such a complete account of the origin and destiny of God's people that, starting (in Genesis) with the beginning of the world, the first moment in the world's history at which no human being was present, it follows it to the end of all things (in the Apocalypse) – a narrative that one could, indeed, expect only from a divinely inspired author – still, the existence of a questionable cabala of numbers regarding the most important epochs of sacred chronology might somewhat weaken one's faith in the authenticity of the *historical narrative* the Bible contains.†

---

* On this point (the reading of the Bible), the Roman Catholic system of dogma is more consistent than the Protestant. – The reformed preacher La Coste[28] says to his co-religionists: "Draw the divine word from the spring itself (the Bible), where you can take it purer and unadulterated; but you must find in the Bible nothing other than what we find there. – Now, dear friends, please tell us what you find in the Bible so that we won't waste our time searching for it ourselves, only to have you explain, in the end, that what we supposed we had found in it is a false interpretation." – Again, when the Catholic Church says: Outside the (Catholic) Church there is no salvation, it speaks more consistently than the Protestant Church when it says: Catholics too can be saved. For if that is so (says Bossuet),[29] then the safer choice is to join the Catholic Church; for no one can ask for *more* salvation.

† 70 Apocalyptic months (of which there are 4 in this cycle), each 29½ years long, equal 2065 years. Subtract every 49th year of this, as the great year of rest (there are 42 of them in this period) and we get exactly 2023 as the year Abraham left the land of Canaan, which God had given him, for Egypt. – From then to the occupation of that land by the children of Israel 70 Apocalyptic weeks (= 490 years) – multiply these week-years by 4 (= 1960) and add 2023, and this gives, according to P. Petaus's[30] reckoning, the year of Christ's birth (3983) so exactly that it is not even a year off. – 70 years after this, the destruction of Jerusalem (also a

[k] first among equals

Now a code of God's *statutory* (and so revealed) will, not derived from   7:63
human reason but harmonizing perfectly with morally practical reason
toward the final end – in other words, the Bible – would be the most
effective organ for guiding human beings and citizens to their temporal
and eternal well-being, if only it could be accredited as the word of God
and its authenticity could be proved by documents. – But there are many
difficulties in the way of validating it.

For if God should really speak to a human being, the latter could still
never *know* that it was God speaking. It is quite impossible for a human
being to apprehend the infinite by his senses, distinguish it from sensible
beings, and *be acquainted with* it as such. – But in some cases the human
being can be sure that the voice he hears is *not* God's; for if the voice
commands him to do something contrary to the moral law, then no matter
how majestic the apparition may be, and no matter how it may seem to
surpass the whole of nature, he must consider it an illusion.*

Now the source from which we draw the credentials of the Bible, as an
evangelical-messianic faith whose teachings and examples serve as a
norm, cannot be the divine learning of its author (for he remained a

---

mystical epoch). – But Bengel (*in ordine temporum*, page 9 and pages 218 ff.)[31] gets 3939 as
the date of Christ's birth? That changes nothing in the sacred character of the *numerus
septenarius;* for the number of years between God's call to Abraham and the birth of Christ is
1960, which comprises 4 Apocalyptic periods each of 490 years, or also 40 Apocalyptic
periods each of 7 × 7 or 49 years. Now if we subtract 1 from every 49th year for the great
year of rest, and 1 for every greatest year of rest, which is the 490th (44 altogether), there
remains exactly 3939. – Hence the dates 3983 and 3939, as different years assigned to the
birth of Christ, differ only in this: that 3939 is obtained from 3983 by subtracting the
number of years of rest from what is included in the time of the 4 great epochs. According to
Bengel, the table of sacred history is as follows:

2023 Promise to Abraham that he would possess the land of Canaan

2502 He takes possession of it

2981 Consecration of the first temple

3460 Command given to build the second temple

3939 Birth of Christ

The year of the Flood, too, can be calculated a priori in the same way: 4 epochs of 490 (70 ×
7) years makes 1960. Subtract from this every 7th (280) and this leaves 1680. From this
1680 subtract every 70th year contained in it (× 24), and this leaves 1656 as the year of the
Flood. – Also, from this to God's call to Abraham are 366 full years, of which 1 is a leap
year.

What are we to say to this? Have the sacred numbers perhaps determined the course of
events in the world? – Frank's *Cyclus iobilaeus* also revolves around the center of this mystical
chronology.[32]

* We can use, as an example, the myth of the sacrifice that Abraham was going to make by
butchering and burning his only son at God's command (the poor child, without knowing it,
even brought the wood for the fire). Abraham should have replied to this supposedly divine
voice: "That I ought not to kill my good son is quite certain. But that you, this apparition, are
God – of that I am not certain, and never can be, not even if this voice rings down to me
from (visible) heaven."

283

human being, exposed to possible error). It must rather be the effect which its content has on the morality of the people, when it is preached to them by teachers from these same people. And since these teachers, themselves, are incompetent (in scientific matters), we must regard the credentials of the Bible as drawn from the pure spring of universal ra-
7:64 tional religion dwelling in every ordinary human being; and it is this very simplicity that accounts for the Bible's extremely widespread and powerful influence on the hearts of the people. – Through certain statutory precepts by which it gave a *form*, as of a government, to the practice of religion in civil society, the Bible was the vehicle of religion. As far as its spirit (its moral content) is concerned, then, this code of laws accredits itself and is itself the document that establishes its authenticity as a divine code (the sum total of all our duties as divine commands). As for the letter of the code (the statutory element), the decrees of this book do not need to be accredited because they do not belong to what is essential in it (*principale*)[*l*] but only to what is associated with this (*accessorium*).[*m*] – But to base the origin of this book on the inspiration of its author (*deus ex machina*),[*n*] in order to sanctify its non-essential statutes as well, must weaken, rather than strengthen, our confidence in its moral worth.

No historical account can verify the divine origin of such a writing. The proof can be derived only from its tested power to establish religion in the human heart and, by its very simplicity, to reestablish it in its purity should it be corrupted by various (ancient or modern) dogmas. The working of the Bible does not thereby cease to be an act of *nature* and a result of advancing moral cultivation in the general course of *providence;* and we must explain it as such, so that we do not attribute the Bible's existence *skeptically* to mere accident or *superstitiously* to a *miracle,* both of which would cause reason to run aground.

Now the conclusion from this is as follows:

The Bible contains within itself a credential of its (moral) divinity that is sufficient in a practical respect – the influence that, as the text of a systematic doctrine of faith, it has always exercised on the hearts of human beings, both in catechetical instruction and in preaching. This is sufficient reason for preserving it, not only as the organ of universal inner rational religion, but also as the legacy (new testament) of a statutory doctrine of faith which will serve us indefinitely as a guiding line. It matters little that scholars who investigate its origin theoretically and historically and study
7:65 its historical content critically may find it more or less wanting in proofs from a theoretical point of view. – The *divinity* of its moral content adequately compensates reason for the *humanity* of its historical narrative

[*l*] what is primary
[*m*] what is auxiliary
[*n*] God from a machine

which, like an old parchment that is illegible in places, has to be made intelligible by adjustments and conjectures consistent with the whole. And the divinity of its moral content justifies this statement: that the Bible deserves to be kept, put to moral use, and assigned to religion as its guide *just as if it is a divine revelation.*

If the government were to neglect that great means for establishing and administering civil order and peace and abandon it to frivolous hands, the audacity of those prodigies of strength who imagine they have already outgrown this leading-string of dogma and express their raptures either in public churches devoted to theophilanthropy or in mysticism, with its lamp of private revelations, would soon make it regret its indulgence. – Moreover, we cannot expect that, if the Bible we have were once discredited, another would arise in its place; for public miracles do not happen twice in the same affair, since the failure of the first one to endure would prevent anyone from believing in the second – nevertheless, we should pay no attention to the outcry raised by *alarmists* (that the state is in danger) when some fault is found with the authors of the Bible in certain of its statutes having to do more with formalities presented in the text than with its inner content of faith; for a prohibition against examining a doctrine is contrary to freedom of belief. – But it is superstition to hold that historical belief is a duty and essential to salvation.*

With regard to what is statutory in religion, we may require biblical   7:66

---

* *Superstition* is the tendency to put greater trust in what is supposed to be non-natural than in what can be explained by laws of nature, whether in physical or in moral matters. The question can therefore be raised: whether biblical faith (as empirical belief) or morality (as pure rational and religious belief) should serve as the teacher's guide? In other words, is the teaching from God because it is in the Bible, or is it in the Bible because it is from God? The first proposition is obviously inconsistent, because it requires us to presuppose the divine authority of the book in order to prove the divinity of its doctrine. Hence only the second proposition is acceptable, though it admits of no proof whatsoever (*Supernaturalium non datur scientia*).⁰ Here is an example of this. – The disciples of the Mosaic-messianic faith saw their hopes, based on God's covenant with Abraham, fail completely after Jesus' death (we had hoped that he would deliver Israel); for their Bible promised salvation only to the children of Abraham. Now it happened that when the disciples were gathered at Pentecost, one of them hit upon the happy idea, in keeping with the subtle Jewish art of exegesis, that pagans (Greeks and Romans) could also be regarded as admitted into this covenant, if they believed in the sacrifice of his only son that Abraham was willing to offer God (as the symbol of the world-savior's own sacrifice); for then they would be children of Abraham in faith (at first subject to circumcision, but later even without it). – It is no wonder that this discovery which, in a great gathering of people, opened so immense a prospect, was received with the greatest rejoicing as if it had been the direct working of the Holy Spirit, and was considered a miracle and recorded as such in biblical (apostolic) history. But religion does not require us to believe this as a fact, or obtrude this belief on natural human reason. Consequently, if a church commands us to believe such a dogma, as necessary for salvation, and we obey out of fear, our belief is superstition.

⁰ There is no science of supernatural matters.

285

hermeneutics (*hermeneutica sacra*)*ᵖ* – which, since it has to do with a scientific system, cannot be left to the laity – to tell us whether the exegete's findings are to be taken as *authentic* or *doctrinal*. – In the first case, exegesis must conform literally (philologically) with the author's meaning. But in the second case the writer is free, in his exegesis, to ascribe to the text (philosophically) the meaning it admits of for morally practical purposes (the pupil's edification); for faith in a merely historical proposition is, in itself, dead. – Now the literal interpretation may well be important enough for biblical scholars and, indirectly, for the people as well, for certain pragmatic purposes. But this kind of interpretation cannot only fail to promote but even hinder the real end of religious teaching – the development of morally better human beings. For even the authors of sacred Scripture, being human, could have made mistakes (unless we admit a miracle running continuously throughout the Bible), as, for example, St. Paul in good faith carried over the doctrine of election to grace from the doctrines of the Mosaic-messianic Scriptures to those of the Gospels, although he was greatly embarrassed over the inconceivability of the reprobation of certain human beings even before they were born. And so, if the

7:67   hermeneutics of scriptural scholars is supposed to be a continuous revelation the interpreter receives, the divine character of religion must be constantly prejudiced. – Hence – *doctrinal* interpretation – which does not seek to know (empirically) what meaning the sacred author may have connected to his words but rather what teaching reason can ascribe (a priori), for the sake of morality, to a biblical text it is presented with – is the only way of handling the Gospels to instruct the people in true, inner and universal religion, which must be distinguished from particular church dogma, as a matter of historical belief. In this way everything takes place honestly and openly, without deception. On the other hand, the people can reproach their teachers for *deceiving* them in their aim (which they must have) if they are given historical belief, which none of them can prove, instead of moral faith (the only kind that brings salvation), which everyone grasps.

    If a people has been taught to revere a sacred Scripture, the doctrinal interpretation of that Scripture, which looks to the people's moral interest – its edification, moral improvement, and hence salvation – is also the authentic one with regard to its religion: in other words, this is how God wants this people to understand His will as revealed in the Bible. For it is not a question here of a civil (political) government keeping the people under discipline, but of a government which has as its end the essence of this people's moral attitude of will (hence, a divine government). The God who speaks through our own (morally practical) reason is an infallible interpreter of His words in the Scriptures, whom everyone

ᵖ sacred hermeneutics

can understand. And it is quite impossible for there to be any other accredited interpreter of his words (one, for example, who would interpret them in a historical way); for religion is a purely rational affair.

· ·

And so the theologians of the faculty have the duty incumbent on them, and consequently the title, to uphold biblical faith; but this does not impair the freedom of the philosophers to subject it always to the critique of reason. And should a dictatorship be granted to the higher faculty for a short time (by religious edict), this freedom can best be secured by the solemn formula: *Provideant consules, ne quid respublica detrimenti capiat.*[q]

Appendix: Historical questions about the Bible concerning the practical use and probable duration of this sacred book

7:68

The government's wisdom guarantees that, whatever changes our opinions may undergo, the Bible will continue to hold a place of honor among us for a long time, since the government's interest in the harmony and peace of people in civil society is closely bound up with it. But to guarantee that the Bible will last forever, or even have it pass over into the millennium of a new kingdom of God on earth, goes far beyond our whole faculty of divination. – What would happen, then, should ecclesiastical faith eventually have to do without this great instrument for guiding the people?

Who edited the books of the Bible (Old and New Testaments), and from what period does the canon date?

Once the norm of faith has been accepted, will philological and antiquarian knowledge always be needed to preserve it, or will reason, by itself and with universal agreement, some day be able to direct it to the use of religion?

Have we documents adequate to establish the authenticity of the so-called Septuagint version of the Bible? From what time can we date it with certainty? And so forth.

The practical use of this book – especially its public use in sermons – is undoubtedly the one that is conducive to the human being's improvement and to quickening his moral motive (his edification). All other aims must give way to this, if they collide with it. – It is surprising, then, that this maxim could have been doubted and that a *periphrastic* treatment of the

---

[q] Let the consuls see to it that no harm befalls the republic.

text should have overshadowed, if not eclipsed, a *hortatory* treatment. – In explaining the Bible to the people the preacher must be guided, not by what scholarship *draws out* of Scripture by philological studies, which are often no more than misleading guesses, but by what a moral cast of mind (according to the spirit of God) *puts into* it, and by teachings that can never mislead and can never fail to produce beneficial results. In other words, 7:69 he must treat the text *only* (or at least *primarily*) as an occasion for anything morally improving that can be made of it, without venturing to search for what the sacred authors themselves might have meant by it. – A sermon directed to edification as its final end (as any sermon should be) must develop its lesson from the *hearts* of the listeners, namely, from the natural moral predisposition that is present in even the most unlearned human being; for only then will the attitude of will it brings forth be pure. The *testimony of* Scripture connected with these teachings should also not be treated as historical arguments confirming their truth (for morally active reason needs no such argument, and besides, empirical cognition could not yield anything of the sort), but merely as examples in which the truth of reason's practical principles is made more perceptible through their application to facts of sacred history. But this, too, is a very valuable gain for peoples and states throughout the world.

Appendix
On a pure mysticism in religion*

I have learned from the critique of pure reason that philosophy is not a science of representations, concepts and ideas, or a science of all the sciences, or anything else of this sort. It is rather a science of the human being, of his representations, thoughts and actions: it should present all the components of the human being both as he is and as he should be – that is, in terms both of his natural functions and of his relations of morality and freedom. Ancient philosophers were quite mistaken in the role they assigned the human being in the world, since they considered 7:70 him a machine within it, entirely dependent on the world or on external things and circumstances, and so made him an all but passive part of the world – Now the critique of reason has appeared and assigned the human being a thoroughly *active* existence in the world. The human being himself

---

* This is a letter by Carol. Arnold. Wilmans, who enclosed it with his dissertation *De similitudine inter Mysticismum purum et Kantianam religionis doctrinam* (Bielefelda-Guestphalo, Halis Saxonum 1797). With his permission I publish it here, except for the salutation and the complimentary close. It singles out this young man – now devoted to the science of medicine – as one from whom much can be expected in other fields of science as well. In doing this, however, I do not mean to guarantee that my views coincide entirely with his.[33]

is the original maker of all his representations and concepts, and ought to be the sole author of all his actions. That "*is*" and this "*ought*" lead to two quite different functions in the human being. Accordingly, we also find in man two quite different elements, namely sensibility and understanding on the one hand, and on the other hand reason and free will; and these two are essentially distinct. In nature, everything *is:* the question of *ought* does not arise there. And since sensibility and understanding aim only at determining what *is* and how it comes to be, they must have their function in nature, in the physical world, and so belong to it. Reason tries constantly to enter the supersensible, to see what there *might be* beyond sensible nature. Although it is a theoretical power, it thus appears not to have its function in what is sensible. Free will, however, consists in independence from external things, since these ought not to be motives in a human being's actions; still less, then, can it belong to nature. But where does this lead us? To the fact that the human being must be destined for two entirely different worlds: for the realm of sense and understanding and so for this terrestrial world, but also for another world, which we do not know – a moral realm.

As for understanding, it is, by its form, intrinsically limited to this terrestrial world; for it consists merely in categories, that is, modes of expression which can refer only to sensible things. Its limits are therefore sharply defined: where the categories stop, so too does understanding: for the categories form and compose it. (It seems to me that we can also find evidence for the merely terrestrial and natural vocation of understanding in the fact that we find in nature a ladder of powers of understanding, from the most intelligent human being to the dumbest beast [since we can consider instinct, too, a kind of understanding insofar as free will does not belong to mere understanding].) But this is not the case with morality, which comes into being along with humanity and which is originally the same thing in all human beings. Understanding must, therefore, belong merely to nature; and if the human being had only understanding, without reason and free will, or without morality, there would be nothing to distinguish him from the beasts – he might merely stand at the top of their ladder. But because the human being 7:71 does have morality he is completely and essentially different, as a free being, from the beasts, even from the most intelligent of them (whose instinct often works more clearly and precisely than the human being's understanding). Understanding, however, is a thoroughly active power of the human being; all his representations and concepts are purely *his* works: he thinks spontaneously with his understanding, and he therefore makes *his* world. External things are only occasional causes for understanding's activity: they stimulate it to act and the products of this action are representations and concepts. Thus the things to which these representations and concepts refer cannot be that which our understanding represents; for understanding can make only representations and *its* own objects, not real things. In other words, we cannot possibly know, by these representations and concepts of understanding as such, things as they might be in themselves. Things that our senses and understanding express are in themselves only appearances, that is, objects of our senses and understanding produced by the cooperation of occasional causes and the activity of understanding. But this does not mean that they are illusions: in practical life we can regard them as real things for us and objects of our representations, just because we must suppose real things as occasional causes. Natural science provides an example. External things work on a body capable of action and, by so doing, stimulate it to act. The result of this is life. – But what is life? Physical recognition of one's existence in the world and one's relation to external things. The body lives insofar as it reacts to external things, takes them for its world, and uses them to its advantage, without concerning itself further about their essence. Without external things, this body would not be a living body; and without the body's capacity for action, external things would not be its world. It is the same with understanding. Its world arises from its encounter with external things, and without them it would be dead. But without understanding there would be no representations, without representations there would be no objects, and without objects its world would not exist. So too, given another understanding, another world would also exist, as the example of insanity makes clear. Understanding, 7:72 therefore, makes its objects and the world that is composed of them, but in such a way that real things are occasional causes of its activity and so of its representations.

This essentially distinguishes these natural powers of the human being from his reason and free will. For while both reason and free will are also active powers, they should not take the occasional causes of their action from the sensible world. So reason as a theoretical power can have no objects in the sensible world; because the occasional causes of its action are not real things but only, perhaps, the play of understanding, it can produce only ideas – that is, representations of reason to which no objects correspond. This is why reason cannot be used as a theoretical, speculative power here in this world of sense (and must, because it nevertheless exists as a power in it, be destined for another world), but only as a practical power on behalf of free will. Now free will is purely and simply practical. Its essence consists in this: that its action should not be reaction but rather a pure objective act, or that the motive and the object of its volition should not coincide; and that it should, accordingly, act independently of understanding's representations, since dependence on them would produce a perverted and corrupt kind of act, just as it should act independently of the ideas of speculative reason, since nothing real corresponds to them and they could easily give rise to a false and unfounded determination of the will. The motive of free will's action must therefore have its ground in the inner being of the human being himself and be inseparable from this very freedom of the will. Now this motive is the moral law, which so thoroughly frees us from nature and raises us above it that, as moral beings, we have no need of natural things as causes and motives in our acts of will and cannot consider them objects of our volition. The moral person of humanity, alone, takes their place. This law, then, guarantees us a specific characteristic that belongs only to the human being and distinguishes him from all the rest of nature: morality, which makes us independent and free beings and which is itself, in turn, based on this freedom. – Thus morality, not understanding, is what first makes us human beings. Although understanding is a fully active power and, to this extent, an independent power, it still needs external things for its action and is limited to them. Free will, on the contrary, is completely independent and should be determined solely by the inner law: in other words, the human being should be determined solely by himself insofar as he has raised himself to his original dignity and independence from everything but the law. Without its external things our understanding would be nothing – at least it would not be *this* understanding; but reason and free will remain the same in whatever realm they might carry on their activity. (Could we, with some plausibility, draw from this the admittedly hyperphysical conclusion: "With the death of the human body, the human being's understanding with all its earthly representations, concepts and knowledge also dies and vanishes, since the use of this understanding is limited to earthly, sensible things and ceases as soon as the human being tries to rise into the supersensible, where it is replaced by the use of reason"? This is an idea that I later found among the mystics too, though they have only an obscure conception of it and do not assert it. Certainly, it would be conducive to the comfort of many human beings, and perhaps also to their moral improvement. The human being is no more responsible for his understanding than for his body. A human being with a defective body consoles himself with the knowledge that a good physical constitution is not essential: it is advantageous only here on earth. Were the same view generally accepted with regard to understanding, should not the morality of human beings profit from it? Modern physiology harmonizes thoroughly with this idea, since it considers understanding dependent on the body and produced by the working of the brain. See Reil's[34] writings on physiology. Even ancient views on the material nature of the soul could, in this way, be reduced to something real.) –

As we continue the critical investigation of the human being's powers of soul, the question naturally arises: is there valid ground for reason's inevitable and irrepressible idea of a moral author of the universe and so

7:73

of ourselves and of the moral law, even though no theoretical ground, by its very nature, can adequately establish and guarantee that idea? From this arises the beautiful moral argument for God's existence, which is bound to be a clear and adequate proof for everyone in private – even for those who are reluctant to have it proved. And from the idea of a world-7:74 creator, which it has now established, there finally issues the practical Idea of a universal moral law-giver who, as the author of the moral law dwelling in us, prescribes all our duties. This Idea presents an entirely new world to the human being. He feels that he was created for another realm than that of sense and understanding – namely, for a moral realm, a kingdom of God. Now he recognizes his duties as divine commands also, and there arises in him a new awareness, a new feeling – namely, religion. – I had reached this point in my study of your writings, venerable father, when I became acquainted with a group of people, called separatists but calling themselves *mystics*, among whom I found your teachings put into practice almost verbatim. It was indeed difficult to recognize your teachings, at first, in their mystical terms, but after persistent probing I succeeded. It struck me as strange that these people live entirely without public worship: that they repudiate all "divine service" that does not consist in fulfilling one's duties: that they consider themselves religious people and indeed Christians, though they take as their code not the Bible, but only the precepts of an inward Christianity dwelling in us from eternity. – I inquired into their conduct and found in them (except for the mangy sheep that, from self-interest, get into every flock) a pure moral attitude of will and an almost Stoic consistency in their actions. I examined their teachings and principles and recognized the essentials of your entire moral and religious doctrine, though with this difference: that they consider the inner law, as they call it, an inward revelation and so regard God as definitely its author. It is true that they regard the Bible as a book which in some way or other – they do not discuss it further – is of divine origin; but, inquiring more closely, one finds that they infer the divine origin of the Bible from the consistency of the doctrine it contains with their inner law. For if one asks their reason, they reply: The Bible is validated in my heart, as you will find it in yours if you obey the precepts of your inner law or the teachings of the Bible. For the same reason they do not regard the 7:75 Bible as their code of laws but only as a historical confirmation in which they recognize what is originally grounded in themselves. In a word, if these people were philosophers they would be (pardon the term!) true Kantians. But most of them are merchants, artisans, and peasants, although I have now and then found them in higher stations, and a few of them among the educated. But I have never found a theologian among them – for to theologians, they are a real thorn in the eye because, while they do not support public worship, their exemplary conduct and complete submission to the civil order put them quite beyond reproach. What distinguishes these separatists from Quakers is not their religious *principles*, but the way they apply them to their everyday life; for example, they adopt no distinctive dress and pay both their state and church taxes. Among the educated members I have never encountered enthusiasm, but rather free, unprejudiced reasoning and judgment in religious matters.

Second part
The conflict of the philosophy faculty with the faculty of law

An old question raised again: Is the human race constantly progressing?

I.
WHAT DO WE *WANT* TO KNOW IN THIS MATTER?

We desire a fragment of human history and one, indeed, that is drawn not from past but future time, therefore a *predictive* history; if it is not based on known laws (like eclipses of the sun and moon), this history is designated as divinatory, and yet natural; but if it can be acquired in no other way than through a supernatural communication and widening of one's view of future time, this history is called *premonitory* (prophetic).* – If it is asked whether the human *race* at large is progressing perpetually toward the better, the important thing is not the natural history of human beings (whether new races may arise in the future), but rather his *moral history* and, more precisely, his history not as a species according to the *generic concept* (*singulorum*), but as the totality of human beings united socially on earth and apportioned into peoples (*universorum*).

2.
HOW *CAN* WE KNOW IT?

As a divinatory historical narrative of things imminent in future time, consequently as a possible representation a priori of events which are supposed to happen then. – But how is a history a priori possible? – Answer: if the diviner himself *makes* and contrives the events which he announces in advance.   4:80

It was all very well for the Jewish prophets to prophesy that sooner or later not simply decadence but complete dissolution awaited their state, for they themselves were the authors of this fate. – As national leaders they had loaded their constitution with so much ecclesiastical freight, and civil freight tied to it, that their state became utterly unfit to subsist of itself, and especially unfit to subsist together with neighboring nations. Hence the jeremiads of their priests were naturally bound to be lost upon the winds, because the priests obstinately persisted in their design for an

* From Pythia³⁵ to the gipsy woman, whoever dabbles in divination (doing it without knowledge or honesty) is said to be a *soothsayer.*

297

untenable constitution created by themselves; and thus they could infallibly foresee the issue.

So far as their influence extends, our politicians do precisely the same thing and are just as lucky in their prophecies. – We must, they say, take human beings as they are, not as pedants ignorant of the world or good-natured visionaries fancy they ought to be. But in place of that *as they are* it would be better to say what they *have made* them – stubborn and inclined to revolt – through unjust constraint, through perfidious plots placed in the hands of the government; obviously then, if the government allows the reins to relax a little, sad consequences ensue which verify the prophecy of those supposedly sagacious statesmen.

Ecclesiastics, too, occasionally prophesy the complete destruction of religion and the imminent appearance of Antichrist; and in doing so they are performing precisely what is requisite to call him up. This happens because they have not seen to impressing on their parishes moral principles which lead directly to the better, but rather fabricate into essential duty observances and historical beliefs which are supposed to effect it indirectly; from this, of course, can grow the mechanical unanimity as in a civil constitution, but none in moral disposition. But then they complain about irreligion, which they themselves have caused and thus could predict even without any special prophetic talent.

3.
DIVISION OF THE CONCEPT OF THAT WHICH WE WISH TO FOREKNOW AS REGARDS THE FUTURE

In three cases one could make predictions. The human race exists either in continual *retrogression* toward wickedness, or in perpetual *progression* toward improvement in its moral destination, or in eternal *stagnation* in its present stage of moral worth among creatures (a stagnation with which eternal rotation in orbit around the same point is one and the same).

The *first* assertion we can call moral *terrorism*, and the *second eudaemonism* (which could also be called *chiliasm* if we view the goal of progress within a broad prospectus); but the *third* we can term *abderitism*[36] because, since a true stagnation in matters of morality is not possible, a perpetually changing upward tendency and an equally frequent and profound relapse (an eternal oscillation, as it were) amounts to nothing more than if the subject had remained in the same place, standing still.

a.
Concerning the terroristic manner of representing human history

Decline into wickedness cannot be incessant in the human race, for at a certain stage of disintegration it would destroy itself. Hence in connection with the increase of great atrocities looming up like mountains, and evils commensurate with them, it is said: now things cannot grow worse; judgment day is at the door; and the pious enthusiast by this time is already dreaming of the restoration of all things and a renovated world after the time that this one will have perished in flames.

b.
Concerning the eudaemonistic manner of representing human history

It may always be conceded that the proportion of good and evil elements inherent in our predisposition remains constant and can be neither augmented nor diminished in the same individual; how then should the quantity of good in our predisposition increase? For that would happen only through the freedom of the subject, for which purpose the subject would in turn require a greater reservoir of good than it now possesses. – The effects cannot surpass the power of the efficient cause; thus the quantum of good in the human being mixed with the evil cannot exceed a certain measure beyond which it would be able to work its way up and thus ever proceed toward the better. Eudaemonism, with its sanguine hopes, therefore, appears to be untenable and to promise little in a prophetic history of humanity in favor of progress endlessly broadening its course toward the good.

4:82

c.
Concerning the abderitic hypothesis of the human race for the predetermination of its history

This opinion may well have the majority of voices on its side. Bustling folly is the character of our species: people hastily set off on the path of the good, but do not persevere steadfastly upon it; indeed, in order to avoid being bound to a single goal, even if only for the sake of variety they reverse the plan of progress, build in order to demolish, and impose upon themselves the hopeless effort of rolling the stone of Sisyphus uphill in order to let it roll back down again.[r] The principle of evil in the natural predisposition of the human race, therefore, does not seem to be amalgamated (blended) here with that of the good, but each appears rather to be neutralized by the other. Inertia (which is called here stagnation) would be the result of this. It is a vain affair to have good so alternate with evil that the whole traffic of our species with itself on this globe would have to be considered as a mere farcical comedy, for this can endow our species with no greater value in the eyes of reason than that which other animal species possess, species which carry on this game with fewer costs and without expenditure of thought.

[r] Princip

299

4.
THE PROBLEM OF PROGRESS IS NOT TO BE RESOLVED DIRECTLY THROUGH EXPERIENCE

Even if we felt that the human race, considered as a whole, was to be conceived as progressing and proceeding forward for however long a time, still no one can guarantee that now, this very moment, with regard to the physical disposition of our species, the epoch of its decline would not be liable to occur; and inversely, if it is moving backwards, and in an accelerated fall into baseness, a person may not despair even then of encountering a juncture (*punctum flexus contrarii*)' where the moral predisposition in our race would be able to turn anew toward the better. For we are dealing with beings that act freely, to whom, it is true, what they *ought* to do may be *dictated* in advance, but of whom it may not be *predicted* what they will do: we are dealing with beings who, from the feeling of self-inflicted evil, when things disintegrate altogether, know how to adopt a strengthened motive for making them even better than they were before that state. – But "miserable mortals," says the Abbé Coyer, "nothing is constant in your lives except inconstancy!"37

If the course of human affairs seems so senseless to us, perhaps it lies in a poor choice of position from which we regard it. Viewed from the earth, the planets sometimes move backwards, sometimes forward, and sometimes not at all. But if the standpoint selected is the sun, an act which only reason can perform, according to the Copernican hypothesis they move constantly in their regular course. Some people, however, who in other respects are not stupid, like to persist obstinately in their way of explaining the phenomena and in the point of view which they have once adopted, even if they should thereby entangle themselves to the point of absurdity in Tychonic cycles and epicycles.38 – But, and this is precisely

the misfortune, we are not capable of placing ourselves in this position when it is a question of the prediction of free actions. For that would be the standpoint of Providence which is situated beyond all human wisdom, and which likewise extends to the free actions of the human being; these actions, of course, the human being can *see*, but not *foresee* with certitude (for the divine eye there is no distinction in this matter); because, in the final analysis, the human being requires coherency according to natural laws, but with respect to his future *free* actions he must dispense with this guidance or direction.

If we were able to attribute to the human being an inherent and unalterably good, albeit limited, will, he would be able to predict with certainty the progress of his species toward the better, because it would concern an occurrence that he himself could produce. But in connection with the

---

' the point of rebound in the opposite direction

mixture of good and evil in his predisposition, with the proportion of which he not acquainted, he himself does not know what effect he might expect from it.

5.
YET THE PROPHETIC HISTORY OF THE HUMAN RACE MUST BE CONNECTED TO SOME EXPERIENCE

There must be some experience in the human race which, as an event, points to the disposition and capacity of the human race to be the cause of its own advance toward the better, and (since this should be the act of a being endowed with freedom), toward the human race as being the author of this advance. But from a given cause an event as an effect can be predicted [only] if the circumstances prevail which contribute to it. That these conditions must come to pass some time or other can, of course, be predicted in general, as in the calculation of probability in games of chance; but that prediction cannot enable us to know whether what is predicted is to happen in my life and I am to have the experience of it. – Therefore, an occurrence must be sought which points to the existence of such a cause and to its effectiveness in the human race, undetermined with regard to time, and which would allow progress toward the better to be concluded as an inevitable consequence. This conclusion then could also be extended to the history of the past (that it has always been in progress) in such a way that that occurrence would have to be considered not itself as the cause of history, but only as an intimation, a historical sign (*signum rememorativum, demonstrativum, prognostikon*)[1] demonstrating the tendency of the human race viewed in its entirety, that is, seen not as [a sum of] individuals (for that would yield an interminable enumeration and computation), but rather as divided into nations and states (as it is encountered on earth).

6.
CONCERNING AN OCCURRENCE IN OUR TIME WHICH DEMONSTRATES THIS MORAL TENDENCY OF THE HUMAN RACE

This occurrence consists neither in momentous deeds nor crimes committed by human beings whereby what was great among human beings is made small or what was small is made great, nor in ancient splendid political structures which vanish as if by magic while others come forth in their place as if from the depths of the earth. No, nothing of the sort. It is

---

[1] a sign of recalling, demonstrating, foretelling

simply the mode of thinking of the spectators which reveals itself *publicly* in this game of great revolutions, and manifests such a universal yet disinterested sympathy for the players on one side against those on the other, even at the risk that this partiality could become very disadvantageous for them if discovered. Owing to its universality, this mode of thinking demonstrates a character of the human race at large and all at once; owing to its disinterestedness, a moral character of humanity, at least in its predisposition, a character which not only permits people to hope for progress toward the better, but is already itself progress insofar as its capacity is sufficient for the present.

The revolution[39] of a gifted people which have seen unfolding in our day may succeed or miscarry; it may be filled with misery and atrocities to the point that a right-thinking human being, were he boldly to hope to execute it successfully the second time, would never resolve to make the experiment at such cost – this revolution, I say, nonetheless finds in the hearts of all spectators (who are not engaged in this game themselves) a wishful *participation* that borders closely on enthusiasm" the very expression of which is fraught with danger; this sympathy, therefore, can have no other cause than a moral predisposition in the human race.

This moral cause exerting its influence is twofold: first, that of the *right*, that a nation must not be hindered in providing itself with a civil constitution, which appears good to the people themselves; and second, that of the *end* (which is, at the same time, a duty), that that same national constitution alone be *just* and morally good in itself, created in such a way as to avoid, by its very nature, principles permitting offensive war. It can 7:86 be no other than a republican constitution, republican at least in essence;* it thus establishes the condition whereby war (the source of all evil and corruption of morals) is deterred; and, at least negatively, progress toward the better is assured humanity in spite of all its infirmity, for it is at least left undisturbed in its advance.

This, then, plus the passionate participation in the good, i.e., an effect

---

* But this is not to say that a nation which has a monarchical constitution should therewith usurp the law, nor even only cherish the secret wish of seeing it changed; for its position in Europe, perhaps very extended, can recommend that constitution as the only one by which that nation can maintain itself among powerful neighbors. Likewise the grumbling of the subjects, provoked not by the internal policy of the government but by the conduct of the latter toward foreigners, if perchance that conduct should hinder the subjects in their republican tendencies, is no proof at all of the nation's dissatisfaction with its own constitution, but rather of love for it; because the nation is the more assured against any danger the more other nations pursue a republican policy. – Nevertheless, some slanderous sycophants, to make themselves important, have sought to pass off this innocuous political twaddle as fondness for innovation, Jacobinism and mob action which would threaten the state; yet, under the circumstances, there was not even the least reason for these allegations, particularly in a country more than a hundred miles removed from the scene of the revolution.
" *Enthusiasm*

(although not to be wholly esteemed, since *enthusiasm* as such deserves censure), provide through this history the occasion for the following remark which is important for anthropology: genuine enthusiasm[v] always moves only toward what is ideal and, indeed, to what is purely moral, such as the concept of right, and it cannot be grafted onto self-interest. Monetary rewards will not elevate the adversaries of the revolution to the zeal and grandeur of soul which the pure concept of right produced in them; and even the concept of honor among the old martial nobility (an analogue to enthusiasm) vanished before the weapons of those who kept in view* the right of the nation to which they belonged and of which they considered themselves the guardians; with what exaltation the uninvolved public looking on sympathized then without the least intention of assisting.   7:87

7.
PROPHETIC HISTORY OF HUMANITY

In the principle there must be something *moral*, which reason presents as pure; but because of its great and epoch-making influence, reason must

---

* Of such an enthusiasm – for upholding justice for the human race we can say: "postquam ad arma Vulcania ventum est, mortalis mucro glacies ceu futilis ictu dissiluit."[w] Why has a ruler never dared openly to declare that he recognizes absolutely no right of the people opposed to him, that his people owe their happiness solely to the beneficence of a government which confers this happiness upon them, and that all presumption of the subject to a right opposed to the government (since this right comprehends the concept of permissible resistance) is absurd and even culpable? – The cause is that such a public declaration would rouse all of his subjects against him; although, as docile sheep, led by a benevolent and sensible master, well-fed and powerfully protected, they would have nothing wanting in their welfare for which to lament. – For a being endowed with freedom is not satisfied with the pleasure of life's comforts which fall to his lot by the act of another (in this case the government); what matters rather is the principle[x] according to which the individual provides such things for himself. But welfare possesses no *principle* either for him who receives it or for him who dispenses it (one places it here, the other there), inasmuch as what matters in welfare is the material of the will, which is empirical, and which is thus unfit for the universality of a rule. A being endowed with freedom in the consciousness of his superiority over the irrational animal, can and should therefore, according to the *formal* principle of his will, demand no other government for the people to which he belongs than one in which the people are co-legislative; that is, the right of human beings who are supposed to obey must necessarily precede all regard for well-being, and this right is a blessing that is exalted above all price (of utility), and one upon which no government, however beneficent it may persistently be, is permitted to infringe. – But this right is still always only an idea of which the realization is restricted to the condition of accord of its means with the morality which the nation may not transgress; and this may not come to pass through revolution which is always unjust. – To *govern* autocratically and yet in a republican way, that is, in the spirit of republicanism and on an analogy with it – that is what makes a nation satisfied with its constitution.
[v] *Euthusiasm* is translated in the passage as "enthusiasm".
[w] "When it met the divine Vulcanian armor, the mortal blade, like brittle ice, snapped in one stroke" (Virgil, *Aeneid* 12:739–41).[40]
[x] *Princip*

present it as the acknowledged duty of the human soul, concerning humanity as a whole (*non singularum, sed universorum*), which hails, with such universal and impartial sympathy, the hopes for its success and the efforts toward realizing it.[41] This occurrence is the phenomenon, not of revolution, but (as Erhard expresses it) – a phenomenon of the evolution of a constitution in accordance with *natural right* which, to be sure, is still not won solely by desperate battles – for war, both civil and foreign, destroys

7:88 all previously existing *statutory* constitutions. This evolution leads to striving after a constitution that cannot be bellicose, that is to say, a republican constitution. The constitution may be republican either in its *political form* or only in its *manner of governing*, in having the state ruled through the unity of the sovereign (the monarch) by analogy with the laws that a nation would provide itself in accordance with the universal principles of legality.

Now I claim to be able to predict to the human race – even without prophetic insight – according to the aspects and omens of our day, the attainment of this goal. That is, I predict its progress toward the better which, from now on, turns out to be no longer completely retrogressive. For such a phenomenon in human history *will not be forgotten*, because it has revealed a tendency and faculty in human nature for improvement such that no politician, affecting wisdom, might have conjured out of the course of things hitherto existing, and one which nature and freedom alone, united in the human race in conformity with inner principles of right, could have promised. But so far as time is concerned, it can promise this only indefinitely and as a contingent occurrence.

But even if the end viewed in connection with this occurrence should not now be attained, even if the revolution or reform of a national constitution should finally miscarry, or, after some time had elapsed, everything should relapse into its former rut (as politicians now predict), that philosophical prophecy still would lose nothing of its force. – For that occurrence is too important, too much interwoven with the interest of humanity, and its influence too widely propagated in all areas of the world to not be recalled on any favorable occasion by the nations which would then be roused to a repetition of new efforts of this kind; because then, in an affair so important for the human race, the intended constitution, at a certain time, must finally attain that constancy which instruction by repeated experience suffices to establish in the minds of all.

Here, therefore, is a proposition valid for the most rigorous theory, in spite of all skeptics, and not just a well-meaning and a commendable

7:89 proposition in a practical respect: the human race has always been in progress toward the better and will continue to be so henceforth. To him who does not consider what happens in just some one nation but also has regard to the whole scope of all the peoples on earth who will gradually come to participate in progress, this reveals the prospect of an immeasurable time – provided at least that there does not, by some chance, occur a second epoch of natural revolution which will push aside the human race to clear the stage for other creatures, like that which (according to Camper and Blumenbach)[42] submerged the plant and animal kingdoms before human beings ever existed. For in the face of the omnipotence of nature, or rather its supreme first cause which is inaccessible to us, the human being is, in his turn, but a trifle. But for the sovereigns of his own species also to consider and treat him as such, whether by burdening him as an animal, regarding him as a mere tool of their designs, or exposing him in their conflicts with one another in order to have him massacred – that is no trifle, but a subversion of the *final end* of creation itself.

8.
CONCERNING THE DIFFICULTY OF THE MAXIMS APPLYING TO WORLD PROGRESS WITH REGARD TO THEIR PUBLICITY

Enlightenment of the people is the public instruction of the people in its duties and rights vis-à-vis the state to which they belong. Since only natural rights and rights arising out of the common human understanding are concerned here, then the natural heralds and expositors of these among the people are not officially appointed by the state but are free professors of law, that is philosophers who, precisely because this freedom is allowed to them, are objectionable to the state, which always desires to rule alone; and they are decried, under the name of *enlighteners,* as persons dangerous to the state, although their voice is not addressed *confidentially* to the people (as the people take scarcely any or no notice at all of it and of their writings) but is addressed *respectfully* to the state; and they implore the state to take to heart that need which is felt to be legitimate. This can happen by no other means than that of publicity in the event that an entire people cares to bring forward its grievances (*gravamen*). Thus the *prohibition* of publicity impedes the progress of a people toward improvement, even in that which applies to the least of its claims, namely its simple, natural right.

Another disguise, which is easily penetrated indeed, but is one to which a nation, nevertheless, is legally committed, is that pertaining to the true nature of its constitution. It would be an insult to its majesty to say of the British nation that it is an *unlimited monarchy:* some rather maintain that a constitution *limiting* the will of the monarch through the two Houses of Parliament, acting as representatives of the people, is supposed to exist; and yet everyone knows perfectly well that the monarch's influence on these representatives is so great and so certain that nothing is resolved by the Houses except what he wills and purposes through his

7:90

minister. The latter then probably even proposes resolutions in connection with which he knows that he will be contradicted, and even arranges it that way (for example, with regard to slave-trade) in order to provide a fictitious proof of the freedom of Parliament. – This representation of the nature of the case has something delusive about it so that the true constitution, faithful to law, is no longer sought at all; for a person imagines he has found it in an example already at hand, and a false publicity deceives the people with the illusion of a *limited monarchy** in power by a law which issues from them, while their representatives, won over by bribery, have secretly subjected them to an *absolute monarchy.*

$$\cdot \; \cdot$$

7:91 The idea of a constitution in harmony with the natural right of human beings, one namely in which the citizens obedient to the law, besides being united, ought also to be legislative, lies at the basis of all political forms; and the body politic which, conceived in conformity to it by virtue of pure concepts of reason, signifies a Platonic *ideal* (*respublica noumenon*), is not an empty figment of the brain, but rather the eternal norm for all civil organization in general, and averts all war. A civil society organized conformably to this ideal is the representation of it in agreement with the laws of freedom by means of an example in our experience (*respublica phaenomenon*) and can be acquired only painfully, after multifarious hostilities and wars; but its constitution, once won on a large scale, is qualified as the best among all others to banish war, the destroyer of everything good. Consequently, it is a duty to enter into such a system of government, but it is provisionally the duty of the monarchs, if they rule *as autocrats,* to govern in a *republican* (not democratic) way, that is, to treat people according to principles^y which are commensurate with the spirit of laws of freedom (as a nation with mature understanding would prescribe them for itself), although they would not be literally canvassed for their consent.

---

* A cause, the nature of which one does directly understand, makes itself known through the effect which unfailingly attaches to it. – What is an *absolute* monarch? He is one at whose command, if he says, "war is necessary," a state of war immediately exists. – What is a *limited* monarch, on the other hand? He who must first consult the people as to whether war is or is not to be; and the people say, "there is to be no war," so there is no war. For war is a situation in which *all* political power must be at the disposal of the sovereign. Now the British monarch has conducted wars aplenty without seeking the consent for them. Therefore, this king is an absolute monarch who ought not to be one, of course, according to the constitution; but he is always able to bypass it because precisely through those political powers, namely, that he has it in his power to dispense all appointments and posts, he can consider assured the assent of the representatives of the people. In order to succeed, however, this system of bribery must certainly not be publicized. Hence it remains under the highly transparent veil of secrecy.

^{y} *Principien*

9.
WHAT PROFIT WILL PROGRESS TOWARD THE BETTER YIELD HUMANITY?

Not an ever-growing quantity of *morality* with regard to intention, but an increase of the products of *legality* in dutiful actions whatever their motives.[z] That is, the profit (result) of the human being's striving toward the better can be assumed to reside alone in the good *deeds* of human beings, which will become better and better and more and more numerous; it resides alone in phenomena constituting the moral state of the human race. – For we have only *empirical* data (experiences) upon which we are founding this prediction, namely, the physical cause of our actions as these actually occur as phenomena; and not the moral cause – the only one which can be established purely a priori – which contains the concept of duty with respect to what ought to happen.

Gradually violence on the part of the powers will diminish and obedience to the laws will increase. There will arise in the body politic perhaps more charity and less strife in lawsuits, more reliability in keeping one's word, etc., partly out of love of honor, partly out of well-understood self-interest. And eventually this will also extend to nations in their external relations toward one another up to the realization of the cosmopolitan society, without the moral foundation in humanity having to be enlarged in the least; for that, a kind of new creation (supernatural influence) would be necessary. – For we must also not hope for too much from human beings in their progress toward the better lest we fall prey with good reason to the mockery of the politician who would willingly take the hope of the human being as the dreaming of an overstressed mind.*

7:92

10.
IN WHAT ORDER ALONE CAN PROGRESS TOWARD THE BETTER BE EXPECTED?

The answer is: not by the movement of things *from bottom to top*, but *from top to bottom*. – To expect not simply to train good citizens but good human

---

* It is sweet, however, to imagine constitutions corresponding to the requirements of reason (particularly in a legal sense), but rash to propose them and culpable to incite the populace to abolish what presently exists.

Plato's *Atlantica*, More's *Utopia*, Harrington's *Oceana* and Allais's *Severambia*[43] have been successively brought on the scene, but have never so much as been tried (Cromwell's abortive monster of a despotic republic excepted). – The same goes for political creations as for the creation of the world; no human was present there, nor could he have been present at such an event, since he must have been his own creator otherwise. However late it may be, to hope someday for the consummation of a political product, as it is envisaged here, is a sweet dream; but that it is being perpetually approached is not only *thinkable*, but, so far as it is compatible with the moral law, an *obligation*, not of the citizens, but of the sovereign.
[z] *Triebfeder*

307

beings who can improve and take care of themselves; to expect that this will eventually happen by means of education of youth in the home, then in schools on both the lowest and highest level, in intellectual and moral culture fortified by religious doctrine – that is desirable, but its success is hardly to be hoped for. For while the people feel that the costs for education of their youth ought to be borne, not by them, but by the state, the state for its part has no money left (as Büsching complains)[44] for the salaries of its teachers who are capable and zealously devoted to their spheres of duty, since it uses all the money for war. Rather, the whole mechanism of this education has no coherence if it is not designed in agreement with a well-weighed plan of the sovereign power, put into play according to the purpose of this plan, and steadily maintained therein; to this end it might well behoove the state likewise to reform itself from time to time and, attempting evolution instead of revolution, progress perpetually toward the better. Nevertheless, since they are also *human beings* who must effect this education, consequently such beings who themselves have to be trained for that purpose, then, considering this infirmity of human nature as subject to the contingency of events which favor such an effect, the hope for its progress is to be expected only on the condition of a wisdom from above (which bears the name of providence if it is invisible to us); but for that which can be expected and exacted from *human beings* in this area toward the advancement of this aim, we can anticipate only a negative wisdom, namely, that they will see themselves compelled to render the greatest obstacle to morality – that is to say *war* which constantly retards this advancement – firstly by degrees more humane and then rarer, and finally to renounce offensive war altogether, in order to enter upon a constitution which by its nature and without loss of power is founded on genuine principles of right, and which can persistently progress toward the better.

CONCLUSION

A doctor who consoled his patients from one day to the next with hopes of a speedy convalescence, pledging to one that his pulse beat better, to another an improvement in his stool, to a third the same regarding his perspiration, etc., received a visit from one of his friends. "How's your illness, my friend," was his first question. "How should it be? *I'm dying of improvement, pure and simple!*" – I blame no one when, considering the ills of the state, he begins to despair of the health of humanity and its progress toward the better; but I would rely on the heroic remedy which Hume prescribes and which would effect a quick cure. "If, at the present time," he says, "I see the nations on the point of war with one another, it is as if I were seeing two besotted fellows beating each other about with cudgels in a china shop. For not only do they have to recover slowly from the bruises

308

they administered to each other, but afterwards they must pay for the damages that they have done."[45] *Sero sapiunt Phryges.* [a] However, the painful consequences of the present war can compel the political prophet to confess a very imminent turn of humanity toward the better that is even now in prospect.

[a] The Phrygians are wise too late (Cicero, *Ad familiam* 7:16).

Third part
The conflict of the philosophy faculty with the
faculty of medicine

On the power of the mind to master its morbid feelings by sheer resolution

A LETTER IN REPLY TO PRIVY COUNCILLOR AND
PROFESSOR HUFELAND[46]

The fact that I am only now, in January of this year [1798], writing to thank you for the gift of your instructive and enjoyable book *On the Art of Prolonging Human Life*, which you sent me on 12 December 1796, might make you think that I am counting on a long life in which to reply. But old age brings with it the habit of postponing important decisions (*procrastinatio*) – just as we put off concluding our lives: death always arrives too soon for us, and we are inexhaustible in thinking up excuses for making it wait.

You ask for my opinion of your "attempt to treat the physical element in the human being morally: to present the whole human being, including his physical side, as a being that is ordered to morality, and to show that moral cultivation is essential to the physical completion of human nature, which exists only in outline." And you add, "At least I can assure you that these were no preconceived opinions, and that it was my work and investigation itself that compelled me to treat human nature in this way." – Such an outlook betrays a philosopher, not a mere subtle reasoner. It is the outlook of a man who is not only, as a director of the French Convention, skilled in applying the means reason prescribes, on the basis of experience (technically), to realize the ends of medical science, but who is also a legislative member of the body of doctors drawn from pure reason and has, along with the skill to prescribe what *cures*, the wisdom to prescribe what is also *duty* in itself. In this way morally practical philosophy also provides a panacea which, though it is certainly not the complete answer to every problem, must still be an ingredient in every prescription. 7:98

This panacea, however, is only a *regimen* to be adopted: in other words, it functions only in a *negative* way, as the art of *preventing* disease. But an art of this sort presupposes, as its necessary condition, an ability that only philosophy, or the spirit of philosophy, can give. The supreme task of the art of formulating a regimen, which refers to this spirit, is contained in the following thesis:

313

ON THE POWER OF THE HUMAN MIND
TO MASTER ITS MORBID FEELINGS MERELY
BY A FIRM RESOLUTION

My examples confirming the possibility of this proposition cannot be drawn from other people's experiences, but, in the first instance, only from what I have experienced in myself; for they come from introspection, and only afterwards can I ask others whether they have not noticed the same thing in themselves. – I am forced, accordingly, to talk about myself; and although this would betray lack of modesty in a dogmatic treatise,* it is excusable if we are dealing, not with common experience, but with an inner experiment or observation that I had to make on myself before I could submit, for others' consideration, something that would not of itself occur to everyone unless his attention were drawn to it. – To want to entertain others with the inner history of the play of my thoughts, which has subjective importance (for me) but no objective importance (valid for everyone), would be presumptuous, and I could justly be blamed for it. But if this sort of introspection and what I found by it is something rather uncommon, which it is worthwhile for everyone to try though it must be pointed out to them, the nuisance of telling others about my private feelings can at least be excused.

7:99 Before attempting to present the results of the self-observation I undertook with a view to a regimen, I must say something about the way Herr *Hufeland* poses the task of *formulating a regimen*, that is, of the art of *preventing* illness, as distinguished from *therapeutics* or the art of *curing* it.

He calls the art of formulating a regimen "the art of prolonging human life."

He derives this term from what human beings desire most ardently, even though it might not be so desirable, though they would, indeed, like to have two wishes fulfilled at the same time: *to have a long life* and to enjoy *good health* during it. But the second wish is not a necessary condition of the first: the wish for long life is unconditioned. Take a sick person who has been lying for years in a hospital bed, suffering and indigent, and hear how often he wishes that death would come soon and deliver him from his misery. Do not believe him: he is not in earnest about it. Though his reason does prompt him to wish for death, his natural instinct is to live. When he beckons to death as his deliverer (*Jovi liberatori*)[b] he always asks for a short respite and has some sort of pretext for *putting off* its peremp-

---

* In treatises of a dogmatic-practical nature – for example, the sort of self-examination that is directed to duties incumbent on everyone – the lecturer speaks in terms of *me* rather than *I*. But if he is describing his private feelings (as a patient to his doctor), or his personal experience as such, he must speak in terms of I.
[b] Jove the liberator

tory decree (*procrastinatio*). The fact that a man may, in a wild rage, decide to end his own life is no exception to this; for his decision results from an emotional agitation' – raised almost to the point of insanity. – Of the two things promised to us for fulfilling our filial duty ("may you prosper and live long on earth"), the second contains the stronger incentive, even in the judgment of reason – that is to say, as a duty the observance of which is *meritorious*.

The duty of *honoring old age*, in other words, is not really based on the consideration that age, because of its frailty, can rightly claim from youth; for weakness is no reason for being entitled to *respect*. Old age, therefore, claims to be considered something *meritorious* besides, since *reverence* is due it. And the reason for this is not that in attaining the age of Nestor one has acquired, by varied and long experience, wisdom for guiding the young; it is only that a man who has survived so long – that is, has succeeded so long in eluding mortality, the most humiliating sentence that can be passed on a rational being ("you are dust and will return to dust")[47] – has to this extent won immortality, so to speak. This is the reason why old people should be honored, as long as no shame has stained their lives – simply because they have preserved their lives so long and set an example.

On the other hand, it is always uncertain whether the human being's second natural wish, for good health, is fulfilled. He can *feel* well (to judge by his comfortable feeling of vitality), but he can never *know* that he is healthy. – Every cause of natural death is illness, whether one feels it or not. There are many people of whom one can say, without really wanting to ridicule them, that they are always *sickly* but can never be *sick*. Their regimen consists in constantly deviating from and returning to their way of life, and by this they manage to get on well and live a long, if not a robust life. I have outlived a good many of my friends or acquaintances who boasted of perfect health and lived by an orderly regimen adopted once and for all, while the seed of death (illness) lay in them unnoticed, ready to develop. They *felt* healthy and did not *know* they were ill; for while the cause of natural death is always illness, *causality* cannot be felt. It requires understanding, whose judgment can err. Feeling, on the other hand, is infallible; but we do not call a human being ill unless he *feels* ill, although a disease which he does not *feel* may lie hidden in him, about to come forth. Hence if he does not feel ill, he is entitled to express his well-being only by saying that he is *apparently* in good health. So a long life, considered in retrospect, can testify only to the health one *has enjoyed*, and the art of a regimen will have to prove its skill or science primarily in the art of *prolonging* life (not *enjoying* it). This is what Herr Hufeland, too, wanted to say.

7:100

' *Affekts*

315

THE PRINCIPLE OF THE REGIMEN

A regimen for prolonging man's life must not aim at a life of *ease;* for by such indulgence toward his powers and feelings he would spoil himself. In other words, it would result in frailty and weakness, since his vital energy can be gradually extinguished by lack of exercise just as it can be drained by using it too frequently and too intensely. Hence *Stoicism* (*sustine et abstine*) belongs, as the principle of a regimen, to practical *philosophy* not only as the *doctrine of virtue* but also as the *science of medicine.* – Medical 7:101 science is *philosophical* when the sheer power of man's reason to master his sensuous feelings by a self-imposed principle determines his manner of living. On the other hand, if medical science seeks the help of external physical means (drugs or surgery) to stimulate or ward off these sensations, it is merely empirical and mechanical.

Warmth, sleep, and *pampering* ourselves when we are not ill are some of these bad habits of a life of ease.

1. From my own experience, I cannot agree with the rule that the head and feet should be kept warm. I find it more advisable to keep them both cold (the Russians include the chest as well), just as a precaution *against being cold.* – Granted it is more comfortable, in winter, to wash one's feet in tepid water than in water that is almost ice-cold: using cold water prevents a slackening of the blood vessels in members far removed from the heart – a condition which, in old age, often results in an incurable disease of the feet. – It may be a precept of a regimen, rather than of comfort, to keep the abdomen warm, especially in cold weather; for it contains the intestines, which have to carry a non-liquid material over a long course. This, rather than warmth itself, is the reason for using what is called a supporting belt in old age (a wide band that holds in the abdomen and supports its muscles).

2. To sleep a *long time* or a *great deal* (intermittently, by midday naps) is, admittedly, to spare ourselves just this much of the inconvenience that waking life inevitably brings with it – and it is rather odd to want a long life in order to sleep most of it away. But what is really to the point here is that this supposed means to a long life, comfort, contradicts its own purpose. For alternate waking and falling asleep again in long winter nights cripples, depresses, and exhausts the entire nervous system in a mere illusion of rest. So in this case comfort contributes to shortening one's life. – The bed is a nest for a whole flock of illnesses.

3. Some elderly people *coddle* themselves, or let themselves be coddled, because they think they can prolong their lives if they *conserve* their energy by avoiding discomfort (for example, going out in bad weather) or, 7:102 in general, by relegating to others work they could do themselves. But their solicitude for themselves brings about the direct opposite: premature old age and a shorter life. – Again, it might be hard to prove that *married*

people have a *better chance* of living to a very old age. – In some families longevity is hereditary, and intermarriage in such a family may well establish a family trait of this kind. Again, it is not a bad political principle to promote marriage by commending married life as a long life, although experience provides relatively few examples of married couples who have lived to an exceptionally old age together. But here we are concerned only with the physiological cause of longevity according to the order of nature, not with the cause that might be assigned to it for political reasons, that is, with what the state's interests require in the way of public opinion. – Besides, *philosophizing*, in a sense that does not involve being a philosopher, is a means of warding off many disagreeable feelings and, besides, a *stimulant* to the mind that introduces an interest into its occupations – an interest which, just because it is independent of external contingencies, is powerful and sincere, though it is merely in the nature of a game, and keeps the vital force from running down. On the other hand *philosophy*, whose interest is the entire final end of reason (an absolute unity), brings with it a feeling of power which can well compensate to some degree for the physical weaknesses of old age by a rational estimation of life's value. – But opening new prospects for increasing our knowledge, even if they do not belong directly to philosophy, serves the same function, or one similar to it; and to the extent that the mathematician takes an *immediate* interest in mathematics (and does not consider it instrumental to some other aim), he is also a philosopher and enjoys the benefit of having his powers stimulated in this way, in a life that is rejuvenated and prolonged without exhaustion.

But for people of limited intelligence, merely puttering about in a carefree situation is a substitute that serves almost the same function, and those who are always busy doing nothing are usually long-lived as well. – A very old man found a great interest in making the numerous clocks in his room strike always one after another, never at the same time – an interest that gave both him and the watchmaker more than enough to do all day and earned the watchmaker a living. For another, feeding and caring for his songbirds served to keep him busy from his own mealtime to   7:103
his bedtime. A wealthy old lady found a way to fill her time with idle chatter at the spinning wheel; and when she was very old she complained, just as if she had lost a good companion, that she was in danger of dying from boredom now that she could no longer feel the thread between her fingers.

But since I am afraid that my discourse on longevity may be boring, and so dangerous, to you, I shall put a limit[d] on the garrulity that one mildly ridicules if one does not censure it, as a fault of old age.

[d] *Grenzen*

1.

On hypochondria

The exact opposite of the mind's power to master its pathological feelings is *hypochondria*, the weakness of abandoning oneself despondently to general morbid feelings that have no definite object (and so making no attempt to master them by reason). Since this sort of melancholia (*hypochondria vaga*)* has no definite seat in the body and is a creature of the imagination, it could also be called *fictitious* disease, in which the patient finds in himself symptoms of every disease he reads about in books. The opposite of the mind's self-mastery, in other words, is fainthearted brooding about the ills that could befall one, and that one would not be able to withstand if they should come. It is a kind of insanity; for though some sort of unhealthy condition (such as flatulence or constipation) may be the source of it, this state is not felt immediately, as it affects the senses, but is misrepresented as impending illness by inventive imagination. And then the self-tormenter (*heautontimorumenos*), instead of pulling himself together, summons the doctor's help. But this does no good, since only he himself, by disciplining the play of his thoughts, can put an end to these harassing notions that arise involuntarily – notions, indeed, of diseases that could not be prevented if they were really forthcoming. – As long as a man is afflicted with this sickness we cannot expect him to master his

7:104 morbid feelings by sheer resolution; for if he could do this, he would not be hypochondric. A reasonable human being does not permit himself any such hypochondria; if uneasiness comes over him and threatens to develop into melancholia*ᶜ* – that is, self-devised illness – he asks himself whether his anxiety has an object. If he finds nothing that could furnish a valid reason for his anxiety, or if he sees that, were there really such a reason, nothing could be done to prevent its effect, he goes on, despite this claim of his inner feeling, to his agenda for the day – in other words, he leaves his oppression (which is then merely local) in its proper place (as if it had nothing to do with him), and turns his attention to the business at hand.

I myself have a natural disposition to hypochondria because of my flat and narrow chest, which leaves little room for the movement of the heart and lungs; and in my earlier years this disposition made me almost weary of life. But by reflecting that, if the cause of this oppression of the heart was purely mechanical, nothing could be done about it, I soon came to pay no attention to it. The result was that, while I felt the oppression in my chest, a calm and cheerful state prevailed in my mind, which did not fail to communicate itself to society, not by intermittent whims (as is usual with

---

* As distinguished from *localized* hypochondria (*hypochondria intestinalis*).
ᶜ Grillen

hypochondriacs), but purposely and naturally. And since one's life becomes cheerful more through what we freely *do* with life than through what we *enjoy* as a gift from it, mental work can set another kind of heightened vital feeling against the limitations that affect the body alone. The oppression has remained with me, for its cause lies in my physical constitution. But I have mastered its influence on my thoughts and actions by diverting my attention from this feeling, as if it had nothing to do with me.

2.
On sleep

The Turks, with their fatalism*[f]* have a saying about moderation: that at the beginning of the world each human being had allotted to him the portion he would have to eat during his lifetime, and to the degree that he squanders his ration in very large meals, he can count on a shorter time *to eat* and so *to exist.* This saying can also serve as a rule in a regimen, when we put this in the form of *elementary school teaching* (for in questions of pleasure, doctors must often treat human beings as if they were children): the rule, namely, that fate in the beginning assigned to each man his portion of *sleep*, and that one who has given too much of his adult life (more than one-third of it) to sleep cannot expect a long time for sleeping, that is, for living and growing old. – If, in order to enjoy the sweet luxury of dozing (the Spanish *siesta*) or to pass the time (in long winter nights), a human being allots much more than a third of his lifetime to sleep, or if he metes it out bit by bit, in naps instead of in one continuous period each day, he miscalculates seriously regarding the *quantity of life* at his disposal, both as to the level and the length of it. – Now hardly anyone would wish that he could dispense with sleep entirely (which shows that we regard a long life as a long drudgery, and the part of it spent in sleep as an escape from this much hardship). So it is more advisable, for both feeling and reason, to set aside completely this third that is empty of enjoyment and activity, and relinquish it to the necessary restoration of nature. However, one should regulate exactly the time it is to begin and how long it is to last.

To be unable to sleep at one's fixed and habitual time, or also unable to stay awake, is a kind of morbid feeling. But of these two, insomnia is worse: to go to bed intending to sleep, and yet lie awake. – Doctors usually advise a patient to drive all *thoughts* from his head; but they return, or others come in their place, and keep him awake. The only disciplinary advice is to turn away his attention as soon as he perceives or becomes conscious of any thought stirring (just as if, with his eyes closed, he turned

7:105

---

[f] *Prädestination*

them to a different place). This interruption of any thought that he is aware of gradually produces a confusion of ideas by which his awareness of his physical (external) situation is suspended; and then an altogether different order sets in, an involuntary play of imagination (which, in a state of health, is *dreaming*). Dreaming is an admirable device of our animal organization by which the body is relaxed for animal movement but stimulated within for vital movement; so, even if we do not remember our dreams when we wake up, they must still have occurred: for otherwise, if they were totally lacking – if the nervous energy that proceeds from the brain, the seat of representations, did not work in unison with the muscular power of the viscera – life could not maintain itself for an instant. This is why we presume that all animals dream when they sleep.

But it can happen to anyone, now and then, that when he lies down in bed ready to sleep he cannot fall asleep, even by diverting his thoughts in this way. When this happens he will feel a kind of spasm (like a cramp) in his brain – a feeling quite consistent with the observation that a man upon awakening is some half-inch taller than if he had only remained in bed awake. – Since insomnia is a failing of weak old age, and since the left side is generally weaker than the right,* I felt, perhaps a year ago, these cramplike seizures and quite sensible stimuli of this kind (though they were not, like cramps, actual visible movements of the affected limb); and from other people's descriptions I had to take them for attacks of gout and consult a doctor about them. But, impatient at feeling my sleep interfered with, I soon had recourse to my Stoic remedy of fixing my thought forcibly on some neutral object that I chose at random (for example, the name Cicero, which contains many associated ideas), and so diverting my attention from that sensation. The result was that the sensation was dulled, even quickly so, and outweighed by drowsiness; and I can repeat this procedure with equally good results every time that attacks of this kind recur in the brief interruptions of my night's sleep. It occurred to me that these might be merely imaginary pains; but the fact that the toes of my left foot were bright red the next morning convinced me that they were not. -

7:106

7:107

* It is sometimes said that exercise and early training are the only factors determining which side of one's body will be stronger or weaker, as far as the use of external members is concerned – whether in combat he will handle the sabre with his right arm or with his left, whether the rider standing in his stirrup will vault onto his horse from right to left or vice-versa, and so forth. But this assertion is quite incorrect. Experience teaches that if we have our shoe measurements taken from our left foot, and the left shoe fits perfectly, the right one will be too tight; and we can hardly lay the blame for this on our parents, for not having taught us better when we were children. The advantage of the right side over the left can also be seen from the fact that, if we want to cross a deep ditch, we put our weight on the left foot and step over with the right; otherwise we run the risk of falling into the ditch. The fact that Prussian infantrymen are trained to *start out* with the left foot confirms, rather than refutes, this assertion; for they put this foot in front, as on a fulcrum, in order to use the right side for the impetus of the attack, which they execute with the right foot against the left.

I am sure that many attacks of *gout* could be checked in the same way, provided one's diet of food and drink is not too great an obstacle, and even *cramps* and *epileptic* seizures (though this does not apply to women and children, who do not have the necessary strength of resolution). Indeed, even cases of *podagra* that have been given up as incurable could be controlled, at each new attack, by a firm resolution (to divert one's attention from the pain), and, indeed, gradually cured.

3.
On food and drink

When someone is healthy and young, his best guide to when and how much to eat and drink is simply his *appetite* (hunger and thirst). But when the weaknesses of old age set in, he can best prolong his life by a disciplinary principle of making a *habit*, to a certain extent, of a manner of living that he has tested and found beneficial; in other words, by uniformity in his daily routine – provided that his diet allows for suitable exceptions when his appetite balks at it. – More specifically, an elderly person's appetite, and especially a man's, refuses large quantities of liquids (soup, or too much drinking water); on the other hand, it demands more stimulating drink (wine, for example) and heartier food, both to bring into the circulatory system stimulating elements which help to keep the machinery of blood circulation working, and to promote the *vermicular* movement of the intestines (which, of all the viscera, seem to have the most *vita propria;* for if they are removed still warm from an animal and cut into pieces, they crawl like worms, and one can not only feel but even hear them working). 7:108

With elderly people, water, once in the blood stream, takes longer to complete the long process of separation from the blood mass through the kidneys to the bladder when it does not contain elements which are assimilated to the blood and stimulate the blood vessels to eliminate it (as wine does). But in this case wine is used medicinally, and because of this its artificial use is not really part of a preventive regimen. Attacks of the appetite for water (thirst) are, for the most part, only habit; and by not giving in to them at once, and adopting a firm resolution about this, one reduces this stimulus to the level of a natural need to add liquids to solid foods. Even natural instinct denies elderly people the use of liquids in great quantities. Moreover, drinking water to excess lowers the temperature of the blood and so prevents one from sleeping well, or at least deeply.

The question is often raised, whether the rules of a regimen permit only one meal, as well as only one period of sleep, in twenty-four hours, or whether it would not be *better* (more healthful) to stint the appetite somewhat at the midday meal and eat something at night. Having an evening meal is, admittedly, better for passing the time. – I also consider it more beneficial in the so-called best years of life (middle age). But in later years it is better to eat only at midday; for since the stages of the digestive process in the intestines undoubtedly take longer to complete in old age, there is reason to believe that setting nature a new task (by an evening meal) when the first stage of digestion is still going on is prejudicial to health. – For this reason, an impulse to have an evening meal after an adequate and satisfying one at midday can be considered a pathological feeling; and one can master it so completely by a firm resolution that one gradually ceases to feel these attacks at all.

7:109

4.

On pathological feelings that come from thinking at unsuitable times

Thinking – whether in the form of *study* (reading books) or *reflection* (meditation and discovery) – is a scholar's food; and *when he is wide awake and alone,* he cannot live without it. But if he taxes his energy by occupying himself with a specific thought when he is eating or walking, he inflicts two tasks on himself at the same time – on the head and the stomach or on the head and the feet; and in the first case this brings on hypochondria, in the second, vertigo. To master these pathological states by a regimen, then, all he has to do is alternate the mechanical occupation of the stomach or the feet with the mental occupation of thinking and, while he is eating or taking a walk (restoring himself), check deliberate thought and give himself over to the free play of imagination (a quasi-mechanical activity). But, in the scholar's case, this requires the adoption, in a general way, of a firm resolution to go on a *diet with regard to thinking.*

The practice of occupying oneself with reading or reflecting when dining alone provokes pathological feelings; for intellectual work diverts vital energy from the stomach and bothers it. Reflecting while taking a walk also brings on these feelings, since the work the feet are doing is already draining one's energy.* (The same thing holds true of *studying by artificial light,* if one is not used to it.) However, these pathological feelings arising from intellectual work undertaken at the wrong time (*invita Minerva*) are not the kind that can be eliminated directly and at once by sheer resolution. One can get rid of them only gradually, by breaking the habit

* When someone of studious habits goes for a walk alone, it is hard for him to refrain from entertaining himself with his own reflections. But if he engages in strenuous thinking during his *walk,* he will soon be exhausted, whereas if he gives himself over to the free play of imagination, the motion will refresh him – the reports of others whom I asked about this confirm my own experience. If in addition to thinking he also engages in conversation while he is walking, he will be even more fatigued, so that he will soon have to sit down to continue with his play of thought. – The purpose of walking in the open air is precisely to keep one's attention moving from one object to another and so *to keep it from becoming fixed* on any one object.

through a principle opposed to it. And here we should be speaking only of those that can be mastered immediately.

5.
On overcoming and preventing pathological seizures by a resolution about breathing

A few years ago I suffered occasionally from catarrh and cough, and these attacks were all the more troublesome because they sometimes occurred when I was going to sleep. Indignant, so to speak, at having my night's sleep disturbed, I resolved, with regard to the attacks of catarrh, to keep my lips closed tight and to breathe only through my nose. At first I could manage only a thin, whistling breath; but as I did not give up or relax my efforts, my breathing grew continually stronger until finally I could inhale fully and freely through my nose. – And when I reached this point, I fell asleep at once. As for *coughing* – a spasm, so to speak, of loud exhalations broken by gasps (not continuous, like laughter) – I was bothered especially by what the ordinary Englishman calls an old man's cough (since the attacks come when one is lying in bed), which was all the more annoying since it sometimes came just after I had got warm in bed, and delayed my sleep. Since this kind of cough is brought on when air breathed through the mouth irritates the larynx,* no mechanical (pharmaceutical) remedy is

---

* Is it not likely that atmospheric air circulating through the Eustachian tubes (when the lips are kept closed) produces the refreshing feeling of increased vigor in the vital organs by depositing oxygen as it makes this circuit that brings it near the brain – a feeling as if one were *drinking* air? And that air, though it has no odor of its own, in this way strengthens the olfactory nerves and the adjacent vessels which absorb it? In some kinds of weather one does not get this refreshment from drinking air; but in others, it is a real pleasure to drink it in long draughts as one strolls along, a pleasure one does not get from inhaling through the mouth. – But it is of the utmost importance, in a regimen, to become so *accustomed* to inhaling through the nose, with closed lips, that one cannot do otherwise, even in the deepest sleep, and wakes up at once, startled out of sleep, so to speak, as soon as one inhales through the mouth. This sometimes happened to me at first, before I made it a habit to breathe in this way. – When one has to walk rapidly or uphill, one needs greater strength of resolution not to depart from this rule, and to moderate one's steps rather than make an exception to the rule. The same thing is true of vigorous exercise; and a teacher who is directing his pupils' exercise should have them do it in silence rather than inhale frequently through the mouth. My young friends (former students) have commended this disciplinary maxim as proved and beneficial, and have not belittled it because it is a simple household remedy by which we can dispense with the doctor's services. – A further point should be noted: though it might seem that one who *speaks* for a long time *inhales* through his mouth every time he opens it and so breaks the rule with impunity, this is not really so; for even then he inhales through his *nose*. For when the speaker's nose is stopped up, we say that he speaks through his nose (a very disagreeable sound) because he is not really speaking through his nose; and vice-versa, he does not "speak through his nose" when he is really speaking through his nose, as Privy Councillor *Lichtenberg* notes humorously and correctly. – It is for the same reason that people who have to speak for a long time and in a loud voice (lecturers and

needed to check it; a mental action can stop it directly – the action, namely, of completely diverting one's *attention* from this irritation by directing it forcibly to some other object[g] (as with convulsive seizures, which I have already discussed), which stops the expulsion of air. I clearly felt it drive the blood to my face. But the flow of saliva brought on by this irritation checked its effect, the expulsion of air, and the saliva subsided. – Such a mental operation requires a very high degree of firmness in one's resolution, but this makes it all the more beneficial.

6.
On the results of this habit of breathing with closed lips

The *immediate* result is that the habit carries over into sleep, and I am startled out of my sleep as soon as I happen to open my lips and draw a breath through my mouth. This shows that sleep, and with it dreaming, is not such a complete absence of the waking state as to exclude attention to one's situation in sleep. The fact that a man does awaken earlier than usual if, the preceding evening, he decided to get up earlier (to go for a walk, perhaps) leads to the same conclusion; for he is presumably awakened by the clocks of the city, which he must have heard and paid attention to in his sleep. – The *mediate* result of this laudable habit is that it prevents involuntary forced coughing (as distinguished from deliberate *coughing up* phlegm) in one's sleep as well as when one is awake, so that sheer force of resolution averts an illness. – I have found that it has even further results. Once, after I had put out the light and gone to bed, I suddenly felt an intense thirst and went, in the dark, to another room to get a drink of water. While I was groping about for the water pitcher, I hit upon the idea of *drinking* air through my nose, so to speak, by taking several deep breaths and expanding my chest. Within a few seconds this quenched my thirst completely. The thirst was a pathological stimulus, which was neutralized by a counteracting stimulus.

7:112

CONCLUSION

All pathological attacks in which one's mind can master these feelings by sheer steadfast will, as the superior power of a rational animal, are convulsive (cramplike) in nature. But we cannot convert this proposition and say

---

preachers) can keep it up for an hour without getting hoarse: namely, that they inhale through the nose and merely *exhale* through the mouth. – An incidental advantage of habitually inhaling with closed lips, when one is alone or at least not engaged in conversation, is that saliva, which is constantly secreted and moistens the throat, is also made to act as a digestive agent (*stomachale*) and perhaps also (when swallowed) as a laxative, if one's decision not to waste it is firm enough.

[g] *Object*

that every convulsive seizure can be checked or eliminated merely by a firm resolution. – For some of them are such that an attempt to subject them to the force of one's resolution aggravates the convulsive ailment. This was true in my own case, when I contracted an illness that the *Copenhagen Newspaper* described, about a year ago, as "an epidemic of catarrh accompanied by *distress in the head*" (I came down with it a year before this, but the symptoms were similar).* The result of it was that I felt disorganized – or at least weakened and dulled – in my intellectual work; and since this ailment has attached itself to the natural weaknesses of my old age, it will end only with life itself.

This pathological condition of the patient, which accompanies and impedes his thinking, insofar as thinking is holding firmly onto a concept (of the unity of ideas connected in his consciousness), produces a feeling of a spasmic state in his organ of thought (his brain). This feeling, as a burden, does not really weaken his thought and reflection itself, or his memory of preceding thoughts; but when he is setting forth his thoughts (orally or in writing), the very need to guard against distractions which would interrupt the firm coherence of ideas in their temporal sequence produces an involuntary spasmic condition of the brain, which takes the form of an inability to maintain unity of consciousness in his ideas, as one takes the place of the preceding one. In every discourse I first prepare (the reader or the audience) for what I intend to say by indicating, in prospect, my destination and, in retrospect, the starting point of my argument (without these two points of reference a discourse has no consistency). And the result of this pathological condition is that when the time comes for me to connect the two, I must suddenly ask my audience (or myself, silently): now where was I? where did I start from? This is a defect, not so much of the mind or of the memory alone, as rather of *presence of mind* (in connecting ideas) – that is, an involuntary *distraction*. It is a most distressing feeling, which one can guard against in writing, though only with great labor (especially in philosophical writing, where it is not always easy to look back to one's starting point); but despite all one's efforts, one can never obviate it completely.

It is different with the mathematician, who can hold his concepts or their substitutes (symbols of quantity or number) before him in intuition and assure himself that, as far as he has gone, everything is correct. But the worker in the field of philosophy, especially pure philosophy (logic and metaphysics), must hold his object hanging in midair before him, and must always describe and examine it, not merely part by part, but within the totality of a system as well (the system of pure reason). Hence it is not surprising if metaphysicians are *incapacitated* sooner than scholars in other fields or in applied philosophy. Yet some people must devote themselves

7:113

7:114

* I think it is a kind of gout that has to some extent penetrated the brain.

entirely to metaphysics, because without it there would be no philosophy at all.

This also explains how a person can boast of being healthy *for his age* though he must put himself on the sick list with regard to certain affairs incumbent on him. For as his *inability* to discharge this business prevents him from using his vital energy, it also prevents him from expending and consuming it. He admits that he is living only on a lower level, so to speak (vegetating): namely, that he can eat, walk, and sleep; and since a state of health in relation to his animal existence can be one of illness in relation to his civil existence (in which he is obliged to transact certain public business), this candidate for death does not contradict himself in the least.

So the art of prolonging human life leads to this: that in the end one is tolerated among the living only because of the animal functions one performs – not a particularly amusing situation.

But in this respect I myself am guilty. For why am I not willing to make way for younger people who are struggling upward, and why do I curtail the enjoyment of life I am used to just to stay alive? Why do I prolong a feeble life to an extraordinary age by self-denial, and by my example confuse the obituary list, which is based on the average of those who are more frail by nature and calculated on their life expectancy? Why submit to my own firm resolution what we used to call fate (to which we submitted humbly and piously) – a resolution which, in any case, will hardly be adopted as a universal rule or regimen by which reason exercises direct healing power, and which will never replace the prescriptions the pharmacist dispenses?

POSTSCRIPT

I might also suggest that the author of the art of prolonging human life (and in particular, literary life) kindly consider the protection of readers' *eyes* (especially the now large number of women readers, who may feel more strongly about the nuisance of glasses). At present our eyes are harassed from all sides by the wretched affectations of book printers (for 7:115 letters, considered as pictures, have no intrinsic beauty at all). In Moroccan cities, a large percentage of the inhabitants are blind because all the houses are whitewashed; and to prevent this evil from spreading among us from a similar cause, printers should be subjected to police regulations in this respect. The current *fashion* in printing, however, would have it otherwise. It dictates:

1) That the text be printed with *gray* ink instead of black (because the contrast of gray ink on fine white paper is softer and more agreeable).

2) That it be printed in *Didot* characters with narrow feet, instead of

Breitkopf characters, which would correspond better to the name *Buchstaben*[h] – (*bucherner Stabe,*[i] as it were, for steadying oneself).

3) That works in the German language be printed with *Roman* (and even italic) type, although, as Breitkopf[48] rightly said, this tires the eyes more quickly than does Gothic type.

4) That printers use the smallest possible type that will allow still smaller letters (even harder on the eyes) to remain legible when used in footnotes.

To control this abuse, I suggest that printers take as their model the *Berlin Monthly* (both its text and its notes); for no matter what page one opens it to, the sight of it will strengthen the eyes perceptibly when they have been strained by reading the kind of print described above.*

I. Kant

---

* When I was forty years old I experienced the first attack of a *pathological condition* of the eyes (not really an opthalmic disease), which used to recur, from time to time, at intervals of some years but now comes several times within a year. The phenomenon is that, when I am reading, a certain brightness suddenly spreads over the page, confusing and mixing up all the letters until they are completely illegible. This condition, which does not last longer than six minutes, could be very risky for a preacher who is in the habit of reading off his sermons from pages. But since, in my courses in logic and metaphysics, I can lecture freely (from my head) after a suitable preparation, my own concern was that these attacks might be the precursor of blindness. But I am no longer worried about this; for, although the attacks now come more frequently than usual, I do not notice any loss of acuity in my one good eye (I lost the sight in my left eye some five years ago). – Once when this phenomenon happened, it occurred to me to close my eyes and even hold my hand over them to keep out external light even better; and then I saw in the darkness a luminous figure outlined in phosphorous, so to speak, on a page, similar to the one that represents the last quarter in the calendar but with a jagged border on the convex side. After gradually diminishing in brightness, it disappeared within six minutes. – I should like to know whether other people have had the same experience and how we can explain this appearance,[49] which might well have its source in the *sensorium commune* rather than in the eyes – for when I moved my eyes, this picture did not move with them: I saw it always in the same place. It is also curious that one can *lose* the sight in one eye without *noticing* it (I estimate the period, with regard to my left eye, at about three years).

[h] letters
[i] beechwood staves

7:115

7:116

Preface to Reinhold Bernhard Jachmann's Examination of the Kantian Philosophy of Religion

Translator's introduction

Reinhold Bernhard Jachmann was Kant's student, in Kant's last years his devoted friend and amanuensis, and one of his first biographers: *Immanuel Kant* (Königsberg, 1804). The full title of Jachmann's treatise on the Kantian philosophy of religion is: *Examination of the Kantian Philosophy of Religion in Respect of the Similarity to Pure Mysticism which Has Been Attributed to It* (Königsberg, 1800). Jachmann's book was a reply to a Latin doctoral dissertation by C. A. Wilmans: *On the Similarity between Pure Mysticism and the Kantian Religious Doctrine* (Halle, 1797). After writing his dissertation Wilmans had pestered Kant with a series of letters, to which Kant made a couple of replies (see AK 12:202, 207, 230, 259, 277, 279).

Kant generously published one of Wilmans's letters as an Appendix to Part One of the *Conflict of the Faculties* (1798) (AK 7:69–75), while also appending a footnote saying that in publishing Wilmans's letter "I do not mean to guarantee that my views coincide entirely with his" (AK 7:69n). It was evidently out of kindness that Kant left it to Jachmann to respond to Wilmans's (absurd) suggestion that there might be an affinity between Kantian moral religion and any form of religious mysticism.

Kant's short Preface to Jachmann's book has not previously been translated into English.

Preface to Reinhold Bernhard Jachmann's Examination of the Kantian Philosophy of Religion

PROSPECTUS TO THE FOLLOWING WORK

Philosophy, as the theory of a science, can like any other doctrine serve as a tool for all kinds of arbitrary ends; but in this regard it has only a *conditioned* worth. – Whoever intends this or that product has to go to work in this or that way, and if one proceeds according to *principles,*[a] then it can also be called a *practical* philosophy, and has a value like any other commodity or labor about which there can be commercial transactions.

But philosophy in the literal meaning of the term, as a doctrine of wisdom,[b] has an *unconditioned* worth; for it is the theory of a *final end* of human reason, which can be only a single end toward which all others strive or to which they must be subordinated; and the complete *practical* philosopher (as an ideal) is he who fulfills this demand in himself.

Now the question is whether wisdom is *infused* into a person from above (by inspiration) or its height is *scaled* from below through the inner power of his practical reason.

He who asserts the former, as a passive means of cognition, is thinking of a chimaera[c] – the possibility of a *supersensible experience* which is a direct self-contradiction (representing the transcendent as immanent) – and bases himself on a certain mysterious doctrine called "mysticism"; this is the opposite of all philosophy and yet just because of this it (like the alchemist) puts the greatest stock in being superior to the labor of all those rational but troublesome investigations of nature, dreaming the while of being blessed with the sweet state of enjoyment.

To eliminate this counterfeit philosophy, or not to let it get started once it raises its head: this is what the author of the present work – formerly an industrious and alert auditor of my lectures, now a most treasured friend – intends in the following text, and with good success. Not that it in any way needs a recommendation on my part; rather, I

[a] *Principien*
[b] *Weisheitslehre*
[c] *Unding*

333

would merely add to this book the seal of my friendship toward the author as an everlasting memento.

Königsberg
14 January 1800

I. Kant

Lectures on the philosophical doctrine
of religion

Editor's introduction

Alexander Gottlieb Baumgarten's *Metaphysica* was the leading text of Wolffian rationalism in the late eighteenth century. Kant lectured nearly every year on the *Metaphysica*, whose fourth part is on natural theology. But he did not often lecture on natural theology by itself. During this critical period he announced lectures on this topic only once, in the winter semester of 1785–86,[a] but J. G. Hamann reports that he lectured on theology to an "astonishing throng" in the winter semester of 1783–84.[b]

Transcriptions from one or both sets of these lectures came into the possession of Friedrich Theodor Rink, the editor during Kant's lifetime of Kant's lectures on physical geography (1802) and pedagogy (1803). After Rink's death in 1810, these materials were purchased, along with other transcriptions of Kant's lectures on metaphysics, by Karl Heinrich Ludwig Pölitz, who first published the *Vorlesungen über die philosophische Religionslehre* in 1817 (second edition, 1830), followed four years later by the *Vorlesungen über die Metaphysik* (1821).

Kant used three texts in his lecture course: the theology section of Baumgarten's *Metaphysica;* the *Vorbereitung zur natürlichen Theologie* by Johann August Eberhard, with whom Kant was involved in a polemical exchange in the early 1790s; and Christoph Meiners, *Historia doctrinae de uno vero Deo* (1780). The introductory section of the lectures seems to refer mainly to Eberhard (see AK 28:1033), but the lectures as a whole are mostly a commentary on Baumgarten's *Metaphysica* §§ 815–982.

In many ways it is evident that the lectures on the philosophical doctrine of religion postdate the *Critique of Pure Reason* (1781). Not only do several passages paraphrase the *Critique,* they also show detailed knowledge of Hume's *Dialogues Concerning Natural Religion,* which was first available in German translation in 1781. Eberhard's *Vorbereitung* was published the same year. It appears that at least a sizeable portion of Kant's text must date from 1783–84. The other two manuscripts of Kant's lectures on natural theology published in AK 28 are dated 13 November 1783 and 19 July 1784.[c] Further, Erich Adickes dates the *Nachlass* mate-

---

[a] According to the reports of Emil Arnoldt. See W. B. Waterman, "Kant's Lectures on the Philosophical Theory of Religion," *Kant-Studien* 2 (1899), p. 306.
[b] Karl Vorländer, *Immanuel Kants Leben* (Leipzig, 1911), p. 121.
[c] AK 28:1363.

rial on Eberhard's *Vorbereitung* at 1783.[d] But there are a few indications that at least parts of them may be later, perhaps dating from Kant's announced series of lectures in 1785–86. Kant's use of the phrase "realm of ends" (AK 28:1088, 1100, 1113, 1116) suggests that the lectures may postdate the *Groundwork* (published early in 1785); and some remarks in Kant's discussion of evil (AK 28:1077–80) are reminiscent of the *Conjectural Beginning of Human History* (1786).

These lectures provide us with a valuable source of Kant's views on many topics relating to Kant's thought about religion and natural theology; it is our principal source about his views on the concept of God and traditional scholastic questions about the divine nature and attributes.

[d] AK 18:504.

Lectures on the philosophical doctrine of religion

Introduction

Human reason has need of an idea of highest perfection, to serve it as a   28:993
standard according to which it can make determinations. In human love,
for example, we think of the idea of highest friendship in order to be able
to determine the extent to which this or that degree of friendship approaches or falls short of it. One can render friendly service to another but
still take one's own welfare into account, or one can offer up everything to
one's friend taking no account of one's own advantage. The latter comes
nearest to the idea of perfect friendship. A concept of this kind, which is
needed as a standard of lesser or greater degrees in this or that case,
regardless of its reality, is called an idea. But are not these ideas (such as
Plato's idea of a republic, for example) all mere figments of the brain? By
no means. For I can set up this or that case so as to accord with my idea.
Thus a ruler, for example, can set up his state to accord with the idea of
the most perfect republic, in order to bring his state nearer to perfection.
For such an idea, three points are required:

1. Completeness in the determination of the subject with respect to all
   its predicates (for instance, in the concept of God all realities are
   encountered);
2. Completeness in the derivation of the existence of things (for instance, the concept of a highest being which cannot be derived from
   any other, but which is rather that from which everything else must
   be derived);
3. Completeness of community, or the thoroughgoing determination
   of community and connection of the whole.

The world depends on a supreme being, but the things in the world, on
the contrary, all depend mutually on one another. Taken together, this
constitutes a complete whole. The understanding seeks to form a unity in
all things, and to proceed to the maximum. Thus for instance we think of
heaven as the highest degree of morality combined with the highest degree of blessedness, and of hell as the highest degree of evil combined   28:994
with the greatest degree of misery. We think of evil, when we think of the
highest degree of it, as an immediate inclination to take satisfaction in evil
with no remorse or enticement, and to carry it out with no consideration
of profit or advantage, *merely because it is evil.* This idea we form in order
to determine the intermediate degrees of evil according to it.

How does an idea of reason differ from an ideal of imagination? An idea is a universal rule *in abstracto*, whereas an ideal is an individual case which I bring under this rule. Thus for example Rousseau's Emile and the education to be given him is a true idea of reason. But nothing determinate can be said about the ideal. A person can have every excellent attribute applied to him regarding the way in which he should conduct himself as ruler, father or friend, but this will not exhaust the account of what these attributes amount to in this or that case (an example of this is Xenophon's *Cyropaedia*).[1] The cause of this demand for completeness lies in the fact that otherwise we could have no concept of perfection. Such is the case, for instance, with moral perfection. Human virtue is always imperfect; but for this reason we must have a standard in order to see how far this imperfection falls short of the highest degree of virtue. It is the same with vice. We leave out of the idea of vice everything which could limit the degree of vice. In morality it is necessary to represent the laws in their moral perfection and purity. But it would be something else again for someone to realize such an idea. And even if this is not completely possible, the idea is still of great utility. In his *Emile*, Rousseau himself admits that a whole lifetime (or the better part of it) would be required to give one single individual the education he describes.[2] – This leads us to the idea of the highest being. We represent to ourselves:

1. a being which *excludes every deficiency*. (If, for example, we imagine a man who is at once learned and virtuous, this may be a great degree of perfection, but many deficiencies still remain);
2. a being which contains all realities in itself; only in this way will the concept be precisely determined. This concept can also be thought of as the most perfect nature, or the combination of everything belonging to a most perfect nature (for example, understanding and free will);
3. can be considered as the highest good, to which wisdom and morality belong. – The first of these is called transcendental perfection, the second physical perfection, the third practical perfection.

28:995

What is theology? It is the system of our cognition of the highest being. How is common cognition distinguished from theology? Common cognition is an aggregate, in which one thing is placed next to another without looking to combination and unity. There is system where the idea of the whole rules throughout. The system of cognition of God signifies the sum total not of all possible cognitions of God but of what human reason encounters pertaining to God. The knowledge[a] of everything in God is what we call *theologia archetypa*, and this occurs *in him*. The system of

---

[a] *Kenntniss*

cognition of that part of God which lies in human nature is called *theologica ectypa,* and it can be very deficient. It does constitute a system, however, since all the insights which reason affords us can always be thought in a unity. – The sum total of *all possible* cognition of God is not possible for human beings, not even through a true revelation. But it is one of the most worthwhile considerations to see how far our reason can go in attaining cognition of God. Rational theology too can be brought to completion in the sense that no human reason has the ability to achieve a more extensive cognition and insight. Hence it is an advantage for reason to be able to point out its boundaries completely. It is in this way that theology relates to the capacity for all possible cognition of God.

All our cognition is of two kinds, positive and negative. Positive cognition is very limited, but this makes the gain of negative cognition so much the greater. As regards positive cognition of God, our cognition is no greater than common cognition. But our negative cognition is greater. Common usage does not see the sources from which it draws its cognition, hence it is uncertain whther there are not more sources from which it can draw it. This comes about because it is not acquainted with the boundaries of its understanding. – What interest does reason have in this cognition? No speculative interest, but a practical one. The object is much too sublime for us to be able to speculate about it. In fact we can be led into error by speculation. *But our morality has need of the idea of God* to give it emphasis. Thus it should not make us more learned, but better, wiser and more upright. For if there is a supreme being who can and will make us happy, then our moral dispositions will thereby receive more strength and nourishment, and our moral conduct will be made firmer. Yet our reason finds a small speculative interest in these matters, which, however, is of very little worth in comparison to this practical one. Our reason always has need, namely, of a highest in order to measure off the less high, and to make determinations. –

28:996

We sometimes ascribe an *understanding* to God. To what extent can we do this? If we do not know the boundaries of our own understanding, then even less can we think of the divine understanding. But here too we must have a maximum, and we can obtain it only by removing all limitations, and saying thus: Our understanding cannot cognize things otherwise than through certain general marks; but this is a limitation of the human understanding, and this cannot occur in God. Thus we think of a maximum understanding, that is, an intuitive understanding. This gives us no concept of all, but such a maximum serves to make the lesser degrees determinate, for the maximum is determinate. If, for example, we want to determine human benevolence, we can do it only by thinking of the highest benevolence, which is found in God. And then it is easy to determine the intermediate degrees according to it. Thus in our cognition the concept of God is not so much extended as determined, for the maximum always has to be determinate. For instance, the concept of right is wholly and precisely determined, just as the concept of equity is, on the contrary, indeterminate. For it means that I should forgo my right to some extent. But how much? If I forgo too much, I violate my own right. – Thus in morality too we are referred to God; for it tells us to aspire to the highest idea of morality in conformity with the highest being. But how can we do this? To this end we must see to what extent our morality falls short of the

28:997 morality of the highest being. In this way the concept of God can be of service to us, and we can also make use of it as a gauge by which we are able to determine the smaller differences in morality. Thus we do have a speculative interest here too. But how insignificant it is! For it is no more than a means enabling us to represent in a determinate way whatever is to be found between the maximum and nothing. How small, then, is this speculative interest compared to the practical interest which has to do with our making ourselves into better human beings, with uplifting our concepts of morality and with placing before our eyes the concepts of our moral conduct!

Theology cannot serve to explain the appearances of nature to us. In general it is not a correct use of reason to posit in God the ground of anything whose explanation is not immediately evident to us. On the contrary, we must first gain insight into the laws of nature in order to be able to cognize and explain its operations from them. In general it is no use of reason, and no explanation, to say that something is due to God's omnipotence. This is a lazy reason, and we will have more to say about it later.[3] But if we ask who has so firmly established the laws of nature and so limited its operations, then we will come to God as the supreme cause of the entirety of reason and nature. Let us ask further: Why does our cognition of God, or our rational theology have dignity? Not because it concerns itself with the highest object; not because it has God as its object;[b] let us rather ask: do we have a cognition of the object which is appropriate to its dignity? In morality we see that not merely the object has dignity, but that the cognition contains dignity too, so theology has absolutely no cause to boast just because the object of its cognition is a being of highest dignity. In any case our cognition is only a shadow in comparison with the greatness of God, and our powers are far transcended by him. The real question is: Does our cognition have dignity just the same? Yes, insofar as it has a relation to religion. For religion is nothing but the application of theology to morality, that is, to good disposition and to a course of conduct well-pleasing to the highest being. *Natural religion is thus the substratum of all religion, the firmest support of all moral principles,* and insofar as it is the hypothe-

28:998 sis of all religion, and gives weight to all our concepts of virtue and

[b] *Objekt*

344

uprightness, to this extent natural theology contains a worth raising it above all speculations.

Are there scholars of the divine' in natural theology? There is no such thing as being a scholar of nature. In revealed religion there is a place for scholarship; revealed religion requires that we become acquainted with it. But in natural religion there is no place for scholarship. For here there is nothing to be done but to prevent errors from creeping in, and this is fundamentally not a kind of scholarly learning. In general no cognition of reason a priori can be called learning. Learning is the sum total of cognition which must be taught. – The theologian or divine scholar must have true learning, since he must interpret the Bible, and interpretation depends on languages and much else which can be taught. In the time of the Greeks, philosophical schools were divided into *physicas* and *theologicas.* But the latter must not be understood as schools in which contemporary religious usages were studied, or in which their sacred formulas and other such superstitious stuff were learned; rather, that is what the inquirers of reason were called. They saw which concepts of God lay in their reason, how far reason could proceed in the cognition of God, where the boundaries in the field of cognition were, and so on. Here it was a matter only of the use of reason; but in the cognition of God it was a matter of scholarly learning.[4]

Now let us ask: What is the minimum of theology required for religion? What is the smallest useful cognition of God that can accordingly move us to have faith in God and thus direct our course of life? What is the smallest, narrowest concept of theology? It is that we need a religion and that the concept is sufficient for natural religion. There is this minimum, however, if I see that my concept of God is *possible* and that it does not contradict the laws of the understanding. – Can everyone be convinced of this much? Yes, everyone can, because no one is in a position to rob us of this concept and prove that it is impossible. Hence this is the smallest possible requirement for a religion. Provided that this alone is made a ground, there can always be religion. But the possibility of the concept of God is supported by morality, since otherwise morality would have no incentives. Moreover, the mere possibility of such a being is sufficient to produce religion in the human being. But this is not the maximum of theology. It would be better if I knew that such a being actually existed. Yet   28:999 it is believed that the Greeks and Romans of antiquity who devoted themselves to an upright life had no concept of God other than the possibility of this concept. And this was sufficient to move them to a religion. – We now have sufficient insight to tell that we will be satisfied from a practical standpoint, but from a speculative standpoint we will find

' *Gottesgelehrten; gelehrt* = "learned"; *Gelehrte* = "scholar." *Gelehrtheit* will be translated either as "scholarship" or as "learning."

little satisfaction. As we strive to present the concept of God we will guard ourselves from errors and contradictions from a speculative standpoint, and we must hold our reason very much in check if we are to be safe from the attacks of the foes of theology. But from a moral point of view we first of all have to guard ourselves against any errors which might have an influence on our morality.

Natural theology is twofold: (a) *theologia rationalis,* which is opposed to (b) *theologia empirica.*[d] But since God is not an object of sense and hence cannot be an object of experience, we can be capable of a *theologia empirica* only through the help of a divine revelation. *But from this it follows that there are no kinds of theology but those of reason and revelation.* The theology of reason is either *speculative* (with theoretical science as its ground) or *moral* (with practical cognition as its object). The first could also be called *speculative theology* and the latter, which we draw from practical principles, would then be called *moral theology.* Speculative theology would further be either:

1. *transcendental,* having its origin independently of all experience, merely from pure understanding and reason;
2. *natural.* The former is distinguished from natural theology because according to the latter we are able to represent God in comparison with ourselves wherever there is something in us founded on a nature from which we can draw attributes applicable to God. But in natural theology there is never the purity of concepts found in transcendental theology, where all concepts are taken from reason alone –

Nature is the sum total of objects of experience. I can consider nature either as the nature of the world in general or as the constitution of everything present. Natural theology can be twofold:

1. a *cosmotheology.* Here I can consider the nature of a world in general and argue from it to the existence of an author of the world;
2. and a *physicotheology,* where I cognize a God from the constitution of the present world. –

This is the division wholly according to logical rules. But to be precise, we should divide rational theology into (a) *transcendentalem,* (b) *naturalem* and (c) *moralem.* In the first I think God from transcendental concepts alone; in the second from physical concepts, and in the last I think God from concepts taken from morality. Now if we want to determine this more closely, we will think of God as the original being, which 1) is no *derivativum,* no being determined from and dependent on another; 2) is the cause of all possible and existing beings. Thus

9:1000

---

[d] (a) Rational theology; (b) empirical theology.

1. I will think of him as the *ens originarium*,[e] as the *ens summum*[f] when I compare him with all things in general and consider him as the highest of all beings and the root of all possible things. The concept of an *ens originarium* as an *ens summum* belongs to transcendental philosophy. This transcendental concept, in fact, is the foundation of transcendental philosophy and there is a special theology in which I think of the original being as the *ens originarium* to which belongs the properties of not deriving from any other thing and of being the root of everything.

2. the *ens originarium* as *summa intelligentia*,[g] which means the highest being considered as the highest rational being. Whoever thinks of God merely as the *ens summum* leaves undecided how this being is constituted. But whoever thinks of God as the *summa intelligentia* thinks of him as a *living* being, as a living God, having cognition and free will. He thinks of him not as a cause of the world, but as an *author of the world*, who had to apply understanding to the production of a world and who also has free will. These first two points are in *theologia rationalis.* – Finally, follows

3. the representation of the *ens originarium* as the *summum bonum*, as the *highest good*, i.e. one must think of God not only as the highest power of cognition but also as the highest *ground* of cognition, as a system of all *ends;* and that is *theologia moralis.*[h]   28:1001

In transcendental theology we represent God as *cause of the world;* in natural theology as *author of the world*, i.e. as a living God, as a free being which has given the world its existence as a free being, out of his own free power of choice, without any compulsion whatever. And finally in moral theology we represent God as *ruler of the world.* For he could indeed produce something from his free power of choice, but without having set any further end before himself; but here we consider him as *lawgiver for the world*, in relation *to moral laws.*

DIFFERENT TERMS FOR THE SUBJECTS OF THESE DIFFERENT SPECIES OF COGNITION

Whoever accepts[i] no theology at all is an *atheist.* Whoever accepts only transcendental theology is a *deist.* The deist will certainly concede that there is a cause of the world; but he leaves it undecided whether this cause is a freely acting being. In transcendental theology we can even apply

[e] original being
[f] highest being
[g] highest intelligence
[h] moral theology
[i] *annimmt*

ontological predicates; for instance, that it has reality. But whoever accepts a *theologia naturalis* is a theist. E.g., The terms "deist" and "theist" are nearly indistinguishable except that the former is of Latin origin and the latter is of Greek origin. But this difference has been taken as the sign distinguishing two species. *Theism* consists in believing not merely in a God, but in a *living* God who has produced the world through knowledge and by means of free will. It can now be seen that *theologia transcendentalis* is set up by pure reason alone, wholly pure of any admixture of experience. But this is not the case with *natural theology*. In it some kinds of experience must be mixed in, since I must have an example such as an intelligence (for instance, the human power of understanding, from which I infer the highest understanding). But transcendental theology represents God to me wholly separate from any experience. For how could experience teach me something universal? In transcendental theology I think of God as having no limitation; there I extend my concept to the highest degree and regard God as a being infinitely removed from myself. But do I become acquainted with God at all in this way? – Hence the deist's concept of God is wholly idle and useless and makes no impression on me if I assume it alone. But if transcendental theology is used as a propaedeutic or introduction to the two other kinds of theology, it is of great and wholly excellent utility. For in transcendental theology we think of God in a wholly pure way; and this prevents anthropomorphisms from creeping into the other two kinds of theology. Hence transcendental theology is of the greatest negative utility in keeping us safe from errors.

28:1002

But what are we to call the kind of theology in which God is thought of as the *summum bonum,* as the highest moral good? Up to now it has not been correctly distinguished and so no name has been thought up for it. It can be called *theismus moralis,*[j] since in it God is thought of as the author of our moral laws. And this is the real theology which serves as the foundation of religion. For if I were to think of God as the author of the world but not at the same time as the ruler of the world, then this would have no influence on my conduct. In moral theology I do not think of God as the supreme principle in the realm of nature but rather as the supreme principle in the realm *of ends.* – But *moral theology* is something wholly different from *theological morality*, namely, a morality in which the concept of obligation presupposes the concept of God. Such a theological morality has no principle;[k] or if it does have one, this is nothing but the fact that the will of God has been revealed and discovered. Morality, however, must not be grounded on theology, but must have in itself the principle[l] which is

---

[j] "moral theism"; but Kant apparently goes on to use the term *moralische Theologie* (moral theology) as a German equivalent to *theismus moralis.*
[k] *Princip*
[l] *Princip*

to be the ground of our good conduct. Afterward it can be combined with theology, and then our morality will obtain more incentives and a morally moving power. In theological morality the concept of God must determine our duties; but this is just the opposite; for here one pictures in one's concept of God all sorts of terrible and frightening attributes. Now of course this can generate fear in us and hence move us to follow moral laws from coercion or so as to avoid punishment, which, however, does not provide any interest in the object.*m* For we no longer see how abominable our actions are, but abstain from them only from fear of punishment. Natural morality must be so constituted that it can be thought independently of any concept of God, and obtain zealous reverence from us solely on account of its own inner dignity and excellence. But further it serves for this if, after we have taken an interest in morals itself, to take an interest also in the existence of God, a being who can reward our good conduct; and then we obtain strong incentives which determine us to observe moral laws. This is a highly necessary hypothesis.   28:1003

Speculative theology can be divided into: (1) *ontotheology*, (2) *cosmotheology* and (3) *physiocotheology*. The *first* considers God merely in terms of concepts (and it is just *theologia transcendentalis*, which considers God as the principle of all possibility). Cosmotheology presupposes something existing and infers a highest being from the existence of a world in general. And finally, physicotheology makes use of experience of the present world in general and infers from this to the existence of an author of the world and to the attributes which would belong to its author as such.

Anselm was the first to try to establish the necessity of a highest being from mere concepts, proceeding from the concept of an *ens realissimum*. Even if this theology is of no great utility from a practical standpoint, it still has *the one* advantage of purifying our concepts and cleansing them of everything which we as human beings belonging to the world of sense might ascribe to the abstract concept of God. It is the ground of every possible theology. – Cosmotheology has been treated primarily*n* by Leibniz and Wolff. In this kind of theology it is presupposed that there exist some object of experience and then the attempt is made to establish the existence of a highest being from this pure experience. Wolff asserted that the existence of a being containing the ground of all possibility can be proved merely from the concept of such a being; accordingly, he said: Something exists; now it must either exist through itself*o* or have a cause as the ground of its existence. The first cause must be the being of all beings. – Hence we see that cosmotheology is just as abstract as ontotheology, for it does not help me much to be told that something exists

---

m . . . *die aber den Gegenstand nicht interessant machen.*
n zuvörderst
o für sich selbst

which either exists for itself or has another cause as the ground of its existence. And if we investigate whether this cause contains every perfection in itself, the result is the concept that there must be a being of all beings, an original being which depends on nothing else.

28:1004   All the world aims at popularity and tries to provide insight into concepts by means of easily grasped examples. So there is good cause to seek an intuitive grasp even as far as the highest concept. But in order to keep a sure foothold as well, and not to wander in labyrinths outside the field of experience, it is also demanded with right that it be possible to represent the absolute idea *in concreto*. This is why we come to physicotheology. It has been treated by many, and it was already the foundation of the teachings of Anaxagoras and Socrates.⁵ Physicotheology has the utility of presenting the highest being as the highest intelligence and as the author of purposiveness, order and beauty. It is adapted to the whole human race, for it can provide an intuitive element, and shed light on our concepts of God. But it must also be remarked that physicotheology cannot have any *determinate* concept of God; for only reason can represent completeness and totality. Here I see power; but can I say determinately: This is *omnipotence* or the highest degree of power? I cannot, therefore, infer a perfection of the highest kind.

THE ONTOLOGICAL PROOF

This gives me ontotheology, in which I can think of the highest perfection as determined in all its predicates. But the judgments our reason makes about things are either affirmative or negative. That is, when I predicate something of a thing, this predicate I apply to the thing expresses either that something is (or is encountered) in the thing, or else that something is not in it. A predicate which expresses being in a thing contains a reality; but one which expresses nonbeing contains its negation. Every negation presupposes some reality. Therefore I cannot cognize any negation unless I cognize the reality opposed to it. For how could I perceive a mere deficiency without being acquainted with what is lacking? – Every thing in the world has realities and negations in it. Something composed only of negations and lacking in everything would be a nothing, a nonentity. Hence every thing, if it is to be a thing at all, must have some realities. Every thing in the world, however, also has some negations, and it is just this relationship between reality and negation that constitutes the difference between things. But we 28:1005   find some negations in things whose corresponding realities are encountered nowhere in the world. How are these negations possible, if they are nothing but limitations on reality? Or how can we judge the magnitude of reality in these things and determine the degree of their perfection? If *that* is what reason wants to do, then since according to the principles of its own nature it can only infer the particular from the universal, it must think of some maximum of reality from which it can proceed and according to which it can measure other things. A thing of this kind, in which all realities are contained, would be the only complete thing, because it is perfectly determined in regard to all possible predicates. And just for this reason such an *ens realissimum*[p] would also be the ground of the possibility of all other beings. For I need only think the highest reality as limited in infinitely many ways and I thereby also think the possibility of infinitely many things. If I retain a certain reality but limit it – totally abstracting from the rest – then I have a thing, which has both reality and negation, and whose limitations presuppose some greater reality. For instance, we can think of a single light, and also of infinite modifications of it by mixing shadow with the light. Here light would be the reality and shadow the negation. Now I can think of much light and little shadow or little light and much shadow, and there will be aspects and modifications in proportion as I think more or less of each. – This is how copper-engraving and etching arose. Just as here the light contains the ground of the possibility of all the modifications arising from it by our mixing shadow with it, so in the same way the *ens realissimum* contains the ground of the possibility of all other things when I limit it so that negations arise. This pure concept of the understanding, the concept of God as a thing having every reality, is to be found in every human understanding; only it is often expressed in other formulas.

But is the object of this concept actual? That is another question. In order to prove the existence of such a being, Descartes argued that a being containing every reality in itself must *necessarily exist,* since existence is also a reality.[6] If I think of an *ens realissimum* I must also think of this reality along with it. In this way he derived the necessary existence of such   28:1006 a being merely out of a pure concept of the understanding. And this would certainly have been a splendid thing, if only his proof had been correct. – For then my own reason would compel me to accept[q] the existence of such a being, and I would have to give up my own reason if I wanted to deny its existence. – Further, I could then prove incontrovertibly that there could be only one such being. For I could not think of more than one being which includes everything real in itself. If there were several such beings, then either they would not be *realissima*[r] or else they would have to be one and the same being. –

THE COSMOLOGICAL PROOF

Here I presuppose that something exists, hence an experience, and thus the proof built on this presupposition is no longer derived from pure

[p] most real being
[q] *annehmen*
[r] most real

reason, as was the transcendental proof already discussed. It is, however, the simplest experience that I can presuppose: the experience *that I am.* Now I infer with Leibniz and Wolff:7 I am either necessary or contingent. But the alterations which go on in me show that I am not necessary; therefore I am contingent. But if I am contingent, then there must be somewhere *outside me* a ground for my existence, which is the reason why I am as I am and not otherwise. This ground of my existence must be absolutely necessary. For if it too were contingent, then it could not be the ground of my existence, since it would once again have need of something else containing the ground of its existence. This absolutely necessary being, however, must contain in itself the ground of its own existence, and consequently the ground of the existence of the whole world. For the whole world is contingent, and hence it cannot contain in itself the ground why it is as it is and not otherwise. But a being which contained in itself the ground of the existence of all things would also have to contain in itself the ground of its *own* existence; for there is nothing from which it could be derived. – And this is God! – Now from the absolute necessity of such a being Wolff inferred its highest perfection. – Except for what pertains to its primary source, this cosmological proof is fundamentally just as abstract as the transcendental one; for this source is empirical, but beyond it we have to do here too only with pure concepts. – One easily sees that in the cosmological proof the transcendental proof is presupposed as correct

28:1007 and gives the cosmological proof all its strength, that conversely if the earlier proof is incorrect, this second proof breaks down of itself; for it is only in case I am able to prove that a most perfect being must necessarily exist that I can infer conversely that an absolutely necessary being must be a most perfect being.

THE PHYSICOTHEOLOGICAL PROOF

The physicotheological proof is the one in which we infer from the constitution of the present world to the nature of its author. This proof is nearly identical with the cosmological one; the only difference is that in the cosmological proof the concept of an author of the world is abstracted from the concept of a world in general, whereas in the physicotheological proof it is abstracted from the *present* world. The source of this proof is wholly empirical and the proof itself very popular and appealing, whereas the ontological and cosmological proofs are rather dry and abstract. – Here we must introduce a correction relating to the systematic application of the proofs for God's existence, and this is necessary because we have not expressed the matter precisely enough above. This correction consists in pointing out that the ontological and cosmological proofs both belong to transcendental theology because both of them are derived from *principii a priori.*8 This has already been made sufficiently clear as regards the ontological proof. But in considering the cosmological proof it might appear as if it were borrowed from experience, as was asserted above. But on closer inspection we find that no experience of a world really need be presupposed in this proof, but rather that it may assume the existence of a world merely as a hypothesis. I infer: If there is a world, it must be either contingent or necessary, etc.; but not: There exists a world, etc. Thus in this inference I need no experience of the world at all, or of the manner in which it is constituted, but I rather make use of the mere concept of a world, whatever sort it might be, the best or the worst. Thus the whole cosmological proof is built on pure concepts of understanding and to this extent it belongs to transcendental theology, which infers from *principia a priori*. But the physicotheological proof is derived wholly from empirical principles, because here I use my actual perception of the existing world 28:1008 as its ground. But if transcendental theology does not succeed, physicotheology will not succeed either. For physicotheology can never give a determinate concept of God without transcendental theology, and an indeterminate concept doesn't help at all. The precise concept of God is the concept of a most perfect thing. But I can never derive such a concept from experience, for the highest perfection can never be given me in any possible experience. For example, I could never prove God's omnipotence through experience, even if I assume a million suns surrounded with a million universes in an immeasurably immense space, with each of these universes occupied by both rational and irrational creatures. For a great power could have produced even a hundred million and a thousand million suns. From anything made' I could infer only a great power, an immeasurable power. – But what is meant by an "immeasurable power"? A power which I have no capacity to measure, over against which my power is extremely' small. That, however, is still not omnipotence. – Likewise, even though I may wonder at the magnitude, order and chainlike combination of all things in the world, I cannot conclude that only one being has produced them. There could just as easily have been several powerful beings, each taking pleasure in working its own field.[9] Or at least I cannot refute this supposition from my experience of the world. This is why the ancients, who founded their proofs of God on what they experienced of the world, produced such contradictory results. Anaxagoras, and later Socrates, believed in one God. Epicurus believed in none, or believed that if there is one, he has nothing to do with the world. Others believed in many gods, or at least in one supreme good and one evil principle." This happened because each considered the world from a different point of view. One saw an order of the highest harmony derived

---

' *Faktum*
' *ganz*
" *Principium*

from an infinite understanding, and the other perceived everything only according to the physical laws of coming to be and perishing. Yet another took notice of wholly contradictory purposes, for instance, earthquakes, fiery volcanoes, furious hurricanes, and the destruction of everything so excellently set up. – The abstract of concepts of God from these empirically founded perceptions can generate nothing but contradictory systems. Our experience of the world is too limited to permit us to infer a highest reality from it. Before we could argue that the present world is the most perfect of all possible ones and prove from this that its author is the highest perfection, we would first have to know the whole totality of the world, every means and every end which is reached by it. The natural theologians have certainly had insight into this; so they follow their proof only *up to that point,* only to where they believe it has been thoroughly established that there exists a *prima causa mundi,*[v] and then by a leap they fall into transcendental theology and prove from it that the *prima causa mundi* (the *ens originarium*)[w] would have to be absolutely necessary, and hence an *ens realissimum*[x] as well. From this we see that physicotheology rests wholly on transcendental theology. If it is correct and well-founded then physicotheology does an excellent service, and all the objections against the highest perfection based on the conflicts in nature will collapse of themselves. For then we already know to the point of complete conviction that the *ens originarium* is an *ens realissimum,* and consequently we known that everywhere he must have left the imprint of his highest perfection. And we know that it can be due only to our limitation and shortsightedness if we do not see the best everywhere, because we are not in a position to survey the whole and its future consequences from which the greatest and most perfect result would certainly have to arise.

There are no speculative proofs of the existence of God except these three. For as to the ancients' concept of the *primo motore*[y] and the necessity of its existence due to the impossibility of matter's having moved itself first, this proof is already contained in the cosmological proof, and in fact it is not even as general, since the cosmological proof is founded on the thoughts of alteration and contingency and not merely on motion in the corporeal world. If, however, one wanted to prove the existence of God from the *agreement of all nations* in believing in him, a proof of this kind would not work at all. For history and experience teach us equally well that all nations have believed in ghosts and witches, and still believe in them.[10] –

Thus all speculation comes down in substance to the transcendental

28:1009

---

[v] first cause of the world
[w] original being
[x] most real being
[y] first mover

concept. But if we suppose that it is not correct, would we then have to   28:1010
give up the cognition of God? Not at all; for then we would only lack the
knowledge that God exists, but a great field would still be open to us, and
this would be the belief or faith[z] that God exists. This faith we will derive
a priori from moral principles.[a] Hence if in what follows we provoke doubt
about these speculative proofs and take issue with the supposed demonstrations of God's existence, we will not thereby undermine faith in God;
but rather we will clear the way for practical proofs. We are merely
throwing out the false presumptions of human reason when it tries from
itself to demonstrate the existence of God with apodictic certainty; from
moral principles,[b] however, we will accept[c] a faith in God as a principle[d] of
every religion.

Atheism (godlessness, denial of God) is divided into *skeptical* or *dogmatic*. *The former* disputes only the proofs for the existence of a God and
especially their apodictic certainty, but not God's existence itself, or at
least its possibility. Hence a skeptic can still have religion, because he
sincerely admits that it is even more impossible to prove that there is no
God than to prove that there is one. He denies only that human reason
can ever prove God's existence with certainty through speculation; but he
sees with equal certainty on the other side that it can never establish that
God does not exist. Now the belief in a merely possible God as ruler of
the world is obviously the minimum of theology; but it is of great enough
influence that it can occasion morality in any human being who already
recognizes the necessity of his duties with apodictic certainty. It is entirely
otherwise with the dogmatic atheist who directly denies the existence of a
God, and who declares it impossible that there is a God at all. Either there
never have been such dogmatic atheists, or they have been the most evil of
human beings. In them all the incentives of morality have broken down;
and it is to these atheists that moral theism stands opposed.

MORAL THEISM

Moral theism is of course critical, since it pursues all the speculative
proofs for the existence of God step by step, and recognizes them to be   28:1011
insufficient; indeed, the moral theist asserts absolutely that it is impossible
for speculative reason to demonstrate the existence of such a being with
apodictic certainty; but he is nevertheless firmly convinced of the existence of this being, and he has a faith beyond all doubt on practical

---

[z] *Glaube* means either "belief" or (in religious contexts) "faith."
[a] *Principien*
[b] *Principien*
[c] *annehmen*
[d] *Princip*

grounds. The foundation on which he builds his faith is unshakeable and it can never be overthrown, not even if all human beings united to undermine it. It is a fortress in which the moral human being can find refuge with no fear of ever being driven from it, because every attack on it will come to nothing. Hence his faith in God built on this foundation is as certain as a mathematical demonstration. This foundation is *morals,* the whole system of duties, which is cognized *a priori* with apodictic certainity through pure reason. This absolutely necessary morality of actions flows from the idea of a freely acting rational being and from the nature of actions themselves. Hence nothing firmer or more certain can be thought in any science than our obligation to moral actions. Reason would have to cease to be if it could in any way deny this obligation. For these actions do not depend on their consequences or circumstances; they are determined for the human being once and for all simply through their own nature. It is only through setting his end in them that he becomes a human being, and without them he would be an animal or a monster. His own reason bears witness against him when he forgets himself so far as to act against them and makes himself despicable and abominable in his own eyes. But if he is conscious of following them, then he is certain that he is also a member of the chain of the realm of ends, and this thought gives him consolation and comfort, makes him most inwardly noble and worthy of happiness, raising him to the hope of constituting a whole with all rational beings in the realm of morality, just as all and each are connected to one another in the realm of nature. Now the human being has a secure foundation on which he can build his faith in God; for although his virtue must be without any selfishness, even after denying the many claims of seductive temptations he still feels in himself a drive to hope for a lasting happiness. He tries to act according to the duties he finds grounded in his own nature; but he

28:1012 also has senses which present the opposite to him with an blinding bedazzlement, and if he had no further incentives and powers to resist it, then he would in the end be blinded by their dazzle. Hence in order that he may not act against his own powers, he is set by his own reason to think of a being whose will is those very commands which he recognizes to be given by themselves^c *a priori* with apodictic certainty. This being he will have to think of as the most perfect, for otherwise his morality would not obtain reality through it. It must be *omniscient* of it is to know the smallest stirrings of his innermost heart and all the motives and intentions of his actions. And for this merely much knowledge will not suffice, but only omniscience. – It must be *omnipotent,* so that it can arrange the whole of nature to accord with the way I act regarding my morality. It must even be *holy* and *just;* for otherwise I would have no hope that the fulfillment of my duties would be well-pleasing to it. From this we see that the moral theist

^{c} *für sich*

356

can have a wholly precise and determinate concept of God by setting up this concept to accord with morality. And he thereby renders superfluous everything that the skeptical atheist attacks. For he needs no speculative proofs of the existence of God; he is convinced of it with certainty, because otherwise he would have to reject the necessary laws of morality which are grounded in the nature of his being. Thus he derives theology from morality, yet not from speculative but from practical evidence; i.e. not through knowledge but from faith.*f* But it is a necessary practical hypothesis in respect of our practical knowledge*g* what an axiom is with respect to speculative knowledge. Hence the existence of a wise governor of the world is a necessary *postulate of practical reason*.

f nicht durchs Wissen, sondern durch den Glauben
g Kenntnisse

First part:
Transcendental theology

In this cognition of God from pure concepts we have three constitutive concepts of God, namely:

1. as *original being* (*ens originarium*). Here I think of God in general as a thing which is not derived from any other, as the original being, the sole one which is not derivative. I represent God as completely isolated from all, as a being that exists for himself and from himself and stands in community with no other being. This concept of an *ens originarium* is the foundation of cosmotheology. For it is from this concept that I infer the absolute necessity and highest perfection of God.

2. as the *highest being* (*ens summum*). Here I think of God as a being that has every reality, and derive precisely from the concept of such an *ens realissimum*, and from its attributes, its originality and absolute necessity. This concept of God, as an *ens maximum*[h] is the foundation of ontotheology.

3. as the *being of all beings* (*ens entium*). Here I think of God not only as the original being for itself which is derived from no other, but also as the highest ground of all other things, as the being from which everything else is derived. This we can call God's *all-sufficiency*. These three concepts of God as the original being, the highest being and the being of all beings are the foundation of all the rest. We will of course ascribe various other predicates to God in what follows, but these will be only *individual*[i] determinations of those fundamental concepts.

First section: Ontotheology

In ontotheology we consider God as the *highest being,* or at least we make this concept our ground. But how will I be able to think of a highest being through pure reason, *merely as a thing?* – Every thing must have something

---

[h] greatest being
[i] *einzelne*

358

positive which expresses some being in it. A mere not-being cannot constitute any thing. The concept *de ente modo negativo* is the concept of a *non entis.*[j] Consequently, since each thing must have reality, we can represent every possible thing either as an *ens realissimum*[k] or as an *ens partim reale, partim negativum.*[l] But in the case of any thing which has only some reality, something is always still lacking, and hence it is not a complete thing. A highest thing, therefore, would have to be one which has all reality. For in this one case I do have a thing whose thoroughgoing determination is bound up with its concept, because it is thoroughly and completely determined with respect to all possible *praedicates opposites.*[m] Consequently, the concept of an *ens realissimum* is the very concept of an *ens summum;*[n] for all things except this being are *partim realia, partim negativa*[o] and just because of this their concepts are not thoroughly determined. For example, in the concept of a most perfect human being as human it is yet undetermined whether this human being is old or young, tall or short, learned or unlearned. Hence such things are not complete things because they do not have all reality, but are instead mixed with negations. – But what are negations? Nothing but limitations of realities. For no negation can be thought unless the positive has been previously thought. How could I think of a mere deficiency, of darkness without a concept of light, or poverty without a concept of prosperity? Thus if every negative concept is derivative in that it always presupposes a reality, then every thing in its thoroughgoing determination as an *ens partim reale, partim negativum*[p] also presupposes an *ens realissimum* with respect to its realities and negations, because they are nothing but limitations of the highest reality. For when I entirely remove some realities from the concept of an *ens realissimum*, there arise negations which give me the concept of an *ens partim reale, partim negativum* when I combine them with the remaining realities; hence the concept of an *ens realissimum* contains simultaneously the ground for every other concept. Consequently it is the fundamental measure according to which I have to think or even judge all other things. Thus for instance I can think of something which does not know only if I previously thought of a being which knows everything and then entirely removed this reality. – From this it equally follows that the concept of an *ens realissimum* is at the same time the concept of an *ens originarium* from which all the concepts of other things are derived. But obviously this is only an *ens*

28:1014

---

[j] The concept of a being negative in every mode is the concept of a non-being.
[k] most real being
[l] a being partly real, partly negative
[m] opposed predicates
[n] highest being
[o] partly real things, partly negative things
[p] a being partly real, partly negative

originarium logice tale,[q] a being whose concept cannot be derived from any other concept because all other concepts of things must be derived from it. Thus an *ens realissimum* is also an *ens logice originarium.*[r] On the contrary, *omne ens limitatum* is also an *ens derivativum.*[s] If one speaks of "mixed realities," one is using an improper expression.[11] For a mixture of a reality and a negation, of something and nothing, cannot be thought. If I am to mix something with something else, then I must have something actual; but negations are mere deficiencies. Hence if a thing has something negative along with what is real (for example, a darkened room, etc.) then in this case there is no mixing in of the negation, but rather a limitation of the reality. Thus in the case cited I could not mix the negation darkness in with the light as something real, but rather the negative darkness arose when I reduced and limited the reality light. But the *logical* mixture of concepts is something wholly different. Here I can certainly say that the concept of a negation is mixed in with my concept of reality, for my concept of something negative is a concept every bit as much as my concept of something real is a concept. Hence here I have things which can be mixed with one another; yet this is not the case with the object[t] itself, but only with my idea of the object.[u]

More important than this is the thesis of those *scholastic theologians* who said that every attribute of God is in fact God himself.[12] Expressed completely and precisely, the thesis is this: any single reality considered as ground without limitation is at the same time my whole concept of God. If we examine this thesis, we find that it is actually well grounded. Every reality, if I think of it without limitation, is God himself, e.g. the Omniscient, the Omnipotent, the Eternal. Here I have only single realities without limitation and I represent God wholly under each of them, because I think of each such unlimited reality equally as a ground from which I understand every other unlimited reality. For example, when I represent omniscience, I equally regard it as a ground through which I posit omniscience, omnipotence, etc., and I rightly infer that the being to which this single reality belongs without limitation is a being to which all the other realities also belong; and hence arises the concept of God. God is a necessary idea of our understanding, because he is the substratum of the possibility of all things. This was already established above in detail. But now the question is whether this idea of ours also have objective reality, that is, whether there actually exists a being corresponding to our idea of God. Some have wanted to prove this because in our concept there

[q] an original being for logic
[r] a logically original being
[s] Every limited being is also a derivative being.
[t] *Objekt*
[u] *Objekt*

360

is nothing which contradicts it. Now this is obviously true, for our whole 28:1016
concept of God consists of realities. But it is impossible for one reality to
contradict another, since a contradiction requires that something be and
also not be. This not-being, however, would be a negation, and nothing of
this kind can be thought in God. Yet the fact that there is nothing contradictory in my concept of God proves only the *logical possibility* of the
concept, that is, the possibility of forming the concept in my understanding. For a self-contradictory concept is no concept at all. But if I am to
give objective reality to my concept and prove that there actually exists an
object corresponding to my concept – for this more is required than the
fact that there is nothing in my concept that contradicts itself. For how can
a concept which is logically possible, merely in its logical possibility, constitute at the same time the real possibility of an object?[v] For this not only an
analytic judgment is required, but also a synthetic one, i.e. I must be able
to know that the effects of the realities do not cancel one another. For
instance, decisiveness and caution are both realities, but their effects are
often of such a kind that the one cancels the other. Now I have no capacity
to judge *a priori* whether the realities combined in the concept of God
cancel each other in their effects, and hence I cannot establish the possibility of my concept directly; but on the other side, I may also be sure that no
human being could ever prove its impossibility.

If we now ask how we come to the concept of a maximum of all
realities, then insofar as the reality is finite we must leave every limitation
out of its concept if we want to apply it to the concept of a *realissimum*. For
fundamentally we can think of God only by ascribing to him without any
limitation everything real which we encounter in ourselves. But it is often
very difficult to separate out every limitation, because we ourselves are
limited creatures and are often unable to represent the real except under
limitations. In such a case, where we are not in a position to remove all the
limitations from our concept, we still do not need to give up the reality
itself; rather we can say that we do ascribe it to God, only without any
limitations, because in fact it is grounded on something real. Thus for 28:1017
example it is very difficult for us to think of eternity without any limitations; but we must nevertheless have it in our concept of God, because it
is a reality. So we ascribe it to God and admit the inability of our reason to
think it in an entirely pure way. – As to God's *understanding*, we must
think of it as intuitive, as opposed to our discursive understanding, which
is able to make concepts of things only from universal marks. But this is a
limitation which must be left out of the reality of understanding if I am to
apply this reality to God. Hence God's understanding will not be a faculty
of thinking but a faculty of intuiting. – The concept of the infinite is taken
from mathematics, and belongs only to it;[13] for this concept never deter-

[v] *Objekt*

361

mines an absolute magnitude, but always only a relative one. It is the concept of a magnitude which in relation to its measure as unity is greater than any number. Hence infinity never determines *how* great something is; for it does not determine the measure (or unity) and a great deal in fact depends on this. For example, if I represent space as infinite, I can assume either miles or diameters of the earth as the measure or unity with respect to which it is infinite. If I assume miles as the measure, then I can say that universal space is greater than any number of miles, even if I think of centillions of them. But if I assume diameters of the earth as my measure, or even distances, to the sun, I will still be able to say here that cosmic space is greater than any number, in this case, of diameters of the earth and distances to the sun, even if I think of centillions of them. But who does not see that in the last case infinity is greater than in the first, because here the unity with respect to which cosmic space is greater than any number is much greater than it was before? But from this we also see that the concept of infinity expresses only a relationship to our incapacity to determine the concept of magnitude, because the magnitude in question is greater than every number I can think of, and hence gives me no determinate concept of the magnitude itself. Fundamentally, therefore, when I call an object infinite the only advantage this gives me is that I gain an insight into my inability to express the magnitude of this object in numbers. I may be very impressed and astonished at the object*w* in this way, but on the other side I can never learn to recognize its absolute

28:1018 magnitude. Thus the concept of infinity can always have much aesthetic beauty, because it moves me deeply. But it does not help me at all to say with precision how great the object itself is. Moreover, if I am to assume an object*x* to be infinite, I must always assume that it is homogeneous with something else. For instance, if I call the divine understanding "infinite" I must assume my understanding as a measure of unity and then admit that the magnitude of the divine understanding is greater than everything I can think of as an understanding. But this does not help me in the least to be able to say determinately *how great* the divine understanding is. Thus we see that I cannot come a single step further in my cognition of God by applying the concept of mathematical infinity to him. For through this concept I learn only that I can never express the concept of God's greatness in numbers. But this gives me no insight into God's absolute greatness. I cannot even find any measure for it; for where is a unity which is homogeneous with God? – Might we perhaps succeed in finding this measure by means of the concept of *metaphysical* infinity? But what is the meaning of "metaphysical infinity"? In this concept we understand perfections in their highest degree, or better yet, without any degree. The

w Objekt
x Objekt

omnitudo realitatis[y] is what is called metaphysical infinity. Now it is true that through this concept we do gain a precise concept of God's greatness. For this total reality does determine only his absolute greatness. But here I need no homogeneous measure, no unity to be compared with God from which to bring out his greatness relative to it. Rather I have here a determinate concept of this greatness itself. For I see that everything which is truly a reality is to be encountered in him. But the concept of totality is always completely precise, and I can never think of it as more or less than it is. On the other side, I cannot see why I ought to express an ontological concept (the concept of totality) in terms of mathematical infinity. Should I not rather use a term congruent with the concepts of this science, instead of permitting an ambiguity by usurping an expression from another science, thus running the risk of letting an alien concept creep in as well? Hence in theology we can easily dispense with the term   28:1019
metaphysical infinity, since the ontological concept expressed is not suitably rendered by a term of mathematical origin, and would be better signified by the term "All of reality." But if we want a special term for this concept, we would do better to choose the expression *all-sufficiency (omnisufficientia).* This expression represents everything real in God to us as a ground *(ens entium),*[z] because *sufficientia* always expresses the relationship of a ground to its consequences. We would also do better to be satisfied with the pure concept of our reason, *omnitudo realitatis.*[a] For this concept is the fundamental measure by which I can determine the absolute greatness of God. –

Above we have already firmly established the universal concept of God, namely that he is an *ens realissimum.* This is the ideal our reason needs as a higher standard for what is less complete. We have further seen that this concept of a most perfect being has to be at the same time the concept of a highest being. Now the question is: Which predicates will we ascribe to this being, and in what way must we proceed in arranging these predicates of God's so that they do not contradict the concept of a being which is the most primary of all?[b] Here we still have to do only with mere concepts, without troubling ourselves whether there is an object[c] corresponding to these concepts! We have thought of a being as the substratum of the possibility of all other beings, and now we are asking how this ideal must be constituted. Hence we want to see which predicates can agree with the concept of this highest and most perfect being. This investigation is most necessary, because otherwise the whole concept is of no help to us and cannot in general

[y] All of reality
[z] being of beings
[a] All of reality
[b] *allerersten*
[c] *Objekt*

be rightly thought by us unless we determine the predicates which are congruent to it. But this investigation will also be of great utility to us in that it teaches us to cognize God as far as human reason is capable of this cognition. It gives us handy rules for speaking of God, and what we are to assert of him; and it will recommend care and caution to us, so that nothing creeps into our concept of God which is contrary to his highest reality.

28:1020 What predicates, then, can be thought in an *ens realissimum?*[d] What are its attributes? We have already seen this much, that nothing can be predicated of the concept of an *ens realissimum* except realities. But where will we find these realities? What are they? And how can we – and how must we – ascribe them to God? Every reality is either given to me through pure reason, independently of any experience, or encountered by me in the world of sense. I may ascribe the first kind of reality to God without hesitation, for realities of this kind apply to things in general and determine them through pure understanding. Here no experience is involved and the realities are not even affected by sensibility. Hence if I predicate them of God I need not fear that I am confusing him with an object of sense. For in this case I am not ascribing anything to him but what is true of him as a thing in general. It already lies in my concept of an *ens realissimum* that he must be a thing, and therefore I have to ascribe to him every reality which can be predicated of him as a thing. Now since these *a priori* realities refer to the universal attributes of a thing in general, they are called *ontological* predicates. They are purely transcendental concepts. To this class of realities belong God's possibility, his existence, his necessity, or whatever kind of existence flows from his concept; also the concept of substance, the concept of unity of substance, simplicity, infinity, duration, presence, and others as well. But these concepts determine only *the concept of a thing* in general. They are only predicates *in abstracto* which the deist ascribes to God. It is impossible for us to be satisfied with them alone, for such a God would be of no help to us; he would indeed be a thing, but one wholly isolated and by itself,[e] standing in no relationship to us. Of course this concept of God must constitute the beginning of all our cognition of God, but it is useless when taken only by itself, and quite superfluous to us if we could not cognize more of God than this. If this concept of God is to be of utility to us, we must see if these ontological predicates cannot be applied to examples *in concreto.* The theist does this when he thinks of God as the *supreme intelligence.* If we are to ascribe predicates to God *in concreto,* we must take materials for the concept of God from empirical principles[f] and empirical information.[g] But in the

---

[d] most real being
[e] *für sich*
[f] *Principien*
[g] *Kenntnissen*

whole of our experience we find nothing which has more reality *than our* 28:1021
own soul. Hence *these* realities too will have to be taken from the cognition
of ourselves; they will be psychological predicates which can be ascribed
to God along with his ontological predicates. But since all these predicates
are borrowed from experience, and since in the whole of experience we
encounter nothing but phenomena, we must exercise great care here not
to let ourselves be blinded by a mere show and ascribe predicates to God
which can be true only of objects of sense. Hence we must note the
following rules of caution:

1. *Regarding the choice of predicates themselves:* What kinds of predicates
   shall we take from experience and be able to unite with the concept
   of God? – Nothing but pure realities! But in the whole world there
   is no thing that has *pure* reality, but rather all things which can be
   given through experience are *partim realia, partim negativa.*[h] Hence
   great difficulties arise here, because many of my concepts are associated with determinations which have some deficiency in them. But
   such negations cannot be ascribed to God; hence I must first proceed *via negationis;* that is, I must carefully separate out everything
   sensible inhering in my representation of this or that reality, and
   leave out everything imperfect and negative, and ascribe to God the
   pure reality which is left over. But this is extremely difficult, for
   often very little or nothing at all is left over after I reject the limitations; or at least I can never think of the pure positive without the
   sensible element which is woven into my representation of it. In a
   case like this I have to say that if I do ascribe this or that *realitas
   phaenomenon* to God, I do it only *insofar* as all limitations have been
   separated from it. But if the negative element cannot be separated
   without cancelling the concept at the same time, then in this case I
   will not be able to predicate the concept of God at all. Thus for
   instance I cannot ascribe extension to God as a predicate, because it
   is only a concept of sense and if I separate everything negative from
   it, nothing real at all is left over. Of the concept of matter, after I 28:1022
   remove everything negative and sensible inhering in it I retain nothing but the concept of an externally active power, and of the concept
   of spatial presence if I leave out the condition of sense (i.e. space)
   nothing but the pure reality of presence. I will be able to apply to
   God, therefore, only the real itself, power and presence. – In this
   way I will be able to determine the quality of divine predicates *via
   negationis;*[i] that is, I can determine which predicates drawn from
   experience can be applied to my concept of God after all negations
   have been separated from them, but in this way I cannot come to

[h] partly real, partly negative things
[i] by the way of negation

cognize the quantity of reality in God; rather, the reality remaining in my concepts after all the limitations have been left out will be quite insignificant and small in degree. Hence if I meet with any reality in any of the attributes of things given to me through experience, I must ascribe this reality to God in the highest degree and with infinite significance. This is called proceeding *per viam eminentiae.*[j] But I cannot proceed in this way unless I have first brought out the pure reality *via negationis.*[14] But if I have neglected this task and have not carefully separated everything negative from my concept, then if I predicate the concept of this reality as it is encountered in appearance with its limitations, then my concept of God will be wholly corrupt. This is how anthropomorphism arises. – Hence first the limits must be left out and only the pure reality which is left over must be ascribed to God; but it must be ascribed *via eminentiae;* for instance, not merely power but *infinite* power, and not merely an understanding but an *infinite* understanding. But we can never arrive fully at the attributes of God so as to be able to cognize *how they* might be constituted *in themselves;* for example, if we take the human understanding, it is not enough to magnify it infinitely *via eminentiae;* for it would still remain a limited understanding and would grow merely in the quickness of its cognition. Rather we must first leave out all the limitations inhering in it as an understanding that can cognize everything only

28:1023 discursively. Now since the purely real, which is then left over (i.e. understanding) cannot in general be comprehended by us at all, there is only one path still left open to us.

2. *Regarding the way of proceeding, by which we are able to ascribe to God realities abstracted from concepts of sense:*

This is the noble way of *analogy.* – But what does this proceeding *per analogiam* consist in? Analogy does not consist in an imperfect similarity of things to one another, as it is commonly taken; for in this case that would be something very uncertain. Not only would we have bad predicates, because we would not be in a position to think of their reality without any limitations, but we could ascribe even these not wholly purified realities to God only insofar as he had something perfectly similar to them in himself. But how would that help me? Could it give me a sufficiently complete concept of God? If, however, we understand analogy to be the perfect similarity of relationships (not of things but of relationships), or in short what the mathematicians understand by *proportion,* then we will be satisfied at once; we can then form a concept of God and of his predicates which will be so sufficient that we will never need anything more. But

[j] by the way of eminence

obviously we will not assume any relations of magnitude (for this belongs to mathematics); but rather we will assume a relation of cause to effect, or even better, of ground to its consequence, so as to infer in an entirely philosophical manner.[15] For just as in the world one thing is regarded as the cause of another thing when it contains the ground of this thing, so in the same way we regard the whole world as a consequence of its ground *in God*, and argue from the analogy. For instance, just as the happiness of one human being (the removal of his misery) has a relationship to the benevolence of another human being, so in just the same way the happiness of all human beings has a relationship to the benevolence of God. The primary ground of proof for the existence of God is the ontological one from pure concepts. But the real possibility of a most perfect being must be proven before I can prove its existence in this way.[16] For the dogmatic atheist absolutely denies the possibility of a God and asserts that there is no God. But here, where we have to do only with pure reason, denying the existence of an *ens realissumum* and denying its possibility are fundamentally the same thing. Hence if the dogmatic atheist denies that there is a God, he takes upon himself the obligation to prove that God is impossible. For all our *a priori* cognition is of such a kind that, when I presume to prove from pure reason that something does not exist, I can do it only by proving that it is impossible for this thing to exist. The reason for this is that, since here I can borrow no proof from experience either for or against the existence of the being in question, it follows that I have no other path before me but to prove from the mere concept of the thing that it does not exist, and that means proving that it contradicts itself. Hence, before he presumees the right to assert that no *ens realissimum* exists, the dogmatic atheist must show that an object corresponding to our idea of such a being would contradict itself in the unification of its predicates. On the other side, if it occurs to us to want to demonstrate *a priori* that God does exist, then we too must undertake the duty to prove through pure reason and with apodictic certainty that God is possible. But there is no way we can do this except by proving that an *ens realissimum* does not contradict itself in the synthesis of all its predicates. But in his proof of the possibility of an *ens realissimum* Leibniz confused the possibility of the concept with the possibility of the thing itself. Namely, he inferred this way: In my concept of an *ens realissimum* there is no contradiction, because one reality cannot contradict another, beacause a contradiction necessarily requires a negation in order for me to say that something both is and is not. But where there are only sheer realities, there is no negation and hence no contradiction either. But if there is no contradiction in the concept of an *ens realissimum*, then such a thing is possible. He should have concluded, however, *only that my idea of such a thing is possible*. For the fact that there is nothing contradictory in my concept of a thing does not prove that it is the concept of something possible, but it does not

28:1024

yet prove the possibility of the object[k] of my idea. The principle of contradiction is only the analytic principle[l] of possibility, by means of which it is established with apodictic certainty whether my concept is possible or impossible. But it is not the synthetic principle[m] of possibility, i.e. by means of it we cannot at all prove whether or not the predicates of a thing would cancel each other in the thing itself. For by means of the principle of contradiction I cannot come to cognize the synthesis of predicates in the object;[n] for this there is required, rather, an insight into the constitution and range of each predicate as regards its operations. Hence if I undertake to prove the possibility of an *ens realissimum* (that is, to prove the possibility of the synthesis of all predicates in one object),[o] then I presume to prove *a priori* through my reason and with apodictic certainty that all perfections can be united in a single stem and derived from a single principle.[p] But such a proof transcends the possible insight of all human reason. Where will I get this cognition? From the world? Well and good, but in the world I will find realities only as they are distributed among objects; for example, a great capacity for understanding in one human being but a certain indecisiveness; in another, on the contrary, very lively affections but only an average amount of insight. In animals I note an astonishing fertility in propagation, but no reason; in human beings I find reason but much less fertility; in short, I see in these cases that where one reality is found in an object,[q] some other reality is not present. Now obviously I cannot infer from them that the one reality cancels the other, and that for instance it is impossible that there is a human being who unites in himself every reality a human being can have; but on the other side I also have no insight as to *how* such a perfect human being could be possible; for I cannot cognize whether in the synthesis (the composition) of all human realities the effects of one perfection would contradict the effects of another. In order to have this insight I would have to be acquainted with all the possible effects of all human realities and their respective relationships. But I cannot, because in all human beings I perceive only individual realities, and consequently also only the effects of these individual realities, but not all possible effects of a synthesis of all human realities. Apply this to God, I must concede even more my incapacity to have insight into how a synthesis of all possible realities is possible with regard to all their effects. For how will my reason presume to cognize how all the highest realities operate, what effects would arise from them,

[k] *Objekt*
[l] *Princip*
[m] *Princip*
[n] *Objekt*
[o] *Objekt*
[p] *Princip*
[q] *Objekt*

and what relationship all these realities would have to have? – But I would   28:1026
have to cognize this if I wanted to have insight into whether all realities
could be united together in one object,[r] and hence into how God is
possible.

On the other side, it is also impossible for human reason ever to
prove that such a combination of all perfections in one thing is *not*
possible; for this would also require an insight into the extent of all the
effects of the All of reality, since the same grounds which make visible
human reason's inability to assert the existence of such a being are also
necessarily sufficient to prove the unworkability of every counter-
assertion. – In short, it is impossible to prove that God is impossible.
Rather, reason does not put the least obstacle in the way of my accepting[s] the possibility of God, if I should feel bound to do so in some other
way. Reason itself is not able to prove with apodictic certainty any such
possibility (and *a priori* proofs must one and all have apodictic certainty,
otherwise they are not proofs). For this would require an insight which
far transcends the bounds of the human faculty of reason. But from this
same inability of my reason follows the impossibility of ever proving that
a most perfect being is not possible. And thus collapses the edifice of the
dogmatic atheist. For if he wishes to deny God's existence and assert
that there absolutely is no God, the atheist must first demonstrate the
impossibility of God. But here reason forsakes him, and everything he
may bring against the possibility of God will be only so much absurdity
and nonsense. From all this we see that human reason can prove neither
the possibility nor the impossibility of God, because it lacks the necessary insight into the domain and effects of all realities; but nothing
prevents us from assuming the possibility of God, if we should be able to
find convincing grounds for it in some other way.

Now just as we can refute the dogmatic atheist and reject his presumptuous assertions of the nonexistence of God before we ourselves have
proven God's existence, so in the same way we can also render fruitless all
the attacks of the skeptical atheist without previously giving a proof for the
existence of a most perfect being. For since the latter doubts that there
can be any proof at all just because speculative reason cannot prove to our
satisfaction the existence of God, he also equally doubts at the same time   28:1027
the existence of God itself. The skeptical atheist can be refuted only if,
granting him the insufficiency of all speculative proofs for the existence of
God as an *ens realissimum*, we nonetheless feel an inner conviction on
practical grounds that *a God must exist.* We must assume a God and we must
believe in him, even though our reason may not venture to assume his
possibility and his existence *a priori.*

[r] *Objekt*
[s] *anzunehmen*

369

The ontological proof for the existence of a God is taken from the concept of an *ens realissimum*. One infers, namely: An *ens realissimum* is one which contains all realities in itself. But existence is also a reality; hence the *ens realissimum* must necessarily exist. If one therefore asserts that God is not, then one thereby denies something in the predicate which lies already in the subject; consequently there is a contradiction here. The great simplicity of this proof by itself provokes a not unfounded suspicion. But we will let the critique of the proof take its course, and see whether the proof holds water. In this proof, everything unquestionably depends on whether the existence of a thing is in fact one of its realities. – But the fact that a thing exists does not by itself make the thing more perfect; it does not thereby contain any new predicate, but in such a way it is rather posited with all its predicates. The thing was already just as complete in my concept when I thought of it as possible as it is afterward when it actually exists; for otherwise, if existence were a special reality belonging to the thing, it would not be the same thing I had thought before, but more would exist in it than was included in the concept of the object. *Being* is thus obviously not a real predicate, that is, the concept of something which could be added to the concept of a thing in order to make it still more perfect. It is only the positing' of a thing, or of certain determinations, in themselves. In its logical use, it is merely the copula of a judgment. The proposition "God is omnipotent" contains sheer concepts which have as their objects God and omnipotence. The little word *is* is not a further predicate, but is only that which posits the predicate (omnipotent) in the subject (God). If I now take the subject (God) together with all

28:1028   its predicates, and say "God is" or "there is a God," then I do not add any new predicate to the concept God, but rather only posit the subject in itself with all its predicates, and more specifically" the object in relation" to my concept. Both the object and the concept must have the same content, and thus nothing can be added to the concept (which expresses mere possibility) by simply thinking its object as given (through the expression "it is"). Hence the actual contains no more than the merely possible. For example, one hundred actual dollars do not contain the least bit more than one hundred possible dollars. For the possible dollars signify the concept, and the actual ones the object of this concept and the positing of it as such. Hence in a case where the object contained more than the concept, my concept would not express the whole object, and thus would not be the suitable concept for it. For the object in its actuality is not contained analytically in my concept, but is added synthetically to my concept (which is a determination of my state) without this additional *being* external to my

' Position
" zwar
" Beziehung

concept thereby increasing in the least the hundred dollars I am thinking of. Whatever our concept of an object may contain and however much it may contain, we must still go beyond it if we are to impart existence to the object. If I think in a thing every reality except one, the missing reality is not added if I say that this defective thing exists, but rather it exists with precisely the same deficiency I have thought in it, for otherwise what exists would be something different from what I was thinking of. Now if I think of some being as the highest reality (without deficiency), it is still an open question whether it exists or not; for it is just as thoroughly determined as an ideal as it would be if it were an actual object. From this we see how rash it would be to conclude that existence is included already in the concept of a possible thing. And thus collapses every argument which says that existence follows necessarily from the concept of an *ens realissimum.*[17] –

The cosmological proof retains the connection of absolute necessity and the highest reality, but instead of inferring necessary existence from supreme reality, it infers from an already given unconditional necessity of some being to its unbounded reality. Leibniz, and later Wolff, called this   28:1029 the proof *a contingentia mundi.*[*] It says that if something exists, then an absolutely necessary being must also exist. But at the very least, I myself exist; therefore, an absolutely necessary being exists. The minor premise of this argument contains an experience, and the major premise contains an inference from experience. This inference rests on the natural law of causality, which says that everything contingent has a cause, which if it is also contingent, must once again have a cause, and so on. This series of things subordinated one to another has to end in an absolutely necessary cause, without which it would not be complete. For a *regress in infinitum,*[x] a series of effects *without* a supreme cause, is absurd. Everything which exists can exist in only one of two ways, either *contingently* or *necessarily.* The contingent must have some cause for its existing as it does and not otherwise. Now I exist (and even the world in general exists) contingently; hence an absolutely necessary being must also exist, in order to be the cause of my being as I am and not otherwise. Thus the proof really does begin from experience and so it is not carried out in a wholly *a priori* manner, or ontologically. And it is called the *cosmological* proof because the object of any possible experience is called a *world.* But since it abstracts from every particular attribute which distinguishes this world from any other possible world and grounds itself only on a world in general without regard to its constitution, the cosmological proof is distinguished in its denomination from the physicotheological proof, which makes use of observations about the *particular* constitution of the sensible world as

---

[*] from the contingency of the world
[x] regress to infinity

ground of proof. Now the cosmological proof infers further from the existence of an absolutely necessary being to the conclusion that this being must also be an *ens realissimum*. The inference is thus: A necessary being can be determined in only one way: this is, with respect *to* all possible *praedicata contradictorie opposita*[y] it must be determined by one of these opposed predicates, consequently it must be thoroughly determined by its concept. But there is only one possible concept of a thing which determines it thoroughly *a priori*, and this is the concept of the *ens realissimum*, since in every possible pair of *praedicata contradictorie opposita* only the reality always belongs to it. Hence the concept of a most real being is the only concept by means of which a necessary being can be thought; i.e. there exists an *ens realissimum* and it exists necessarily.

28:1030

This cosmological proof is based on experience and gives itself the appearance of arriving step by step at the existence of a necessary being in general. But the empirical concept can teach us nothing about the attributes of this being, but rather at this point reason says goodbye to experience and searches only among concepts. For if I ask, namely, what attributes a necessary being must have, the answer can be only: those attributes from which its absolute necessity flows. But reason believes that the requisites needed for absolute necessity are met with solely in the concept of a most real being. So it concludes that the absolutely necessary being is the most real being. But how could reason conclude this if it had not already *presupposed* that the concept of a being of the highest reality is fully adequate to the concept of absolute necessity? And what does this amount to except that it is possible to argue from the highest reality to an absolutely necessary being? This is the proposition which the ontological argument asserted, and the cosmological takes as a ground, even though there was an attempt to avoid it. – Now since we cannot succeed in proving from the concept of the highest reality the absolutely necessary existence of the object[z] corresponding to this idea, it will also be impossible conversely to demonstrate successfully the supreme reality of a thing from its absolute necessity; for absolute necessity is an existence from mere concepts. If I say that the concept of an *ens realissimum* is a concept of this kind and in fact the only concept fitting and adequate to necessary existence, then I must also admit that existence can be inferred from the concept of a most real being. *It is thus really only the ontological proof* from sheer concepts which truly contains demonstrative power in the so-called cosmological proof, and *the alleged experience is entirely pointless,* [serving] perhaps to lead us to the concept of absolute necessity, but not to establish this concept as pertaining to any determinate thing. For as soon as this is our intention, we immediately leave all experience behind and seek among pure concepts for those containing the condition

28:1031

[y] contradictorily opposed predicates
[z] *Objekt*

for the possibility of an absolutely necessary being. If it were correct to say that every absolutely necessary being is also a most real being, then it would also be possible to convert this proposition, as with every affirmative judgment, and say that every most real being is a necessary being. Now since this proposition is determined *a priori* from mere concepts, the mere concept of an *ens realissimum* must carry its own absolute necessity along with it, and this is what the ontological proof asserts. The cosmological proof does not want to recognize it, even though it secretly underlies its inferences just the same.[18]

But what sort of concept do we have of an absolutely necessary being or thing? – In all ages one has spoken of an absolutely necessary being, but human beings have taken less trouble to understand whether and how one could think of such a thing at all than they have rather to prove its existence. A nominal definition of this concept is quite easy to give: it is something whose nonexistence is impossible; but this makes us none the wiser as to the conditions which might make it impossible for such a thing not to be.[19] For the human understanding cannot grasp how the nonexistence of a thing might be impossible,[a] since it has a concept of impossibility only through the principle of contradiction. For every contradiction, two things are required, for a single thing cannot contradict itself. Hence there can never be a contradiction in the nonexistence of a thing, consequently also never a contradiction in the nonexistence of an *ens realissimum*. In his explanation of the absolute necessity of an *ens realissimum*, Wolff used examples of absolute necessity: that a triangle has three angles is absolutely necessary.[20] But the absolute necessity of this judgment is only a conditioned necessity of the matter or predicate in the judgment. The proposition in question does not say that three angles necessarily exist, but rather that under the condition that a triangle exists (is given), three angles exist along with it in a necessary manner. If in an ideal judgment I remove the predicate and retain the subject, a contradiction results. For example, to posit a triangle and remove three angles is contradictory. Hence I say that this predicate belongs necessarily to the subject. But if I remove the subject together with the predicate, then there is no contradiction, for nothing is left which could be contradicted. Thus, for example, there is no contradiction in removing the triangle together with its three angles. And this is exactly how it is with the concept of an absolutely necessary being. If I remove its existence, I remove the thing itself with all its predicates. So where can the contradiction come from? There is nothing external which would be contradicted, for the thing is not supposed to be externally necessary; but not internally either, for by removing the thing itself I have at the same time removed everything internal to it.

28:1032

---

[a] Pölitz's text reads *möglich*, but the sense seems to require *unmöglich*.

Example "God is omnipotent." This is a necessary judgment. Omnipotence cannot be removed as long as I posit a deity with whose concept this predicate is identical. Here I have logically unconditioned necessity. But now what would an absolute real necessity have to be? It would have to consist in the fact that it is absolutely necessary that God must be. But if I say, "God does not exist," then neither omnipotence nor any of his other predicates is given; for they are all removed along with the object,[b] and this thought does not exhibit the least contradiction. It is no more possible for an internal contradiction ever to arise if I remove the predicate of a judgment along with the object[c] – no matter what the predicate may be – than it is possible for me to form the least concept of a thing which would leave a contradiction behind if it were removed along with all its predicates; and without a contradiction I have through mere pure concepts *a priori* no mark of impossibility. Hence in this case it is possible that God does not exist. It costs speculative reason nothing at all to remove God's existence in thought. The entire task of the transcendental ideal depends on either finding a concept for absolute necessity or finding absolute necessity for the concept of some thing. If the one can be done, then the other must be able to be done as well; for reason cognizes absolute necessity only in what is necessary from its concept. But both tasks totally exceed every effort to satisfy our understanding on this point; yet at the same time they exceed every attempt to appease it on account of this incapacity. The absolute necessity which we indispensably need as the final ground of all things is the

28:1033 true abyss[d] for human reason. Even eternity, as described in its dreadful sublimity by a Haller, does not long make a dizzying impression on the mind;[21] for it only does away with the duration of things, but it doesn't sustain them. One can neither resist nor tolerate the thought of a being represented as the highest of all possible things, which may say to itself, "I am from eternity to eternity, and outside me there is nothing except what exists through my will; *but whence then am I?*" – Here everything falls away beneath us, and the greatest perfection, as much as the smallest, hovers without any support before speculative reason, and it costs reason nothing to let them both disappear, nor is there the least obstacle to this. In short, an absolutely necessary thing will remain to all eternity an insoluble problem for the human understanding. –

Up to this point we have followed Eberhard in his *Propaedeutic to Natural Theology*. But now he proceeds immediately to the physicotheological proof, and it seems to us more systematic not to get to this quite yet, but instead, now that we have treated the concept of a highest being and the

---

[b] *Objekt*
[c] *Objekt*
[d] Ground = *Grund*, abyss = *Abgrund*, i.e. as at a precipice, where the ground falls away.

proof for the existence of this being from pure reason, we will proceed to *the ontological predicates* of this being, so that we can have transcendental theology in its proper connection. The first thing here is the *possibility* of God, which no one either can deny or prove, because the cognition of it surpasses all human reason. As was shown above, the objective reality of the synthesis which generates this concept rests on principles[e] of possible experience; for by "experience" we understand the sum total of all the objects of sense. But how am I going to have *a priori* insight into the possibility of this thing without being able to perceive the synthesis of its predicates? As long as my concept does not contradict itself, it is possible. But this principle of analysis (the principle of contradiction) is only the *logical mark* of possibility, by means of which an object can be distinguished from a *nihil negativum!*[f] But how, from the possibility of a concept (logical possibility), can I straightway infer the possibility of a thing (real possibility)? – Let us now go on to the proof that the *ens realissimum* must also be the *ens entium;* or, as we expressed it earlier, that the most perfect being must contain in itself the ground of the possibility of all other things. This we have already established, because everything which is a *partim reale, partim negativum*[g] presupposes a being containing all realities in itself and constituting these things through a limitation of its realities: for otherwise we could not think where either the realities or the negations in things come from, because even a negation always presupposes some reality and arises through the limitation of this reality. On this point rests the only possible ground of proof for my demonstration of God's existence, which was discussed in detail in an essay I published some years ago.[22] Here it was shown that of all possible proofs, the one which affords us the most satisfaction is the argument that if we remove an original being, we at the same time remove the substratum of the possibility of all things. – But even this proof is not apodictically certain; for it cannot establish the objective necessity of an original being, but establishes only the subjective necessity of assuming such a being. But this proof can in no way be refuted, because it has its ground in the nature of human reason. For my reason makes it absolutely necessary for me to assume a being which is the ground of everything possible, because otherwise I would be unable to know what in general the possibility of something consists in. – Now from the fact that the highest being is also the original being, from which the essence of all things is derived, it follows that the order, beauty, harmony and unity which are encountered in things are not always contingent, but can rather inhere necessarily in their essence. If, for example, we find that our earth is flattened at the poles but

28:1034

---

[e] *Prinzipien*
[f] "negative nothing," or an individual thing whose concept entails its impossibility
[g] partly real, partly negative thing

elevated between the tropics and the equator, this follows from the necessity of its nature, that is, from the equilibrium of the fluid masses of which the earth was once composed.[23] Hence Newton could prove the shape of the earth reliably a priori and prior to experience, before the astronomers had measured its elevation at the equator, merely from the fact that it once must have been in a fluid state. But now this oblateness of the spherical earth has its great advantage, since it alone prevents the projections of solid earth (or even smaller mountains perhaps raised by earthquakes) from continuously displacing the earth's axis, perhaps to a noticeable degree over a long period of time; the rotation of the earth at the equator is such a mighty mountain that the vibration of all the other mountains will

28:1035 neer noticeably alter the earth's position in regard to its axis, or even be able to alter it. But wise as this arrangement is, I may not derive it straightway from the divine will, as something contingent, but I must rather consider it as a necessity of the earth's nature, just as has actually been demonstrated in this case. Yet this takes nothing away from God's majesty as creator of the world; for since he is the original being from whose essence the nature of all things is derived, the necessity of this natural arrangement is also derived from his essence, not from his will, for otherwise he would be only the world's architect, not its creator. Only the contingent in things can be derived from the divine will and its arbitrary directives. But now everything contingent lies in the *form* of things; consequently only the form of things can be derived from the divine will. To say this is not to make things themselves independent of God, nor is it to withdraw them in any way from his highest supreme power. For by regarding God as the *ens originarium* containing in itself the ground of all possible things, we derive their matter, in which their reality itself lies, from the divine essence. Thus we make the essence of things themselves derivative from God, that is, from his essence. For it is unthinkable that a special divine volition could be necessary to produce certain effects in a thing which follow necessarily from its nature; for instance, how could a special divine volition be necessary to give a spheroid shape to a fluid body revolving on its axis, when this is a necessary effect of the body's own nature? If we wanted to derive everything from the divine will, we would have to make everything inhering necessarily in the nature of things independent of God. We would have to recognize a creator for only what is contingent, that is only for the *form of things* and not for their matter or for what belongs necessarily to the things themselves. Hence if the laws and arrangements in nature which flow from the essence of things themselves are to be dependent on God (and they must be dependent on him, since otherwise we would be unable to find any ground for their possibility), then they can be derived only from his original essence. –

From everything that has been brought forth from pure reason thus far in favor of God's existence, we see that we are justified in assuming and

presupposing an *ens originarium,* which is at the same time an *ens*   28:1036
realissimum, as a necessary transcendental hypothesis; for to remove a
being which contains the data for everything possible is to remove all
possibility; such a most real original being is, because of its very relationship to the possibility of things, a necessary presupposition. For in addition to the logical concept of the necessity of a thing (where something is
said to be absolutely necessary if its nonexistence would be a contradiction, and consequently impossible), we have yet another rational concept
of real necessity. This is where a thing is *eo ipso* necessary if its nonexistence would remove all possibility. Of course in the logical sense possibility always precedes actuality, and here I can think the possibility of a thing
without actuality. Yet we have no concept of real possibility except through
existence, and in the case of every possibility which we think *realiter* we
always presuppose some existence; if not the actuality of the thing itself,
then at least an actuality in general which contains the data for everything
possible. Hence every possibility presupposes something actually given,
since if everything were merely possible, then the possible itself would
have no ground; so this ground of possibility must itself be given not
merely as possible but also as actual. But it must be noted that only the
subjective necessity of such a being is thereby established, i.e. that our
speculative reason sees itself necessitated to presuppose this being if it
wants to have insight into *why* something is possible, but the objective
necessity of such a thing can by no means be demonstrated in this matter.
For here reason must come to know its weakness, its inability to soar over
the boundaries of all possible experience. And insofar as it does presume
to continue its flight beyond these boundaries, it only falls into whirlpools
and turbulent waters, plunging it into a bottomless abyss where it is wholly
swallowed up. – Hence the totality of what speculative reason can teach
us concerning the existence of God consists in showing us how we must
necessarily hypothesize this existence, but speculative reason does not
show us how God's existence could be demonstrated with apodictic certainty. Even this much, however, is quite fortunate for us, since it removes
every obstacle which might stand in the way of our assuming a being of all
beings; indeed, if we can be convinced of such a being in some other way,
we can believe in it firmly and unshakably. For even in the speculative use   28:1037
of reason, the highest being remains a faultless ideal, a concept which
brings to a close and crowns the whole of human cognition.

All God's attributes (according to Baumgarten) are *quiescentes* or *op-
erativae.*[24] *Perfectiones quiescentes* are those in which we think of an action
which can be represented without a *nota actionis;*[h] *operatives,* on the contrary, cannot be thought without a mark of activity. Let us first consider
God's *perfectiones quiescentes;* for his ontological predicates belong to them.

[h] mark of activity

In addition to God's possibility and actuality, which we have already treated as far as reason can teach us about them, we further maintain that God is *a substance*. This predicate belongs to God merely as a thing, since all things are substances. A substance is understood to be a reality existing merely for itself, without being a determination of any other thing. Substance is opposed to accident, which can exist only by inhering in another thing. *Accidentia* are therefore not particular things, but only different ways[i] or *modi* of the existence of substance. God, however, is a thing for itself and *eo ipso* a substance. If we would dispute God's substantiality, we would have to deny him thinghood as well, and thus remove the whole concept of God. But if God is assumed to be an *ens realissimum*, then it follows already just from the concept of a thing that God is a substance.

Another of God's ontological attributes is *unity*.[25] This follows from the concept of an *ens realissimum;* for God is thoroughly determined in that in each pair of *praedicatis contradictorie oppositis* only the reality belongs to him. Now this concept of a being having every reality can only be *singularis*, and can never be thought of as a species, for in every species the individuals must somehow be distinguished from one another if they are to be particular things. But this difference can take place only through a distribution of reality, or one thing must have something in itself which the others do not. But that contradicts our concept of a *realissimum*.

28:1038   From God's unity follows his *simplicity*.[26] For every *compositum reale*[j] is to be regarded as reality composed of substances external to each other yet standing *in commercio*.[k] Hence if God were a *compositum*, he must consist of many parts, and then either each of them must be an *ens realissimum* (and then there would be many *realissima*, which is a contradiction) or else the parts would be *partim reale, partim negativa*. But then the whole which consisted in these parts would itself be only *partim reale, partim negativum*, consequently not a *realissimum*, consequently not God. For an unlimited reality can never arise out of many limited realities, because in order for a thing to have unlimited realities, all realities must be united in one subject. It is just this unification, therefore, which constitutes the form of an *ens realissimum*. But as soon as realities are distributed (and there must be such a distribution among the parts of the *compositum* if the *ens realissimum* is to be an *end compositum*), then limitations arise. For whenever a reality is distributed among several things, the whole reality cannot be in each of them, and consequently each part lacks some of the missing reality. The unity of a *compositum* is always only a contingent unity of combination, i.e. the parts of every composite can always be presented separately; and if in fact they are combined, it still could have been

[i] *Arten*
[j] composite of real things
[k] in reciprocal interaction

otherwise; but the unity of a simple substance is necessary. Thus the simplicity of the *ens realissimum* can also be proven from its absolute necessity. For if the *ens realissimum* were an *ens compositum*, then all its parts would have to be absolutely necessary if the whole is to be absolutely necessary, insofar as the whole cannot be constituted in a manner different from the parts of which it consists. But then there would be many *entia absolute necessaria,*[l] which contradicts the concept of absolute necessity. A third proof for the simplicity of God is derived from the fact that every *compositum* is also *divisibile,* in that it consists of parts. But divisibility always involves the inner alterability of a thing, since the relation between the parts of an *ens compositum* can always be altered. Every composite substance is thus internally alterable; but that contradicts the concept of an *ens realissimum.* – Now just because the most real being must be simple, it follows also that it must be immaterial as well; for matter is what constitutes the composite.

To God there further pertains *immutability.* This too belongs to his 28:1039 *perfectiones quiescentes.* But one must not confuse the *immutabile* as concept with the *immutabile* as thing. This difference Baumgarten has not duly observed; hence he infers the unalterability of God from the fact that every determination of a most real being is absolutely and internally unalterable.[27] But from this follows only the unalterability of the concept of God, which consists in the fact that God is thoroughly determined through his concept. – What is mutation? A succession of states. But alterations can be thought possible only in time, for only here is there succession. If we want to prove the unalterability of God, then we first have to prove that God is not in time. But this can be seen clearly from the concept of an *ens realissimum;* for if God were in time he would have to be limited. But now he is a *realissimus,* and consequently he is not in time. His real unalterability also follows from his absolute necessity; for if he were so constituted that something could arise in him which was not already actual in him, then it could not be said that he is necessary in his actual constitution, but rather that he could be otherwise than he is, since he could be sometimes in this state and sometimes in that one. From this highest immutability of God with respect to all his realities it follows that it is anthropomorphic to represent God as able to be gracious after he was previously wrathful. For this would posit[m] an alteration in God. But God is and remains always the same, equally gracious and equally just. It depends only on us whether we will become objects of his grace or of his punitive justice. The alteration, therefore, goes on *within us;* it is the relation[n] in which we stand to God which is altered whenever we improve

---

[l] absolutely necessary beings
[m] *supponiren*
[n] *Relation*

ourselves, in such a way that, whereas previously our relation to God was that of culpable sinners to a just God, afterward, after our improvement, this relation is removed and the relation of righteous friends of virtue takes its place. It does not accord with the concept of an unchangeable God that God should be more effective in us just because we make moral improvement our end; rather, when we work for our own improvement it is we ourselves who are more susceptible to the influence of his power, and we participate in it to a higher degree. His influence itself does not become stronger or increase; for that would be a change *in him;* but
28:1040 rather, *we* feel it to be stronger because we no longer resist it; the influence itself remains the same.

The author next discusses polytheism.[28] It doubtless arose because human beings could not comprehend the apparent conflict of purposes in the world, the mixture of good and evil; so they assumed several beings as the cause of this conflict and assigned to each a special department. Nevertheless, in addition to these lower gods every heathen people has the thought of a special original source out of which they flowed. But they made this supreme principle in and for itself so blessed that it has nothing at all to do with the world. Examples of this are the Tibetans and other existing heathen peoples of inner Asia. And in fact they follow the course of human reason, which needs a thoroughgoing unity in its representation and cannot stop until it has reached the One which is higher than everything. Polytheism as such, not combined with a supreme original source, would be in conflict with common human understanding; for common sense teaches monotheism by taking as its supreme principle a being which is all in all. Thus one should not think that the doctrine of one God needs to be built on a very advanced degree of human insight; rather it is a need of the most common reason. Hence the insight was universal even in the beginning. But because human beings subsequently perceived many kinds of destructive forces in the world, they did not believe that these forces along with the agreement and harmony in nature could be derived from God, so they assumed various lower gods to which they ascribed those particular effects. And since everything in the world carries with it something which can be put under the rubric either of good or of evil, they assumed a *duality* of God, a *principium bonum et malum.*[o] And that was *manichaeism.*[29] But this doctrine does not seem so wholly nonsensical and absurd if we consider that the manichaeans also posited a supreme principle[p] beyond this duality from which it arose. For if they had made each of the two principles[q] into a *realissimum,* then it would have been a contradic-

[o] principle of good and of evil
[p] *Prinzip*
[q] *Principia*

tion that an *ens realissimum* should be a *principium malum.*[r] Yet they did not think of either principle[s] as a *realissimum,* but gave some realities to one and other realities to the other; consequently, negations could be thought in both. But above these *principia partim reales, partim negatives*[t] they thought of an original source of everything, an *ens realissimum.* From this one can see[u] that polytheism did not cancel monotheism, but both could be combined without contradiction, since different concepts were bound up with the word "God." 28:1041

Now we proceed to another ontological predicate of an *ens realissimum,* which is also one of its *perfectiones quiescentes,* namely that it is *extramundanum.*[30] To this belongs:

1. That God is an *ens a mundo diversum,* or that God is external to the world in an intellectual way, This proposition is opposed to Spinozism, for Spinoza believed that God and the world were one substance and that apart from the world there is no substance anywhere. This error flowed from his faulty definition of substance. As a mathematician he was accustomed to finding arbitrary definitions and deriving propositions from them. Now that works fine in mathematics, but as soon as one tries to apply this method to philosophy, one falls into errors.[31] For in philosophy we must first seek out the marks themselves and acquaint ourselves with them before we can construct their definitions. But Spinoza did not do this; instead he constructed an arbitrary definition of substance. *Substantia,* he said, *est cujus existentia non indiget existentia alterius.*[32] Assuming this definition he correctly inferred that there is only one substance, God. Everything in the world is an *accidens* inhering in this divinity, since each thing has need of God's existence for its own existence; consequently everything existing is in God and nothing can be thought as external to God. But that is as much as to say that *God and the world are one.* For the whole world is in God and nothing is outside him. Now this argument is just as mistaken in content as it is correct in form; for it is derived from a wholly false principle,[v] from a faulty definition of a substance. But we have already given another definition of substance, and its correctness is clear because it is not assumed arbitrarily, like Spinoza's, but is derived instead from the concept of a thing itself. This concept of a thing in general, however, teaches us everything real which *exists for itself, without being a determination of any other thing, is a substance;* consequently all things 28:1042

---

[r] principle of evil
[s] *Prinzipien*
[t] partly real and partly negative principles
[u] *einsehen*
[v] *Principe*

are substances. For my own self-consciousness testifies that I do not*" relate all my actions to God as the final subject which is not the predicate of any other thing, and thus the concept of a substance arises when I perceive in myself that I am not the predicate of any further thing. For example, when I think, I am conscious that my I, and not some other thing, thinks in me. Thus I infer that this thinking in me does not inhere in another thing external to me but in myself, and consequently also that I am a substance, i.e. that I exist for myself, without being the predicate of another thing. I myself am a thing and hence also a substance. But now if I am a substance, then I must be either God himself, or God is a substance distinct from me, and hence also distinct from the world. The first is absurd, because it contradicts the concept of an *ens realissimum;* consequently there must exist apart from me some other thing existing for itself which is not a predicate of any other existing thing, i.e. a substance subsisting for itself. Indeed, there can be outside me still other distinct substances, because infinitely many things outside me are possible. But every thing, just because it is a thing, is *eo ipso* not the predicate of another thing, but it exists for itself and is thus a substance. All these things, however, will be distinct from one another, because otherwise they would not be particular things. Thus an *ens realissimum,* which is already considered as a thing having the highest reality, must also exist for itself and not be a predicate of another thing, i.e. it must be a substance, which is distinct from all others. The world comprehends things within itself which are all substances, because otherwise they would have to cease being things if they were mere determinations of another thing; consequently the whole world will not be a determination of God, but the *ens realissimum* has to be distinct from it.

2. that God is an *ens extramundanum,* i.e. he does not belong to the world at all, but is entirely external to it. This is opposed to the stoic proposition that God is the *world soul.* If this were so, then the two, God and the world, would have to stand *in commercio,* that is, each would have to have influence on the other; God would have to be not *only active,* but also *passive.* But this reciprocal effect would contradict God and the concept of him as an *ens realissimum* and *necessarium.* For an *ens absolute necessarium* is *independens,* hence also *impassibile* (not passive). If the world is to have influence on God so as to affect him, then *eo ipso* he would have to be dependent on the

28:1043

---

*" Pölitz's text reads: *Denn das Bewusstsein meiner selbst zeugt, dass ich alle Handlungen auf Gott, als auf das letzte Subject . . . beziehe . . .* But Kant's sense would seem to be the negation of this; so I assume that a *nicht* has been omitted from the sentence.

world. The human being, of course, can intuit an object only insofar as he has the receptivity enabling him to be affected by it; yet such an intuition cannot be predicated of God, because a limitation is comprehended in it. –

Thus God is isolated; i.e. not as if he stands in no connection with the world at all, but rather only this much: he does not stand in *the connection of a reciprocal effect* (of a *commercium*). Thus God has an influence on he world, he is active; but the world has no influence on him, that is, he is not passive. We have already dealt with God's *infinity* in the metaphysical sense, and it was shown above that instead of this one could better say that God has *all-sufficiency;* for the latter is a concept of the pure understanding, while the former is borrowed from mathematics and even belongs only to it. –

Of the eternity of God.[33] The magnitude of existence is duration; thus we can combine with existence the concept of magnitude, and this only by means of time. Hence this is the measure of duration. – *Duration without beginning and end is – eternity.* – But what is beginning? – What is end? – Beginning is an existence. Good. But what does this mean if not that *before* the beginning of a thing there was a time when it was not, or that *after* its end there will be a time when it is no more? Here, therefore, I still have a concept of time, and we cannot find a concept of eternity which would not still be affected with the concept of time; for beginning and end are possible only in time. The divine existence, however, can never be thought of as determinable through time; for then we would have to represent God as a *phaenomenon.* But this would be an anthropomorphic predicate, unthinkable in an *ens realissimum* because it contains limitations in it. For the existence of a thing in time is always a succession of parts in time, one after the other. Duration in time is, so to speak, a continuous disappearing and a continuous beginning. We can never live through[x] a certain year without already having lived through a previous one. But none of this can be said of God, since he is unalterable. Hence since it is a continuous limitation, time must be opposed in quality to an *ens realissimum.* But if I represent eternity as a duration without beginning or end, which is just about the most minimal definition of eternity I can give, then the concept of time is still mixed with it. For duration, beginning and end are all predicates which can be thought only of things in time. Of course it is true that I am negating beginning and end in relation to God; but I do not gain much by this, since my concept of eternity is not the least enlightened or purified through such negations. Fundamentally I am still representing

28:1044

_____

[x] *erleben*

God as a being within time, even if I do remove beginning and end from him. But it is most necessary to leave all the conditions of time out of the concept of God, because otherwise we could be misled and accept a number of anthropomorphic consequences. For example, if I think of God as existing within time but having no beginning or end, it is impossible for me to think how God could have created the world without suffering any alteration, or what he had been doing before the world was. But if I reject all the conditions of time, then this *before* and *after* are concepts which cannot be thought in God at all, hence even if I must be content to have very little comprehension of God's eternity, my concept will still be pure and free from errors, even though it is deficient. – Some have tried to prevent the difficulties which arise from representing God's existence as within time by insisting that all the consecutiveness of time be thought as simultaneous in God; yet this is a pretension which requires us to think a contradiction: *Consecutive* states of a thing, which are nevertheless *simultaneous*. What is this, if not a *contradictio in adjecto?* For what does *simultaneously* mean, if not at *one* time? And to think of parts of time which follow one upon the other as at one time – this is contradictory. From all this we can see that if eternity is to be represented as a particular attribute of God, it is still impossible to think of it apart from time, because time itself is a condition of all our representation, a form of sensibility. If we nevertheless want to exclude time from the concept of God, then nothing remains of eternity except a representation of the necessity of his existence. But we must make do with this because, on account of the weakness of our reason, it would be impertinent for us to want to lift the curtain which veils in holy darkness him who is invariably and forever. – And so *to be eternal* means (if we want to eliminate every sensible representation of time from the concept of God, as we must because such representations can easily corrupt a concept which is supposed to be free from all limitation), *to be eternal* means only as much as to be *absolutely necessary*. Now although we have seen that we are unable even to think this absolute necessity conceptually, it is nevertheless a concept which reason necessitates us to assume before it can find rest. Eternity has a great similarity to *omnipresence.* For just as eternity fills all of time, according to our sensible representations, so too is God's presence, according to our sensible representation, a filling up of *space.* Spatial presence or the presence of God in space, is subject to just the same difficulties as his eternity when it is conjoined with time; for it is a contradiction that a thing should be in more than one place in space at the same time.

Under the *omnipotence* of God one usually understands the capacity *to make all possible things actual.*[34] But it would be most presumptuous to test the power of God on things which are in themselves contradictory. e.g. a circle with four corners, and conclude that God obviously cannot do them; but it is foolish frivolity to think a being with supreme dignity and

28:1045

majesty in relation*y* to *non entia.*^z In general it is very improper when human reason presumes to dispute stubbornly about God, the most sublime thing, which it can think only feebly, and wants to represent everything of him, even the impossible; for whenever reason wants to venture into thoughts of this magnitude, it ought first to make a modest retreat and, fully conscious of its own incapacity, to take counsel with itself how it might worthily think of Him – of God. Hence all such expressions are presumptuous, even if they are posited only as hypotheses; if one, for instance, undertakes to portray God as a tyrant who makes the punishments of hell eternal, or according to the doctrine of predestination, who unconditionally determines some human beings to blessedness and others   28:1046
to damnation!

Anthropomorphism is usually divided into the *vulgar* kind, when God is thought of in human shape, and the *subtle* kind, where human perfections are ascribed to God but without separating the limitations from them.[35] The latter kind of anthropomorphism is a particularly dangerous enemy of our pure cognition of God; for the former is too obvious an error for human beings to be fooled by it very often. But we have all the more to turn our power against *anthropomorphismus subtilis*, since it is all the easier for it to creep into our concept of God and corrupt it. For it is better not to be able to represent something at all than only to be able to think of it confused with errors. – This is the reason that the transcendental theology we have been treating is of such great utility: it puts us in a position to remove from our cognition of God everything sensible inhering in our concepts, or at least by its means we become conscious that if we predicate something of God which cannot be thought apart from the conditions of sensibility, then we must give a proper definition of these predicates, even if we are not always in a position to represent them in a manner wholly free from faults. It would be easiest to deal successfully with all the consequences of anthropomorphism if only our reason voluntarily relinquished its claim to have cognition of the nature of God and his attributes, as to how they themselves are constituted internally, and if, mindful of its weakness, it never tried to exceed its bounds but were content to cognize only so much about him, who must always remain the object of an eternal quest, as it has need of. This interest of humanity is best furthered and attained *per viam analogiam*, as we will see below. – With this we conclude ontotheology,^a in which we have considered *God as the original being.* At times we have inferred this originality from the concept of the *ens realissimum*, and sometimes we have inferred conversely from the concept

---

y im Verhältnisse
^z nonbeings, i.e. contradictory beings.
^a The text reads *Ontologie*, but this seems to be a mistake, since the title of the section being concluded is *Ontotheologie*.

of the *ens originarium* to its highest reality, etc. Our effort and caution in the cognition of this speculative part of theology have been rewarded in that we may henceforth accept God as an *ens realissimum* and all the predicates flowing from this concept at least *as an undoubted hypothesis* for our speculative reason, and we can be sure that no rational human being will ever prove the opposite, or be able to tear down this support of ours for all human reason. Is this not better than boasting that we can cognize God and his attributes with apodictic certainty through pure reason, and yet having to fear each attack of our opponents? For what reason has taught us about God is faultless and free from error. We may without hesitation found our further investigation on this modest but correct cognition, and we may build on it with trust. It is true that all we have cognized of God in transcendental theology is the mere concept of a highest original ground; but as useless as this concept might be for itself and without any additional cognition, it is nonetheless just this splendid when it is applied as the substratum of all theology.

28:1047

Second section:
Cosmotheology

In our treatment of the ontological proof for the existence of God we have already taken the opportunity to deal with the cosmological proof; but we did this only in order to compare both proofs of transcendental theology, and to show the close kinship between them. Now we will set forth a more detailed account of the whole concept of God insofar as it can be derived from a foundation in experience, yet without determining more closely the world to which this experience belongs. Cosmotheology teaches us a theistic concept of God, since in this concept we come to cognize God as supreme intelligence, as highest being who is author of all things through understanding and freedom. The deist understands by the concept of God only a blindly working eternal nature as the root of things, an original being or a highest cause of the world; but he does not venture to assert that God is the ground of all things through freedom. Since we are interested only in the concept of an author of the world, that is, the concept of a living God, let us see whether reason can provide us with this theistic concept of God as a *summa intelligentia*.[b] This cognition will not be entirely pure and independent of experience; but the experience which has to be its foundation is the simplest experience there could be, namely the knowledge[c] of our self. Hence we now proceed to the psychological

28:1048

[b] highest intelligence
[c] *Erkenntniss*

386

predicates borrowed from the nature of our own soul, and we ascribe them to God after separating all the limitations from them. Yet if in the case of ontological predicates derived *a priori* much caution was necessary to avoid mixing in external sensible representations, think how much more care will be necessary now, when we are founding everything only on empirical principles,[d] or at least when it is from objects of sense, such as we ourselves are, that we must abstract the determinations from which we are to form the concept of a highest intelligence. Now we will have to apply all our attention if the reality is not to escape from us along with the limitations, and if, instead of making our concept of God more perfect, we are not to make it impure by bringing negations into it. If we meet with any reality in ourselves which we are able to ascribe to a being which has all reality, then we must be very careful to avoid predicating of God the negative element inhering in that reality in us. This separation of everything limited from the real is often very difficult for us, and nothing of the whole reality may be left over. In this case, where nothing remains after the careful testing of the reality and the removal of every limit, it is self-evident that we cannot think of such a thing in God. But if the reality which is brought out *via negationis* from some perfection in us is even ever so small, we yet should not omit it from God as long as it contains a true reality; instead, we must predicate it of God *per viam eminentiae*. Here the way of analogy is especially appropriate; for it teaches us the perfect similarity between the relation[e] of things in the world, where one is regarded as ground and the other as consequence, and between God and the world which has its being from him. First we find in our soul the faculty of cognition. That this is a reality no one can doubt. Every human being holds it to be a great perfection in which he shares in some part. Hence we must also introduce it into our concept of an *ens realissimum*, after all the limitations inhering in it have been carefully separated out. From this it follows that no contradiction will arise from the addition of this reality to our concept of a most perfect being, since one reality does not remove the other in the concept. But if we unite a faculty of cognition with other perfections in our concept of God, it still does not follow that this reality belongs to the thing itself in the synthesis of all other predicates; for as was shown above for this we would have to be able to cognize all the predicates of the thing and all their effects, as they relate[f] to one another in the actual composition, which is not possible for the human understanding regarding an all-perfect being. Thus we cannot prove with apodictic certainty that the reality of a faculty of cognition does not remove any of the other realities

28:1049

---

[d] *Principien*
[e] *Verhältnisses*
[f] *sich verhalten*

when put together with them; but neither can any human being ever prove the contrary, that in fact some reality in the thing itself, if it were put in composition with a faculty of cognition, would be *removed* or limited in its effects. For both surpass the faculty of human reason. In such cases, where it is equally impossible to prove either side apodictically, we are free to choose the alternative which has the most probability for us; and no one can deny that the concept of an *ens realissimum* itself gives us a much greater right to ascribe a faculty of cognition to it than to exclude such a faculty from the total reality. For here we already have one undoubted reason on our side in the fact that nothing contradictory shows itself in our concept, and while it does not follow that the object[g] itself is possible in reality, still we cannot see any reason why this reality should not belong to the synthesis of attributes of a most perfect being, even if we cannot prove it with apodictic certainty from our concept of an *ens realissimum*. The deist has nothing on his side when he denies it, because such a denial would require an insight into the nature of an *ens realissimum* which would surpass all human reason.

28:1050 We have, however, a much stricter ground of proof that God has a faculty of cognition, namely a ground derived from the *constitution* of an *ens realissimum;* and the grounds of proof derived from that always have more strength than proofs taken merely from the concept of an *ens realissimum*. We infer, namely, that an *ens originarium* that contains within itself the ground of the possibility of all things must have a faculty of cognition because it is the original source of beings which do have this faculty, e.g. human beings. For how could something be derived from a being unless this original being had it? Thus the original being of all beings must have a faculty of cognition. Of course the deist may reply that there could be another kind of reality in the original source of things which might give rise to a faculty of cognition inhering in human beings. This faculty of cognition would not itself, therefore, be the original reality, but only a consequence of some reality, unknown to us, in the original being. Thus the Tibetans, for example, represent God as the highest source from which all other beings emanate, and to which they will again return, without this original being having the same perfections that pertain to the things derived from it. But where will the deist find a reason for asserting such a thing? It is true that we can never refute him with apodictic certainty, but neither will he ever be in a position to prove his position. Rather, we will always have a greater right to assume a faculty of cognition as one of the realities in the original being. – Yet not, to be sure, a faculty like the one encountered in human beings; but rather a faculty of an entirely different kind. We cannot in the least think how a reality could be in an effect without already being in its cause – how beings with under-

[g] *Objekt*

standing could be derived from an original source which is dead and without a faculty of cognition. We do not have the least concept of the way in which one reality could produce other realities without having any similarity to them. From what could the human faculty of cognition be derived if not from such a faculty in the original being? – Thus we see that speculative reason not only presents no obstacle to our assuming a faculty of cognition in a highest being, but it even urges us to assume it, since otherwise we would have to search for another reality in this being as the cause of our power of cognition. Yet that would be a reality of which we could make no concept at all, indeed which must not only remain completely unknown to us, but also be thought up without any ground at all.   28:1051

Why, then, would we take refuge in such an unknown, incomprehensible reality in God when we can much more easily explain our faculty of cognition by deriving it from the supreme intelligence of the highest original being? Hence God has a faculty of cognition; but all the limitations found in our faculty of cognition must be carefully separated out if we are to think of such a faculty in the highest being. Hence the faculty of cognition in God will be:

First: not sensible, but pure understanding. We therefore have to exclude sensibility from an *ens originarium,* because as an *ens independens* it cannot be affected by any object.[h] But sensible cognition is obtained from objects which have some influence on us. But in the case of God, there can be no influence of any object[i] on him and therefore no sensible cognition; in an original being all cognition must necessarily flow from a pure understanding not affected by any representations of sense. Hence it is not because sensible representations are obscure, as is commonly said, that they cannot be ascribed to God; for we often find that a representation of sense is much more distinct than certain cognitions gained through the understanding; but rather, everything sensible must be removed from God because, as we have shown above, it is impossible for objects to influence an independent being.

Second: The understanding of God is intuitive. It is a limitation of our understanding that we can infer the particular only from the universal, and this limitation cannot in any way be ascribed to a most real being. This being must rather intuit all things immediately through its understanding, and cognize everything at once. To be sure, we are unable to form any concept of such an intuitive understanding, because *we* can intuit only through the senses. But it follows from God's supreme reality and originality that such an understanding must be present in him.

[h] *Objekt*
[i] *Objekt*

Third: God cognizes everything a priori. We can cognize only a few things
28:1052 without previous sensible intuitions; indeed it is impossible in the case of
any thing of which we are not ourselves the author. For example, we can
represent a garden we have planned a priori in our thought before it
actually exists; but this is not possible for things which lie outside our
sphere of operation. – The original being is the ground of everything
possible. Everything existing is dependent on it and derives from it.
Hence it must cognize every possibility *a priori* even before it exists. –
God cognizes all things by cognizing himself as the ground of all possibility; this is what has been called *theologia archetypa* or *exemplaris,* as we have
mentioned previously.[36] Thus God has no empirical cognition because
this would contradict independent, original being. – We human beings
cognize very little *a priori* and have our senses to thank for nearly all our
cognition. Through experience we cognize only appearances, the *mundum
phaenomenon* or *sensibilem,*[j] but not the *mundum noumenon* or *intelligibilem,*[k]
not things as they are *in themselves.* This is shown in detail in the theory of
being (ontology). God cognizes all things as they are *in themselves* immediately and *a priori* through an intuition of the understanding; for he is the
being of all beings and every possibility has its ground in him. If we were
to flatter ourselves that we cognize the *mundum noumenon,* then we would
have to be in community with God so as to participate immediately in the
divine ideas which are the authors of all things in themselves. *To expect this
in the present life is the business of mystics and theosophists.* Thus arises the
mystical self-annihilation of China, Tibet and India, in which one deludes
oneself that one is finally dissolved into the Godhead.[37] Fundamentally
one might *just as well call Spinozism a great enthusiasm as a form of atheism.*
For Spinoza affirms two predicates of God: *extension* and *thinking.* Every
soul, he says, is only a modification of God's thinking, and every body is a
modification of his extension. Thus Spinoza assumed that everything that
exists is to be found in God. But he thereby fell into crude contradictions.
For if only a single substance exists, then either I must be this substance,
and consequently I must be God – but this contradicts my dependency –
or else I am an accident – but this contradicts my concept of my I, in
28:1053 which I think myself as the ultimate subject which is not the predicate of
any other thing. Attention, abstraction, reflection and comparison are only
aids to a discursive understanding; hence they cannot be thought in God;
God has no *conceptus* but pure *intuitus,* through which his understanding
immediately cognizes every object as it is in itself, whereas every concept
is something mediate, in that it originates from universal marks. But an
understanding which cognizes everything immediately, an intuitive understanding, has no need of reason; for reason is only a mark of the limits of

[j] phenomenal or sensible world
[k] noumenal or intelligible world

an understanding and provides it with concepts. But an understanding which receives concepts through itself has no need of reason. Thus the expression "reason" is beneath the dignity of the divine nature. One should leave this concept entirely out of the most real being, and it would be better to ascribe to it only an intuitive understanding as the highest perfection of cognition. Of such an immediate intuition of the understanding *we* have *now* no concept at all; but whether the *separated* soul, as an intelligence, could perhaps contain a similar intuition instead of sensibility, through which it might cognize things in themselves in their divine ideas – this can neither be denied nor proven.

The author[38] divides God's cognition into: (1) *scientia simplicis intelligentiae,*[l] (2) *scientia libera,*[m] and (3) *scientia media.*[n] As for the expression "science"[o] (*scientia*), it is improper as applied to God. For in God we should make no distinction between *knowledge, belief* and *opinion,*[p] because all his cognition is intuitive and thus excludes opinion. Thus it is not necessary to apply the anthropomorphic term "scientific knowledge" to God's cognition. It is better to call it simply "cognition." And [Baumgarten's] division itself will hardly hold water if we try to think of it in relation to God. For the term *scientia simplicis intelligentiae* is understood by the author to mean the cognition of everything possible, while *scientia libera* means the knowledge of everything actual. Yet in regard to God there is no distinction between the possible and the actual; for a complete cognition of the possible is simultaneously a cognition of the actual. The actual is already included within the possible, since what is actual must also be possible, for otherwise it could not be actual. – Thus if God is thinking of everything possible, he is already thinking of everything actual. The distinction between *scientia simplicis intelligentiae* and *scientia libera* is to be found only *in our* human representation of God's cognition, and not in this cognition itself. We represent to ourselves, namely, that in cognizing his own essence (*simplex intelligentia*) God must also cognize everything possible, since he is the ground of all possibilities. Thus we derive the cognition of all possibilities from his nature and call it *cognitio simplicis intelligentiae.* – We think of *scientia libera* as God's cognition of the actual, insofar as he is simultaneously conscious of his free choice of things; for either all things are actual *by the necessity of God's nature* – which would be the principle[q] of *emanation;* or else they exist *through his will* – which would be the system of *creation.* We think of a *scientia libera* in God to the

28:1054

[l] knowledge of simple intellect
[m] free knowledge
[n] middle knowledge
[o] *Wissenschaft*
[p] *Wissen, Glauben und Meinen;* cf. *Critique of Pure Reason* A820/B848.
[q] *Princip*

extent that in his cognition of everything possible, God is at the same time conscious in his free will of those possible things which he has made actual; hence this representation is grounded on the system of creation, according to which God is the author of all things through his will. But so too according to the principle[r] of emanation. For since everything that exists is actual through the necessity of the divine nature, God must be conscious of all things – not, however, as he is conscious of his choice of things, but rather as he is conscious of them insofar as he is conscious of his own nature as a cause of all things. All God's cognition is grounded on his being an *ens entium*, an independent original being. For if God were not the cause of things, then either he would not cognize them at all, because there would be nothing in his nature which could supply him with knowledge of things external to him, or else things would have to have some influence on him in order to give him a mark of their existence. But then God would have to have sensible cognition of things, consequently he would have to be *passibilis*,[s] which contradicts his independence as an *ens originarium*. If, therefore, God is able to cognize things apart from sensibility, he cannot cognize them except by being conscious of himself as the cause of everything. And consequently the divine cognition of all things is nothing but the cognition God has of himself as an effective power. – The author further divides *scientia libera* into *recordatio*,[t] *scientia visionis*[u] and *praescientia*.[v] Yet this division is again expressed according to human representations and cannot be thought in

28:1055 the divine cognition itself. For him, the unalterable, nothing is past or future, since he is not in time at all. He cognizes everything simultaneously, whether it is present to our representation or not. If God cognizes everything, he also cognizes our free actions, even those we will perform only at a future time. But the freedom of our actions is not removed or limited by the fact that God foresees them; for he foresees simultaneously the whole nexus in which our actions are comprehended, the motives for which we do them and the aims we strive to attain by means of them. Now in foreseeing all this, God does not at all determine that it has to happen as it does. Through his prevision, he does not at all make our future actions necessary, as some have falsely believed; but he only sees that these or those actions will happen. Besides, the concept of prevision is anthropomorphic, and cannot be thought in God himself. Rather there is not the least further difficulty in representing how God cognizes the future free actions of a human being. Insight into the one is just necessary for our reason as insight into the other.

[r] *Princip*
[s] capable of being passive
[t] memory
[u] science of vision
[v] foreknowledge

The so-called *scientia media,* or the cognition of that which could happen in other possible worlds outside the present actual one, is an entirely useless distinction. For if God cognizes everything possible, then he cognizes it as much in itself as *in nexu,*[*m*] and consequently in just this way he cognizes every possible world as a whole. – A cognition is *free* if the object[*x*] itself depends on this cognition. Hence our cognition is not free, because the objects[*y*] themselves are *given* and our cognition of the objects depends on this. The freedom of God's cognition presupposes that God is the cause of the world *through freedom,* or the author of the world.

All errors presuppose illusion and deception.[*z*] They are not a mere lack of cognition, for that would be ignorance; but they are a consequence of some positive obstacles to truth. Now God cognizes nothing *a posteriori;* no object[*a*] can have any influence on him, because he is independent, the original being, and consequently *impassibilis.* But just because no object can influence God, no object[*b*] can mislead[*c*] him. God is therefore *infallibilis.* Proofs such as this one, which are derived from certain predicates belonging to God, are always better than proofs derived merely from the concept of an *ens realissimum.*[39] For in the latter case it is often difficult to decide whether something is in fact a pure reality. 28:1056

The author calls the *scientia visionis* or *scientia libera* an *analogon modi,*[40] as if the cognition of an actual thing contained more than the cognition of something possible. But the difference between something's being first possible and then becoming actual is only a distinction with respect to temporal relationships and does not pertain to God at all. – Now the author goes on to another property of God, the divine *wisdom.* But this is premature, because wisdom presupposes a faculty of desire, and this faculty has not yet been proven in God.[41] For as a *summa intelligentia*[*d*] God has *three* predicates which we have ascribed to him from psychology, namely *cognition, pleasure* and *displeasure,* and a *faculty of desire.* For the sake of economy we should therefore spare ourselves this treatment of God's wisdom; but since we don't want to leave the author's order behind altogether, we will now deal with it provisionally. – A being which has cognition must have the following two properties of its cognition:

1. *Theoretical perfection of its cognition.* This would belong to it insofar as the cognition is common cognition or science. But neither of these

---

[*m*] in connection [with other things]
[*x*] *Objekt*
[*y*] *Objekte*
[*z*] *Schien und Verleitung*
[*a*] *Objekt*
[*b*] *Objekt*
[*c*] *hintergehen*
[*d*] highest intelligence

is suitable for God, but apply only to human beings. For common cognition is an aggregate, while science on the contrary is a system of cognitions. Both comprise a collection*e* of cognitions in themselves, only with the difference that in the former cognition is just accumulated without being ordered by any principle,*f* whereas in the latter it is bound up in common as a unity. – The theoretical perfection of the cognition of God is called *omniscience*.

2. *Practical perfection* of cognition. To this belongs:

a) *Skill*, i.e. perfection in the cognition of choosing the means to arbitrary ends, which are still problematic.

b) *Prudence*. This is the cognition of the means to given ends, insofar as the means to them are not completely in my power. These means are rational beings. Hence prudence is nothing but a skill in making use of freely acting beings for given ends.

c) *Wisdom*, i.e. perfection of cognition in the derivation of every end from the system of all ends. On the unity of ends rests contentment. It is easy to see that the first two kinds of perfection (skill and prudence) cannot be predicated of God, because they involve too much which is similar to the human and moreover whatever is real in them is already contained in omniscience. How, for example, is prudence to be ascribed to God? For he has the full perfection of power, and consequently no end can ever be given whose means are not fully in his power. It is beneath the dignity of the divine nature to think of God as skillful or prudent; wisdom, on the contrary, when properly understood, can apply only to a being of the highest perfection. For who else cognizes the system of all ends, and who else is in a position to derive every end from it? If we predicate wisdom of human beings, then this can mean no more than the positing of all one's ends in harmony with morality. For morals has as its object precisely to consider how each end can stand together with the idea of a whole of all ends, and it estimates all action as common rules. – Insofar as our cognition of human actions is derived from the principle*g* of a possible system of all ends, it can be called human wisdom. Hence we are even able to give an example *in concreto* of a highest understanding which infers from the whole to the particular, namely our conduct in morals, because here we determine the worth of each end by means of an idea of a whole of all ends. In the idea of happiness, on the contrary, we have no concept of the whole, but rather we *only compose it out of parts. And just for this reason we cannot direct our actions according*

28:1057

e Menge
f Princip
g Princip

to an idea of happiness, because such a whole cannot be thought by us. –   28:1058
But the human being does have an idea of a whole composed of *all*
ends, even though he never fully attains to this idea and thus is not
himself wise. Accordingly, the divine wisdom is distinguished from
human wisdom not only in quantity but also in quality, just as God's
absolute necessity is distinguished from the existence of all other
things. – God's wisdom consists also in the agreement of divine
choice with itself. A plan involving *selection,*[h] which in its execution
would produce collisions and thus require exceptions, cannot be
the most perfect plan. Hence God's plan for the arrangement of
nature has to be conjoined with the divine will as a whole. And this
complete unity in the choice of means to his ends is a property of
God's wisdom. But we must postpone further discussion of this
until after our treatment of the divine will, where it really belongs.

The author also speaks of the divine *omniscience,* and treats it as a
property distinct from divine cognition.[42] But we cannot take special note
of God's knowledge, so as to distinguish it from belief, opinion and
conjecture. For the latter do not apply to God at all, since he cognizes
everything; his cognition is knowledge just because of this; for this knowledge flows from an all-sufficiency of cognition. Since we do not always
cognize things completely, our cognition is often not a knowing but a
believing; God's complete cognition of everything, on the contrary, is
precisely his omniscience.

To conclude [Baumgarten's] treatment of divine cognition, we add one
more remark concerning the Platonic idea. The term *idea* properly signifies
simulacrum, and therefore in human philosophy it signifies a concept of
reason insofar as no possible experience can ever be adequate to it. Plato
thought of the divine ideas as the archetypes of things, according to which
these things are established, although, to be sure, they are never posited as
adequate to the divine idea. For example, God's idea of the human being, as
archetype, would be the most perfect idea of the most perfect human being.
Particular individuals, as particular human beings, would be formed in
accord with this idea, but never in such a way that they completely corre-   28:1059
sponded to it. – In consequence, Plato was blamed for treating these ideas
in God as pure substances. And in the second century there finally emerged
a so-called "eclectic" school which dreamed of *the possibility of participating
in the divine ideas.*[43] *The whole of mystic theosophy based itself on this,* so it was
fundamentally nothing but a corrupt Platonic philosophy.

We have now dealt with the first of God's predicates drawn from
psychology, the faculty of cognition or understanding; the author now
proceeds to discuss the *will* of God,[44] which is a practical perfection, just

[h] *Auswahl*

as the understanding is a theoretical perfection. Here many difficulties show themselves right away at the beginning, as soon as we ask: Does God have a faculty of desire? And how is it constituted? All desires are either immanent or transient, i.e. either they relate to the very thing which has them and remain in this thing or else they relate to something which is external to the thing. But neither can be thought in a being of all beings. First, an all-sufficient being cannot have immanent desires, simply because it is all-sufficient. For every desire is directed only to something possible and future. But since God has all perfections actually, there is nothing left over for him to desire as a future possibility. But neither can God be represented as desiring something external to him; for then he would need the existence of other things in order to fulfill the consciousness of his own existence. But that is contrary to the concept of an *ens realissimum*. Thus the big question is: How can we think of a most perfect being as having desires? To answer this question, let us undertake the following investigations. The powers of our mind are (1) *cognition;* (2) the feeling of pleasure and displeasure, or better, since the word *feeling* appears to connote something sensible, the faculty of *being well-pleased and displeased;*[i] and (3) the *faculty of desire.*

There are only a few beings which have a faculty of representation. If a being's representations can become the cause of the objects of representation (or of their actuality), then the being is called a *living* being. Hence a faculty of desire is the causality of the faculty of representation with 28:1060 respect to the actuality of its objects. The will is the faculty of ends. – Well-pleasedness cannot consist in the consciousness of perfection, as our author defines it,[45] because perfection is the harmony of a manifold in a unity. But here I do not want to know *in what* I take pleasure, but rather *what* pleasure itself is. Now pleasure itself does not consist in the relation of my representations to their object;[j] it consists rather in the relation of my representations to the subject, insofar as these representations determine the subject to actualize the object. Insofar as it first determines the subject to the desire, it is called *faculty of desire;* but insofar as it first determines the subject to desire, it is called *pleasure.* Thus one obviously sees that pleasure precedes desire. Well-pleasedness with one's own existence, when this existence is dependent, is called *happiness. Thus happiness is contentment with my own dependent existence.* But a complete well-pleasedness with one's independent existence is called *acquiescentia in*

---

[i] Pleasure and displeasure = *Lust und Unlust;* well-pleased and displeased = *Wohlgefallen und Missfallen.* The former pair translate Baumgarten's *voluptas et taedium,* and imply sensible feelins; the latter pair translate Baumgarten's *complacientia et displacientia* and do not imply sensation. *Wohlgefallen* also has Biblical connotations: e.g. "Thou art my beloved son, in whom I am well-pleased" (Luke 3:22).
[j] *Objekte*

semetipso[46] or self-sufficiency (*beatitudo*). This blessedness of a being consists therefore in a *well-pleasedness* with one's own existence *apart from any
need*, and thus it belongs solely to God alone; for he alone is independent.
Hence if the will of God has to be represented as the will of a self-
sufficient being, then it follows that before treating of the divine will, it
will be necessary first to discuss the faculty of the object of well-
pleasedness and displeasedness, and then also the self-sufficiency of God.
This attempt is new; but it is founded on the natural sequence of ideas,
according to which something must be discussed first if the matter at hand
cannot be cognized clearly without it. Thus in order to answer the main
question as to the manner in which a faculty of desire could be found in a
most real being and how this faculty of desire would have to be constituted, we must first deal with God's faculty of pleasure and displeasure,
and with his blessedness. – If there is to be a conjunction of the divine
understanding with volition, then it must be shown how a self-sufficient
being could be the cause of something external to itself. For God's will is
derived from the fact that he is supposed to be the creator of the world. –
We see very well that things in the world can be the cause of something
else; this quality, however, does not relate to the things themselves, but
only to their determinations; not to their substance but only to their form.   28:1061
It follows that the casuality by which God is supposed to be the author of
the world must be of a wholly different kind. For it is impossible to think
God's causality, his faculty of actualizing things external to himself, otherwise than as in his understanding; or in other words, a being which is self-
sufficient can become the cause of things external to itself only by means
of its understanding; and it is just this causality of God's understanding,
his actualization of the objects of his representation, which we call "will."
The causality of the highest being as regards the world, or the will
through which he makes it, rests on his highest understanding, and cannot
rest on anything else. We can think of the opposite of an understanding, of
a blindly working eternal root of all things, a *natura bruta*. But how can the
divine will lie in this causality? Without understanding it would have no
faculty at all for relating itself, its own subject, to something else, or for
representing something external to itself; and yet it is only under this
condition that anything can be the cause of other things external to itself.
From this it follows that an all-sufficient being can produce things external to itself only through will and not through the necessity of its nature.
The self-sufficiency of God, connected to his understanding, is *all-
sufficiency*. For in cognizing himself, he cognizes everything possible which
is contained in him as its ground. The well-pleasedness of a being with
itself as a possible ground for the production of things is what determines
its causality. – The same thing can be expressed in other words by saying
that the cause of God's will consists in the fact that despite his highest
self-contentment, things external to him shall exist insofar as he is con-

scious of himself as an all-sufficient being. God cognizes himself by means of his highest understanding as the all-sufficient ground of everything possible. He is most well-pleased with his unlimited faculty as regards all possible things, and it is just this well-pleasedness with himself which causes him to make these possibilities actual. Hence it is just this which is God's desire to produce things external to himself. The product of such a will must be the greatest whole of everything possible, that is the *summum bonum finitum,* [k] the most perfect world. If we make such a repre-

28:1062   sentation of the divine will, one which is suitable to the highest being, then the usual objections to the possibility of volition in a highest being will collapse. For objections are directed only to an anthropomorphic conception of God's will. It is said, for example, that a being which desires something external to itself can be contented only if what it desires actually exists. Hence volition or the desire for something presupposes that the well-pleasedness or contentment of a being with such desires can be complete only through the existence of other things. And indeed it is true of every created being that the desire for something always presupposes a need, and it is because of this need that I desire it. But why is this? *Simply because no creature is self-sufficient,* and so each one always has need of many things. Just for this reason it always reaches a higher degree of self-contentment when what it desires is produced. But in a being which is independent and thus self-sufficient as well, the ground of its volition and desire that things external to itself should exist is just that it knows its own faculty of actualizing things external to itself. – Hence according to pure reason, we see that a faculty of desire and volition may be found in a self-sufficient being. In fact, it is impossible to think of a being which combines the highest self-contentment with a supreme understanding unless we also think in it a causality as regards the objects of its representations. Of course here we must stay away from an anthropomorphic concept of volition; for otherwise vain contradictions will result instead of agreement. – Now before we proceed to our proper treatment of the divine will, we must first consider an introduction to it borrowed from *physicotheology*.

Third section:
Physicotheology

28:1063   The question, namely, is: From the purposive order of nature can one infer an intelligent author of this order? In his *Dialogues,* Hume raises an objection to this inference which is by no means weak. He says that even assuming there is a supreme cause which has brought about all the order in nature through understanding and freedom, we still cannot compre-

[k] "the highest *finite* good." The phrase as a whole is italicized because it is in Latin, but Kant also stresses the word "finite."

hend how this supreme intelligence could have all the perfections necessary to produce such a harmony, or where all these excellences in such a
being might come from. We can no more comprehend this, he says, than
we can comprehend the origin of the perfections of the world apart from
the presupposition of an intelligent author.[47] We can feel the full force of
Hume's objection only after we have come to see that it is quite impossible
for us either to assert that a supreme original being is absolutely necessary
or to cognize whence God himself is. For *this* question is equally unanswerable: "Where do all the perfections of God come from?" – On the
other hand, however, we have already shown that we can have no insight
through our reason into the existence of a being whose nonexistence is
impossible, in a word, we have no insight into an existence which is
absolutely necessary, and yet our reason urges us on *to assume* to such a
being as a *hypothesis which is subjectively necessary for us,* because otherwise
we could provide no ground why anything in general is possible. But if it is
a true need of our speculative reason to assume a God, nevertheless from
the fact that human beings cannot prove this apodictically, nothing follows
except that *such a proof exceeds our faculty of reason.* But now as regards
Hume's objection, it is mistaken despite its apparent strength; for let us
now compare two hypotheses with each other. The first is this: A supremely perfect being is the author of the world through understanding.
The second is: A blindly working eternal nature is the cause of all the
purposiveness and order in the world. Now let us see whether we are able
to accept[l] this latter hypothesis. Can we think without contradiction that
the purposiveness, beauty and harmony of the world have arisen from a
natura bruta, even though these things obviously have to be predicates of
an understanding? How could nature, simply of itself, arrange the various
things in harmony with its determinate final aims, using so many united
means? Everywhere in the world we find a chain of effects and causes, of   28:1064
ends and means, of regularity in arising and perishing; how could this
whole, just of itself, come to be in its present state? Or how could merely a
blind, all-powerful nature be the cause of it? – Purposiveness in the effects always presupposes understanding in the cause. Or what cooperation
of blind accidents could produce a moth, with its purposive structure?
Hume says: A mere fecundity is certainly in a position to produce harmony in its effects.[48] We can see this right now in the way things come to
be in the world; we ourselves, as intelligent beings are generated by our
parents through the senses and not through understanding. Very well; but
what about the whole of things, the totality of the world? Is it therefore
generated by some fertile cause? What a sophistry! – Could a being have
understanding when, like the world, it is a composite of true substances? –
Is it possible for us to think an understanding distributed [among things]?

l annehmen

399

It is certainly more comprehensible to us if we assume that a highest understanding of the world, rather than to assume that a fertile cause without understanding generated all this from the necessity of its nature. The latter supposition cannot even be thought without contradiction; for assuming that we think of nature as such a blindly working original being, it would never have had the capacity to relate itself to subjects, to things outside it. How, then, could it have the causality or the capacity to actualize things outside it, and indeed things which are to agree with a plan? But if the things of the world are generated simply through fertility, then what is generated are only the *forms* of things. As regards their first origin, the things themselves which are already contained in the sense could have been produced only by some being with freedom and understanding. But if on the contrary we do assume a highest intelligence which has caused the whole of creation through its will, then it is not at all incomprehensible to me how a purposive order could be found in nature, since I derive it from a supreme understanding. And if we ask *how* this supreme being has sufficient perfections and *whence* it gets them, the answer can be only that they follow from its absolute necessity – into which, to be sure, on account of the limitations of my reason I really have no insight, but which for the same reason I also cannot deny. – After this preliminary introduction, we will now turn to our real treatment of the divine will, and in it we will follow the author in regard to the order of his §§.[49]

28:1065

The author first talks about the fact that God's faculty of desire cannot be sensible.[50] This follows because God, as an *ens originarium independens*, cannot be affected by objects. But we have already given a detailed treatment of this point, and also of the author's discussion of the *acquiescentia Dei in semetipso*.[51] But if we ask what the divine will is, we can answer: It is the divine understanding determining God's activity to the production of the objects he represents. In human beings, well-pleasedness is pleasure in an object. Thus, for example, I can be well-pleased with a house, even if I can see only the plans. But well-pleasedness in the *existence* of an object is called *interest*. I cannot predicate either one of God. He has no pleasure and no interest; for his is self-sufficient and has a complete self-contentment in his independent existence; he needs no thing external to him, and nothing outside him could increase his blessedness. Hence we can ascribe to God only an analogue of interest, that is, a similarity of relation. The relation of everything good in the world to the will of God is the same as the relation of a benevolent deed to the will of the being who does the deed for me, when this being from whom I receive the benevolence is happy and has no need of me; all good in the world is related in this way to the will of God, which beyond this is unknown to me. I know only this much: that his will is *pure goodness*,[m] and that is enough for me. –

---

[m] *Güte*

Thus the Stoics thought the ideal of the sage, as one who would feel no compassion for distress, but would feel no greater delight in anything than in remedying all distress. This ideal is not possible for human beings; for an incentive must be added to my cognition of the good before I can actually will to produce the good. This is becuase my activity is limited, and thus if I am to apply my powers to the production of some good I must first judge whether in this way I am not using up resources" which might have produced some other good. Therefore I need certain incentives to determine my powers to this or that good, since I do not have resources sufficient for the actual production of everything I cognize to be good. – Now these incentives consist in certain subjective relations which must determine my being well-pleased in choosing, subsequent to the determination of my *well-pleasedness* in judging or my cognition of the good. If this subjective relation were taken away, then my choice of the good would be removed. But with God it is entirely different. He has the greatest power combined with the highest understanding. Since his understanding cognizes his capacity to actualize the objects of his representation, he is *eo ipso* determined to activity and to the production of the good, and indeed to the production of the greatest possible sum of all good. For God the mere representation of a good is all that is required to actualize it. He does not need to be motivated, and in his case there are no particular incentives; indeed, no subjective relations are possible for him at all, because he is already all-sufficient in himself and has the highest blessedness. If, therefore, we talk about God's motives, nothing but the goodness of the object° can be understood by it, but no subjective relations, as if God were out for praise or glory. For this would not be suitable to the dignity of the most blessed being, but rather God knows through his understanding simultaneously both the possible good and his capacity to produce it. In this cognition lay simultaneously the ground why he actually produced it.

28:1066

The divine will is *free*. Freedom of the will is the capacity to determine oneself to actions independently of *causae subjectae*ᵖ or sensuous impulses, or the capacity to will *a priori*. But since with us inclinations are the subjective conditions of self-contentment, the concept of human freedom is subject to many psychological difficulties. For the human being is a part*q* of nature, and belongs to the sensible world, thus he is therefore also subject to the laws of appearances. All appearances are determined among themselves by certain laws, and it is just this determination of everything

---

" *Vermögen*

° *Objekte*

ᵖ "Subjective causes," i.e. causes in the subject. Kant's Latin phrase, *causis subjectis,* is in the ablative.

q *Glied*

given in nature by universal laws which constitutes the *mechanism* of nature. The human being, therefore, as a part^r of nature is subject to this natural mechanism, or at least to a psychological mechanism. But how, then, can his actions be thought of as indpendent of the natural occurrences? To be sure, the human being is conscious of himself as an intellectual object,^s but this consciousness too has its difficulties, with which

28:1067 psychology must deal. – But *here* these difficulties do not concern us; for they do not apply to God at all. God is wholly distinct from the world *and has no connection at all with space and time*, is therefore not subject to the laws of appearances and is not determined by anything whatever. Consequently it is self-evident that his will is not determined by other things as incentives. Just as little is it possible for God to have inclinations to change his state; for he is the self-sufficient one. Hence if we want to think of the concept of divine freedom purified of every limitation, then it consists in nothing but the complete independence of God's will both from external things and from inner conditions. But as little as we need to fear that this concept of freedom will be exposed to any psychological difficulties (since these apply only to human freedom), we yet cannot any the less avoid the contrary defect that this concept cannot be represented *in concreto*. For from where will we draw an example from which to put the concept distinctly before our eyes? Indeed, a freedom such as God has applies to no one; but it is the case in general that if we purify divine predicates of all negations, then we have no means of thinking them *in concreto*, since all sensible conditions have been taken away. Now just because this concept cannot be illustrated by an example, the suspicion might arise that the concept itself is obscure or even false; yet once a concept has been introduced *a priori* with apodictic certainty, then we need fear no error even if our incapacity or even all our reason forbids us to set up a case of it *in concreto*. For it can be proven that the divine will has to be entirely free, for otherwise God could not be an *ens originarium*, or in other words, could not be God. For as *prima causa mundi*^t his will must be independent of all things, because there is nothing which could serve as an incentive to determine him to anything. Just as little could any inclination toward something arise in him, since he possesses supreme self-contentment. To God pertains transcendental freedom, which consists in an absolute spontaneity, as well as practical freedom, or the independence of his will from any sensuous impulses. The latter cannot be proven at all in regard to the

28:1068 human being, indeed its possibility cannot be cognized, because we human beings belong to the world and are affected by things; but in God it can be thought without the least difficulty. It is just the same with practical

---

^r *Glied*
^s *Objekt*
^t first cause of the world

freedom which must be presupposed in human beings if the whole of morality is not to be abolished. The human being acts according to the idea of freedom, he acts *as if he were free, and eo ipso he is free.* This capacity to act according to reason must certainly be in God, since sensuous impulses are impossible in him. One might raise the objection that God cannot decide otherwise than he does, and so he does not act freely but from the necessity of his nature. The human being, however, can always decide something else, e.g. a human being, instead of being benevolent in this case, could also not be that. But it is precisely this which is a lack of freedom in the human being, since he does *not always* act according to his reason; but in God it is not due to the necessity of his nature that he can decide only as he does, but rather it is true freedom in God that he decides only what is in conformity with his highest understanding. – Fatalism predicates blind necessity of God, thus contradicts the concept of a highest intelligence.[52] This wrongheaded opinion does of course deserve to be called "fatalism," just as we give the name "chance" to a blind accident. Fatalism arises *when the blind necessity of nature is not distinguished from physical and practical necessity.* Of course the fatalist appeals to examples where God is supposed to have acted only according to a necessity of nature, e.g. that God created the world only so and so many years ago, but did nothing in a whole long eternity before that.[53] This, says the fatalist, can be explained only by saying that God *had to* create the world just at that time. But how anthropomorphic this representation is! No years can be thought in God, and no time. He is not in time at all; and to limit his efficacy to the conditions of time is to think contrary to the concept of God.

The author appeals to a distinction in the divine volition between *voluntas antecedens* and *voluntas consequens.*[54] The *voluntas antecedens*[u] refers to the object of my will according to universal concepts. For example, the king wills to make his subjects happy, because they are his subjects. The *voluntas consequens*[v] refers to the object of my will in its thoroughgoing determination. For example, the king wills to reward his subjects only insofar as they are worthy subjects. In both kinds of volition we must remove the human concept of time, according to which the will precedes what follows it, and applied to God in this way it is proper to the majesty of a highest being. This division in volition has a foundation in every rational being; only in God all succession must be left out. In the human being the *voluntas antecedens* is a provisional opinion of the will, but the *voluntas consequens* is the resolution. In God, however, the *voluntas antecedens* is always already in the *decreto,*[w] and refers only to what the object has in common with other things not willed by God.

28:1069

It is clear that everything which happens in the world conforms to a divine decree, because otherwise it would not exist. But now suppose we try to gain insight into the motives of the divine will; suppose we want to know what there was in the world that made God arrange it as he did, and to gain insight into the ends of God's will; then we will of course find that God's will is *inscrutable*.[55] We may indeed make use of the analogy with a perfect will and apply some of its aims to help us in particular cases; but these judgments can be only problematic and we must not flatter ourselves that they are apodictically certain. It would be presumption, and a violation of God's holy right, to want to determine precisely that this or that is and had to be God's end in the production of a certain thing. In a few cases the wise will of God and his intentions are obvious, e.g. the whole structure of the human eye shows itself to be a wise means to the end of seeing. But it is not possible for our reason to decide whether in a certain thing we are encountering an end in itself or only with a consequence of still higher ends, which constitute the connection of all ends. For the presupposition that everything in the world has its utility and its good intention, if it is supposed to be constitutive, would go much farther than our observations up to now can justify; yet as a regulative principle[x] it serves very well for the extension of our insight and can therefore always be useful to reason and yet never harm

28:1070 it. For if we approach the world assuming the wise intention of its author in a thousand ways, then we will make a host[y] of discoveries. In any case the only error which can result from this is that where we expected a teleological connection (a *nexus finalis*), we will encounter only a mechanical or physical one (a *nexus effectivus*); through which in such a case we merely miss one more unity, but do not spoil the unity of reason in its empirical use. In a *nexus effectivus* the end is always last and the means, on the contrary, is first; but in a *nexus finalis* the aim always precedes the use of the means. When a sick person, by means of medications, attains his end (health), this is an example of a *nexus effectivus; a nexus finalis,* on the contrary, is where the sick person first sets himself the aim of becoming healthy before he applies the means to it. – Of the will of God we always cognize only the conditioned aim, e.g. if human beings are to exist they must see and hence their eyes must be arranged thus and not otherwise; but never the final aim, e.g. why human beings exist at all. Of course we can be sure that human beings are ends, and not just the consequence of still higher ends; for the latter would be to downgrade rational beings; but this is the only case where we can be certain of such a thing. In the case of every other thing in the world, it is impossible to

[x] *Princip*
[y] *Menge*

cognize whether its existence is a final aim of God or only something necessary as a means to still higher ends. –

The recognition that from the primary constitution of nature we can infer a supreme principle*z* as a highest intelligence shows in general both the possibility and necessity of a physicotheology. Indeed, the proposition that everything good and purposive comes from God can itself be called a universal physicotheology. But if we find that a great deal of the order and perfection in nature has to be derived from the essence of things themselves according to universal laws, still in no way do we need to withdraw this order from God's supreme governance; but rather these universal laws themselves always presuppose a principle*a* connecting every possibility with every other. But to say that God's will is directed to ends is to ascribe a psychological predicate to it; and thus the nature of his will must remain incomprehensible to us, and its aims inscrutable. – The other predicates of his will were *ontological;* those which are still left to us are the *moral* ones.

28:1071

z *Princip*
a *Princip*

Second part:
Moral theology

First section:
On the moral attributes of God

The concept of God is no natural concept and not necessary from a psychological standpoint. For in psychology and in the cognition of nature I must nowhere appeal directly to God whenever I perceive beauty and harmony. For this is a kind of lazy reason,[56] which would gladly dispense with all further investigations into the natural causes of natural effects. Rather in such cases I must turn to a method which can further the cultivation of my reason, and I must seek out the proximate causes of such effects in nature itself. In this way I may come to know*b* the universal laws according to which everything in the world proceeds. Earlier I saw that it was necessary for me to assume the hypothesis of a being containing in itself the ground of these universal laws; but even without this hypothesis I can still make great progress in physics by endeavoring to find all the intermediate causes. Physicotheology also does not give me a determinate concept of God as an all-sufficient being, but only teaches me to recognize him as a very great and immeasurable being. But in this way I still am not entirely satisfied regarding what I need to cognize of God. For I can always ask further: Is not perhaps another being possible, which might possess even more power and cognition than this recognized supreme principle of nature? But an indeterminate concept of God does not help me at all. Yet on the contrary the concept of God is a *moral* concept, the *practically necessary;* for morality contains the conditions, as regards the conduct of national beings, under which alone they can be worthy of 28:1072 happiness. These conditions, these duties, are apodictically certain; for they are grounded in the nature of a national and free being. Only under these conditions can such a being become worthy of happiness. But if in the case of a creature who has conducted himself according to these eternal and immediate laws of nature and who has thus become worthy of happiness, no state can be hoped for where he participates in this happiness; if no state of well-being thus follows his well-doing; then there would be a contradiction between morality and the course of nature. Yet

b kennen

406

experience and reason show us that in the present course of things the precise observation of all morally necessary duties *is not always connected with well-being*, but rather the noblest honesty and righteousness is often misunderstood, despised, persecuted, and trodden underfoot by vice. But then there must exist a being *who rules the world according to reason and moral laws*, and who has established, in the course of things to come, a state where the creature who has remained true to his nature and who has made himself worthy of happiness through morality will actually participate in this happiness; *for otherwise all subjectively necessary duties which I as a rational being am responsible for performing will lose their objective reality.* Why should I make myself worthy of happiness through morality if there is no being who can give me this happiness? Hence without *God* I would have to be either a visionary or a scoundrel. I would have to deny my own nature and its eternal moral laws; I would have to cease to be a rational human being. – Hence the existence of God is not merely a hypothesis about contingent appearances, as it was in physicotheology, but rather a *necessary postulate for the incontrovertible laws of my own nature.* For morality not only shows that we have need of God, but it also teaches us that he is already present in the nature of things and that the order of things leads us to him. Of course *this* proposition must first be firmly established: that moral duties are necessarily grounded in the nature of everyone's reason and hence that they have a bindingness for me which is apodictically certain. For if moral duties are based only on feelings, or on the prospect of happiness – so that just by fulfilling them I would become *happy already*, not merely *worthy of happiness*, but through them an actual participant in happiness – then well-being would already exist in the present course of things as the effect of good conduct and I would not need to count only on a happy state in the future or assume a being who could help me attain it. But the ungroundedness of Hume's proposition, when he wants to derive all morality from particular moral feelings,[57] is sufficiently demonstrated by morality; and *this* proposition: that here virtue is already sufficiently rewarded, has experience against it. Hence the duties of morality are apodictically certain, since they are set before me by my own reason; but there would be no incentives to act in accord with these duties as a rational human being if there were no God and no future world.

28:1073

Morality alone, moreover, gives me a *determinate* concept of God. It teaches me to recognize him as a being having every perfection; for that God who has to judge, according to the principles of morality, whether I am worthy of happiness, and who in that case must also make me actually participate in happiness, must be acquainted even with the most secret stirrings of my heart, because this chiefly determines the worth of my conduct; he must also have the whole of nature under his power if he is to be able to order my future happiness in its course according to a plan;

finally, he has to arrange and direct the consequences of the different states of my existence. In short, he must *be omniscient, omnipotent, eternal,* and *not in time.*

A being who is to give objective reality to moral duties must possess without limit the moral perfections of *holiness, benevolence and justice.*[58] *These attributes constitute the entire moral concept of God.* They belong *together* in God, but of course *according to our representations* they have to be *separated from one another.* Thus through morality we recognize God as a *holy lawgiver,* a *benevolent sustainer of the world,* and a *just judge.* We must think of the holiness of the laws *as first,* even though our interest commonly beguiles us into placing God's benevolence above it. But a restric-

28:1074 tive condition always precedes God's benevolence, under which human beings are to become worthy of the happiness flowing to them. This condition is that they conduct themselves in accord with the holy law, which must therefore be presupposed if well-being is to follow upon it. A supreme principle of legislation must be altogether *holy,* and it must allow no vice or sin or declare them less punishable than they are. For it should be an eternal norm for us, departing at no point from what is in accord with morality. – *Benevolence,* once again, is a special idea whose object is happiness, just as the object of holiness can be nothing but strictly good conduct or the highest virtue.[59] Benevolence in and for itself is without limit, but it has to express itself in the apportionment of happiness *according to the proportion of worthiness in the subject.* And just this *limitation of benevolence by holiness* in apportioning happiness is *justice.*[60] I must not think of a judge as benevolent, as if he could somewhat relax the holiness of the law and spare something of it. For then he would not be a judge at all, since a judge must weigh and apportion happiness strictly according to the measure in which the subject has become worthy of it through his good conduct. The justice of the judgment must be unexceptionable and unrelenting. – We meet with a symbol of this in the well-ordered government of a land; only with this difference, that in such a government the powers of legislation, government and justice are found in different persons, whereas in God they are all combined. – In a state the legislator must be sovereign, one whom nobody can evade. The administrator of the laws (who provides for and proportionately rewards whose who have become worthy of his benevolence by following the laws) must be subordinate to the legislator, because he too must conduct himself in accord with the same laws. Finally, the judge must be most just and must look closely to see whether the apportionment of rewards is really in accord with desert. Now if we separate every human representation from this symbol, the pure concept we obtain will be precisely that which constitutes the moral perfections of God. This idea of a threefold divine function is fundamentally very ancient and seems to ground nearly every religion. Thus the Indians thought of Brahma, Vishnu and Shiva; the Persians of

Ormuzd, Mithra and Ahriman; the Egyptians of Osiris, Isis and Horus; and the ancient Goths and Germans of Odin, Freya and Thor: as three powerful beings constituting one divinity, of which world-legislation belongs to the first, world-government to the other and world-judgment to the third. 28:1075

Reason leads us to God as a holy legislator, our inclination for happiness wishes him to be a benevolent governor of the world, and our conscience represents him to our eyes as a just judge. Here one sees the needs and also the motives for thinking of God as holy, benevolent and just. Happiness is a system of ends which are contingent because they are only necessary on account of the differences between subjects. For everyone can participate in happiness only in the measure that he has made himself worthy of it. Morality, however, is an absolutely necessary system of *all ends*, and it is just this agreement with the idea of a system which is the *ground of the morality of an action*. Hence an action is *evil* when the universality of the principle from which it is performed is contrary to reason. Moral theology convinces us of God's existence with far more certainty than physicotheology. For the latter teaches us only that we have need of the existence of God as a hypothesis for the explanation of contingent appearances, as has been sufficiently shown in that part of cosmology which deals with contingent ends. But morality leads us to the principle of *necessary ends*, without which it would itself be only a chimaera.

Holiness is the absolute or unlimited moral perfection of the will.[61] A holy being must not be affected with the least inclination contrary to morality. It must be *impossible* for it to will something which is contrary to moral laws. So understood, no being but God is holy. For every creature always has some needs, and if wills to satisfy them, it also has inclinations which do not always agree with morality. Thus the human being can *never* be *holy, but of course* [he can be] *virtuous.* For virtue consists precisely in *self-overcoming.* But one also calls someone "holy" if he has an aversion to something as soon as he recognizes it to be morally evil. Yet this concept of holiness is not sufficiently dignified for the thing itself which it is 28:1076 supposed to designate. It is always better, therefore, not to call any creature perfectly holy, however perfect it may be; or at least not in the sense that God is. For he is the moral law itself, as it were, but thought as personified.

Benevolence is an immediate well-pleasedness with the welfare of others. Except for God, pure and complete is nowhere to be found. For every creature has needs which limit its inclination to make others happy, or its *de facto* ability to exercise these inclinations in such a way as to have no regard at all for its own welfare. But God is independent benevolence. He is not limited by any subjective ground, because he himself has no needs; though to be sure the application of his benevolence is limited *in concreto* through the constitution of the subject in which it is to be shown. This benevolence is something positive, but *justice* is fundamentally only a negative perfection, because it limits his benevolence in the measure that we have not made ourselves worthy of it. God's justice therefore consists in the *combination of benevolence with holiness*. In other words, one could also call it a true benevolence. – Against these moral perfections of God, reason makes objections whose strength have driven many human beings crazy and plunged them into despair. It is just on this account that these perfections have been made the object of extensive philosophical investigations. Among others, Leibniz has attempted in his *Theodicy* to weaken these objections, or rather to do away with them entirely. Let us now look carefully at these objections ourselves and test our powers on them.

> The first objection is against God's *holiness*. If God is holy and hates evil, then whence comes this *evil*, which is an object of aversion to all rational beings and is the ground of all intellectual aversion?

> The second objection is against God's *benevolence*. If God is benevolent and wills that human beings be happy, then whence comes all the *ill* in the world, which is an object of aversion to everyone who meets with it and constitutes the ground of physical aversion?

> The third objection is against God's *justice*. If God is just, then whence comes the unequal apportionment of good and evil in the world, standing in no community with morality? –

28:1077

Concerning the first objection – namely: Where does the evil in the world come from if the sole original source of everything is holy? – this objection gains its strength primarily through the consideration that nothing can arise without its first predisposition being made by its creator. What, then? Has a holy God himself placed a predisposition to evil in human nature? Because they were unable to make sense of this, it occurred to human beings long ago to assume a *special* evil original being, who had wrested part of all things from the holy original source and impressed its own essence on that part. Yet this manichaeism conflicts with human reason, since reason leads us to one single being of all beings, and it can think of this being only as supremely holy. What, then? Shall we derive evil from a holy God? – The following considerations will settle the matter for us. First, one must note that among the many creatures, the human being is the only one who has to work for his perfections and for the goodness of his character, producing them from within himself. God therefore gave him talents and capacities, but left it up to the human being how he would employ them. He created the human being free, but gave him also animal instincts; he gave the human being senses to be moder-

410

ated and overcome through the education of his understanding. Thus created, the human being was certainly perfect both in his nature and regarding his predispositions. But regarding their education he was still uncultivated.ᶜ For this the human being had to have himself to thank, as much for the cultivation of his talents as for the benevolence of his will. Endowed with great capacities, but with the application of these capacities left to himself, such a creature must certainly be of significance. One can expect much of him; but on the other hand no less is to be feared. He can perhaps raise himself above a whole host of will-less angels,[62] but he may also degrade himself so that he sinks even beneath the irrational animals. To begin his cultivation he must step forth out of his uncultivated state and free himself from his instincts. – But what then will be his lot? Only false steps and foolishness. Yet who but the human being is responsible for them? This way of representing things agrees completely with the mosaic story, which describes the same thing in a sensible way. In paradise the human being here appears as a darling of nature, great in his predispositions but crude in his cultivation. Thus he lives undisturbed, led by his instincts, until finally he feels his humanity, and in order to prove his freedom, he *falls*. Now he no longer *is* an animal, but he has *become* an animal. He proceeds to educate himself, but with each new step he takes some new false steps, and in this way he approaches ever nearer to the idea of perfection in a rational being, which he will nevertheless perhaps not attain to for millions of years.[63] – In this earthly world there is only progress. Hence in this world goodness and happiness are not things to be possessed, they are only paths toward perfection and contentment. Thus evil in the world can be regarded as *incompleteness in the development of the germ toward the good*. Evil has *no special* germ; for it is *mere negation* and consists only in the *limitation of the good*. It is nothing beyond this, other than incompleteness in the development of the germ to the good out of uncultivatedness. *The good, however, has a germ; for it is self-sufficient.* This predisposition to good, which God has placed in the human being, must be developed by the human being himself before the good can make its appearance. But since at the same time the human being has many instincts belonging to animality, and since he has to have them if he is to continue being human, the strength of his instincts will beguile him and he will abandon himself to them, and *thus arises evil*, or rather, when the human being begins to use his reason, he falls into foolishness. *A special germ toward evil cannot be thought*, but rather *the first development of our reason toward the good is the origin of evil*. And that remainder of uncultivatedness in the progress of culture is again evil. – Is evil therefore inevitable, and in such a way does God really will evil? –

Not at all; but rather God wills the *elimination* of evil *through the all-*

28:1078

ᶜ *roh*

powerful development of the germ toward perfection. He wills that evil be removed through the *progress toward good.* Evil is also *not a means to good,* but rather arises as a *by-product,* since the human being has to struggle with his own limits, with his animal instincts. The means to goodness is placed in *reason;* this means is the striving to tear himself out of uncultivatedness. When the human being makes this beginning, he first uses his reason in the service of instinct; finally he develops it *for its own sake.* Hence he finds evil *first* when his reason has developed itself far enough that he recognizes his obligations. St. Paul says that sin follows upon the law.[64] When he human being has finally developed himself completely, *evil will cease of itself.* As soon as the human being recognizes his obligation to the good and yet does evil, then he is *worthy of punishment,* because he could have overcome his instincts. And even the instincts are placed in him *for the good;* but that he exaggerates them is his own fault, not God's.

28:1079

This *justifies* God's holiness, because by following this path the whole species of the human race will finally attain to perfection.[65] But if we ask where the evil in individual human beings comes from, the answer is that it exists on account of the limits necessary to every creature. It is just as if we were to ask: Where do the parts of the whole come from? – But the human race is a class of creatures which through their own nature are someday to be released and set free from their instincts; during their development many false steps and vices will arise. But the whole is *someday to win through to a glorious outcome,* though perhaps only after enduring many punishments for their deviation. If one went so far as to ask why God created me, or humanity in general, this would certainly be *presumptuousness,* for it would be as much as to ask why God completed and joined together the great chain of natural things through the existence of a creature like the human being. Why did he not instead leave a *gap?* Why didn't God make the human being into an angel instead? But then would he have still been human?–The objection that if God has the actions of human beings in general under his power and guides them according to general laws, then he must be the author of evil actions, is transcendental and hence does not belong here, but to rational psychology, which deals with human freedom. Later on in our theory of providence we will show how we are to understand the claim that God concurs in the free actions of human beings.[66]

28:1080

The other objection, taken from the *ill* that is in the world, goes up against God's *benevolence.* Hence now we want to investigate where the ill in the world comes from. – We do, to be sure, have an idea of the complete entirety of well-being and of the highest contentment; but we cannot cite a case *in concreto* where this idea of happiness is *entirely* realized. There is a twofold happiness:

1) A happiness consisting in the *satisfaction of desires.* But desires al-

ways presuppose needs, which is why we desire something, hence also pains and ill. – But there also may be thought as a possibility:

2) A happiness *without any desires*, consisting merely in *enjoyment*. Any human being who wanted to be happy in this way would be the most useless human being in the world. For he would be completely lacking in any incentives to action, since incentives consist in desires. Fundamentally we cannot even frame a correct concept of happiness for ourselves except by thinking of it as a *progress toward contentment*. This is why we are uneasy about the lifestyle of those human beings who do almost nothing except eat, drink and sleep. It would not occur to any human being who is aware of the powers and impulses in himself toward activity to exchange his state for this supposed happiness, even if he had to struggle with all sorts of discomforts. Hence a novelist always permits his hero to withdraw from the stage once he has overcome his many difficulties and has finally achieved tranquillity. For the novelist is quite conscious of the fact that he cannot describe happiness as mere enjoyment. Rather it is labor, difficulty, effort, the prospect of tranquillity and the striving toward the achievement of this idea which is happiness for us and a proof already of God's benevolence. The *measure* of happiness for a creature cannot be determined *for one point* of its existence. Rather God's aim is the happiness of creatures *throughout their entire duration. Ill* is only a special arrangement *for leading the human being toward happiness.* We are acquainted with too little of the outcome of suffering, of God's purposes in it, of the constitution of our nature and of happiness itself, to be able to determine the measure of happiness of which the human being is capable in this world. It is enough that it is within our power to render most ill harmless to ourselves, indeed to make our world into a paradise, and to make ourselves *worthy* of an uninterrupted happiness. But ill is necessary if the human being is to have a wish and an aspiration toward a better state, and at the same time to learn how to strive to become worthy of it. If the human being must someday die, then he must not have only sweetness here. Rather, the sum, the whole *facit* of his sufferings and his joys must finally be brought into relation.[d] Is it possible to think of a better plan for human destiny?

28:1081

The third objection is against God's *justice,* and has this question as its object: Why in this world is there no proportion between good conduct and well-being? If we investigate this closely we find that the disproportion between the two is not really so large, and in the end *honesty is the best policy.*[e] We must not be blinded by the outward glitter that frequently surrounds the vicious person. If we look within, we read constantly, as Shaftesbury says, his reason's admission: *You are nevertheless a villain.*[67]

---

[d] *Verhältnis*
[e] *Positio*

The restlessness of his conscience torments him constantly, agonizing reproaches torture him continually, and all his apparent good fortune is really only self-deceit and deception. Nevertheless we cannot deny that at times even the most righteous human being would seem to be a ball in the hands of fate, as regards the external circumstances of fortune. But all morality, that is, all good conduct which is done merely because our reason commands it, would come to nothing if our true worth were determined by the course of things and the fate we meet with in it. Moral conduct would be transformed into a *rule of prudence;* self-interest would be the incentive for our virtues. But to sacrifice one's peace, one's powers and one's advantage when the eternal laws of morality demand it, *that is true virtue, and worthy of a future recompense*! If there were no disproportion at all between morality and well-being here in this world, there would be no opportunity for us to be truly virtuous.

28:1082

Second section
Of the nature and certainty of moral faith

Probability has a place only regarding cognition of things in the world. For a thing of which I am to have probable cognition must be homogeneous with (or a thing of the same kind as) some other thing of which my cognition is certain. For example, I cognize with probability that the moon is inhabited because I discover many similarities between it and the earth (mountains, valleys, seas, and perhaps also an atmosphere). But this cognition of the moon's habitability is *probable* only because I see with certainty that the earth is homogeneous with it in many ways, and from this I infer that it would also be similar to it in this way. But when it is a question of a thing that does not belong to this world at all, then no homogeneity and hence no probability can apply to it. So I cannot say that it is probable that God exists. Such an expression would also be unsuited to the dignity of this cognition; and it is improper too because no analogy between God and the world is thinkable. Hence in this case I must either be entirely modest about cognizing something or else have complete conviction of its existence.

All conviction is of two kinds: either dogmatic or practical. The former must be sought in mere concepts *a priori* and has to be apodictic. But we have already seen that by the path of mere speculation we cannot convince ourselves with certainty of God's existence. At most the speculative interest of our reason compels us to assume such a being as a subjectively necessary hypothesis; but nowhere has reason sufficient capacity *to demonstrate it.* Our need makes us wish for this being, but our reason cannot grasp it. It is true that I can infer from the existence of the world and from its contingent appearances to the existence of some supreme original being; but I cannot sufficiently cognize its nature and attributes. Yet there still remains to us another kind of conviction, the *practical*. This is a special field which gives us far more satisfying prospects than dry specula- 28:1083 tion can ever yield. For if something presupposed on subjective grounds is only a hypothesis, *then*, on the contrary, *a presupposition from objective grounds is a necessary postulate*. These objective grounds are either theoreti- cal, as in mathematics, or *practical*, as in morals. For moral imperatives, since they are grounded in the nature of our being as free and rational creatures, have as much evidence and certainty as ever could be had by mathematical propositions originating in the nature of things. Thus a necessary practical postulate is the same thing in regard to our practical interest as an axiom is in regard to our speculative interest. For the practical interest which we have in the existence of God as a wise ruler of the world is, on the contrary, *the highest* there can ever be, since if we remove this fundamental principle, we renounce at the same time all prudence and honesty, and we have to act against our own reason and our conscience.

Such a moral theology not only provides us with a convincing certainty of God's existence, but it also has the great advantage that it leads *to religion*, since it joins the thought of God firmly to our morality, and in this way it even makes *better* human beings of us. This moral faith is a practical postulate, in that anyone who denies it is brought *ad absurdum practicum.ᶠ* An *absurdum logicumᵍ* is an absurdity in judgments; but there is an *absur- dum practicum* when it is shown that anyone who denies this or that would have to be a scoundrel. And that is the case with moral faith. This moral belief is not equivalent to saying that my opinions occur only as hypothe- ses, i.e. as presuppositions such that they are grounded on contingent appearances. If one infers from the contingency of the world to a supreme author, this is only a hypothesis, even if it is one which is necessary for us as an explanation, and hence something like a highly probable opinion. But such presuppositions, which flow from some absolutely necessary datum, as in morals and mathematics, are not mere opinions but demand of us a firm belief. Hence our faith is not knowledge, and thank heavenʰ it 28:1084 is not! For divine wisdom is apparent in the very fact that *we do not know but rather ought to believe that a God exists*. For suppose we could attain to knowledge of God's existence through our experience or in some other way (although the possibility of this knowledge cannot immediately be thought); suppose further that we could really reach as much certainty through this knowledge as we do in intuition; then all morality would

---

ᶠ to a practical absurdity
ᵍ logical absurdity
ʰ *Heil uns!*

break down. In his every action the human being would represent God to himself as a rewarder or avenger; this image would force itself involuntarily on his soul, and his hope for reward and fear of punishment would take the place of moral motives; the human being *would be virtuous from sensible impulses.*

If the author talks about God's *sincerity,*[68] this expression is far beneath the dignity of the highest being. For negative perfections like sincerity, which consist only in God's not being hypocritical, could be predicated of God only insofar as *it might occur to someone to deny them.* But sincerity and truth are already contained in the concept of God in such a way that anyone who rejected these attributes would have to deny God himself as well. Such perfections, moreover, are already contained in God's holiness, since a holy being would certainly never lie; and why set up a particular rubric and classification for each of the *corollaria?* If we really want to cite sincerity and truth as particular attributes of God, it would be better to define them in terms of the sincerity and truth God demands *from us.* So there are still only three moral attributes of God, the three we have treated above: holiness, benevolence and justice.

We can think of divine *justice* in two ways: either as justice within the order of nature or justice by special decree. But as long as we have no instruction concerning the latter, or as long as we can make everything given in nature harmonize with God's holiness and benevolence, it is our duty *to stop with a justice which gives us what our deeds are worth in the present course of things.* This justice within the order of nature consists in the fact that God has already laid down in the course of things and in his plan for 28:1085 the world, the way in which a human being's state will be proportioned to the degree of morality he has attained. Well-being is inseparably combined with good conduct, just as punishment is combined with moral corruption. Moral perfection in this life will be followed by moral growth in the next, just as moral deterioration in this life will bring a still greater decline of morality in that life. After death the human being will continue with his development and predisposition of his capacities, and thus if in this world he strives to act in a morally good way and gradually attains to moral accomplishment, he may hope to continue his moral education there too; on the other side, if he has acted contrary to the eternal and necessary laws of morality and has gradually made himself worse by frequent transgressions, then he must fear that there too his moral corruption will continue and increase. Or at least he has no reason to believe that a sudden reversal will occur in the next life. Rather, the experience of his state in the world and in the order of nature in general gives him clear proofs that his moral deterioration, and the punishments essentially necessary with it, will last indefinitely or eternally, just as will moral perfection and the well-being inseparable from it.

God's justice is usually divided into *justitiam remunerativam et punitivam,*[i] according as God punishes evil and rewards good.[69] But the rewards God bestows on us proceed not from his justice but from his benevolence. For if they came to us from justice, then there would be no *praemia gratuita,*[j] but rather we would have to possess some right to demand them, and God would have to be bound to give them to us. Justice gives nothing gratuitously; it gives to each only the *merited* reward. But even if we unceasingly observe all moral laws, we can never do more than is our duty; hence we can never expect rewards from God's justice. Human beings may certainly merit things of *one another* and demand rewards based on their mutual justice; but we can give nothing to God, and so we can never have any right to rewards from him. If, according to a sublime and moving text, it says: "He that hath pity on the poor lendeth to the Lord,"[70] then here the reward which is due us for the sake of the unfortunate is ascribed to God's benevolence, and God himself is re-   28:1086
garded as our debtor. It is represented that when God bestows a promise on us we are justified in demanding what he has promised us and expecting from his justice that it will be fulfilled. But promises of this kind, where someone pledges a wholly undeserved benefit to another, do not appear actually to bind the promisor to grant this benefit to the other; at least they give him no right to demand it. For they always remain benefi-cent deeds, bestowed on us undeservedly, and they carry the mark not of justice but of benevolence. Hence in God there is no *justitiam remunera-tivam* toward us, but all the rewards he shows us must be ascribed to his benevolence. His justice is concerned only with punishments. These are either *poenae correctivae,*[k] *poenae exemplares,*[l] or *poenae vindicativae.*[m] The first two are given *ne peccetur,*[n] the third *quia peccatum est.*[o] But all *poenae correctivae* and *poenae exemplares* are always grounded on *poenae vindica-tivae.* For an innocent human being may never be punished as an example for others unless he deserves the punishment himself. Hence all correc-tive punishments which have as their aim the improvement of the pun-ished, as well as those which have been ordained for the guilty as a warning to others, must always accord with the rules of justice. They must at the same time be *avenging* punishments. But the expression *poenae vindicativae,* like the expression *justitia ultrix,*[p] is really too hard.[71] For

[i] rewarding justice and punitive justice
[j] gifts of grace
[k] corrective punishments
[l] exemplary punishments
[m] vindictive punishments
[n] so that there will not be sin
[o] because there has been sin
[p] avenging justice

vengeance cannot be thought in God, because vengeance always presupposes a feeling of pain impelling one to do something similar to the offender. So it is better to regard the punishments inflicted by divine justice on sins in general as an *actus* of *justitiae distributivae,*[q] that is, as a justice limiting the apportionment of benevolence *by the laws of holiness.* Hence we see that there must be *poenae vindicativae,* because they alone constitute what is proper to justice; if they were rejected, this attribute could not be assumed in God at all. For *poenae correctivae* and *exemplares* are really acts of benevolence, because they promote what is best either for the individual human beings improved by them or for the entire people for whom the punishment serves as a warning. How, then, is the essence of divine justice to be posited in them? God's justice must limit benevolence so that it distributes good only *according to the subject's worthiness,* hence justice will not ordain punishments for the criminal merely in order to teach what is best for him or for someone else, but rather it does so in order to punish the offense by which he has violated the law and made himself unworthy of happiness. These retributive punishments will become obvious only when our whole existence is considered, and hence can be correctly determined and appraised only in it. *It is from this we get the majestic idea of a universal judgment of the world.* There it is to be made well known before all the world how far the human race has made itself *worthy* of a determinate happiness or unworthy of it through transgression of holy moral laws. At the same time, the conscience, that judge in us which is not to be bribed, will place before the eyes of each one the whole world of his earthly life and convince him himself of the justice of the verdict. And then, in accord with the constitution of our striving here in the world, there too there will follow either eternal progress from good to better or an interminable decline from the bad into the still worse. –

28:1087

The *patience* of God consists in the fact that he executes his punishment of evil in the criminal only after he has given him the opportunity to improve himself.[72] But after that, God's justice is unrelenting. For a judge who *pardons* is not to be thought of! He must rather weigh all conduct strictly according to the laws of holiness and allow each only that measure of happiness which is proportionate to his worthiness. It is enough to expect from God's benevolence that in this life it gives us the capacity to observe the laws of morality and to become worthy of happiness. God himself, the all-benevolent, can make us worthy of his good deeds; but that he shall yet make us partakers of happiness without our becoming worthy of his good deeds in virtue of morality – *that* he, the Just One, cannot do.

Impartiality belongs to those attributes which should not be specifically predicated of God,[73] since no one could doubt that it pertains to him,

---

[q] act of distributive justice

because it lies already in the concept of a holy God. God's impartiality consists in the fact that God has no favorites; for this would be to presuppose some predilection in him and that is only a human imperfection, e.g. when parents have a special love for a child which has not especially distinguished itself. But it cannot be thought of God that he would choose some individual subject over others as his favorite with no regard to the subject's worthiness; for this would be an anthropomorphic representation. But if it should happen that one nation becomes enlightened sooner than another and is brought nearer to the destination' of the human species, then this (far from being a proof that God had a special interest in, and cares with special favor for this people) would belong rather to the wisest plan of universal providence, which we are in no position to survey. For in the realm of ends as in the realm of nature, God governs according to *universal* laws which do not appear to be in connection with our short-sighted understanding. The human being is certainly in the habit of taking any special bit of undeserved good fortune which may befall him for a special testimony of the favor of divine providence. But this is the work of our love of self, which would gladly persuade us that we are really worthy of the happiness we enjoy.

28:1088

Equity is also an attribute which is beneath the majesty of the supreme being;74 for we can think of genuine equity only among human beings. Equity is an obligation arising from the right of another insofar as it is not combined with a warrant to compel someone else. Hence it is distinguished from strict right, where I can compel someone else to fulfill his obligation. For example, if I have promised to give a servant a certain allowance, then I must pay it to him whatever happens. But now suppose there comes a time of scarcity, so that the servant cannot live on the agreed wages; here according to strict right I have no obligation to accord him more for his maintenance than I have promised him; he cannot compel me to do so, since he has no further obligation as a ground for his right. But it is only equitable that I not let him go hungry, and that I add to his wages a proportion large enough that he can live from it. Before the bar of conscience it counts as a strict right that I owe to others what is due them merely from equity; and even if everyone were to think me just because I fulfill everything to which I can be compelled and to which I have an external obligation, my conscience will still reproach me if I have violated the rules of equity. God judges according to our conscience, which is his representative here on earth.

28:1089

Absolute *immortality*, the impossibility of perishing, is ascribed to God.75 This attribute belongs by right only and solely to him, as a consequence of the absolute necessity of his existence. But the expression "immortality" is unsuitable, because it is only a mere negation of an

' *Bestimmung*

anthropomorphic representation. It is to be remarked in general that in theory the concept of God must be carefully purified and freed of all such human ideas; from a practical point of view, though, we may momentarily represent God using such predicates whenever by this means the thought of God affords more power and strength to our mortality. But in the present case it is much better to use the expression *eternal* instead of "immortal," since it is nobler and more appropriate to the dignity of God.

When the author praises God as *the most happy*,[76] it will be necessary for us to investigate the true concept of happiness' to see whether it fits God. Pleasure in one's state is called *welfare;* insofar as this pleasure applies to the entirety of our existence it is called "happiness." This is consequently *pleasure in our state as a whole.* Pleasure in *one's own person is called self-contentment.* But what is distinctive about us is constituted by freedom. Consequently, self-contentment is a pleasure in one's own freedom, or in the quality of one's will. If this self-contentment were to extend to our *entire existence,* it would be called *blessedness.'* The difference between self-contentment and happiness is just as necessary as it is important. For one can be fortunate without being blessed, even though the *consciousness of one's own dignity,* or self-contentment, belongs to a perfect happiness. But self-contentment can certainly be found without good fortune, because at least in this life good conduct is not always combined with well-being. Self-contentment arises from morality, while happiness depends on *physical* conditions. No creature has the powers of nature in its control, so as to be able to make them agree with its self-contentment. Hence the highest degree of self-contentment, or in other words blessedness, cannot be ascribed to any creature. But we are more fortunate if our whole state is such that we are able to be well-pleased with it. Yet in the present life happiness itself *will hardly be our lot,* and the Stoics probably exaggerated things very much when they believed that in this world virtue is always coupled with being well-pleased. The most infallible witness against this is experience.

28:1090

Human good fortune is *not a possession, but a progression toward happiness.* Yet full self-contentment, the consoling consciousness of rectitude, is a good which can never be stolen from us, whatever the quality of our external state may be. And in fact all earthly happiness is far outweighed by the thought that as morally good human beings we have made ourselves worthy of an uninterrupted future happiness. Of course this inner pleasure in our own person can never compensate for the loss of an externally happy state, but it can still uplift us even in the most troubled

---

' *Glükseligkeit;* "the most happy" translates *den Glücklichsten.* The noun *Glück* means both "happiness" and "good fortune," and the same is true of the adjective *glücklich.* In the following passage, these words will be translated in either or both ways as seems most suitable.
' *Seligkeit*

life when it is combined with the prospect for the future. If now the question is whether happiness may be ascribed to God, since happiness relates only to one's external state, the question must first be raised whether one can think of God as *in a state*. Here we must first see what a *state* is. The ontological definition of a "state" is this: the coexistence of the alterable determinations of a thing along with the persisting ones; in the human being, for example, the persisting determination is that he is human, whereas what alters is whether he is learned or ignorant, rich or poor. This coexistence of his alterable determinations, such as wealth or poverty, with the persisting one, humanity, constitutes his state. But in God *everything* is permanent; for how could changeable determinations be thought in him, existing along with what is persisting in his essence? Or how, then, can the Eternal be thought of as in a state? But if no state can be predicated of God, then a state of happiness cannot be ascribed to him either. But supreme blessedness, the greatest possible self-contentment with himself belongs to him, and indeed in a sense that no creature can ever boast of anything even similar to it. For with creatures many external, 28:1091 sensible objects have an influence on their inner pleasure; but God is completely independent of all physical conditions. He is conscious of himself as the *source* of all blessedness. He is, as it were, the moral law itself personified; hence he is also the only blessed one. –

At the conclusion of moral theology it should be remarked that the three articles of moral faith, *God, freedom of the human will,* and *a moral world,*[77] are the only articles in which it is permissible for us to transport ourselves in thought beyond all possible experience and out of the sensible world; only here may we assume and believe something from a practical point of view for which we otherwise have no adequate speculative grounds. But however necessary or dependable this procedure may be on behalf of our morality, we are in no way justified in admitting ourselves further into this idea and venturing to go with our speculation to a region with which only our practical interest is concerned. If we do so, *then we are enthusiasts.* For here the limits of our reason are distinctly indicated, and whoever dares to transcend them will be punished by reason itself for his boldness with both pain and error. But if we remain within these boundaries, then our reward will be to become wise and good human beings.

Third section
Of God, regarding his causality

God's causality, or his *relation*" *to the world,* can be considered in *three* respects:

" *Verhältnis*

1. *in nexu effectivo,*[v] insofar as God is in general the cause of the world, and the latter is an *effectus* of him;
2. *in nexu finali,*[w] insofar as God has willed the attainment of certain aims by his production of the world. Here God is considered as an author of the world, i.e. as a cause of the world according to aims;
3. *in nexu morali.*[x] Here we become acquainted with God as the ruler of the world.

28:1092

1) OF GOD AS THE CAUSE OF THE WORLD

All the concepts in which human beings have ever thought of God as the world's cause can be brought under the following classification:

1. One has represented things as if the world itself were God.
2. Or God has been thought as an *ens extramundanum,*[y] but as to his causality, either:

     (a) One has sought to explain it according to the necessity of his nature. This is the *systema emanationis,*[z] which is either *crassior,*[a] as when one represents the substances of the world as arising through division. But this is absurd, or *subtilor,*[b] where one considers the origin of all substances to be an emanation of God,[78]

     (b) Or: according to freedom. This is the *systema liberi arbitrii,*[c] in which God is represented as the creator of the world.

The system of emanation of the subtler kind, according to which God is regarded as the cause of substances by the necessity of his nature, has one ground of reason opposed to it, which at once overthrows it. This ground is taken from the nature of an absolutely necessary being and consists in the fact that the actions which an absolutely necessary being undertakes from the necessity of its nature can never be any but those internal actions which belong to the absolute necessity of its essence. For it is unthinkable that such a being should produce anything outside itself which is not also absolutely necessary. But how can something produced by something else be thought of as absolutely necessary? Yet if it is contingent, then how could it have emanated from a nature which is absolutely necessary? Every action performed by such a being from the necessity of

---

[v] "in effective connection," i.e., regarding efficient causality
[w] "in final connection," i.e., regarding final causality
[x] in moral connection
[y] a being outside the world
[z] system of emanation
[a] more vulgar
[b] more subtle
[c] system of free will

its nature is immanent and can concern only its essence. Other things external to it can be produced by it only *per libertatem,*[d] otherwise they are not things external to it but belong to the absolute necessity of its own essence and are therefore *internal* to it. – This ground sets up a resistance on the part of reason toward the system of emanation, which regards God as cause of the world by the necessity of his nature, and discovers the cause of the unwillingness to accept this system, which everyone feels even if he is not able to develop it distinctly. It is an altogether different matter when we see one thing arise from another by the necessity of its nature within the world itself. For here cause and effect are homogeneous, as for instance in the generation of animals and plants. But it would be absurd to think of God as homogeneous with the totality of the world, because this would contradict entirely the concept of an *ens originarium*, which, as we have shown above, has to be isolated from the world. Hence there remains to our reason only the opposite system of causality, the *systema per libertatem.*[e]

28:1093

2) OF GOD AS THE AUTHOR OF THE WORLD[79]

As *autor mundi*[f] God can be thought of either:

1. merely as the author of the forms of things; in this way we regard God as only the *architect* of the world; or

2. as the author of the very matter of substance in the world as well; and then God is the *creator of the world.*

In the world itself, only the forms of things arise and perish; substances themselves are permanent. For example, an apple arises because the tree forces fluids up through its stems and composes them. But the fluids themselves, where did the tree get them? From the air, the earth, the water, and so on. This matter is found in the apple too; but it exists in a different composition, a different form. Another example is an example of perishing. For example, when we remove the phlogiston from iron, its whole form is changed; it decomposes into dust and is no longer iron at all to ordinary eyes.[80] But the substance of the iron remains undisturbed. For when now phlogiston is blown into it, the old form is restored and the iron dust becomes firm and solid. This form is contingent; its alternations testify to this. Hence it must have an *author,* who gave it its initial arrangement. But the substances in the world, even if we do not perceive any alterations in them, are just as contingent as the forms. This is clear from

28:1094

---

[d] through freedom
[e] system [of causality] through freedom
[f] author of the world

their reciprocal *commercium*[g] the relationship in which they stand to each other as parts of a whole world. Indeed, in ancient times it was assumed that the matter of things, the fundamental material out of which all their forms arise, is eternal and necessary. Hence God was considered only as the world's *architect*, and matter was considered to be the material out of which he formed all things. Fundamentally, therefore, one assumed two principles:[h] *God* and *nature*. This served excellently for blaming the greater part of the world's ills on the original properties of matter, without detracting from the wisdom and benevolence of the architect. Matter was held responsible because the eternal attributes of its nature were supposed to have placed many obstacles in the way of God's will when he tried to form it to his ends. Yet this opinion was rejected, and rightly, as soon as philosophical ideas were further determined and refined. For it was seen that if matter occasions the ill in the world owing to its being unsuitable for certain aims, then it might also occasion much that is good through its fitness and agreeableness with other ends of the author, and that it might accordingly be difficult to determine the extent to which God as the world's architect is responsible for what is good and bad in the world and the extent to which matter, as its fundamental material, is responsible. Such indeterminate ideas are useless in theology. Also, one finally noted the contradiction between saying that substances are eternal and necessary and yet that they nevertheless have an *influxum mutuum*[i] on each other. The confusion and absurdity in the view that the whole world consists of many necessary beings finally put human reason on the track of *creation* from nothing, a doctrine of which the ancients hardly had the least concept. Matter was now viewed as a product of God's free will, and God was thought of not only as the world's architect but also as its creator. But for a long time the idea of an independent matter persisted in the heads of philosophers, even of the orthodox. Hence there were zealous outcries against anyone who ventured to explain part of the world's order and beauty from universal laws of nature. For some were concerned that in this way such arrangements would be snatched away from God's supreme
28:1095   rule. But this could be believed only by someone who thinks of matter as independent of God, like a coordinated principle.[j] If, on the contrary, it is assumed that every substance receives its origin from God, then all matter is subordinated to God and all its laws in the last analysis have their origin in him. This creating out of nothing appears to contradict the metaphysical proposition: *ex nihilo nihil fit.*[k] Yet this proposition can be true only of

---

[g] community, in the sense of mutual causal influence
[h] *Prinzipien*
[i] mutual influence
[j] *Prinzip*
[k] Nothing is made out of nothing.

what is highest in the world itself. In this world it can be rightly said that no substance can arise which has not already previously existed. And only *that* is what the above proposition means to say. But if we are talking about the origin of the world-whole, and this creation itself is not thought of as an occurrence in time, since time itself, indeed, began only *with* it, then there is no difficulty in thinking that the whole universe might have arisen through the will of an extramundane being, even if nothing previously existed. But at this point we must guard against mixing in the concepts of time, arising, and beginning; for this would only introduce confusion. We must even admit that such a production of substances, hence the possibility of creation, is something which cannot be comprehended by human reason, since we are not in a position to cite any similar case *in concreto* where the arising of a substance could be put before our eyes. In general the question how one substance can be produced by another, whether through emanation or through freedom, makes for many difficulties, which may well remain in part insoluble. But this is certainly not a sufficient ground for doubting the system of creation itself, since the subject matter here is of such a kind that, chained as we are to sensible representations, we can probably never attain to a clear insight into it. It is enough we feel in some way the urge to assume it as something given and to have a firm belief in it. For speculative reason must always admit that this idea is the most rational of any, and the one most suited to reason's own use.

Creation, or the making actual out of nothing, relates merely to substances; their forms, however different they may be, arise from the particular modifications of their composition. Hence one calls every substance produced out of nothing a *creature*. Now if, therefore, even the substance itself as well as its form comes from God, the question still remains: Can one substance be thought as the *creatrix* of another? And to this the answer is: Absolutely not! For all substances, as part of the world-whole, are in reciprocal *commercium* and have a mutual influence on one another. If this were not so, then all the substances together could not constitute a whole with each substance as a part of the whole. But if this is so, then it is unthinkable that one substance could be the author of another, since the second substance must act on the first as well as being passive to it. But that is a *contradictio in adjecto*.[1] For example, if someone built a house and then was killed when it collapsed, then one could think of him as having been here the cause of his own passivity. But in fact he made only a mere form through the composition of the building materials, and did not himself generate the substance, the matter. But it was just this matter, of which he was not the author or cause, which worked its influence on him and caused his death. Hence even God cannot be thought as having a reciprocal influence on the world. He effects everything, but cannot be

28:1096

---

[1] contradiction in the adjective

passive to anything. Creation cannot have been other than completed at once in an instant. For in God only one infinite act can be thought, a single, enduring force which created an entire world in an instant and preserves it in eternity. Through this act, many natural forces were poured out, as it were, in this world-whole, which they gradually formed in accordance with general laws.

Creation of the world, as we have remarked already, applies merely to substances. Hence if it is said that the creation of the world happened all at once, it is only the creation of substances that is to be understood. Now these substances also remain always persisting and their number neither increases nor decreases. God creates *only once.* Hence one cannot assert that *even now* God is creating a world, at least in the sense we mean here, that new substances can arise, even though many *new forms* can arise in the *world,* when the matter already present is put together*ᵐ* in some different way. Fundamentally only one action can be thought in God; for in him there is no succession; but nevertheless this one act may have an infinite number of relations and expressions according to the constitution of the subjects to which it relates, and it actually does have them too.

28:1097 Hence God's power is not at all visible to us at one time while at another it is sensed by us.

God acts in no way but *freely.* Nothing has any influence on him, so as to be able to move him to act in any particular way and not otherwise. For in an absolutely necessary being all determinations that might impel him to actions other than those he wills out of his highest freedom are done away with. – That the world created by God is the *best* of all possible worlds is clear from the following reason.[81] If a better world than the one willed by God were possible, then *a better will* than the divine will would also have to be possible. For indisputably that will is better which chooses what is better. But if a better will is possible, then so is a being who could express this better will. And this being would therefore be more perfect and better than God. But that is a contradiction; for in God is *omnitudo realitatis.*ⁿ – There is more on this subject in Kant's "Attempt at Some Considerations on Optimism."[82]

According to Leibniz, all the objections to the theory based on the existence of so much ill in the world can be briefly dismissed in that since our earth is only a part of the world, and since each part must be incomplete in itself, because only the *whole* totality of the world is supposed to be the best, it is impossible to determine whether ill would have to belong even to the best world as regards the plan for the whole. For whoever demands that our earth be free of all ill, and hence wholly good, is acting as if he wanted one part to be the whole.[83] Thanks be to the astronomers,

ᵐ zusammengesetzet
ⁿ the all of reality

who by their observations and inferences have elevated our concept of the world as a whole far above the small circle of our world, for they have not only provided us with a broader acquaintance with the whole, but they have also taught us modesty and caution in our estimation of it. For surely if our terrestrial globe were the whole world, it would be difficult to know it to be the best and to hold by this with conviction; for, to speak with sincerity, on this earth the sum of pain and the sum of good might just about *balance each other.* Yet even in pain there are incentives to activity, and so one might even call it beneficial in itself. Thus the stinging flies in a swampy place are nature's call to human beings to drain the mires and make them arable in order to get rid of these disagreeable guests. Or if we 28:1098 did not feel the pain of a wound and were not thus driven to concern ourselves with healing it, we might bleed to death from it. But it is possible to recognize the doctrine of the best world from maxims of reason alone, independently of all theology and without its being necessary to resort to the wisdom of a creator in proof of it. And specifically in the following way: In the whole of organized nature it must be assumed as a necessary maxim of our reason that in every animal and plant there is not the least thing which is useless and without purpose; on the contrary, it must be assumed that everything contains a means best suited to certain ends. This is an established principle in the study of nature, and it has been confirmed by every experiment made in this case. Set these experiments aside and the field of discoveries is foreclosed to the anatomist. Hence the cultivation of our own reason urges us to assume and use this maxim. But if the whole of organized though irrational nature is arranged in anything like the best way, then we should expect things to be similar in the nobler part of the world, in rational nature. But the same law is valid also for organized creatures and for the mineral realm, for the sake of the necessary harmony in which everything is combined under the supremely necessary principle of unity. Thus we can and must assume for reason's sake that everything in the world is arranged for the best, and that the whole of everything existing is the best possible one. This doctrine has the same influence on morality as it has on natural science; for if I cannot be sure that the laws governing the course of nature are the best ones, then I must also doubt whether in such a world true well-being will eventually be combined with my worthiness to be happy. But if this world is the best, then my morality will stand firm and its incentives will retain their strength. For now I can be certain that in a best world it is impossible for good conduct to exist apart from well-being; and that even if for a certain part of my existence the course of things does not look this way, it would certainly have to hold for my existence as a whole if this world is to be the 28:1099 best. Hence even *our practical reason* takes great interest in this doctrine and recognizes it as a necessary presupposition for its own sake and without founding it only theology. For how the best[o] in a best world can obtain as a by-product of the progress toward the morally good, is already clear from our above theory of the origin of evil.[84]

On the end of creation. It is possible to think of a double end for it, first an objective end, consisting in the perfection which made the world an object of God's will, and then a subjective end. Yet what kind of incentive, if one may so express it, could move God to create a world? But the next section[85] will deal with this latter end; the first end is the object of our present investigation.

Now what is the perfection for which the world was created by God? We may not seek such an end in irrational creatures. For everything in these creatures is only a means to higher ends which can be reached only by correct use of these means. The true perfection of the world-whole has to lie in the use *rational creatures* make of their reason and freedom. Only here can absolute ends be proposed, since reason is always required for something intentional. But what is the right use which rational creatures are to make of the will? It is a use such as can stand under the principle of the system of all ends. A universal system of ends is possible only in accord with the idea of morality. Hence the only rightful use of reason is that according to which the moral law is fulfilled. The perfection of the world will therefore consist in the fact that it is congruent with morality, which alone is what makes possible a system of all ends. –

A *twofold* system of all ends may be thought: either *through freedom* or *according to the nature of things.* A system of ends through freedom can be attained by means of the principles of morality, and this is the moral perfection of the world; only insofar as they can be regarded as members of this universal system do rational creatures have personal worth. For a good will is something good in and for itself, therefore something *absolutely* good. Everything else is only a conditioned good. For example, acuteness of mind, or health, is good only under the right condition, namely that of its right use. But morality, through which a system of all ends is possible, gives to the rational creature a worth in and for itself by making it a member of this great realm of all ends. The possibility of such a universal system of all ends *is dependent solely on morality alone.* For it is only insofar as *all* rational creatures act according to these eternal laws of reason that they can stand under a principle of community and together constitute a system of all ends. For example, if all human beings speak the truth, then among them a system of ends is possible; but if only one should lie, then his end is no longer in connection with the others. Hence the universal rule for judging the morality of an action is always this: If all

28:1100

[o] *Beste;* it is possible that the text is corrupt at this point and the word intended is *Böse* (evil).

428

human beings did this, could there still be a connection of all ends? The system of all ends in accordance with the nature of things is attained along with the rational creature's worthiness to be happy, and it is the physical perfection of the world. It is only in this way that the state of a creature may obtain a preeminent value. Without this the rational creature might certainly have an excellent worth in itself, but its state could still be bad, and vice versa. But if both moral and physical perfection are *combined*, then this is the best world. The objective end of God in creation was the perfection of the world and not merely the happiness of creatures; for this constitutes only the [world's] physical perfection. A world with it alone would still be lacking in moral perfection, or the worthiness to be happy. Or is the perfect world supposed to be one whose members overflow with pleasure and good fortune while nevertheless being conscious that their own existence is *without worth?*

But apart from objective grounds for being well-pleased with some thing itself and its constitution, there are also *subjective* grounds for pleasure in the existence of a thing. The two must be distinguished from each other, for I can find a thing to be very fine indeed on objective grounds, but still be indifferent to its existence as far as I myself am concerned. Here a subjective ground for my pleasure, or in a word, my interest, would be lacking. Just this often holds even of moral motives which, if they are objective, obligate me to do something, but still do not bestow on me the 28:1101 powers and incentives to do it. For in order to perform the actions recognized to be good and right, certain subjective motives in me are also required to put them into practice. For this it is necessary not only that I find the deed to be noble and fine, but that my choice be determined accordingly. Now it is asked: Did God in creating the world have, in addition to the objective ground of its perfection, also a subjective determining incentive determining his choice, and if so what was it? In God, however, no incentives except the objective motives may be thought! His pleasure which he has in the idea of a perfect object, combined with the consciousness of himself as a sufficient ground of every perfection, already determines his causality. – For if before God actualized anything some further subjective pleasure in the existence of this thing had to be added as an incentive to his causality, then a part of his blessedness would have to depend on the existence of the thing in which he takes this interest. For his pleasure in the perfection of the thing in its idea alone would not be strong enough to move him to produce it, and God would have need of a special interest that the thing should actually exist. This interest would not have been there if the thing, however perfect it may be in the idea, had not also actually existed; consequently God would have needed the existence of a world in order to have his perfect blessedness. But this contradicts his highest perfection. – Hence one must make a distinction between a *voluntas originaria*[p] and a *voluntas derivativa.*[q] It is only the latter which has need of special incentives to determine it to the choice of something good. Thus, for example, a human being can find a deed thoroughly noble on objective grounds, but he may nevertheless hesitate to perform it because he believes he has no particular subjective motives for doing so. A completely perfect will, on the contrary, would do the deed merely *because it is good.* The perfection of the thing it wills to produce is by itself a sufficient motive for it actually to put the deed into practice. Hence God created a world because he was most well-pleased with its highest perfection, where every rational creature would participate in happiness to the measure in which he had made himself worthy of it; in short, he created the world for the sake of its physical as well as its moral

28:1102 perfection. Thus one must not say that God's motive in creating the world *was merely the happiness of his creatures,* as if God could take pleasure in seeing other beings happy without their being worthy of it; God's infinite understanding, on the contrary, recognized the *possibility of a highest good* external to himself in which morality would be the supreme principle.[r] He was conscious at the same time of having all the power needed to set up this most perfect of all possible worlds. His well-pleasedness in this consciousness of himself as an all-sufficient ground was therefore the only thing determining his will to actualize the greatest finite good. Hence it would be better if one said that God created the world for the sake of his honor because it is only through obedience to his holy laws that God can be honored.[86] For what does it mean to honor God? What, if not to serve him? – But how can he be served? Certainly not by trying to entice his favor by rendering him all sorts of praise; for that is at best only a means of preparing ourselves and elevating our own hearts to a good disposition; instead the service of God consists simply and solely in *following his will* and observing his holy laws and commandments. *Thus morality and religion stand in the closest combination,* and are distinguished from each other only by the fact that the former moral duties are carried out from the principles of every rational being, which is to act as a member of a universal system of ends; whereas *here* [in religion] these duties are regarded as commandments of a supremely holy will, because fundamentally the laws of morality are the only ones that agree with the idea of highest perfection. –

The whole world can be regarded as a universal system of all ends, whether through nature or through freedom. This doctrine of ends is called "teleology." But just as there is a physical system of ends in which every thing in nature has a relation as a means to some end found in rational creatures, so there is also a practical system of ends, that is, a

---

[p] original will
[q] derivative will
[r] *Prinzip*

430

system in accordance with the laws of free volition. In this system every rational creature stands in connection with every other as reciprocal end and means. The former system of ends is the object of *theologia physica;*[s] the latter is treated by *theologia practica seu pneumatica.*[t] There all rational beings are themselves regarded as possible means to the attainment of ends of rational creatures, and in this way the world may be exhibited not merely *in nexu effectivo*[u] as a combination of causes and effects like a machine, but also in *nexu finali*[v] as a system of all ends. In *theologia practica*[w] we see that rational creatures constitute the *center* of creation, and everything in the world relates to them. But they also have some relation to one another as mutual means. Yet however disordered and purposeless as history may describe human conduct, yet we should not let this drive us crazy, but should rather believe nevertheless that the human race is grounded on *a universal plan* according to which it will in the end *attain to its highest possible perfection.* For up to now we have surveyed the plan *only in its individual parts and fragments.*

28:1103

To conclude our consideration of God as creator of the world, we must yet try to solve the cosmological problem as to whether he created the world *in time or from eternity.* – Now would it not be an internal contradiction to say that God created the world form eternity? For then the world would have to be eternal, as God is; and yet it is also supposed to be dependent on him. Yet if "eternity" here means the same as infinite time, then I become guilty of a *regressus in infinitum*[x] and commit an absurdity. But then can we think of the creation of the world only as in time? No, not this either. For when I say that the world had a beginning, I am thereby asserting that there was a time *before* the origin of the world, because every beginning of something is the end of a time just past, and the first moment of a subsequent time. But if there was a time before the world existed, then it must have been an empty time. Again an absurdity! And God himself must have been in this time. – Now how can reason emerge from this conflict between its ideas?[87] What is the cause of this dialectical illusion? It lies in the fact that I am regarding time, a *mere form of sensibility,* a mere formal condition and a phenomenon, as a determination of the *mundus noumenon.*[y] All appearances, to be sure, are given only in time; but when I try to bring under the rule of time even the actuation of the substances themselves which are the substratum of all appearances and consequently also of my sensible representations, then I commit a striking

28:1104

---

[s] natural theology
[t] practical or spiritual theology
[u] in the connection of efficient causes
[v] in the connection of final causes
[w] practical [or moral] theology
[x] regress to infinity
[y] noumenal world

error, a μετάβασις εἰς ἄλλο γένος.[z] For I confuse things which do not belong together at all. At this point my reason recognizes its incapacity to raise itself above experience, and although it is in a position to show that all the objections of its opponents are fruitless and vain, it is still too weak to settle anything itself with apodictic certainty.

Of providence

The actuation of the beginning of the world is *creation*. The actuation of its duration is *conversation*. Both apply only to substances. For of that which adheres to them as something accidental, I can say neither that it was created nor that it is conserved. It is also good if one makes a distinction between the concepts of God as the architect of the world and as the world's creator. This distinction is just as cogent as the one between accident and substance. For in God only one act can really be thought, which never ceases but expresses itself without variation or interruption. For in God no succession of states takes place, and consequently no time. So how could his power operate only for a certain time and then cease or be interrupted? Hence the same divine power which actuated the beginning of the world constantly actuates its duration. The same power required for the creation of substances is also needed for their conservation. Yet if every substance in the world can have duration only through a continuous *actus divinus*,[a] then it would appear that this deprives it of its very substance. But here it is fundamentally only the expression *subsistentia*[b] (self-sufficiency[c]) which causes the difficulty and the apparent contradiction. Of course we cannot substitute a more suitable expression for it because language does not have one; but we can prevent it from being misunderstood by explaining it. A substance, a thing subsisting for itself, is one *quod non indiget subjecto inhaerentiae*,[d] that is, it exists without being the predicate of anything else. For example, I am a substance because I refer everything I do to myself, without needing something else to which to ascribe my actions as something inhering in it. – But I myself may

28:1105 nevertheless always have need of some other being for my own existence. This being may be the author of my existence and duration without its having to be at the same time the author of my actions. Hence substance and accident must be carefully distinguished from cause and effect. For the two relationships are entirely different. A thing can be a *causatum*

[z] a change to another kind
[a] divine act
[b] subsistence
[c] *Selbständigkeit*
[d] which does not need a subject of inherence

*alterius*ᵉ (or have need of the existence of something else for its own existence) and still subsist for itself. But subsisting and existing *originarie*ᶠ have to be distinguished from one another; for subsistence would involve a contradiction if something existing *originarie* also had to exist as a *causatum alterius*. This would be the false definition of substance like the one sketched out by the well-meaning Spinoza; for through too great a dependence on Cartesian principles he understood a substance to be a thing *quod non indiget existentia alterius*.[88] – The result of all thing is that it is incomprehensible how substances should have duration through the power of God; but it is not contradictory.

The causality of more than one *causa* is a *concursus*. Several causes, that is, can be united to produce one effect. If this happens, then several *concausae*ᵍ concur. In such a case none of these cooperating causes is in itself sufficient to produce the effect; for otherwise its unification with another cause would not be necessary to give it a *complementum ad sufficientiam*.ʰ But where there is a *causa solitaria* or solitary cause, there can be no *concursus*. For firstly, several causes are required for a *concursus;* but these causes also have to be *concausae*, that is, they must be coordinated with one another and not subordinated one to another. For if the causes are subordinated one to another and constitute a chain or series of causes in which each is a particular link, then each link in the chain is the complete cause of the next, even if all together they have a common ground in the first cause. But then each considered in itself is still a *causa solitaria* and there is no *concursus*. If this is to take place, then causes have to be united and coordinated with one another; and one cause must make up for what the other fails to produce. Thus the effect is produced only by the causes being unified and working in community with one another. – Applying this to God, it is clear firstly that he does not concur in the existence of substances; for substances contribute nothing to their own duration, and therefore cannot themselves operate in union with God as *concausae* of their own conservation.[89] – In this case there is only a subordination of causes, so that every substance has its ground in God as the *prima causa*,ⁱ since the matter of every substance itself is created by him; but just for this reason there can be no *concursus*, for if there were, then the substance would have to be coordinated with God. – In the same way, there takes place no *concursus* of God with natural occurrences. For just because they are supposed to be natural occurrences, it is presupposed already that their first proximate cause is in nature itself, and it must be

28:1106

ᵉ being caused by another
ᶠ "originally," i.e. without need of an external cause
ᵍ cooperating or joint causes
ʰ complement to the point of sufficiency
ⁱ first cause

sufficient to effect the occurrence, even if the cause itself (like every natural cause) is grounded in God as the supreme cause. – Yet a *concursus* between God and natural occurrences in the world is still not impossible; for it is always thinkable that a natural cause is not sufficient by itself to produce a certain effect. In such a case God might give it a *complementum ad sufficientiam;* but whenever he did this, he would *eo ipso* perform a *miracle.* For we call something a miracle *when the cause of an occurrence is supernatural,* as it would be if God himself operated as *concausa* in the production of such a miracle. – Hence if one ascribes to God special turns and twists of affairs in the world, then one is only predicating so many miracles of him. –

But how does it stand with free actions? Can a *concursus divinus* be affirmed of them?[90] Now in general speculative reason cannot comprehend the freedom of creatures, nor can experience prove it; but our practical interest requires us to presuppose that we can act according to the idea of freedom. Yet even if it is true that our will can decide something independently of every natural cause, it is still not in the least conceivable how God might concur in our actions despite our freedom, or how he could concur as a cooperating cause of our will; for then *eo ipso* we would not be the author of our own actions, or at least not wholly so. Of course this idea of freedom is one which belongs to the intelligible world, and we are acquainted with nothing of it beyond the fact that it exists, so we also do not know the laws by which it is governed. But even if our reason cannot deny the possibility of this *concursus,* it still sees that such an effect would have to *be a miracle of the moral world,* just as God's acts of cooperation with occurrences in the sensible world are God's miracles in the physical world.

28:1107

God's *omnipresence* is closely bound up with *conservation;*[91] the former, indeed, consists precisely in God's immediate operation in the duration of every thing in the world. It is, in the first place, something *immediate.* God does not act through intermediate causes in his conservation of substances; for if he did, then these causes would once again have to be substances which were his effects, and consequently one substance would have to operate in conserving the others, and thus one substance would be dependent on another. But that one substance in the world cannot cause the existence of another had already been shown where we dealt with the impossibility of substances in the world standing *in commercio* with each other so as to be able to create each other.[92] Just as impossible is that substances could mutually contribute to the conservation of one another or the duration of each other's existence. For creation and conservation are one and the same act. Further, God's omnipresence is an *inward* presence; i.e. God conserves what is substantial, the very inwardness of substances.[93] For it is just this which is necessary for the duration of substances, and unless God unceasingly actuated this inwardness and essential substantiality, things in the world would all have to cease being. We have an example of such a thing in Newton's theorems about the mutual attraction of all things in the world; for things attract one another immediately, or as he expressed it, in empty space, consequently they operate reciprocally on one another and thus they are all present to one another, but not inwardly; for this is only a case of reciprocal influence, that is, an operation on the state of things or a modification of their alterable determinations by one another. An inward presence, however, is an action of the duration of the very substance in a thing. Hence one cannot, as the author does, call conservation a "constant influence";[94] for by speaking of an influence, he is saying that God conserves only the state of substances (their alterable determinations) and not the substances themselves; hence we would be asserting that matter is independent of God. God's omnipresence is therefore *immediate* and *inner* but *not local;* for it is impossible for a thing to be in two or more places at the same time, because then the thing would be external to itself (which is a contradiction). Suppose, for example, that *A* is in place *a;* then *A* is wholly in *a;* if one said now that it is in place *b* too, then it cannot be wholly in place *a* or in place *b,* but there must be a part of it in each place. Hence if one wants to assert that God is in all places, then he has to be thought of as a composite being, as a mass extending throughout the whole world, something like the air. But then God would not be wholly in any place in the world; part of him would be in each place, just as the whole atmosphere is not in any place on the earth but in each place there is always only a collection of little particles of air. Yet if God is the most perfect spirit, then he cannot be thought of as in space. For space is only a condition of the sensible appearance of things. – Newton says in one place that space is the *sensorium* of God's omnipresence.[95] Of course one can think of such a *sensorium* in the human being, where the *seat* of the soul is located and where all the impressions of sense concur; but this would be the soul's organ, the point from which it disperses its powers and operations to the whole body. Such a representation of God's omnipresence, however, is most inappropriate; for it would regard God as the *soul of the world,* and space as his *sensorium.* For if God were the soul of the world, then he would have to stand *in commercio* with the world and all the things in it, i.e. he would not only operate on those things but receive their operations as well. Or at least our only concept of a soul is that of an intelligence united with a body in such a way that both *reciprocally* influence each other. It is not easy to see how such a thing could be brought into agreement with the impassibility of a highest being. It would be better to say that space is a phenomenon of God's omnipresence, although even this expression is not entirely suitable, though it cannot be avoided on account of the poverty of language, which lacks words signifying such thoughts, not to mention expressing them clearly. But space is only an appearance of our senses and

28:1108

a relation^j of things to one another; and the relation between things themselves is possible only insofar as God conserves them through his immediate and inner presence; thus he determines the place of each through his omnipresence; so to this extent God himself is the cause of space, and space is a phenomenon of his omnipresence. The omnipres-

28:1109 ence of God is consequently not local but virtual; i.e. God's power operates constantly and everywhere on all things; thus he conserves substances themselves as well as governing their state. But we must be *careful* to guard ourselves *against all enthusiasm* in this representation, for although God's omnipresence expresses itself in each of us by the actuation of our very existence, this omnipresence cannot be felt by any of us, nor can any of us be certain for himself that God is operating in him in any particular case. For how am I to experience or be sensible of what is the cause of my own existence? – Indeed, if it were only a question of some change in my state, it might very well be possible for me to feel it. Yet no experience of the actuation of my own existence is possible. This is of great importance, and a caution^k *protecting us from all fanatical madness and delusion.*

If we affirm a *concursum divinum* as regards things as well as occurrences in the world, then this is usually called a *concursum physicam.* But from what we have already said about God's "cooperation" with natural occurrences, can it not be recognized how inappropriate it is to use this expression in place of "divine conservation." For how can I regard substances as concurring with God in their own preservation, since they are not coordinated with him but wholly depend on him as their *causa solitaria absolute prima?^{l}* Would I not then be asserting that their existence is not actuated by God and that they do not have need of him for their duration as their sole cause, since he is only a cooperating cause of it? – It is equally wrong to posit a *concursus Dei* for natural occurrences. For we can always think of a *causa proxima^m* for these occurrences, operating in accord with laws of nature; since otherwise they would *eo ipso* not be natural occurrences. So it is likewise unthinkable that God, who is the *causa prima^n* of the whole of nature, might also cooperate as a *concausa* in each particular occurrence. For then these occurrences would be just so many miracles; for every case where God himself acts immediately is *an exception to the rule of nature.* But if God is to cooperate as a special *concausa* of every particular natural occurrence, then every occurrence would be an excep-

^{j} *Relation*
^{k} *Cautele*
^{l} absolutely first solitary cause
^{m} proximate cause
^{n} first cause

tion to the laws of nature, or rather there would be no order at all in nature, because the occurrences would not happen according to general rules but in each case God would have to give a *complementum ad suffi-* 28:1110 *cientiam* to anything which was to be set up according to his will. What imperfection in a world, totally irreconcilable with a wise author!

But as regards a *concursum moralem*⁰ or God's free cooperation in the free actions of human beings, such a thing cannot be comprehended in the nature of freedom, but at the same time it cannot be regarded as impossible. For if it is presupposed that every rational being could from itself act even against the plan of God, hence entirely free and independently of the whole mechanism of nature, then it is indeed possible that God, in order to make rational creatures use their freedom in a manner agreeable to his highest will, could cooperate as a *concausa.*

Providence is in God one single act; but we can think of it as having three separate functions, namely *providence,ᵖ government* and *direction.*⁹⁶ Divine *providence*⁹ consists in the institution of the laws according to which the course of the world is to proceed. *Government* is the conservation of the course of the world in accord with these laws, and divine *direction* is the determination of individual occurrences according to these decrees. Insofar as God's providence is benevolent, it is called *provision.ʳ* These expressions are deceptively infected with the concept of time; but one nevertheless has to use them, after separating all sensible limitations, for lack of anything more suitable.

God's providence is usually divided into *providentiam generalem* and *providentiam specialem.ˢ* By the former is understood God's conservation of all types and kinds (*genera*); by the latter, however, his caring for *species,* a word used here in its juridical sense to indicate care for individuals. At this point the expression *generalis* is distinguished from *universalis,* as if many exceptions may be made in a general providence, as for example it is said of a king that he cares for his subjects in general.ᵗ Yet this concept of divine providence is obviously wholly anthropomorphic. For such general provision is extremely imperfect, and in fact could be found only in beings 28:1111 who have to be acquainted through experience with needs. But experience furnishes only an aggregate, and hence the rules abstracted from it can

---

⁰ moral cooperation
ᵖ *Providenz*
⁹ *Providenz*
ʳ *Vorsorge*
ˢ general providence and special providence
ᵗ The German word *allgemein* translates both *generalis* (general) and *universalis* (universal). We will continue to translate it as either "general" or "universal," as the context dictates, but in the following passage it is well for the reader to keep in mind that the term translated in these ways is ambiguous in the original.

never be universal, because a portion of the possible perceptions are always lacking. Consequently, it is impossible for every law whose beneficence rests on principles of experience to suit every individual in the state and to work equally for the well-being of all and the common utility. For how could the lord of a country be acquainted with every single one of his subjects and with all the circumstances under which his laws might be of great advantage to one but detrimental to another? God, however, has no need of experience at all; rather he knows everything *a priori* because he himself created everything he provides for, and everything is possible only through him. Hence God formulated the laws governing the world in light of a thorough acquaintance with every single occurrence in it, and in the establishment of the course of the world he certainly had the greatest possible perfection in view, because God himself is the all-wise and is all in all. For certainly in his omniscience he foresaw every possible individual, as well as every *genus*, even before there was anything at all. And in actualizing them he provided for their existence as well as their welfare, through the establishment of suitable laws. Hence because God cognizes everything *a priori*, his providence is *universalis*, or general enough to comprehend everything: *genera*, *species* and individuals. In one glance God surveys all of existence and he conserves it by his power. This universality of divine providence is not a logical generality, as with general rules we draw up in order to classify the marks in things; rather it is *real* [universality], for God's understanding is intuitive, whereas ours, on the contrary, is discursive. Hence it is foolish to think of a divine providence "on the whole" (*generalis*) as coming from a highest being; for such a being could not fail to cognize the totality in every single part. Rather God's providence is wholly universal (*universalis*), and thus the distinction of a *providentia generali* from a *providentia speciali* collapses of itself.

Since every occurrence in the world is directed by God, supreme will, the divine *direction* is partly *ordinary* and partly *extraordinary*. *The former* consists in God's setting up an order in nature, so that its laws accord with what he decrees for the world; *the latter* consists in the fact that he sometimes determines in accord with his aims that individual occurrences should not correspond to the order of nature. It is not at all impossible that even in the best world the powers of nature may sometimes require 28:1112 the immediate cooperation of God in order to bring about certain great ends. It is not impossible that the lord of nature might at times communicate to it a *complementum ad sufficientiam* in order to carry out his plan. Or who would be so presumptuous as to want to cognize how everything God intends for the world could be attained in accord with universal laws and without his extraordinary direction? – Hence God can of course use natural causes merely as means for bringing about certain occurrences which he has put before himself as an end, and for the sake of the greater perfection of the whole are applied to the production of this or that occurrence. Such exceptions to the rules of nature may be necessary because without them God might not be able to put many great aims to work in the usual course of nature. Only we must guard ourselves from trying to determine without further instruction whether God's extraordinary direction" has taken place in *this or that case;* this is sufficient for us to place an immeasurable trust in God.

Nevertheless, not everything happens through divine direction, even if everything stands *under* it. For as soon as an occurrence is produced immediately through the divine will, then it is a miracle and an effect of his extraordinary direction. Now every miracle either was woven by God into the laws of nature during the creation of the world, or else he works it in the course of the world in order to bring about some necessary aim of his. In either case they are miracles, which we cannot expect, but neither can we deny them. To reassure ourselves in the face of life's contingencies, we may think of every occurrence as fundamentally a consequence of God's government and direction.[v] What is it to us whether these events happen in accord with the order of nature or in an extraordinary way? Everything still stands under his provision. – Only we must never regard our *prayer* as a means of getting something, but rather, as regards corporeal advantages, we ought to offer it both with a trust in God's wisdom and with submission to this wisdom. The greatest utility of prayer is indisputably a *moral* one, because through prayer both thankfulness and resignation toward God become effective in us. But if an investigation is required into whether this or that occurrence is an immediate end of God, something he has arranged or effected in an extraordinary way, then here *great reserve and caution* are necessary, so that we do not, at the bidding of a lazy reason, derive anything from God as its immediate cause when more acute reflection might convince us that it was only a natural effect; and even if all our researches on this score should be in vain, it is still the case that our fruitless seeking fulfills our great vocation and furthers the cultivation of our reason. –

    28:1113

If, in our discussion of the truth that God created the whole world for the best, it was necessary to reply to the objection how moral evil could be found in such a best world, then it is now also our duty to show why God has *not prevented* evil, since everything is subject to his government. – The possibility of deviating from the moral law must adhere to every creature. For it is unthinkable that any creature could be without needs and limits. God alone is without limitations. But if every creature has

" *Lenkung*
[v] *Lenkung*

needs and deficiencies, then it must also be possible that impulses of sense (for these derive from the needs) can seduce it into forsaking morality. It is self-evident that we are speaking here only of free creatures, since the irrational ones have no morality. If the human being is to be a free creature and responsible for the development and cultivation of his abilities and predispositions, then it must also be within his power to follow or shun the laws of morality. His use of his freedom has to depend on him, even if it should wholly conflict with the plan God designed for the moral world. By divine decree God could have given the human being overriding powers and motives sufficient to make him a member of the great realm of ends. Hence if God does not prevent evil in the world, this never sanctions evil; it only permits it.

3) OF GOD AS THE RULER OF THE WORLD

28:1114　God is the only *ruler of the world.* He governs as a monarch, but not as a despot;[97] for he wills to have his commands observed out of love, not out of servile fear. Like a father, he orders what is good for us and does not command out of mere arbitrariness, like a tyrant. God even demands of us that we reflect on the *reason*[w] for his commandments, and he insists on our observing them because he wants first to make us worthy of happiness and then make us participate in it. – God's will is benevolence and his end is the best. If God commands something for which we cannot understand the reason, then this is because of the limitations on *our* cognition, and not because of the nature of the commandment itself. God carries out his rulership over the world *alone;* for he surveys everything with one glance. Of course he may often use wholly incomprehensible means to carry out his benevolent aims.

Since God governs everything, we are warranted in assuming a teleological connection in nature. For governing presupposes aims, and God's government presupposes the wisest and best ones. To be sure, in many cases our efforts must be in vain, because the true ends of the highest understanding are too much concealed from our insight for us to be able to descry them. Great care is required on our part if we are not to take some natural occurrence to be part of a divine end when it is really either only a means or a by-product of a higher end. But even if we sometimes engage in these researches without success, still we have exercised our reason and at least discovered something. And even if we go entirely wrong, no greater harm results than that we take something to be the work of an intention when it is only a mechanism of nature. A need of our own reason requires that we search everywhere for universal laws according to

---

w Grund

which certain occurrences are ordered. For in this way we bring unity and harmony into our cognition of nature, instead of destroying all order in nature, as we would do if we regarded every single thing in the world as an effect of God's special providence. – In the same way, in world history we can also think of the occurrences which are consequences of human freedom as connected with and carried out by God's government according to a plan. Only here too according to the nature of our reason we have to hold on to the universal and not try to determine how divine providence has proven itself effective in particular cases. – For although for God's understanding, which cognizes everything intuitively, the whole is a whole fundamentally only insofar as it consists of every particular; for this, consequently, divine providence is also completely universal, in the sense that it includes every individual in its plan; but it would be perverse of us and contrary to our discursive reason if we too tried to rise from the particular directly[x] to the universal and survey the whole. The nature of our reason lays on us the duty of first reflecting[y] on *general* laws and then, as far as possible, of grasping every individual and then every species under them, and in such a way of forming some sketch of the whole, which is to be sure very defective, but nevertheless sufficient for our needs.

28:1115

What the author says about *divine decrees* is obviously only a human representation; for in God the decree and its execution are one.[98] But it is necessary to our concept, as long as we think of it in a worthy manner. Yet an *absolutum decretum* is absolutely improper regarding God;[99] for such a thing would make of God not only a despot but a complete tyrant, as if without any regard to the worthiness of his subjects he elected some to happiness and condemned the others straightway to reprobation, providing all sorts of remedies for the first and withdrawing from the others every power and opportunity to make themselves worthy of happiness, so as to do all this with a show of right. It would be almost unthinkable that any men of heart and insight could come to such dishonorable thoughts about God, unless it is assumed for their honor's sake either that they have not thought over the terrible consequences of such corrupt doctrines or have not shunned them merely out of bewilderment. For through this the concept of God would become a scandal and all morality would become a figment of the brain. This would also wholly conflict with the idea of human freedom, since in this way all actions can be considered to accord with the necessity of nature. Hence speculative philosophers may always be forgiven for having fallen into such notions,[z] since human freedom and its possibility will always be something insoluble for them. But in any theology which is to be a princi-

[x] *erst*
[y] *nachsinnen*
[z] *Vorstellungen*

441

28:1116 ple[a] for religion it is both puzzling and senseless to make such concepts of God the ground. *If the human soul as an intelligence is free* (for as appearance it belongs to be sure in the series of natural things), *then it also depends on the soul itself whether it will be worthy or unworthy of happiness.*

Insofar as its object is the reprobation of one whole part of humankind, the doctrine of *predestination* presupposes an *immoral* order of nature. For it is thereby asserted that in the case of some human beings the circumstances of their lives are so ordered and connected that they could not but be unworthy of blessedness. Hence simply according to the order of nature, these unfortunates would be *sacrifices* to *misery*. But how could such a thing be compatible with the concept of a benevolent, wise and holy creator and governor of the world? It is one of the great advantages provided by the doctrine of God from the point of view of our cognition and reassurance that this doctrine *brings the realm of nature into exact harmony with the realm of ends!* It is precisely through it, indeed, that we infer that the whole order of nature is arranged in accordance with God's ends and agrees with them! – How, then, should we suppose that one of God's ends is the misery of a portion of his creation? – God's government of the world in accordance with moral principles is an assumption without which all morality would have to break down. For if morality cannot provide me with the prospect of satisfying my needs, then it cannot command anything of me either. Hence it is also necessary that God's will should not be made the principle[b] of rational morality; for in this way we could never be sure what God had in mind for the world. How can I know by reason and speculation *what* God's will is, and what it consists in? Without morality to help me here, I would be on a slippery path, surrounded by mountains which afford me no prospect. How much danger I would be in of having my foot slip, or, because no clear horizon ever meets my eyes, of wandering lost in a labyrinth!

The cognition of God must therefore complete morality, but it must not first determine whether something is morally good or a duty for me! This I must judge from the nature of things in accordance with possible system of ends; and I must be just as certain of it as I am that a triangle has three angles. But in order to provide my heart with conviction, weight and 28:1117 emphasis, I have need of a God who will make me participate in happiness in accordance with these eternal and unchangeable laws, if I am worthy of it. – In the same way, the cognition of God and his providence must be the goal of our natural science, crowning all our endeavors in it; but not the principle from which we derive every single occurrence without inquiring into its general laws.

[a] *Princip*
[b] *Princip*

Fourth section
Of revelation

The author defines[100] *revelationem latius dictam*[c] as *significationem mentis divinae creaturis a Deo factam.*[d] Yet this definition of a revelation in general is *angustior suo definito.*[e] For divine revelation must be able to furnish us with convincing cognition of God's existence and attributes as well as his will. The former have to be the motives and incentives impelling us to fulfill the latter. Revelation is divided into the *outer* and the *inner.* An *outer* revelation can be of *two kinds:* either through works, or through words. *Inner* divine revelation is God's revelation to us through our own reason; this latter must *precede all other* revelation and serve for the estimation of outer revelation. It has to be the touchstone by which I recognize *whether an outer revelation is really from God,* and it must furnish me with proper concepts of him. For as we have seen above, nature by itself can never give me a complete and determinate concept of God unless I bring reason to its aid. Nature teaches me to fear that one being, or several beings, who might have produced the world, but not to honor and love without flattery a God who has all perfection. But now if I make into a principle[f] of religion a concept of God such as nature gives me, namely the concept of a very mighty being (for I would hardly come to be acquainted with him as a benevolent being in this way, on account of the apparent conflict of ends in the world) – in short, if I take as this principle not the concept of God as an all-perfect being but only the mere concept of a very perfect being, then from this little or nothing can be deduced toward the confirmation and awakening of a true morality. And of what use, then, is the entire natural concept of God? Certainly for nothing else than that actually made of it by most peoples: as a *terrifying picture of fantasy,* or a superstitious object of ceremonial adoration and hypocritical high praise! But now if before I turn to physicotheology, my reason has already taught me that God is all in all,[101] and that in accordance with my cognition of moral laws I have gained insight into the concept of God as a being who governs the world according to the highest morality, then in this case my knowledge of nature serves me admirably to give the pure concepts of my understanding greater intuitiveness[g] and to make a stronger impression on the sensible human being. I will no longer be in danger of forming an incomplete concept of God from mere nature; for now I have already received from my reason a thoroughly determinate concept; and in accord with this

28:1118

[c] revelation in the wide sense
[d] a signification by the divine mind to the creature made by God
[e] narrower than what is defined
[f] *Principe*
[g] *Anschaulichkeit*

concept I can judge all God's works in this world insofar as he has revealed himself in them. In just the same way, the revelation of God through words presupposes an *inner* revelation through my own reason. For words are only the sensible signs of my thoughts; how by means of them will I therefore attain to an entirely pure concept of God? But if my own reason has already abstracted such a concept from things, if with the help of morality it has already come to an entirely determinate concept of God, then I have a norm in accordance with which I can measure and explain the verbal expressions of a divine revelation. Even if God were to make an immediate appearance, I would still need a previous rational theology. For how will I become certain here whether it is God himself who has appeared to me, or only another powerful being? Thus I have need of a pure idea of the understanding, an idea of a most perfect being, if I am not to be blinded and led astray. Thus we can have no correct insight into the external revelation of God, and we can make no right use of it, until we have made an entirely rational theology our property. But on

28:1119 the other side an external divine revelation can be an occasion for the human being to come for the first time to pure concepts of God which are pure concepts of the understanding; and it can also give him the opportunity to search for these concepts. A verbal revelation will always become more and more a matter of scholarly learning the longer it lasts, even if in the beginning it was something quite simple. For with time it becomes a matter of tradition, whether it is transmitted orally or in writing; and then there can be only a few whose scholarly learning is broad enough that they can go back to its very first origins and carefully test its genuineness. Here the religion of reason always has to remain the *substratum* and foundation of every investigation; it is *according to this religion* that the value of that verbal revelation must be determined. So it must precede every other revelation and serve as a gauge.

In rational theology there are many *credenda*[h] which reason itself urges us to assume; and it is an important duty for us to believe them with conviction. The object[i] of this cognition – God – is of such a kind that, since it transcends the bounds of every possible experience and belongs to the intelligible world, there can be no knowledge of it. For I can have knowledge only of what I myself experience. But regarding our morality, it is very good that our cognition is not knowledge but faith; *for in this way the fulfillment of my duty will be far purer and more unselfish.* But the matters of faith pertaining to rational religion extend their obligation to the whole human species; for every rational being must assume them unfailingly from a moral standpoint even if he cannot prove them with apodictic certainty.

[h] things believed
[i] *Objekt*

444

Now it can be asked whether there are also *credenda* given in a higher revelation, which have to be accepted[j] even though reason does not recognize the necessity of believing them. But reason can *neither deny nor prove* the possibility of such things. First, no human being can hold it impossible that in order to bring the human species to the highest stage of perfection in its vocation, God might have given to it, in a higher revelation, certain truths necessary to happiness into which reason, through its own cultivation, can perhaps never come to have insight. For who dares to specify the plan or the means by which God might help human beings to become what their vocation determines them to be? – But on the other side my reason has *just as little insight* as to how something not lying in reason but transcending all reason could be necessary to the welfare of humanity. Thus a pagan philosopher[102] once said: *Quod supra nos, nihil ad nos.*[k] The precise cognition of and adherence to the path reason prescribes is all that God himself teaches to make us worthy of any higher insight which might be provided to supplement reason's deficiencies. For how could I reckon on additional gifts and presents even before I have applied and used that with which I am already endowed?

28:1120

Mysteries, properly so called, are those doctrines which are not to be made public;[103] for they are truths into whose possibility reason cannot have insight, but which are to be accepted[l] from other causes. There are many natural mysteries; but there are also many mysteries in rational religion, for example, the absolute necessity of God, to believe which reason is urged for its own sake, but concerning which reason comes to a standstill as soon as it is a question of gaining insight into the possibility of such a thing. Further: [it is a mystery that] a just God in his benevolence can distribute happiness only according to the object's worthiness to be happy; yet he can make a human being happy even when this human being finds himself unworthy of happiness, since before the bar of conscience his best striving is never adequate to the whole of the moral law. Here our reason is profoundly silent. For even if it says, "Do as much good as you can," this is still a long way from being sufficient to reassure me. For where is there a human being who can determine how much good he can do? Where is the human being bold enough to say: "I have done everything I could"? I cannot rely upon God's beneficence here, for my reason has to think of God's judgment as supremely just, limiting benevolence by his strict holiness, so that no one unworthy might participate in it. What kind of means God has here to replace what is lacking in my worthiness to be happy – this is for my reason an impenetrable mystery. It is enough that I have a duty to strive as much as possible to act in accord with the moral

28:1121

---

[j] *angenommen*
[k] What is above us is nothing to us.
[l] *angenommen*

law, and make myself susceptible and worthy of such a means. Accordingly, that mysteries are possible in God's revelation through words is, according to what we have already said, not to be denied; but whether *there actually are such mysteries, no longer belongs to rational theology.*

Appendix
History of natural theology
according to
Meiners's historia doctrinae de uno
vero Deo[104]

In considering what human reason has up to now cognized about God, one has fallen into two extremes, which have been used as principles of rational theology according to the difference in one's systems.

1. Some have wanted to deny reason any faculty which is able to cognize something true and reliable about God.
2. Others have praised their reason so highly that they have wanted to derive from it all the cognition of God which is necessary for human beings.

At every instant the former have needed some verbal revelation from God, and the latter have despised it. Both have appealed to history but both erred. For if we go to work with sincerity and an impartial spirit of investigation, we find that reason does in fact have the capacity[m] to form a morally determinate concept of God, a concept which is as complete as possible for it. But on the other hand we have to admit that from a variety of causes this pure concept of the Deity did not occur easily in any ancient people. To blame for this was not reason, but rather the obstacles which stood in the way of its making use of its ability in this respect. But now reason is also far from having the right to be proud of this ability, and perhaps even to believe that it *is able to cognize everything having to do with the infinite and its own relationship to the infinite.* If it is honest and free of prejudices, how many deficiencies and weaknesses now might it not still discover even in the complete system of a theology which is possible to it? Surely it may not boast with its cognition of God, and if a higher revelation has made known some clearer insights into its relationship to God, it   28:1123

---

[m] *Vermögen*

must, instead of rejecting them, rather accept" and use them with thanks. It is true that the moral concept of God reason gives us is so simple and obvious to the ordinary human understanding that not much cultivation is required for faith in a supreme governor of the world; it is also necessary that any cognition which is of interest to the whole human species must be intelligible to every human being; but someone would have to be very little acquainted with the error's of the human understanding if he seriously asserted that this concept of God is safe from misinterpretation and disfigurement by hypocritical speculation, and that it is therefore unnecessary to keep it safe from corruption through a critique of all speculative reason, which is required by acute and profound reflection. – The chief cause that the concept of God was so corrupt even among the Greeks and Romans was that they knew so little of morality that was pure and certain. They commonly held their duty to be their own advantage, thus eliminating moral worth from their actions, or grounding the beauty and magnitude of virtue on mere feeling, and not [to be] the principle° itself which their reason makes determinate and firmly established as an unalterable norm and condition of all their obligations. Hence they were not acquainted with any moral need to postulate a most perfect legislator for the world. – Only from a speculative standpoint did the ancients assume a supreme cause, in order to complete the series of causes and effects. But since nature can lead us only to a powerful and intelligent author and never to one who has all reality, they fell into polytheism, which could be endlessly multiplied to infinity with such natural concepts. And even if a few for the sake of greater harmony assumed only one single cause for the world, still their concept was fundamentally only a deistic one, because they were not thinking of a higher moral author and governor of the world but only of a supreme original source for everything. For fundamentally no ancient people had any concept of God which could have been used as a foundation for morality. Here Meiners is certainly correct; but if he believes that they could not have arrived at such concepts because a great deal of culture and an acquaintance with science is required for it, then *that* cannot possibly be said about the simple moral concept of God. For almost nothing is easier in itself than the thought of a being who is supreme above all and who is all in all.[105] It is much more difficult to divide perfection, and to ascribe one perfection to one being and another perfection to another, because then one never knows how much each is to be given. But if one understands by this that it takes much information and a reflection practiced in science in order to secure the concept of the divine from the side of speculation, then that much must be conceded. But this reflection was not necessary before human wit and acuteness had begun to venture

28:1124

" *annehmen*
° *Princip*

speculating about the divine, and some culture was required for that. The Egyptians had for a concept of God only that of deism, or rather that of the most wretched polytheism. It is in general a prejudice, established according to the sayings of Herodotus,[106] to believe that all of Greek science and culture came from Egypt, since the situation and constitution of the country, the tyranny of the pharaohs and the usurpation of the priests must rather have formed this people into a gloomy, melancholy and ignorant mass. It is also unproven that the Egyptians had surpassed any other people of that time in any field of useful knowledge, unless one is to count soothsaying and the interpretation of dreams. Rather, since their land was populated and made habitable, some science must already have been present among humans, such as geometry, because with it all property would have ceased with every annual inundation of the Nile. Besides, their priests truly monopolized all the arts they might have had and never let them serve the common utility, since otherwise their own reputation and greed would have suffered shipwreck. The most credible historians of the ancient world inform us as to which sciences were invented by the Greeks, and among them we find the very ones which one has been under the delusion that they were communicated to them by the Egyptians.

The worship of animals, as regards its origin, may be explained in a tolerable way. Perhaps in the beginning these animals were merely part of the coat of arms used by each city to distinguish itself from the others, and subsequently the peoples retained them, but finally, blinded by superstition, they accepted[p] them as protective gods and worshipped them. It does not hold of these peoples, what Hume says quite correctly in his natural religion about polytheism, namely that they were tolerant.[107] For since one city among them often had a protective god directly opposed to the god of another, for example, the one a dog and the other a cat, so the inhabitants were hostile just for this reason. For they believed that one deity would always try to encroach on the other's powers and prevent much good which it would otherwise have given its clients. – The Greeks and certain others were tolerant enough of other heathen peoples, and certainly of one another as well; for they found their own deities in those of other peoples, only the names were different, since for the most part the attributes were the same. But it was on this account that all heathen peoples held a terrible hatred for the Jews, because the Deity of this people was raised above all [others] and, as regards its essence and will, could have nothing in common with them. Hence it was also natural that monotheism, or rather the Jews who had it, should have been so intolerant against all heathens.

28:1125

The Persians, Indians and other heathen peoples of antiquity had a theology far more bearable than the Egyptian one was. It is true that they

---

[p] annahm

prayed to many gods, but the concepts they formed of these gods were nevertheless in some measure worthy of their object, even if they were quite corrupt. In general we must admit that nearly all these peoples probably had at least an obscure thought of a supreme Deity above their idols, as an original source from which everything, even the lower divinities, arose, but which was wholly unconcerned about the world. Even now this is still the notion[q] of God which heathens have of God. It was also entirely natural that, since their concepts of God were only abstracted from the world, that by analogy of nature they regarded him as a fertile cause from which everything had emanated.

Among the Greeks we find no natural theology earlier than the time of the so-called Seven Sages. But for a long time their concepts of God were deistic until finally Anaxagoras and Socrates made God the foundation of morality.[108] But by then morality itself had already been grounded on secure principles;[r] hence it was easy to establish a moral concept of God, the only one truly useful for humanity. But as soon as one wanted to cognize God as a principle[s] of nature and began speculating about him, then it was easy for them to be led astray again. Plato and Aristotle did maintain a pure and morally determinate concept of God, because they applied it only in behalf of morality; but Epicurus and others wanted to ground the natural sciences on this concept as well, and so they nearly gave up morality or else lost themselves in skepticism.[t] For how much knowledge and discernment would have been required of them here, if they were going to unite science with morality and yet not be led astray by the apparent conflict of ends in the world! Yet one must admit that Epicurus preserved a concept of the Deity which is quite pure, considered from the speculative point of view from which he drew it. Yet the greatest utility of this concept was lost to him and his disciples; for such a God cannot be used as an incentive to morality. The Stoics probably had the purest concept of God, and they did apply it with a practical aim. Yet they could not raise themselves far enough to regard God as the creator of the world. For even if they did use the term *creator* of him, if we consider this precisely we will see that only the concept of an architect was combined with this term. They always assumed a matter co-eternal with God, from which Jupiter, a name designating not the poetic god of thunder but the highest Deity above everything, had formed and arranged the things of the world. But if one blames them for asserting a necessity of things in the world and its alternations, then one does them an injustice; for they distinguished fate carefully from necessity, and understood by it nothing

28:1126

[q] *Vorstellung*
[r] *Principien*
[s] *Princip*
[t] *Zweifelsucht*

but the divine government and provision. Yet in order to justify the supremely perfect God against all the ill and evil found in the world, they attributed the blame for them to the unfitness of matter, which could not always be used for the supreme aims of the architect.

How happy we are that neither moral nor physical evil can shake our faith in one God who governs the world in accord with moral laws!

Editorial notes

Editorial notes

What does it mean to orient oneself in thinking?

1 Moses Mendelssohn, *Gesammelte Schriften* (Jubiläumsausgabe) (Stuttgart and Bad Cannstatt, 1929–) 3:2, 81–2, 198, 211.

2 The author of the *Results* was Thomas Wizenmann (1759–87). Cf. AK, 5:143.

3 See Jacobi, *On the Doctrine of Spinoza, Jacobis Werke* (Leipzig, 1812–25, reprint: Darmstadt, 1980) 4/1:176, 192.

4 Spinoza holds that thoughts are modes of God, considered as a thinking substance (*Ethics* IIP1 Proof), and that the human mind is the idea of an existing (extended) thing (viz. the human body), so that both minds and bodies are modes of the divine substance (*Ethics* IIP11, IIP13).

5 This may be a reference either to Spinoza's proof that there cannot be more than one substance with the same nature or attribute (*Ethics* IP5); or, more generally, to his argument that it is impossible for there to be more than one substance (*Ethics* IP10 Scholium); or, still more broadly, simply to Spinoza's willingness to infer real possibility from lack of contradiction.

6 This may be a reply to criticisms of Kant made by the popular Enlightenment philosophers J. G. Feder and G. A. Tittel. Or the target may be Christoph Meiners, *Outline of a Doctrine of the Soul* (Lemgo, 1786).

7 Cf. Ecclesiastes 1:1.

8 This became Jacobi's most prominent contention in the dispute with Mendelssohn, especially in *Reply to Mendelssohn's Imputations in His Writings to the Friends of Lessing, Werke* 4/2.

On the miscarriage of all philosophical trials in theodicy

1 "For my thoughts are not your thoughts, nor are your ways my ways, saith the Lord." Isaiah 55:8.

2 Count Pietro Verri (1728–97), economist, politician, moralist, and literary man. ("Verri" is the usual spelling of the name.) The reference is to *Sull'indole del piacere* (1773), which was translated into German by Christoph Meiners as *Gedanken über die Natur des Vergnügens* (Leipzig, 1777; *Thoughts Concerning the Nature of Pleasure*). Count Verri was a pioneer in the movement to abolish torture. For another reference to Verri, cf. AK 8:232. For a modern edition of *Sull'indole*, cf. *Sull'indole del piacere e del dolore, con altri scritti di filosofia e di economia*, ed. R. De Felice (Milan: Feltrinelli, 1964).

3 "But he is in one mind, and who can turn him? and what his soul desireth, even that he doeth."

4   "But ask now the beasts, and they shall teach thee: and the fowls of the air, and they shall tell thee: / Or speak to the earth, and it shall teach thee: and the fishes of the sea shall declare unto thee. / Who knoweth not in all these that the hand of the LORD hath wrought this? / In whose hand is the soul of every living thing, and the breath of all mankind. / Doth not the ear try words? and the mouth taste his meat?" "With him is strength and wisdom: the deceived and the deceiver are his."

5   The reference is to "the enlightened Berlin High Consistory which retained its liberal policies even under [the reactionary] King Friedrich Wilhelm II." AK 8:500. Cf. Wilhelm Dilthey, "Drittes Stück der Beiträge aus den Rostocker Kanthandschriften," *Archiv für Geschichte der Philosophie*, 3(1890) 418–50, reprinted as "Kant's Dispute with the Censors over the Right of Free Research in Religion," in *Wilhelm Dilthey: Gesammelte Schriften*, Vol. IV (Stuttgart and Göttingen: Teubner, Vandenhoech & Ruprecht, 2nd ed., 1959), pp. 285–309, cf. p. 288.

6   "God forbid that I should justify you: till I die I will not remove mine integrity from me. / My righteousness I hold fast, and will not let it go: my heart shall not reproach me so long as I live."

7   For Kant's claim that it is not legitimate to irrevocably bind oneself under oath to uphold a historical creed, since future progress in enlightenment might cast doubt on the reliability of the creed, see *Beantwortung der Frage: Was ist Aufklärung? (Answer to the Question: What Is Enlightenment?* 1784, AK 8:38–39). For the significance of Kant's footnote, see the Translator's Introduction to the present text.

8   Jean-André de Luc (1727–1817; Swiss scientist and moralist), *Lettres physiques et morales sur les Montagnes, et sur l'Histoire de la terre et de l'Homme* (La Haye, 1778–80, 6 vols).

9   Mountain range in Germany.

Religion within the boundaries of mere reason

1   Kant is reacting to H. A. Pistorius's review of his *Groundwork of a Metaphysics of Morals* (1785), in *Allgemeine Deutsche Bibliothek*, 66.2(1786): 447–63.

2   In what follows Kant is very likely reacting to August Wilhelm Rehberg's criticism of his moral theory – specifically to Rehberg's rejection of his claim that the law can be itself an effective principle of action, and to Rehberg's denial that the feeling of respect for the law can be more than just an empirical quantity. Rehberg developed his criticism in *Über das Verhältniß der Metaphysik zur Religion* (Berlin: Mylius, 1787; *Concerning the Relationship of Metaphysics to Religion*), and in his review of Kant's *Critique of Practical Reason*, in *Allgemeine Literatur-Zeitung*, Nr 188.a.b. (August 6, 1788): 345–60. Kant had already reacted to Rehberg in at least another place, namely the *Critique of Judgment*, AK 5:177, footnote.

3   Roman law, as distinguished from the common law of the Anglo-Saxon tradition, is the basis of the legal system in much of Europe. Roman civil law (*corpus juris civilis*), which governs the relations between citizens, was codified and published by the Emperor Justinian in A.D. 528–534.

4   The *Berlinische Monatsschrift* was an influential Berlin journal published un-

der various titles from 1783 to 1811 under the editorship of Johann Erich
Biester (1749–1816), who was at some time Frederick II's librarian. Friedrich Gedike (1754–1803) was also its editor up to January 1792. For the
history, see pp. 41–46 and notes b and m in the Translator's Introduction.

5   Johann David Michaelis (1717–91), orientalist, biblical scholar, and professor of philosophy in Göttingen; the work *Moral* (in its German title) was
posthumously edited and published by F. Stäudlin in 1792.

6   Gottlieb Christian Storr (1746–1805), dogmatic theologian, Tübingen professor of theology, and author of *Annotationes ad philosophicam Kantii de
religione doctrinam,* (1793; *Observations Concerning Kant's Philosophical Doctrine
of Religion*), in response to Kant. The book was translated into German by
Storr's follower Johann Friedrich Flatt (1759–1821), as *D. Gottlob Christian
Storr's Bemerkungen über Kant's philosophische Religionslehre. Aus dem Lateini-
schem. Nebst einigen Bemerkungen des Übersetzers über den aus Prinzipien der
praktischen Vernunft hergeleiteten Überzeugungsgrund von der Möglichkeit und
Wirklichkeit einer Offenbarung in Beziehung auf Fichtes Versuch einer Kritik der
Offenbarung* (Tübingen: Cotta, 1794).

7   *Neueste Kritische Nachrichten,* (1793) 225–9. This annual journal was published and edited from 1779–1807 by J. G. P. Möller (1729–1807), professor of rhetoric and history at the University of Greifswald since 1765.

8   John 5:19: "*And* we know that we are of God, and the whole world lieth in
wickedness."

9   According to Bohatec, Kant drew his information from Johann Ith,
*Übersetzung und Kommentar über den Ezour-Vedam, oder die Geschichte, Religion
und Philosophie der Indier (Translation and Commentary of the Ezour-Vedam, or
the History, Religion and Philosophy of the Indians;* Bern, no date) pp. 10 ff., and
from Pierre Sonnerat (French natural scientist and explorer, 1749–1814),
*Reise nach Ostindien und China auf Befehl des Königs unternommen (Voyage to
East-India and China, Undertaken at the King's Request;* 2 vols; Zürich, 1783),
1, pp. 166, 249, both of which he had read. Cf. Bohatec, pp. 166–7, and AK
8:505. The whole imagery of this passage, however, is drawn from the Christian apocalyptic writers, notably Bengel, with whose work, *Ordo temporum
(The Order of Time;* Tübingen, 1741), Kant was acquainted. Cf. *The Conflict of
the Faculties,* AK, 7:62, 80–81. J. A. Bengel (1687–1752) was a mystical
theologian who predicted the end of the world for 1836.

10 Elsewhere, Kant speaks of a "heroic faith in virtue," AK, 8:332.

11 Cf. J.-J. Rousseau (1712–1778), *Discours sur l'origine et les fondemens de
l'inégalité (Discourses on the Origin and Grounds of Inequality,* 1755; German
tr., 1756): "Men are evil. Grim and constant experience dispenses us from
the effort of providing a proof of this. I have however proven, as I believe,
that man is by nature good." Part I, Note IX (second paragraph).

12 The denominations "latitudinarian" and "indifferentist" come from J. F.
Stapfter, *Institutiones theologiæ polemicæ universæ ordine scientifico dispositæ,* 5
vols. (Zürich, 1743–47), 84 and 599 (cited after Bohatec, p. 176, footnote).
Baumgarten refers to an *ethica rigida* as contrasted to a "lax one," in *Ethica
philosophica* (eds. 1740, 1751, 1763), stating that "the more severe an ethics,
the more perfect" (§ 4). Cf. also *Eine Vorlesung Kants über Ethik,* ed. Paul
Menzer (Berlin: Heinse, 1924), p. 93; English trans. Infield/Macmurray,

Lectures on Ethics: "The man who conceives the moral law in such a [lax] way that it allows his feeble conduct to pass muster, who fashions lenient precepts for himself, we call a *latitudinarius*" (London: Methuen, 1930), p. 75. Many of Kant's theological notions and terms derive from the cited work of Stapfter, and from his *Grundlegung zur wahren christlichen Religion (Groundwork of the True Christian Religion)*, 12 Parts (Zürich, 1746–53).

13   Cf. *Metaphysics of Morals*, AK 6:384; also, *Reflexion* 7234, AK 19:291.

14   J. C. F. Schiller (1759–1805), *Über Anmut und Würde in der Moral.*

15   This was a basic principle of rigorist ethics. Kant could have found it stated in Heilmann's *Dogmatics*, a book which (according to Bohatec) he possessed and had certainly read. (Bohatec, p. 177, and footnotes.) J. D. Heilmann, *Compendium theologiæ dogmaticæ* (Göttingen, 1761), § 196.

16   "Only through this independent power of a self-determining will alone – a power which indeed cannot suppress the impulse of needs but can steer them according to its law and through its capacity – can we and must we, as rational beings which should not be looked at or used as *things*, think of ourselves as *persons*." Anonymous (but in fact, C. L. Reinhold), "Über die Grundwahrheit der Moralität und ihr Verhältnis zur Grundwahrheit der Religion" ("Concerning the Fundamental Truth of Morality and its Relation to the Fundamental Truth of Religion"), *Der neue Teutsche Merkur*, 2.3(1791): 225–80, 231. Reinhold further developed his distinction between "practical reason," as the law-giving faculty, and "will" understood as power of choice and as faculty of personality in volume two of his *Kantian Letters*, Nos. 7, 8, 9, 10: *Briefe über die Kantische Philosophie*, 2 vols. (Leipzig: Göschen, 1790 and 1792).

17   Cf. AK 8:19.

18   Cf. J.-J. Rousseau: "We have love *for oneself*, which is only concerned with ourselves, when our true needs are satisfied; self-love, however, which is an object of *comparison*, is never satisfied – nor can it be, because this sentiment, *in preferring ourselves to others*, also requires that others prefer us to themselves." *Émile ou de l'éducation*, (1762) Part 4, ed. John S. Spink, *Oeuvres complètes* (Paris: Gallimard, 1969), Vol. 4, p. 493.

19   Romans 7:15: "For that which I do I allow not: for what I would, that I do not; but what I hate, that do I."

20   Romans 14:23: "And he that doubteth is damned if he eat, because *he eateth* not of faith: for whatsoever *is* not of faith is sin."

21   Sonnerat, *Reise nach Ostindien und China*, describes the customs of these places. Cf. AK 6:505.

22   Samuel Hearne (1745–1792), an English traveler at the service of the Hudson Bay Company. A brief account of Hearne's travels was to be found in Douglas's Introduction to *Cook's Third Voyage*, London, 1784. Cf. Wobbermin, AK 6:501. Perhaps Kant was familiar with Georg Förster, *Geschichte der Reisen die seit Cook an der Nordwest- und Nordöstküste von Amerika und in dem nördlichsten Amerika unternommen worden. . . . (History of the Voyages Undertaken since Cook [. . .] in the Northwest and Northeast Coast of America and in Northmost America;* 3 vols; Berlin, 1792).

23   La Rochefoucauld, *Maximes* (1678), No. 583: "Dans l'adversité de nos

meilleurs amis, nous trouvons toujours quelque chose qui ne nous déplaît pas."

24 There is very likely a reference here to La Rochefoucauld. Cf. *Maximes* (1678), No. 207, "La folie nous suit dans tous les temps de la vie. Si quelqu'un paraît sage, c'est seulement parce que ses folies sont proportionnées à son âge et à sa fortune." ("Folly follows us throughout every stage of life. If someone appears wise, that's only because his follies are proportionate to this age and fortune.")

25 Kant repeats the same idea in *Toward Perpetual Peace* (*Zum ewigen Frieden*, 1795), where he attributes it to an ancient Greek; cf. AK 8:365. However, the identity of the author has not been established. Wobbermin, AK, 6:502.

26 The saying is attributed to Sir Robert Walpole, referring to "certain patriots" and not to human beings in general: "All those men have their price."

27 Romans 3:9–10: "What then? are we better *than they*? No, in no wise: for we have before proved both Jews and Gentiles, that they are all under sin; As it is written, There is none righteous, no, not one."

28 "And the Lord God commended the man, saying, Of every tree of the garden thou may freely eat: But of the tree of the knowledge of good and evil, thou shalt not eat of it: for on the day that thou eatest thereof thou shalt surely die."

29 "And when the woman saw that the tree was good for food, and that it was pleasant to the eyes, and a tree to be desired to make one wise, she took of the fruit thereof, and did eat, and gave also unto her husband with her; and he did eat."

30 Cf. Revelation 12:9: "Satan, which deceiveth the whole world . . ."

31 Romans 5:12: "Wherefore, as by one man sin entered into the world, and death by sin; and so death passed upon all men, for that all have sinned." That "in Adam we all sinned" is the Augustinian interpretation of this verse based on the Vulgate (Latin) translation. This interpretation was also common in the early Lutheran churches. Cf. Wobbermin, AK 6:502.

32 "How art thou fallen from heaven, O Lucifer, son of the morning! how art thou cut down to the ground, which didst weaken the nations!" Isaiah 14:12. Cf. Luke 10:18; Revelation 8:10. The church Fathers interpreted this fall of the morning star (*Luciferus*, in the Latin of the Vulgate) as the fall through sin of the prince of the angels.

33 Cf. Genesis 3:3–5, where the serpent tempts the woman to eat the fruit from the tree of knowledge of good and evil.

34 Cf. Martin Luther: "From the inception of sanctity up to its perfection there are infinite degrees." "Dictata super Psalterium: Psalmus LXXIV [LXXV]" *Kritische Gesammtausgabe* (Weimar, 1883–), Vol. 3, p. 512.

35 Colossians 3:9–10: "Lie not to one another, seeing that ye have put off the old man with his deeds; and have put on the new man, which is renewed in knowledge after the image of him that created him"; also Ephesians 4:22, 24.

36 "Verily, verily, I say unto thee, Except a man be born of water and of the Spirit, he cannot enter into the kingdom of God."

37 "And the earth was without form and void; and darkness was upon the face of the deep. And the spirit of God moved upon the face of the waters."

38 Colossians 2:9–10.

39 Cf. verse 15: "And it came to pass, that when [the nobleman] was returned, having received the kingdom, then he commanded these servants to be called unto him, to whom he had given the money, that he might know how much every man had gained by trading."

40 "Virtue (*virtus*) is named after man (*vir*); fortitude, however, pertains most to a man." Cicero, *Tusculanæ Disputationes*, II:18.43. *aner* ['ἀνήρ] in Greek means "man"; *andreios* ['ἀνδρεῖος] means both "male" and "valiant."

41 "They [the Stoics] say that the fountain-head of all disorders is intemperance, which is a desertion from all guide of the mind and right reason, so adverse to the precepts of reason that the cravings of the soul can in no way be reined or contained." Cicero, *Tusculanæ Disputationes*, 6:9.22.

42 Kant had been accused of not having been altogether fair to the Stoics in his *Critique of Practical Reason*. Cf. A. W. Rehberg's review of this work in *Allgemeine Literatur-Zeitung*, August 6, 1788, 188a and 188b, column 358 (last paragraph).

43 The saying *virtutes gentium, splendida vitia* (the virtues of the nations are splendid vices) has been traditionally attributed to Augustine and is consistent with the general tendency of his thought, even though it has never been found in any of his extant writings. Cf. Wobbermin, AK 6:502.

44 Cf. *Critique of Practical Reason*, AK 5:127, footnote.

45 Cf. Ephesians 6:12: "For we wrestle not against flesh and blood, but against principalities, against powers, against the rulers of the darkness of this world, against spiritual wickedness in high places."

46 Cf. A. G. Baumgarten (1714–1762), *Metaphysica*, 7th ed. (Halle, 1779), § 946: "God's end in creating the world was the perfection of creatures, so far as it is possible in the best world." However, Baumgarten's conclusion is that "therefore the ends of creation are the cult of God and religion," § 947. God's ultimate end in creating the universe was "his own glory," § 943.

47 John 1:1–2: "In the beginning was the Word, and the Word was with God, and the Word was God. The same was in the beginning with God."

48 John 1:3: "All things were made by him; and without him was not any thing made that was made."

49 Hebrews 1:3: "Who being the brightness of *his* glory, and the express image of his person, and upholding all things by the word of his power."

50 John 3:14: "For God so loved the world, that he gave his only begotten Son, that whosoever believeth in him should not perish, but have everlasting life." Cf. also I John 4:9–10: "In this was manifested the love of God toward us, because that God sent his only begotten Son into the world, so that we might live through him."

51 John 1:12: "But as many as received him, to them gave he power to become the sons of God, even to them that believe on his name."

52 Cf. Philippians 2:8.

53 Albrecht Haller (1708–1777), in his poem "Über den Ursprung des Übels" ("Concerning the Origin of Evil," 1734), 2:33–34. Kant alludes to the same line in his *Lectures on the Philosophical Doctrine of Religion*, 28:1077.

54 John 3:16: "For God so loved the world that he gave his only begotten Son, that whosoever believeth in him should not perish, but have everlasting life."

55 John 8:46: "Which of you convinceth me of sin? And if I say the truth, why do ye not believe me?"

56 Matthew 5:48: "Be ye therefore perfect, even as your Father which is in Heaven is perfect." Cf. Leviticus 11:44 and I Peter 1:16.

57 Matthew 6:33: "But seek ye first the kingdom of God, and his righteousness; and all these things shall be added unto you."

58 Romans 8:16: "The Spirit itself beareth witness with our spirit, that we are the children of God."

59 Philippians 2:12: "Wherefore, my beloved, as ye have always obeyed, not as in my presence only, but now much more in my absence, work out your own salvation with fear and trembling."

60 Francis Moore, *A New Collection of Voyages and Travels*, 1745; translated into German by G. J. Schwabe as *Allgemeine Historie der Reisen (A General History of Voyages)*, 3 vols. (1748). Cf. Wobbermin, AK 6:503.

61 Cf. Colossians 3:9-10.

62 Genesis 3:15-19.

63 Nicolas Malebranche (1638-1715), *De la recherche de la vérité (Concerning the Search of Truth,* 1674-75), Bk. IV, ch. 11.

64 Cf. Colossians 3:9-10.

65 Romans 6:6: "Knowing this, that our old man is crucified with *him,* that the body of sin might be destroyed, that henceforth we should not serve sin."

66 Galatians 5:24: "And they that are Christ's have crucified the flesh with the affections and lusts."

67 Romans 8:1: "There is therefore now no condemnation to them which are in Christ Jesus, who walk not after the flesh, but after the Spirit."

68 Matthew 5:25.

69 "And God blessed them, and said unto them, Be fruitful, and multiply, and replenish the earth, and subdue it: and have dominion over the fish of the sea, and over the fowl of the air, and over every living thing that moveth upon the earth."

70 Pierre-François Xavier de Charlevoix (1682-1761) wrote an account of his experiences as a Jesuit missionary in Canada entitled *Histoire et description générale de la Nouvelle-France (General History and Description of New France),* Paris, 1744. Wobbermin, AK 6:503.

71 John 14:30: ". . . for the prince of the world cometh, and hath nothing in me."

72 Cf. Luke 4:5-7: "And the devil, taking him up into an high mountain, shewed unto him all the kingdoms of the world in a monent of time. And the devil said unto him, All this power will I give thee, and the glory of them: for that is delivered unto me: and to whomsoever I will give it. If thou therefore wilt worship me, all shall be thine."

73 Karl Friedrick Bahrdt (1741-92), a popular rationalist and voluminous writer. *System der moralischen Religion zur endlichen Beruhigung für Zweifler und Denker. Allen Christen und Nichtchristen lesbar.* (*System of Moral Religion for the Ultimate Pacification of Doubters and Thinkers. Readable by All Christians and Non-Christians,* Berlin, 1787; 3rd ed., 1791), cf. chapters 9 and 10. Cf. Wobbermin, AK 6:503.

74 The "fragmentarist" is the deist Hermann Samuel Reimarus (1694-1768),

sometime professor of oriental languages at Hamburg and popular author. Reimarus was the author of a stinging attack on the reliability of the biblical narratives conducted along the customary lines of rationalistic interpretation. The attack was so radical in tone that Reimarus himself had kept it secret during his lifetime. Fragments of it, however, were posthumously published by Lessing, without attribution, as part of his program of making public materials discovered at the Wolfenbüttel library, where he was then librarian. Lessing prefaced each fragment with a rebuttal of its attack on the reasonableness of Christian beliefs. These fragments (seven in number, 1774–8) eventually forced Lessing into a bitter dispute with the orthodox pastor Goeze. The "Fragment" at issue here is the seventh in the series.

75 Luke 22:19.

76 Cf. John 1:11–12.

77 Titus 2:14: ". . . that he might redeem us from all iniquity and purify unto himself a people for his own possession, zealous of good works."

78 Matthew 16:18: ". . . thou art Peter, and upon this rock I will build my church; and the gates of hell shall not prevail against it."

79 Mark 9:39–40: "But Jesus said, Forbid him not: for there is no man which shall do a miracle in my name, that can lightly speak evil of me. For he that is not against us is on our part."

80 John 4:48.

81 Johann Konrad Pfenniger (1747–92), pastor at Zürich; cf. his work, *Appellation an den Menschenverstand, gewisse Vorfälle, Schriften und Personen betreffend, (An Appeal to Common Sense, With Reference to Certain Events, Writings, and Persons;* Hamburg, 1776), especially No. 8. Wobbermin, AK 6:504.

82 Johann Kaspar Lavater (1741–1801), Swiss poet, physiognomist, and pietist theologian. He preached a religion of feeling and inner inspiration which brought God to the level of man. He advocated a literal reading of the Bible and was a great believer in the power of prayer, and in the possibility of miracles. He is notorious for his challenge to Moses Mendelssohn to convert to Chrisitanity. Lavater fitted Kant's image of the "enthusiast" perfectly. For Kant's correspondence with Lavater, see the Translator's Introduction above, pp. 49–50.

83 Cf. Genesis 22.

84 *Der höllische Proteus oder tausend-künstige Versteller (nebenst vorberichtlichen Grundbeweis der Gewissheit, daß es wirklich Gespester gebe),* abgebildet durch Erasmum Francisci, Nürnberg, 1708: *The Hellish Protheus, or The Deceiver of a Thousand Arts (Together with a preliminary justification of the certainty that ghosts truly exist),* depicted by Francis Erasmus. AK 6:504.

85 Romans 6:18: "Being then made free from sin, ye became the servants of righteousness."

86 Cf. Thomas Hobbes (1588–1679), *De cive* (1642) 1:12. Hobbes's full text reads: "Negari non potest, quin status hominum naturalis antequam in societatem coiretur, bellum fuerit; neque hoc simpliciter, sed bellum omnium in omnes." ("It cannot be denied that the natural state of men before they come together in society is war – not war in an ordinary sense but a war of all against all.")

87 *De cive,* 1:12.

88 Acts 5:29.

89 Acts 1:24: "Thou, Lord, which knowest the hearts of all men . . ."; Acts 15:8: "And God, which knoweth the hearts . . ."; Luke 16:5: ". . . but God knoweth your hearts."

90 I Peter 2:10: "Which in time past *were* not a people, but *are* now a people of God."

91 Titus 2:14: ". . . that he [Jesus Christ] might redeem us from all iniquity, and purify unto himself a peculiar people, zealous of good works."

92 Cf. "Idea for a Universal History," Prop. 6; AK 8:23.

93 Matthew 6:10: "Thy kingdom come. Thy will be done in earth, as it is in heaven." Luke 11:2: "Thy kingdom come. Thy will be done, as in heaven, so in earth."

94 Here Kant gives an interpretation of the traditional attributes of the Church: one, holy, catholic, apostolic. Cf. AK 6:504.

95 Matthew 7:21: "Not every one that saith unto me, Lord, Lord, shall enter into the kingdom of heaven; but he that doeth the will of my Father which is in heaven."

96 *Alphabetum Tibetanum missionum apostolicarum commodo editum . . .* , studio et labore Fr. Augustini Antonii Georgii emeritae Augustinui (Romae, 1762). Cf. AK 6:504.

97 According to Wobbermin, this etymological explanation is certainly erroneous. *Ketzer* is more likely to derive from *Kathari*, i.e., the "Catharans" or "pure ones," the most significant heretical sect in Medieval Europe in the twelfth and thirteenth century. The presence in the movement of an ancient manichean element is unmistakable. AK 6:504.

98 Here Kant is dealing with a problem to which Lessing had given the classical formulation: "Accidental truths of history can never become a proof of necessary truths of reason"; and again, "But to jump over from that historical truth [of the gospel] into a totally different class of truths; and to demand that I should construct all my metaphysical and moral concepts accordingly. . . . That, that is the broad and terrible ditch that I cannot overcome, however often and earnestly I have tried to make the jump." On *"The Proof of the Spirit and the Power" (Über den Beweis des Geistes und der Kraft*, 1777), *Gotthold Ephraim Lessing: Sämmtliche Werke*, ed. K. Lachmann and F. Muncker (Stuttgart/Leipzig/Berlin: Göschen, 1886–1924), Vol. 13, pp. 5, 7.

99 Cf. verse 13: "Consume them in wrath, consume them, that they may not be: and let them know that God ruleth in Jacob unto the ends of the earth."

100 Cf. Preface to the Second Edition, pp. 64–65 above, and the reference there.

101 Matthew 5:21ff., 44ff.

102 Romans 12:19; cf. Deuteronomy 32:35: "To me belongeth vengeance, and recompense."

103 Adrian Reland (1676–1718), a Dutch Orientalist, wrote *De religione mohammedica libri duo*, 2nd ed. (Trajecti ad Rhenum: 1717). Cf. II, Paragraph xvii. AK 6:504.

104 Hindu, or orthodox, sacred scriptural texts. They originated in the north of India around 1500 B.C.

105 Kant is very likely relying on Ith, *Übersetzung und Kommentar über den Ezour-*

Vedam, oder die Geschichte, Religion und Philosophie der Indier (Translation and Commentary of the Ezour-Veda, or the History, Religion, and Philosophy of the Hindus): "*Shasta* truly means science or cognition, *explanation*, clarification. According to this derivation, the *Shastri* cannot be anything but explanations, clarifications, of the Veda. We believe we can say that the intention of their authors was to present the Hindu religion from a rational perspective, to convince that its fables were all philosophical allegories."; pp. 87 ff. Cited after Bohatec, p. 431.

106 James 2:17: "Even so faith, if it hath not works, is dead, being alone."

107 II Timothy 3:16: "All scripture is given by inspiration of God, and is profitable for doctrine, for reproof, for correction, for instruction in righteousness."

108 John 16:13: "Howbeit when he, the Spirit of truth, is come, he will guide you into all truth."

109 John 5:39: "Search the scriptures; for in them ye think ye have eternal life: and they are they which testify of me."

110 Cf. *Die Metaphysik der Sitten (The Metaphysics of Morals)*, AK 6:327.

111 John 7:17: "If any man will do his will, he shall know of the doctrine, whether it be of God. . ."

112 *fides mercenaria, servilis, ingenua:* apparently these are terms coined by Kant. Cf. Bohatec, p. 440, note.

113 Cf. G. Achenwall, *Prolegomena iuris naturalis,* 5th ed. (Göttingen: 1781), § 85. Cited after Bohatec, p. 442, note.

114 Colossians 3:9–10.

115 Colossians 3:9–10; Ephesians 4:22,24.

116 Romans 9:18: "Therefore hath he mercy on whom he will have mercy, and whom he will he hardeneth."

117 *Salto mortale,* i.e. an upward leap accompanied by a rotation of the body that brings the head below the feet. Jacobi had recommended such a leap to Lessing, in order to gain the freedom of faith and thereby escape the determinism which – as Jacobi thought – is the inevitable consequence of a philosophy based on reason alone. In direct opposition to Jacobi, Kant here claims that faith (not reason) leads to a deterministic view of human destiny. Cf. F. H. Jacobi, *Concerning the Doctrine of Spinoza in Letters to Herr Moses Mendelssohn (Über die Lehre des Spinoza in Briefen an Herrn Moses Mendelssohn;* Breslau: Löwe, 1785), pp. 32–3.

118 I Corinthians 15:28: "And when all things shall be subdued unto him, then shall the Son also himself be subject unto him that put all things under him, that God may be all in all."

119 Cf. I Corinthians 13:11: "When I was a child, I spake as a child, I understood as a child, I thought as a child: but when I became a man, I put away childish things."

120 I Corinthians 13:11.

121 Matthew 12:28: "But if I cast out devils by the Spirit of God, then the kingdom of God is come unto you."

122 Cf. Jewish religion is "a public national religion, which was always implicated with *civil society*, and always had a political purpose." J. S. Semler (died 1791; the major exponent of Enlightenment theology), *Letztes Glaubensbekenntnis*

über natürlicher und christlicher Religion, (A Recent Profession of Faith Regarding Natural and Christian Religion; Königsberg, 1792), p. 10. Cited after Bohatec, p. 461.

123   Cf. Semler, *Letztes Glaubensbekenntnis über natürliche und christliche Religion,* pp. 116, 126, where Semler sharply divides Christianity from Judaism. (Cited after Bohatec, p. 460.) Semler's book was a reply to one of Dr. Bahrdt's many books (cf. above, Part II, Kant's note on p. 120).

124   Cf. Matthew 5:48: "Be ye therefore perfect, even as your Father which is in heaven is perfect"; I Peter 1:16: "Because it is written, Be ye holy; for I am holy."

125   Cf. Matthew 28:20: "Teaching them to observe all things whatsoever I have commanded you: and, lo, I am with you always, even unto the end of the world."

126   The Sibylline books were a body of prophetic literature accumulated, according to tradition, by female seers (the first of whom, Sibyl, gave her name to her descendants) under the influence of a deity, usually Apollo. These books in Greek hexameter, which disappeared in A.D. 83, exerted a strong influence on Roman religion.

127   Revelation 12:9: "And the great dragon was cast out, that old serpent, called the Devil, and Satan, which deceiveth the whole world: he was cast out into the earth, and his angels were cast out with him."

128   Matthew 5:12. Greene and Hudson note that Kant uses *vergolten* (repaid) as opposed to the *belohnet* (rewarded) in Luther's Bible. Greene/Hudson, p. 125, note.

129   Cf. I Corinthians 15:26: "The last enemy that shall be destroyed is death."

130   I Corinthians 15:28. Cf. above, p. 151, note 118.

131   Cf. Matthew 26:64: "Jesus saith unto him. . . . Hereafter shall ye see the Son of man sitting on the right hand of power, and coming in the clouds of heaven."

132   Kant apparently derived his information on Zoroaster from Sonnerat, *Reise,* to which he explicitly refers in *The End of All Things,* AK 8:328–9, footnote.

133   Cf. above, Part I, translator's note 9, p. 59.

134   Ith, *Übersetzung und Kommentar,* Introduction, pp. 6 ff., 58, 88. Bohatec, p. 167, note 10.

135   Cf. Matthew 26:61–5.

136   Mark 3:28: "Verily I say unto you, All sins shall be forgiven unto the sons of men, and blasphemies wherewith soever they shall blaspheme"; also Ephesians 3:5.

137   I John 4:8: "He that loveth not knoweth not God; for God is love"; I John 4:16: "And we have known and believed the love that God hath to us. God is love; and he that dwelleth in love dwelleth in God, and God in him."

138   John 15:26: "But when the Comforter is come, whom I will send unto you from the Father, even the Spirit of truth, which proceedeth from the Father, he shall testify of me." This is the Western (Augustinian) formula of the dogma of the Trinity. Cf. Wobbermin, AK 6:505.

139   John 16:13: "Howbeit when he, the Spirit of truth, is come, he will guide you into all truth."

140 II Timothy 4:1: "I charge thee therefore before God, and the Lord Jesus Christ, who shall judge the quick and the dead at his appearing and his kingdom."

141 John 16:8: "And when he is come, he will reprove the world of sin, and of righteousness, and of judgment."

142 On Kant's interpretation of the Trinity, cf. *Reflexionen* 6092, 6093, AK 18:448–9.

143 "In those days came John the Baptist, preaching in the wilderness of Judæa, And saying, Repent ye: for the kingdom of heaven is at hand." Matthew 3:1–2.

144 "But I say unto you, That whoever looketh on a woman to lust after her hath committed adultery with her already in his heart."

145 "Be ye therefore perfect, even as your Father which is in heaven is perfect."

146 "But I say unto you, That whoever is angry with his brother without a cause shall be in danger of the judgement: and whosoever shall say to his brother, Raca, shall be in danger of the council: but whosoever shall say, Thou fool, shall be in danger of hell fire."

147 "Leave there thy gift before the altar, and go thy way: first be reconciled to thy brother, and then come and offer thy gift."

148 "But I say unto you, Swear not at all. . . . But let your communication be, Yea, yea; Nay, nay: for whatsoever is more than these cometh of evil."

149 "But I say unto you, That ye resist not evil; but whosoever shall smite thee on the right cheek, turn to him the other also. And if any man will sue thee at the law, and take away thy coat, let him have thy cloak also."

150 "But I say unto you, Love your enemies, bless them that curse you, do good to them that hate you, and pray for them that despitefully use you, and persecute you."

151 "Think not that I have come to destroy the law, or the prophets . . ."

152 "Enter ye in at the strait gate: for wide is the gate, and broad is the way, that leads to destruction, and many there be that go in thereat."

153 Cf.: "Strive to enter in at the narrow gate; for many, I say unto you, will seek to enter in, and shall not be able." Luke 13:24.

154 "Ye shall know them by their fruits. Do men gather grapes of thorns, or figs of thistles?"

155 "Not everyone that saith unto me, Lord, Lord, shall enter into the kingdom of heaven; but he that doeth the will of my Father which is in heaven."

156 "Let your light so shine before men, that they may see your good works, and glorify your Father which is in heaven."

157 "Moreover when ye fast, be not, as the hypocrites, of a sad countenance: for they disfigure their faces, that they may appear unto men to fast. Verily I say unto you. They have their reward."

158 "The kingdom of heaven is like a grain of mustard seed, which a man took, and sowed in his field: Which indeed is the least of all seeds: but when it is grown, it is the greatest of all herbs, and becometh a tree, so that the birds of the air come and lodge in the branches thereof. . . . The kingdom of heaven is like unto leaven, which a woman took, and hid in three measures of meal, till the whole was leavened."

159 "For unto every one that hath shall be given, and shall have abundance: but from him that hath not shall be taken away even that which he hath."

160 "Blessed are ye, when men shall revile you, and persecute you, and shall say all manner of evil against you falsely, for my sake. Rejoice, and be exceeding glad: for great is your reward in heaven."

161 "Then the steward said within himself . . . I am resolved what to do, that, when I am put out of the stewardship, they may receive me into their houses. So he called every one of his lord's debtors unto him, and said unto the first, How much owest thou my lord? And he said, a hundred measures of oil. And he said unto him, Take thy bill, and sit down quickly, and write fifty. . . . And the lord commended the unjust steward, because he had done wisely: for the children of this world are in their generation wiser than the children of light."

162 "For I was hungered, and ye gave me meat: I was thirsty, and ye gave me drink: I was a stranger, and ye took me in. . . . Then shall the righteous answer him, saying: Lord, when saw we hungered, and fed thee? or thirsty, and gave thee drink? When saw we thee a stranger, and took thee in? . . . And the King shall answer and say unto them, Verily I say unto you, Inasmuch as ye have done it unto one of the least of these my brethren, ye have done it unto me."

163 Cf. Ephesians 2:15–21.

164 The source of this citation is unknown.

165 Moses Mendelssohn (1729–86), renowned Enlightenment philosopher and a close friend of G. E. Lessing. With Lessing and C. F. Nicolai he contributed to *Briefe, die neueste Literatur betreffend (Letters Concerning the Most Recent Literature)*, one of the most important catalysts in the formation of the German Enlightenment. In 1763 his essay, *Abhandlung über die Evidenz in den metaphysischen Wissenschaften (Essay on Evidence in the Metaphysical Sciences)*, won first prize from the Berlin Academy. Kant's submission in the same competition, *Untersuchung über die Deutlichkeit der Grundsätze der natürlichen Theologie und der Moral (Inquiry Concerning the Clarity of the Principles of Natural Theology and Morality*, AK 2:273 ff.), was only awarded an honorable mention. In *Phädon oder über die Unsterblichkeit der Seele*, 1767 *("Phaedo," or on the Immortality of the Soul)*, Mendelssohn set out his argument for the immortality of the soul which Kant sought to refute in the second edition of the *Critique of Pure Reason* (B 395 ff.). In *Morgenstunden, oder Vorlesungen über das Dasein Gottes*, 1785 *(Morning Hours, or Lectures on the Existence of God)*, Mendelssohn elaborated once more the Cartesian argument for the existence of God and the argument from design. From 1783 until his death in 1786 he became involved in a correspondence with F. H. Jacobi on the question whether Lessing (who had died in 1781) had been a Spinozist. The correspondence eventually deteriorated into an open and bitter dispute in which reason itself, and its relation to faith, became the central issue. Kant's 1786 essay, *Was heißt: Sich im Denken orientiren? (What Does It Mean To Orient Oneself in Thinking?* AK 8:131 ff.), is his contribution to the dispute.

The reference in the present note is to Mendelssohn's 1783 political treatise *Jerusalem oder über religiöse Macht und Judentum* (*Jerusalem, or on Religious Power and Judaism*, cf. *Gesammelte Schriften, Jubiläumsausgabe*, Vol. 8 [Stuttgart-Bad Cannstatt: Fromann, 1983], p. 145). A similar comment by Kant concerning Mendelssohn can be found in *Der Streit der Fakultäten*, 1798 (*The Conflict of the Faculties*, AK 7:52, note). Section III of Kant's *Über den Gemeinspruch: Das mag in der Theorie richtig sein, taugt aber nicht in die Praxis*, 1793 (*On the Common Saying: That May Be Correct in Theory, but It Is No Use in Practice*, AK 8:307 ff.) is dedicated to a criticism of one of the theses defended by Mendelssohn against Lessing in the treatise *Jerusalem*.

166 Cf. *What Does It Mean to Orient Oneself in Thinking?* AK 8:142.

167 Kant is very likely referring here to August Willhelm Rehberg (political man in Hanover and writer, 1757–1836) who reviewed Kant's *Critique of Practical Reason* in the *Allgemeine Literatur-Zeitung*, August 6–7, 1788, Nos. 188a–188b, columns 345–60. Rehberg accused Kant of falling victim to the same amphiboly of reason of which he had accused the Leibnizians in his first *Critique* (columns 353–4). Specifically, Rehberg argued that pure Critique reason can indeed be the formal principle for morality but not the efficient cause of the actions that occur in the sensible world in accordance with it; hence some other motive must be sought for such actions than the law itself as formally stipulated by pure reason. Kant had tried to give evidence for the efficacy of pure reason in the sensible world by pointing to the feeling of respect for the law which he assumed every moral subject to have, and which he took to be the fundamental temporal determination of that subject attributable to the law itself. Rehberg argued that, on the contrary, that feeling could not be an effect of pure reason without the latter being thereby subjected to the conditions of space and time. To the extent that this supposed "respect" is a genuine feeling, it must be sensible and hence not the product of reason, i.e. either it is not a feeling at all or it must be a case of self-love (354). Just as the concept of creation can meaningfully apply only to a causal relation holding between two beings, one infinite and the other finite yet both equally noumenal, so too any moral efficacy of pure reason would have to be conceived as devolving into an effect just as noumenal as its cause. The concept of a sensible event brought about by pure reason would on the contrary entail just as much of an illicit transition from one level of categorization to another as the concept of a created appearance (356–7). Rehberg also accused Kant of courting enthusiasm. "The thought," he argued, "that the law itself must be the incentive of morality is itself enthusiasm (*Schwärmerei*). For what else can it possibly be but enthusiasm (which consists in the fabrication of supersensible objects) if respect for the law is to be a feeling yet not a sensible feeling (*sinnliche Empfindung*)? And this enthusiasm immediately leads to another kind of enthusiasm, the worst of them all – the deadening of the senses" (355). The fundamental problem bedeviling Kant's position according to Rehberg is that whatever self-consciousness we can have of the law as effective in the sensible world would have to be empirical, hence not fit to detect a moral object. To claim any other self-consciousness would be to project into a supersensible world a consciousness which in fact can only be sensible. For Rehberg's review, cf. Christian Gottfried Schütz's letter to Kant of June 23,

1788 (Schütz, professor of rhetoric at Jena, was the founder of the *Jena Literaturzeitung*).

Also intended might be Johann August Heinrich Ulrich (1744–1807; professor of philosophy at Jena), whose book *Eleutheriologie oder über Freyheit und Nothwendigkeit* (Jena: Cröker, 1788) attacked Kant's attempt at reconciling causality through freedom and natural causality. Christian Jakob Kraus (1753–1807; professor of moral and political philosophy at Königsberg, sometime student of Kant and close friend) reviewed the book anonymously in the *Allgemeine Literatur-Zeitung*, April 25, 1788, No. 100, columns 177–84. For how much Kant might have had a hand in this review, cf. AK 8:524. For Ulrich's campaign against Kant, cf. Carl Leonhard Reinhold's letter to Kant of March 1, 1788, and Kant's reply of March 7, 1788.

168 *Fables*, 2:5,1–3:

> Est ardelionum quædam Romæ natio,
> Trepide concursans, occupata in otio
> Gratis anhelans, multa agendo nil agens.

"There is a class of busybodies at Rome, hurriedly running in concourse, employed in idleness, out of breath for no reason, doing nothing while doing many things."

169 These practices were reported by Lepechin, *Tagebuch der Reise durch verschiedene Provinzen des Russischen Reiches*, 1776, I, p. 280 *(Diary of a Voyage through Various Provinces of the Russian Empire)*, and by P. S. Pallas, *Reise durch verschiedenen Provinzen des Russischen Reiches*, 1771, I, p. 354 *(A Voyage through Various Provinces of the Russian Empire)*. Cited after Bohatec, p. 510, note 6a.

170 "The wind bloweth where it listeth, and thou hearest the sound thereof, but canst not tell whence it cometh, and whither it goeth: so is every one that is born of the Spirit." John 3:8.

171 The Tunguses were a people of Siberia; the Wogulites, a Finnish people living in the Urals. According to Bohatec (p. 516, notes 24–25), Kant derived his knowledge of shamanism, and of the customs of such peoples as the Tunguses and the Wogulites (including their cult of the bear), from the works of J. G. Georgi, *Bemerkung einer Reise im Russischen Reich*, 1775 *(Report of a Voyage in the Russian Empire)*, *Beschreibung aller Nationen des Russischen Reiches*, 1776 *(Description of All the Nations of the Russian Empire)*, and from J. G. Gmelin, *Reisen durch Sibirien*, 1751 *(Voyages through Siberia)*.

172 The "Independents" were a Christian sect founded by John Robinson in 1610.

173 "For my yoke is easy, and my burden is light." Matthew 11:30.

174 "For this is the love of God, that we keep his commandments: and his commandments are not grievous." I John 5:3.

175 "For ye see your calling, brethren, how that not many wise men after the flesh, not many mighty, not many noble, are called." I Corinthians 1:26.

176 "But God hath chosen the foolish things of the world to confound the wise; and God hath chosen the weak things of the world to confound the things which are mighty." I Corinthians 1:27.

177 *Epistles*, 1:18. The saying is cited totally out of context. Pliny is writing to a client who wishes to postpone a court hearing because of a menacing

dream. After encouraging him to give the dream a good interpretation, as he had once done himself to a dream that had frightened him, Pliny goes on: "See then if you can follow my example, and give a happy interpretation to your dream; but if you still think there is more safety in the warning given by all cautious folk, 'When in doubt do nothing,' you can write and tell me." Tr. Betty Radice (Cambridge: Harvard, 1969), p. 55.

178 The thesis of probabilism was defined in 1577 by the Salamancan Dominican Bartolomeo de Medina with the now classical formula: "Si est opinio probabilis, licitum est eam sequi, licet opposita, se est probabilior." ("It is legitimate to follow a probable opinion even if there is an opposite and more probable one.") Cf. AK 6:506. The original intention of this moral doctrine was to prevent the proliferation of obligations by limiting their basis to laws of undoubted authority. The doctrine was especially favored by the Jesuit moralists but bitterly opposed by the Jansenists. Pascal satirized its abuses in *Lettres provinciales*, § 5 ff. Cf. *Oeuvres complètes*, ed. Louis Lafuma (Paris: Aux editions du seuil, 1963), pp. 387 ff.

179 "And the Lord said unto the servant, Go out into the highways and hedges, and compel them to come in, that my house may be filled." Luke 14:23. The Gospel injunction, "compel them to come in," was used by Augustine as proof of the state's obligation to use force agains idolaters, heretics, and schismatics. Cf. *Epistles* Nos. 93 and 95. AK 6:506.

180 Genesis 22.

181 Cf. above, p. 6:173 (of Kant's text) and Kant's note.

182 A "hadji" is one who has undertaken the pilgrimage to Mecca (the "hadj"). Bohatec tried in vain to locate Kant's source for this proverb (p. 519, note 35a).

183 "And straightway the father of the child cried out, and said with tears, Lord, I believe, help thou mine unbelief." Mark 9:24.

184 Cf. Ovid, *Metamorphoses*, I, 128–55:
Last came the race of iron. In that hard age
Of baser vein all evil straight broke out . . .
Honour and love lay vanquished, and from earth,
With slaughter soaked, Justice, virgin divine,
The last of the immortals, fled away.
    Tr. A. D. Melville (Oxford: Oxford University Press, 1986), p. 5.
Astræa, daughter of Jupiter, was often considered the goddess of justice like her mother Themis.

185 "Pray without ceasing." I Thessalonians 5:17.

186 Ephesians 2:15–21.

187 "And Jesus said unto them. . . . If ye have faith as a grain of mustard seed, ye shall say unto this mountain, Remove hence to yonder place; and it shall remove; and nothing shall be impossible unto you." Matthew 17:20; cf. Luke 17:6.

188 The authorship of many psalms is traditionally attributed to King David.

189 "Having abolished in his flesh the enmity . . . to make in himself of twain one new man, so making peace. . . . Now therefore ye are no more strangers and foreigners, but fellow citizens with the saints, and of the household of God; And are built upon the foundation of the apostles and prophets,

Jesus Christ himself being the chief corner stone; In whom all the building fitly framed together groweth unto an holy temple in the Lord." Ephesians 2:15–21.

190 The reference is probably to the story of Amphion and Zethus, twin sons of Zeus by Antiope. The two brothers slew Lycus, the commander in chief of the Theban army who had maltreated their mother, and thereupon gained sovereignty over the city. They then began to fortify it. According to the story, Amphion walked around the city playing his lyre, and at its sound stones began to gather on their own accord until a wall rose. Cf. Apollodorus, *The Library*, 3.5.

191 Exodus 20:4.

192 "Not every one that saith unto me, Lord, Lord, shall enter into the kingdom of heaven; but he that doeth the will of my Father which is in heaven." Matthew 7:21.

193 "Neither do men light a candle, and put it under a bushel, but on a candlestick; and it giveth light unto all that are in the house." Matthew 5:15.

The end of all things

1 Victor Albrecht von Haller, *Imperfect Poem on Eternity* (1736). See *Hallers Gedichte*, edited by Ludwig Hirzel (Bibliothek alterer Schriftwerke der deutschen Schweitz, 1882), Volume 3, p. 151. cf. KrV A613/B641 and AK 2:40.

2 "And the stars of heaven fell to earth, as a fig tree drops its late figs when it is shaken by a mighty wind. Then the sky receded, as a scroll when it is rolled up" (Rev. 6:13–14).

3 "Then death and Hades were cast into a lake of fire. This is the second death. And anyone not found written in the Book of Life was cast into the lake of fire. And I saw a new heaven and a new earth, for the first heaven and the first earth had passed away" (Rev. 20:14–21:1).

4 Pierre Sonnerat (1749–1814), French naturalist and traveler. Kant is referring to the German edition of his *Travels to East India and China Undertaken by Royal Command from 1774 to 1781* (Zurich, 1783), in two volumes. In Volume 2, pp. 38ff., "Godeman" is mentioned as one of the gods of the Papuans and Burmese.

5 Cf. 2 Kings 2:11: "Then it happened, as they [Elijah and Elisha] continued on and talked, that suddenly a chariot of fire appeared with horses of fire, and separated the two of them; and Elijah went up by a whirlwind into heaven."

6 Cf. Numbers 16:32: "And the earth opened its mouth and swallowed them up, with their households and all the men with Korah, with all their goods."

7 The King James version reads: "And the angel whom I saw standing on the sea and on the land lifted up his hand to heaven and swore by him who lives forever and ever, who created heaven and the things that are in it, the earth and the things that are in it, and the sea and the things that are in it, that there should be delay no longer" (Rev. 10:5–6).

8 Presumably a reference to the Chinese philosopher Lao-Tsu (c. 600–531 B.C.), founder of Taoism, to whom the *Tao Te Ching* is attributed.

9 This paragraph alludes to a German translation of writings by the French Jesuit Gabriel F. Coyer (1707–82), *Moralische Kleinigkeiten* (Berlin, 1761). Cf. AK 7:83.

10 Matthew 5:12.

The conflict of the faculties

1 Johann Christoph Wöllner (1732–1800). See General Introduction.

2 According to Arthur Warda, the friend was Kant's later biographer Andreas Christoph Wasianski, with whom he had been close since 1790 (see Vorländer's note, AK 7:343).

3 Compare AK 11:508–11.

4 Johann David Michaelis (1717–91), Professor of Theology at Göttingen.

5 Eberhard Julius von Massow, the newly appointed Minister of Justice, head of the state department of church and schools and Ober-Kurator of the universities in Prussia. Kant was personally acquainted with him (see AK 12:187–8).

6 Claudius Salmasius (1588–1655), French historian and jurist, author of *De annis climacteriis et de antiqua astrologia* (1648).

7 This story, told of the French minister Colbert, is supposedly the origin of the phrase *laissez faire* (August Oncken, *Die Maxime laissez faire et laissez passer* (Bern, 1886)).

8 "Search the scriptures, for in them ye think ye have eternal life" (John 5:39).

9 Cicero *Ad familiam* 12:4: *Nunc me reliquiae vestrae exercent* ("Now your remains weary me").

10 Religion 6:60–6.

11 This is not a scriptural quotation; there are no explicit biblical sources for the doctrine of incarnation, which was formally defined as Church doctrine at the Council of Chalcedon (451).

12 Guillaume Postel (c.1505–81), a French mystical writer.

13 "And if Christ is not risen, then is our preaching vain and your faith is also vain" (I Corinthians 15:14).

14 "But we were hoping that it was he who was going to redeem Israel" (Luke 24:21).

15 The most prominent Pauline statement of the doctrine of predestination (election) is to be found in Romans 11:1–10.

16 Emanuel Swedenborg (1688–1772) was discussed by Kant in *Dreams of a Spirit Seer* (1766), cf. AK 2:354–64.

17 "Arise, go your way. Your faith has made you well" (Luke 17:19).

18 "Thy sins be forgiven thee" (Luke 5:23); "And the sin which he has done shall be forgiven him" (Leviticus 19:22; cf. Numbers 15:25–8).

19 Christoph Wieland, *Peregrius Proteus* (1791).

20 Moses Mendelssohn, *Jerusalem, or on religious power and Judaism* (1783).

21 Lazarus ben David was a follower of Kant, who propagated his philosophy in Vienna between 1794 and 1797.

22 Philip Jacob Spener (1635–1705), whose *Pia desideria* (1675) was the chief document of Pietism.

23 Cf. *Religion* 6:29 and Romans 7:15.

24 A. H. Franck (1663–1727), pastor and Professor in Halle, a leading Pietist.

25 Count Nikolaus Ludwig von Zinzendorf (1700–1760), leader of the Bohemian Brethren (founded 1467) reconstituted as the Moravian Brethren (1722).

26 Johann Georg Hamann (1730–88), resident of Königsberg, Kant's sometime friend, a critic of the Enlightenment's attempt to separate reason from tradition, history, and language.

27 Christian Friedrich Nicolai (1733–1811), publisher and one of the leading Berlin popular philosophers.

28 Pierre la Coste, a pastor of the French-speaking Reformed Church in Leipzig.

29 Jacques Benigne Bossuet (1627–1704), renowned preacher and writer, Bishop of Meaux, author of many theological works, including *Exposition of the Catholic doctrine on matters of controversy* (1671).

30 Denis Petau (1583–1652), a French Jesuit theologian.

31 Johann Bengel (1687–1752), a Württemberg theologian, author of *Ordo temporum a principio per periodos oeconomiae divinae historicus atque propheticus* (1741), proclaimed the year 1738 as the beginning of the millennium.

32 Johann Georg Frank (1705–84) published a mystical chronology in 1774; cf. *Anthropology* 7:194–196.

33 Regarding Wilmans, see translator's introduction to "Preface to Reinhold Bernhard Jachmann's *Examination of the Kantian Philosophy of Religion.*"

34 Johann Christian Reil (1759–1813), professor of medicine in Halle and later in Berlin, founded *Archiv fur Physiologie* in 1796.

35 Pythia: the legendary oracular priestess of Apollo at Delphi.

36 Abdera was the ancient Greek city, home of the atomistic philosophy of Democritus and the relativistic one of Protagoras. But Kant is doubtless thinking of Christoph Wieland's satirical novel *History of the Abderites* (1774).

37 Gabriel François Coyer (1707–82), French Jesuit, author of *Dissertation on the difference of ancient religions* (1755).

38 The Danish astronomer Tycho Brahe (1546–1601) attempted a compromise between the Ptolemaic and Copernican systems, holding that the five known planets revolve around the sun, but that this whole system revolves around the earth.

39 The "event of our time" to which Kant is referring, of course, is the *public reaction* to the French Revolution, which began in 1789. Note that the event is not the revolution itself, about whose prospects Kant is not particularly optimistic.

40 The reference is to the sword of Meliscus, which Aeneas snatched in his battle with Turnus.

41 The reference is to Johann B. Erhard (1766–1827), *On the Right of the People to a Revolution* (Jena and Leipzig, 1795), p. 189.

42 Petrus Camper (1722–89), *On the Natural Difference of Facial Features* (Berlin, 1792) and Johann F. Blumenbach (1752–1840), *Manual of Natural History* (Göttingen, 1779).

43 Thomas More, *Utopia* (1516); James Harrington (1611–77), *Oceania* (1656), Denis Vairasse d'Allais (fl. 1665–81), *History of Severambes* (1675). Oliver Cromwell's protectorate lasted from 1653 to 1658.

44 Anton F. Büsching (1724–93) was the author of extensive writings on geography, history, education, and religion, and the editor of two journals in the fields of geography and history.

45 David Hume (1711–76), "Of Public Credit," in *Essays Moral, Political and Literary* (1741–42).

46 C. W. Hufeland was Professor of Medicine at the University of Jena and author of *Macrobiotics: Or the art of prolonging human life* (1796), a copy of which he sent to Kant (see AK 12:137). Hufeland made several comments on Kant's essay (see AK 7:345–7).

47 "All are from the dust, and all return to dust" (Ecclesiastes 3:20).

48 The Leipzig publisher Johann Gottlieb Breitkopf (1719–94) advocated the development of Fraktur type, whereas the Didot firm in Paris had, since 1713, published its Antiqua in very small type.

49 Hufeland here added a note confirming Kant's view that this condition is not an opthalmic disease, and suggesting that it results from a temporary circulatory or gastric irritation (AK 7:346–7).

Lectures on the philosophical doctrine of religion

1 The *Cyropaedia* is a historical novel by Xenophon (c. 430–355 B.C.) purporting to describe the education of Cyrus the Great of Persia (died 529 B.C.); its real (moralistic) purpose is to set forth Xenophon's conception of the ideal ruler, statesman, and general. The point of Kant's illustration is clearer in another manuscript of the lectures: "The idea in an *individuum* is an ideal. e.g., the Cyrus of Xenophon is an idea of a perfect prince, which Xenophon here sets forth *in concreto*" (AK 28:1223).

2 What Rousseau actually says is that a single tutor should educate one pupil to maturity, and should never attempt to educate more than a single pupil during his life (Rousseau, *Émile,* Book I, *Oeuvres complètes;* Paris: Gallimard, 1969; 4:265).

3 See below AK 28:1071. This is the error of *ignava ratio* which Kant criticizes in the *Critique of Pure Reason* A689/B717.

4 Kant's discussion here is clearly intended as a criticism of Eberhard's use of the term *Gottesgelehrtheit,* as applied to natural theology: "[In theology] the cognition of God has to be taken in the greatest perfection possible for human beings; that is, it must be the richest, most correct, clearest, most evident, and most living cognition, or, in short, it must be most scientific or learned. Such cognitions, even the more limited ones, contain *religion.* We do well to distinguish two kinds of cognition of God. For every human being has to have religion but not every human being needs to be a divine [*Gottesgelehrte*]" (J. A. Eberhard, *Vorbereitung zur natürlichen Theologie;* Halle, 1781, p. 4).

5 Cf. *Phaedo* 97–98, where Socrates describes his enthusiasm over Anaxagoras's view that mind (*nous*) is the cause of everything, producing and ordering everything for the best.

6 Descartes, *Meditations of First Philosophy,* Meditation 5.

7   Kant's version of the proof is closest to Wolff, *Metaphysik* (Halle, 1751) §
928, 1:574-5, and *Theologia naturalis* (Frankfurt and Leipzig, 1730) § 69,
1:55.

8   Following Eberhard, Kant first classified the Wolffian proof *a contingentia
mundi* as an a posteriori proof. His own opinion, however, is that it is just as
much an a priori proof as the ontological proof is (cf. Eberhard, *Vorbereitung*,
p. 28).

9   Compare the following passage from Hume: "And what shadow of an argument, continued Philo, can you produce from your hypothesis to prove the
unity of the Deity? A great number of men join in building a house or ship, in
rearing a city, in framing a commonwealth: why may not several deities
combine in contriving and framing a world? This is only so much greater
similarity to human affairs" (Hume, *Dialogues concerning Natural Religion* Part
V; New York: Hafner, 1948, p. 39). Hume's *Dialogues* were published posthumously after Hume's death in 1776. Kant, who did not read English, may
very well have been acquainted with them through the German translation
published in 1781.

10   Cf. Eberhard's remarks: "The proof of God's existence drawn from the
agreement of nations has too many difficulties to be used with certainty. For
(1) it gets entangled in historical investigations pertaining to the minor prem-
ise, and (2) the major premise will also be disputed, because the cognition of
God in many nations is mixed with error and superstition" (Eberhard,
Vorbereitung, p. 60). Eberhard probably takes the argument to go something
like this:
Major premise: Whatever all nations agree on is true.
Minor premise: All nations agree that God exists.
Therefore, God exists.

11   The target here seems to be the following passage from Eberhard's textbook:
"Realities are either pure or mixed. . . . The latter are realities which include
negations in themselves. . . . In this case we have to separate the negative
element from our concept if we are to retain something real" (Eberhard,
Vorbereitung, pp. 14-15).

12   This is the doctrine of divine simplicity, which is found (for example) in St.
Anselm (*Monologion* 16-18, *Proslogion* 12, 17) and St. Thomas Aquinas,
Summa Theologiae Ia Q. 3, aa. 3,7. Earlier sources of the doctrine include
Pseudo-Dionysius (*On the Divine Names* 4.1) and St. Augustine (*On the
Trinity* 6:7-8, *The City of God* 11:10).

13   Eberhard claims that God is both "mathematically" (or "indeterminately")
infinite and "metaphysically" (or "determinately") infinite (*Vorbereitung*, pp.
15-17).

14   Both the way of negation and the way of eminence are discussed by Eberhard, *Vorbereitung*, p. 26 and Baumgarten, *Metaphysica* (Halle, 1963) § 826.

15   Kant's preference for the ground/consequence over the cause/effect relationship is probably a critical reflection on Eberhard's discussion of the "way
of causality" (*via causalitatis*) (Eberhard, *Vorbereitung*, p. 26).

16   Duns Scotus seems to have been the first to maintain that the ontological
argument, in order to be demonstrative, requires the premise that God is
possible; and he claimed the argument was not demonstrative because this

premise is neither self-evident nor demonstrable (Scotus, *Commentaria Oxoniensis* (Quaracchi, 1912–14) 1.2.2.32). Leibniz, accepting the challenge, offered a proof that necessarily God is possible because the concept of God, consisting solely of realities and of no negations, is necessarily free of contradiction (Leibniz, *Philosophische Schriften*, ed. Gerhardt, 7:261–2. Cf. Loemker (ed.), *Leibniz: Philosophical Papers and Letters* (Dordrecht: Reidel, 1969), p. 167). Kant accepts Leibniz's proof but claims it settles only the question of logical possibility, not of real possibility.

17 With the above critique of the ontological argument cf. *Critique of Pure Reason* A598–600/B626–8.

18 With the above critique of the cosmological argument cf. *Critique of Pure Reason* A605–6/B633–4.

19 Cf. *Critique of Pure Reason* A592–6/B621–4.

20 Wolff does not use this illustration, but it is strongly reminiscent of Descartes in *Meditation* 5.

21 Victor Albrecht von Haller (1708–77) was a Swiss anatomist, physiologist, novelist and poet. The allusion is to Haller's *Imperfect Poem on Eternity* (1736), which Kant quotes in *The End of All Things;* see above (8:327).

22 AK 2:63–204.

23 Cf. *Critique of Pure Reason* A637/B715.

24 Cf. Baumgarten, *Metaphysica* § 815.

25 "To God belongs the highest unity, which is inseparable from the plurality of the highest realities" (Baumgarten, *Metaphysica* § 815).

26 "Every substance is a monad. God is a substance. Hence God is a monad and a simple being. But if the highest simplicity of God is granted, then it is denied that there could be any ground for his being a composite made up of external parts" (Baumgarten, *Metaphysica* § 838).

27 "The determinations of every necessary being are absolutely and internally immutable. Therefore, God is absolutely and internally immutable" (Baumgarten, *Metaphysica* § 839).

28 "Many gods are impossible.... God is unique. POLYTHEISM is the proposition positing more than one god, and is an error" (Baumgarten, *Metaphysica* § 846).

29 "MANICHAEISM is the proposition positing an equally powerful god as the author of evil, and is an error" (Baumgarten, *Metaphysica* § 844).

30 "God is a being outside the world [*ens extramundanum*]. And the world is not something essential to him, nor is it his essence, nor one of God's attributes, nor modes, nor modifications, nor accidents. THEOLOGICAL SPINOZISM is the proposition denying that God is a being outside the world, and is an error" (Baumgarten, *Metaphysica* § 855).

31 Cf. *Critique of Pure Reason* A727–8/B755–6.

32 "Substance is that whose existence does not require the existence of anything else." Cf. Spinoza, *Ethics* I, Def. 3: *Per substantiam intelligo id, quod in se est et per se concipitur: hoc est id, cujus conceptus non indiget conceptu alterius rei, a quo formari debet.* "By substance, I understand that which is in itself and is conceived through itself; it is that whose concept can be formed without requiring the concept of any other thing" (Spinoza, *Opera* (The Hague: 1882) 1:39).

33 "In God there are no successive states. Hence God is not in time. . . . If a contingently eternal being be posited, its eternity differs in many ways from God's eternity. For (1) its duration as a continuous modification of successive states is obnoxious [to the divine nature]. (2) Its eternity has no protensive end; yet such an eternity could not really be called infinite. And (3) its eternity would be time without beginning or end (and could be called infinite for this reason); yet it is not really infinite mathematically. For a being having successive states is never actually all that it can be in its internal determinations" (Baumgarten, *Metaphysica* §§ 849–50).

34 "Omnipotence is the power sufficient to actualize everything" (Baumgarten, *Metaphysica* § 832).

35 "God has no shape (*figuram*). VULGAR ANTHROPOMORPHISM (*Anthropomorphismus crassior*) is the error of attributing some shape to God (e.g. the human). SUBTLE ANTHROPOMORPHISM (*Anthropomorphismus subtilor*) is the error of attributing to God the imperfections of finite things (e.g. of human beings)" (Baumgarten, *Metaphysica* § 848).

36 "The cognition of God is THEOLOGY IN THE WIDER SENSE. That theology by which God cognizes himself is EXEMPLARY THEOLOGY (*Theologia exemplaris*) (*archetypos*)" (Baumgarten, *Metaphysica* § 866).

37 Cf. *The End of All Things* AK, 8:335.

38 "God knows (*scit*) every determination of every thing, insofar as mere possibility pertains to it. This is KNOWLEDGE OF SIMPLE INTELLECT. . . . God knows every determination of what is actual in (1) this world, and this is his FREE KNOWLEDGE (or vision) of (a) the past (the *divine memory*) (b) the present (knowledge of vision) and (c) the future (*foreknowledge*) . . . God knows every determination of what is actual in (2) other [possible] worlds, which is MIDDLE KNOWLEDGE" (Baumgarten, *Metaphysica* §§ 874–6). The distinctions drawn here were first devised by the sixteenth-century Jesuit theologian Luis de Molina. According to Molina, God knows everything possible through his "knowledge of simple intellect" and everything absolutely existing through his "knowledge of vision." But God also knows, prior to any absolute decree on his part, what he will decree concerning future contingents. This knowledge, falling midway between knowledge of mere possibles and knowledge of absolute existents, is what Molina calls "middle knowledge." Molina's purpose is to show how God's infallible foreknowledge can be reconciled with real contingency, especially with human free choice.

39 Baumgarten appears to infer God's infallibility simply from the fact that the possibility of error in God would be a defect (Baumgarten, *Metaphysica* § 879), hence to prove it in a way Kant regards as less than satisfactory.

40 "God's free knowledge is one of his perfections. And since he is an absolutely necessary being, this knowledge in him must be most true. Yet God causes this world to exist in such a way that it is in and for itself contingent. For this reason it is absolutely necessary that [God's free knowledge] be necessary only hypothetically. Therefore, God's free knowledge is a modal analogue (*analogon modi*)" (Baumgarten, *Metaphysica* § 881).

41 Baumgarten, like Kant, includes in wisdom (*sapientia*) the ability to perceive final ends (*sapientia generatim*), particular ends (*sapientia speciatim*), and the means to them (*prudentia*) (*Metaphysica* § 882).

42   "Omniscience is the knowledge of everything (*scientia omnium*)" (Baumgarten, *Metaphysica* § 889). Baumgarten first attributed knowledge (*scientia*) to God at *Metaphysica* § 873.

43   This is a reference to the movement now usually called "neo-Platonism," centered in Alexandria, Egypt, in the third century A.D. Its founder was Ammonius Saccas (d. 243), and its most prominent representatives were Plotinus (c. 205–70), Porphyry (d. 304), and Iamblichus (d. 333). The term "eclecticism" was first applied to it by Jakob Brucker, *Historia critica philosophiae* (Leipzig, 1742–4) 2:193; this work was Kant's principal source for the history of philosophy.

44   Part 4, Section 3 (§§ 890–925) of Baumgarten's *Metaphysica* is a treatise on the *Voluntas Dei*.

45   Baumgarten defines well-pleasedness as "a state of the soul occasioned by the intuition of perfection" (Baumgarten, *Metaphysica* § 655). Kant's real reason for objecting to this is that Baumgarten followed Wolff in holding that perfection of character was an end desirable *a priori* which serves as the determining ground or motive of moral volition. Kant holds, on the contrary, that the relation between any pleasure and its object, when the pleasure is caused by the object, is *a posteriori*, contingent and hence sensible. This is his reason for denying that any "material" practical principle (any principle presupposing an object of desire as the motive of the will) must be contingent and cannot be a categorical imperative (*Critique of Practical Reason* 5:21). In the present context, however, this point seems moot, since Kant would presumably agree that in the case of God, whose well-pleasedness and displeasedness are not empirical, there could be an *a priori* connection between well-pleasedness and a necessary or *a priori* motive.

46   "Because God intuits himself most distinctly as the good and the supreme holiness, . . . the acquiescence of God in himself is the exemplary theology, and the greatest delight" (Baumgarten, *Metaphysica* § 892).

47   "How therefore shall we satisfy ourselves concerning the cause of that Being, whom you suppose the Author of Nature, or, according to your system of anthropomorphism, the ideal world, into which you trace the material? Have we not the same reason to trace that ideal world into another ideal world, or new intelligent principle? But if we stop, and go no farther, then why go so far? Why not stop at the material world? How can we satisfy ourselves without going on *in infinitum*? And after all, what satisfaction is there in that infinite progression?" (David Hume, *Dialogues Concerning Natural Religion*, Part 4, New York: Hafner, 1969, p. 34).

48   In Hume's *Dialogues*, Cleanthes proposes to explain the purposiveness of living things in nature through the hypothesis that their cause is an intelligent designer; in Parts 6 and 7 of the *Dialogues*, Philo cleverly proposes the rival hypothesis that it results from a generative process like that through which individual living specimens are reproduced.

49   See note 44.

50   "God's well-pleasedness and displeasedness are not pleasure or displeasure, nor does he have sensitive appetites and aversions" (Baumgarten, *Metaphysica* § 891).

51   See note 46.

52 "FATALISM, the proposition denying God's freedom, is an error" (Baumgarten, *Metaphysica* § 898).

53 Cf. Leibniz, *Correspondence with Samuel Clarke,* Third letter, § 6, *Philosophical Essays,* trans. Ariew and Garber (Indianapolis: Hackett, 1989), p. 325.

54 "THE WILL OF GOD, insofar as it is the object of his free knowledge, or he desires the actual things of the universe, is called his CONSEQUENT WILL; insofar as it is turned toward universals and actual things in other universes, it is called his ANTECEDENT WILL" (Baumgarten, *Metaphysica* § 899).

55 "An INSCRUTABLE WILL is one whose impelling causes are incomprehensible. But the impelling causes of the divine will are most distinctly at God's own discretion (*ipsius lubitus*). For this reason [God's will] is to God internally perfect but to us incomprehensible" (Baumgarten, *Metaphysica* § 900).

56 See above, note 3.

57 Cf. Hume, *Enquiry Concerning the Principles of Morals,* ed. J. Schneewind (Indianapolis: Hackett, 1983), especially Appendix 1: Concerning Moral Sentiment, pp. 82–8.

58 Cf. *Religion* 6:139.

59 "BENEVOLENCE (kindness) is the determination of the will to doing good to another. . . . God wills to confer benefit on others. Therefore, he is kind" (Baumgarten, *Metaphysica* § 903–904).

60 "JUSTICE is benevolence proportionate to a person or spirit" (Baumgarten, *Metaphysica* § 906). But Baumgarten does not systematize God's moral attributes in triadic form as holiness, benevolence and justice. He dealt with God's holiness earlier (see next note). Kant seems to be following his practice in the table of categories, which are arranged in triads, with the third member consisting in some sort of combination of the first two (see *Critique of Pure Reason* B110–11).

61 "HOLINESS is the reality of a being by which all imperfections are denied in it" (*Metaphysica* § 828).

62 The allusion is to a line from Albrecht von Haller's *Über den Ursprung des Übels* (*On the Origin of Evil*) (1734), 2:33–4:

> *Denn Gott liebt keinen Zwang, die Welt mit ihren Mängeln*
> *Ist besser als ein Reich von Willen-losen Engeln.*
> For God loves no compulsion, the world with all its faults
> Is better than a realm of will-less angels.

Kant also quotes these lines at *Religion* 6:65n.

63 Cf. *Conjectural Beginning of Human History* (1786), AK 8:115–16.

64 "I would not have known sin except through the law" (Romans 7:7).

65 Cf. *Idea for a Universal History with a Cosmopolitan Aim* AK 8:18.

66 See below 28:1106–7.

67 This does not appear to be an exact quotation. Perhaps Kant has in mind the following passage:

> There scarcely is, or can be any Creature, whom Consciousness of Villainy, as such merely, does not at all offend; nor anything opprobrious or heinously imputable, move, or affect. If there be such a one; 'tis evident he must be absolutely indifferent towards moral Good or Ill. If this indeed be his Case, 'twill be allow'd he can be in no way

capable of natural Affection: If not of that, then neither of any social Pleasure, or mental Enjoyment, as shewn above; but on the contrary, he must be subject to all manner of horrid unnatural and ill Affection. So that to want CONSCIENCE, or *natural Sense of the Odiousness of Crime and Injustice,* is to be most miserable of all in Life; but where Conscience, or Sense of this sort, remains; there, consequently, whatever is committed against it must of necessity, by means of Reflection, as we have shewn, be continually shameful, grievous and offensive" (Anthony Ashley Cooper, Third Earl of Shaftesbury, *Characteristics of Men, Manners, Times,* Volume 2, Treatise 4: An Inquiry concerning Virtue or Merit (London, 1699) 2:2:1, pp. 121–2).

68 "SINCERITY is benevolence concerning what is signified in one's mind, and this is in God" (Baumgarten, *Metaphysica* § 919).

69 "A REWARD (remuneration) is some good contingent on the moral goodness of a person. Justice in conferring rewards is REMUNERATIVE JUSTICE (*Iustitia Remuneratoria*), which we venerate in God in the highest degree" (Baumgarten, *Metaphysica* § 907). "Justice in imposing punishment is PUNITIVE JUSTICE (*Iustitia Punitiva*) (vindictive, avenging, vindicating, nemesis); punitive justice belongs to God" (Baumgarten, *Metaphysica* § 910).

70 Proverbs 19:17.

71 These are expressions used by Baumgarten, see note 69 above.

72 "FORBEARANCE (the patience of a judge) is justice which does not look for occasions to punish. God infallibly knows all the opportunities for punishment and all the proximate matters for punishment where they are real; but he wills [punishments] proportionately. Hence he is the most forbearant" (Baumgarten, *Metaphysica* § 916).

73 God's *impartialitas* is spoken of by Baumgarten in *Metaphysica* § 917.

74 "Impartial justice is EQUITY. God is most just and most impartial, so he is most equitable" (Baumgarten, *Metaphysica* § 918).

75 "Since God's highest life is absolutely necessary (for it is his essence itself and his existence), God is not only immortal, but *only he has absolute immortality*" (Baumgarten, *Metaphysica* § 922).

76 Cf. Baumgarten, *Metaphysica* § 924.

77 Cf. *Critique of Pure Reason* B xxx, where the three postulates of practical reason are identified as God, freedom and immortality; immortality is also presented in the *Critique of Practical Reason* as the first postulate of practical reason (KpV 5:121–4). But in Reflexion 8101 (AK 19:644) he describes faith in immortality as "faith of the second rank," suggesting that it may not be as necessary for the moral life as faith in God.

78 "CREATION BY EMANATION is the actualization of the universe from the essence of God" (Baumgarten, *Metaphysica* § 927).

79 "An AUTHOR (*Auctor*) is a cause of free actions, and such actions as are caused by it are the effects of an author are DEEDS (*Facta*). Now God is the author of creation and of this world" (Baumgarten, *Metaphysica* § 940).

80 Here as in the second edition of the *Critique of Pure Reason* (B xii–xiii) Kant follows Stahl's phlogiston theory of combustion and other chemical processes (such as the rusting of iron) which are now regarded as processes of oxidation. Kant followed with interest the revolution in chemistry brought about by Antoine Lavoisier in the 1790s, and exhibits awareness of it in his *Opus postumum.* See AK 22:508–9 and *Opus Postumum,* ed. Eckart Förster,

Cambridge Edition (New York: Cambridge University Press, 1993), pp. 150, 275.

81 "In creating this world, God decreed according to his most proportional will. Hence he decreed the existence of this world for the sake of the good he recognized in it. . . . Therefore, this world is of all possible ones the most perfect" (Baumgarten, *Metaphysica* §§ 934–5). Kant defended this Leibnizian doctrine in "An Attempt at Some Reflections on Optimism" (1759), AK 2:27–35. But compare *On the Miscarriage of All Philosophical Trials in Theodicy* 8:258, 263–4.

82 Kant is referring to his 1759 essay; see previous note.

83 Cf. Leibniz, *On the Ultimate Origin of Things* (1697), *Philosophischen Schriften* 7:303–4; cf. Leibniz, *Philosophical Essays*, tr. R. Ariew and D. Garber (Indianapolis: Hackett, 1989), pp. 153–4. The argument is stated most precisely in *Theodicy* §§ 213–15: "That part of the best whole is not necessarily the best which could have been made of that part. For the part of a beautiful thing is not always beautiful, since it can be extracted from the whole or taken in the whole in an irregular manner. If goodness and beauty always consisted in something absolute and uniform. . . . it would be necessary to say that the part of what is good and beautiful would also be good and beautiful. But this is not so with things involving relations (*choses relatives*). . . . In some parts of the universe, we find defects which the author of things allowed because otherwise, if he had reformed the faulty part and made a satisfactory composite out of it, the whole would not be as beautiful as it is. . . . [Hence] I answer that since God chooses the best possible, one cannot object to any limitation in its perfections. And not only does good surpass evil in the universe, but in fact the evil serves to augment the good" (*Philosophischen Schriften* 6:245–7).

84 See above, 28:1077–9.

85 See 28:1100–2.

86 "HONOR is the recognition of a higher perfection in something. Greater honor is GLORY. God's glory therefore is the greater cognition of his own highest perfection" (Baumgarten, *Metaphysica* § 942). Clearly Kant is strongly inclined to reject the traditional idea that God created the world for the sake of his own glory, in the sense of the praise and honor bestowed on him by his creatures: cf. 28:1002, 1102, 1118. But he also tries to save this doctrine by reinterpreting it, as he does here and also at KU 5:449n.

87 The problem raised here is the temporal half of the First Antinomy of Pure Reason. Cf. *Critique of Pure Reason* A426–35/B454–63.

88 See above, note 32. In the *Principles* Descartes defines substance as "that which so exists that it needs no other thing in order to exist," and adds that so understood, the term applies strictly only to God, so that it must have a different sense when applied to creatures (Descartes, *Principles of Philosophy* 1:51).

89 "God concurs mediately as efficient cause in all the actions of finite substances, and . . . concurs immediately as efficient cause . . . actuating and conserving them" (Baumgarten, *Metaphysica* § 954). Kant rejects this doctrine of a "GENERAL PHYSICAL COOPERATION OF GOD (*Concursus Dei Physicus Generalis*)" (Baumgarten, *Metaphysica* § 958).

90 This is, in contrast to the *physical* cooperation of God (see previous note) the "MORAL OR SPECIAL COOPERATION OF GOD (*Concursus Moralis seu Specialis*)" (Baumgarten, *Metaphysica* § 960).

91 "God is close to every monad in this world and is inwardly present to every body. And it is by this moment that every creature is actual. Therefore, God is most omnipresent" (Baumgarten, *Metaphysica* § 956).

92 See above, 28:1095–6.

93 "What is proximately present as a whole and singly to the substantial parts of a thing, the same is called an INWARD PRESENCE to it. Now God is proximately present to all substantial parts of all bodies in this universe. Therefore, God is inwardly present to all bodies in this universe" (Baumgarten, *Metaphysica* § 955).

94 "Conservation is God's constant influence" (Baumgarten, *Metaphysica* § 951).

95 "The first Contrivance of those very artificial Parts of Animals . . . and the Instinct of Brutes and Insects, can be the effect of nothing else than the Wisdom and Skill of a powerful ever-living Agent, who being in all Places, is more able by his Will to move the Bodies within his boundless uniform Sensorium, and thereby to form and reform the Parts of the Universe, than we are by our Will to move the Parts of our own Bodies" (Newton, *Opticks* (London: 1931), p. 403). Newton's conception of space as a manifestation of God reflects the influence of Henry More on his theology. Kant's criticism of Newton here follows Leibniz's in his first, second, third, and fourth letters to Samuel Clarke.

96 Providence = *Vorsehung*, providing = *Providenz* (cf. *providentia*, Baumgarten, *Metaphysica* § 974). Governing = *Gubernation* (cf. *gubernatio*, Baumgarten, *Metaphysica* § 963). Directing = *Direction* (cf. *dirigere strictius*, Baumgarten, *Metaphysica* § 963).

97 Baumgarten describes God as *despotes*, and his rule of the world as a *monarchia despotica*, since he has not only "supreme power" but also "plenary power" over creatures (Baumgarten, *Metaphysica* § 974).

98 Baumgarten distinguishes between (1) the *propositum* in which God represents the best complex of compossible beings, (2) the *praevisio* in which he knows it as the best possible world and (3) the *decretum* through which this best world receives existence. But Baumgarten himself admits that this account is only "a way in which [God's decree] may be conceived according to a human fashion" (Baumgarten, *Metaphysica* § 976).

99 Baumgarten too insists that God's decrees are not "absolute," rejecting the doctrines of eternal predestination and reprobation which seem to follow from this *absolutismus theologicas* (Baumgarten, *Metaphysica* § 980).

100 "Revelation in the wide sense is the signification by the divine mind to the creature made by God" (Baumgarten, *Metaphysica* § 982).

101 "Now when all things are made subject to Him, then the Son Himself will also be subject to Him who put all things under Him, that God may be all in all" (1 Corinthians 15:28). Cf. *Religion* 6:135.

102 This classical proverb is probably most often attributed to Socrates.

103 "Holy mysteries are things set above the reason of creatures, and included in the objects of holy faith" (Baumgarten, *Metaphysica* § 906).

104 Christoph Meiners (1747–1810) was a prolific German writer on a wide variety of historical topics. The *Historia doctrinae de uno vero Deo* (History of the doctrines of the one true God) (1780) was the first of his many writings on the history of religions, culminating in his two-volume *Allgemeine kritische Geschichte der Religionen* (Universal critical history of religions) (1806).

105 See above, note 101.

106 Herodotus, *The Persian Wars* 2:35–182, which has much to say about the influence of Egyptian religious practices on the Greeks.

107 David Hume, *The Natural History of Religion* (Stanford: Stanford University Press, 1967), Sec. 9, pp. 48–51.

108 See above, note 5.

Glossary

Glossary

German–English

Aberglaube	*superstition*
Abhandlung	*treatise*
abnehmen	*extract*
ableiten	*derive*
Absicht	*aim; intention*
Abweichung	*deviation*
Achtung	*respect (*reverentia*)*
Actus	*act*
Affekt	*affect, emotional agitation*
Afterdienst	*counterfeit service*
All	*(the) all (*omnitudo*)*
allgemein	*universal; general (*universalis, generalis*)*
Allgemeingültigkeit	*universal validity*
Allgenugsamkeit	*all-sufficiency (*omnisufficientia*)*
Allheit	*totality*
Allmacht	*omnipotence (*omnipotentia*)*
alter Mensch	*old man*
Anbetung	*worship; adoration*
Andacht	*devotion*
anerkennen	*recognize; acknowledge*
angenehm	*agreeable*
Angriff	*assault; attack*
Anlage	*predisposition*
Anlaß	*occasion (cf.* Gelegenheit*)*
Anmerkung	*remark (cf.* Bemerkung*)*
Anmut	*gracefulness*
annehmen	*assume; accept*
Annehmung	*assumption; adoption*
Anordnung	*regulation*
Anschauung	*intuition (*intuitus*)*
Anspruch	*claim (cf.* Behauptung*)*
Antrieb	*impulse*
Armseligkeit	*wretchedness*
Art	*way, species, kind*
auffordern	*require (cf.* erfordern*)*
Aufforderung	*requirement, demand*
Aufgabe	*problem; task*

aufgeben	*propose, set up*
aufheben	*remove; abolish; cancel*
auflösen	*resolve, solve*
aufsuchen	*seek out*
Ausbildung	*education, training (cf.* Bildung*)*
ausdehnen	*extend*
Ausführung	*execution*
ausführlich	*exhaustive*
Auslegung	*interpretation; exegesis (cf.* Deutung*)*
ausrotten	*eradicate (cf.* vertilgen*)*
ausüben	*execute*
Auswahl	*selection*
Bedeutung	*significance, signification; meaning (cf.* Sinn*)*
Bedingung	*condition*
Bedürfnis	*need*
Befehl	*order*
Befolgung	*compliance*
Befriedigung	*satisfaction*
Befugnis	*warrant, authorization; title*
Begebenheit	*occurrence (cf.* Ereignis*)*
Begehrungsvermögen	*faculty of desire*
Begeisterung	*exaltation*
Begierde	*desire*
begreifen	*comprehend*
Begriff	*concept (conceptus)*
behaftet	*encumbered*
Behaglichkeit	*complacency*
beharrlich	*persisting; abiding*
Beharrlichkeit	*persistence; perseverance*
Beherrscher	*ruler*
beilegen	*attribute; apply (to)*
Beimischung	*admixture (cf.* Vermischung*)*
Beistand	*assistance*
Bekehrung	*conversion (cf.* Sinnesänderung*)*
beleben	*stimulate, give life*
Bemerkung	*observation (cf.* Anmerkung*)*
Benutzung	*utilization*
Beschaffenheit	*constitution; property; characteristic; nature (cf.* Eigenschaft, Natur*)*
Beschäftigung	*concern; business*
besonder(-)	*particular; peculiar; special*
beständig	*constant*
bestimmen	*determine*
Bestimmung	*determination; vocation (determinatio)*
Beweis	*proof*
Beziehung	*relation; reference (cf.* Verhältnis*)*

Bild	*image*
Bildung	*education; formation (cf.* Ausbildung*)*
billig	*equitable, fair*
Billigkeit	*equity (*aequitas*)*
billigen	*approve*
Blendwerk	*semblance, mirage, illusion (cf.* Illusion, Schein, Wahn*)*
Böse	*evil (cf.* Übel*)*
Bösartigkeit	*depravity; malignancy*
Bosheit	*malice*
bürgerlich	*civil (*civilis*)*
büßen	*atone*
Cultus	*cult*
Darstellung	*presentation; exhibition; display*
dartun	*establish*
Dauer	*duration*
Deutlichkeit	*distinctness; clarity*
Deutung	*interpretation*
durchgängig	*thorough(going)*
Ehrfurcht	*awe*
Ehrbegierde	*ambition (*ambitio*)*
Eifersucht	*jealousy*
Eigenschaft	*attribute; property*
eigentümlich	*peculiar*
einsehen	*have insight into*
Einsicht	*insight*
Einwilligung	*consent*
Empfänglichkeit	*receptivity*
Empfindung	*sensation, feeling*
Endabsicht	*final aim*
Endzweck	*final end*
entäussern	*divest*
Entschließung	*decision*
Entsündigung	*remission of sin*
Erfahrung	*experience*
ergänzen	*make up for; supplement*
Ergänzung	*supplement*
erhaben	*sublime*
Erhaltung	*conservation (*conservatio*)*
erkennen	*cognize; recognize*
Erkenntnis	*cognition (*cognitio*)*
Erläuterung	*illustration; elucidation*
Erlaubnis	*permission*
erreichen	*attain*
Erscheinung	*appearance*

489

erteilen	*grant*
Erweiterung	*expansion*
Erziehung	*upbringing; education*
fähig	*able, capable*
Fähigkeit	*capacity*
Falschheit	*deceit*
fürwahrhalten	*hold (true)*
Festigkeit	*firmness; stability*
Fleck	*stain*
Folge	*consequence*
Fortschritt	*progress; advance*
Frohndienst	*compulsory service*
Gattung	*genus; species*
Gebot	*command*
Gebrauch	*use, employment (cf.* Benutzung*)*
Gebrechlichkeit	*frailty; fragility*
Gedankending	*thought-entity (*ens rationis*)*
Gegenstand	*object*
Gefühl	*feeling*
Geheimnis	*mystery*
Geist	*spirit, mind*
Geistlicher	*clergyman*
Gelehrte(r)	*scholar*
Gelehrtheit	*scholarship; learning*
Gemeinschaft	*community (*communio*); interaction (*commercium*)*
gemeines Wesen	*community; commonwealth*
Gemeinde	*congregation*
Gemüt	*mind*
Genugtuung	*satisfaction*
Genuß	*enjoyment*
Gerechtigkeit	*justice; righteousness*
Geschäft	*concern, business; practical affairs*
Geschicklichkeit	*skill*
Geschöpf	*creature*
Gesetzgeber	*legislator; lawgiver*
Gesetzgebung	*legislation*
Gesetzmäßigkeit	*lawfulness*
Gesinnung	*disposition*
Gewalt	*power, authority; coercive power*
gewahr	*aware*
Glaube	*belief, faith*
Glück	*(good) fortune; luck*
Glückseligkeit	*happiness*
Gnade	*grade (*gratia*)*
Gnadenwahl	*election (*electio*)*

490

Gottmensch	*God-man*
Grad	*degree*
Grenze	*bound(ary)*
Grund	*ground*
gründlich	*well-grounded*
Grundsatz	*principle (cf.* Prinzip*)*
Gültigkeit	*validity*
Gütigkeit	*generosity; benevolence*
Handlung	*act(ion)*
Hang	*propensity*
Heide	*heathen; pagan*
Heiligkeit	*holiness*
Herrschaft	*dominion, mastery*
hervorbringen	*produce; bring forth*
hinreichend	*sufficient*
Hochschätzung	*esteem*
Illusion	*illusion (cf.* Blendwerk, Schein, Wahn*)*
Inbegriff	*sum total*
Jammertal	*vale of tears*
Kampf	*battle*
Keim	*germ*
kennen	*know, have cognizance of, be acquainted with*
Kenntnis	*cognizance, acquaintance*
klar	*clear*
Klugheit	*prudence* (prudentia*)*
Kraft	*power; force*
Kritik	*critique, criticism*
Kunst	*art*
Langmut	*patience*
Laster	*vice*
Lebenswandel	*course of life; life conduct*
Legalität	*legality*
Lehre	*doctrine; teaching*
Leiden	*suffering, passivity*
Leidenschaft	*passion*
Lust	*pleasure* (voluptas*)*
Macht	*might, power*
Mannigfältigkeit	*manifold*
Materie	*matter*
meinen	*hold or express opinion(s); opine*
Meinung	*opinion; estimation*

Mensch	*human being*
Menschheit	*humanity*
menschlich	*human*
Merkmal	*mark (*nota*)*
mißbilligen	*disapprove*
Mißfallen	*dislike*
Nachteil	*disadvantage*
Nebenbuhlerschaft	*rivalry*
Nebenfolge	*by-product*
Nebenzweck	*incidental end*
Neigung	*inclination*
neuer Mensch	*new man*
Notwendigkeit	*necessity*
Oberhaupt	*head, chief*
Object	*object*
Offenbarung	*revelation*
Pfaffentum	*priestcraft*
Pflicht	*duty*
Prinzip	*principle (cf.* Grundsatz*)*
Probierstein	*touchstone*
Quelle	*source*
Ratschluß	*decree (*decretum*)*
Recht	*right (n.) (*ius*)*
Regierer	*governor*
Regierung	*government, governance*
Reich	*kingdom, realm*
Schein	*illusion (cf.* Blendwerk, Illusion, Wahn*)*
scheinen	*seem*
Scheinwissen	*illusory knowledge*
schliessen (auf)	*infer*
Schluß	*inference (cf.* Vernunftschluss, Verstandeschluss*)*
Schmerz	*pain*
Schöpfer	*creator*
Schranke	*limit(ation)*
Schrift	*scripture; writing*
Schuld	*guilt*
Schwärmerei	*enthusiasm*
Seele	*soul*
Seelsorger	*clergyman; spiritual advisor*

Selbständigkeit	*self-sufficiency; independence*
Selbstzufriedenheit	*self-contentment*
Seligkeit	*blessedness*
Sinn	*sense; meaning (cf.* Bedeutung*)*
sinnlich	*sensible, sensory, sensuous, of the senses*
Sinnlichkeit	*sensibility, the senses*
Sitten	*manners*
Sittlichkeit	*morals*
Streit	*conflict*
Streitigkeit	*dispute*
Tapferkeit	*valor*
Tat	*deed; what one does*
Tätigkeit	*activity*
Tierheit	*animality*
Torheit	*folly*
Trieb	*drive; impulse*
Triebfeder	*incentive*
Tücke	*perfidy*
Tugend	*virtue*
tunlich	*feasible*
Übel	*ill, evil (cf.* Böse*)*
übereinstimmen	*agree*
Übergewicht	*preponderance*
Überlegung	*reflection*
Überredung	*persuasion*
Übertretung	*transgression*
überwältigen	*overpower*
Überzeugung	*conviction*
Umfang	*extent; domain*
Umwandlung	*transformation*
unabläßig	*unremitting*
unerforschlich	*inscrutable*
ungereimt	*absurd*
unkenntlich	*unrecognizable*
Unlauterkeit	*impurity*
Unlust	*displeasure; aversion (tædium)*
Unparteilichkeit	*impartiality*
Unredlichkeit	*dishonesty*
Unschuld	*innocence*
Unsterblichkeit	*immortality*
Unterschied	*difference; distinction*
Untersuchung	*investigation*
Unvermögen	*incapacity*
Urbild	*prototype; archetype*

493

Urgrund	*original ground*
Urheber	*author*
Ursache	*cause (*causa*)*
Urteilskraft	*(faculty of) judgment*
Urwesen	*original being (*ens originarium*)*
verabscheuen	*abhor*
verachten	*despise*
Verachtung	*contempt*
Veränderung	*alteration*
Verbindlichkeit	*obligation*
Verbindung	*combination (*conjunctio*);*
	association
Verbot	*prohibition*
Verderbnis	*corruption (cf.* Verderbtheit*)*
Verderbtheit	*corruption (cf.* Verderbnis*)*
Verdienst	*merit*
Vereinigung	*unification; union*
Verehrung	*reverence*
Vergehen	*transgression (cf.* Übertretung*)*
Verhältnis	*relationship*
Verkehrtheit	*perversion*
Verknüpfung	*connection*
Vermessenheit	*presumptuousness*
Vermögen	*faculty (*facultas*); capacity*
Vernunft	*reason*
Vernunftschluß	*syllogism (cf.* Schluß*)*
vernünftelnd	*rationalizing; sophistical*
Verschuldung	*guilt*
versöhnen	*reconcile*
Verstand	*understanding (*intellectus*)*
Verstandeschluß	*inference of the understanding (cf.* Schluß*)*
verwerflich	*reprehensible*
Volk	*people; nation*
Vollendung	*completion; fulfillment*
Völlerei	*gluttony*
vollführen	*carry out*
vollkommen	*perfect (v.)*
Vollkommenheit	*perfection (*perfectio*)*
vollständig	*complete*
Voraussetzung	*presupposition*
Vorsatz	*intention; resolution*
Vorsehung	*providence (*providentia*)*
Vorsorge	*provision*
vorstellen	*represent*
Vorstellung	*representation (*repræsentatio*)*

wählen	*choose*
Wahn	*delusion (cf.* Blendwerk, Illusion, Schein*)*
Wahrnehmung	*perception*
Wahrscheinlichkeit	*probability*
Wechsel	*change*
wechselseitig	*reciprocal*
Wesen	*being, entity (*ens*); essence (*essentia*)*
Wille	*will (*voluntas*)*
Willkür	*(power of) choice (*arbitrium*)*
willkürlich	*arbitrary; voluntary*
wirklich	*actual; real*
Wirkung	*effect; operation*
Wissen	*knowing, knowledge (*scientia*)*
Wissenschaft	*science (*scientia*)*
Wohl	*welfare*
Wohlergehen	*well-being*
Wohlgefallen	*good pleasure; well-pleasedness*
Wohltun	*benefaction*
Wohlwollen	*benevolence*
wollen	*will*
Wollen	*volition*
Wollust	*lasciviousness; lust*
Wunder	*miracle*
Würde	*dignity*
Würdigkeit	*worthiness*
zufällig	*contingent*
Zufriedenheit	*contentment*
zurechnen	*impute*
Zusammenhang	*connection*
Zusammensetzung	*composition; synthesis*
Zustand	*state, condition*
Zwang	*coercion*
Zweck	*end, purpose*
Zweckmäßigkeit	*purposiveness*
Zweckwidrigkeit	*counterpurposiveness; unsuitableness*

English–German

abhor	*verabscheuen*
abiding	*beharrlich*
able	*fähig*
abolish	*aufheben*
absurd	*ungereimt*
acquaintance	*Kenntnis*
act(ion)	*Handlung*

activity	*Tätigkeit*
actual	*wirklich*
act	*Actus*
admixture	*Beimischung*
adoption	*Annehmung*
adoration	*Anbetung*
advance	*Fortschritt*
affect	*Affekt*
agree	*übereinstimmen*
agreeable	*angenehm*
aim	*Absicht*
all	*All*
all-sufficiency	*Allgenugsamkeit* (omnisufficientia*)*
alteration	*Veränderung*
ambition	*Ehrbegierde (*ambitio*)*
animality	*Tierheit*
appearance	*Erscheinung*
approve	*billigen*
arbitrary	*willkürlich*
archetype	*Urbild*
art	*Kunst*
assault	*Angriff*
assistance	*Beihilfe*
assume	*annehmen*
assumption	*Annehmung*
atone	*büßen*
attack	*Angriff*
attain	*erreichen*
attribute (n.)	*Eigenschaft*
attribute (v.)	*beilegen*
author	*Urheber*
authority	*Gewalt*
authorization	*Befugnis*
aversion	*Unlust (*Tædium*)*
aware	*gewahr*
awe	*Ehrfurcht*
battle	*Kampf*
being	*Wesen (*ens*), Sein*
belief	*Glaube*
benefaction	*Wohltun*
beneficence	*Wohltun*
benevolence	*Wohlwollen*
blessedness	*Seligkeit*
bound(ary)	*Grenze*
bring forth	*hervorbringen*
business	*Geschäft, Beschäftigung*
by-product	*Nebenfolge*

496

cancel	*aufheben*
capable	*fähig*
capacity	*Fähigkeit*
carry out	*vollführen*
cause	*Ursache*
change	*Wechsel*
character	*Character*
characteristic	*Beschaffenheit*
choice (power of)	*Willkür*
choose	*wählen*
civil	*bürgerlich*
claim	*Anspruch*
clear	*klar, deutlich*
clergyman	*Geistlicher, Seelsorger*
coercion	*Zwang*
cognition	*Erkenntnis*
cognizance	*Kenntnis*
cognize	*erkennen*
combination	*Verbindung*
command	*Befehl*
commonwealth	*gemeines Wesen*
community	*gemeines Wesen*
complacency	*Behaglichkeit*
complete	*vollständig*
completion	*Vollendung*
compliance	*Befolgung*
composition	*Zusammensetzung*
comprehend	*begreifen*
compulsory service	*Frohndienst*
concept	*Begriff*
concern	*Beschäftigung, Geschäft*
condition	*Bedingung, Zustand*
conflict	*Streit*
congregation	*Gemeinde*
connection	*Verknüpfung*
consent	*Einwilligung*
consequence	*Folge*
conservation	*Erhaltung*
constant	*beständig*
constitution	*Beschaffenheit*
contempt	*Verachtung*
contentment	*Zufriedenheit*
contingent	*zufällig*
conversion	*Bekehrung, Sinnesänderung*
conviction	*Überzeugung*
corruption	*Verderbtheit*
counterfeit service	*Afterdienst*
counterpurposiveness	*Zweckwidrigkeit*

497

course of life	*Lebenswandel*
creator	*Schöpfer*
creature	*Geschöpf*
criticism	*Kritik*
critique	*Kritik*
cult	*Cultus*
deceit	*Falschheit*
decision	*Erschließung*
decree	*Ratschluß* (decretum)
deed	*Tat*
degree	*Grad*
delusion	*Wahn*
demand	*Aufforderung*
depravity	*Bösartigkeit*
derive	*ableiten*
desire	*Begierde*
despise	*verachten*
determination	*Bestimmung*
determine	*bestimmen*
deviation	*Abweichung*
devotion	*Andacht*
difference	*Unterschied*
dignity	*Würde*
disadvantage	*Nachteil*
disapprove	*mißbilligen*
dishonesty	*Unredlichkeit*
dislike	*Mißfallen*
display	*darstellen*
displeasure	*Unlust* (Tædium)
disposition	*Gesinnung*
dispute	*Streitigkeit*
distinctness	*Deutlichkeit*
divest	*entäussern*
doctrine	*Lehre*
domain	*Umfang*
dominion	*Herrschaft*
drive	*Trieb*
duration	*Dauer*
duty	*Pflicht*
education	*Bildung, Ausbildung, Erziehung*
effect	*Wirkung*
election	*Gnadenwahl*
elucidation	*Erläuterung*
emotional agitation	*Affekt*
employment	*Gebrauch*

498

encumbered	*behaftet*
end	*Zweck*
enjoyment	*Genuß*
enthusiasm	*Schwärmerei*
entity	*Wesen (*ens*)*
equitable	*billig*
equity	*Billigkeit*
eradicate	*ausrotten*
essence	*Wesen (*essentia*)*
establish	*dartun*
esteem	*Hochschätzung*
estimation	*Meinung, Schätzung, Beurteilung*
event	*Ereignis*
evil	*Böse*
exaltation	*Begeisterung*
execute	*ausführen*
execution	*Ausführung*
exegesis	*Auslegung*
exhaustive	*ausführlich*
exhibition	*Darstellung*
expansion	*Erweiterung*
experience	*Erfahrung*
extend	*ausdehnen, ausbreiten*
extent	*Umfang*
extract	*abnehmen*
faculty	*Vermögen*
faculty of desire	*Begehrungsvermögen*
fair	*billig*
faith	*Glaube*
feasible	*tunlich*
feeling	*Gefühl, Empfindung*
final aim	*Endabsicht*
final end	*Endzweck*
firmness	*Festigkeit*
folly	*Torheit*
force	*Kraft*
fragility	*Gebrechlichkeit*
frailty	*Gebrechlichkeit*
fulfillment	*Vollendung*
general	*allgemein*
generosity	*Gütigkeit*
genus	*Gattung*
germ	*Keim*
give life	*beleben*
gluttony	*Völlerei*

God-man	*Gottmensch*
good fortune	*Glück*
good pleasure	*Wohlgefallen*
government	*Regierung*
governor	*Regierer*
grace	*Gnade*
gracefulness	*Anmut*
grant	*erteilen*
ground	*Grund*
guilt	*Schuld, Beschuldung*
happiness	*Glückseligkeit*
have insight into	*einsehen*
head	*Oberhaupt*
heather (n.)	*Heide*
hold opinion	*meinen*
hold (true)	*fürwahrhalten*
holiness	*Heiligkeit*
human	*menschlich*
human being	*Mensch*
humanity	*Menschheit*
illusion	*Schein, Illusion*
illusory knowledge	*Scheinwissen*
illustration	*Erläuterung*
image	*Bild*
immortality	*Unsterblichkeit*
impartiality	*Unparteilichkeit*
impulse	*Trieb, Antrieb*
impurity	*Unlauterkeit*
impute	*zurechnen*
in itself	*an sich*
incapacity	*Unvermögen*
incentive	*Triebfeder*
incidental end	*Nebenzweck*
inclination	*Neigung*
independence	*Selbständigkeit*
infer	*schließen*
inference	*Schluß*
inference of the understanding	*Verstandeschluß*
innocence	*Unschuld*
inscrutable	*unerforschlich*
insight	*Einsicht*
intention	*Absicht, Vorsatz*
interaction	*Wechselwirkung*
interpretation	*Auslegung, Deutung*
intuition	*Anschauung (*intuitus*)*
investigation	*Forschung*

jealousy	*Eifersucht*
judgment	*Urteil, Urteilskraft*
justice	*Gerechtigkeit*
kind	*Art*
kingdom	*Reich*
know	*wissen, kennen*
knowledge	*Wissen, Kenntnis*
lasciviousness	*Wollust*
lawfulness	*Gesetzmäßigkeit*
lawgiver	*Gesetzgeber*
learning	*Gelehrtheit*
legality	*Legalität*
legislation	*Gesetzgebung*
legislator	*Gesetzgeber*
life conduct	*Lebenswandel*
limit(ation)	*Schranke, Einschränkung*
luck	*Glück*
lust	*Wollust (*voluptas*)*
make up for	*ergänzen*
malice	*Bosheit*
malignancy	*Bösartigkeit*
manifold	*Mannigfältigkeit*
manners	*Sitten*
mark	*Merkmal (*nota*)*
mastery	*Herrschaft*
matter	*Materie*
meaning	*Sinn, Bedeutung*
merit	*Verdienst*
might	*Macht*
mind	*Gemüt, Geist*
miracle	*Wunder*
mirage	*Blendwerk*
morality, morals	*Sitten, Sittlichkeit, Moral*
mystery	*Geheimnis*
nation	*Volk*
nature	*Natur, Beschaffenheit*
necessity	*Notwendigkeit*
need	*Bedürfnis*
new man	*neuer Mensch*
object	*Gegenstand, Object*
obligation	*Verpflichtung*
observation	*Bemerkung*
occasion	*Anlaß, Gelegenheit*

501

occurrence	*Begebenheit*
old man	*alter Mensch*
omnipotence	*Allmacht*
operation	*Wirkung*
opinion	*Meinung*
order	*Befehl*
original being	*Urwesen (*ens originarium*)*
original ground	*Urgrund*
overpower	*überwältigen*
pagan (n.)	*Heide*
pain	*Schmerz*
particular	*besonder(-)*
passion	*Leidenschaft*
passivity	*Leiden*
patience	*Langmut*
peculiar	*eigentümlich*
people	*Volk*
perception	*Wahrnehmung*
perfect	*vollkommen*
perfection	*Vollkommenheit*
perfidy	*Tücke*
permission	*Erlaubnis*
perseverance	*Beharrlichkeit*
persistence	*Beharrlichkeit*
persisting	*beharrlich*
persuasion	*Überredung*
perversion	*Verkehrtheit*
pleasure	*Lust*
power	*Gewalt, Macht, Kraft*
practical affairs	*Geschäft*
predisposition	*Anlage*
preponderance	*Übergewicht*
presentation	*Darstellung*
presumptuousness	*Vermessenheit*
presupposition	*Voraussetzung*
priestcraft	*Pfaffentum*
principle	*Grundsatz, Prinzip*
probability	*Wahrscheinlichkeit*
problem	*Aufgabe, Problem*
produce	*hervorbrigen*
progress	*Fortschritt*
prohibition	*Verbot*
proof	*Beweis*
propensity	*Hang*
proper	*eigen*
property	*Eigenschaft*
propose	*aufgeben*

prototype	*Urbild*
providence	*Vorsehung*
provision	*Vorsorge*
prudence	*Klugheit*
purpose	*Zweck*
purposiveness	*Zweckmäßigkeit*
rationalize	*vernünfteln*
real	*wirklich, real*
realm	*Reich*
reason	*Vernunft*
receptivity	*Empfänglichkeit*
reciprocal	*wechselseitig*
recognize	*anerkennen, erkennen*
reconcile	*versöhnen*
reference	*Verweisung, Beziehung*
reflection	*Überlegung*
regulation	*Anordnung*
relation	*Beziehung, Verhältnis*
relationship	*Verhältnis*
remark	*Anmerkung*
remission of sin	*Entsündigung*
remove	*aufheben*
reprehensible	*verwerflich*
represent	*vorstellen*
representation	*Vorstellung*
require	*auffordern*
requirement	*Aufforderung*
resolution	*Vorsatz*
resolve	*auflösen*
respect	*Achtung*
revelation	*Offenbarung*
reverence	*Verehrung*
right (n.)	*Recht*
righteousness	*Gerechtigkeit*
rivalry	*Nebenbuhlerschaft*
ruler	*Beherrscher*
satisfaction	*Befriedigung*
scholar	*Gelehrte(r)*
scholarship	*Gelehrsamkeit*
science	*Wissenschaft*
scripture	*Schrift*
seek out	*aufsuchen*
soul	*Seele*
seem	*scheinen*
selection	*Auswahl*

self-contentment	*Selbstzufriedenheit*
self-sufficiency	*Selbständigkeit*
semblance	*Blendwerk*
sensation	*Empfindung*
sense(s)	*Sinne, Sinnlichkeit*
sensibility	*Sinnlichkeit*
sensible	*sinnlich*
sensory	*sinnlich*
sensuous	*sinnlich*
set up	*aufgeben*
significance	*Bedeutung*
signification	*Bedeutung*
skill	*Geschicklichkeit*
solve	*auflösen*
sophistical	*vernünftelnd*
source	*Quelle*
species	*Art, Species, Gattung*
spirit	*Geist*
stability	*Festigkeit*
stain	*Fleck*
state	*Zustand*
stimulate	*beleben*
sublime	*erhaben*
suffering	*Leiden*
sufficient	*hinreichend*
sum total	*Inbegriff*
superstition	*Aberglaube*
supplement	*ergänzen*
syllogism	*Vernunftschluß*
synthesis	*Synthesis, Zusammensetzung*
task	*Aufgabe*
teaching	*Lehre*
thing	*Ding, Sache*
thorough(going)	*durchgängig*
thought-entity	*Gedankending (*ens rationis*)*
totality	*Allheit*
touchstone	*Probierstein*
transformation	*Umwandlung*
transgression	*Übertretung*
treatise	*Abhandlung*
understanding	*Verstand*
unification	*Vereinigung*
union	*Vereinigung*
universal	*allgemein*
universal validity	*Allgemeingültigkeit*
unrecognizable	*unkenntlich*

unremitting	*unabläßig*
unsuitableness	*Zweckwidrigkeit*
upbringing	*Erziehung*
use	*Gebrauch*
vale of tears	*Jammertal*
validity	*Gültigkeit*
valor	*Tapferkeit*
vice	*Laster*
virtue	*Tugend*
vocation	*Bestimmung*
volition	*Wollen*
voluntary	*willkürlich*
warrant	*Befugnis*
way	*Art, Weise*
welfare	*Wohl*
well-being	*Wohlergehen*
well-grounded	*gründlich*
well-pleasedness	*Wohlgefallen*
will	*Wille*
worship	*Anbetung*
worthiness	*Würdigkeit*
wretchedness	*Armseligkeit*
writing	*Schrift*

Index of names

Abbott, T. K., 51–2
Abraham, 124, 204, 282–5
Achenwall, G., 464
Adam, 118, 459
Adickes, E., 337
Aeneas, 473
Ahriman, 166, 222, 409
Allais, D. V., 307, 474
Amphion, 471
Anaxagoras, 350, 450
Anchor, R., 220, 236
Anselm, St., 349, 475
Apollodorus, 471
Aristotle, 450
Arnoldt, E., 41, 43, 45–8
Astraea, 206, 470
Augustine, St., 102, 460, 465, 470

Bahrdt, K. F., xvi–xvii, 120, 461, 465
Baumgarten, A. G., 240–1, 337–8, 377,
    380, 395, 400, 403, 418–20, 441–3,
    457, 460, 475–82
Beck, J. S., 6, 23, 50–1
Beck, L. W., 6, 220, 236
ben David, L., 375, 472
Bengel, J. A., 283, 457, 473
Biester, J. E., xv, xx–xxi, 4–5, 21, 41–5, 47,
    219–20, 456–7
Bischoffwerder, R., xv
Blumenbach, J. F., 305, 473
Bohatec, J., 49, 457–8, 464–5, 469, 470
Born, F. G., 50
Borowski, L. E., 43, 45, 48–9
Bossuet, J. B., 282, 473
Brahe, T., 300, 473
Brahma, 69, 166, 408
Breitkopf, J. G., 326–7, 474
Brucker, J. J., 478
Büsching, A., 474

Campe, J. H., xviii
Camper, P., 305, 473
Charlevoix, P-F. X., 118, 461
Cicero, 263, 309, 320, 460, 472
Colbert, J.-B., 249, 472
Colquhoun, J. C., 236
Coyer, G. F., 300, 472, 473

Confucius, xii
Cromwell, O., 307
Cyrus, 474

David, 212, 470
Democritus, 473
Descartes, R., 351, 433, 474, 476, 481
Despland, M., 23
Dilthey, W., 41–7, 456
Dione, 73
Dönhoff, S., xv

Eberhard, J. A., 45, 337–8, 374–5, 474–5
Elijah, 225
Epicurus, 353, 450
Epstein, K. xvi–xix, xxii
Erasmus, F., 125, 462
Erhard, J. B., 304, 473
Ernesti, J. A., xvi

Fackenheim, E., 220
Feder, J. G. H., 22, 455
Flatt, J. F., 457
Förster, G., 458
Franck, A. H., 277, 473
Frank, J. G., 283, 473
Frederick II (the Great), xii, xv–xvii, 5, 21,
    42, 47, 457
Frederick William I, xii
Frederick William II, xv, xx–xxii, 5, 21, 42–
    5, 48, 235, 239–43, 456
Freya, 166, 409
Fromm, E., 41, 45, 48
Furies, 28

Galileo, 61
Gedike, F., 43, 457
Genghis Khan, 28
Georgius, A. A., 141, 463, 469
Gmelin, J. G., 469
Goeze, J. M., 462
Greene, T. M., 51–3, 62
Gregor, M., 236
Grillo, F., 50
Gulyga, A. xviii

507

Index of subjects

Abdera, 298
abderitism, in history, 298–301
accountability, 71, 75, 80, 82, 87–8, 102,
   105, 122, 147, 149, 150, 160, 166, 181,
   194; *see also* punishment; God, justice of
agreement of nations, argument from, 354–5
alteration (*Veränderung*), 379–80
America, 80
analogy, 107, 130, 165, 166, 206, 208, 214,
   366–7, 385–7, 393, 477
animality, predisposition, 74–5, 82, 114,
   210, 411–12
animals, worship of, 449
anthropomorphism, 107, 166–7, 189, 200,
   348, 384–5, 403, 419–20, 437, 477
Antichrist, 163, 231, 298
Arabia, 163
archetype, 115, 135; *see also* idea
argument from possibility, 375–6
ascension, 157
atheism, 143, 347–8; dogmatic, 355, 369;
   skeptical, 355, 369
atonement, 86, 112–17, 201; *see also* justification; satisfaction

Babylon, 163
baptism, 208, 213, 267
belief (*Glaube*), 414–16; ethics of, 17–18;
   historical, 13–14; *see also* faith
best of all possible worlds, 426–427
Bible, 47, 54, 61, 63, 88, 107, 114, 142,
   181, 185, 240–2, 251–2, 262–4, 282–
   8, 292, 345; interpretation, 264–72,
   345; *see also* Scripture, Holy
blessedness (*Seligkeit*), 420–1
boredom, 317
breathing, 323–4
Burma, 222

call, divine, 167–8
Carthusians, 72
catechism, 65, 140
Catholicism, 140–1, 273, 282
causality, 96, 404; choice as, 74, 79, 190;
   concurrence, 433–4; empirical, 165;
   and freedom, 85, 87, 148, 168–9 (*see
   also* freedom); incomprehensible, 108,

137, 148, 168–9, 190; of gravity, 125,
   165; and law, 60, 82, 103; and miracles,
   124, 126; and morality, 59, 115, 137,
   145, 147, 169, 197, 211; natural, 71,
   86–7, 90; in time, 85, 108–9; *see also*
   God, causality
censorship, xvii–xx 41–7, 50, 60–2, 239,
   248, 456
chiliasm, 81, 219–31, 298
China, 163, 228, 390
choice (*Willkür*), 54, 57–8, 60, 70–94, 102,
   105, 132, 159, 165, 181, 190, 200; *see
   also* will
Christianity, 47–9, 186–7, 156–8, 160,
   163, 187, 229–31, 240–3, 264–7, 272–
   8, 467
church, xiv, 135–6, 138–9, 140–1, 151,
   156–61, 180–5, 187–9, 190–5, 213–
   15; and state, 145; universality, 142–4,
   146, 152–5, 162, 180; visible, 135, 152,
   175–80; *see also* community, ethical;
   faith, ecclesiastical
church-going, 212–13
clergy, xv–xvi, xix, 70, 110–11, 120, 134,
   139, 144–5, 150, 151, 154, 156, 158,
   180, 185, 198, 211, 214; celibacy of,
   158
cognition, a priori, 59–60, 64, 70, 82, 208,
   256
communion, 209, 213
community (*gemeines Wesen*), 62, 123; ethical, xiv, 130, 132–6, 139, 155, 176–7,
   180, 198 (*see also* church); political,
   130, 132, 135, 213
conscience, 22, 28, 32, 34–6, 84, 110–11,
   117, 145, 150, 160–1, 166, 181, 170,
   187, 191, 197–8, 201, 203–6, 207,
   213; erring, 34–5
conservation of substances, 432–4, 482
contingency, 352, 371
conversion, 91–2, 108, 111–12, 113–14,
   116, 122, 125, 148, 186, 211; *see also*
   new man
conviction, 414
cosmological argument, 349–50, 351–2,
   371–3, 476
cosmotheology, 346, 349, 386–98

Index of biblical references

- don't understand God's will → no sin
  ↳ yes mere is
- sinfulness in predetermined nature
  ↳ we no responsible
- God allowed it
  ↳ again, no responsibility

- prefer to live than die
  ↳ world has more pain
  ↳ not guaranteed life w/ pleasure
- life bad for heaven good
  ↳ arbitrary

- God makes you feel guilty
  ↳ NO
- seeing injustice makes me virtuous
  ↳ only notice it if virtuous already
- hey
  ↳ no know
- insight into God from evil

- Son of God mythological description of perfection
- Crucifixion represents all our sins

- what is grace? hope?
- religion: historically grounded way of expressing moral commitment

Printed in the United States
65598LVS00003B/5-30